THE KINGDOM OF GOD IN THE TEACHING OF JESUS

THE KINGDOM OF GOD IN THE TEACHING OF JESUS

IN 20TH CENTURY THEOLOGY

BY

MARK SAUCY

WORD PUBLISHING
Dallas•London•Vancouver•Melbourne

Library of Congress Cataloging-in-Publication Data
Saucy, Mark.
  The kingdom of God in the teaching of Jesus : in 20th
century theology / by Mark Saucy.
      p. cm.
  Includes bibliographical references and indexes.
  ISBN: 0-8499-1329-2
  1. Kingdom of God—History of doctrines.   2. Jesus
Christ—Teachings.   3. Eschatology—History of doctrines.
I. Title.
BT94.S28   1997
231.7'2—dc21   97-33713
                                                              CIP

Printed and bound in the United States of America
789 QKP 9 8 7 6 5 4 3 2 1

For Bonnie,
my dear wife and closest partner
in the work of the Kingdom

TABLE
OF CONTENTS

PART 1:
FOUNDATIONS FOR THE STUDY
OF THE KINGDOM SINCE 1960

1. Issues in the Interpretation of the Kingdom of God Prior to 1960

Part 2:
New Testament Trends Since 1960

PART 3:
SYSTEMATIC PRESENTATION
OF THE KINGDOM SINCE 1960

PART 4:
CONTRIBUTION TO THE STUDY OF THE KINGDOM

FOREWORD

A compendious yet balanced work on the teaching of Jesus relating to the Kingdom of God is a timely publication. Unlike many scholars who have and are still engaged in the so-called Third Quest of the Historical Jesus, Mark Saucy has recognized that the essential element in the life and teaching of Jesus is precisely the Kingdom of God, as the earliest evangelist Mark made plain in his summary of the proclamation of Jesus (Mark 1:15).

From the exodus onwards, the history of the Jewish nation was dominated by the consciousness of the kingship of God. Under the prophets their hopes became centered on the redemptive rule of God that would bring about a second exodus for them, and the subjugation of all the nations to his judgment. Some, notably Deutero-Isaiah, extended the redemptive element of God's rule to the whole world. The burden of the message of Jesus was in harmony with that.

Jesus proclaimed that God's saving sovereignty was in process of initiation, its reality was demonstrated in his acts of power, and it would lead to the consummation of God's gracious purpose of his own people and for all nations. The teaching of Jesus on the Kingdom of God, accordingly, was essentially Christological. Naturally his insight into his own destiny to suffer death—and resurrection—that the gate of the Kingdom be opened for all, and ultimately his part in the consummation of the Kingdom through his parousia, was not part of his public proclamation, but it was communicated to his disciples, to their mystification, and made known to the Jewish authorities in his trial, to their fury.

Mark Saucy has described at length the endeavors of scholars since the rise of modern biblical criticism to interpret the message of Jesus and has evaluated the results of their research. In so doing, he has cast his net widely and provided a multitude of valuable insights on the continuing debate. He is wise enough not to claim infallibility for his findings, but his contribution deserves to be taken seriously by the academic community, and by the proclaimers of the Word of God who look to that community for guidance in their ministry.

George R. Beasley-Murray
May 1997

PREFACE

The proliferation of literature in the fields of New Testament studies and theology virtually guarantees a certain obsolesce to any work once it is printed. This obsolesce factor is magnified in attempts to survey the state of current research especially when the field is as vast as the Kingdom of God and the Historical Jesus. In the case of this work, new studies pertaining to the Kingdom of God in the teaching of Jesus have appeared in the months since this book entered the printing process and which have not been considered herein. One of the most significant of these recent publications is Jürgen Moltmann's definitive statement on eschatology in *The Coming of God*, which is only mentioned here in chapter six as a forthcoming work. Any study of his view of the Kingdom of God must necessarily be informed by this book. Several of the other scholars whose works are considered here have also made recent contributions to the study of the Kingdom. Among these N. T. Wright, Bruce Chilton and Robert Funk deserve mention and further consideration.

A work of this nature certainly is not the product of one individual. Thanks are deserved to too many to name individually but special thanks must go first to my faithful and loving wife, Bonnie, whose partnership in the work of the Kingdom and loving genius created the environment necessary for this book. Second, eternal thanks to my parents who first and patiently showed me the way into the Kingdom. Third, heartfelt thanks go to Colin Brown of Fuller Seminary who taught me the scholarship of the Kingdom. Only the positive features of this present work must reflect on him. Finally, thanks to my co-workers of SEND International laboring for the Kingdom in Ukraine and the Russian Federation. Their timely help and encouragement at many stages of this project, not to mention their own personal dedication to the message of the Kingdom, has been an inspiration to me.

Mark R. Saucy
Kiev, Ukraine
June 1997

ABBREVIATIONS

ANCIENT SOURCES

Apocrypha

Tob	Tobit
WisSol	Wisdom of Solomon

Old Testament Pseudepigrapha

AsMos	*Assumption (Testament) of Moses*
1En	*1 (Ethiopic Apocalypse of) Enoch*
PssSol	*Psalms of Solomon*
SibOr	*Sibylline Oracles*
TAb	*Testament of Abraham*
TAsh	*Testament of Asher*
TLev	*Testament of Levi*

Dead Sea Scrolls

1QS	*Rule of the Community*
1QSa	*Rule of the Congregation*
1QM	*War Scroll*
4Q400–407;	
11Q Shir Shabb;	
Masada Shir Shabb	*Songs for the Holocaust of the Sabbath*
11QTemple	*Temple Scroll*
11QMelch	*Melchizedek*

New Testament Pseudepigrapha

GThom	*Gospel of Thomas*

Rabbinic Writings

Ber	*Berakhot*
mAb	*Aboth (Mishnah)*
SLev	*Sifra on Leviticus*
SNum	*Sifra on Numbers*
MekEx	*Mekilta (Exodus)*
Men	*Menakhot*

MODERN SOURCES

AAS	Acta apostolicae sedis
ANRW	*Aufstieg und Niedergang der Römischen Welt. Geschichte und Kultur Roms im Spiegel der neueren Forschung.* Ed. Hildegard Temporini and Wolfgang Haase. Berlin/New York: Walter de Gruyter, 1972-
BaptQ	Baptist Quarterly
BiRes	Biblical Research
BibTB	Biblical Theology Bulletin
BS	Bibliotheca Sacra
BZ	Biblische Zeitschrift
CJT	Calvin Theological Journal
CanadJT	Canadian Journal of Theology
CBQ	Catholic Biblical Quarterly
ChSchR	Christian Scholar's Review
ChrC	Christianity and Crisis
ChH	Church History
ConcordTM	Concordia Theological Monthly
DRev	Downside Review
EcuR	Ecumenical Review
EvQ	Evangelical Quarterly
EvT	Evangelische Theologie
ExpTim	Expository Times
Forum	Foundations and Facets Forum
HarTR	Harvard Theological Review
HeythJ	Heythrop Journal
HibbJ	Hibbert Journal
HorBibT	Horizons in Biblical Theology

HUT	Hermeneutische Untersuchungen zur Theologie
IntRMiss	International Review of Mission
Interp	Interpretation
JStJud	Journal for the Study of Judaism
JStNT	Journal for the Study of the New Testament
JBiRel	Journal of Bible and Religion
JBL	Journal of Biblical Literature
JChrE	Journal of Christian Education
JChrRec	Journal of Christian Reconstruction
JEcuSt	Journal of Ecumenical Studies
JSNTSS	Journal for the Study of the New Testament Supplement Series
JSOT	Journal for the Study of the Old Testament
JRel	Journal of Religion
JRelEth	Journal of Religious Ethics
JEvTS	Journal of the Evangelical Theological Society
JTS	Journal of Theological Studies
JTChu	Journal of Theology and Church
Loeb	Loeb Classical Library
LonQR	London Quarterly and Holburn Review
LuthQ	Lutheran Quarterly
ModChu	Modern Churchman
MPL	*Patrologiae cursus completus. . . . Series prima in qua prodeunt patres, doctores Scriptoresque Ecclesiae Latinae a Tertulliano ad Gregorium Magnum.* Ed. J.-P. Migne. Parisiis: Venit apud editorem, in Via Dicta D'Amboise, près la Barrière D'Enfer, ou Petit-Montrouge, 1845
NS	New Series
NIDNTT	*New International Dictionary of New Testament Theology.* Ed. Colin Brown. 3 vols. Grand Rapids: Zondervan, 1976
NTS	New Testament Studies
NRT	Nouvelle Revue Théologique
NovT	Novum Testamentum
OTP	*The Old Testament Pseudepigrapha.* Ed. James H. Charlesworth. 2 vols. New York: Doubleday, 1983, 1985
PerspRelSt	Perspectives in Religious Studies

RGG	*Die Religion in Geschichte und Gegenwart*, 3d ed. Ed. Kurt Galling. Tübingen: J. C. B. Mohr (Paul Siebeck), 1957–1965
RelSt	Religious Studies
RestQ	Restoration Quarterly
RQum	Revue de Qumrân
RTLv	Revue Thèologique de Louvain
ScotBEv	The Scottish Bulletin of Evangelical Theology
ScotJT	Scottish Journal of Theology
SBL	Society of Biblical Literature
SEAJT	South East Asia Journal of Theology
Str-B	H. Strack and P. Billerbeck. *Kommentar zum Neuen Testament aus Talmud und Midrash*. 6 vols. Munich: Beck, 1922–1928
SR	Studies in Religion/Sciences Religieuses
TDNT	*Theological Dictionary of the New Testament*. Ed. G. Kittel. Trans. Geoffrey Bromiley. 10 vols. Grand Rapids: Eerdmans, 1964–1968
TS	Theological Studies
TRE	*Theologische Realenzyklopädie*. Ed. Gerhard Müller and G. Krause. Berlin/New York: Walter de Gruyter, 1986-
TRu	Theologishe Rundschau
TToday	Theology Today
TrinJ	Trinity Journal
USemQR	Union Seminary Quarterly Review
VT	Vetus Testamentum
WestTJ	Westminster Theological Journal
WUNT	Wissenschaftliche Untersuchungen zum neuen Testament
ZTK	*Zeitschrift für Theologie und Kirche*

INTRODUCTION

In 1963 two books bearing the same title—*The Kingdom of God in the Teaching of Jesus*—were published; both attempted to survey and critically assess the history of the modern scholarly discussion of Jesus' doctrine of the Kingdom of God. One was by Norman Perrin, one by Gösta Lundström; both were the products of earlier doctoral studies (Lundström's at Uppsala and Perrin's at Göttingen under Joachim Jeremias), and both sought to satisfy a critical need of scholarship. By the late fifties and early sixties the Kingdom of God had long been recognized by scholars as the central focus of the historical Jesus, and consensus about some points of the Kingdom's nature and chronology was gradually emerging under the Already/Not Yet rubric. However, current, wide-ranging summaries of the modern scholarly inquiry into the Kingdom were available only as articles in journals and encyclopedias or as abbreviated components of monographs.[2] Complete treatments of the subject were wholly lacking.

---

[1] Norman Perrin, *The Kingdom of God in the Teaching of Jesus* (London: SCM, 1963); Gösta Lundström, *The Kingdom of God in the Teaching of Jesus: A History of Interpretation from the Last Decades of the Nineteenth Century to the Present Day*, trans. Joan Bulman (London: Oliver and Boyd, 1963). The two works are complementary in some senses. Lundström's focus is primarily continental scholarship from Albrecht Ritschl to the discussion in 1960, including the works of several systematicians. Perrin, on the other hand, concentrates on New Testament scholars from the works of Schleiermacher through the post-Bultmannian quest of the historical Jesus.

[2] See the brief survey by Otto Knoch, "Die eschatologische Frage, ihre Entwicklung und ihr gegenärtiger Stand," *BZ* 6 (1962): 112-20; the articles "Reich Gottes," in *RGG* by Kurt Galling et al.; and "Reich Gottes," in *Bibeltheologisches Wörterbuch* (1959) (Eng. ed. *Sacramentum Verbi: An Encyclopedia of Biblical Theology*, ed. Johannes B. Bauer [New York: Herder and Herder, 1970], s.v. "Kingdom of God," by Rudolf Schnackenburg); and the introductory chapters of Herman Ridderbos, *The Coming of the Kingdom*, trans. H. de Jongste (Philadelphia: Presbyterian and Reformed, 1962); and George E. Ladd, *The Presence of the Future* (Grand Rapids: Eerdmans, 1974), which all survey the history of the interpretation of the Kingdom of God through the early 1960s.

The recent history of inquiry into the Kingdom of God has shown Perrin's and Lundström's works to be important gathering points for an academy that would soon launch out in new directions in quest of Jesus' meaning of the Kingdom. In New Testament studies some of these emergent trajectories were only a few years old in Europe and just making their way across the Atlantic. For example, it was in 1959 that James Robinson excitedly announced "a new quest" of the historical Jesus.[3] In it he extolled the promise of the new way a group of Bultmannian scholars were dealing with the "pastness of the past" and bringing the message of the historical Jesus to new life. Parts of this "new quest" were heavily informed by the philosophical and linguistic contributions of Martin Heidegger and Hans-Georg Gadamer in the field of hermeneutics. This philosophical input, which took theological form in the works of the New Testament scholar Ernst Fuchs and the systematician Gerhard Ebeling, brought forth what would be known in the early 1960s as the New Hermeneutic.[4] It was from this protean bed of the New Hermeneutic that literary theory began its ascendent role as an exegetical tool from which other language-based methodologies would emerge. New treatments of the Kingdom of God in Jesus' teaching followed, precipitating, as one recent commentator of the Kingdom has noted, a "major shift in this century in the interpretation of Jesus' teaching of the Kingdom of God."[5]

Systematic interpretations of the Kingdom of God were also bursting into new forms in 1963 when Perrin and Lundström wrote. With the ravages of World War II still fresh in mind, a new generation of German theologians began considering the future prospects of a world threatened by nuclear war, environmental contamination, and oppressive social and

---

[3] James M. Robinson, *A New Quest of the Historical Jesus* (London: SCM, 1959). See also the 1983 edition, which includes several other important essays on the same topic (James M. Robinson, *A New Quest of the Historical Jesus and Other Essays* [Philadelphia: Fortress, 1983]).

[4] Robinson wrote an important description and apology for this as well ("Hermeneutic Since Barth," in *The New Hermeneutic*, ed. James M. Robinson and John B. Cobb, New Frontiers in Theology 2 [New York: Harper & Row, 1964], 1-77). Here, he anticipates the New Hermeneutic would become "a whole new understanding of theological scholarship" (63).

[5] Wendell Willis, "The Discovery of the Eschatological Kingdom: Johannes Weiss and Albert Schweitzer," in *The Kingdom of God in Twentieth-Century Interpretation*, ed. Wendell Willis (Peabody, Mass.: Hendrickson, 1987), 1, states this in reference to Norman Perrin's later work on the Kingdom embodied in his *Jesus and the Language of the Kingdom: Symbol and Metaphor in New Testament Interpretation* (Philadelphia: Fortress, 1976).

political structures. Moved by collective guilt for past sins, disillusionment with the all-powerful state as a tool for the Kingdom of God, growing dialogue with utopian Marxist ideology, and the perceived inadequacy of theologies built around the individual's existential existence, theologians began to articulate worldly, social, and political aims for the church in the name of the Kingdom of God. In the early sixties Harvey Cox's *The Secular City* and Jürgen Moltmann's *Theology of Hope* appeared with great acclaim, along with a number of theologies of liberation.[6] Eschatology had reached new heights of popularity through the ruin of the past.[7]

The mere passage of thirty years since Perrin and Lundström does not in itself establish the case for a new undertaking in surveying the Kingdom.[8] That case obviously has something to do with the importance of

---

[6] Harvey Cox, *The Secular City* (New York: Macmillan, 1965); Jürgen Moltmann, *Theologie der Hoffnung. Untersuchungen zur Begründung und zu den Konsequenzes einer christlichen Eschatologie* (Munich: Christian Kaiser, 1964). See the excellent account of the rise of political theology during this period in Alfredo Fierro, *The Militant Gospel: A Critical Introduction to Political Theologies*, trans. John Drury (Maryknoll, N.Y.: Orbis, 1977).

[7] See also the eschatological focus of Wolfhart Pannenberg, "Dogmatische Thesen zur Lehre von der Offenbarung," in *Offenbarung als Geschichte*, ed. Wolfhart Pannenberg (Göttingen: Vandenhoeck & Ruprecht, 1961), 91-114; Eng. ed. *Revelation as History*, ed. Wolfhart Pannenberg, trans. David Granskou (London: Collier, 1968); Pannenberg, *Grundzüge der Christologie* (Gütersloh: Gerd Mohn, 1964); Eng. ed. *Jesus—God and Man*, trans. Lewis L. Wilkins and Duane A. Priebe (Philadelphia: Westminster, 1968); Gerhard Sauter, *Zukunft and Verheissung. Das Problem der Zukunft in der gegenwärtigen theologischen und philosophischen Diskussion* (Zürich: Zwingli, 1965); and Walter Kreck, *Die Zukunft des Gekommenen. Grundprobleme der Eschatologie* (Munich: Christian Kaiser, 1961).

[8] This is not to say that various summaries and assessments of scholarship on the Kingdom are not available since Perrin and Lundström, only that there is nothing comparable to them in breadth and depth. For significant recent summaries of the scholarship on the Kingdom, see Bruce Chilton's introduction in *The Kingdom of God*, ed. Bruce Chilton, Issues in Religion and Theology 5 (Philadelphia: Fortress, 1984), 1-26; Jacques Schlosser's survey of New Testament Kingdom study from 1960-1980 in his *Le règne de Dieu dans les dits de Jésus*, Études Bibliques (Paris: J. Gabalda, 1980), 47-86; and Willis, ed., *Kingdom of God in Twentieth-Century Interpretation*, which itself seems to have been mistitled as only four of the fourteen contributions are helpful as surveys of the topic in this century (1-66). Of these four only one addresses developments since the early sixties (53-66). The rest of the articles represent recent approaches to the Kingdom in the various New Testament sources, for example, Old Testament, Qumran, Apocrypha, Pseudepigrapha, and so on, as they appeared in papers presented in the New Testament section of the Central States Society of Biblical Literature, spring 1985. Chilton has recently written a review of the scholarship through 1993. See "The Kingdom of God in Recent Discussion," in *Studying the Historical Jesus: Evaluations of the State of Current Research*, ed. Bruce Chilton and Craig A. Evans (Leiden: E. J. Brill, 1994), 255-80.

the subject under consideration. And according to this criterion of overall importance, few would argue that the Kingdom of God does not have vital significance to New Testament studies. However, our quest is also propelled by the appearance in the last thirty years of a new wave of critical methodologies arising from the disciplines of philosophy, historiography, and the human sciences. These new methodologies have become paradigms for scholars to exegete the documents of the New Testament. At bottom, this study really grows out of hermeneutics and is driven by developments that have taken place here.[9] In a sense the need for this study is best viewed in the context of the historical development of ideas germane to the Kingdom itself and also developments of hermeneutical methods of biblical inquiry. Consequently, part of the introductory chapter that follows will consider the significant issues in hermeneutics that prepare the stage for at least part of the last thirty years' discussion of the Kingdom.

PROCEDURES AND LIMITATIONS

The major aim of this study is much the same as that of Lundström and Perrin: "to follow the interpretation of the Kingdom of God in the teaching of Jesus down to the present day."[10] In Perrin's volume especially this immediate goal was pursued with the added purpose of grounding his own view of the Kingdom. That added goal is also my own. Specifically, I propose to use the findings from the study of the Kingdom in the last generation to fund yet another venture in understanding the Kingdom of God in Jesus' teaching. I have presented the results of my quest in the last chapter.

Because of the importance of the topic and the immensity of the material available, even when limited to the last thirty years, our goal needs

---

[9] The discipline of hermeneutics embodies our task for two reasons: (1) It is the "central problem" of hermeneutics to be concerned with the distance between primitive Christian teaching and our own (cf. Wolfhart Pannenberg, *Basic Questions in Theology*, trans. George H. Keim [London: SCM, 1970], 1:96). Perrin dedicated his last book *(Jesus and the Language of the Kingdom)* "to Amos Wilder and Paul Ricoeur who taught me to look at the problem of hermeneutics in new ways." (2) "The hermeneutic question is interdisciplinary. It is correlated to philosophy, theology, exegesis, literary criticism, the human sciences in general," as R. Lapointe has noted in "Hermeneutics Today," *BibTB* 2, no. 2 (1972): 107.

[10] Lundström, *Kingdom of God*, 1.

refinement. Perrin and Lundström certainly saw this to be true, and their self-imposed limitations are readily visible in their works. The following are the key procedures and limitations under which this study will be carried out.

1. Unlike Perrin and Lundström, who did not discuss the Kingdom of God and the church as far as the implications of Jesus' ethics are concerned, I will survey such contributions. They have been categorized as "systematic theology," with the general understanding of systematic theology as that discipline which, from the platform of the other biblical disciplines, seeks modern application or reformulation of the ancient biblical message.[11] The scope of this survey of the Kingdom of God theme then will not only be exegetical but historical as well.[12]

2. Since literally everything written about Jesus in New Testament or systematic theology during the last thirty years concerns the Kingdom of God in one way or another, this study must be limited primarily to major published works in which the Kingdom of God has a central place or which attempt to advance understanding of the Kingdom theme specifically. In New Testament studies, this means inclusion of works on the Synoptic Gospels, the historical Jesus, and works about the Kingdom from the other ancient sources, that is the Old Testament Apocrypha and Pseudepigrapha, Qumran, the Targums, Josephus, and so on.

Much the same approach will be used to consider the contributions of systematic theologians; that is, the focus will be on those writers and new movements which depend significantly on the theme of the Kingdom of God to define their task and identity. Most attention will be given to the

---

[11] See Osborne's discussion of the nature of systematic theology in *The Hermeneutic Spiral: A Comprehensive Introduction to Biblical Interpretation* (Downers Grove, Ill.: InterVarsity Press, 1991), 286-317. He describes systematic theology as a "contextualization of biblical theology, filtered through the history of dogma but recontextualized for the contemporary situation and both organized and expressed in current thought patterns" (309).

[12] Historical in the sense of the realization of doctrine in history. Note Pannenberg's statement about the nature of systematic theology: "Traditional dogmatics, by treating God, election, creation, man, redemption, church and sacraments as items of doctrine, has all too often lost sight of the fact that these concepts are real only in the movement of a history in which both their nature and their truth are still being determined. A systematic theology of Christianity must express the historical nature of Christianity and its truth in order to match its material" (Wolfhart Pannenberg, *Theology and the Philosophy of Science*, trans. Francis McDonagh [Philadelphia: Westminster, 1976], 420).

political and liberation theologies, including those of the World Council of Churches, but post-Vatican II Roman Catholicism and Protestant evangelicalism will be considered also. Political theology will be dealt with almost entirely through its most influential thinker, Jürgen Moltmann,[13] and the Kingdom of God in liberation theologies will be discussed in terms of the first liberation theology, that of Latin America.

3. The categorization of the different viewpoints is an important feature of this study in its approach to both the New Testament studies and those of systematic theology. On the New Testament side, I have not classified views according to a particular hermeneutical methodology that an author may have used, though a method's contribution to the results will be noted; nor have I made classifications according to any particular ancient source which may have been probed concerning the Kingdom. Rather, I have chosen to classify scholars by their conclusions about the historical Jesus' proclamation of the Kingdom of God, particularly as to whether he preached an *apocalyptic* or a *nonapocalyptic* Kingdom.

These two terms naturally call for further refinement and explanation.[14] Toward that end, it should be noted first that *apocalyptic* and *nonapocalyptic* will be understood generally in light of the discussion of Jesus' message inaugurated by Johannes Weiss and Albert Schweitzer earlier this century. In this context, *apocalyptic* delineates a Jesus who acted and spoke out of an

---

[13] That is, influential in actualizing the transitional role of political theology vis-à-vis liberation theology. Moltmann's fathering role to Latin American liberation theology is well known. Several important writers express their debt to Moltmann's work, including José Bonino, *Doing Theology in a Revolutionary Situation* (Philadelphia: Fortress, 1975), 144; Hugo Assmann, *Theology for a Nomad Church* (Maryknoll, N.Y.: Orbis, 1976), 225; and Gustavo Gutiérrez, *A Theology of Liberation*, trans. Caridad Inda and John Eagleson (Maryknoll, N.Y.: Orbis, 1973), 94.

[14] "Apocalyptic" is a notoriously amorphous term in biblical studies, as it is used to describe specific eschatological issues and also a literary genre. See Klaus Koch, "What is Apocalyptic? An Attempt at a Preliminary Definition," in *Visionaries and Apocalypses*, ed. Paul D. Hanson (Philadelphia: Fortress, 1983), 16-36; Koch, *The Rediscovery of Apocalyptic*, Studies in Biblical Theology, second series 22 (London: SCM, 1972); D. S. Russell, *The Method and Message of Jewish Apocalyptic* (Philadelphia: Westminster, 1964); "Apocalypse: The Morphology of a Genre," ed. J. J. Collins, *Semeia* 14 (1979); H. Anderson, "A Future for Apocalyptic?" in *Biblical Studies in Honor of William Barclay*, ed. J. R. McKay and J. F. Miller (Philadelphia: Westminster, 1976), 56-71; Christopher Rowland, *The Open Heaven: A Study of Apocalyptic in Judaism and Early Christianity* (New York: Crossroad, 1982). See also J. Carmignac, "Les dangers de l'eschatologie," *NTS* 17 (1970-71): 388-90, who points out the confusing imprecision of eschatological terms in scholarly discussion since Weiss and Schweitzer.

awareness of an eschatological calendar or sequence of events. This calendar included traditional themes of Jewish apocalyptic literature, including cosmic battles between heavenly and demonic forces, the tribulation of the earth, a final judgment of evil, resurrection, and the disclosure of the Kingdom of God as an end of this present world. The apocalyptic Kingdom of God is something that comes at a precise time in the future in one of two ways; it is the supernatural end to the natural world, as Weiss and Schweitzer saw it, or it is the supernatural invasion of the natural world that establishes a restored Jewish state within history.[15] *Nonapocalyptic*, in contrast, will be used in this study as the broad category for views which either deemphasize or eliminate altogether this temporal view of the Kingdom. In this category will be those whose understanding is that Jesus' primary concern was not with a cosmic timetable. Jesus and his message must be more broadly conceived. He is the herald and seal of something that is indeed transcendent, but of something that is also immanent. Consequently,

---

[15] At this point the use of "apocalyptic" in this study becomes more inclusive than that of Weiss and Schweitzer, who understood the apocalyptic Kingdom as something on a "supersensuous plane" only. The substance of the inclusion being added here may be seen in Schweitzer's review of Hermann Reimarus, "Von dem Zwecke Jesu und seiner Jünger," in *Noch ein Fragment des Wolfenbüttelschen Ungenannten*, ed. Gotthold Ephraim Lessing (1778). After praising Reimarus for grasping the essence of the eschatological issue in Jesus from which everyone else until Weiss "appears retrograde," Schweitzer takes umbrage with Reimarus's "sole mistake," namely, "the assumption that the eschatology was earthly and political in character" (*The Quest of the Historical Jesus: A Critical Study of Its Progress from Reimarus to Wrede*, introduction by James M. Robinson, trans. W. Montgomery [New York: Macmillan, 1968], 23).

In truth, the inclusion of a historical Kingdom with "apocalyptic" fits the original paradigm of Jewish pseudepigraphal literature, which often mingled the Kingdom as the transcendental end of history and the Kingdom as the final period of history of unspecified duration. See D. S. Russell, *Apocalyptic: Ancient and Modern* (Philadelphia: Fortress, 1978), 24, who cites George Caird's helpful distinction between *das Ende* and *die Endzeit* when discussing Jewish pseudepigraphal eschatology. See G. B. Caird, "Eschatology and Politics: Some Misconceptions," in *Biblical Studies in Honour of William Barclay*, ed. Johnston R. McKay and James F. Miller (Philadelphia: Westminster, 1976), 72-86.

The Kingdom as "end to the world as we know it," therefore, often, but not necessarily, includes Jesus' consistent expectation of the Kingdom's *imminent* appearance. Weiss and Schweitzer conceived of the Kingdom as imminent, and Borg affirms, "The eschatological Jesus is one who thought [the end of the world] was imminent " (Marcus Borg, "A Temperate Case for a Non-Eschatological Jesus," *Forum* 2, no. 3 [1986]: 81, n. 1). However, see Ladd, *The Presence of the Future*, 323, whose picture of Jesus would be thoroughly "apocalyptic" and "eschatological," but who would interpret the Kingdom-as-imminent passages as proleptically fulfilled in Jesus.

the Kingdom message on this side is mainly one of the Kingdom as some kind of present reality.[16]

Second, it should be understood that *apocalyptic* and *nonapocalyptic* are not necessarily as strongly antithetical to each other as their nomenclature may indicate. As Koch has noted that the otherworldly Kingdom so typical of Jewish apocalyptic could also be present in a concealed form in the present age, so the question of what divides the two categories often becomes one of emphasis. The position of Marcus Borg would be an example of one who retains the Kingdom-as-end as a feature of Jesus' meaning of the Kingdom, which would be still "apocalyptic" as defined above, but who would not see this as the predominant feature of Jesus' message:

> The final kingdom is part of Israel's story about the Kingship of God, but kingdom-as-end was not the central element in Jesus' message. . . . [The kingdom] refers to the kingship of God at the beginning of time, in the present, and at the end of time, and to life in that kingdom, i.e., to a way of being created by the kingship of God. . . . The most satisfactory understanding of the Kingdom of God is one in which "end of the world" becomes one nuance among many, rather than being the defining nuance.[17]

For this reason, though he has retained elements of the apocalyptic view, Borg sees himself in a nonapocalyptic category for Jesus' understanding of the Kingdom. This study will follow similar patterns of categorization: namely, where the Kingdom is understood, in Borg's terms, as "kingdom-as-end," or, as I would add, as "kingdom-as-endtime," it will be termed "apocalyptic." Views in which the other-worldly kingdom diminishes in importance, though not necessarily disappearing altogether, will be labeled "nonapocalyptic."

Third, it should be noted that categorization by the apocalyptic or

---

[16] In this century the nonapocalyptic Jesus has been championed in the Anglo response to the Teutonic hegemony of the apocalyptic Jesus. Scholars like C. H. Dodd, G. B. Caird, and T. F. Torrance have held various nonapocalyptic views of Jesus, compared to those of R. Bultmann, W. G. Kümmel, J. Jeremias, E. Käsemann, H. Conzelmann, and G. Bornkamm.

[17] Borg, "A Temperate Case," 94-95.

nonapocalyptic content does not mean the study will be completely disengaged from chronology. While it is true that certain interpretations continue uninterrupted from scholarship predating 1960, throughout this period there are still certain discernable forks in the road. Norman Perrin's consideration of the Kingdom in the terms of language in the early 1970s would be one such fork. The decline in popularity of the eschatological Jesus in the early 1980s would be another. Where possible, significant authors in these trends will be grouped together with some concern for chronology.

4. In addition to the presentation of recent Kingdom research, the study will seek to critically interact with the views presented. In general this analysis will proceed in greatest detail immediately following the presentation of the various writers or groups. In the last chapter, the preceding critical assessments will be united to generate a presentation of my own view of the Kingdom of God in the teaching of Jesus. This final chapter will be an attempt to build Jesus' teaching upon the results of the last thirty years of scholarly effort much like the study of Perrin thirty years ago.

5. Finally, it is necessary to set the stage in more detail for the period immediately preceding our own. As we have already seen, the New Quest, which fed into the newer literary critical approaches, grew out of the Bultmannian school of interpretation. But as Perrin's and Lundström's works show us, this was only one of the interpretations of the Kingdom to arise from the previous century of critical reflection. The first chapter covers introductory matters that comprise the intellectual context for discussion of the Kingdom in the last thirty years. This chapter includes a brief recapitulation of Perrin's and Lundström's survey of the Kingdom in the biblical disciplines, a survey of the pertinent issues for the Kingdom in philosophical hermeneutics, and the social and political factors that shaped the Kingdom's application in systematic theology.

After this introduction our study will address these five procedures and limitations in three parts. The four chapters of part two (chapters two through five) comprise the various interpretations of the Kingdom in important New Testament and historical Jesus studies of the last thirty years. This section commences with the various nonapocalyptic approaches to the Kingdom, taking first the heritage of the newer literary criticism in the new hermeneutic. It moves then to those scholars who both anticipate and follow the influential work of Norman Perrin in literary criticism. In chapter three I have discussed the nonapocalyptic views I have entitled *regnum Christi:* those writers who understand the Kingdom primarily in terms of Jesus' personal inauguration and enduring leadership in the spiritual salvation of his people. Chapter four considers the nonapocalyptic Kingdom from various historical Jesus studies associated especially with the Third Quest. The diminished interest in Christology of those in this chapter when combined with the interdisciplinary methodologies of the Third Quest yields a Kingdom that is earthly, social, and political. Part two concludes in chapter five with the representatives of New Testament studies still retaining the apocalyptic Kingdom in one form or another.

Part three (chapters six through eight) takes us into the systematic interpretations of the Kingdom since the advent of political theology in the early 1960s. As a way into political theology, chapter six presents a detailed examination of Jürgen Moltmann's thought on the Kingdom. Chapter seven follows with an example of the reified Kingdom contextualized to the social and political constraints typical of the liberation theologies. As already noted, this will be handled through the liberation theology of Latin America, the first and most prominent of the liberation theologies. Finally, part three concludes in chapter eight with the systematic expressions of the Kingdom of post-Vatican II Roman Catholicism, the World Council of Churches, and three newer streams of evangelicalism.

The presentations of parts two and three yield numerous observations that serve as both warnings and guides to discoverers seeking the meaning of the Kingdom in Jesus' teaching. In part four I have utilized these warnings and guides to approach anew the teaching of the Kingdom of God by Jesus. The ground of my own presentation of Jesus' teaching is found in the following observations I believe are evident from the last generation's work on the Kingdom of God.

TRENDS IN RECENT STUDY OF THE KINGDOM

The first observation of the last thirty years is really about a nontrend. That is, there has been no movement in eschatological terminology in the last thirty years, but there should be. Much confusion and obfuscation abounds because of the many ways words like *apocalyptic, otherworldly,* and *eschatological* are thrown about without clarification. *Otherworldly*, for example, can refer to the nature of the Kingdom's advent in history or the nature of the Kingdom itself as nonhistorical. The variety of referents for *apocalyptic* is well attested and is similar to *otherworldly*. In some writings the Kingdom is apocalyptic if it is nonhistorical but comes in a sudden cataclysmic way, while in others, as in the representations by Weiss and Schweitzer, the apocalyptic Kingdom was meant for something after the end of time, something transcendent. The confusion in terminology becomes magnified within the debates of the apocalyptic and the nonapocalyptic sides. Some, like many categorized in our study under the *regnum Christi* view, contend for the nonapocalyptic Kingdom but only mean to address the supramundane, transcendent Kingdom of Weiss and Schweitzer and would allow for some "apocalyptic" events associated with the Kingdom's advent at the end of time, like the Parousia of Christ for instance. As will be noted more fully in the next observation, N. T. Wright was no doubt correct in his comment to John Collins that, had Schweitzer heard the latter's presentation of the earthly, historical hope of Israel in the first century, New Testament studies would have been different, and we might add here, spared some confusion of terms.[18] Carmignac's call almost twenty years ago for clarifying the terminology is still relevant today.

Second, Wright's commendation to Collins elicits comment at another point. That is to say, the last thirty years have seen considerable progress in refining the milieu of ancient eschatological texts pertinent to first-century Judaism. Work on the Pseudepigrapha alone, not to mention the Qumran writings, the Targums, and later rabbinic work, has progressed in such a way as to have significant bearing on the study of the Kingdom. One of the critical conclusions coming out has concerned the eschatological hopes of the apocalyptic texts in the Pseudepigrapha. As Wright and Collins and others like Rowland and Sanders are noting, these writings were far less dualistic, otherworldly (in Schweitzer's meaning), and nontemporal than is commonly believed. For all their symbolism and fantasy, the apocalyptic writers still wrote in the context of an historical and earthly hope for the Kingdom. The Kingdom expectation within Judaism was not the timeless realms of eternity that Schweitzer and Weiss supposed.

---

[18] N. T. Wright, *The New Testament and the People of God* (Minneapolis: Fortress, 1992), 333-34.

These advances in the knowledge of the ancient sources have also meant a clearer identification of the environment of the historical Jesus. In the first place, as Wright, Collins, and others evidence, the fundamental eschatological hope of Judaism is being recognized as not so diverse as it had been thought to be. The eschatological differences of the various Jewish philosophies of the first century are not differences of essence but differences of lesser and somewhat more peripheral matters. Jewish eschatology, it is now appearing, was fairly monolithic in the main substance of its hopes. Jews of the first century looked forward to an earthly and historical manifestation of God's covenant promises. This means, in the second place, that the prevailing eschatological hopes of Jesus' time were not so diverse as to constitute a broad array of options available to Jesus for the meaning of the Kingdom. Of course he could have transformed the Kingdom into anything he wanted, but justifying such a transformation according to the diversity of the options available to him is less and less appearing to be an option.

Third, the past thirty years have witnessed a significant modification of New Testament methods typically founded on the atomization of the New Testament texts. The attempt to uncover the aims and purposes of Jesus solely by means of reconstructing the history of individual pericopes is giving way in the Third Quest of the historical Jesus to more syncretistic methods that look at social factors by means of the tools of the social sciences. New ways of looking at the texts themselves have also risen from the literary disciplines. Within the sphere of narrative criticism in particular, the source critical assumptions of form criticism are not being allowed to occlude the view of the New Testament documents as complete and reliable literary units in themselves.

A fourth observation concerns a conclusion obtained by Perrin and Lundström in their reviews of the Kingdom prior to 1960. At that time they noted the beginnings of the narrowing of the Kingdom's polarized past. Some years after the battles of realized and consistent eschatologies, a growing consensus was speaking of the Kingdom as having inherited features of both positions. The Kingdom was an Already and at the same time a Not Yet phenomenon. At a most general level of New Testament scholarship, this consensus is still intact thirty years later, though there is detectable movement in favor of the Kingdom's Already at the expense of its Not Yet. For the most part, this movement still appears to be a matter of degree or emphasis, as Borg and others have said, and while it may be attributable in part to a general interest in the Kingdom's application for the present, it is still an emphasis built on the supposed demise of New Testament apocalyptic, the apocalyptic Son of Man in particular.

The movement away from the futuristic Kingdom is also visible in the groups who would eradicate calendaric notions for the Kingdom altogether. These are the spiritual heirs of Bultmann in the New Hermeneutic and the New Literary Criticism, those who would attempt to supplement their more radical historical criticism with existential philosophy. For them the Kingdom is existentially realized in the present only through the vehicle of language. There is no particular future course for anything other than the personal "world" of the individual. This was the real subject of Jesus' concern.

Perrin wrote a eulogy for this proposal of the New Hermeneutic before it had even finished adolescence, but his own attempt to complete what it lacked through literary criticism has not won the day either. It is true his "tensive-symbol" terminology has some popularity in New Testament studies today, but it is a term emptied of its original meaning and filled anew with notions Perrin would not have abided. The real substance of the New Literary Criticism has not taken the lead in discussion of the Kingdom. Kingdom research that would be "more towards the poet and the critic of the poet" has not delivered as Perrin had hoped. It remains just one of many methodologies currently being used to understand the Kingdom in the New Testament.

The rise of new methodologies as supplements of historical criticism is a fifth feature of the New Testament horizon since Perrin and Lundström. Two observations follow on this point that have bearing for the Already/Not Yet paradigm of the Kingdom. First, the great variety of methodologies has meant a variety of conclusions about the nature of the Kingdom. In some cases the Kingdom is social only, in others it is social and political; some still paint it only in terms of spiritual salvation. Second, the advance of this diverse methodology in the Third Quest has meant a general reification of the Kingdom and, hence, the adduction of the question of temporality in the discussion. In both the apocalyptic and nonapocalyptic approaches within the Third Quest, the Kingdom is viewed as having societal connotations. While there is difference as to when this community called the Kingdom was to be manifested, no longer is the Kingdom only a matter for the individual, as in the existentialism of the New Hermeneutic. It is the perfect egalitarian society evolving toward fulfillment in the present age (nonapocalyptic Third Quest), or it is the perfect society that will cataclysmically inaugurate the age to come (apocalyptic Third Quest). In either case the temporal Already and the Not Yet of the Kingdom appear to be established over the Kingdom's more existential version.

A sixth observation of New Testament trends relates to the Kingdom's general reification under the auspices of the Third Quest. The wealth of new background information to the political and social setting of first-century Palestine has contributed to the concretization of the Kingdom in terms of a just society evolving gradually or cataclysmically unveiled. But this Kingdom remains in tension with the yet-dominant contention in most circles as to the Kingdom's dynamic nature. Over and over the survey emphasizes (still largely on the strength of Dalman) that *basileia* connotes first and foremost the notion of the act of ruling, a reign, and then only secondarily, very secondarily in most cases, anything concrete like a realm.[19] Carmignac buttressed the dynamic concept by noting the linguistic limitations of Greek in comparison with Hebrew and modern languages like English, French, and German. Perrin also was a champion of the dynamic meaning for *basileia,* playing it to the full in his literary criticism. Yet any lopsided conclusions in favor of the dynamic over the concrete are threatened or at least muddled by the various visions of the Kingdom's reification in the Third Quest. When Perrin agrees with Walter Rauschenbush, the father of the American Social Gospel movement, that the Kingdom finally is the "energy of God realizing itself in human life," he highlights the Kingdom's dynamic but also assumes the Kingdom's progressive concretization.[20] At worst, as is the case for many in the Third Quest, the usual association of the dynamic rule of God with personal salvation is lost in the concretization of the Kingdom in a just society. At best, the remaining voices of the Third Quest call for caution in overplaying the dynamic aspect of the Kingdom that occurs in so much of the

---

[19] A fact that is evident simply by the need for four chapters dealing with "nonapocalyptic" interpretations and only one for the "apocalyptic."

[20] Perrin, *Language of the Kingdom,* 70-71.

other nonapocalyptic views. The Kingdom does not only mean spiritual salvation or a change in personal circumstances. Whether in his age or the next one, Jesus intended earthly consequences for the Kingdom. This is a message coming louder from the New Testament and historical Jesus studies.

Seventh, the last thirty years indicates that the great multiplication of methods has obviously wrought a multiplication of Kingdoms. This variety has been noted already, but the point now is to call attention to the tendency that where methods and the Kingdom are concerned, like begets like. That is, linguistic methods tend to beget a linguistic Kingdom, sociological methods beget a social Kingdom, anthropological methods beget an anthropological Kingdom, and so on. Particular social models for the historical Jesus, whether they are the Cynic-sage, the Pharisaic rabbi, or the charismatic prophet, also tend to produce a Jesus and hence a Kingdom that correlates to the model. To the outside observer the range of possibilities for the meaning of the Kingdom must seem infinite. A similar state of affairs attained in the Old Quest of the nineteenth century, and Albert Schweitzer and Johannes Weiss brought it to a halt with their call for serious attention to the biblical record, specifically to biblical eschatology. In his day Schweitzer figured New Testament study had only two roads down which it could go: the road of consistent eschatology or the road of consistent skepticism embodied then in the writings of William Wrede. Schweitzer said we must either take the Gospels seriously and see Jesus as a deluded prophet caught in the wheels of his own apocalyptic vision or doubt the Gospels at every point and return to the myriad of biblically and humanly manufactured gestalts of Jesus and his Kingdom.

Time, of course, has demonstrated the false option in Schweitzer's scenario, but only at the point of his consistent eschatology. Where he was correct was in identifying the locus of the real issue: New Testament scholarship can either function with a general trust of the New Testament documents or a general mistrust of them. Where the tendency is toward trust, the available options for Jesus and the Kingdom he proclaimed become markedly reduced. Certainly, some sectors of New Testament studies are working from such a posture of trust, holding in abeyance many of the negative presuppositions about the nature of the biblical record. However, where there is mistrust of Scripture, the key is turned and the door is open to clever innovation, plurality, and the same subjectivity Schweitzer saw embedded in the Old Quest that virtually guarantees a new Kingdom every time a new method or ancient gestalt might be applied to it. Boundless subjectivity is the certain breeding ground of relativity, which is also the necessary end of Wrede's road. One is mindful of a favorite saying of Perrin to his students in New Testament research: "Today's assured results are tomorrow's forgotten hypotheses." That Wrede's road is the option most operative in New Testament studies in the last thirty years seems evident from the variety of forms of the Kingdom, and especially in the most recent formulations for the Kingdom in the Third Quest. It is also poignantly reiterated in Perrin's 1966 reflections on the Dodd Festschrift, which he prophetically entitled "The *Wredestrasse* Becomes the *Hauptstrasse*."[21] If there is to be an end to the multiplied variety of forms for Jesus and his Kingdom it will not be because of a new method or a new ancient model; it will be when these and forthcoming methods and models start with a different view of the Gospel data.

Part three of this study will reveal further progress in what theologian Langdon Gilkey in 1969 identified as the Modern *Geist* behind the contemporary "ferment in theology."[22] There are four features to the Modern *Geist*, and all of them are visible in the last thirty years' rush to the praxis of the Kingdom. *Contingency* is that feature suggesting that the world is the result of causes that are neither necessary, rational, or purposive. Reality is the result of accidental events. Contingency represents the penetration of the modern mind of Darwinian antiteleology. There is nothing behind the immediately given. There is no ultimate intention, plan, or explanation. All reality is the result of the accidents of chance. The second characteristic is one that Gilkey considers as undergirding all the rest as either a cause or a result. It is *relativism*—the idea that all reality is bound to the flux of history, the passage of time. All reality is shaped by its immediate historical context. No ideas or events are truly timeless. The third feature is *transience or temporality*, which recognizes the transitory nature of reality. All

[21] Norman Perrin, "The *Wredestrasse* Becomes the *Hauptstrasse*: Reflections on the Reprinting of the Dodd Festschrift," *JRel* 46 (1966): 296-300.
[22] Langdon Gilkey, *Naming the Whirlwind: The Renewal of God-Language* (New York: Bobbs-Merrill, 1969), 40-61; see chapter one, "The Present Ferment in Theology," 3-29.

things have their time of ending. Nothing is enduring. Finally is *autonomy*, the freedom of humanity and concomitant belief in humanity's innate capacity to know its own truth.

Relativism appears first through its cousin subjectivity in the ease with which political and liberation theologies deny or emphasize only select parts of the Christian Scriptures. The most outstanding instance here is one of omission, namely the omission of the praxis of the first Christians in the early church. Time and again, the center of Kingdom praxis in the political and liberation theologies is found to lie in the Gospel records about Jesus or the Old Testament paradigms of the Exodus or the prophets. Whether it is admitted forthrightly or left unsaid altogether, the rest of the New Testament is thought to have little to contribute to the modern political and social visions of the Kingdom's praxis. It should be noted that this particular focus has shed some light on the politics of Jesus, and in principle there is validity to investigating the background of the New Testament. It is the modern interpreter's responsibility to penetrate the thought world of the writer and relate it to our world. However, the penetrating process has gone too far if it marginalizes certain New Testament authors altogether. Apart from the illogicality inherent to this view (since the writers of the paradigmatic Jesus of the Gospels were themselves members of the nonparadigmatic apostolic church of the epistles), if the apostolic Christians cannot speak to us today, at least in principle, Christianity becomes free-floating and anchored nowhere but in the machinations of the modern mind.

Beyond the *prima facie* selectivity exhibited in the omission of the early church, relativism is manifest in political and liberation theologies in the fact that such an omission poses little or no problem. This survey reveals well enough the various strategies employed to circumvent any need for the early Christian paradigm in the theology of the Kingdom. These strategies receive succor from a New Testament academy distrustful of the historicity of the first Christian records. Commonplace are the views that the New Testament was either a complex of historically contingent and contradictory theologies or the record of one theology historically contingent on the personal problems of its leaders or on the problems of the different communities at large. Help in marginalizing the New Testament's voice is also found in the sociology of knowledge articulated in the social sciences. Whatever the justification given, one is left with the strong impression that it is apparently not difficult in the present milieu to come up with some reason why the New Testament church is not normative today, at least in regards to the Kingdom's praxis.

This contemporary neglect of the early church's role for guidance as to the modern church's role reflects another one of Gilkey's observations about the modern *Geist*. Temporality or transience, as Gilkey said, relates to contingence and relativism in the suggestion that validity decreases with time. This is because old things and old ideas may have been good and appropriate in their own day, but they are anachronistic to the present day. One cannot but speculate that the way the modern contextual theologies spurn the *earliest* church's history is further evidence of the invasion of the modern *Geist* into theology.

Gilkey's mention of the modern sense of autonomy is intricately interwoven with all of the preceding features of the modern relativism in these theologies. That modern theologians would exploit the supposed freedom bequeathed to them by modern philosophy and certain strains of New Testament scholarship the way they have is testimony in itself to Gilkey's accuracy here. It is one of the ironies of theologies claiming the Christian label that the newly contextualized Jesus, though he is hailed as the chief paradigm, in many cases bears only the vaguest of resemblance to the Jesus of Matthew, Mark, Luke, and John. One wonders, for example, how well the crucified Jesus whose own proclamation of the Kingdom never developed a program of social action would be received in many meetings of the World Council of Churches. How does the Jesus whose own proclamation developed themes of repentance, faith, humble openness to God (Luke 10:38–42), love for enemies, and power through weakness fit in today's world? Some will relativize Jesus according to the exigencies of his day, but it can be argued this is just more evidence of the autonomy of the modern *Geist* at work.

Of course appeal to the Jesus of *every* part of the Gospels or the Kingdom of *every* part of the New Testament is no longer as compelling in the modern world as it once was, but this fact in itself is the dangerous consequence for theology when relativism encroaches. If Hertz is correct and theology's chief end is universal truth,[23] then relativism by definition must

---

[23] Karl Hertz, "An Investigation of Ecumenical Theology," *Mid-Stream* 19 (October 1980): 407.

be theology's archenemy. And so it is. Any theology built on the foundations of relativism is necessarily marginalized under the weight of its own
argument. At the simplest level the thought here would be: if the bulk of
New Testament Christianity is contingent upon the unique circumstances
of its day, then so must be the case for modern Christianity. Modernity
cannot therefore claim universality for its own systematic applications of
the Kingdom. Furthermore, this relativized Christianity takes to itself the
added and contradictory facade of still trying to justify the universal claim
of those witnesses of the New Testament it considers paradigmatic. This of
course entails the assumption of universal truths and by definition the falsehood of bonafide Relativism. Theology so concerned becomes hopelessly
trapped in the futility of its own maxims. Relativized theology by definition is an oxymoronic dilemma. It is the silent face behind the present
ferment in theology identified by Gilkey more than twenty years ago.

As we will see, for the Kingdom's praxis, selective, relativized application of the New Testament has contributed to the modern confusion of
the lines between the Kingdom's indicative and the Kingdom's imperative.
More and more the last thirty years have seen groups of all stripes taking
matters of social involvement into their own hands and doing it all under
the banner of the Kingdom. In some cases this is a necessary corrective to
an overly individualized and otherworldly faith, but in other cases the pull
of the eschatological Kingdom on history has the effect of gradually transforming history into the eschatological Kingdom and subverting the consensus of the Kingdom as some part Already and some part Not Yet. For
many of those in the theological portion of our study the Already is definitely eclipsing the Not Yet as they seek to approximate all dimensions of
the coming Kingdom in their work. Professing the consensual maxim of
the Kingdom's Already and Not Yet is becoming harder and harder to
those straying from the New Testament on the longest tethers.

It needs to be noted that this tendency in modern theology to focus on
the Kingdom's realization at the expense of its futurity is neatly paralleled
in many of the New Testament studies we surveyed. The "vanishing
eschatological Jesus" of Jesus Seminar fame necessarily means the "appearing realized Jesus," as the writings of Borg, Mack, Crossan, and others will
attest. It also means that the myriad of political and liberation theologies
are walking in lockstep with these similar developments in other biblical

fields. However, there is irony in this modern twosome. The great variety of competing portraits for Jesus and the praxis of the Kingdom coming from the New Testament and systematic quarters indicates that political theology's original quest to assert the horizontal dimension of the Kingdom over the individual's vertical (i.e., relative/subjective) experience has not really undone the relativistic paradigm. Rather, the last thirty years of theology have done their work within the relativistic stream. The only element added now is that relativism has been moved from the personal level of existentialism to the collective and social level of praxis.

Finally, the danger of relativism in Christian theology is not only that the integrity of theology as a legitimate discipline is eroded; there is a threat to the very nature of Christian theology as *Christian*. The point here is that, as we will see in part three of our survey, relativized eschatology of the Kingdom contains within it the seeds to relativize other doctrines along with it. If the early Christian's view of the Kingdom's praxis was a mistake for today because of its historical contingency, the possibility is raised that it was equally mistaken about the Kingdom's soteriology and Christology. The fact that this is no conspiratorial domino theory but simple reality is evident in some of the defenders of liberation theology like Arthur McGovern and Leonardo Boff. The orthodox doctrine of justification becomes denigrated because of its supposed contingency upon St. Paul's personal problems with the Mosaic law. Traditional Christology is likewise eroding in some of the ecumenical dialogue we see taking place in the World Council of Churches.

Within the domain of systematic theology Christian theology is most securely established as to its nature as *theology* and its subject as *Christian* when it can make sense out of the greatest portion of the Christian Scriptures. Conversely, Christian theology that is most insecurely placed is characterized by having to explain away greater and greater portions of the Christian Scriptures. Claims to universality and persuasive power tend to be substantiated in the former state, not the latter. The result of the latter condition is, in Gilkey's words, contingency, relativism, temporality, and autonomy.

PART ONE

*Foundations for the Study
of the Kingdom Since 1960*

CHAPTER ONE

Issues in the Interpretation
of the Kingdom of God Prior to 1960

MODERN CRITICAL STUDY OF THE KINGDOM

Historical Criticism and the Kingdom of God: Hermann Reimarus

Critical study of the Kingdom of God begins with the critical study of the life of Jesus.[1] On this count, the work of Hermann Samuel Reimarus (1694–1768) is most often credited with inaugurating the discussion.[2] Although he is not especially known for his contributions to eschatology,[3] Reimarus

---

[1] For a review of the interpretation of the Kingdom of God before the Enlightenment, see the first chapters of Louis Berkhof, *The Kingdom of God: The Development of the Idea of the Kingdom Especially Since the Eighteenth Century* (Grand Rapids: Eerdmans, 1951); Benedict T. Viviano, *The Kingdom of God in History* (Wilmington, Del.: Glazier, 1988); Henry Martyn Herrick, *The Kingdom of God in the Writings of the Fathers* (Chicago: Chicago University Press, 1903); Christian Walther, *Typen des Reich-Gottes Verständnisse* (Munich: Christian Kaiser, 1961); Ernst Staehelin, *Die Verkündigung des Reiches Gottes in der Kirche Jesu Christi. Zeugnisse aus allen Jahrhunderten und allen Konfessionen*, vols. 1-5 (Basel: Friedrich Reinhardt, 1957-1964); Rudolf Mau, "Herrschaft Gottes," *TRE*, 15:218-24; and the bibliographical survey of John E. Groh, "The Kingdom of God in the History of Christianity: A Bibliographical Survey," *ChH* 43 (June 1974): 257-67.

[2] As is recognized in Schweitzer's work *The Quest of the Historical Jesus: A Critical Study of Its Progress from Reimarus to Wrede*, trans. W. Montgomery (New York: Macmillan, 1968).

[3] As Colin Brown has noted, Reimarus really was not interested in eschatology at all (*Jesus in European Protestant Thought 1778-1860* [Grand Rapids: Baker, 1985], 53); he did not "make any deep penetration into the thought-world of apocalyptic," and "little attempt was made to understand eschatological language." This is probably the reason Reimarus was overlooked in Perrin's and Lundström's surveys. Lundström begins his study with Albrecht Ritschl, and Perrin starts with Friedrich Schleiermacher, who, he says, was the first to give the Kingdom a "central place in his theology and did make some attempt to relate his use of the concept to the teaching of Jesus" (Norman Perrin, *The Kingdom of God in the Teaching of Jesus* [London: SCM, 1963], 13). Perrin's rationale for beginning with Schleiermacher here is curious in light of the fact that of the seven *Fragments*, *Von dem Zwecke Jesu und seiner Jünger* was the most famous and by far the longest. The omission of Reimarus is not uncommon in surveys of the Kingdom's modern interpretation.

stirred up a significant controversy on the relationship of history, revelation, and faith, while he was attempting a historical conception of the life of Jesus. In the last and most notorious of the *Fragments* that were published from 1774 to 1777 by the drama critic Gotthold Lessing, Reimarus considered *The Aims of Jesus and His Disciples*.[4] Reimarus held that Mark 1:15 was the best place to start in arriving at Jesus' understanding of his mission, including the meaning of the Kingdom: "Repent, and believe the gospel, the Kingdom of God is at hand." Reimarus observed that where the Kingdom was concerned, Jesus never offered his own definition of the Kingdom; he simply announced it. From this Reimarus deduced that Jesus used "the Kingdom" according to the common understanding of his Jewish audience. Since the contemporary Jewish hopes for the Kingdom of the Messiah were grandly physical, national, and spiritual, he concluded that this must have been Jesus' understanding of the Kingdom as well.[5] Furthermore, Reimarus said that Jesus did not see the Kingdom as coming to "end the world" in the manner that has dominated the eschatological or apocalyptic views since Weiss and Schweitzer. When the disciples asked Jesus about the "end of the age" (Matt. 24:3), they were speaking from their Jewish context and asking about the end of the period preceding the establishment of the earthly Jewish kingdom.[6]

The significance of Reimarus for the Kingdom was not his detailed study of ancient Jewish eschatological hopes but the fact that he construed the historical mission of Jesus as basically eschatological and, beyond that, more provincial, that is, Jewish, than had been assumed throughout much of Christendom. Although Reimarus's proposition has been marginalized

---

[4] Published originally as the *Fragmente des Wolfenbüttelsche Ungenannten*. See the English translation, *Reimarus: Fragments*, trans. Ralph S. Fraser, ed. Charles H. Talbert (Philadelphia: Fortress, 1970). Schweitzer wrote that the *Aims of Jesus* is a magnificent piece of work; "not only one of the greatest events in the history of criticism, it is also a masterpiece of general literature" (*Quest of the Historical Jesus*, 15). See Buchanan's discussion of the *Aims of Jesus* and the Kingdom (G. W. Buchanan, *The Consequences of the Covenant* [Leiden: E. J. Brill, 1970], 42-43, and his introduction to his translation of the seventh of the *Fragments*: H. S. Reimarus, *The Goal of Jesus and his Disciples*, trans. G. W. Buchanan (Leiden: E. J. Brill, 1970), 1-32.

[5] *Reimarus Fragments*, ed. Talbert, 136-38.

[6] Ibid., 216.

within scholarship since he wrote,[7] his earthly, eschatological view of the Kingdom did command the attention of Albert Schweitzer, who built on it in his own portrait of the historical Jesus. Schweitzer's *Quest of the Historical Jesus* went on to effect a major change in the scholarly approach to the Kingdom, but he gives credit to Reimarus for being "the first, after eighteen centuries of misconception, to have an inkling of what eschatology really was."[8]

The Ethical Kingdom of Ritschlian Liberalism

For more than one hundred years that followed, Reimarus's eschatological, let alone political and messianic, Kingdom was left to languish in the wings of the critical discussion while the spiritualized Kingdom of Schleiermacher and his influential successor, Albrecht Ritschl, had center stage.[9]

It is true that Friedrich Schleiermacher (1768–1834) is not remembered as one of the premier commentators on Jesus' understanding of the Kingdom of God, but nonetheless he did see the Kingdom of God as something "all-inclusive for Christianity."[10] In the context of his total theological system, with its basic anthropological orientation, he construes all human

---

[7] In 1970 Buchanan noted, "No adequate study, however, has been made of the Jewish teaching which, Reimarus said, was still in his day similar to the teaching of Jesus about the political kingdom he hoped to reestablish in Palestine" (introduction to *The Goal of Jesus and His Disciples*, 2). For discussion of the limited influence of Reimarus in the one hundred years that followed, see Ernst Bammel, "The Revolution Theory from Reimarus to Brandon," in *Jesus and the Politics of His Day*, ed. Ernst Bammel and C. F. D. Moule (Cambridge: Cambridge University Press, 1984), 11–69.

[8] Schweitzer, *Quest of the Historical Jesus*, 23.

[9] In the survey that follows I am largely indebted to the works of Perrin, Lundström, Bruce Chilton (*The Kingdom of God*, Issues in Religion and Theology 5 [Philadelphia: Fortress, 1984], 1–26), George Eldon Ladd (*The Presence of the Future: The Eschatology of Biblical Realism* [Grand Rapids: Eerdmans, 1974], 3–42), Herman Ridderbos (*The Coming of the Kingdom*, trans. H. de Jongste, ed. Raymond O. Zorn (Philadelphia: Presbyterian and Reformed, 1962], ix–xxxiv), Geoffrey Wainwright (*Eucharist and Eschatology* [New York: Oxford University Press, 1981], 7–17), and Helmut Merkel ("Die Gottesherrschaft in der Verkündigung Jesu," in *Königsherrschaft Gottes und himmlischer Kult im Judentum, Urchristentum und in der hellenistischen Welt*, ed. Martin Hengel and Anna Maria Schwemer [Tübingen: J. C. B. Mohr (Paul Siebeck), 1991], 120–35).

[10] Friedrich Schleiermacher, *The Christian Faith*, ed. H. R. Mackintosh and J. S. Stewart, (Edinburgh: T. & T. Clark, 1928), 43. This is the English translation of the 1830 edition of *Der Christliche Glaube*, which was first published in 1821. On the Kingdom in Schleiermacher see especially Perrin, *Kingdom of God in the Teaching of Jesus*, 13–14.

reality in terms of humanity's innate God-consciousness. Against this backdrop, the Kingdom of God takes shape as the corporate expression of the human God-consciousness.[11] This corporate expression has its ground in the perfect God-consciousness of Jesus as he communicates the blessings and perfections of the manifested God-consciousness to the redeemed.[12] Thus, in Schleiermacher, the Kingdom is entirely a spiritual reality that is in evidence wherever the blessings of redemption are enjoyed by God's people.

Albrecht Ritschl (1822–1889) developed Schleiermacher's spiritualized thesis with an added teleological dimension. In his view, Schleiermacher's discussion of the Kingdom as the "all-inclusive" theme of reality was justified but for one thing: it had neglected the goal. Like too much of Protestantism before him, Schleiermacher had defined Christianity and the Kingdom only in terms of personal redemption through Christ. Every facet of the Christian life had become realized as radii of a circle that had redemption in Christ as its center. In contrast, Ritschl proposed Christianity in the form of an ellipse with two focal points, one towards the individual (redemption in Christ) and one towards the world of humanity (the Kingdom of God, the final end of all of God's designs).[13] According to the pattern of Jesus, who "saw in the Kingdom of God the moral end of the religious fellowship He had to found,"[14] the Kingdom of God needed to stand on its own as the end towards which even personal redemption inexorably moves. Leaning heavily on the intellectual shoulder of the philosopher Immanuel Kant, for whom the Kingdom of God was "an association of men bound

---

[11] Schleiermacher states, "We shall come immediately to the point that to regard our corporate life as divinely-created, and to derive it from Christ as a divinely-given One, are the same thing; just so, at that time, to believe that Jesus was the Christ, and to believe that the Kingdom of God (that is, the new corporate life which was to be created by God) had come, were the same thing. Consequently, all developing blessedness had its ground in this corporate life" (*Christian Faith*, 360).

[12] Ibid., 386-88.

[13] Albrecht Ritschl, *The Christian Doctrine of Justification and Reconciliation*, ed. H. R. Mackintosh and A. B. Macaulay (Edinburgh: T. & T. Clark, 1900), 9-10. This is the English translation of the third edition of the third volume of Ritschl's *Rechtfertigung und Versöhnung*, originally published in 1870-1874. The third edition of the third volume was published in 1888.

[14] Ibid., 12.

together by laws of virtue,"[15] Ritschl saw the Kingdom as the morally ordered human society initiated in the world by those who had become beneficiaries of God's love. He states,

> The Kingdom of God, then, is the correlate of God's love in so far as it is the association of men for reciprocal and common action from the motive of love. . . . And this does not mean merely that the individuals combined in the Kingdom of God are subject to Divine action as creatures and members of the natural world; it means besides, that, as possessed of moral freedom and in accordance with their spiritual constitution and destiny, they stand in the line of that purpose which, from our interpretation of love, we have found to be the content of God's personal end. Accordingly, the instances of human action from love which are comprehended under the Kingdom of God constitute, as the correlate of God's personal end and as His specific operations, the perfect revelation of the truth that God is love.[16]

Thus, for Ritschl the Kingdom of God was always a sociological phenomenon before it was an individual or national one.[17] Through emulation of God's example in Jesus, humankind would engage the task of realizing God's Kingdom on the earth through deeds of love. Perrin has noted Karl Barth's apt summary of Ritschl's whole project:

> With Ritschl reconciliation . . . means the realized ideal of humanity. . . . All Ritschl's thinking springs from this result. . . . Completed reconciliation consists in God's confronting the believer as his Father and justifying him in his child-like feeling of utter truth, giving

---

[15] Ibid., 11.

[16] Ibid., 290-91. See Chilton, *Kingdom of God*, 5; Gösta Lundström, *The Kingdom of God in the Teaching of Jesus*, trans. Joan Bulman (London: Oliver and Boyd, 1963), 3-9; Philip Hefner, "The Concreteness of God's Kingdom: A Problem for the Christian Life," *JRel* 52 (1971): 190-91.

[17] The nationalized kingdom, which Ritschl admits of the Old Testament, was universalized by New Testament Christianity: "In Christianity, the Kingdom of God is represented as the common end of God and the elect community, in such a way that it rises above the natural limits of nationality and becomes the moral society of nations" (Ritschl, *Justification and Reconciliation*, 10).

him spiritual dominion over the world and engaging him in the work in the kingdom of God.[18]

During the nineteenth century Ritschl's ethical/sociological interpretation of the Kingdom enjoyed a huge following. The idea of a virtuous society that was being ordered by loving deeds dovetailed nicely with the portrait of Jesus as the teacher of morality and ethics that was coming from the liberal Quest for the Historical Jesus. Systematic applications of Ritschl's ethical, this-worldly thesis were also forthcoming in the social gospel movement of Walter Rauschenbusch (*A Theology for the Social Gospel* [1912]) and Shailer Mathews (*The Social Teaching of Jesus* [1897]).[19] Even after the apocalyptic thunderbolt of Weiss and Schweitzer had sent the discussion feverishly in another direction, Ritschl's lineage lived on in the liberalism of Adolf von Harnack (*What Is Christianity?* [1901]) and Wilhelm Hermann (*Systematic Theology* [1927]), albeit with some shift of emphasis back toward the individual. For these, Ritschl's ethical influence is still basic, but it is augmented by a more individualistic interpretation of the Kingdom of God. The essential element of the Kingdom is its activity within the souls of men and any societal effects are secondary.[20]

Eschatological Views

In 1892 cracks began to appear in the Ritschlian facade with the publication of a modest sixty-seven page booklet, *Die Predigt Jesu vom Reich Gottes* (rev. 1900), written by none other than Ritschl's student and son-in-law, Johannes Weiss.[21] Weiss waited some three years after his

---

[18] Perrin, *Kingdom of God*, 16, citing Karl Barth, *Protestant Thought: From Rousseau to Ritschl*, trans. Brian Cozens (New York: Harper & Row, 1959), 393.

[19] Chilton, *Kingdom of God*, 6, has observed that much of the theological application of Ritschl in the social gospel strayed from him by making the Kingdom more of a human endeavor than a divine one. Ritschl wanted to protect the inherent otherness of the Kingdom; it was not simply a matter of transforming the world through practice of the ethical teaching of Jesus.

[20] See the discussion in Ridderbos, *Coming of the Kingdom*, xviii.

[21] Göttingen: Vandenhoeck & Ruprecht, 1982. The English translation of the first edition appeared as *Jesus' Proclamation of the Kingdom of God*, trans. and ed. Richard H. Hiers and David L. Holland (Philadelphia: Fortress, 1971). See also Wendell Willis, "The Discovery of the Eschatological Kingdom: Johannes Weiss and Albert Schweitzer," in *Kingdom in Twentieth-Century Interpretation*, 1-14; and David Larrimore Holland, "History, Theology and the Kingdom of God: A Contribution of Johannes Weiss to 20th Century Theology," *BiRes* 3 (1968): 54-66.

influential father-in-law's death and then allowed his work to be published because of the moral support of other recent studies of the Kingdom of God by Otto Schmoller and Ernst Issel.[22] *Die Predigt Jesu* was driven by three nagging reservations Weiss held concerning Ritschl's doctrine of the Kingdom.[23] First, Weiss said that Ritschl was not satisfying in his explanation of the antithesis between the Kingdom of Satan and the Kingdom of God, an antithesis that is parallel in Jesus' teaching (Matt. 12:25–29) and Jewish apocalyptic (e.g., *AsMos* 10.1ff.). This was the first hint that the Jesus of the Gospels had more in common with Jewish apocalyptic than he did with nineteenth-century liberalism.[24] Second, in Weiss's mind Ritschl had placed far too much emphasis on the activities of human beings in building the Kingdom of God, whereas for Jesus the Kingdom was the irruptive work of God alone.[25] Finally, Weiss interpreted Ritschl as making Jesus' aim more continuous with preceding history than could be justified from the Gospel record (Mark 1:15; Matt. 10:7; Luke 10:7, 9). Weiss contended that Jesus was in fact conscious that he stood on the brink of history and eternity. The end of the world was imminent and all that remained was Judgment and new and glorious Palestine.[26]

For Weiss, the fact that the Kingdom of God was a decisive event according to the paradigm of the apocalyptists meant there was no middle ground for the Kingdom: it was either present or it was not. With the

---

[22] See Weiss's preface to the first edition in *Jesus' Proclamation of the Kingdom of God,* 56.

[23] Perrin, *Kingdom of God,* 17-18.

[24] See Weiss, *Proclamation,* 74-79; 101-4.

[25] "[T]he actualization of the Kingdom of God has yet to take place. In particular, Jesus recognized no preliminary actualization of this rule of God in the form of the new piety of his circle of disciples, as if there were somehow two stages, a preliminary one, and the Kingdom of Completion. In fact, Jesus made no such distinction. The disciples were to pray for the coming of the Kingdom, but men could do nothing to establish it" (ibid., 129).

[26] Ibid., 129. In light of the "otherworldliness" ascribed to the "apocalyptic" Kingdom, it is interesting that Weiss consistently identified the supramundane, transcendent Kingdom Jesus taught as the earthly and territorial messianic kingdom. In one of his concluding polemics with Ritschlian liberalism he states, "The Kingdom of God as Jesus thought of it is never something subjective, inward, or spiritual, but is always the objective messianic Kingdom, which usually is pictured as a territory into which one enters, or as a land in which one has a share, or as a treasure which comes down from heaven" (ibid., 133).

apocalyptists, Weiss opted for the latter situation: though Jesus saw it as near, very near, the Kingdom had not yet come.[27] The implications for this conclusion were twofold. First, Weiss had to deal with the passages in the Gospels that spoke of the Kingdom's presence, such as, for example, the parables and the confrontations with Satan (e.g., Matt. 12:28). His solution was to see such sayings as either the ecstatic exclamations of a Jesus inspired by his own consciousness of victory over Satan or as the work of the early church, which mistakenly had believed Jesus did start the Kingdom in their midst.[28] Second, the fact that the Kingdom had not yet come meant that Jesus was not the king. Indeed, in his first advent he was more of a forerunner, a herald, like John the Baptist had been.[29] In all, Weiss's understanding of the Kingdom featured six characteristics notable in their comparison to Ritschl:

> The kingdom was transcendent and supramundane; it belonged to the future; Jesus was not the founder or inaugurator but waited for God to bring it; the kingdom was not identified with the circle of Jesus' disciples; it did not come gradually by growth or development; its ethics were negative and world-denying.[30]

Even though Weiss's views had run roughshod over the prevailing Ritschlian doctrine of the Kingdom (in terms of history if not theology),[31] it took the help of a world war and the lively prose of Albert Schweitzer to

---

[27] Ibid., 114-29.

[28] Ibid., 67-74.

[29] Ibid., 81-82.

[30] Colin Brown, "Historical Jesus, Quest of," in *Dictionary of Jesus and the Gospels,* ed. Joel B. Green, Scot McKnight, and I. Howard Marshall (Downers Grove, Ill.: InterVarsity Press, 1992), 331.

[31] Weiss had no problem separating his historical results from their application. Even though his results had rendered Jesus' apocalypticism an unwieldy burden for the modern Christian, when it came to theology Weiss still retreated to the domain of his nemesis, Ritschl: "I am still of the opinion today that his [Ritschl's] system and precisely this central idea [the Kingdom of God] present that form of dogmatic statement which is best suited to draw our race to the Christian religion and, correctly understood and correctly expressed, to awaken and nurture a healthy and powerful religious life such as we need today" (foreword to the 1900 edition of *Die Predigt Jesu,* v, [cited by Holland, "History, Theology and the Kingdom of God," 55]).

signal the demise of the ethical Kingdom of God.[32] In *Vom Reimarus zu Wrede. Eine Geschichte der Leben-Jesu-Forschung* (1906), Schweitzer, with his usual aplomb, hailed the eschatological thesis first conceived in Reimarus and now reborn in Weiss. Johannes Weiss, he said, was the sure ground for the weary explorer who had passed through the billowy seas and swampy reed-grass of the nineteenth-century Quest for the Historical Jesus.[33] In Schweitzer's mind, Weiss was right on target to see Jesus against the background of Jewish apocalyptic,[34] to reject any idea of the "growth" of the Kingdom in this present age,[35] and to reject taking the Kingdom from any moral point of view. The Kingdom has nothing to do with this age and is, in fact, "supermoral."[36]

There were some points where Schweitzer took exception with Weiss. The foremost of these was in regards to the impact of eschatology on the ministry of Jesus. On this subject Schweitzer considered that Weiss had not gone as far as he ought. For Weiss the element of an eschatological timetable of the Kingdom was not of foremost importance for Jesus' ministry. Whether the Kingdom was present or future was to Weiss an "unfruitful debate" compared to the miracle of the Kingdom as God's intention for the world.[37] Schweitzer, on the other hand, had taken on liberalism for not reckoning with the eschatological element in Jesus, but he also engaged Weiss for not letting the apocalyptic timetable of the events of the Kingdom be more crucial for understanding all of Jesus' ministry. For Schweitzer Jesus was an apocalyptic prophet who looked forward to and announced the imminent inbreaking of God into history with himself playing the role of the "Son of

---

[32] See Holland, "History, Theology and the Kingdom of God," 54, n. 3, who notes that Weiss's rebuttal to Ritschl was largely unnoticed until the 1920s. Willis, "The Discovery of the Eschatological Kingdom," 3, cites W. G. Kümmel, "Die 'Konsequente Eschatologie' Albert Schweitzers im Urteil der Zeitgenossen," in *Heilsgeschen und Geschichte: Gesammelte Aufsätze* (Marburg: N. G. Elwert, 1965), 338, for the disastrous effects of World War I on liberal eschatology.

[33] Schweitzer, *Quest of the Historical Jesus*, 238.

[34] Albert Schweitzer, *The Mystery of the Kingdom of God: The Secret of Jesus' Messiahship and Passion*, trans. Walter Lowrie (New York: Schocken, 1964), 101.

[35] See his treatment of the parable of the leaven, which, he contends, is about not growth but the fact that there is a sign present in Jesus that points to consummation (ibid., 109-10).

[36] Ibid., 102.

[37] Chilton, *Kingdom of God*, 7-8.

Man coming on the clouds of the sky" (Matt. 24:30). The twelve disciples, far from being the passive men of prayer of Weiss's version, were the "men of violence" (Matt. 11:12) who would provoke the coming of the Kingdom. Theirs was a suicide mission in Matthew 10.[38] When the intervention of God's Kingdom never came, Jesus tried to force its arrival by going to the cross himself. In all, his effort was a pathetic failure, but it was quite clear to Schweitzer that a "thoroughgoing eschatology" colored all Jesus did.[39]

Early Responses to the Eschatological Jesus

In the history of interpretation of the Kingdom of God it is difficult to overstate the impact of Weiss and the eschatological hypothesis he articulated. "In retrospect one can see that the whole modern interpretation of Jesus and his teaching stems from those sixty-five pages," was the way Norman Perrin assessed the impact after some seventy years of hindsight.[40] Yet a theory's impact is not measured by the number of its advocates alone[41]

---

[38] See Brown's discussion of differences between Weiss and Schweitzer in "Historical Jesus," 331.

[39] Schweitzer's own "life" of Jesus is laid out in *Quest of the Historical Jesus,* 330-97. In his opinion, Jesus' misunderstanding of the Kingdom begins to be righted in the theology of Paul. Accordingly the modern church must follow the pattern of Paul and transform the Kingdom to a wholly interior rule of God in his people's hearts. "Paul the thinker recognized as the essence of the Kingdom of God which was coming into existence that it consists in the rule of the Spirit. We learn from this knowledge which comes to us through him that the way in which the coming of the Kingdom will be brought about is by the coming of Jesus Christ to rule in our hearts and through us in the whole world. In the thought of Paul the supernatural Kingdom is beginning to become the ethical and with this to change from the Kingdom to be expected into something which has to be realized. It is for us to take the road which this prospect opens up" (Schweitzer, *The Kingdom of God and Primitive Christianity,* ed. Ulrich Neuenschwander, trans. L. A. Garrard [New York: Seabury, 1968], 183).

[40] Norman Perrin, *Jesus and the Language of the Kingdom* (Philadelphia: Fortress, 1976), 66.

[41] The eschatological Jesus of Weiss and Schweitzer made a tremendous impression on Anglo scholarship in the early twentieth century. See the works of Burkitt (*Gospel History and Its Transmission,* 1906), E. F. Scott (*Kingdom and Messiah,* 1910), E. G. Selwyn (*Teaching of Christ,* 1915), and James Moffatt (*Theology of the Gospels,* 1912). According to Ladd in *Presence of the Future,* 10, the consistent or futuristic eschatology of Schweitzer had great influence in America as late as 1958, with able defenders such as Alan Richardson (*An Introduction to the Theology of the New Testament)* and R. H. Fuller (*The Mission and Achievement of Jesus,* 1954) putting forward this view. W. G. Kümmel also considers the work of Martin Werner (*Die Entstehung Des Christlichen Dogmas Problemgeschichtlich Dargestellt,* 1941) as a relatively recent proponent of consistent eschatology (W. G. Kümmel, *Promise and Fulfillment: The Eschatological Message of Jesus,* trans. Dorothea M. Barton [Naperville, Ill.: Alec R. Allenson, 1957], 15).

but by the intensity of the debate that follows. On this count there is no doubt that the eschatological Jesus of Weiss and Schweitzer has been a touchstone, positive or negative, for every twentieth-century interpretation of the Kingdom of God.

One of the first reactions to Weiss came out of the History-of-Religions School of which he himself was a part.[42] Later in the same year as *Die Predigt Jesu*, Wilhelm Bousset published *Jesu Predigt in ihrem Gegensatz zum Judentum* (*The Proclamation of Jesus in Contrast to Judaism*).[43] The title by itself indicates the ground he was attempting to defend. In distinction to Weiss, Bousset argued the case of liberalism that said, yes, Jesus was to be understood in terms of the thought and speech patterns of the Jewish apocalyptic, but Jesus was far more than a Jewish preacher of apocalyptic dualism. At many points Jesus repudiates the worldview of the apocalyptists, a worldview that included rigid asceticism, an abstract and distant view of God, and a decidedly negative opinion of the world. In contrast to these Jewish ideas of his day, Bousset contended that (1) Jesus was actually positive towards this world because he could hear the rush of the coming one, and (2) the fundamental element of Jesus' message was the heavenly Fatherhood of God to his creation. For the Kingdom this meant that on one level Jesus accommodated the times and spoke in apocalyptic language of a coming, transcendent Kingdom, but on another level he carefully transformed the concept before his hearers by means of the parables and the statements of the Kingdom's presence.

In a essay written in 1894, "Die Predigt Jesu vom Reiche Gottes," Wilhelm Wrede took a different path from Bousset.[44] In many ways a prelude to his more well-known *Das Messiasgeheimnis in den Evangelien* (1901), "Die Predigt Jesu" was Wrede's response to Bousset's transformation theory of Jesus and the Kingdom of God. Beginning from the simple observation of Reimarus more than a century earlier, Wrede took as his point of departure the fact that Jesus never gave a definition of what he meant by the Kingdom of God. On these grounds Wrede felt it unwarranted to read anything into the Kingdom other than the customary

---

[42] O. Merk, "Bibelwissenschaft II," *TRE*, 6:386ff.

[43] Göttingen, 1892. See Merkel, "Die Gottesherrschaft in der Verkündigung Jesu," 121-24.

[44] This essay was published in *Vorträge und Studien* (Tübingen: 1907). See Merkel, "Die Gottesherrschaft," 124-26.

understanding of the time.[45] Answering the spiritualizations of Bousset, Wrede countered that if Jesus intended to transform the meaning of the Kingdom, he would have certainly been more clear about it. The end result is that Wrede's view came close to that of Weiss: the Kingdom is a purely eschatological reality. Jesus was indeed driven by an eschatological calendar, but not a calendar which had him in the role of the Messiah of the endtime.[46] Something like John the Baptist, Jesus is only a herald of the Kingdom's nearness, its dawn. All of the Kingdom-as-present passages need to be understood this way,[47] and Jesus' ethical teaching set forth the conditions for participation in that final, eschatological Kingdom.

Realized Eschatology

Two other reactions to the eschatological Jesus in the earlier decades of this century are also noteworthy. The first became known as realized eschatology.[48] Though the name commonly associated with realized eschatology is C. H. Dodd, numerous works preceded him in calling Schweitzer's and Weiss's futuristic eschatology to recognize the teaching of Matthew 12:28 and Luke 17:20, where the Kingdom for Jesus is clearly

---

[45] "Jesus never gave a discourse as to what he meant by the Kingdom. He never said to his disciples that his perspective of the Kingdom of God was anything other than the customary understanding. Overall there is the impression that he used the term in the same sense in which it was generally understood" (Wrede, *Vorträge und Studien,* 88 [quoted in Merkel, "Die Gottesherrschaft," 124, author's translation]).

[46] The suspicions Wrede had about the early church's meddling with the story of Jesus appears to have deep roots, beginning with the meaning of the Kingdom of God. Since Jesus himself was not the Messiah, all of the high christological statements of the Gospels must have come from the church. In *The Quest of the Historical Jesus,* 330ff., Schweitzer referred to Wrede's later *Das Messiasgeheimnis in den Evangelien* as "thorough-going skepticism."

[47] Wrede also employs the parables to introduce a universalistic element to the Kingdom that contrasted with the nationalistic one of Jesus' contemporary audiences (Wrede, *Das Messiasgeheimnis,* 113 [cited by Merkel, "Die Gottesherrschaft," 125]).

[48] See Ladd, *Presence of the Future,* 11-23; Richard H. Hiers, "Pivotal Reactions to the Eschatological Interpretations: Rudolf Bultmann and C. H. Dodd," in *The Kingdom of God in Twentieth Century Interpretation,* 15-34; Lundström, *The Kingdom of God in the Teaching of Jesus,* 104-26; Kümmel, *Promise and Fulfillment,* 144-45; Chilton, *Kingdom of God,* 10-12; and Perrin, *Kingdom of God,* 58-78.

a present reality.[49] Nonetheless, Dodd galvanized the issue with publication of his 1935 Shaffer Lectures, *The Parables of the Kingdom,* and his later *The Apostolic Preaching and Its Developments.*[50] To Dodd's way of thinking, these Matthean and Lucan passages, along with the parables, revealed that Jesus only expected the Kingdom to be active in his person and the events of his life. Consequently, where Jesus is, there is the fullness of the Kingdom. Great exegetical effort is put forth in his famous argument that *ephthasen* ("has come") in Matthew 12:28 is synonymous with *ēngiken* of Matthew 4:17. If this is correct, then Dodd has a case that Jesus' proclamation is not "The Kingdom of God has come near," but "The Kingdom of God has come." The so-called eschatological events partial to the futurists should be seen as symbols of the "ultimates" of the transcendent world that absolutely and finally confronts humanity through Jesus.[51] Other later writers who had great affinity with Dodd were A. T. Cadoux (*The Theology of Jesus,* 1940) and F. C. Grant (*The Gospel of the Kingdom,* 1940).

In 1945 T. F. Glasson contributed to Dodd's case from the point of view of the Parousia doctrine.[52] Contending that the Parousia was an invention of the early church, Glasson was able to reassert with Dodd the major view

---

[49] See Lewis Muirhead, *The Eschatology of Jesus* (1904), and E. von Dobschütze, *The Eschatology of the Gospels* (1910), as examples here (Ladd, *The Presence of the Future,* 11-12).

[50] *The Parables of the Kingdom,* 3d rev. ed. (London: Nisbet, 1936); C. H. Dodd, *The Apostolic Preaching and Its Developments* (London: Hodder and Stoughton, 1936).

[51] In subsequent works, Dodd moderated his anti-eschatological rhetoric to accept some residue of unrealized or futuristic eschatology in the Kerygma. "The Kingdom of God, while it is a present experience, remains also a hope, but a hope directed to a consummation beyond history" (Dodd, *The Founder of Christianity* [New York: Macmillan, 1970], 115). See Ladd, *Presence of the Future,* 20; and G. R. Beasley-Murray, "A Century of Eschatological Discussion," *ExpT* 64 (1952-1953): 315.

[52] *The Second Advent: The Origin of the New Testament Doctrine* (London: Epworth, 1945). Glasson has been a persistent voice against the apocalyptic Jesus of Schweitzer and Weiss throughout his scholarly career. See T. F. Glasson, "Apocalyptic: Some Current Delusions," *LonQR* (1952): 104-10; "The Kingdom as Cosmic Catastrophe," in *Studia Evangelica III* (Berlin: Akademie Verlag, 1964), 187-200; "Schweitzer's Influence—Blessing or Bane?" *JTS,* NS 28 (1977): 289-302; *Jesus and the End of the World* (Edinburgh: St. Andrews, 1980), and more recently, "The Temporary Messianic Kingdom and the Kingdom of God," *JTS,* NS 14 (1990): 517-25.

of church history that Jesus had transformed the material Jewish hope into a "spiritual" one. He said that the spiritual Kingdom was realized in Jesus' ministry and in the Spirit's coming at Pentecost to inaugurate the era of redemption enjoyed in the church on earth and in heaven. The Kingdom of God that Jesus taught was realized in the first century, and no further manifestations of it are to be expected. The early church's failure to relate the coming of the Spirit at Pentecost to their preconceived notions of the glorious reign of the Messiah is what motivated their composing the Gospels to include a second coming of the Son of Man.[53]

Existential Eschatology

Despite the resistance of Dodd and Anglo scholarship in general, the eschatological Jesus of Schweitzer marched on.[54] In the other twentieth-century reaction to it, Rudolf Bultmann chose to deal with the consistent eschatology of Jesus differently than Dodd.[55] Instead of denying future eschatology to Jesus as realized eschatology had done, Bultmann's Gospel criticism led him to the conclude that Jesus had in fact embraced the apocalyptic ideas of later Judaism.[56] Like Weiss, his teacher, Bultmann believed that for Jesus

> the kingdom of God transcends the historical order. It will come into being not through the moral endeavor of man, but solely through the supernatural action of God. God will suddenly put an end to the world

---

[53] See especially *The Second Advent*, 63-105; 161-178; 194; 202-205.

[54] Glasson, "Schweitzer's Influence," 296-97, offers interesting reasons for the success of the other-worldliness of Schweitzer's Kingdom, including the catastrophe of apocalyptic proportions that was World War I, the world-denying/world-affirming categories of the philosophies of Nietzsche and Schopenhauer, and the lack of a viable alternative to Ritschlian ethics.

[55] See Rudolf Bultmann, *Jesus and the Word*, trans. Louise Pettibone Smith and Erminie Huntress (New York: Scribner's, 1934; *Theology of the New Testament*, trans. Kendrick Grobel (New York: Scribner's, 1951; *The Presence of Eternity* (New York: Harpers, 1957); *Jesus Christ and Mythology* (New York: Scribner's, 1958). For secondary literature on Bultmann and the Kingdom of God see Hiers in *Kingdom of God in Twentieth-Century Interpretation*, ed. Willis, 24-31; Perrin, *Kingdom of God*, 112-29; Lundström, *Kingdom of God*, 146-55; Merkel, "Die Gottesherrschaft," 128-30.

[56] In *Theology of the New Testament*, 1:22, Bultmann stated that Dodd's realized eschatology "cannot be substantiated by a single saying of Jesus."

and to history, and he will bring in a new world, the world of eternal blessedness.[57]

However, unlike Weiss, who retreated into Ritschlian ethics when it came time to apply this Kingdom theologically, Bultmann took the meaning of the apocalyptic Kingdom in another direction. According to theological hermeneutics based in the existential paradigm of human Being, Bultmann did not grimace and withdraw from the poor, deluded, apocalyptic Jesus. Rather, he considered that Jesus' apocalyptic was to be welcomed by the exegete, but only if it was demythologized. According to Bultmann, the Kingdom of God was in fact dawning (*im Anbruch*) in Jesus' ministry, but modern humanity needed to understand what this meant. Bultmann assured his readers that Jesus was really speaking about human existence and the realization of Being via decision about God. Jesus' interests were not chronological, but existential. The Kingdom apocalyptically breaks in through the timeless confrontation of individuals in their world and challenges them to make a decision. Will they say yes to God and no to the world, or not? Both Jesus and the Kingdom of God he preached come back to this existential yes or no. The "myth" of the Kingdom, therefore, is the completely nontemporal, "transcendent event, which signifies for man the ultimate Either-Or, which constrains him to decision."[58]

> Jesus Christ is the eschatological event not as an established fact of past time but as repeatedly present as addressing you and me here and now in preaching. . . . Every instant has the possibility of being an eschatological instant and in Christian faith this possibility is realized.[59]

---

[57] *Jesus Christ and Mythology*, 12. Bultmann believed that Jewish apocalyptic literature also contained the traditional messianic hope of a renewed, earthly kingdom ruled by the Davidic king, but this was superseded by the other-worldly Son of Man in later Judaism. See "History and Eschatology in the New Testament," *NTS* 1 (1954-1955): 6. This "apocalyptic" Jesus, existentially interpreted, was still the view of Bultmann's more famous *Schüler* in the New Quest. See Perrin, *Kingdom of God*, 119-29, however, for a discussion of the movement in the New Quest towards a more realized understanding of the Kingdom than that of Bultmann.

[58] Bultmann, *Jesus and the Word*, 41.

[59] Bultmann, *Presence of Eternity*, 152, 154.

In Bultmann's project, the chasm separating faith and history started in Martin Kahler reaches its most radical point,[60] for neither the historical Jesus nor the ancient language of the Gospels matters in the true Christian message. While the docetic threat motivated a New Quest that was less radical towards the historical Jesus, the existential theology of Bultmann continued to enjoy popularity in Bultmann's students in, for example, the New Quest[61] and the more recent work of Herbert Braun.[62]

Realized and Future Eschatology

Partly in reaction to the suprahistorical school of Bultmann, and partially in an attempt to deal fairly with both future and present sayings of the Kingdom of God, a mediating position for the Kingdom of God arose after World War II. The Kingdom of God that Jesus preached came to be seen by many as both realized in the present *and* awaited in the future. In the person of Jesus the Kingdom is present as evidenced in his powers over the domain of Satan (as in Matt. 12:28/Luke 17:20, 21), but Jesus himself also looked forward to its eschatological and historical irruption in the future. Oscar Cullmann likened the situation to the memorable dates of the conclusion of World War II, D-Day, and VE-Day.[63] He said that Jesus, in casting out demons and in other activities of his ministry, demonstrated the decisive defeat of Satan's Kingdom by God's Kingdom (Luke 10:18— "I saw Satan fall like lightning from heaven"). This was D-Day for Satan's kingdom, just as June 6, 1944, was D-Day for the Third Reich. However, just as D-Day did not end the war immediately (VE-Day was eleven months later—May 8, 1945), so the Kingdom of God is now performing

---

[60] Martin Kahler, *The So-called Historical Jesus and the Historic Biblical Christ*, trans. and ed. Carl E. Braaten (Philadelphia: Fortress, 1988).

[61] For example, Hans Conzelmann, *An Outline of the Theology of the New Testament* (New York: Harper and Row, 1969), 114: "The contradiction between the 'present' and 'future' sayings is only an apparent one. The two have the same significance for human existence: man's attitude of the moment towards the kingdom of God. . . . Jesus concentrates the statements made in this imagery [signs of future and immediate inbreaking] on the meaning for existence." See also Günther Bornkamm, *Jesus of Nazareth*, trans. Irene and Fraser McLusky with James Robinson (New York: Harper & Row, 1960).

[62] Herbert Braun, *Jesus of Nazareth*, trans. E. R. Kalin (Philadelphia: Fortress, 1979).

[63] Oscar Cullmann, *Christ and Time*, trans. Floyd V. Filson (Philadelphia: Westminster, 1950).

"mopping up" activities until the day of final and complete defeat at the coming of the Kingdom of God in glory and power. This will be Victory-Day for the Kingdom of God.

While Cullmann's memorable metaphor struck a certain popular chord, the work of W. G. Kümmel[64] made the most impact in the scholarly world in initiating the mediating position.[65] Through careful exegesis, Kümmel tried to establish that the ideas of the presence and the future of the Kingdom of God were side-by-side in Jesus' message. Matthew 11:12 ("From the days of John the Baptist until now the Kingdom of heaven suffers violence and violent men take it by force") is a clear indication that the Kingdom is present, because men can attack it.[66] He also sought to establish Jesus as a legitimate "futurist" who looked for one final redemptive act of God in history, even within his own generation.[67] He held that Jesus, of course, was wrong at this point, but the fulfillment of the Old Testament promise in Jesus allows the Kingdom of God to become a reality and still remain as a promise of God that history will be consummated.

Another early voice seeking to make sense of the Kingdom as both present and future was Joachim Jeremias. In his monograph *Jesus als Weltvollender*,[68] Jeremias clearly ties the Kingdom of God to the person of Jesus. Jesus, Jeremias said, claimed to be and also acted as the inaugurator of the long-promised era of the world's salvation. Possessed of the Holy Spirit, calling himself the Son of Man ("the new man"), purifying his temple, and, above all, breaking the power of the one who had enslaved the world to evil, Jesus was the unique bearer of the ultimately future dominion of God in the present.[69] Jesus was thoroughly eschatological, but in his person that

---

[64] See his *Promise and Fulfillment: The Evangelical Message of Jesus*, trans. Dorothea M. Barton, Studies in Biblical Theology 23 (Naperville, Ill.: Alec R. Anderson, 1957).

[65] See Eldon Jay Epp, "Mediating Approaches to the Kingdom: Werner Georg Kümmel and George Eldon Ladd," in *Kingdom of God in Twentieth-Century Interpretation*, 35-52.

[66] See the third chapter of *Promise and Fulfillment*, "The Presence of the Kingdom of God," 105-40.

[67] Kümmel's discussion of the linguistic differences between *ēngiken* and *ephthasen* (*Promise and Fulfillment*, 105-9) is generally credited with having laid to rest the contention of Dodd that the two terms were synonymous.

[68] Joachim Jeremias, *Jesus als Weltvollender*, Beiträge zur Förderung christlicher Theologie 28 (Gütersloh: Bertelsmann, 1930). See also the comments of Lundström, *Kingdom of God*, 204.

[69] *Jesus als Weltvollender*, 60 (cited by Lundström, *Kingdom of God*, 204).

eschatological Kingdom of God is on earth. Jesus is now gathering the community of the last days about him; in the final consummation the evil one will be completely destroyed. In his office as Savior, the Kingdom Jesus brought is visible right now to his faithful ones, whom he nourishes and protects.

Later in his career Jeremias produced a landmark study on the parables in which he modified the position of Dodd by means of the oft-quoted tag: "eine sich realisierende Eschatologie" (eschatology in the process of realization).[70] To Jeremias, the parables left no doubt as to the Kingdom's presence, but it was not so easy, as Dodd had maintained, to remove all references to the future from their original form. In fact, two bodies of evidence demanded a future eschatology from the parables. First, there were the parables which looked forward to the future culmination of something begun in the present. These parables, such as those of the mustard seed, the leaven, the sower, and the patient husbandman, teach hope from the assurance of the approach of God's final solution.[71] In the second category establishing the future eschatology of the parables, Jeremias included the parables of crisis in which Jesus warns of the imminence of catastrophe. The parables of the children in the marketplace (Matt. 11:16–19) and the signs of the times (Luke 12:54–56), and the references to Sodom and Gomorrah (Luke 17:28–30) and the Flood (Matt. 24:37–39), are all warnings to Jesus' contemporaries of a coming cataclysmic rearrangement of the world's systems under the Kingdom of God.[72]

An Emerging Consensus

Modern discussion about the nature of the Kingdom of God that Jesus preached was particularly spirited during the first sixty years of the

---

[70] Joachim Jeremias, *Die Gleichnisse Jesu* (Zürich: Zwingli, 1947). The English edition is *The Parables of Jesus*, 2d rev. ed., trans. S. H. Hooke (New York: Scribner's, 1966), 230. See Perrin, *The Kingdom of God*, 80–81. Jeremias credits the German form of the expression to Ernst Haenchen, who communicated it to him in a letter (*Parables of Jesus*, 230, n. 3). Here he also notes with pleasure that Dodd found the term agreeable in his *Interpretation of the Fourth Gospel* (Cambridge: Cambridge University Press, 1953), 447, n. 1.

[71] Jeremias, *Parables of Jesus*, 146–60.

[72] Ibid., 160–69.

twentieth century. During this time the eschatological pendulum swung from the one extreme of a purely eschatological Kingdom to the other extreme of a totally realized one, with many stops in between. However, since World War II, the positions of those like Cullman, Kümmel, and Jeremias began gaining momentum towards forging a scholarly consensus about an Already-but-Not-Yet Kingdom of God. The amassed evidence was seen as pointing to the Kingdom as having multiple temporal dimensions. In some way it was present with Christ and in some way it was still future. In just what way the Kingdom was present and future was still a matter for debate, but at least this issue seemed settled by the early 1960s.[73] George E. Ladd and Hermann Ridderbos, who wrote in the early sixties as adherents of this mediating position, both note the ascendency of the Already/Not Yet Kingdom among the commentators at that time. Ladd considered it "an emerging consensus,"[74] while Ridderbos noted this view is finding "expression in all kinds of ways in recent literature."[75] In 1963, Perrin was more hesitant to say that a consensus had been reached, but he does comment that most scholars of his day view the Kingdom as somehow both present and future.[76]

A look at the debate over the last thirty years reveals what was only in the ascent at the time of Ladd and Ridderbos now is much more solidly entrenched. In his more recent summary of the history of the Kingdom of God research (1985), I. Howard Marshall has noted no change in the

---

[73] There was even a shifting of the ground beneath the existential interpretation of Bultmann. Whereas Bultmann had derived his existential theology from the Kingdom as a purely future entity, his student and member of the New Quest Ernst Fuchs admitted that the presence of the Kingdom in the parables was also historical, kerygmatic ground for the existential meaning of the Kingdom in the present (Ernst Fuchs, "Jesus' Understanding of Time," in *Studies of the Historical Jesus*, trans. Andrew Scobie, Studies in Biblical Theology 42 [Naperville, Ill.: Alec R. Allenson, 1964] 122-23). See Perrin, *Kingdom of God*, 122-23.

[74] Ladd cites an impressive list of more than thirty scholars taking this view from the early 1950s to 1968 (*Presence of the Future*, 38-39, n. 161).

[75] Ridderbos, *Coming of the Kingdom*, xxvii, classifies this position as "christological" for those who see the Kingdom of God present in the person of Christ.

[76] Perrin, *Kingdom of God*, 159.

consensus of the "present or fulfilled and future or consummated" position.[77] Such a statement may appear bold, especially to some like Bruce Chilton, Marcus Borg, and the members of the Jesus Seminar who have been recently advocating a nontemporal and noneschatological Jesus, but even these will concede their battle against the eschatological consensus is uphill right now.[78]

HERMENEUTICAL ISSUES: PREUNDERSTANDING AND LANGUAGE

Many of those challenging the consensual view of the Kingdom in the last thirty years have been profoundly affected by developments in philosophical hermeneutics. Two developments in particular have challenged the historical-critical hermeneutic practiced by most of those in the preceding survey of the Kingdom: (1) the nature and impact of the interpreter's preunderstanding to the hermeneutical process, and (2) the priority of language as the locus of hermeneutical meaning. Before discussing the impact of these two themes in recent biblical studies of the Kingdom, I will chronicle their intellectual lineage through the modern period. The following account is admittedly selective of thinkers in philosophical hermeneutics, but the works of Friedrich Schleiermacher, Wilhelm Dilthey, Martin Heidegger, and Hans-Georg Gadamer have particular importance for the two themes of preunderstanding and language. They are the intellectual forefathers of significant discussions of the Kingdom of God since 1960.

---

77 I. Howard Marshall, "The Hope of a New Age: The Kingdom of God in the New Testament," *Themelios* 11, no. 1 (1985): 5. On the consensus more recently, see Marinus de Jonge, "The Christological Significance of Jesus' Preaching of the Kingdom of God," in *The Future of Christology: Essays in Honor of Leander E. Keck*, ed. Abraham J. Malherbe and Wayne A. Meeks (Minneapolis: Fortress, 1993), 7; and G. N. Stanton, *The Gospels and Jesus* (Oxford: Oxford University Press, 1989), 191-92.

78 Of this group, many are not trying to overthrow the consensus, but are attempting to work within it to deemphasize the eschatological in favor of the present or transcendent. Chilton, for example, admits the present and future in Jesus (i.e., the "eschatological consensus"), but sees this "flexibility" in the Kingdom's timing as a sign that the Kingdom is ultimately transcendent and nontemporal (Chilton, introduction to *Kingdom of God*, 26).

Biblical hermeneutics, the science of biblical interpretation, entered the modern period through the work of Friedrich Schleiermacher (1768–1834).[79] Schleiermacher was the first to advocate a hermeneutical method that was sensitive to both author and reader. A correct interpretation, Schleiermacher contended, required both in-depth knowledge of the cultural/historical context of the author and a grasp of the author's subjective consciousness. Accomplishment of this last object meant the reader needed to relive the author's experience and find common ground in his or her own experience.[80] Schleiermacher suggested the priority of language as the medium for the reader to return to the experience of the author, and, consequently, that the nature of language was the crucial theoretical issue confronting hermeneutics.[81] Schleiermacher also argued that an important place also needed to be given to the reader's preunderstanding of reality if common ground with the author could be recognized.

Wilhelm Dilthey (1833–1911), philosopher and literary historian, is most

---

[79] Friedrich Schleiermacher, *Hermeneutics: The Handwritten Manuscripts*, ed. Heinz Kimmerle, trans. James Duke and Jack Forstman, American Academy of Religion Texts and Translations 1 (Missoula, Mont.: Scholars, 1977). Schleiermacher is credited with having inaugurated the *philosophical* discussion of hermeneutics (Dilthey referred to him as the "Kant of Hermeneutics." Cf. Van A. Harvey, "Hermeneutics," in *Encyclopedia of Religion*, ed. Mircea Eliade [New York: Macmillan, 1987], 6:281) wherein reflection begins to encompass broader issues of human understanding, which traditionally had been considered under epistemology. See Randy L. Maddox, "Contemporary Hermeneutic Philosophy and Theological Studies," *RelSt* 21 (1985): 517-29. Important surveys of modern hermeneutics include Josef Bleicher, *Contemporary Hermeneutics* (London: Routledge and Kegan Paul, 1980); Roy Howard, *Three Faces of Hermeneutics* (Berkeley: University of California Press, 1982); Richard Palmer, *Hermeneutics: Interpretation Theory in Schleiermacher, Dilthey, Heidegger, and Gadamer* (Evanston, Ill.: Northwestern University Press, 1969); Anthony C. Thiselton, *The Two Horizons: New Testament Hermeneutics and Philosophical Description* (Grand Rapids: Eerdmans, 1980); Thiselton, *New Horizons in Hermeneutics: The Theory and Practice of Transforming Biblical Reading* (Grand Rapids: Zondervan, 1992); and Claus v. Bormann, Ludwig Schmidt, and Henning Schröer, "Hermeneutik," *TRE*, 15:108-56.

[80] Schleiermacher, *Hermeneutics*, 42, n. 8; 44, n. 19.

[81] "Language is the only presupposition in hermeneutics, and everything that is to be found, including the other objective and subjective presuppositions, must be discovered in language" (Schleiermacher, *Hermeneutics*, 50, n. 55). See H.-Georg Gadamer, "The Problem of Language in Schleiermacher's Hermeneutic," *JTChu* 7 (1970): 68-95. Schleiermacher's influence on modern hermeneutics at this point is evident from Lapointe's assessment that "language constitutes a veritable cross-roads of modernity" (Lapointe, "Hermeneutics Today," 119).

known for his reflections on the hermeneutical foundation of the human sciences (*Geisteswissenschaften*).[82] For Dilthey, the different nature of the human sciences when compared to the natural sciences was the locus for solving the hermeneutical problem of the human sciences. Since the human sciences study agents moved by intentions, purposes, wishes, and individual character traits, the universal human nature shared by the interpreter is key for interpretation in the human sciences. The universal human nature meant that the modern interpreter could relive the past experiences of the subject and make them their own. Like Schleiermacher before him, Dilthey said this reliving of the past was central to the hermeneutic act of understanding.[83] Dilthey also agreed with Schleiermacher on the priority of language as the means of recovering the inner life of the human agents of the past. To his way of thinking, the hermeneutical task had to focus on written texts because "in language alone does what is inside man finds its complete, exhaustive and objectively intelligible expression. Hence the art of understanding has its center in the interpretation of the remains for human Beings which are contained in writing."[84]

The work of the great philosopher of Being (*Dasein*), Martin Heidegger (1889–1976), next advances the hermeneutical discussions of Schleiermacher

---

[82] Wilhelm Dilthey, *Gesammelte Schriften* (Stuttgart: Teubner, 1962). For important studies of Dilthey see Rudolf A. Makkreel, *Dilthey, Philosopher of Human Studies* (Princeton: Princeton University Press, 1975); H. A. Hodges, *The Philosophy of Wilhelm Dilthey* (London: Routledge & Kegan Paul, 1952); Hodges, *Wilhelm Dilthey: An Introduction* (London: Kegan Paul, Trench & Trubner, 1944); and H. N. Tuttle, *Wilhelm Dilthey's Philosophy of Historical Understanding: A Critical Analysis* (Leiden: E. J. Brill, 1969).

[83] "Verstehen" (understanding) and "Erklaren" (explaining) are the two categories Dilthey assigned to the task of the human sciences and the natural sciences respectively. "Understanding" has been the recognized objective of philosophical hermeneutics ever since (Maddox, "Hermeneutic Philosophy and Theological Studies," 518, n. 1). Dilthey stated, "Understanding is a rediscovery of the I in the Thou; Mind is found in higher degrees by relationship; this identity of mind in the I, in the Thou, in every subject of a community, in every system of culture, finally in the totality of mind and of world history, makes possible the joint result of the various operations performed in the human studies. The knowing subject is here one with its object, and this is true for all gradations of objectification" (Dilthey, *Gesammelte Schriften*, 6:191 [author's translation]).

[84] Dilthey, *Gesammelte Schriften*, 5:319 (author's translation).

and Dilthey.[85] From the side of the interpreter, Heidegger acknowledges and even welcomes the "World"[86] the interpreter brings to the hermeneutic process. In his mind, this preunderstanding happens only as new material is matched to something that has already been understood.[87] This is the nature of human Being.[88] From the side of the text or author, in his later works Heidegger also focuses on the importance of language because of its significance "in the sharing of communication between human persons."[89] Language is the medium or "event" through which Being becomes

---

[85] The phenomenological method of investigating the "fundamental ontology" that is *Dasein* remained Heidegger's project throughout his life. In the introduction of *Sein und Zeit* (1927), Eng. ed. *Being and Time*, trans. John Macquarrie and Edward Robinson (New York/Evanston, Ill.: Harper & Row, 1962), Heidegger first treats the necessity, structure, and priority of the question of Being (1-35), and then moves to the discussion of his methodology and nature of his program proper (36-66). In one of his later works, *Unterwegs zur Sprache* (1959), Eng. ed. *On the Way to Language*, trans. Peter D. Hertz (San Francisco: Harper & Row, 1971), 30, which is considered in the period of the "later" Heidegger (see Thiselton's discussion in *Two Horizons*, 327-29), Heidegger reiterates, "What mattered then [in *Being and Time*], and still does, is to bring out the Being of beings—though no longer in the manner of metaphysics, but such that Being itself will shine out, Being itself—that is to say: the presence of present beings, the two-fold of the two in virtue of their simple oneness. That is what makes its claim on man, calling him to essential being."

[86] "World" for Heidegger does not consist of the entities of nature but of the ontological reality of those natural things (*Being and Time*, 91ff.). See also the discussion of "World" and "Worldhood" in Thiselton (*Two Horizons*, 154-61) and Palmer (*Hermeneutics*, 132-34).

[87] In Heidegger's work "Understanding" signifies the deeper ontological structures which make the *Verstehen* of Dilthey possible (Heidegger, *Being and Time*, 182ff.). For Dilthey understanding was the level of comprehension involved in grasping something as an expression of the "inner realities" of people. Heidegger, on the other hand, would see understanding ontologically as the "structure in being which makes possible the actual exercise of understanding on an empirical level" (Palmer, *Hermeneutics*, 131).

[88] The "World" of individuals is a "unitary phenomenon" with *Dasein*. It is one of the structures through which *Dasein* exists or "takes on character" (Heidegger, *Being and Time*, 78).

[89] Thiselton, *Two Horizons*, 168. See Heidegger, *Being and Time*, 205, "Communication is never anything like a conveying of experiences, such as opinions or wishes, from the interior of one subject into the interior of another. Dasein-with is already essentially manifest in a co-state-of-mind and a co-understanding. In discourse Being-with becomes 'explicitly' *shared;* that is to say, it *is* already, but it is unshared as something that has not been taken hold of and appropriated." Major works of the later Heidegger that consider language are *An Introduction to Metaphysics*, trans. Ralph Manheim (New Haven: Yale University Press, 1959), and *On the Way to Language*.

most visible in another person.[90] As such, language has a "gathering power" to collect the reality of the author beyond the symbols of language.[91] Texts, therefore, have a life of their own. They call out for readers to listen to the disclosure of Being expressed in them.

In 1960 Hans-Georg Gadamer published his magisterial *Wahrheit und Methode: Grundzüge einer philosophischen Hermeneutik.*[92] Central to Gadamer's resolution of the hermeneutic problem is his belief that all interpretation takes places within a polarity of what is familiar to the interpreter and what is not. As Heidegger before him, Gadamer held that the presuppositionless interpreter was an impossibility, but at the same time, not necessarily something negative.[93] Literary texts, in Gadamer's understanding, are not lifeless and static entities to be deciphered by the historian. This indeed was the whole problem with the hermeneutics of the Enlightenment as typified by Dilthey, who "ultimately conceives inquiring in to the historical past *as deciphering and not as historical experience.*"[94] Interpretation as experience (*Erfahrung*) speaks to what Gadamer means about the dynamic life or "presentness" of texts to the modern reader. As language (along with other art forms) is one of the means Being is disclosed, the language of the text is the window into the "world" implicit in the individual words used.[95] Texts therefore are events (*Ereignis*) of Being; they gather and communicate the meaning of Being beyond even what the

---

[90] We note here Heidegger's memorable concept of language as the "house of Being." See, for example, Heidegger, *On the Way to Language*, 5, 21, 22, 26. See Thiselton, *Two Horizons*, 335-42.

[91] See "Language in the Poem" in *On the Way to Language*, 159-98, where Heidegger demonstrates the gathering power of Georg Trakl's poetry.

[92] Hans-Georg Gadamer, *Wahrheit und Methode: Grundzüge einer philosophischen Hermeneutik* (Tübingen: J. C. B. Mohr [Paul Siebeck], 1960); English edition, *Truth and Method*, 2d rev. ed., trans. Joel Weinsheimer and Donald G. Marshall (New York: Crossroad, 1989).

[93] The key concept with one's presuppositions was not to deny or try to discard them but to use them: "it is right for the interpreter not to approach the text directly, relying solely on the fore-meaning already available to him, but rather explicitly to examine the legitimacy-i.e., the origin and validity—of the fore-meaning dwelling within him" (Gadamer, *Truth and Method*, 267).

[94] Ibid., 214 (italics his).

[95] Gadamer develops these ideas in the third part of *Truth and Method*, "The Ontological Shift of Hermeneutics Guided by Language," 381ff.

author understood at the time of writing.[96] Consequently, texts have an existence of their own independent of the original occasion, which may be "experience" as the interpreter steps into the text's world and confronts the reality of Being contained there.[97] A "fusion of horizons" takes place when the interpreter has a "conversation" with the text. True understanding happens as both text and interpreter make their contributions to the disclosure of Being.[98]

In the pages of *Truth and Method* philosophical hermeneutics attained new heights that would affect the disciplines of aesthetics, law, philosophy, and theology for years to come.[99] In New Testament hermeneutics Gadamer is ultimately significant because he represents a movement where meaning is less and less concerned with the author and more and more a feature of the reader. As the last thirty years will demonstrate, this element of this particular movement would eventually eliminate the author's voice altogether[100] and at the same time increasingly marginalize itself from the mainstream of New Testament studies. Nevertheless, in 1960 the "fusion of horizons" and language as the medium for the disclosure of Being were indeed powerful medicine for New Testament scholars suffering malaise from existing trends in hermeneutics. The ontological importance of language, as enunciated by Heidegger and Gadamer, would

---

[96] "It sounds at first like a sensible hermeneutical rule-and is generally recognized as such—that nothing should be put into a text that the writer or the reader could not have intended. But this rule can be applied only in extreme cases. For texts do not ask to be understood as a living expression of the subjectivity of their writers. This, then, cannot define the limits of a text's meaning" (ibid., 395).

[97] Gadamer sees the act of play as a model for this dynamic. Players and games both have worlds of their own that interface in the act of playing a game. Play happens as the player submits to the game's world, that is, the rules. The game proceeds according to the player effecting decisions and behavior from his own world in light of the game's world. See ibid., 101ff.

[98] Ibid., 306-7; 374-75.

[99] Von Bormann recognizes *Truth and Method* as the dominating statement on the issue in Germany throughout the 1960s and 1970s (*TRE*, 15:125).

[100] See the excellent review of the development of the reader's perspective in structuralist, poststructuralist, and deconstructive thought in Grant Osborne, *The Hermeneutical Spiral: A Comprehensive Introduction to Biblical Interpretation* (Downers Grove, Ill.: InterVarsity Press, 1991), 369-85.

motivate these scholars to kindle afresh the quest for something they thought they had lost forever: the historical Jesus.

THE QUEST OF THE HISTORICAL JESUS

Ernst Käsemann's call to his fellow old Marburgers in 1954 for a "new quest of the historical Jesus" was the watershed event for what would ultimately be a striking marriage of philosophical hermeneutics and study of the life of Jesus and the Kingdom he proclaimed.[101] What made the event so stunning was that prior to this announcement the quest for the historical Jesus topped the list of all things thought obsolete because of Bultmann's form criticism and demythologizing program. For Bultmann, not only was the historical Jesus unrecoverable from the New Testament documents, but such a project was neither necessary nor profitable for faith.[102] Consequently, in Germany there had been relative disinterest in the historical Jesus for decades.[103] However, as Käsemann explained, the years of disinterest had precipitated an uneasiness among New Testament scholars that radical demythologization undermined something fundamental to Christianity. Cutting the anchor of the Christian religion from the historical

---

[101] See Ernst Käsemann, "Das Problem des historischen Jesus," *ZTK* 51 (1954): 123-53. The English edition was published as "The Problem of the Historical Jesus," in *Essays on New Testament Themes* (Philadelphia: Fortress, 1982), 15-48.

[102] Bultmann's ideas on the subject of the historical Jesus are detailed in these important works: *Jesus and the Word*; "New Testament and Mythology," in *Kerygma and Myth: A Theological Debate*, ed. H. E. Bartsch (London: SPCK, 1953), 1-44; along with his rejoinder to the New Quest in "The Primitive Christian Kerygma and the Historical Jesus," in *The Historical Jesus and the Kerygmatic Christ*, ed. and trans. C. E. Braaten and R. A. Harrisville (Nashville: Abingdon, 1964), 15-42.

[103] Though this is not so in French and Anglo-Saxon scholarship, as is evidenced by Robinson's extensive bibliography of various "lives of Christ" written in the first half of this century (James M. Robinson, *A New Quest of the Historical Jesus and Other Essays* [Philadelphia: Fortress, 1983], 9-10, n. 2). Nevertheless, it is commonplace to consider Albert Schweitzer's *Von Reimarus zu Wrede* (1906) as having ended the "first" quest of the historical Jesus (cf. Stephen Neill and N. Thomas Wright, *The Interpretation of the New Testament 1861-1986* [New York: Oxford University Press, 1988], 379-403), though his work actually added one more portrait to the nineteenth-century gallery.

personage whose name it bore threatened to set Christianity adrift into the murky waters of a docetic sea.

Käsemann's call to his fellow Marburgers was answered first by Günther Bornkamm, whose *Jesus von Nazareth* appeared in November 1956.[104] Firmly fixed in the conclusions of form criticism as to the nature of the Gospel documents,[105] Bornkamm nevertheless broke ranks in contending that the sources were not totally negligible in yielding the "personality and career of Jesus." As he saw it, the task he was optimistically undertaking was "to compile the main historically indisputable traits, and to present the rough outlines of Jesus' person and history."[106] The result was the existentially robed Jesus of Bultmann who brings an end to the world each hearer knows and makes possible "a new present" through decision about the future.[107]

The New Hermeneutic

While Bornkamm and others[108] took up Käsemann's gauntlet to search for the authentic Jesus from the Gospel record of Jesus' deeds and teaching, Ernst Fuchs and Gerhard Ebeling approached the challenge from another angle. Guided by the philosophical hermeneutics of Heidegger and Gadamer, they began to look for the historical Jesus through the

---

[104] Günther Bornkamm, *Jesus von Nazareth* (Stuttgart: W. Kohlhammer, 1956); Eng. ed. *Jesus of Nazareth*.

[105] The third chapter begins: "The nature of the sources does not permit us to paint a biographical picture of the life of Jesus against the background of the history of his people and his age" (Bornkamm, *Jesus of Nazareth*, 53).

[106] Ibid., 53.

[107] "The story told by the Gospels signifies the end of the world, although not, it is true, in the sense of an obvious drama and a visible catastrophe. . . . In the encounter with Jesus, time is left to no one: the past whence he comes is no longer confirmed, and the future he dreams of no longer assured. But this is precisely why every individual is granted his own new present. For life, work and the existence of every individual now stand in the sudden flash of light of the coming God, in the light of his reality and presence. This is the theme which Jesus proclaims" (ibid., 62-63).

[108] For example, Braun, *Jesus of Nazareth*, Hans Conzelmann, *Jesus*, ed. J. Reumann, trans. J. R. Lord (Philadelphia: Fortress, 1973); and W. Marxsen, *The Beginnings of Christology*, trans. P. J. Achtemeier and L. Nieting (Philadelphia: Fortress, 1979).

linguistic phenomena of the Gospels.[109] Under the auspices of a "New Hermeneutic,"[110] Fuchs and Ebeling considered the Gospels not as repositories of the actual words of Jesus but as legitimate guides to the *word* of Jesus. They reasoned that because of the nature of language as the revealer of true Being, it ought to be possible to work backwards from the language-events of the Gospels, that is, the early church's Kerygma, to the aims, the decisions, and the conduct of their ultimate author: the historical Jesus.[111]

Thus, in two important ways the New Hermeneutic builds upon the foundation laid in Schleiermacher that continued through the work of Heidegger and Gadamer. First, the preunderstanding of the interpreter is critical to the hermeneutical process. Especially reflective of Gadamer's "fusion of horizons," Fuchs and Ebeling considered the hermeneutical process as a dialogue between the world of the text and the world of the interpreter, where the interpreter's presuppositions were admitted and welcomed. Understanding[112] was achieved as both "worlds" questioned back and forth

---

[109] Fuchs's important works here are *Zum hermeneutischen Problem in der Theologie* (Tübingen: J. C. B. Mohr [Paul Siebeck], 1959); *Zur Frage nach dem historischen Jesus* (Tübingen: J. C. B. Mohr [Paul Siebeck], 1960) (partly translated as *Studies of the Historical Jesus*, [London: SCM, 1964]); "The New Testament and the Hermeneutical Problem" in *The New Hermeneutic*, 111-45; *Marburger Hermeneutik* (Tübingen: J. C. B. Mohr [Paul Siebeck], 1968); *Hermeneutik* (Tübingen: J. C. B. Mohr [Paul Siebeck], 1970); "The Hermeneutical Problem," in *The Future of Our Religious Past: Essays in Honour of Rudolf Bultmann*, ed. James M. Robinson (London: SCM, 1971), 267-78. For Ebeling see "Hermeneutik," *RGG*, 3: cols. 242-62; *The Nature of Faith*, trans. Ronald Gregor Smith (Philadelphia: Muhlenberg, 1961); *Word and Faith*, trans. James W. Leitch (Philadelphia: Fortress, 1963); *Theology and Proclamation: A Discussion with Rudolf Bultmann*, trans. John Riches (Philadelphia: Fortress, 1966); *God and Word*, trans. James W. Leitch (Philadelphia: Fortress, 1967); *The Problem of Historicity in the Church and Its Proclamation*, trans. Grover Foley (Philadelphia: Fortress, 1967); *The Word of God and Tradition: Historical Studies Interpreting the Divisions of Christianity*, trans. S. H. Hooke (Philadelphia: Fortress, 1968); "Time and Word," in *The Future of Our Religious Past*, 247-66; *Introduction to a Theological Theory of Language*, trans. R. A. Wilson (London: Collins, 1973).

[110] The singular term *hermeneutic* is thought to reintroduce the true depth and fullness of the Greek *hērmēneia*, which originally encompassed the "the interpretive interrelatedness of language, translation, and exegesis." *Hermeneutics*, on the other hand, came to represent the narrowed focus of exegesis alone (Robinson, "Hermeneutic Since Barth," 9-10; 39ff.)

[111] Fuchs, "The Quest of the Historical Jesus,"in *Studies*, 30, says, "The so-called Christ of faith is none other than the historical Jesus." See also Robinson, *New Quest of the Historical Jesus*, 39-41, 69.

[112] "Understanding" in the terms of Heidegger, not Dilthey.

in what Fuchs called the phenomenon of *Einverständnis*.[113] *Einverständnis* has been variously translated as "common understanding," "mutual understanding," and even "empathy"; for Fuchs it signifies the precognitive interface of text and interpreter that grounds all understanding. Similar to Gadamer's "world" of playing a game, Fuchs illustrates *Einverständnis* in terms of the "world" of a home. He observes that a close-knit family, because of its common assumptions, ideas, and experiences, shares a common language. The common language means therefore, that "at home one does not speak so that people may understand, but because people understand."[114] As Fuchs sees it, the hermeneutical process is the wrestling of the text and the interpreter until this phenomenon of *Einverständnis* occurs and the possibilities of understanding can be realized.

The result of the New Hermeneutic's concept of *Einverständnis* has bearing on the subject-object relationship of the text and the interpreter. Namely, since text and interpreter are equal partners in the process of understanding, both are equally the subjects and objects of interpretation. Thus, as Fuchs contends, "The text is itself meant to live,"[115] which means consequently, "*The truth has us ourselves as its object.*"[116] When the text interprets the interpreter, then the message of the text speaks anew and is relevant.[117]

This last concept of the interpreter as listener depends on a prior hermeneutical proposition upon which the New Hermeneutic builds: the meaning and role of language. Again reiterating a theme first introduced to the modern discussion by Schleiermacher, Fuchs and Ebeling look to language as the key to the hermeneutic process. On this count, Ebeling makes a significant statement in the New Hermeneutic when he declares, "*The primary phenomenon in the realm of understanding is not understanding OF language, but understanding THROUGH language.*"[118] Understanding

---

[113] Fuchs, "The Hermeneutical Problem," in *Studies*, 267-68.

[114] Fuchs, "The New Testament and the Hermeneutical Problem," in *Studies*, 124.

[115] Fuchs, "Theology of the New Testament and the Historical Jesus," in *Studies*, 193.

[116] Fuchs, "The New Testament and the Hermeneutical Problem," in *Studies*, 143 (italics his).

[117] That the New Testament be relevant to the modern reader was the driving passion of Fuchs and Ebeling, who both spent many years in the pastorate. See Anthony C. Thiselton, "The New Hermeneutic," in *New Testament Interpretation*, ed. I. Howard Marshall (Grand Rapids: Eerdmans, 1977), 308.

[118] Ebeling, *Word and Faith*, 318.

through language comes from the belief that, as in Heidegger, "Language . . . makes being into an event."[119] In the New Testament we are not confronted with mere words, but the *word* of faith (i.e., a word-event) embedded in the early Christian Kerygma. This language-event (*Sprachereignis*) has a performative function of communicating the reality of God who promises, demands, or gives something in the present.[120] Thus, "the text is . . . not just the servant that transmits kerygmatic formulations, but rather a master that directs us into the language-context of our existence."[121] The words of Jesus recorded in the text, while not his words, still encompass the event of Being of which he did take part. So, not only does New Testament language have impact for the reader's reality, it is the window through which Jesus' reality is also visible.

As might be suspected, the parables of Jesus were the most fruitful quarries for the methodology of the New Hermeneutic. Fuchs and several of his students produced extensive studies probing the language-events of the parables for the realities of human existence that gripped not only the historical Jesus but the modern reader as well.[122] In Fuchs's thinking, the parables are the perfect example of the meaning of language in New Testament hermeneutics.[123] In them one observes Jesus enter the "world" of his first-century listeners by his reference to common features of their life. The "world" of the businessman, the farmer, or the housewife in the "picture-part" of the parable is where Jesus creates *Einverständnis* with his hearers. He engages them in what is common in their respective "worlds." Once the hearer's horizon has been entered, Jesus can then challenge and shatter the hearer's presupposition about reality through the substance of

---

[119] Ernst Fuchs, "What Is a Language-Event?" in *Studies*, 207.

[120] Ernst Fuchs, "What Is Interpreted in the Exegesis of the New Testament?" in *Studies*, 91, 93.

[121] Fuchs, "What Is a Language-Event?" 211.

[122] See for example, Ernst Fuchs, "The Parable of the Unmerciful Servant," in *Studia Evangelica I*, ed. Kurt Aland et al. (Berlin: Akademie Verlag, 1959), and the work of his students, Eta Linnemann, *Jesus of the Parables: Introduction and Exposition*, trans. John Sturdy (New York: Harper & Row, 1966), and Eberhard Jüngel, *Paulus und Jesus. Eine Untersuchung zur Präzierung der Frage nach dem Ursprung der Christologie* (Tübingen: J. C. B. Mohr [Paul Siebeck], 1967). See also James M. Robinson, "Jesus' Parables as God Happening," *Jesus and the Historian*, ed. F. Thomas Trotter (Philadelphia: Westminster, 1968), 134-50.

[123] Fuchs, "The New Testament and the Hermeneutical Problem," 126.

the parable. In the parable of the laborers in the vineyard (Matt. 20:1–16),[124] the crowds know well the exigencies of casual day labor as the vineyard owner goes about hiring for the day. However, when it comes time to receive wages, the crowds' expectations are challenged because those who worked little received the same as those who worked longest. The audience is opened up to true reality of human Being as the effect of the language-event is brought home in Jesus' challenge: "Is your eye evil because I am kind?" Far better than any discourse on grace or the kindness of God, the parable as a language event reached out and grasped the hearer with the reality that hope can only be based on an act of God's kindness.[125]

The parables also reveal the historical Jesus in his own intentions, decisions, and understanding of his situation. Proponents of the New Hermeneutic are prepared to speak of Jesus' personal faith and his own decisions. Jesus' challenge to the crowd in the parable of the laborers and the vineyard reveals his own decision to wager everything on the grace of God. For the New Hermeneutic, this was no mere psychologizing. Ebeling's answer to the psychologizing charge from Bultmann contended that because of the word-event feature of language, the subject is necessarily involved in the object, and the person is necessarily involved in his word. When Jesus calls for a decision, that call is a reflection of a decision he himself has already made.[126]

The Importance of the New Hermeneutic and New Quest for the Kingdom of God Since 1960

When Norman Perrin finished his work on *The Kingdom of God and the Teaching of Jesus* in the early 1960s, the New Quest of the historical Jesus as pursued through the New Hermeneutic was just getting underway. At that time Perrin's qualified judgment could only be that "it is far too soon to be able to judge the long-term significance of the approach of which [Fuchs] is the leading representative, but one tribute must be paid to it: it offers a

---

[124] See Ernst Fuchs, "The Reflection Which Is Imposed on Theology by the Historical-Critical Method," *Studies*, 32-38; Fuchs, "Jesus' Understanding of Time," *Studies*, 154-56.

[125] Fuchs, "The Reflection Imposed on Theology," 33-37.

[126] "The nature of the word-event of the proclamation of faith cannot be defined without a close examination of the way in which the preacher is drawn into the event of the proclamation in which 'person' and 'subject-matter' are interrelated" (Ebeling, *Theology and Proclamation*, 128-29).

most challenging presentation of Jesus."[127] Even though the mark of the
New Hermeneutic did appear on Perrin's later work on the Kingdom
theme,[128] it was only fifteen years after *The Kingdom of God and the Teaching of Jesus* that he was offering the New Hermeneutic's postmortem in
Jesus and the Language of the Kingdom. In this later assessment, the New
Hermeneutic is eulogized for its concern for the historical Jesus as the
author of the parables[129] but criticized for its rush to theological conclusions. In Perrin's mind, the attention paid to New Testament language for
the disclosure of Being was right on target, but the New Hermeneutic
failed by being satisfied with something short of the goal. He states,

> There can be no doubt of the validity of [Heidegger's] insight that
> reality with power to shape men's lives, with the ability to transform
> men's perceptions of meaning in existence, can and does disclose itself
> in certain kinds of language, especially in the primordial language of
> the poet. But this point again has ramifications at the level of literary
> criticism. If poetic language is, or can be, primordial language with
> the power to disclose being, then Heidegger will not have been the
> first to notice this. . . . The next step from this insight should therefore have been a step toward poets and critics of poetry, to learn how
> far and in what ways they could help us to understand this dimension
> of language. . . . But the "New Hermeneutic" is primarily a Christian
> theological movement, so the next step taken was not toward a better
> understanding of the power of poetic language to mediate an ultimate
> reality, to disclose being.[130]

This fatal omission of literary criticism by the New Hermeneutic demonstrated to Perrin and others that merely identifying the oral traditions

---

[127] Perrin, *Kingdom of God*, 127. Lundström's survey and assessment does not treat the New Hermeneutic.

[128] The concern for the language of the biblical writers established another point of contact to the disclosure of Being that was also the concern of Jesus as well as the basis of modern self-understanding. See Norman Perrin, *Rediscovering the Teaching of Jesus* (New York: Harper & Row), 1967; and Perrin, *What Is Redaction Criticism?* Guides to Biblical Scholarship Series (Philadelphia: Fortress, 1969).

[129] Perrin, *Language*, 121.

[130] Ibid., 124.

which lay behind the written text, or the author's theological agenda, did not go far enough in the hermeneutical task. As Amos Wilder emphasized in his introductory essay for *Semeia,* more energy was needed to consider the sociological character of the linguistic forms "involving language-codes and communication factors."[131] As with the New Hermeneutic, the parables became the focus of intense scholarly scrutiny in certain circles of New Testament scholarship.[132] In Perrin's own career, literary criticism governed his vision for the future of Kingdom research that would be more "towards the poet and the critic of the poet." He began the project himself in *Jesus and the Language of the Kingdom,* and the results have had considerable influence in present opinion about the Kingdom.[133]

The influence of Perrin's literary-critical analysis of the Kingdom of God represents only one of the justifications for the present study. General dissatisfaction with the New Quest in more than just the New Hermeneutic has moved scholarship in other more original directions. Colin Brown, for example, notes the failure of the New Quest in its questionable Bultmannian assumptions and conclusions (i.e., that Jesus was essentially an existential philosopher), its indifference to first-century Judaism as seen through Josephus, Qumran, and rabbinic literature, and its ignorance of the interplay between religion, theology, politics, economics, and the other cultural factors that are necessary for a thorough historiography.[134] Consequently,

---

[131] See "*Semeia:* An Experimental Journal for Biblical Criticism: An Introduction," *Semeia* 1 (1974): 5. His argument throughout the article is that New Testament studies give more attention overall to "a better understanding of language in all aspects."

[132] See for example the works of Robert Funk (*Language, Hermeneutic and Word of God: The Problem of Language in the New Testament and Contemporary Theology* [New York: Harper & Row, 1966]), Dan O. Via (*The Parables: Their Literary and Existential Dimension* [Philadelphia: Fortress, 1967]), and John Dominic Crossan (*In Parables: The Challenge of the Historical Jesus* [New York: Harper & Row, 1973]) during this period.

[133] In the New Testament contributions to Willis's recent *The Kingdom of God in Twentieth-Century Interpretation,* four of the six writers give credit to Perrin's concept of "tensive symbol" as constituting their presuppositions.

[134] Brown, "Historical Jesus," 337. For other assessments of the New Quest see R. P. Martin, "The New Quest of the Historical Jesus," in *Jesus of Nazareth: Saviour and Lord,* ed. C. F. H. Henry (Grand Rapids: Eerdmans, 1966), 25-45; James I. H. McDonald, "New Quest-Dead End? So What About the Historical Jesus?" in *Studia Biblica 1978,* vol. 2, *Papers on the Gospels,* ed. E. A. Livingstone JSNTSS 2 (Sheffield, U.K.: JSOT, 1980), 151-70.

since the first attempts by Perrin and other scholars in literary criticism, use of other disciplines within the social sciences to unveil the world of the first century has burgeoned—with each making its own contribution to the historical Jesus' understanding of the Kingdom of God. So vigorous is this movement, that it is now being described as the "third quest" of the historical Jesus.[135] At the Society of Biblical Literature national meeting in Chicago in 1984, Bernard Brandon Scott prophetically announced: "The historical quest of the historical Jesus has ended; the interdisciplinary quest has just begun."[136] It will be a great part of this essay to survey and assess the results of the "Third Quest" to the present.

POLITICAL AND SOCIAL DIMENSIONS OF THE KINGDOM

The theological developments that brought forth the New Quest and its subsequent theological responses germinated in the seedbeds of the dialectical theology of the 1920s. For these theologians, for whom the biblical documents contained the "Word of God," hermeneutics had become the proper task of theology.[137] The living Word that addressed all people had to be liberated from the historical confines of the Bible to speak anew and afresh to the modern person. For Bultmann, of course, the demythologizing program sought to make that theological expression of the Word in terms of Heideggerian existentialism. As we have already seen, despite all its promise of being "a new understanding of theological scholarship as a whole,"[138] the New Hermeneutic's Bultmannian presuppositions gave it similar theological conclusions—namely, the modern voice of the ancient Word is directed toward the heart of the individual as

---

[135] Neill and Wright, *The Interpretation of the New Testament,* 379-403. See Brown, "Historical Jesus," 37-341.

[136] Quoted by Marcus Borg, "Portraits of Jesus in Contemporary North American Scholarship," *HarTR* 84, no. 1 (1991): 2, n. 6. Borg also notes that by 1988 Daniel Harrington's bibliographical survey cites over 250 works employing interdisciplinary approaches in New Testament study (cf. "Second Testament Exegesis and the Social Sciences: A Bibliography," *BibTB* 18 (1988): 77-85.

[137] As in the writings of Karl Barth, E. Thurneysen, F. Gogarten, Emil Brunner, and Rudolf Bultmann. See von Bormann's discussion of "Hermeneutische Theologie" in "Hermeneutik I," *TRE,* 15:127ff.

[138] Robinson, "Hermeneutic Since Barth," 63.

a call to human authenticity or openness to Being. Theology primarily became the provenance of the individual, with theological reflection seldom exploring implications of the Word beyond the individual's own life. Increasingly, voices began to call for the liberation of theology from its privatized ghetto. The church, the state, and the individual had to be critiqued from a new perspective if any progress would be made in dealing with society's problems. One of these voices of the early 1960s was Dorothee Sölle, whose "political theology"[139] arose from a hermeneutic that included not only the individual but the society of all individuals. She states:

> Political theology begins with a modified preunderstanding. Its guiding hermeneutical principle is the question of authentic life for all men. This does not mean that the question about individual existence must be suppressed or thrust aside as nonessential. But surely even the question can be answered only in terms of social conditions and in the context of social hopes. No one can be saved alone. Subjectivity is injected into even this process of social understanding, but not for the purpose of seeking understanding for itself alone; rather it believes in and calls for the indivisible salvation of the whole world.[140]

Thus, the emphasis on the individual coming from existential theology had to be replaced with the question of society, the community of individuals. It is no surprise, therefore, that Sölle saw all of her theological work as "a conversation with Rudolf Bultmann."[141]

Another seminal voice in the call to make theology more responsive to the circumstances of human society was the Roman Catholic theologian Johann Baptist Metz. In a 1966 essay entitled "The Church and the World in the Light of a 'Political Theology,'" he inaugurated an extended discussion of his new political theology.[142] Metz's Thomistic approach had

---

[139] For a bibliography of political theology of this period, see Wolfgang Darshin, "Bibliographische Hinweise zur 'Politische Theologie,'" in *Diskussion zur "Politischen Theologie,"* ed. Helmut Peukert (Munich: Christian Kaiser, 1969), 302-27.

[140] Sölle, *Political Theology,* 60.

[141] Ibid., 3.

[142] See in Johann Baptist Metz, *Theology of the World,* trans. William Glen-Doepel (New York: Herder & Herder, 1971), 107-24.

led him to see the world in the context of human history. As such the world was inexorably a matter of human existence in community, and this meant politics. A genuine theology of the world was a political theology and a theology of the forces within human society that change the world. The scholarly debate of Metz's ideas over the next ten years allowed for him to sharpen and refine his own position. In 1969 one important response to his critics identifies what he sees as three essential features of his political theology, and we note the reiteration of Sölle's "conversation with Bultmann" in the second one. In Metz's understanding, political theology was (1) a theological hermeneutic in a social context, (2) a correction to the privatizing tendency in recent theology, and (3) in inextricable relationship to the church due to the church's political importance.[143]

Jürgen Moltmann's theological project in *Theologie der Hoffnung* (*Theology of Hope*) was a third conspicuous European voice of the 1960s calling for a theology useful to society. He likewise sees his message as a challenge to current theological trends. Existentialist theology, in his estimation, is justly criticized for its "inability to make anything of the world of objects."[144] Consequently, Christian ethics is only understood in the vague notion of taking responsibility for the world in general. Because of this, Moltmann thinks that existentialism "is no longer able to give any pertinent ethical instructions for the ordering of social and political life."[145] In no uncertain terms he states:

> A theology which settles faith in the "existence" of the individual, in the sphere of his personal, immediate encounters and decisions, is a theology which from the viewpoint of sociological science stands at the very place to which society has banished the *cultus privatus* in order to emancipate itself from it. This faith is in the literal sense socially irrelevant."[146]

---

[143] Johann Baptist Metz, " 'Politische Theologie' in der Diskussion," in *Diskussion zur "Politischen Theologie,"* 274-77.

[144] Moltmann, *Theology of Hope,* 314, quotes here from E. Topitsch, "Zur Soziologie des Existentialismus," in *Socialphilosophie zwischen Ideologie und Wissenschaft,* 1962, 86.

[145] Ibid., 315.

[146] Ibid., 316.

For Christian faith to be relevant to the world it needed a new theological base—a base that would bring Christian faith into the political arena. *Theology of Hope* was the first installment of Moltmann's political theology. Later, in an essay entitled "Political Theology," published in 1971, Moltmann would reemphasize the impetus behind his work. Again he describes the necessary movement beyond existentialist dogma:

> Responsible theology must therefore engage in institutional criticism as it reflects on the "place" of the churches "in the life" of modern society and in ideological criticism as it reflects on itself. It can no longer self-forgetfully screen out its own social and political reality as the old metaphysical and personalistic theologies did. . . . Political theology designates the field, the milieu, the environment, and the medium in which Christian theology should be articulated today.[147]

At about the same time as Moltmann, Metz, and Sölle were beginning to attract attention in Europe, similar ideas were taking shape in America through Harvey Cox's best-seller, *The Secular City*. Like his European counterparts, Cox denigrated existentialism's reformulated metaphysical answers to the issues of modern humanity.[148] He notes that the existentialist rightly sees the problem that modern humanity is not reached by metaphysical language, but existentialism fails by continuing to trying to find its answers through metaphysics. In Cox's way of thinking, something other than metaphysics had to serve as medium to talk about God in the secular culture. For him, talking about God *politically* was the answer, because politics

> brings unity and meaning to human life and thought. In today's world, we unify the various scholarly and scientific specialities by focusing them on specific human issues. Intellectual teamwork does not replace the lonely grind of the disciplined mental laborer, but truth is not unified today in metaphysical systems. Rather it is functionally unified by bringing disparate specialities to bear on concrete political perplexities.[149]

---

[147] Jürgen Moltmann, *The Experiment Hope*, ed. and trans. M. Douglas Meeks (Philadelphia: Fortress, 1975), 102-3.

[148] Cox, *The Secular City*, 251-54.

[149] Ibid., 254.

The new political agenda these writers prescribed for theology naturally had much to do with the Kingdom of God as the center of the New Testament message. How does the Kingdom of God address the constraints of contemporary human society? The answer was found in the one biblical personality who perfectly embodied and represented the Kingdom—Jesus. The Kingdom's inherent relationship to Jesus makes the fundamental theological issue of the Kingdom really a christological one. How did the divine Kingdom relate to the world of humanity? The answer is found in christology: "If Jesus personifies the Kingdom of God, then the elements of divine initiative and human response in the coming of the Kingdom are totally inseparable."[150] Thus, the case for human participation in the activity of the Kingdom is not only justified but modeled: "the Kingdom of God, concentrated in the life of Jesus of Nazareth, remains the fullest possible disclosure of the partnership of God and man in history. Our struggle for the shaping of the secular city represents the way we respond faithfully to this reality in our own times."[151]

Armed with the fiat of the Kingdom of God, political theology came to practical fulfillment first in the "theologies of liberation" of the late sixties and early seventies.[152] Influential early works appeared in the Latin American context with publication of Gustavo Gutiérrez's *Teología de la liberación, Perspectivas*[153] and in the Black American context with James

---

[150] Ibid., 111.

[151] Ibid., 112.

[152] The nature of political theology as a transition to liberation theology is noted by Sölle: "The development of a political theology over against a personal existentialist one was a transition; we made a first cautious step" ("Resistance: Toward a First World Theology," *ChrC* 23 [July 1979]: 178).

A concrete application to a particular human situation is one criterion used by liberation theologians to differentiate liberation theology from political theology. According to these theologians, European political theology is only an academic and intraecclesial activity, while liberation theology is a mass movement. See Michael L. Cook, "Jesus from the Other Side: Christology in Latin America," *TS* 44, no. 2 (1983): 260, n. 5 and 6. Another criteria of differentiation is the respective community of origin. Political theology has as its context white Europe and America, while the contexts of liberation theologies are the marginalized and oppressed. See, for example, John B. Cobb, *Process Theology as Liberation Theology* (Philadelphia: Westminster, 1982), vii-viii.

[153] Eng. ed. *A Theology of Liberation: History, Politics and Salvation*, trans. and ed. Caridad Inda and John Eagleson (Maryknoll: Orbis, 1973).

Cone's *A Black Theology of Liberation*.[154] Both of these works placed the Kingdom of God in the experience of Jesus at center stage to call for a new action within Christendom on behalf of the world's oppressed and marginalized. Moreover, these would be only the first of many modern "theologies of liberation" that would seek to drape various forms of human endeavor with the paradigm of the Kingdom of God in Jesus.[155] To this day, liberation theology of one sort or another remains the enduring expression of those theologically turbulent days in the early sixties.

The Kingdom of God in the understanding of the historical Jesus has without doubt had a varied recent past. From the New Quest to the New Hermeneutic and Language, to the Third Quest in New Testament studies; and from the personalized Kingdom of the existentialist to the social and concrete presence of the Kingdom for the liberation theologian, the Kingdom of God has a more diverse appearance than ever. It will be the task of this study to not only describe these developments in particular detail, but to offer reasoned critique along the way with an eye toward suggesting new areas of investigation that should prove profitable in the meaning and praxis of the Kingdom of God.

---

[154] James H. Cone, *A Black Theology of Liberation* (Philadelphia: J. B. Lippincott, 1970).

[155] The range of options for the praxis of the Kingdom in liberation theology goes from violent revolution against the Kingdom's enemies, as in Samuel Ryan, "Your Kingdom Come," *SEAJT* 21:1 (1980): 72, to less radical calls for the church to champion fair legal procedures, denounce violence and torture, and seek justice for the oppressed, as in Orlando Costas, *Christ Outside the Gate* (Maryknoll: Orbis, 1982), 94.

PART TWO

*New Testament
Trends Since 1960*

CHAPTER TWO

The Non-Apocalyptic Kingdom of the New Hermeneutic and the New Literary Criticism

THE KINGDOM IN THE NEW HERMENEUTIC

Fuchs

The New Hermeneutic, as championed by Ernst Fuchs and Gerhard Ebeling plus their influential students, was one of the two post-Bultmannian "quests" that comprised the New Quest of the historical Jesus commissioned by Ernst Käsemann in the early 1950s. These scholars took the quest of the historical Jesus in a new direction through their use of hermeneutics, particularly in the understanding of language. The premise of this New Hermeneutic is that the words of the four Gospels are not important as the actual words of the historical Jesus but that their significance is found in their capacity as language-events. As language-events they not only exegete the modern interpreter but can also be used in reverse to look at the past and reveal the aims, motives, and decisions of the historical Jesus behind the New Testament kerygmatic proclamation.

Though Ernst Fuchs himself is not sure the historical Jesus ever spoke explicitly of the "Kingdom of God," there is no question in his mind that Jesus had often pondered the rule of God and, therefore, that he would have given expression to it in his ministry.[1] That Fuchs would deign to

---

[1] The radical skepticism of his teacher, Rudolf Bultmann, shows through as Fuchs says that because of the stylized-character of Mark 1:15 and Matthew 4:17 it is likely these were creations of the community. Therefore, he concludes, "it is by no means certain, and in my opinion not even likely, that Jesus proclaimed the rule of God, or preached repentance" (Ernst Fuchs, "The Theology of the New Testament and the Historical Jesus," in *Studies of the Historical Jesus*, trans. Andrew Scobie [Naperville, Ill.: Alec R. Allenson, 1964], 179).

speak of the historical Jesus at all, of course, was a hallmark of the New Quest's departure from its Bultmannian roots, but where the Kingdom was concerned, Fuchs did share key ideas with his teacher. First, he speaks of the Kingdom of God solely as an abstraction. Eliminating any notion of a territorial realm, Fuchs fell in line with the current scholarly consensus that the biblical terms for "kingdom" primarily intended a dynamic concept of God's rule and reign.[2] Second, with Bultmann, Fuchs held that the sovereign activity of God could be spoken of as an eschatological or apocalyptic reality. The Kingdom was cataclysmic and other-worldly. Just as Weiss and Schweitzer had proven, the Kingdom of God did not come through the machinations of human effort; it was the work of God alone.[3] Third, the language of the Kingdom of God in the New Testament is meant to speak today through an existential hermeneutic. This is where the modern faith finds its foundation in the ancient biblical documents. Through existential philosophy, the "what" of the New Testament turns into the "how" of faith.[4] Like Bultmann before him, Fuchs saw the mechanism that justifies this hermeneutic in the Pauline transformation of the theology of the Gospels. To his way of thinking, Paul had completely reformulated the apocalyptic language of the Gospels in his understanding of *pneuma* and the presence of the *pneuma* in the church.[5] If Paul can legitimately reconfigure the Kingdom language in terms of the Spirit's operation, then the Kingdom is not at all about the timing of some mythical eschatological events; it is about "the *'existentiell'*"

---

[2] The twentieth-century scholarly consensus for the Kingdom of God as an abstraction was forged on the strength of Gustaf Dalman's studies of Aramaic terms in first-century Palestine (*The Words of Jesus*, trans. D. M. Kay [Edinburgh: T & T Clark, 1909]). No serious examination of Dalman's work has been attempted at this point, but some are calling for a reappraisal of his sources and methodology. See George W. Buchanan, *The Consequences of the Covenant* (Leiden: E. J. Brill, 1970), passim, but especially 50-51.

[3] See Fuchs's discussion of the Lord's Prayer as an "eschatological prayer" (Ernst Fuchs, "Language in the New Testament," in *Studies of the Historical Jesus*, 72-73.

[4] Fuchs, "Theology of the New Testament and the Historical Jesus," 186-87.

[5] Fuchs comments, "We know that Paul proceeded to make the entire apocalyptic conception of the rule of God subservient to his message about Christ." A little later he speaks of "Pneuma, which for Paul was entirely bound up with the rule of God" (Fuchs, "Language in the New Testament," 69-70).

situation of thinking faith."[6] It is individual and personal operation of Spirit putting down the old man.

It is interesting in light of the existentialists' dogmatic denial of the temporal in the Gospel record of the Kingdom that temporal language would be the locus of Fuchs's disengagement from his mentor's understanding of the Kingdom. Yet this is exactly what happened. As Perrin noted in 1963, Fuchs had been one of the early participants of the New Quest to part ways with Bultmann on the presence of the Kingdom.[7] Bultmann's critical reflection of the Gospels allowed only of a Kingdom *im Anbruch* (breaking in), not of one that was really here yet. Though a Kingdom in this stage had existential impact for the present in its ability to evoke decision in those who heard its proclamation, as Bultmann claimed, Fuchs was not content to deny the Kingdom's presence in Jesus and his church that came after him. Not only had Paul admitted of the Kingdom's presence in the church with his retooled terminology of the Spirit,[8] but the nature of New Testament language as *Sprachereignisse* (language-events) demanded the Kingdom was a present reality.

It is here at the point of the Kingdom's presence in the New Testament events of language that Fuchs extends himself into new domains by means of hermeneutics. In his essay "Language in the New Testament" he states his thesis for the Kingdom of God as a language-event: "Jesus spoke of the rule of God. It is not true that the Church came *instead* of the rule of God. Nor is it true that the Church came *with* the rule of God. Rather: *the New*

---

[6] Fuchs, "Theology of the New Testament and the Historical Jesus," 188; cf. also Fuchs, "Language in the New Testament," 70-71. An oft-repeated statement of Fuchs to this effect is: "The *'proton pseudos'* of our present research situation might well consist of the fact that from the outset we accommodate the *nature* of the Basileia within a secondary temporal context of phenomena" (Ernst Fuchs, "Jesus' Understanding of Time," in *Studies of the Historical Jesus*, 123).

[7] Norman Perrin, *The Kingdom of God in the Teaching of Jesus* (London: SCM, 1963), 122-23.

[8] After Fuchs states that Paul made "the entire apocalyptic conception of the rule of God subservient to his message about Christ," he defends the apostle against the charge of spiritualizing: "However, the Apostle cannot be accused of spiritualization of the expectation of the rule of God, because the central Pauline concept of pneuma is in no sense spiritually conceived—quite the contrary. Pneuma, which for Paul was entirely bound up with the rule of God, implies that for the Apostle Christian faith already operates within the rule of God" (Fuchs, "Language in the New Testament," 69-70).

Testament came through the rule of God.[9] According to Fuchs's understanding of the power of language to disclose essential human Being, which he often describes in terms of true freedom and justice,[10] the language of the New Testament documents are the product of the awareness of God's rule in the first century. That is, the revelation of the Kingdom or the rule of God which brought forth the realization of true human freedom and justice in the early Christian communities is that which they have expressed in the language of the New Testament documents.[11] Consequently, like Jesus' own enunciation of the Kingdom's essence, the words of the New Testament writers do not really *explain* the Kingdom, but rather the Kingdom is *proclaimed,* or experienced, throughout the entire fabric of all they wrote.[12] The text interprets the reader as the reader hears the text speak to the reader's existence. Fuchs expresses the result this way: "The text is therefore not just the servant that transmits Kerygmatic formulations, but rather a master that directs us into the language-context of our existence."[13]

For the Kingdom of God in the teaching of Jesus, Fuchs sees the nature of language-events as meaning that the New Testament documents should not be scoured for "concepts" about the Kingdom. In fact "Kingdom" in the Gospels does not even stand for the Kingdom itself, but it is Jesus'

---

[9] Ibid., 69 (emphasis his).

[10] In relationship to Jesus' proclamation of the Kingdom, Fuchs says, "The justice created by Jesus' word is in truth the free *essence* of the rule of God, God's sentence in the present. Here man grows towards his destiny of being God's image in freedom. Thus God's power or justice is in Jesus' case full authority for freedom" (ibid., 75).

[11] James Robinson has put Fuchs's understanding of the Kingdom this way: "the understanding of language as that which presents the possibilities from which reality is actualized identifies in Jesus' language itself the locus of God's reign—not in the present as a reality, nor as an apocalyptic reality near or far, but as the structuring of reality that reveals it as immediate to God, God's 'creation.' God's reign is not the Establishment, but its truth to which it is to be reformed. Nor is God's reign some mythical reality, but rather the truth of real reality. Put still more abstractly, God's reign is the true being of all that is, all the beings' true 'world'" (James Robinson, "Jesus' Parables as God Happening," in *Jesus and the Historian,* ed. F. Thomas Trotter [Philadelphia: Westminster, 1968], 145).

[12] Fuchs makes a big point of distinguishing Jesus' *proclamation* of the Kingdom's presence from John's *explanation* of the Kingdom's imminent arrival. Jesus does not need to explain the Kingdom; the people already know about it. See Ernst Fuchs, "What Is Interpreted in the Exegesis of the New Testament?" in *Studies of the Historical Jesus,* 87–91.

[13] Ernst Fuchs, "What Is a 'Language-Event'?" in *Studies of the Historical Jesus,* 211.

preaching about the Kingdom—something more of a process, than a concept.[14] Even if the writers themselves identify the Kingdom in terms of "present" or "future," or even try to relate it explicitly to parables,[15] it is fruitless to try to confine the transcendent power of language to rigid categories like eschatological timing and territory. The end result for the presentation of the Kingdom in the Gospels is that when the presence of the Kingdom is referred to (as in Luke 6:20–21; 11:20; Matt. 5:3ff.; 12:28) we understand the Kingdom's *efficacy*, not its temporality.[16] When the future of the Kingdom is presented (as in Mark 13 and Matthew 24–25), we again do not understand temporality but that the future is entirely God's concern and care, and by this we are released into freedom.[17]

The process through which Jesus revealed the sovereignty of God in relation to Being is most clearly seen in the parables, which Fuchs also accorded the highest critical acclaim to authenticity. In the daring images the parables present of resolution, certain reward, surprise of unexpected compensation, and so on, the Kingdom grabs hold of the hearer, past and present, to expose authentic human existence of which it is the structuring reality. The parables inspire in us "confidence in God's action" by which our attitude is changed so that we can move in true freedom and meet our neighbor anew.[18] This is the true essence of the Kingdom's presence. Fuchs's reading of a couple of the parables may serve as examples of his hermeneutic. The parable of the treasure (Matt. 13:44), for example, has as its "point of comparison" the joyful recognition that the *basileia* comes, the certainty

---

[14] Fuchs, "What Is Interpreted in the Exegesis of the New Testament?" 94.

[15] Fuchs believes Matthew is mistaken in trying to link the rule of God to parables. Though the parables are the process of the Kingdom's revelation of Being, to explicitly say so is to not understand the nature of Jesus' language (Fuchs, "Jesus' Understanding of Time," 122; cf. also Fuchs, "What Is a 'Language-Event'?" 220). Similarly, the idea of the delay of the Parousia is the result of a mistaken interpretation of Jesus' language (Fuchs, "Theology of the New Testament and the Historical Jesus," 180).

[16] That is, efficacy to release man now to true human freedom and justice. See Fuchs, "Jesus' Understanding of Time," 122, and Fuchs, "Theology of the New Testament and the Historical Jesus," 183.

[17] Fuchs, "Theology of the New Testament," 183.

[18] Fuchs understands the change of attitude the Kingdom effects to be "conversion" (Fuchs, "Language in the New Testament," 73-74).

of God's call. The hearers can *"joyfully* recognize that something great is under way: the Basileia comes, it comes indeed."[19] The parable of the mustard seed that grows (Matt. 13:31-32) has to do with our own individual growth (for the Kingdom elsewhere does not grow, cf. the Kingdom of the Sermon on the Mount) that comes from the freedom of realizing God's miracle comes to our need.[20]

Fuchs's portrait of Jesus as herald of a Kingdom that is a real and dynamic force in the world in some ways makes an attractive contribution to the study of the Kingdom. The desire to apply the biblical message to the present age that we see in the efforts of Fuchs and the other scholars of the New Hermeneutic are laudable. Inherent within the New Hermeneutic's understanding of the power of language to change the reader's reality is an important concern for the application of the biblical message, which should not be overlooked by any interpreter of the Kingdom of God. However, it is just at the point of Fuchs's creative application of the Kingdom that his results merit challenge.[21] That is, the results of Fuchs's New Quest tends to suffer the same criticism as that often made of the Old Quest, namely, with his own modern biblical criticism and existential philosophy, the Kingdom of Fuchs's Jesus resembles more the Kingdom of a twentieth-century existentialist philosopher than a first-century prophet/preacher. The nagging question for Fuchs and the New Hermeneutic will always be: Would this Kingdom, that is, the structure of all human Being, have been understood in the first century? Fuchs and the other members of the New Hermeneutic all admit that if the Kingdom was so intended by Jesus and so understood by some of his hearers, this meaning did not prevail very long in the early church and was soon lost entirely to the temporal prison of the delay of the Parousia. Indeed, Fuchs himself is somewhat mystified as to how a church that so heavily reworked the stories about Jesus could even

---

[19] Contrary to even Bultmann's view that the parable was concerned with the need for sacrifice in a decision for God (Fuchs, "What Is Interpreted in the Exegesis of the New Testament?" 94-95).

[20] Ibid., 92; cf. Fuchs, "Jesus' Understanding of Time," 136ff.

[21] The critique of the broader hermeneutical issues in Fuchs's and the New Hermeneutic's approach has been made by others. See for example, Carl E. Braaten, "How New Is The New Hermeneutic?" *TToday* 22:2 (1965): 218-35; and Anthony C. Thiselton, "The New Hermeneutic," in *New Testament Interpretation*, ed. I. Howard Marshall (Grand Rapids: Eerdmans, 1977), 308-33.

leave such contradictory notions about the Kingdom's apocalyptic future and immanent presence in the final products.[22] What is puzzling to Fuchs is precisely what indicts his project.

Linnemann

After Fuchs, parable study supposedly takes a significant step forward in Eta Linnemann's best-selling introduction and exposition of the parables of Jesus.[23] According to Fuchs's comments in the foreword, his student's revelation of the phenomenon of "interlocking" in parables was an important breakthrough in enlightening both the historical context of the parable and the parable's meaning for the modern reader.[24] Using a concept similar to Fuchs's *Einverständnis*, Linnemann sees interlocking as the way the narrator of a parable engages the view of reality held by his hearers with that of his own. The narrator "concedes" some of the hearers' worldview with the context of the parable, for example, common practices of business, labor, domestic life, and so on, in order to draw the hearer in to take his new view of the situation. This new view will have its locus in the one point of comparison the parable makes, but Linnemann contends it will not be exhausted there. The parables are in fact language-events capable of revealing the true structures of human existence on a level far more impacting than just the one point made explicit by the parable.[25]

The parables of Jesus are said to reveal the Kingdom of God as the true organizing principle of all reality—again reminiscent of Linnemann's teacher, Fuchs. In this regard the parables act as Jesus' arguments to oppose contemporary notions of the Kingdom that had been so clouded with

---

[22] Fuchs, "Theology of the New Testament and the Historical Jesus," 182.

[23] Eta Linnemann, *Gleichnisse Jesu. Einfuhrung und Auslegung* (Göttingen: Vandenhoeck & Ruprecht, 1961). The English edition, *The Parables of Jesus: Introduction and Exposition*, was translated by John Sturdy from the third (1964) edition. A later expression of Linnemann's position is "Zeitansage und Zeitvorstellung in der Verkündigung Jesu," in *Jesus Christus in Historie und Theologie*, ed. Georg Strecker (Tübingen: J. C. B. Mohr [Paul Siebeck], 1975), 237-63. In her most recent writings, Linnemann has repudiated these earlier works and the historical-critical methodology upon which they were based. See Linnemann *Historical Criticism of the Bible: Methodology or Ideology?* trans. Robert W. Yarbrough (Grand Rapids: Baker, 1990).

[24] See Linnemann, *Parables of Jesus*, xi. On "interlocking," see 27-28.

[25] Ibid., 29-30.

hope. According to Linnemann, the truth of the Kingdom as the dynamic organizing principle of all reality may be seen in the Old Testament, where Yahweh is recognized as the universal king, for example, "The Lord is king forever and ever" (Exod. 18:15), and other similar statements, mostly in the Psalms of Enthronement.[26] Alongside this language, the Old Testament also expressed this ultimate reality in terms of a hope that Yahweh's reign would one day appear and smite all the powers of evil once for all. However, in the intervening years, up to the time of Jesus, the suffering of the people of Israel under alien domination succeeded in configuring the reign of God almost totally on the side of the hope. The Kingdom became bound up with hopes for the nation. Its true dynamic essence became lost in the physical, in the apocalyptic, in the talk of timing and irruption. John the Baptist even succumbed to the constraints of this milieu as he proclaimed the nearness of the Kingdom in an apocalyptic scheme.

Jesus, however, returns to the more balanced and dynamic view of God's reign, particularly in the parables. He does not preach the near-expectation of the Kingdom of God as the apocalyptists did, and he has nothing to do with a restored Jewish state.[27] It is true Jesus did use temporal language which appeared paradoxical in its present and future statements, but in fact it only endorsed his existential understanding of the Kingdom. "Jesus' paradoxical time-announcement meant just this, that the question had to be answered by the decision of faith or unbelief, by a 'subjective' decision, a decision of the 'subject' which itself was decisive for him."[28] In Jesus' proclamation "Repent and believe the gospel, the Kingdom of God

---

[26] Ibid., 36.

[27] Linnemann states, "An examination of the passages cited in support of the near expectation seems to me, however, to show that this assumption has no adequate support in them. In my opinion there is not one saying of Jesus that speaks expressly of the nearness of the Kingdom of God the authenticity of which is not at least disputed." She then conducts an exegesis of verses she considers in this "near expectation" category: Mark 1:15; 9:1; 13:28; 13:30; 14:25; Matthew 10:7; 10:23; 13:33-36; 24:43-51; Luke 12:36-38; 12:54-56 (ibid., 132ff.). She continues by quoting Fuchs's line, "The 'proton pseudos' of our present research situation might well consist of the fact that from the outset we accommodate the nature of the Basileia within a secondary temporal context of phenomena" (ibid., 136).

[28] Ibid., 39. Linnemann is critical of efforts to remove either the present or future logia (except of course all the passages of the near expectation) as was attempted in realized and consistent eschatology (ibid., 132, n. 26).

is at hand" (Mark 1:15), the main point is not temporal, but substantial. The emphasis is on what needs to be decided ("repent and believe"), not on the calendar. God's ever-present and dynamic rule means salvation is possible now in the decision.[29] The parables were the primary means of Jesus to bridge the gap between his own view of the reality of God's rule and that of his audience. The Pharisees, for example, did not believe in the presence of God's reign, so Jesus pulls the parable of the great supper (Luke 14:15–24; Matt. 22:2–14) from his arsenal and shows the Kingdom is present in Jesus' table-fellowship with the lost.[30]

Unfortunately, according to Linnemann, after Jesus the dynamic presence of the Kingdom does not come through as clearly as it should in the early church's transmission of the parables or in its presentation of the Kingdom in general. Because the later New Testament documents have evidently reconfigured the Kingdom in futuristic terms, Linnemann has to admit the early Christians eventually returned to the position of the Pharisees, who did not believe in the Kingdom as present.[31] As she explains it, in the process of the Kerygma's transmission, the original conflict between Jesus and his hearers on the Kingdom became occluded by the dulling passage of time. Linnemann points out that the early Christians became more interested in the person of Jesus and his ministry of salvation at Calvary than in the particular hopes of his first hearers. The church's language for the Kingdom's dynamic presence was expressed in terms of the cross and the salvation purchased there. Belonging to the community of salvation that was called by the risen Lord was the presence of the Kingdom in the emerging church.[32]

Linneman's focus on the parables as the locus of Jesus' meaning of the

---

[29] Jesus did believe in a future salvation that included resurrection and judgment, but it was not a future qualified by the calendar. This kind of generalized future determines the present and the present likewise reveals the salvation and judgment of the future. At this point Linnemann cites Bornkamm's *Jesus of Nazareth* on the blending of the present and the future in Jesus and concludes, "There was no longer a basic difference between present and future, they belonged together" (Linnemann, *Parables*, 102).

[30] Linnemann, *Parables*, 91.

[31] Ibid., 92. "[The early church] only spoke of the kingdom of God, however, as future, and differed very little in its language about this from the Pharisees."

[32] Ibid., 92.

Kingdom, as already seen in Fuchs and as to be discussed in Jüngel, is the hallmark of the New Hermeneutic's method. Several issues are raised by this selectivity with the Gospel data. First, the heavy-handed, foundational role of modern biblical criticism threatens the entire superstructure built upon it. Can the temporal and growth elements of the Kingdom really be removed from consideration as easily Linnemann and the others of the New Hermeneutic contend? W. G. Kümmel, for example, has taken Linnemann to task for her historical-critical extrication of all the Kingdom's "near-future" passages from the Gospel record.[33] Similarly, bias and the critical question surfaces in Fuchs's work. On what grounds, for example, does the Kingdom of the Sermon on the Mount become paradigmatic for a nongrowing Kingdom? Why should not the parables of growth inform the Kingdom of the Sermon instead of vice-versa? More fundamentally, must the Sermon and the parables really contradict at all? The selective excising of temporal language within the New Hermeneutic not only lacks the ring of truth, but it also casts doubt on the fundamental premise of the New Hermeneutic: that all language, not just selected portions, has meaning.

Beyond this, Linnemann and the New Hermeneutic must be pressed as to whether the parables really constitute a sufficient basis for a comprehensive definition of the Kingdom, let alone an existential one. If one believes the Gospels are witnesses not just to the words of Jesus but also to his actions, should not Jesus' deeds, which comprise a large percentage of the Gospel material, also be factored into the final conclusions about his view of the Kingdom?[34] Do not actions with accompanying interpretation also project and reveal Being? On miracle-stories Linnemann and the others make little comment, but a Bultmannian hypothesis is most probably operant.[35] Still, the quiet is strangely consistent with other questions for the New Hermeneutic, because if the miracles and miracle-discourses of Jesus

---

[33] W. G. Kümmel, "Jesuforschung seit 1963," *TRu* 41 (1976): 329-30; and *TRU* 43 [1978]): 124-25.

[34] Morton Kelsey notes that almost one-fifth of the Gospels are healings or the discussions raised by them, and that there is more data in the Gospels concerning physical transformation than moral and spiritual transformation (*Healing and Christianity* [New York: Harper & Row, 1973], 53-54). More doubts about the primacy of parables in historical Jesus research are raised by John Meier, *A Marginal Jew: Rethinking the Historical Jesus,* vol. 2, *Mentor, Message and Miracle* (New York, N.Y.: Doubleday, 1994), 290.

[35] That is, the miracles are remnants of prescientific myth in need of demythologizing.

could be allowed to point us towards the Kingdom's meaning in the first century, they would point right into the Old Testament prophetic hope[36]— the locus of some concern for the New Hermeneutic's exegesis in general as we shall observe further in the works of Jüngel.

Jüngel

Another of Fuchs's students, Eberhard Jüngel, took up the study of the Kingdom's existential proclamation in the apostolic church. Attempting to understand the sources and process of the early Christian christology, Jüngel charted the relationship between Jesus' proclamation of the Kingdom and Paul's teaching of justification.[37] Like his mentor before him, Jüngel's working premise was that the Pauline modification of Jesus' Kingdom proclamation is the main warrant for an existential interpretation of Jesus' announcement. The doctrine of justification with its clear statements of Jesus as the Christ, which predicated more of Jesus than Jesus had himself, shows the New Testament is in fact the record of *bewegenden Sprachereignissen* (underlying language events).[38] It shows that the New Testament has departed the realm of the historical Jesus for the realm of theology.[39]

---

[36] Jesus' miraculous deeds as narrated in the Gospels point to the Old Testament in their fulfillment of the prophetic hope of physical restoration and the proclamation of the Gospel (e.g., Isa. 61:1-2 in Matt. 11:5; Luke 4:16-30); their Sabbath occasion, the objects of their concern, their inherent connection to the Holy Spirit; their conflict with Satan; their relationship with the law, and their association with the messianic figure. Of the many works that could be cited here see especially O. Betz and Werner Grimm, *Wesen und Wirklichkeit der Wunder Jesu* (Frankfurt: Peter Lang, 1977); James D. G. Dunn, "Spirit and Kingdom," *ExpTim* 82 (1970-1971): 36-40; W. Grimm, *Weil Ich dich Liebe. Die Verkündigung Jesu und Deuterojesaja* (Frankfurt: Peter Lang, 1976); Klaus Berger, "Jesus als Pharisäer und Frühe Christen als Pharisäer," *NovT* 30 (1988): 231ff.; Hendrick Van Der Loos, *The Miracles of Jesus* (Leiden: E. J. Brill, 1965); *Gospel Perspectives 6: The Miracles of Jesus*, ed. David Wenham and Craig Blomberg (Sheffield, U.K.: JSOT, 1986); and Birger Gerhardsson, *The Mighty Acts of Jesus According to Matthew*, trans. Robert Dewsnap (Lund: W. K. Gleerup, 1979).

[37] Eberhard Jüngel, *Paulus und Jesus. Eine Untersuchung zur Präzisierung der Frage nach dem Ursprung der Christologie* (Tübingen: J. C. B. Mohr [Paul Siebeck], 1962).

[38] Jüngel, *Paulus und Jesus*, 3. Romans 14:17 ("for the kingdom of God is not eating and drinking, but righteousness and peace and joy in the Holy Spirit") shows that Paul knew of Jesus' terminology of the Kingdom but recast it in terms of righteousness (*Paulus und Jesus*, 267).

[39] Ibid., 16.

Working backwards from the Kingdom's coming-to-language in Paul's theology (e.g., Rom. 14:17) brings us to the Kingdom in Jesus' teaching. Like Paul, Jesus was not interested in the Kingdom so much as a distinct concept to be explained, but rather his words themselves were demonstrations of the Kingdom. By means of language Jesus opened his hearers to the ever-present reality of God's kingship. Of course, this means Jesus did not speak of the Kingdom as an eschatological event governed by notions of time.[40] This is most immediately evident from the observation that Jesus offers no definition of the Kingdom of God.[41] It also fits the abstract nature of the *basileia* that Dalman had demonstrated from the Aramaic linguistic domain behind the Greek *basileia* along with the well-known rabbinic idea of assuming the "yoke of the Kingdom."[42]

The existential interpretation is also indicated for Jüngel by the fact that Jesus took on the language of the apocalyptic literature of his day, particularly the doctrine of the two ages. The apocalyptists saw all of God's working in terms of "this age" and "the coming age." According to this scheme, "this age" was eminently temporal, historical, and earthly. It was the present era of suffering under foreign domination, when evil spirits oppressed the righteous. "The coming age" was different. It was the experience of God's people *after* the Messiah's arrival. According to Jüngel's contention, where time is concerned the "coming age" takes on new, otherworldly qualities. After the Messiah, he notes, time can be "hastened," as in the Syriac Apocalypse of Baruch 20:1, and it can be filled up so that it must "wait for fulfillment" as in Esdras 4:36–37.[43] These are not the expressions of temporality and intervals of time. The coming age is in fact

---

[40] At this point (ibid., 141) Jüngel quotes Fuchs's dictum: "The *'proton pseudos'* of our present research situation might well consist of the fact that from the outset we accommodate the *nature* of the Basileia within a secondary temporal context of phenomena."

[41] Ibid., 87.

[42] Ibid., 177. Jüngel asserts that the reality of the Kingdom's yoke takes literary form in the prayers and confession of ancient Israel starting with the Shema in Deuteronomy 6:4. To say the Shema was to assume the Kingdom's yoke. According to Jüngel, this rabbinic idea means the Kingdom is a nontemporal or temporary reality: "The reign of God had no temporary sense; the intended phenomenon has its place not in time, but in the word of confession, prayer" (ibid., 177 [translations of quotations are the author's]).

[43] Ibid., 141.

detemporalized, theological, and, in Jüngel's opinion, not even explicitly associated with the Kingdom of God.[44] Jesus shows up in this milieu and preaches the near presence of this new, detemporalized age; only he does not call it the "coming age" but refers to it as the "Kingdom of heaven."[45] Jesus in essence substitutes Kingdom language for "coming age" language while still retaining "coming age" meaning:

> Thus with his proclamation of the rule of God, Jesus had taken over an idea which was unencumbered by apocalyptic and future nationalistic expectations. Instead, in his proclamation Jesus used "a terminology from his Jewish environment which was not bound with God's kingdom, but with the new eons, of the *olam ha-ba*" [coming age], in which case "he replaced the coming *olam* [age] with the kingdom of God."[46]

The result is that Jesus' eschatology conceives the Kingdom as the consequence of God's rule for human existence. It still may be said to be eschatological, and indeed Jesus speaks of a real future for the Kingdom that presses in and impacts the present,[47] but the *essence* of the Kingdom is the *existential* nearness of God's rule.[48]

At this point Jüngel devotes considerable attention to the parable discourses of Jesus, since *"in the parables the Basileia comes into language as parable."*[49] Jesus brings the timeless sovereignty of God into the presence of his hearers with parables. According to Jüngel's reading, the parables

---

[44] "So far as I see, the eschatological concept of the reign of God *(Gottesherrschaft)* is not used in conjunction with Olam-terminology so as to identify the coming Age with the kingdom of God" (ibid., 178).

[45] Ibid., 179.

[46] Ibid., 179. The citations within Jüngel's statement come from P. Vielhauer, "Gottesreich und Menschensohn in der Verkündigung Jesu," in *Festschrift for Günther Dehn*, ed. W. Schneemelcher (Munich: Neukirchen, 1957), 77.

[47] Jüngel, *Paulus und Jesus*, 180.

[48] Like Linnemann and Fuchs, Jüngel sees the tension of the Kingdom's imminence and its future in the Gospels as evidence that the Kingdom is about a *process* and not a concept. "The eschatology of Jesus is in no way to be taken from the religious-historical terms of his day that he uses; rather it is more evident in the manner he uses these terms; that is, in the way he sets these terms in relationship to each other, and in the way he brings these terms into language" (ibid., 265).

[49] Ibid., 135 (italics his). For more on Jüngel's understanding of the parables, see Norman Perrin, *Jesus and the Language of the Kingdom* (Philadelphia: Fortress, 1976), 117-20.

of the hidden treasure and the pearl of great price (Matt. 13:44–46) set the pattern for the existential message of the Kingdom. In both of these instances the overwhelming value of what was found controls the behavior of the finder to such a degree that it may be said that the finders were themselves "found" by the Kingdom, not vice versa.[50] Being "found" by the Kingdom is the existential foundation to which the other Kingdom parables give appropriate nuances. The point of the parable of the dragnet (Matt. 13:47–48) is the Kingdom's challenge to decision to the "gathered ones" in light of the coming "sorting." Thus, Jesus "*guarantees* to man (those who had been 'gathered') the opportunity to decide."[51] The seed growing by itself (Mark 4:26–29) is also a guarantee for Jesus' hearers of freedom from the past and freedom for the future (the harvest). Again the guarantee is based on the certain opportunity for decision God's rule provides through Jesus' words.[52] The parable of the mustard seed (Mark 4:30–32) invites the audience to consider the present in light of the tremendous future of God's work. So certain is Jesus of this grand future of God that he can use the parable of the mustard seed to call together people to even now become part of that "wonderful end."[53]

Jüngel's treatment of the Kingdom now brings up two points for comment with regard to not only his own work but the whole program of the New Hermeneutic. First, as Jüngel's work shows, much of the justification for the Kingdom-as-language-event in the four Gospels comes from a perceived transformation of the Kingdom in Paul's doctrine of justification, but it needs to be asked if this interpretation must *necessarily* follow from the biblical data. Fuchs and Jüngel are no doubt right to conclude that Paul's doctrine of justification is integrally related to the theme of the Kingdom, but this does not in itself establish the fact that Paul transformed Jesus' message and thereby confirmed the Kingdom as a timeless, existential language-event. Indeed, we should note that the doctrine of justification is not absent from Jesus' teaching (Luke 18:14; Matt. 20:1–16; and related teachings on the necessity of repentance and faith plus the inadequacy of the law). And other causes may also explain the paucity of

---

[50] Jüngel, *Paulus und Jesus*, 145.

[51] Ibid., 147 (italics his).

[52] Ibid., 152.

[53] Ibid., 154.

Kingdom-language in Paul's writings. The difference in terminology may just as well be a matter of *emphasis* (as in a Pauline realized eschatology) not *transformation*. The case for this is substantial, especially when we consider that Paul did continue some use of *basileia*-language alongside and within his doctrine of justification. Furthermore, where *basileia*-language is used, it is still conditioned temporally in terms of a *future* inheritance.[54] Likewise, the summary statements in the early Christian sermons of Acts (8:12; 19:8; 20:25; 28:23, 31) indicate the proclamation about Jesus is not a transformation of the proclamation about the Kingdom. To preach the gospel of Jesus is to preach the Kingdom (cf. esp. Acts 20:24–25).

Second, Jüngel's work highlights anew the anachronism inherent to the New Hermeneutic. Not only was the Kingdom as language-event not a category comprehensible during the time of Jesus or the early church, but such a view is even more unlikely in the milieu of the Old Testament and the Pseudepigrapha. To be sure, both Jüngel's and Linnemann's discussions of the Kingdom's antecedents in the Old Testament and the Pseudepigrapha do well to note the abstract component of Yahweh's reign in his kingship of Israel, but both neglect the way the Old Testament and the Pseudepigrapha consistently make Yahweh's sovereign rule visible in the land and people of Israel. At the Exodus, Yahweh's covenant with the nation is nothing less than a "theo-political act," as Martin Buber has stated.[55] It required that his dynamic rule be exercised visibly in the land and people of Israel. When the people call for a king like the other nations, they reject Yahweh as their king (1 Sam. 8:5–7). At the inauguration of the monarchy, the human king reigns as Yahweh's son over Yahweh's kingdom in Israel.[56] Similarly, at the time of the exile, the prophetic hope was for

---

[54] As J. Eichler notes, the inheritance of the kingdom in 1 Corinthians 6:9-10; 15:50; Galatians 5:21; Ephesians 5:5; and Colossians 1:12-13 "embraces all those promises [in the Holy Spirit] the fulfillment of which is yet future" ("Inheritance," *NIDNTT*, 2:300).

[55] Martin Buber, *The Kingship of God* (New York: Harper, 1967), 124ff.

[56] In 1 Chronicles 17:11-14, the Chronicler ties Yahweh's kingdom in Israel to the Davidic offspring, Solomon, who is also Yahweh's son. Buchanan summarizes the Chronicler's understanding of Yahweh's kingdom: "For the Chronicler, at least, the Lord's kingdom was the whole *Davidic* kingdom, with the center of the government at *Jerusalem* and a Davidic king on the throne" (Buchanan, *Consequences of the Covenant*, 58; cf. also Günther Klein, "The Biblical Understanding of the Kingdom of God," *Interp* 26 [October 1972]: 396, and Walter Dietrich, "Gott als König," *ZTK* 77 [September 1980]: 251-68, esp. 259-62).

Yahweh's hidden rule to become visible, as Jüngel says, but this was a longing that was to be realized in a restored nation on the earth for the people of Israel.[57] The hope for an earthly, temporal, and messianic kingdom survives through the writings of the Apocrypha and Pseudepigrapha as well.[58] Later, into the first century, the New Testament itself, along with other external sources, attests to the endurance of these same hopes for God's kingly rule to be made visible in their land.[59]

---

[57] Donald E. Gowan summarizes the Old Testament prophetic hope by saying, "God must transform the human person; give a new heart and a new spirit. . . . God must transform human society; restore Israel to the promised land, rebuild cities, and make Israel's new status a witness to the nations. . . . And God must transform nature itself" (*Eschatology in the Old Testament* [Philadelphia: Fortress, 1986], 2). See also Sigmund Mowinckel's similar conclusions regarding the content of the prophetic hope in *He That Cometh*, trans. G. W. Anderson (New York: Abingdon, 1954), 133, 137. At the conclusion of his study of the Kingdom of God in the Old Testament Dale Patrick states, "the kingdom language of the OT is historical and contains an irreducibly national strain" ("The Kingdom of God in the Old Testament," in *The Kingdom of God in Twentieth-Century Interpretation*, ed. Wendell Willis [Peabody, Mass.: Hendrickson, 1987], 79).

[58] While it is true the eschatology of the Apocrypha and Pseudepigrapha is more apocalyptic (i.e., fanciful, cataclysmic, cosmic, and dualistic) in its total presentation, Collins can say of the Kingdom ruled by the messiah of *Psalms of Solomon* 17 that it "is essentially the restoration of a national Jewish kingdom" (J. J. Collins, "The Kingdom of God in the Apocrypha and Pseudepigrapha," in *Kingdom in Twentieth-Century Interpretation*, 91). Similar conclusions could be made about the Kingdom of the *Sibylline Oracles* (3:47; 767) and the *Testament (Assumption) of Moses* (8-10, especially, 10:1) which replaces the earthly kingdoms of Egypt and Rome (See ad loc. *OTP*, and the analysis of Meier in *A Marginal Jew*, 245-65. After his study of the Kingdom at Qumran, B. Viviano compares Jesus' view of the Kingdom with that of Qumran. He concludes, "The Qumran kingdom vision is also social and political, but differs as national rather than universal in its aims; militaristic, vindictive, violent, and somewhat more deterministic in its means with no hint of love of enemies or forgiveness of sins" (B. Viviano, "The Kingdom of God in the Qumran Literature," in *Kingdom in Twentieth-Century Interpretation*, 107).

[59] This is clearly what is behind the misplaced requests and expectations of Acts 1:6 and Luke 19:11, along with the popular uprisings against the Romans in A.D. 66-70 and 135, as well as the propensity of large numbers to follow after messianic figures in the first century. See R. A. Horsley and John S. Hanson, *Bandits, Prophets, and Messiahs: Popular Movements in the Time of Jesus* (San Francisco: Harper & Row, 1985). J. Ramsey Michaels summarizes the general Jewish belief about the Kingdom of God at the time of Jesus. "Actually the kingdom of God in Jewish expectation was both spiritual and national, *both* universal and ethnic" ("The Kingdom of God and the Historical Jesus," in *Kingdom in Twentieth-Century Interpretation*, 114 [emphasis his]). See also the endurance of these views in later rabbinic theology in Solomon Schecter, *Aspects of Rabbinic Theology: Major Concepts of the Talmud* (New York: Schocken, 1961), 97-115.

In sum, the New Hermeneutic, while praiseworthy in motive, suffers most from a severe anachronism in result. Its Jesus lacks precedent in Israel, and his Kingdom was thoroughly unknown in the first century. Rather than validating the hermeneutics of language and Being, as the New Hermeneutic suggests, the fact that Jesus did not define the Kingdom at the outset of his ministry seems to argue for something other than twentieth-century existentialism being at the heart of the Kingdom of God.

AMERICAN LITERARY CRITICISM OF THE KINGDOM

The next three sections follow the tendrils of the New Hermeneutic across the Atlantic into the sphere of American New Testament scholarship. The fulcrum of the three sections is the second, which addresses the Kingdom in the understanding of Norman Perrin, who is the single most influential commentator on the Kingdom of God since 1960. The sections before and after this second section are presented as providing the foundation and the extension of his work.

Wilder

Amos Niven Wilder (1895–1993)[60]—poet, literary critic, theologian and exegete—for a long time stood a lonely watch in American New Testament studies. His call for a more language-sensitive approach to the eschatology of the New Testament began with his Yale doctoral dissertation, "The Relation of Eschatology to Ethics in the Teaching of Jesus in Matthew" (1933). In the rewritten and expanded version of that dissertation, published as *Eschatology and Ethics in the Teaching of Jesus,*[61] Wilder argued that Jesus' apocalyptic language of the Kingdom was the vehicle for a this-worldly mission of redemption where the Kingdom is a social

---

[60] Wilder was honored with a biographical monograph in the Society of Biblical Literature's Biblical Scholarship in North America Series. See John Dominic Crossan, *A Fragile Craft: The Work of Amos Niven Wilder,* Biblical Scholarship in North America 3 (Chico, Calif.: Scholars, 1981). See also the brief autobiography in Wilder's *Jesus' Parables and the War of Myths: Essays on Imagination in the Scripture,* ed. J. Breech (Philadelphia: Fortress, 1982), 19–29.

[61] Amos N. Wilder, *Eschatology and Ethics in the Teaching of Jesus,* rev. ed. (1950; reprint, Westport, Conn.: Greenwood, 1978).

creation of God.[62] With a slight bit of "demythologizing" of this apocalyptic language, the whole social world of the first century as well as Jesus' true intent may be unveiled to the modern reader.[63]

In Wilder's view, all eschatology is dogmatized myth about the unknown future.[64] Behind the fanciful but inconsistent language of the apocalyptic symbols and images lies the "essential intuition" of the culture's beliefs about the future. In the Judaism of the first century, these fundamental intuitions included the hope that God would act for the annulment of worldly power and for the fulfillment of the promises of righteousness and salvation for all peoples.[65] This transformed world was idealized in terms of the Kingdom—itself a mythical term from the dogmatizations in the Old Testament.[66] When Jesus speaks of the Kingdom he is "evoking archaic motifs of the wars of Yahweh and the hostility of Satan and the demons, all in relation to the calling of Israel in a time of crisis."[67] Jesus speaks of the Kingdom as a poet, and his mythical language means the Kingdom cannot be conceptualized according to any sort of "literalized" readings of the Gospels.[68]

Believing that he was a participant and witness to a great redemptive transaction effected by God on his generation, Jesus speaks of the Kingdom as present and future. God was beginning the superhuman transformation

---

[62] Ibid., 47, 239. Schweitzer's interim ethic and Bultmann's existential ethic were Wilder's main foils in this work. His concern for a this-worldly ethic in the teaching of Jesus and the early church occupied a great deal of Wilder's attention throughout his career. See, for example, his "Kerygma, Eschatology, and Social Ethics," in *The Background of the New Testament and Its Eschatology*, ed. W. D. Davies and David Daube (Cambridge: Cambridge University Press, 1954), 509-36; reprinted in Facet Books Social Ethics Series 12 (Philadelphia: Fortress, 1966); and Wilder, "Albert Schweitzer and the New Testament," in *In Albert Schweitzer's Realms*, ed. A. A. Roback (Cambridge, Mass: Sci-Art, 1962), 348-62.

[63] See Wilder's efforts to awaken the American and European academies to what he calls this mythopoetic character of the New Testament eschatological texts in Amos Wilder, "Scholars, Theologians and Ancient Rhetoric," SBL Presidential Address 1955, *JBL* 75 (1956): 1-11, and Wilder, "Eschatological Imagery and Earthly Circumstance," *NTS* 5 (1958): 229-45.

[64] Wilder, *Eschatology and Ethics*, 4-5.

[65] Ibid., 19, 27.

[66] Ibid., 17.

[67] Wilder, foreword to *Kingdom in Twentieth-Century Interpretation*, ix.

[68] This idea of the Kingdom being nonconceptual had important ramifications later in the work of Norman Perrin. See the introduction to Perrin's *Jesus and the Language of the Kingdom*.

of society, so the Kingdom is present. The Kingdom was also future because there was a real future to God's powerful acts. The process of realizing God's rule had begun in the world and would continue to its inexorable conclusion.[69] To speak of this future action of God as imminent was also part of the allowable "irrationality" of the apocalyptic figure. Jesus proclaims the Kingdom as imminent because of the intensity of his faith:

> It seems a natural corollary of faith's immediate grasp on the supernatural world that in the category of time also the apprehended object should be sensed as close. Even a modern finds an inseparable connection between his hours of profoundest insight and his sense of the immediate and present and continuous divine assize and sifting in human affairs.[70]

So while there is a timeless dimension to the Kingdom-as-imminent teaching of Jesus, the Kingdom was not intended to be completely detemporalized. The confrontation between Jesus and Satan, for example, was inseparably tied to an eschatological timetable.[71] The issue was knowing when to detemporalize and when not to and what sort of force to give to temporal statements.[72]

Wilder viewed the nature of mythical language as the central hermeneutical principle for understanding the Gospel literature. This did not mean, however, a mere reinterpretation of the premodern forms, but, along

---

[69] Wilder, *Eschatology and Ethics*, 39-41.

[70] Ibid., 8. Wilder sees the language of imminence in Jesus consistent with the sociological characteristics of all utopian-millennial groups (Wilder, foreword to *Kingdom in Twentieth-Century Interpretation*, ix). The irrationality of the eschatological type was specifically that "he could announce the imminent end of the world, but live and teach as if it were to go on" (Wilder, *Eschatology and Ethics*, 41). This eschatological irrationality was the rationale for Wilder's belief that Jesus' ethics were neither "interim" nor existential.

[71] Wilder, foreword to *Kingdom in Twentieth-Century Interpretation*, x. This is where Wilder finds fault with the postmodern hermeneutics of deconstructionists like Jacques Derrida and Roland Barthes, who make the meaning of New Testament language completely unrelated to the New Testament era. See Wilder, *War of Myths*, 34-37.

[72] Wilder doubts that the delay of the Parousia was as critical an issue in the early church as it is often made out to be in New Testament studies. Given the particular mythical time-conception of apocalyptic language, disappointments with the schedule would not have been catastrophic (Amos Wilder, *The Bible and the Literary Critic* [Philadelphia: Fortress, 1991], 80).

the lines of the New Hermeneutic, Wilder urged that attention be given to the metaphysical power of language. In *The Language of the Gospel*[73] Wilder developed this latter concern with an obvious debt to Ernst Fuchs.[74] He noted that the symbols and metaphors of language were both revelatory and effective for impacting reality beyond just communication. Wilder said that language communicated notions of the past but also had power to effect the reality of the present,[75] an idea much on the order of the New Hermeneutic's "language-event" concept. The dynamics of the language demanded hermeneutics to account for both aspects. Thus, "to merely reproduce the words of the New Testament is to falsify their original meaning and to defraud modern hearers of that meaning."[76] When put in terms of New Testament eschatology, Wilder contended the rich symbolisms of Kingdom, Prince of Peace, Son of Man, and so on, should not be *factualized* to accomplish their purpose of calling forth myth in crisis. Like all of the other images and metaphors Jesus employed, the Kingdom is not a rigidly defined concept.

The parables of Jesus are important to the apocalyptic role Jesus played. Not only are they generally agreed to have high claims to authenticity on matters of form,[77] but their parallel to wisdom literature has a unique status in the apocalyptic genre.[78] Contrary to many interpreters, who tend to separate the parables from Jesus' eschatological statements, Wilder urges that the two be seen as integral to one another. Parables were powerful tools Jesus used to apocalyptically present and effect the realities of the

---

[73] Subtitled *Early Christian Rhetoric* (New York: Harper & Row, 1964); reissued as *Early Christian Rhetoric: The Language of the Gospel* (Cambridge, Mass.: Harvard University Press, 1971). On the impact of *Early Christian Rhetoric* in literary criticism of the Kingdom of God see W. Emory Elmore, "Linguistic Approaches to the Kingdom: Amos Wilder and Norman Perrin," in *Kingdom in Twentieth-Century Interpretation,* 53-66.

[74] Fuchs is the modern writer most often cited in *The Language of the Gospel.* Wilder also wrote introductory essays for the New Hermeneutic for English-speaking audiences. See Wilder, "New Testament Hermeneutics Today," in *Current Issues in New Testament Interpretation,* ed. W. Klassen and G. F. Snyder (New York: Harper, 1962), 38-52; and "The Word as Address and the Word as Meaning," in *The New Hermeneutic,* ed. J. M. Robinson and J. Cobb (New York: Harper, 1964), 198-218.

[75] Wilder, *Rhetoric,* 84.

[76] Ibid., 122-23.

[77] It is presumed that tightly framed and coherent metaphors are less vulnerable to revision (ibid., 82).

[78] Wilder observes the Hebrew mashal-form in *1 Enoch* (ibid., 79-81).

transformation that God's actions were producing: "Now we know that a true metaphor or symbol is more than a sign, it is a bearer of the reality to which it refers. The hearer not only learns about that reality, he participates in it."[79] In the discussion that follows concerning the parables of the Kingdom (Mark 4 and Matt. 13), Wilder casts the reality of the Kingdom in terms of faith in God's work throughout one's daily life (the sower, the seed growing by itself)—"a sense of God at work and the wonder and promise of the outcome,"[80] and joy (the treasure and the pearl). In each case the message of the parable confirms the message of the rest of Jesus' mythical language. The messianic banquet, the Son coming in the clouds, and the life of the age to come, were mythical representations of the essential intuitions of Israel, that is, the Kingdom, that Jesus presented in parables.[81]

Parable Studies: Funk, Via, and Crossan

Wilder's lonely crusade for literary criticism was joined in the mid 1960s in North America by the parable studies of Robert W. Funk, Dan O. Via, and John Dominic Crossan.[82] Their collaboration with Wilder and others would later produce the Parables Seminar within the Society of Biblical Literature and the accompanying journal *Semeia*.[83] From the outset, this

---

[79] Ibid., 84.

[80] Ibid., 86.

[81] Ibid., 86.

[82] Interest in analysis of language continued in Europe primarily through the efforts of Erhardt Güttgemanns and his generative poetics group at the University of Bonn. See their journal, *Linguistica Biblica* (since 1970), and its companion monograph series, *Forum Theologiae Linguisticae* (since 1972).

[83] See Amos Wilder's introduction to the first issue of *Semeia* for details on the history and charter of that journal and seminar (*Semeia* 1 [1974]: 1-16). Other important discussions of parable research during this period include: G. V. Jones, *The Art and Truth of the Parables* (London: SPCK, 1964); E. C. Blackman, "New Methods of Parable Interpretation," *CanadJT* 15 (1969): 3-13; J. D. Kingsbury, "Ernst Fuchs' Interpretation of Parables," *LuthQ* 22 (1970): 380-95; Kingsbury, "Major Trends in Parable Interpretation," *ConcordTM* 42 (1971): 579-96; Kingsbury, "The Parables of Jesus in Current Research," *Dialog* 11 (1972): 101-7; N. Perrin, "The Parables of Jesus as Parables, as Metaphors, and as Aesthetic Objects: A Review Article," *JRel* 47 (1967): 340-47; Perrin, "The Modern Interpretation of the Parables of Jesus and the Problem of Hermeneutics," *Interp* 25 (1971): 131-48; Perrin, "Historical Criticism, Literary Criticism, and Hermeneutics: The Interpretation of the Parables of Jesus and the Gospel of Mark Today," *JRel* 52 (1972): 361-75; W. J. Harrington, "The Parables in Recent Study (1960-1971)," *BibTB* 2 (1972): 219-41.

group would have strong ties to the New Hermeneutic in terms of an existential hermeneutic driven by the concept of language-events.[84] For the Kingdom, the results would be very similar to those we have already seen in Fuchs, Linnemann, and Jüngel, while the angle of approach varies according to the individual scholar.

The idea of metaphor is the primary means for Funk to frame his investigation in *Language, Hermeneutic, and Word of God*.[85] With an introductory nod to the language-as-event theology that he takes from Bultmann, Heidegger, Fuchs, Ebeling, Van Buren, Ogden, and Ott, Funk takes up with Eberhard Jüngel's contention that it is in the parables, more than any other mode of language, that the Kingdom of God is brought to existence in language.[86] The existential hermeneutic comes to the fore, with the Kingdom of God again being understood as the ultimate paradigm of reality, the "mystery of being." The expanded metaphors of the parables function to allow the hearer to look beyond the looking glass, so to speak, and grasp

---

[84] This is the context for the way "literary criticism" or "New Literary Criticism" is used in this chapter. A distinction needs to be made in this understanding of literary criticism and study of the literary sources of the Gospels that has been going on for decades. The newer literary criticism employed by Funk, Via, Crossan, and Perrin is dedicated to doing more justice to the text in its own right. Its interest goes beyond the literary history of texts. Funk has argued this criticism should be called "literary literary criticism" and that the older literary criticism is more correctly called "source criticism" (Robert W. Funk, "Literary Critical Study of Biblical Texts," *Semeia* 8 [1970]: viii). For an overview of this recent literary criticism and other discussions of terminology, see William A. Beardslee, "Recent Literary Criticism," in *The New Testament and Its Modern Interpreters*, ed. Eldon Jay Epp and George W. MacRae (Philadelphia: Fortress/Atlanta: Scholars, 1989), 175-200; Edgar Krentz, *The Historical-Critical Method*, Guides to Biblical Scholarship (Philadelphia: Fortress, 1975), 49-50; Norman R. Petersen, *Literary Criticism for New Testament Critics*, Guides to Biblical Scholarship (Philadelphia: Fortress, 1978), 10; and more recently, Stephen D. Moore, *Literary Criticism and the Gospels: The Theoretical Challenge* (New Haven and London: Yale University Press, 1989). Mercer has an excellent survey of the contribution of the nonbiblical New Criticism of the 1920s to this current methodology (Calvin R. Mercer, *Norman Perrin's Interpretation of the New Testament*, Studies in American Biblical Hermeneutics 2 [Macon, Ga.: Mercer University Press, 1986], 46-57). However, Mercer's idea that the New Criticism is the important antecedent of Wilder, Funk, Via, and Crossan needs to be reconsidered. If these writers' works are any gauge, they clearly reckon their indebtedness to Europe through the New Hermeneutic.

[85] Robert W. Funk, *Language, Hermeneutic, and Word of God: The Problem of Language in the New Testament and Contemporary Theology* (New York: Harper & Row, 1966).

[86] Ibid., 129.

the essence of the Kingdom's reality. The parable of the great supper, for example, shows the Kingdom's nearness through Jesus' own invitation to follow after him.[87] The "world"[88] of the parable of the good Samaritan, that is, the Kingdom, shines through as the world of love.[89] The parable of the mustard seed is intended to show how the reality of the Kingdom will arrive in a "disenchanting, disarming form." It will feel uncomfortable to the religiously righteous but will be embraced by the religiously disinherited. The Kingdom is "an unpretentious venture of faith, not a towering empire. . . . The parable is full of promise and assurance, but these become available only in the context of what the kingdom really is; viz. the faith to dwell in the kingdom."[90]

Dan Via's understanding of the parables as "aesthetic objects" was another approach that comported well with the New Hermeneutic's existential doctrine of the Kingdom.[91] By means of aesthetic theory,[92] Via

---

[87] Ibid., 197. Metaphor allows the mystery of the Kingdom to be open-ended where time is concerned. The parables really are timeless because of their status as language-events fusing past and present. On the basis of this parables, Funk asserts that Jesus needs to be seen as one "governed by a different mode of temporality than that current in the marketplace" (Robert W. Funk, *Parables and Presence: Forms of the New Testament Tradition* [Philadelphia: Fortress, 1982], 79). This is not the apocalyptic temporal horizon of the early church, nor is it the complete elimination of "real" time advocated by others in an attempt to solve the question of the imminent Kingdom. Rather, much on the order of Wilder, Funk sees Jesus' statements about the Kingdom's imminence as representing "an ecstatic mythical intensity" that dissolves and transcends the common temporal categories" (Funk, *Parables*, 78).

[88] "World" here as used in the context of Heidegger's works (Funk, *Language*, 235).

[89] Ibid., 216.

[90] Robert W. Funk, *Jesus as Precursor*, Semeia Supplements 2 (Philadelphia: Fortress/Missoula, Mont.: Scholars, 1975), 23-24.

[91] Daniel O. Via, *The Parables: Their Literary and Existential Dimension* (Philadelphia: Fortress, 1967.

[92] Via favors the works of Murray Krieger (*The New Apologists for Poetry* [Minneapolis: University of Minnesota Press, 1956]; *A Window to Criticism* [Princeton: Princeton University Press, 1963]; *The Tragic Vision* [New York: Holt, Rinehart, and Winston, 1960]), Eliseo Vivas (*The Artistic Transaction* [Columbus: Ohio State University Press, 1963]; *D. H. Lawrence: The Failure and Triumph of Art* [Evanston, Ill.: Northwestern University Press, 1960]); Michael Polanyi (*The Study of Man* [Chicago: University of Chicago Press, 1963]; *Personal Knowledge*, rev. ed. [New York: Harper Torchbooks, 1964]); and G. Ingli James ("The Autonomy of the Work of Art: Modern Criticism and the Christian Tradition," *The New Orpheus: Essays Toward a Christian Poetic*, ed. Nathan A. Scott Jr. [New York: Sheed and Ward, 1964], 187-209).

determines that the aesthetics of parables is evident from their organic unity and qualified autonomy.[93] By organic unity Via understands a pattern of connections between form and content wherein the parable, in this case, is referential both "in" and "through" itself. The "through" reference of a parable is Via's nomenclature for the point outside of the parable which the parable signifies. Traditionally, historical critical scholarship, typified by Dodd and Jeremias, has focused its efforts here in the "life-setting of Jesus," producing not only mixed historical results but missing the dominant inner meaning of the parable.[94] The inner meaning of the parable is implicit from the world of the parable itself, that is, the parable's own "perspective on life or understanding of existence."[95] In the aesthetic experience, the reader who would dialogue with the parable's world is grasped in the "total psychosomatic man" by the parable's aesthetic qualities, which effects a change of the reader's own "happening existence."[96] The inner meaning of the parables of the Kingdom demands that the futuristic apocalyptic trappings characteristic of Jesus' other discourses are to be demythologized in accordance with Bultmann's existential paradigm.[97] The Kingdom's presence is nothing less than the presence of God himself, that is, the reality of God's rule—the ultimate

---

[93] Via, *Parables*, 73-78.

[94] Ibid., 86.

[95] Ibid., 82-83.

[96] In a way similar to Heidegger's ontological understanding of *Dasein*, Via uses the term "happening existence" as "a brief way of suggesting that in Jesus' parables, as well as in such other literature, human existence is not static but is always occurring through dramatic encounters, the acquiring of new insights, and the gaining and losing of possibilities" (ibid., 92, n. 68).

[97] "The juxtaposition of sayings expressing both realized and futuristic eschatology suggests that present and future are inherently related. Each is seen in light of the other, and human existence is a movement from the present to the future. . . . Because the kingdom of God is future, man is waiting; but because it is also present, the man who responds is fulfilled. The man who lives the existence envisioned by Jesus' eschatology both has and has not; thus he is man in movement, in movement toward having what he has; being is becoming" (ibid., 187-88).

reality.[98] The parable of the talents (Matt. 25:14–30), for example, negatively nuances the true nature of the divine-human relationship by highlighting the need to accept risk and personal responsibility in the Kingdom.[99] The parable of the ten maidens (Matt. 25:1–13) shows present time as a gift and a demand.[100]

John Dominic Crossan's scholarly interest in the historical Jesus that has now apparently culminated in his voluminous *The Historical Jesus: The Life of a Mediterranean Jewish Peasant* (1991), of which more will be said later, began in the early 1970s in a study of the parables.[101] His first book, *In Parables: The Challenge of the Historical Jesus*, begins with a chapter entitled "Parables and the Temporality of the Kingdom" in which the essential paradigms for his study are laid out. Shades of the New Hermeneutic's Heideggerian ontology color Crossan's description of the parables as "poetic metaphors," which "seek to express what is permanently and not just temporarily inexpressible, what one's humanity experiences as Wholly Other."[102] Crossan asserts the power of metaphor to provoke the hearer to participate in the Wholly Other truth much on the order of language-events:

---

[98] "In Jesus' sayings and parables he brought together the presence of God and the context of daily living. That does not mean that the parables give enlightenment about the constitution of the rule of God (even when they begin 'The kingdom of heaven is like') but that they portray an existential state and show the listener what he must now do" (ibid., 52).

[99] Ibid., 121.

[100] Ibid., 128.

[101] See the brief autobiographical comments in the introduction to Crossan's *In Fragments: The Aphorisms of Jesus* (San Francisco: Harper & Row, 1983). Crossan's works on parables include *In Parables: The Challenge of the Historical Jesus* (New York: Harper & Row, 1973); *The Dark Interval: Towards a Theology of Story* (Niles, Ill.: Argus Communications, 1975); *Raid on the Articulate: Comic Eschatology in Jesus and Borges* (New York: Harper and Row, 1976); *Finding is the First Act: Trove Folktales and Jesus' Treasure Parable*, Semeia Supplements 9 (Missoula, Mont.: Scholars; Philadelphia: Fortress, 1979); *Cliffs of Fall: Paradox and Polyvalence in the Parables of Jesus* (New York: Seabury, 1980).

[102] Crossan, *Parables*, 13. See also Crossan's discussion of "Time and Philosophy" (31–32), which closely follows Heidegger's *Time and Being*.

"A true metaphor is one whose power creates the participation whereby its truth is experienced."[103] This means a modification of the abstract/concrete polarity of the Kingdom's nature[104] and temporal character.[105] The paradigm has an individual, existential, and realized dimension. The *advent* of the Wholly Other *reverses* the individual's entire past and gives his world new life and *action*.[106] The *advent-reversal-action* pattern of the Kingdom's effect is demonstrated in the parables. The canonical parables of the treasure and the pearl and the noncanonical (*GThom* 81:28–82:3) parable of the great fish demonstrate the pattern in microcosm. For each of these "key parables," the advent of the treasure, pearl, or great fish shatters the future that the finders had envisioned for themselves, as myriads of new possibilities are suddenly present. In the face of this new future, the finders then reverse the prior course of their lives and proceed on an entirely new course of action.[107]

---

[103] Crossan, *Parables*, 18.

[104] "The Kingdom of God is the power of God expressed in deeds; it is that which God does wherein it becomes evident that he is king. It is not a place or community ruled by God; it is not even the abstract of reign or kingship of God. It is quite concretely the activity of God as king" (Crossan, *Parables*, 23, apparently following Perrin's *Rediscovering the Teaching of Jesus*. He does not give exact sources of most of his citations or allusions in *Parables*).

Crossan finds support for his agenda from what he calls the permanent eschatology of the Old Testament. Permanent eschatology is Crossan's nomenclature for Jesus' own revival of the ancient "prophetic eschatology" of Israel's traditions. In Crossan's reading of the pertinent documents, the canonical prophetic eschatology was considerable different from the eschatology of the apocalypticists current to Jesus' day. Prophetic eschatology was not so much concerned with the end of *this* world-a characteristic of the later apocalyptic thought—but simply the end of the world. Prophetic eschatology "had no concept of another world above or beyond this one (for example, heaven), while the latter [apocalyptic eschatology] could only accept the ending of the this one so easily because it envisaged a far better one elsewhere" (Crossan, *Parables*, 25-26).

[105] It would be mistaken to say that Crossan completely detemporalizes or dehistoricizes the Kingdom of the parables, as he does deny this (Crossan, *Parables*, 32). In a way more reminiscent of Fuchs and his approach to the New Quest, Crossan claims the parables do not dehistoricize the Kingdom completely because they at least show the historical Jesus' own experience and response to the Kingdom. The actions Jesus takes in even relating the parables indicate the contours of his world. Moreover, in the parables, the "ontological ground" for all of Jesus' other words and acts also becomes evident (ibid., 32).

[106] Ibid., 33-34.

[107] Ibid., 34.

THE KINGDOM AS TENSIVE SYMBOL: NORMAN PERRIN

Norman Perrin's contribution to the modern investigation of the Kingdom is an important benchmark within our survey for several reasons. First, his contribution has been such that he still merits comment from anyone seriously working on the Kingdom in this continent or in Europe.[108] Second, in contrast to those scholars just considered, with the possible exception of Wilder, the Kingdom of God has been a major subject of Perrin's career, beginning with his dissertation (*The Kingdom of God in the Teaching of Jesus* [1963]) to one of the last major works before his untimely death (*Jesus and the Language of the Kingdom* [1976]). Within the approaches of the New Hermeneutic and the Parables Seminar, the Kingdom is something of a side issue subsumed beneath a particular linguistic project, but their literary work is important to set the stage for Perrin, as we shall see. Finally, at a deeper level, Perrin's scholarly pilgrimage coming up through the ranks of historical criticism and then crossing over into the newer literary criticism embodies the transition of many New Testament scholars from the historical methodology of the Enlightenment into the various multidisciplinary approaches found today in New Testament studies. To one degree or another, modern interest in semiotics and the Third Quest is driven from the start by a certain scholarly dissatisfaction with a radical historical critical method. Perrin shared this dissatisfaction.

The Apocalyptic Kingdom

In many ways one of Norman Perrin's favorite maxims to his students, "Today's assured results are tomorrow's abandoned hypotheses," serves as a rubric for

---

[108] In the European context, see for example the comments from Odo Camponovo in *Königtum, Königsherrschaft und Reich Gottes in den Frühjüdischen Schriften* (Göttingen: Vandenhoeck & Ruprecht, 1984), 55-60, 437-38, Martin Hengel and Anna Maria Schwemer in *Königsherrschaft Gottes und himmlischer Kult im Judentum, Urchristentum und in der hellenistischen Welt* (Tübingen: J. C. B. Mohr [Paul Siebeck], 1991), 5-6, and Jacques Schlosser in *Le règne de Dieu dans les dits de Jésus* (Paris: J. Gabalda, 1980), 54-55.

the evolution of his own thought about the Kingdom.[109] Accordingly, there are at least two angles from which his work may be approached. There is a possible focus upon the differing hermeneutical methodologies Perrin experimented with throughout his scholarly pilgrimage.[110] There is also the apparent driving motivation of Perrin's own question about the relationship of the historical Jesus to Christian faith.[111] Both these theological and hermeneutical concerns impact Perrin's discussion of the Kingdom.

Beginning with his education in England (M.Th. under T. W. Manson at Manchester, 1956) and Germany (D.Theol. under Joachim Jeremias at Göttingen, 1959), Perrin enters an academy freshly charged with the New Quest of the historical Jesus. He also enters, escorted with his teachers, more conservative judgments as to the relevance of the quest for Christian

---

[109] As recalled by one of his students, Dennis C. Duling, "Norman Perrin and the Kingdom of God: Review and Response," *JRel* 64 (October 1984): 468. This entire volume of the *Journal of Religion* was dedicated as a memorial tribute to Norman Perrin. It contains several articles by his students and colleagues, including a complete bibliography of his works compiled by John R. Donahue and Robert M. Fowler, "A Bibliography of the Works of Norman Perrin," *JRel* 64 (October 1984): 548-57. Major discussions of Perrin's work include Welton O. Seal Jr., "The Parousia in Mark: A Debate with Norman Perrin and 'His School'" (Ph.D. diss., Union Theological Seminary, 1981); Seal, "Norman Perrin and His 'School': Retracing a Pilgrimage," *JSt NT* 20 (February 1984): 87-107; Calvin R. Mercer Jr., "Norman Perrin: A Scholarly Pilgrim" (Ph.D. diss., Florida State University, 1983); Mercer, *Norman Perrin's Interpretation;* Werner H. Kelber, "The Work of Norman Perrin: An Intellectual Pilgrimage," *JRel* 64 (October 1984): 452-67. Excluding *Jesus and the Language of the Kingdom* (1976), Perrin ("Interpretation of a Biblical Symbol," *JRel* 55 [July 1975]: 360, n. 12) considers the following works the most important in his discussion of the Kingdom: *The Kingdom of God in the Teaching of Jesus* (1963); *Rediscovering the Teaching of Jesus* (New York: Harper & Row, 1967); "Wisdom and Apocalyptic in the Message of Jesus," *Society of Biblical Literature One Hundred Eighth Meeting* [1972] *Proceedings* (Missoula, Mont.: SBL, 1972), 2:543-70; *The New Testament: An Introduction. Proclamation and Paranesis, Myth and History* (New York: Harcourt Brace Jovanovich, 1974), 288-99; "Eschatology and Hermeneutics" (SBL presidential address, 1973) *JBL* 93 (1974): 3-14.

[110] Perrin notes (*A Modern Pilgrimage in New Testament Christology* [Philadelphia: Fortress, 1974], 1), "It has been a feature of my academic pilgrimage that 'one thing has led to another.' I began with life of Jesus research and that led me to the Son of Man and New Testament Christology. The Son of Man is most prominent in the Gospel of Mark and that fact led me to Markan research and redaction criticism. In its turn redaction criticism led me to literary criticism and hermeneutics, the most recent phases of my interest and concerns."

[111] Perrin's own statements to his motive are not the most explicit, but Mercer, *Norman Perrin's Interpretation,* 34, makes a convincing case that the question of the relationship between faith and history is a helpful category to assess Perrin's work. See also the similar observation by Kelber, "The Work of Norman Perrin," 462.

faith and the nature of the New Testament documents. For both Manson and Jeremias, the historical Jesus was critical to true Christian faith and this Jesus was indeed retrievable from the New Testament. In questions of authenticity, both held the burden of proof to be on the skeptic.[112] Perrin's first discussion of the Kingdom bore the marks of these presuppositions.

In *The Kingdom of God in the Teaching of Jesus*, Perrin viewed the Gospels essentially as repositories of the historical memoirs of the Jesus of history. In this context Perrin drew conclusions under three broad categories concerning the Kingdom of God. (1) Jesus' understanding of the Kingdom is basically in line with the Jewish apocalyptic ideas of his day. This meant the "Kingdom of God" referred to a nonspatial, nonterritorial, and therefore nonpolitical, nonnationalistic concept that should be translated "reign," "sovereignty," or "kingly rule" of God.[113] Along with Weiss and Schweitzer, Perrin saw Jesus' proclamation as an end-of-the-world message. (2) In contrast to Jewish apocalyptic, however, Jesus teaches that the Kingdom is both present and future. It is present in his interpretation of exorcisms and spiritual forgiveness of sins, and it is future in the consummation in terms of "judgment, the vindication of Jesus himself, the establishment of the values of God, and the enjoyment of all the blessings to be associated with the perfect relationship with God."[114] The Kingdom's presence gave the Kingdom a this-worldly tenor more in line with the hope of prophetic eschatology than that of apocalypticism. Thus, Perrin saw God's reign broadly defined around two poles: God's "decisive intervention in history and human experience," and "the final state of the redeemed to which that intervention leads (Mark 1:15; Matt. 10:7;

---

[112] Manson states: "If God did in fact speak through the prophets we cannot absolve ourselves from the task of finding out as exactly as we can what was said and what it meant. If God did in fact speak to us through the life, death, and resurrection of Jesus it is vitally important to know as fully and as accurately as possible what sort of life and death and resurrection became the medium of the divine revelation. There is no escaping from the historical inquiry" ("The Life of Jesus: Some Tendencies in Present-Day Research," in *The Background of the New Testament and Its Eschatology* [Cambridge: Cambridge University Press, 1956], 221). On methodological assumptions, Jeremias says: "In the synoptic tradition, it is the inauthenticity and not the authenticity of the sayings of Jesus that must be demonstrated" (Joachim Jeremias, *New Testament Theology*, trans. John Bowden [London: SCM, 1971], 37).

[113] Perrin, *Kingdom of God*, 158.

[114] Ibid., 186, 199 (quotation from 199).

73

Luke 10:9–11).[115] (3) Jesus' ethical teaching illustrates a proclamation-response pattern intended to show what kind of response enables an individual to enter into the new and perfect relationship with God which is the ultimate aim of God's intervention into history and human experience.[116]

The Existential Kingdom

While Perrin's methodology in *The Kingdom of God in the Teaching of Jesus* was conservative, there are nonetheless signs of an increasing existential-ism in his theology even at this early date. In *Kingdom* Perrin is drawn toward existentialism in his attempt to express the presence of the Kingdom in human experience. Jesus uses apocalyptic language not because he believes in the apocalyptic division of history into epochs, its calculations, signs, visions, and mythological portrayal of events, but only as it serves to mediate his real intentions of impressing his hearers with the themes of divine intervention and human response.[117] The existential understanding of the present/future dialectic held promise for making the first-century message of Jesus relevant to today.

Given this initial interest in Bultmann's existentialist theology, Perrin's next major project, *Rediscovering the Teaching of Jesus*, was conducted in full accord with a Bultmannian form-critical methodology that paved the way for even more existential conclusions about the Kingdom. In practice Perrin now is fully convinced of the discontinuity between "Jesus the Proclaimer" and "Jesus the Proclaimed" in the New Testament documents.[118] In questions of authenticity, his mottos are "When in doubt discard," and "The burden of proof always lies on the claim to authenticity."[119]

---

[115] Ibid., 167.

[116] Ibid., 167.

[117] Ibid., 124, 91. See Mercer's discussion of Perrin's early attraction to Bultmann for the question of Christian faith and the historical Jesus (*Norman Perrin's Interpretation*, 80).

[118] At the conclusion of *Rediscovering*, 244, Perrin writes, "The main source [for faith] will always be the proclamation of the Church, a proclamation arising out of a Christian experience of the risen Lord."

[119] In 1962, a few years after his work for *Kingdom*, Perrin writes, "The evangelists have no interest whatsoever in the factuality of that which they are recording" for "it does not matter to them in the slightest degree that their presentation of the teaching of Jesus is very different from what Jesus had actually said in Galilee and Judea" ("Faith, Fact and History," *Christian Advocate* 6 [December 20, 1962]: 7-8).

In *Rediscovering* Perrin proposes his well-known methodology for reconstructing the teaching of Jesus by first "writing a history of the tradition of which a given saying is a part,"[120] and then testing the earliest form of the saying by certain "criteria for authenticity."[121] Perrin advocates three criteria, beginning with the fundamental criterion of *dissimilarity*. By this test, for a saying to be considered as authentic it must be "dissimilar to characteristic emphases both of ancient Judaism and of the early church."[122] The second criterion is that of *coherence*, which means that a saying may be accepted if it can be shown to "cohere" with sayings that have been shown already to be dissimilar by the first criterion.[123] The last criterion for authenticity is that of *multiple attestation*. Accordingly "a motif which can be detected in a multiplicity of strands of tradition and in various forms" may be authentic so long as it also passes the criterion of dissimilarity.[124]

The remainder of *Rediscovering* is comprised of Perrin's application of these criteria to reveal the "irreducible minimum of historical knowledge" of Jesus. For the Kingdom of God this irreducible minimum does not yield any drastically new conclusions from those in *Kingdom* except that now Perrin is working with a much smaller core of sayings and adding more existential flavor. From his work with the three sayings that he considers to

---

[120] Perrin, *Rediscovering*, 32. He arrives at a history of the tradition by examining the catechetical or parenetic teachings of the early church (15).

[121] Mercer, *Norman Perrin's Interpretation*, 21, considers this to be Perrin's most notable contribution as a form-critic. It should be noted with Erich Grässer ("Norman Perrin's Contribution to the Question of the Historical Jesus," *JRel* 64 [October 1984]: 491, n. 33), that Perrin was not the originator of any of his criteria. The idea of dissimilarity as the standard by which distinctive teaching of Jesus is established can be found before Perrin in Bultmann (*The History of the Synoptic Tradition* [1921]) and Käsemann ("The Problem of the Historical Jesus," in *Essays on New Testament Themes* [1954]), or contemporaneously to Perrin in Reginald H. Fuller (*A Critical Introduction to the New Testament* [1966]). The issue seems to be that the common designation of the test as "the criterion of dissimilarity" is first proposed by Perrin (Perrin, *Rediscovering*, 39) and his nomenclature became the standard.

[122] Perrin, *Rediscovering*, 39.

[123] Ibid., 43.

[124] Ibid., 46. Kelber perceptively notices a fourth criterion at work in *Rediscovering*. He calls it the "criterion of vividness" and notes Perrin's frequent appeal to a saying's "quality of freshness" and "acute and sympathetic observation of Palestinian peasant life" (Perrin, *Rediscovering*, 81, cf., also 95, 120, 127-28, 138, 141-42, 159, and 163) as a claim to authenticity (Kelber, "The Work of Norman Perrin," 456).

have highest claim to authenticity and which also "present the fundamental emphases of the teaching of Jesus concerning the Kingdom" (Matt. 11:2; 12:28/ Luke 11:20; Luke 17:20, 21), Perrin sees the Kingdom as (1) a comprehensive term for the blessings of salvation which are available in the present, and not just in the apocalyptic hope for the age to come; (2) the final act of God redeeming his people which "fills" the present; (3) in "dissimilarity" to Jewish texts which spoke of the Kingdom's "establishment," Jesus speaks of the Kingdom as "coming."[125] Within the same existential theology that will govern his discussion of the parables, Perrin highlights the meaning of Luke 17:20–21 ("The kingdom of God is not coming with signs to be observed; nor will they say, 'Look, here it is!' or, 'There it is!' For behold, the kingdom of God is in your midst"):

> We may claim that the meaning is: "the Kingdom is a matter of human experience." It does not come in such a way that it can be found by looking at the march of armies or the movement of heavenly bodies; it is not to be seen in the coming of messianic pretenders. Rather, it is to be found wherever God is active decisively within the experience of an individual and men have faith to recognize this for what it is.[126]

In addition to the prophetic eschatological direction of *Kingdom* now becoming decidedly more individualistic, the existential program surfaces further in Perrin's notice of the New Hermeneutic and the concerns of language. Though at this time he is still wary of the bolder contentions of Jüngel that the Kingdom is manifested in the hearer of the parables, he cites with approval the "less ambitious" and "less dramatic" statement of Amos Wilder that "true metaphor or symbol is more than a sign; it is a bearer of the reality to which it refers."[127] The stage is set for the most

---

[125] Perrin, *Rediscovering*, 54-63.

[126] Ibid., 74. See also 204-5, where Perrin discusses the issue of time: "The whole tenor of the teaching of Jesus at this point is that the experience of the present is an anticipation of the future. Further, the experience of the present is a guarantee of the future, as the parables we discussed earlier in this chapter show, in that they challenge men to learn from their experience in the present to have confidence in the future. . . . In any statement of this theme we must use the words 'present' and 'future,' but let us be careful to remind ourselves that the emphasis is not temporal, but experiential."

[127] Ibid., 82, citing Wilder's *Language of the Gospel*, 92.

dramatic shift in the Kingdom's interpretation Perrin would offer in *Jesus and the Language of the Kingdom.*

Prior to *Language,* however, Perrin would take his form-critical presuppositions to their natural limits in redaction criticism.[128] Viewing the author as the final stage of the biblical document's history unfortunately proved to be just one more factor occluding the text's window to the historical Jesus, and, therefore, shrinking the foundation of Christian faith. Perrin's small book in the Guides to Biblical Scholarship series entitled *What Is Redaction Criticism?*[129] is decidedly negative towards the biblical texts as reliable witnesses upon which one can build faith in Jesus. He wrote that redaction criticism

> makes clear the fact that the voice of the Jesus of the Gospels is the voice of living Christian experience, and that the evangelists and the tradition they represent are indifferent as to whether this experience is ultimately related to anything said or done in Galilee or Judea before the crucifixion.[130]

For the Gospel of Mark, which was the primary locus of Perrin's redactional efforts, the conclusions were indeed stark: "If the Jesus of the Gospel of Mark is the Jesus of Mark's own Christian experience and that of the church before him, then the claim that the 'historical' Jesus is the center and source of Christian faith would seem to have no necessary basis in the New Testament."[131]

The Symbolic Kingdom

Perrin's next major contribution to the study of the Kingdom of God and the one that most impacts current discussion of the Kingdom came within the context of his last methodological shift, that of literary criticism. In

---

[128] Perrin's interest in redaction criticism is evident as early as 1966. See his brief article, "The *Wredestrasse* Becomes the *Haupstrasse:* Reflections on the Reprinting of the Dodd Festschrift," *JRel* 46 (1966): 296-300.

[129] Norman Perrin, *What Is Redaction Criticism?* (Philadelphia: Fortress, 1969). The debt to Bultmann is fully realized during this period as well when Perrin writes *The Promise of Bultmann: The Promise of Theology,* ed. Martin Marty (1969; reprint, Philadelphia: Fortress, 1979).

[130] Perrin, *Redaction Criticism,* 74.

[131] Ibid., 74.

Jesus and the Language of the Kingdom, his understanding of the Kingdom of God undergoes significant revision in line with the concept of "tensive symbol" gleaned from Philip Wheelwright's studies of language, *Metaphor and Reality*[132] and *The Burning Fountain.*[133] Wheelwright distinguishes between two kinds of symbols used in language, steno symbols and tensive symbols. Steno symbols are typified as "closed," "static," having a stipulated meaning, a "public exactitude, uncompromising identity of reference for all who use them correctly."[134] Scientific language and the language of logic necessarily employ steno symbols. Steno symbols have one referent and are conceptual. Examples of steno symbols would be the mathematical symbol for *pi,* and the words "cat," *gato, Katze,* and *chat.* Tensive symbols, on the other hand, may be termed "poetic," "alive," and "built on tension in life." They address what in human experience are more vague, shifting, problematic, and paradoxical phenomena. Wheelwright says,

> The tensive symbol cannot be entirely stipulative, inasmuch as its essential tension draws life from a multiplicity of associations, subtly and for the most part subconsciously interrelated, with which the symbol, or something like it and suggested by it, has been joined in the past, so that there is a stored up potential of semantic energy and significance which the symbol, when adroitly used, can tap.[135]

Tensive symbols are found readily in the work of poets, and they in fact determine whether a work is poetic or not.

---

[132] Philip Wheelwright, *Metaphor and Reality* (Bloomington: Indiana University Press, 1962).

[133] Philip Wheelwright, *The Burning Fountain* (Bloomington: Indiana University Press, 1968). Paul Ricoeur's discussions of sign and symbol also influenced Perrin's thought at this time, as did Mircea Eliade's writings on myth and eschatology. See Paul Ricoeur, *The Symbolism of Evil* (Boston: Beacon, 1969) and *Conflict of Interpretations: Essays in Hermeneutics* (Evanston, Ill.: Northwestern University Press, 1974); Mircea Eliade, *Myth and Reality,* trans. Willard R. Trask (New York: Harper & Row, 1963), 54-74, and *Images and Symbols* (New York: Sheed and Ward/London: Horvil, 1961); Norman Perrin, "Eschatology and Hermeneutics: Reflections on Method in the Interpretation of the New Testament," *JBL* 93 (1974): 3-14, and "Wisdom and Apocalyptic in the Message of Jesus," *Proceedings of the 108th Annual Meeting of the Society of Biblical Literature,* ed. L. C. McGaughty (Missoula, Mont.: SBL, 1972), 2:543-72.

[134] Wheelright, *Metaphor,* 35, 94 (the citation comes from 94).

[135] Ibid., 94.

Following on Wheelwright's terminology, Norman Perrin came to see that the symbol "Kingdom of God" in ancient Judaism was tensive and not steno.[136] As a tensive symbol, the words "Kingdom of God" on the lips of Jesus (as recorded for us in Matt. 11:2; 12:28; Luke 17:20, 21) evoked the myth of God who created the world and was active on behalf of his people in that world.[137] According to this understanding, the Kingdom, Perrin contended, was not *conceptual*, but more voluminous and capable of accommodating many concepts. There was not one single referent that it symbolized:

> "Kingdom of God" is not an *idea* or a *conception*, it is a *symbol*. As a symbol it can *represent* or *evoke* a whole range or series of conceptions or ideas, but it only becomes a conception or idea if it constantly represents or evokes that one conception or idea, and we then take the step of creating a kind of verbal shorthand in speaking of the "conception of the Kingdom."[138]

The evolution of Perrin's understanding of the Kingdom of God is at this point readily visible. Whereas in *Kingdom* Jesus denies the apocalyptic activity in favor of the prophetic/eschatological divine events, in *Rediscovering* he speaks of those divine events only in terms of individual human experience, and now in *Language* the Kingdom of God is even more individually responsive and open-ended through the vehicle of the tensive symbol. In *Language* Luke 17:20–21 means:

> Jesus categorically rejected the seeking after "signs to be observed" and in so doing necessarily equally categorically rejected the treatment of the myth as allegory and its symbols as steno-symbols. In the

---

[136] Perrin does this by tracing the development of the Kingdom in ancient Jewish literature. He began with the Near Eastern myth of God being the king of the earth in renewing and creating. This myth was celebrated by the Hebrews in the enthronement Psalms and repeatedly rehearsed by the prophets in their interpretation of the events of the exodus, conquest and settlement of Canaan, and judgment of the southern and northern kingdoms in 721 and 587 B.C. respectively. See Perrin, *Language*, 16–32, and Perrin, "The Interpretation of a Biblical Symbol," 348–59.

[137] Perrin, *Language*, 45.

[138] Ibid., 33 (emphasis his).

message of Jesus the myth is true myth and the symbols of God's redemptive activity are tensive symbols.[139]

The Kingdom now evokes any number of psychological and semantic associations of divine intervention and creatorship in the existential experience of the hearer. Perrin illustrates what he means in his discussion of the Lord's Prayer:

> Once it is recognized that Kingdom of God is being used as a tensive symbol in the opening petition of the prayer, then the remaining petitions become particularly interesting; they represent realistic possibilities for the personal or communal experience of God as king. God is to be experienced as king in the provision of "daily bread," in the experienced reality of the forgiveness of sins, and in support in the face of temptation.[140]

After discussing the Kingdom of God in Jesus' teaching, in *Language* Perrin pursues the use of the symbol in early Christianity. He concludes here that the early church had made Jesus' tensive symbolism unmistakably steno by its associating the Kingdom symbol to the apocalyptic concept of the coming Son of Man (Luke 17:22, 23), for example.[141] Since that first era, Perrin claims that Christendom has mistakenly understood Jesus' tensive language as steno and run into all sorts of interpretive problems with the Kingdom because of it.[142]

Jesus and the Language of the Kingdom was the final, major step in Norman Perrin's academic pilgrimage prior to his untimely death in 1976. It was a step motivated by interest in the continuing impact and relevance

---

[139] Ibid., 45.

[140] Ibid., 47.

[141] Ibid., 60. Perrin also admits that apocalyptic Judaism of the centuries immediately preceding Jesus also understood the "kingdom of God" as a steno symbol. There is a natural progression at work here as well. Tensive language naturally tends to degenerate into steno language the more it is used.

[142] Ibid., 69-80. One problem Perrin avoids is that of the time of the Kingdom. Tensive symbols are timeless.

of symbol derived from his adoption of literary criticism. It also reflected his continuing quest to find a true basis for faith. Yet, despite his earlier conclusions in *Rediscovering* that faith-knowledge could be grounded on historical data,[143] the newer literary approach in *Language* seems to stretch the history-to-faith thread even thinner. Though there is little doubt Perrin wanted to retain some ultimate importance for the historical Jesus,[144] his later efforts tended to lead him down the path of an increasingly ahistorical perspective on the nature of faith.[145]

The roots of these latter conclusions in Perrin stem in part from the fundamental shift of the locus of meaning from the text to the reader that characterizes the New Literary Criticism and postmodernism in general.[146] It is this shift that accounts for both the new possibilities for contemporary hearing visible in the works of the SBL Parables Seminar and *Semeia* and also for the growing belief of textual autonomy. Implicit in this shift has also been a gnawing skepticism of the adequacy of the historical critical method to bring out the meaning of the biblical documents. Challenges to historical critical exegesis punctuate the writings of the newer literary critics of the

---

[143] In the last chapter of *Rediscovering*, 234ff., Perrin proposes three different kinds of knowledge about Jesus. First, there is *historical knowledge*, which encompasses the raw data of what actually happened. This knowledge is subject to constant revision as historical methods become more precise. Second there is *historic knowledge*, which occurs when historical knowledge becomes significant for the present. This knowledge is possible when some point of contact is made in such a way with a past figure or event that present understanding of human existence is enhanced. Finally, *faith knowledge* refers to knowledge of some figure or event that becomes meaningful at the level of religious belief. For the Christian, faith-knowledge of Jesus is related to the confession of Christ as Lord. Such a confession of faith-knowledge could come from the historical knowledge of Jesus, but did not necessarily have to.

[144] Grässer makes this point clear in "Norman Perrin's Contribution to the Question of the Historical Jesus,"499-500.

[145] Mercer, *Norman Perrin's Interpretation*, 89.

[146] I will not attempt here to comment on the larger hermeneutical matrix within which Perrin's work is found and will leave the evaluation of the philosophical and critical intricacies of postmodernism to others. See for example, Anthony C. Thiselton, *New Horizons in Hermeneutics: Theory and Practice of Transforming Biblical Reading* (Grand Rapids: Zondervan, 1992) and Stephen D. Moore, *Literary Criticism and the Gospels*. Both have extensive recent bibliographies.

Bible.[147] The course of Perrin's own scholarly pilgrimage that had moved from more conservative to the most radical practice of historical criticism and then on into literary criticism represents in microcosm this larger hermeneutical shift. Perrin believed historical-critical methodology should not be made the end-all for interpretation. Needed was the final grid of the nature and function of language as studied in literary criticism, because, as Perrin noted, "such literary-critical considerations offer *new* and *valid* possibilities for interpreting the texts concerned."[148]

It is, however, the very *newness* of the meaning of the Kingdom in Perrin and the New Literary Criticism that should arouse our caution. This is because the very novelty of the literary program for the Kingdom disparages the role of good historiography in the hermeneutical process, and, more importantly, it compromises the historical basis of the Christian religion. For example, when Perrin admits that Jesus' symbolic language was missed by the earliest Christian communities and "lost until it was recovered by modern scholarship in the twentieth century,"[149] something shudders deep within the historical roots of the Christian church. One wonders in what sense Perrin would say the church prior to the modern era (really, the last half of the twentieth century) was "Christian."

---

[147] See for example Leander Keck, "Will the Historical Critical Method Survive? Some Observations," in *Orientation by Disorientation: Studies in Literary Criticism and Biblical Literary Criticism*, Pittsburgh Theological Monograph Series 35, ed. Richard A. Spencer (Pittsburgh: Pickwick, 1980), 115-28; also Roland Mushat Frye, "A Literary Perspective for the Criticism of the Gospels," *Jesus and Man's Hope II*, ed. Donald G. Miller and Dikran Y. Hadidian (Pittsburgh: Pittsburgh Theological Seminary, 1971), 193-221; and Daniel Patte, *What Is Structural Exegesis?* (Philadelphia: Fortress, 1976).

This is not to say the New Literary Criticism is uniformly ahistorical in its approach; this should surely be denied in the case of those we have studied on the Kingdom. Historical criticism informs the exegesis of Wilder, Funk, Via, Crossan, and Perrin. "Historico-literary criticism" is the first state of Via's interpretation of the parables. See part two of *In Parables* (110ff.).

[148] Perrin, *Language*, 9 (emphasis his). Perrin's four steps to the hermeneutical process were textual criticism (establishing the text to be interpreted), historical criticism (understanding the nature of the text as a historical and literary artifact, the intent of the author and the meaning understood by the original hearers), literary criticism ("the nature and natural force of both the literary form and language of a text"), and hermeneutics ("the act of interpretation itself"; see *Language*, 2-9).

[149] Perrin, "Interpretation of a Biblical Symbol," 362.

Moreover, the *validity* of the new interpretations is subject to question beneath the weight of the New Literary Criticism's own paradigm. To speak of the "polyvalence" or "plurisignificance" of written texts because of their unlimited potential to create different meaning to every possible reader through language as event, significantly compromises the *a priori* justification for hermeneutics. Truly, it is pushing the limits of logic for Perrin, in the best tradition of the New Hermeneutic's language-event, Funk's metaphor, Via's aesthetic object, Crossan's poetic metaphor, and so on, to *put into print* that "once a text is 'published' and begins to circulate at large, then the meaning intended by the author, or the meaning natural to it in its original historical context, is no longer the meaning necessarily given to that text."[150] It is indeed an interesting twist of logic that Perrin must assume the falsehood of his proposition in order to propose it in writing in the first place!

Other issues may be raised about Perrin's justification for the tensive nature of Jesus' discourse about the Kingdom of God. With regards to sources, Charlesworth has aptly noted Perrin's survey of the intertestamental Judaism on the Kingdom includes only the *Testament of Moses* and the Qaddish prayer (cf. Perrin, *Language*, 26–29).[151] Omitted by Perrin are *Sibylline Oracles* 3:47; 3:767; Tobit 13:2(1); Wisdom of Solomon 6:4; 10:10; *Testament of the Twelve Patriarchs* (*TBen* 9:1); and the *Testament of Abraham* 8:3—all of which make reference to the *basileia* and all of which point to an earthly form of the Kingdom commensurate with Israel's eschatological hope.[152] In the Gospels, Perrin is similarly vulnerable to the charge that his

---

[150] Perrin, *Language*, 7. See Mercer's discussion of this inherent problem for the New Literary Criticism in *Norman Perrin's Interpretation*, 110. Mercer also cites recent critiques of the philosophical foundations of methodologies that sever the text from objective spheres of meaning.

[151] James H. Charlesworth, "The Historical Jesus in Light of Writings Contemporaneous with Him," *ANRW* 25, no. 1: 464, n. 54. In regards to the Qaddish, Meier presents evidence to challenge Perrin's assertion that the Qaddish was in use in the Jewish synagogues before the time of Jesus. See Meier, *A Marginal Jew*, 361-62, n. 36).

[152] After extensive discussion of the sources, Meier summarizes the view of the intertestamental period this way: "the symbol of God ruling as king was alive and well in the 'intertestamental' period and was often connected with eschatological hopes (sometimes with apocalyptic elements) concerning the restoration of all Israel gathered around Mt. Zion or Jerusalem" (Meier, *A Marginal Jew*, 264). See the appropriate summaries of the Kingdom in Tobit, the *Sibylline Oracles*, and the *Testament of the Twelve Patriarchs* on pages 248, 254, 260-61, and 269 of *A Marginal Jew*.

radically reduced core of Kingdom sayings has determined his particular conclusions and at the same time betrayed them. On the one hand, it is far easier to cull existential hermeneutics from a Jesus whose authentic statements only reject apocalypticism (Luke 17:20–21, Matt. 11:12) and assert the Kingdom's presence (Luke 11:20),[153] than it is from a Jesus who himself gives signs of the end (Mark 13, Matt. 24), who speaks in temporal terms of the Kingdom as future and, beyond that, in terms of the hope of Israel (Matt. 19:28).[154] On the other hand, since the limited sampling of three authentic sayings points to Kingdom activity within one's personal life, with what certainty can Perrin assert the Kingdom as a symbol for Israel's tribal myth of God's activity in creation and redemption—activities having some reality beyond the individual?[155]

A final question for Perrin and the entire new literary-critical agenda in which he takes part also concerns the sources of our knowledge of the historical Jesus. Specifically, is it enough to determine the meaning of Jesus' proclamation and ministry from his words alone? When a good portion of the ancient record of Jesus contains description of his deeds—apocalyptic and prophetic deeds—is Perrin's thesis that "all our knowledge of [Jesus']

---

[153] Perrin, *Language*, 41. See the meaning of these three most reliable Kingdom sayings in the following pages (42-46).

[154] On Matthew 19:28 anticipating a restoration of the people of the twelve tribes, see Ingo Broer, "Das Ringen der Gemeinde um Israel: Exegetischer Versuch über Mt. 19,28," in *Jesus und der Menschensohn: Für Anton Vögtle*, ed. Rudolf Pesch and Rudolf Schnackenburg (Freiburg/Basel/Vienna: Herder, 1975), 152-53. The critical scissors of Perrin displayed in *Rediscovering* have come under intense scrutiny since Perrin wrote. See, for example, Neil J. McEleney, "Authenticating Criteria and Mk 7:1-23," *CBQ* 34:4 (October 1972): 431-60; David L. Mealand, "The Dissimilarity Test," *ScotJT* 31 (1978): 41-50; D. G. A. Calvert, "An Examination of the Criteria for Distinguishing the Authentic Words of Jesus," *NTS* 18 (1971-1972): 209-18; R. S. Barbour, *Traditio-Historical Criticism of the Gospels* (London: SPCK, 1972); Erhardt Güttgemanns, *Candid Questions Concerning Gospel Form Criticism*, trans. William G. Doty (Pittsburgh: Pickwick, 1979); Morna D. Hooker, "Christology and Methodology," *NTS* 17 (1970-1971): 480-87; Hooker, "On Using the Wrong Tool," *Theology* 55 (November 1972): 570-81; Gerd Theissen, "Historical Skepticism and the Criteria of Historical Jesus Research *or* My Attempt to Leap Across Lessing's Yawning Gulf," *ScotJT* 49, no. 2 (1996): 147-76; and Robert H. Stein, "The 'Criteria' for Authenticity," in *Studies of History and Tradition in the Four Gospels*, Gospel Perspectives 1, ed. R. T. France and D. Wenham (Sheffield: JSOT, 1980), 225-63.

[155] This observation comes from I. Howard Marshall, "The Hope of a New Age: The Kingdom of God in the New Testament," *Themelios* 11:1 (September 1985): 7-8.

use of the symbol Kingdom of God has to be derived from these sayings [Luke 17:20, 21; Matt. 11:12; and Luke 11:20] and parables, and from the [Lord's Prayer]" adequate?[156]

LANGUAGE AND THE KINGDOM AFTER PERRIN

The tentacles of Perrin's understanding of the Kingdom as a tensive symbol have reached far into New Testament studies, achieving a consensual status in the minds of many.[157] Three recent works, Bernard Brandon Scott, *Jesus, Symbol-Maker for the Kingdom*, James Breech, *The Silence of Jesus*, and Odo Camponovo, *Königtum, Königsherrschaft und Reich Gottes in den Frühjüdischen Schriften*, will serve as recent representatives of Perrin's influence.

Scott

Though Perrin had little interest in structuralist analysis, Bernard Scott has taken up Perrin's work as a point of departure and return to apply the basic structuralist readings of D. Patte, A. J. Greimas, and C. Lévi-Strauss to Jesus' language as a whole. Assuming the symbolic nature of Jesus' language about the Kingdom, Scott believes it is possible to analyze the interior structure of Jesus' own experience of God through the signatory characteristics of his speech. According to the structuralist project, Jesus' language and deeds are

> performances playing upon the potential of [Jesus'] language. As such, individual sayings imply a system of signs. By analogy, a sentence as performance implies undergirding structures, one aspect of which is syntax whose rules can be deduced from the examples of a number of performances. Thus, Jesus' utterances can be explored so as to deduce a grammar of their symbolic organization.[158]

---

[156] Perrin, *Language*, 56.

[157] For example, James Breech (*The Silence of Jesus: The Authentic Voice of the Historical Man* [Philadelphia: Fortress, 1983], 34) and Wendell Willis ("The Discovery of the Eschatological Kingdom: Johannes Weiss and Albert Schweitzer," in *Kingdom in Twentieth-Century Interpretation*, 1).

[158] Scott, *Jesus, Symbol-Maker for the Kingdom* (Philadelphia: Fortress, 1981), 2.

Jesus' organization of the symbols in his language is governed by his "world."[159] Scott's thesis then is realized in terms of describing a metalanguage to filter Jesus' "world" from Jesus' language.[160] The parables are the most direct and primary source of Jesus' experience of God. Their function as metaphor (Funk) betrays their plurisignificant nature and thus their inherent openness to potential meanings. Because of their dynamic ability to enter and change the world of the reader, they must not be closed off from their hermeneutical potential through discursive methods.[161] This is where Perrin went wrong with his own "genetic mode of interpretation."[162] To Scott's way of thinking, Perrin's insistence that the Kingdom had two referents (God's kingly activity and the future state of God's people) undercut his achievement of the Kingdom as symbol over concept. Even these two referents are too "steno" and discursive for a true symbol. True parables are autonomous of particular referents: "We cannot state what a parable means, for it has no meaning separate from itself."[163]

Scott believes that for Jesus' language in the parables we are left only to outline the "horizons" of meaning that constitute the parables' unified insight into the experience of God.[164] As long as we limit our scope to horizons and general fields of insight we have not betrayed ourselves with discursive renderings.[165] Scott's structural analysis yields the horizons of the parabolic world through his testing the following five theses: (1) "the

---

[159] Scott, *Symbol-Maker*, 15, uses "world" according to Funk *(Jesus as Precursor)*, who follows the later Heidegger.

[160] Scott, *Symbol-Maker*, 16.

[161] Ibid., 15. Scott contends that history has demonstrated the unfortunate tendency of the Christian church to close off the parables' hermeneutical potential and vitiate their true nature as parables.

[162] Ibid., 11.

[163] Ibid., 15. Parables must also be treated autonomously because their historical context within the ministry of the historical Jesus cannot be known (24). Scott, however, denies that he has abandoned the "historical method."

[164] Ibid., 16.

[165] Scott still believes that the best we can do is only approximate the parables' insight through discursive description (ibid., 18). Because of parables' polyvalent nature, any discursive description is immediately obsolete.

cosmic appears under the guise of tragedy"; (2) "grace comes to those who have no alternative"; (3) "in the world of the parable the secular and religious are congruous"; (4) "the World of the hearer is questioned by the World of parable"; (5) "faith appears here as the ability to trust the depiction of World in the parable."[166]

Where does Scott's attempt at a nondiscursive correction of Perrin conclude? In the last chapter, he admits the possibility that we may never know what Jesus meant by the symbol "Kingdom of God." Because the various forms of Jesus' speech are metaphoric, that is, tensive, and consequently full of hermeneutical potential, "there is no single interpretation of his language."[167] Add to this that Jesus chose the Kingdom symbol because it was only vaguely similar to its referent, and the final result is confused even more.[168] Compounding the problem is the terrible weight of trying to reduce to discussion that which can never be replaced by discussion.[169] In the light of these hurdles, Scott musters as much finality as he can for Jesus, "the symbol maker for the Kingdom": "Ultimately, it may be so simple as to say that Jesus' referent [for the Kingdom] represents a radical restoration of the first commandment: the creator claiming his creation."[170]

It is precisely results such as these of Scott's that have strained validity in the New Literary Criticism and driven the New Testament academy, including some former advocates of the newer literary quest (like Crossan), more and more in the direction of a wholistic interdisciplinary approaches to the historical Jesus and not into greater dialogue with literary criticism. If the dynamic, living power of language is consistently upheld and pushed too far, then the interpretations and contentions of those in New Literary Criticism, including Scott, are necessarily obsolete the moment they are written. Two conditions are also created for exegesis in such a conundrum, and Scott is mired in both of them. First, we must despair at the hope of recovering the meaning of any ancient words, let alone those of

---

[166] Ibid., 30-32.
[167] Ibid., 171.
[168] Ibid. The choice was the most adequate but still "arbitrary."
[169] Ibid., 175.
[170] Ibid.

THE KINGDOM OF GOD IN THE TEACHING OF JESUS

the historical Jesus. Twenty centuries has surely lost his meaning forever.[171] Scott comes the closest to admitting this of the writers I have discussed, but even his contention that certain broad "horizons" or "insights" of Jesus' meaning are possible must lack logical cogency.[172]

The second condition the student of the New Literary Criticism must endure is the infinite variety of potential results in exegesis. Few controls are available to judge validity in any one interpretation if true human Being is the ultimate referent of everything Jesus said. Given these circumstances, who is to say Scott is off the mark when he says the meaning of the parable of the Good Samaritan is found with the wounded figure lying in the ditch: "The parable can be summarized as follows: to enter Kingdom one must get into the ditch and be served by one's mortal enemy"?[173] It is this dizzying possibility of results that has dissatisfied many with Scott's, and, as we saw earlier, Perrin's understanding of the Kingdom as a tensive symbol.[174]

Breech

Less radical in the appropriation of Perrin's work is the venture of James Breech. Breech was a student of Amos Wilder's at Harvard and delivers a

---

[171] In his recent academic work, *Jesus and Postmodernism* (Minneapolis: Fortress, 1989), 29, James Breech contends rightly that the ultimate effect of polyvalence is to stamp out all meaning in texts except one: the nihilistic one.

[172] See his explanation of his method given the paradigm of language he assumes in *Symbol-Maker*, 17-18.

[173] Ibid., 29.

[174] See, for example, Robert O'Toole's comment that Perrin's "tensive symbol tends towards relativity. For instance, how much meaning can one drop from 'the kingdom of God' before it ceases to be a 'tensive symbol'? Perrin has not attended sufficiently to the objective content or limited nature of a symbol. A symbol cannot say everything, nor can it be deprived of some definite content" ("The Kingdom of God in Luke-Acts," in *Kingdom in Twentieth-Century Interpretation*, 147, n. 2; cf. also Hengel and Schwemer, foreword to *Königsherrschaft Gottes*, 6). Furthermore, one must also ask here if tensive symbols can evoke *contradictory* steno symbols. For example, when Perrin sees the beginnings of the existential hermeneutic in the Qaddish (*Language*, 29) in the presence of the other steno symbols of the intertestamental period (like clouds and thrones and the returning Son of Man), his case for the existential hermeneutic is weakened. There is a great difference between the end of "world" and the end of the world, but as both are apparently possible referents of the tensive Kingdom Jesus preached, Perrin puts himself at a disadvantage to then have to assert the legitimacy of the existential and the illegitimacy of the apocalyptic/eschatological.

critique of Perrin reminiscent of Wilder at several points.[175] He can appreciate Perrin's suggestion that the parables of Jesus are metaphors of the Kingdom and that the "Kingdom of God" is a symbol; but, with Wilder, Breech wants to give the symbol more immediate existential impact than Perrin. Breech proceeds with his existential agenda along two lines. First, he notes that when Perrin says the Kingdom symbol in Jesus' language evoked the myth of God as King in his hearers, he "drains the symbol of its own power" contrary to Wilder's contention that

> a true metaphor or symbol is more than a sign, it is a bearer of the
> reality to which it refers. The hearer not only learns about that reality,
> he participates in it. He is invaded by it. Here lies the power and
> fatefulness of art. Jesus' speech had the character not of instruction
> and ideas but of compelling imagination, of spell, of mythical shock
> and transformation.[176]

Perrin simply had not taken full advantage of the power of symbol to invade real everyday life.

Second, and more significantly, Perrin has mistaken the referent of the Kingdom symbol. The Kingdom parables and sayings that Perrin had exegeted as pointing to the ancient myth of God's kingship in fact do not evoke the myths Perrin admits his hearers already knew. To the contrary, Breech's exegesis of Matthew 11:16–19; Luke 17:20–12; and Luke 11:20 shows that Jesus used the symbol of the Kingdom to *challenge* the existing myths of his audience.

We have seen that these sayings do use language that evokes a whole range of mythological associations, but we have also seen that it is questionable whether Jesus used kingdom language in order to evoke those mythological associations. Indeed, there is ample evidence for asserting that Jesus used Kingdom language in order to challenge the validity of those experiences which facilitated stock responses to such language.[177]

---

[175] See Breech's article, "Kingdom of God and the Parables of Jesus," *Semeia* 12 (1978): 15-40, that preceded *The Silence of Jesus* and deals directly with Perrin's conclusions in *Jesus and the Language of the Kingdom*.

[176] "Kingdom of God and the Parables of Jesus," 18, 22, citing Wilder, *Rhetoric*, 92.

[177] Breech, "Kingdom," 21. Thus Breech calls Perrin on his own criterion of dissimilarity ("Kingdom," 26-27).

Breech's existential agenda is made clear as a corollary when he continues:

> It appears that Jesus uses Kingdom language not in association with historical experience, nor in order to evoke the tribal memories, expectations, and attitudes of a people, but rather in order to identify personal life as the sphere where he located the reality borne by the symbol Kingdom of God.[178]

Jesus in effect uses the Kingdom to reinterpret or demythologize the Kingdom symbol as it was perceived by his first-century Jewish audience. The locus of the symbol was not in the current kingly myths but the individual. Put this way, Breech takes exception to the conventional scholarly wisdom and denies that the Kingdom was the subject of Jesus' proclamation.[179]

What Jesus really understood to be the reality beneath the Kingdom language was divine power, a transpersonal power "which establishes humans in the mode of being as free persons."[180] Both he and John the Baptist experienced this power; the intent of their proclamation functioned not on the level of beliefs and concepts but as dimensions of human experience. Thus the experience of the Kingdom they manifested is distinguished as living in a mode of free giving and free receiving, forgiving one another, enjoying openness to others in fellowship, and so on.[181]

In both Scott and Breech we now have two different directions in which Perrin's work can be taken. On the one hand, Scott's structuralist method takes Perrin's conclusions and slides further out on the limb of textual autonomy than Perrin himself was comfortable to go. Scott's results are much less optimistic for understanding the meaning of the Kingdom from the historical Jesus. Breech, on the other hand, uses Perrin's most recent findings to return to the existential conclusions Perrin had just come from in *Rediscovering the Teaching of Jesus.* His efforts would certainly comport well with Perrin's own concern for the historical Jesus as well as with the

---

[178] Breech, "Kingdom," 21. See also *Silence,* 32–42.

[179] "Far from *proclaiming* the kingdom of God . . . Jesus totally reinterprets the meaning and significance of the traditional symbol 'kingdom of God'" (Breech, *Silence,* 218). Jesus did not preach the Kingdom, he manifested it in his activity (38).

[180] Ibid., 39, 42.

[181] Ibid., 49, 55, and 62 respectively.

general existential categories that permeated Perrin's work throughout his career. But again, Breech must inherit the questions given to Perrin and others of the newer literary hermeneutic. Is Jesus the existential philosopher a realistic *Gestalt* for first-century Palestine? Breech's apparent satisfaction with the notion that Jesus "uses this language [of the kingdom] in a way that differs explicitly from the usage of his contemporaries, predecessors, and successors"[182] in fact paints the historical Jesus as something of a "bolt from the blue" who failed to communicate his essential message to even his closest followers. According to Breech, Jesus' ideas were missed by his contemporaries and by the church that followed him, and "it was only in the twentieth century that New Testament scholars began to recognize the full importance of this kind of language among those who produced the earliest Christian literature."[183] As already noted with Perrin, such statements as these give cause to wonder whether what has preceded the twentieth-century New Testament scholar in the church's history is really "Christian" at all according to the literary critic.

Breech, like Perrin, must also be asked if investigation of a radically reduced list of Kingdom-sayings is likely to let us know what we want to about the Kingdom of God in the teaching of Jesus. Breech's thesis, "that the historical Jesus is discovered in his sayings and parables," leaves out the greater portion of the earliest church's record of her Lord, namely Jesus' miraculous deeds.[184] As Meier has recently observed and as we shall consider in the last chapter, something critical is missed in the historical Jesus if his status as a miracle-worker is isolated from the picture. The various strains of Jesus as the prophet of the last days, the gatherer of Israel, the teacher of general and moral truths, and the exorcist and healer all converge and mutually reinforce one another to present Jesus' understanding of the Kingdom of God.[185]

Camponovo

Our last representative, while holding true to the final conclusions of Perrin's literary criticism, finds more immediate value in the study of the Kingdom

---

[182] Ibid., 37.
[183] Ibid., 34.
[184] Ibid., 217.
[185] Meier, *A Marginal Jew*, 3-4.

by advancing our knowledge of the first-century sources. Almost a direct answer to James Charlesworth's judgment in 1982 that the "intertestamental literature is almost an unexplored mine for possible background to Jesus' teaching, . . . there are impressive parallels in it to Jesus' concept of the Kingdom of God,"[186] Odo Camponovo's 1983 doctoral dissertation from the University of Freiburg was published for the "compilation and interpretation of the early Jewish materials on the kingship of God."[187] Camponovo's study included the canonical Hebrew Scriptures, Pseudepigrapha, Septuagint, Targums, and the writings of the Qumran sect, and it has been influential as a scholarly treatment of all the materials pertaining to the subject.[188] His interest for us at this point also stems from the way his conclusions relate to those of Norman Perrin.

Camponovo's attraction to Perrin is first visible in his overview of the history of the research on the Kingdom of God. Assessing Perrin's *The Kingdom of God in the Teaching of Jesus* and *Jesus and the Language of the Kingdom*, Camponovo is drawn to the discussion of symbol and myth, and it is here that he hopes to make a contribution:

> The indication of the "reign of God" as a symbol is very interesting. It explains two things well: how eschatological images can be realized over and over, and how the texts which discuss God's reign practically never yield exact descriptions of the subject. A question mark needs to be placed behind the outline of the myth. Without question, the symbol evoked a myth, a network of beliefs. But the question may not be one of a rigidly outlined whole as is the trend in Old Testament research. Therefore, it is to be noted in the following what features of the belief-traditions are referred to in the early Jewish texts.[189]

---

[186] "The Historical Jesus in Light of Writings Contemporaneous with Him," *ANRW* II, 25, no. 1 (1982), 464, n. 52.

[187] *Königtum, Königsherrschaft und Reich Gottes in den Frühjüdischen Schriften*, Orbis Biblicus et Orientalis 58 (Göttingen: Vandenhoeck & Ruprecht, 1984), 2 (translations of quotations are the author's). Camponovo's special interest is to study how the changing social and political circumstances in Palestine during his period effected the understanding of God's kingship (*Königtum*, 3).

[188] Camponovo's conclusions inform, in large measure, A. Lindemann's article, "Gottesherrschaft II," in *TRE*, 15:196-218 (cf. 200).

[189] Camponovo, *Königtum*, 60.

Starting with the Old Testament, Camponovo advances three propositions about the kingship of God which he believes apply broadly to all of the early Jewish materials. First, even though in the Old Testament the concrete expression of Yahweh's kingship (realm) and the dynamic aspect of his reigning authority tend to be held closer together, the dynamic aspect should prevail.[190] This abstract understanding is even more outstanding in the literature that followed, including the New Testament.[191] Second, along with many others, Camponovo observes that the theme of God's rule does not play a major role in the early Jewish literature.[192] Presumably this is because the notion of God's rule was so deeply enmeshed into the Jewish world view that it was an assumed feature in the Jewish texts.[193] Third, the "dominion of God" (Camponovo prefers *Herrschaft* to *Reich*)[194] is in fact a symbol for the saving purposes of God *(Heilswillen Gottes)*. It is not a precisely defined concept, as Perrin had demonstrated; it had a multiplicity of referents. For the Old Testament these referents were primarily: (1) the salvation of Israel, (2) the different destiny of the righteous and the unrighteous, and (3) the fact of divine activity.[195] With the passage of time and change of political climate, other referents having to do with piety, repentance, and political liberation were added to the list of what the "reign of God" could evoke. These later

---

[190] Ibid., 443.

[191] Ibid.

[192] Hengel and Schwemer (foreword to *Königsherrschaft Gottes*, 1-2) take exception to Camponovo here as his work fails to include the recently published *Songs of the Sabbath Sacrifice* (4Q 400-407; Masada Shir Shabb; 11Q Shir Shabb). The critical edition was done by Carol A. Newsom, Harvard Semitic Studies 27 (Harvard: Harvard University Press, 1985). We will consider later what they contend these documents mean for understanding the Kingdom of God.

[193] Camponovo, *Königtum*, 437, 442.

[194] Ibid., 443.

[195] Ibid., 126-27. Camponovo adds, "The eschatological texts exhibit no interest in a detailed description of the results of salvation. There are no 'paradise-accounts.'" The prophets were more concerned to answer the pressing circumstances than to give exact concepts of the coming age of salvation. For this reason also Camponovo sees it wise not to press the national/ political elements of the prophetic picture. "This element plays only an incidental part," he says (127).

additions are reflected in the literature corresponding to these particularly tumultuous times.[196]

The "Reign of God" symbol, thus pregnant with its related associations, comes into the New Testament period, and Camponovo is emboldened to offer brief comments on Jesus' use of *basileia*. Jesus, Camponovo believes, was a true child of his age. His language was indeed symbolic, and, like those before him, he felt free to add his own content to the symbol of the Kingdom. To the other variety of referents to *Kingdom* available, Camponovo believes Jesus added his own experience of God's fatherhood. The hoped-for salvation, when God's reign would be complete, was a time when God's people would know him as Father just as Jesus did.[197]

Camponovo's discussion of the early Jewish literature represents just one side of the debt contemporary New Testament studies owe Norman Perrin. As previously mentioned, no serious study of the Kingdom can ignore his work, and the Kingdom understood as a tensive symbol is very widespread in current scholarship. However, it is Camponovo's use of the tensive symbol language that gives cause to question the validity of the term itself. Specifically, when Camponovo contends that the Kingdom symbol was tensive throughout both the Old Testament and Intertestamental literature, he finds himself at odds with Perrin himself on the meaning of tensive and steno symbols. Camponovo's conflict with Perrin on this last point raises the question as to how useful the steno/tensive categories are to advancing the discussion of the Kingdom of God.

What exactly is a tensive symbol? The more time that passes since Perrin introduced the Kingdom as a tensive symbol, the more his terminology has been adulterated in the continuing discussion. For example, in Perrin's terminology Jesus' tensive symbol "Kingdom of God" was made steno by the early Christians when they ossified it around temporal categories (e.g.,

---

[196] Literature from the period of Antiochus IV and the Maccabees (e.g., *AsMos*) discusses God's kingship in terms of the pietistic conditions necessary for God to act on Israel's behalf. In later literature (e.g., *PssSol*), loss of Jewish sovereignty to Rome evoked the politically charged referents for God's reign (ibid., 440–41).

[197] Ibid., 445.

the coming Son of man).[198] But temporal categories are just what many of those who follow Perrin want to retain in Jesus' proclamation. M. Boring, for example, after many pages reviewing Perrin's position and ultimately accepting the Kingdom as a tensive symbol in Mark, goes on to propose that "the kingdom of God as a tensive symbol does not make irrelevant the question of the time of the kingdom's arrival."[199] R. Farmer similarly departs from Perrin on the point of temporality in Matthew: "I agree that as a tensive symbol the kingdom of God should not be conceived of as exclusively present or exclusively future, but I see no reason to eliminate the category of time altogether."[200]

As it is unlikely Perrin himself would have viewed the augmentations of Boring, Farmer, and Camponovo as a legitimate understanding of tensive symbols, perhaps it is time to admit that this terminology does not provide the best description of the Kingdom. Since many want to have real boundaries for the Kingdom's referents, the choice between only the narrow, single-referent, steno symbol and the inexhaustible tensive symbol seems to be on the wrong track. In fact, it appears as if the "tensive symbol" has become scholarly technical jargon that has fallen prey to its own plurisignificance and that finally today means just "symbol."[201] Gone is the notion that this is an inexhaustible symbol for God's kingly activity; back are the more familiar referents of Jewish apocalypticism and prophetism. While some will question the whole notion of the Kingdom

---

[198] Perrin, *Language*, 40, 60.

[199] Boring, "The Kingdom of God in Mark," in *Kingdom in Twentieth-Century Interpretation*, 134.

[200] Farmer, "The Kingdom of God in the Gospel of Matthew," in *Kingdom in Twentieth-Century Interpretation*, 123, n. 18. Meier is another prominent recent interpreter who retains the tensive-symbol terminology but also retains the category of temporality in his discussion of the Kingdom (Meier, *A Marginal Jew*, 242).

[201] Bruce Chilton's work on the Kingdom in the Targums would be a good example here (*God in Strength: Jesus' Announcement of the Kingdom*, Studien zum Neuen Testament und seiner Umwelt, Series B, vol. 1 [Freistadt: F. Plöchl, 1979]). Though he says he has reached similar conclusions to Perrin when he concludes the Kingdom is a symbol for the personal God revealing himself in strength (introduction to *Kingdom of God*, 24), it is clear he does not mean "tensive" symbol in the same manner as Perrin did. For him the Kingdom is capable of subsuming all Jesus' proclamation, but it is not an inexhaustible, "tensive" symbol.

of God as a symbol from the start,[202] tensive symbol terminology appears to serve some modern interpreters like Camponovo best to deemphasize the apocalyptic elements of Jesus' proclamation and to broadly summarize the Jewish hope of God's restoration of the human heart, human society, and the whole creation. However great the scope of the Kingdom's impact in these three realms, scholars today are using "tensive" to denote a tighter field of associated and consistent ideas than Perrin himself would admit, causing one to wonder if Perrin has just given scholarship another way of talking about what it already knew, that is, that the Kingdom is primarily dynamic and abstract versus static and concrete.[203]

---

[202] See the criticism of Perrin's unsophisticated literary critical use of "symbol" in the reviews of *Language* by Crossan and Via (J. D. Crossan, "Literary Criticism and Biblical Hermeneutics," *JRel* 57 [1977]: 76-80; Dan O. Via, "Kingdom and Parable: The Search for a New Grasp of Symbol, Metaphor, and Myth," *Interp* 31 [1977]: 181-83). Hengel and Schwemer speculate that "Kingdom of God" terminology is a metaphor too intricately joined to the reality of the referent to be separable from and ultimately unimportant to the reality to which it points, as is the case with symbols. Is it possible to know the Kingdom's reality without the Kingdom terminology? See Hengel and Schwemer, foreword to *Königsherrschaft Gottes*, 5-6.

[203] This is not an uncommon criticism of "outsiders" to newer literary-critical exegesis. Note the response of David Roberson to the conclusions of structuralism on parables: "when I add up the data supplied by your methods of computation, the answers seem quite precisely the answers I already had" ("Structuralist Criticism of the Parables: A Brief Response," in *Semiology and Parables: An Exploration of the Possibilities Offered by Structuralism for Exegesis*, ed. Daniel Patte, Pittsburgh Theological Monograph Number 9 [Pittsburgh: Pickwick, 1976], 187).

CHAPTER THREE

The Nonapocalyptic
Kingdom of the Regnum Christi

In the fall of 1986 thirty-nine scholars of the Jesus Seminar met at the University of Notre Dame to consider the authenticity of the Kingdom sayings of Jesus.[1] The record of this meeting was written up in *Foundations & Facets Forum* and discloses what the reviewer, James R. Butts, considered numerous "remarkable results."[2] The second of four summarizing propositions of the seminar's work given by Butts is of particular interest: it states the conclusion of the scholars present that "for Jesus the kingdom of God was *not* an eschatological nor an apocalyptic phenomenon."[3] Butts went on to cite this as evidence of a growing trend in biblical scholarship he termed the "vanishing eschatological Jesus."[4]

---

[1] At this particular meeting the focus was the Kingdom sayings from Q, the *Gospel of Thomas*, and the Gospel of Mark. See the publication of the Jesus Seminar: *The Five Gospels: The Search for the Authentic Words of Jesus*, trans. and ed. Robert W. Funk, Roy W. Hoover, and the Jesus Seminar (New York: Polebridge, Macmillan, 1993).

[2] James R. Butts, "Probing the Polling: Jesus Seminar Results on the Kingdom Sayings," *Form* 3, no. 1 (March 1987): 98-128.

[3] As evidence for this proposition Butts cites the fact that most seminar members voted heavily in favor of the statement that Jesus did not expect the end of the world in his lifetime or the lifetime of his contemporaries, plus the fact that the seminar excluded almost all Markan Kingdom sayings from Jesus because in Mark the Kingdom is thoroughly apocalyptic in nature (ibid., 112). No Kingdom saying the seminar considered received unequivocal assent to authenticity (110-11).

[4] Ibid., 110. See the similar assessment of Bruce Chilton three months later in "Kingdom Come, Kingdom Sung: Voices in the Gospels," *Forum* 3, no. 2 (1987): 51-75. Chilton, however, arrives at his assessment another way, via the Targums, thus distancing himself from what he has recently noted as the Jesus Seminar's confusion of antidispensationalism and antifundamentalism (Bruce Chilton, "The Kingdom of God in Recent Discussion," in *Studying the Historical Jesus: Evaluations of the State of Current Research*, ed. Bruce Chilton and Craig A. Evans (Leiden/New York/Cologne: E. J. Brill, 1994), 268-70. See also James G. Williams, "Neither Here Nor There: Between Wisdom and Apocalyptic in Jesus' Kingdom Sayings," *Forum* 5, no. 2 (1989): 7-30, especially 25-27.

As we have seen in the last chapter, one arm of the "vanishing eschatological Jesus" has been the course of Funk and the others in the newer literary criticism. We also noted that the newer literary critical studies appear to play only a limited role in this trend. Far more influential seem to be the works of those operating more in line with traditional historically critical methodologies in hermeneutics. We shall now consider these works in two categories. First in this chapter are those works which essentially continue the belief, held throughout the major part of Christian history, that the Kingdom is the *regnum Christi* or the domain of spiritual salvation. This Kingdom is not spatial, political, or national, but spiritual, finding expression in the present earthly and heavenly church. Jesus was eschatological only to the extent that he used apocalyptic language; his intentions were not to announce the end of the world but the inauguration of the age of God's activity in personal redemption.[5] The second category, to be discussed in the next chapter, is comprised of those scholars who by means of multidisciplinary methods are seeing the locus of the Kingdom's influence primarily in earthly and social dimensions.[6] The Kingdom of Jesus is a social or an economic movement with immediate impact on social structures and entire classes of people. This is the variegated approach of the Third Quest.[7]

---

[5] This position is the one essentially described and advocated by T. F. Glasson ("Schweitzer's Influence—Blessing or Bane?" *JTS* NS 28 [1977]: 290). See also R. A. Muller, "Regnum Christi," *Dictionary of Latin and Greek Theological Terms* (Grand Rapids: Baker, 1985), 259-61.

[6] This is not to say those in the first category do not have some sort of praxis that correlates to the personal appropriation of the Kingdom's rule in this life. The question again between the two categories seems to be one of emphasis.

[7] I have attempted to differentiate the *regnum Christi* from the Third Quest according to Marcus Borg's distinctions of the Third Quest. Again the difference is often a matter of emphasis. For example, N. T. Wright could also be placed under the category of the Third Quest methodologically, though his christological conclusions separate him from those of the next chapter.

Marcus Borg distinguishes the interdisciplinary approach of the so-called Third Quest three ways: "First, though scholars recognized long ago that early Palestinian Christianity was a sect, the significance of this fact has now been more thoroughly explored. Many of the characteristics of sectarian movements also characterize it; in particular, like most sects, it originated in protest and sought to create a new world, both a new social world and a new way of perceiving reality. Second, there is a new awareness of the social function of religious norms and practices, and of the effect of social factors (especially socio-religious norms) on the psyches of people. Third, there is a sharper perception of the social realities behind the texts, which in turn leads to the realization that many of these texts, whatever trans-cultural dimensions of meaning they may also have, initially had a pointed connection to the social matrix of the day" (Borg, *Conflict, Holiness & Politics in the Teachings of Jesus*, Studies in the Bible and Early Christianity 5 [New York: Edwin Mellen, 1984], 18-19).

CHILTON: GOD IN STRENGTH

Bruce Chilton's work on the Kingdom leads off our discussion of the nonapocalyptic Kingdom for two reasons. First, though he comes by a different route, Chilton's conclusions about the Kingdom arrive at nearly the same place and at the same time as those of Norman Perrin.[8] Second, because of this similarity to Perrin, Chilton is attempting to understand the eschatological statements of the New Testament in ways other than those who follow in this chapter. He, therefore, is a convenient transition between the scholars of the previous chapter and those who follow him in this one.

Chilton begins his doctoral dissertation, *God in Strength: Jesus' Announcement of the Kingdom*,[9] by carefully laying the groundwork for his contention that a study of the eleven announcement sayings of the Kingdom (Mark 1:14, 15; Matt. 4:12–17; Luke 4:16–21; Matt. 8:11, 12; Luke 13:28, 29; Luke 16:16; Matt. 11:12, 13; Luke 12:32; Mark 9:1; Matt. 16:28; Luke 9:27) will reveal the heart of Jesus' proclamation of the Kingdom of God. His choice of the announcement sayings of the Kingdom is justified three ways: (1) the announcement sayings comprise a discernable group of sayings;[10] (2) the simple declarations of the announcement sayings avoid the complications of more unwieldy figures of speech inherent to the catechetical and controversy kinds of sayings; (3) the announcement sayings is the most manageable group in terms of number.[11]

With his target identified, Chilton proceeds to "write a history of the tradition" of the announcement sayings through the *via negativa* of redaction criticism.[12] After identifying the dominical elements, Chilton's unique

---

[8] Chilton himself notes this in Bruce Chilton, ed., *The Kingdom of God*, Issues in Religion and Theology 5 (Philadelphia: Fortress; London: SPCK, 1984), 24. His dissertation was finished the same year Perrin's *Jesus and the Language of the Kingdom* was published (1976).

[9] Studien zum Neuen Testament und seiner Umwelt, series B, vol. 1 (Freistadt: F. Plöchl), 1979.

[10] Chilton, *God in Strength*, 13–18, 21, follows C. F. D. Moule's argument distinguishing *kērygma* and *didachē* in the formation of the New Testament documents (*The Birth of the New Testament* (London: A & C Black, 1962). The initial proclamation was spoken, but when it came time to be written in the Gospels, it served the apologetic and didactic needs of the church. The three interrelated activities of proclamation, catechesis, and controversy came to constitute the New Testament.

[11] Chilton, *God in Strength*, 21.

[12] The possibility of writing the history of the tradition is inspired by Perrin's *Rediscovering*, which Chilton follows but criticizes for a simplistic critical technique. Perrin only used the tools of dissimilarity and coherence to isolate the authentic sayings. Chilton felt this was in the right direction but too imprecise compared with what could be gleaned from studies of syntax, vocabulary, and content. See Chilton, *God in Strength*, 20.

contribution to the Kingdom exegesis comes to the fore in his discussion of extant sources which may be links to the first century. Specifically, he contends that the Targums (particularly *Jonathan* and Isaiah) represent material that seems to have been a formative influence on the thoughts and language of the Kingdom announcement sayings.[13] At Mark 1:15, for example, Targum of Isaiah has strong links to three of the four key dominical terms (*plēroō kairos*, and *basileia*).[14] What is most important from all of this, however, is the way Targum Isaiah urges us to understand the temporal element of the Kingdom's proclamation.

> In reference to time, we are not to think in terms of aeons or epochs, but to see it as the moment in which God acts (Is. 60:22) . . . that God comes or is revealed in strength. His own might is near to disclosure (*[engiken]*, in the sense of Is. 56:1); "the kingdom of God" refers to God's dynamic presence.[15]

As Chilton is able to derive similar conclusions for all the announcement sayings,[16] *God in Strength* concludes with the integration of his findings into the contemporary discussion of the Kingdom. Chilton says that the Targums show Jesus' proclamation is not primarily about an apocalyptic timetable inherent to a "spatial" conception of the Kingdom. It is about the personal revelation of God who acts in the present and the future.[17] Jesus is announcing the Kingdom as the experience of the God whose actions elicit responses of joy. In a very real sense the Kingdom of God is nothing other than God

---

[13] The Targums' relationship to the Kingdom is the focus for much of Chilton's writing in the next decade after *God in Strength*. These works include: "Regnum Dei Deus Est," *ScotJT* 31 (1978): 261-70; Chilton, *The Glory of Israel: The Theology and Provenience of the Isaiah Targum*, JSOT supp. 23 (Sheffield: JSOT, 1982); Chilton, *A Galilean Rabbi and His Bible: Jesus' Use of the Interpreted Scripture of His Time*, Good News Studies 8 (Wilmington, Del.: Michael Glazier, 1984).

[14] Chilton, *God in Strength*, 88.

[15] Ibid., 89.

[16] See the summary of Luke 16:16-17: "Jesus announces that from the time of John God comes in strength. . . . Because he is making himself felt, there is no further need for legal mediation between God and man: we may enter His very presence because He is present with us" (ibid., 230).

[17] Ibid., 285. The temporal element of the Kingdom is not done away with, as in the more existential interpretations; it is simply deemphasized. The important point is that God acts. See also Chilton, "Regnum Dei Deus Est," 268.

himself *(regnum dei deus est)*.[18] This was understood by the early church and incorporated into its subsequent traditions, which are found throughout the rest of the New Testament.[19] Chilton notes further that the self-revelation of God as an important common theme of the Targums and the New Testament was an idea proposed nearly a hundred years ago by Johannes Weiss in his famous *Predigt* but subsequently neglected.[20] Chilton hopes his work will return this lost observation to center stage of the discussion.

More work on the Kingdom in the Targums follows *God in Strength*. In *The Glory of Israel* (1982) Chilton examines the Kingdom of God in the Prophetic Targums, and in *A Galilean Rabbi and His Bible* (1984) he considers Jesus' own preaching of the Kingdom in light of the Targums' theology of the Kingdom. Chilton is aware that the case for the Targum-to-Jesus link is not without its difficulties,[21] but in the end he thinks the Targum material solves more problems than it creates.

One sensitive area taken up in *A Galilean Rabbi and His Bible* is the apparent divergence of Kingdom theology Chilton posited for Jesus in *God in Strength* and that which the Targums represent in general. Though the Targums appear to preserve the idea of the Kingdom as the dynamic

---

[18] Chilton sees the use of "Kingdom" for a personal reference to God himself in the parables of the unforgiving servant (Matt. 18:23-35), the marriage feast (Matt. 22:1-14), and the growing seed (Mark 4:26-29). He contends that Jesus utilized the Targumic equation of God and Kingdom, citing as evidence Jesus' use of Kingdom in similar festal contexts to the Isaiah Targum (e.g., Matt. 8:11, 12 = Luke 13:28-29; Chilton, "Regnum Dei Deus Est," 266-67). Passages like Mark 9:1, Matthew 16:28, and Luke 9:27, where Jesus speaks of the Kingdom's appearance *en dynamei*, also relate the Kingdom to "God's strong assertion of Himself" (Chilton, *God in Strength*, 274).

[19] Chilton thus accounts for the rise of the doctrine of the Parousia in the early church. The first Christians were drawn to the personal revelation of God in the person of Christ and therefore made his personal return one of their abiding hopes (Chilton, *God in Strength*, 286-87).

[20] Ibid., 279. The neglect was due in no little part to Weiss's own mistaken encouragement of his followers to interpret the Targums in light of Jewish apocalyptic (ibid., 279, n. 3, citing Weiss, *Die Predigt Jesu vom Reich Gottes* [1964 German ed.], 16).

[21] Chilton, for example, admits that the late date of the Targums prevents him from making too many direct links to pre-A.D. 70 Judaism through them. However, on the strength of the arguments of McNamara (Chilton, *The New Testament and the Palestinian Targum to the Pentateuch* [1966] and *Targum and Testament* [1972]), Chilton believes that the Targums may preserve pre-A.D. 70 concepts. The fact that the Targums represent the more popular piety of synagogue worship is another point Chilton sees in their favor. See his discussion of these matters in the introductory chapter of *A Galilean Rabbi*, especially 38ff.

THE KINGDOM OF GOD IN THE TEACHING OF JESUS

eschatological self-revelation of God, Chilton concedes that the general understanding of the Targums on the Kingdom is of a this-worldly, social, and political, that is, spatial, Kingdom, as others like Klaus Koch have pointed out.[22] This difference could be a problem, since the very foundation of Chilton's earlier argument seems to be pulling him away from his conclusions at this point. How can the Targums present the Kingdom as both the revelation of God *and* the spatial, political, national Kingdom? Chilton answers the issue by contending that the messianic, nationalistic, and vindictive Kingdom crept into the traditions of the Targums following the events of A.D. 70 and do not represent the oldest traditions of the Targums. The oldest is, in fact, the revelation of the mighty King of Israel: God in strength.

> The theology of messianic vindication which the Targum expresses was occasioned by the hard events around 70 A.D., a generation after Jesus' death, so it is only to be expected that he did not echo this aspect of the Targumic kingdom theology. Indeed he challenged the scribal notion that the messiah was to be a triumphal figure in the manner of David.[23]

Chilton's struggle with the theology of the Kingdom in the Targums is evidence of other questions that his approach to the Targums engenders. For instance, because of his criticism of the facile use of rabbinic materials to inform Jesus (as in Glasson or Vermes),[24] Chilton must argue hard for the Targums being the exception, even though he admits they are from the

---

[22] Klaus Koch, "Offenbaren wird sich das Reich Gottes," *NTS* 25 (1979): 158-65. For the prophet-Targums Koch concludes: "In the prophet-Targums Yahweh is already the king of this age, but his malkuta is however primarily evident eschatologically. Malkuta is better understood as 'kingdom' *[Reich]* than 'kingly dominion' *[Königsherrschaft]*. Although the prophet-Targums recognize neither an imminent expectation nor a pre-announcement of the kingdom in the events of the present, as Jesus does, the connection of Jesus' Kingdom of God sayings to contemporary literature is never so close as it is in the prophet-Targums" (author's translation).

On the Targums as presenting an eschatological Kingdom of the restored nation of Israel around Jerusalem, see also George W. Buchanan, *The Consequences of the Covenant* (Leiden: Brill, 1970), 62-63, and Paul Meier, *A Marginal Jew: Rethinking the Historical Jesus*, vol. 2, *Mentor, Message, and Miracle*, Anchor Bible Reference Library (New York, N.Y.: Doubleday, 1994), 262-65.

[23] Chilton, *A Galilean Rabbi*, 63-64.

[24] In "Regnum Dei Deus Est," 261-62, Chilton says that T. F. Glasson's nonapocalyptic understanding of the kingdom as "the divine authority which one takes on oneself by obedience," based on the rabbinic phrase "the kingdom of the heavens," is stalemated by the late date of those materials. Similarly, in *A Galilean Rabbi*, 30, Chilton thinks that Vermes (*Jesus the Jew* [1973]) has erred in his portrait of Jesus by using the rabbinic materials as if they were contemporary to the first century.

same period as the rabbinic literature.[25] The Targums must uniquely preserve these older traditions. But the potential for his success in this venture raises questions as to why the other rabbinic genres of Midrash and Mishnah are not just as likely to preserve older traditions. If this is possible, then criticism of those who use the later literature to construct the historical Jesus deflates accordingly. Chilton's whole case is dependent on the notion that the Targums are not like the other rabbinic material of their time.[26]

A second critical point for Chilton concerns the stages of Targumic development. Not only must the Targums preserve old tradition, but Chilton must prove the older tradition is what demonstrates the Kingdom as simply God's revelation of himself. What is puzzling in all of this is the way Chilton deals with the nationalistic and messianic tenor of the Targums in general. To say that such ideas only enter the Targums after the insults of A.D. 70 and therefore could not have bearing on Jesus' message virtually requires the nonexistence of such insults or ideas prior to A.D. 70, otherwise we cannot presume these ideas also did not infiltrate before that time and ultimately inform the historical Jesus. But surely the insults to Jewish pride, the nationalistic, and the messianic ideas do predate A.D. 70, as seen in the Old Testament,[27] the Apocrypha and Pseudepigrapha, Qumran, the New Testament, and Josephus.[28] The ancient hope of Israel was for renewal that would be national, personal, and universal.

---

[25] Chilton, *Galilean Rabbi*, 23ff.

[26] In *The Kingdom of God*, 13, Chilton charges that the Already/Not-Yet eschatological consensus lacks a contemporary-to-Jesus Jewish document speaking of the Kingdom in this way. But it must be noted that Chilton is in the same dilemma, being able to claim only certain strata within two documents (*Targum of Isaiah* and *Jonathan*) for his own view.

[27] Chilton's own discussion of the source of the Targums' and Jesus' understanding of the Kingdom in effect admits the nationalistic/messianic position of the Old Testament. The Targums' nationalistic/messianic understanding of the Kingdom, he says, is *exegetically* derived (from the Old Testament), while Jesus' nonnationalistic view is *experientially* derived (Chilton, *Galilean Rabbi*, 166-67).

[28] On the hope of Israel prior to the New Testament era, see the important recent works of N. T. Wright, *Christian Origins and the Question of God*, vol. 1, *The New Testament and the People of God* (Minneapolis: Fortress, 1992), 281-338; Christopher Rowland, *Christian Origins: From Messianic Movement to Christian Religion* (Minneapolis: Augsburg, 1985); and E. P. Sanders, *Judaism: Practice and Belief, 63 BCE–66 CE* (Philadelphia: Trinity Press International, 1992), 298 (summary). On the Roman assaults to Jewish nationalism prior to A.D. 70 see Richard Horsley, *Jesus and the Spiral of Violence: Popular Jewish Resistance in Roman Palestine* (San Francisco: Harper & Row, 1987).

This last observation brings us to the larger question for Chilton's thesis: why must the Kingdom for the Targums be an either-or proposition—either the self-revelation of God *or* the nationalistic/messianic manifestation of God's authority? Neither option seems to demand exclusivity in terms of the other. At least the final redactors of the Targums, whoever they were (assuming Chilton's stages of Targumic development) apparently considered the two concepts compatible in some way. Other modern exegetes of the Targums have voiced the same idea.[29] Perhaps the messianic Kingdom was the *particular form* of God's self-revelation the Jews expected. If this is so, it would be anachronistic of Chilton to empty the Kingdom of content more specific to the first century.[30] Chilton's later works show him to be very amenable to the plurisignificance of the Kingdom symbol and the existential hermeneutic we find in Perrin and the others of the New Literary Criticism before him,[31] but he also inherits their weaknesses. Specifically, it must be asked whether the Kingdom's interpretation has been advanced significantly if it ends up meaning simply "what its users make it mean"[32] in terms of the dynamic, abstract, rule of God.[33]

---

[29] For example Buchanan, *Consequences of the Covenant*, 62-63. Unfortunately Chilton does not consider Buchanan's work in any of his writings.

[30] See the conclusion of Riches and Millar that "at the end of the day, Chilton has remarkably little to say on the content of Jesus' preaching. Notwithstanding the value of his inquiry into sources, we are still left with questions about what God's self-revelation amounts to, about what sorts of power and strength he manifests and about what exactly those who look forward to the coming of his Kingdom expect to happen" (Riches and Millar, "Conceptual Change," 48-49).

[31] A monograph Chilton authored with J. I. H. McDonald, *Jesus and the Ethics of the Kingdom* (Grand Rapids: Eerdmans, 1987), 59, cites Perrin's *Jesus and the Language of the Kingdom* ("religious symbols can never be exhausted in any one apprehension of meaning," [29]). Existentialism appears in a discussion of Jesus' temporal language: "The language of imminent approach subtly shades into that of present invitation. The Kingdom that intersects time is 'at hand' in the sense that it may be entered; it is a realm of meaning and existence into which one can move" (61).

[32] Chilton and McDonald, *Jesus and the Ethics of the Kingdom*, 59, quote J. P. Mackey, *Jesus: The Man and the Myth* (London: SCM, 1979), 127. The full quotation reads: "the reign of God means what its users make it to mean; it does not have a set meaning by which all users are expected to abide." See similar statements in Chilton's "Kingdom Come, Kingdom Sung," 62. Chilton's most recent discussion of the Kingdom is understandably calling for a "much more nuanced application of a language of kingship to God than the modern fixation upon eschatology would allow"

Certainly Chilton's scholarship on the Targums has made a significant contribution in our knowledge of those ancient sources. Their application to the Kingdom in Jesus' teaching, as Chilton would have it, appears more dubious. Less dubious seems to be the Kingdom, at least in part, as the dynamic activity of the sovereign God, which Chilton's conclusions do reinforce, but which do not in themselves demand a totally non-eschatological Jesus.[34] Following are two more scholars who also emphasize this dynamic aspect of Jesus' teaching of the Kingdom, thus deemphasizing the Kingdom as an apocalyptic concept. In so doing, however, these writers also make more specific reference to the *regnum Christi* than Chilton's "God in strength" would allow. They begin our consideration of the Kingdom as the domain of personal redemption.

MERKLEIN AND CARMIGNAC: ACTIVE-DYNAMIC EVENT OF THE KINGDOM

Helmut Merklein and Jean Carmignac both write from within the Roman Catholic tradition, and their similar conclusions about the Kingdom's dynamic character derive from their own discussions of Jesus within the Judaism of his day. In his "sketch" of Jesus' message of the Kingdom,[35] Merklein begins with the words of the historical Jesus that come out of what he calls the scholarly consensus about the sayings of Jesus in the last

---

(Chilton, "Kingdom of God in Recent Discussion," 273). His own first steps in this direction begin with a brief analysis of the nuances of the kingship language of the Psalms and Daniel ("Kingdom of God in Recent Discussion," 273-80).

[33] Chilton's almost-anything-goes understanding of the Kingdom for early Judaism is not universally shared. See the more delimited conceptions of James H. Charlesworth, "The Historical Jesus in Light of Writings Contemporaneous with Him," *ANRW* (Berlin: Walter de Gruyter, 1982), 25:1:451-76; and Wright, *The New Testament and the People of God,* 281-338.

[34] See many like Jeremias who see Jesus' view of the Kingdom as very eschatological, but also as very dynamic (Joachim Jeremias, *New Testament Theology,* trans. John Bowden [London: SCM, 1971], 96-102).

[35] Helmut Merklein, *Jesu Botschaft von der Gottesherrschaft. Eine Skizze,* Stuttgarter Bibelstudien III (Stuttgart: Katholisches Bibelwerk, 1983). Merklein's other major works on the Kingdom are *Die Gottesherrschaft als Handlungsprinzip. Untersuchung zur Ethik Jesu* (Würzburg: Echter, 1978); and *Studien zu Jesus und Paulus* (Tübingen: J. C. B. Mohr [Paul Siebeck], 1987), 127-55.

few years.[36] After his first brief section examining the history of the Synoptic sources of the Kingdom sayings, he reaches three conclusions, which mark his own "history of the tradition": (1) the oldest (and likely most authentic) strata of Kingdom sayings is preserved in those statements that picture the Kingdom as an "active-dynamic concept" *(aktiv-dynamische Größe)*,[37] (2) logia which present the Kingdom as the fruit or circumstances of salvation came later from the traditions of the early church,[38] (3) the listing of the Synoptic sayings which have no parallel to the contemporaries of Jesus, does not in itself lead to the conclusion that Jesus is responsible for them. "At the very least a good part of these usages can be explained tradition–historically in the course of the development of a uniquely Christian terminology."[39]

Jesus' "active-dynamic" view of the Kingdom does not preclude its expression in eschatological language or its essentially eschatological character. Indeed, as Merklein argues, Jesus' eschatological language is very ancient and mediated chiefly by Deutero-Isaiah, then the postexilic

---

[36] The critical methodology of Perrin's *Rediscovering* is the model Merklein takes as the root of the "sure consensus" *(gewisser Konsens;* Merklein, *Jesu Botschaft,* 14, n. 9). On this point Merklein is representative of a great host of exegetes who attempt to unearth the authentic Kingdom-sayings by means of various criteria of authenticity and opt for a nonapocalyptic Jesus from the results. See, for example, Helmut Merkel, who advocates a "criteria of consistency," similar to Perrin's principle of coherence, against the criteria of dissimilarity ("Die Gottesherrschaft in der Verkündigung Jesu," in *Königsherrschaft Gottes und himmlischer Kult im Judentum, Urchristentum und in der hellenistischen Welt,* ed. Martin Hengel and Anna Maria Schwemer [Tübingen: J. C. B. Mohr (Paul Siebeck), 1991], 133, n. 77), as well as the rise of the so-called social formation criteria among the scholars of the Jesus Seminar (Butts, "Probing the Polling," 110-12). Another important work on the Kingdom that is in general agreement with Merklein as to conclusions and methodology is Jacques Schlosser, *Le règne de Dieu dans les dits de Jésus,* Études Bibliques (Paris: J. Gabalda, 1980). See also T. F. Glasson, *Jesus and the End of the World* (Edinburgh: Saint Andrews, 1980). For others, see the bibliography in Merkel, "Die Gottesherrschaft," 131, n. 74.

[37] These are in particular the parables (Mark 4:26-29, 30-32 par.; Luke 13:18-21 par.; Matt. 13:31-33), the first Beatitude (Luke 6:20b/Matt. 5:3) and the Q-sayings that present the *basileia* as the subject of a verb of movement (Luke 10:9/Matt. 10:7; Luke 11:2/Matt. 6:10; Luke 11:20/Matt. 12:28; Luke 16:16b/Matt. 11:12a; cf. Mark 1:15; 9:1; Merklein, *Jesu Botschaft,* 23).

[38] The church used the "Kingdom of God" ostensibly as a terminus technicus for the eschatological salvation, in analogy to the early rabbinic traditions about the coming age and eternal life (Merklein, *Jesu Botschaft,* 24).

[39] Merklein, *Jesu Botschaft,* 24.

prophets, and finally the apocalyptic writers.[40] However, Jesus' own meaning of this language reflects more the core of Old Testament belief found in the prior concept of Yahweh's kingship. Because of this, it follows that

> "the ['kingdom of heaven'] can never designate God's kingdom *[das Königreich Gottes]* as that territory ruled by him. Since the expression describes solely the fact *that* God is king, thus it designates instead His kingly being, or kingship *[das Königsein, Königtum Gottes]*" . . . the kingly dominion of God *in actu.*[41]

Jesus demonstrates this clearly when his authentic sayings show him departing from the static kingdom of the national dream.[42] These sayings demonstrate that Jesus' mission has a horizon much broader than the particular pilgrimage of Israel. Jesus, in fact, came to do business with the real enemy of all humankind. He understood clearly that this enemy was not the Roman oppressors in the political arena; the real enemy was Satan, whom Jesus did battle and ultimately defeat.[43] Jesus thereby means to effect the liberation from the ultimate bondage affecting not only Israel,[44] but the whole world as well.

For Merklein the Kingdom of God that Jesus proclaimed amounts to the inauguration in history of God's kingly rule through his Christ over the creation held in bondage to the Evil One. This Kingdom's nearness is not primarily temporal, as in some apocalyptic scheme, rather it is personal, as

---

[40] Ibid., 25. These works are also responsible for Yahweh's kingship becoming more and more national and concrete. The historical situations of these writers lent themselves to this (40). Merklein also does not see the eschatological language of Jesus or these writers admitting the rabbinic notion of taking upon oneself the "yoke of the Kingdom" as reflecting Jesus' time period (25).

[41] Ibid., 38. The quotation is from Kuhn, *basileia, TDNT,* 1:570-71 (emphasis his).

[42] The Kingdom's ultimate expression no doubt will encompass all the earth, but a specific Jewish denouement is unwarranted in light the development of the idea of God's kingship throughout history (Merklein, *Jesu Botschaft,* 41).

[43] Ibid., 42-44. At this point, Merklein does find great parallel with the spiritualizing characterizations in the apocalyptic writers (e.g., *TestDan* 5:10b-13 and *AsMos* 10:1, 7-10).

[44] Israel's status as a spiritually lost group *(Unheilskollektiv)* is important for Merklein's understanding of the Kingdom. Their first need was for righteousness, as John had proclaimed, not political liberation (Merklein, *Jesu Botschaft,* 44ff.).

near as one's own conversion to the salvific rule of God.[45] Authentic statements announcing the nearness of the Kingdom such as Mark 1:15 and Luke 10:9 need to be interpreted in light of this understanding of the Kingdom latent in all the other authentic sayings.[46]

While it could be easily charged that Merklein's own application of the historical critical method has determined his results in both the Old and New Testaments, similar to the New Hermeneutic and Perrin, a greater question remains for him and others of this view about the present reign of Yahweh's Christ. Namely, if the Old Testament eschatological hope for the Kingdom is spiritually fulfilled in the ministry of Jesus, climaxing in the resurrection-ascension event, then the postascension status of Christ must be that of a ruling king. Several observations need to be made in regards to this apodosis, including (1) the New Testament notably restricts usage of the *basileia*-language group when addressing the function of the risen Christ. It is arguable that after Acts, Christ is not called "king" or pictured as currently "reigning" until in Revelation.[47] It is also a curious

---

[45] Ibid., 52-53.

[46] Ibid., 56-57.

[47] The *ho basileus tōn basileuontōn* title in 1 Timothy 6:15 is seen by many as referring to God the Father, not the Son (I. Howard Marshall, *Jesus the Saviour* [Downers Grove, Ill.: InterVarsity Press, 1990], 209). So also the reference *dei gar auton* [Christ] *basileuein* (1 Cor. 15:25) is not without its assailants. See W. Bousset, *Die Religion des Judentums im spāthellenistischen Zeitalter,* 3d ed. (Tübingen: J. C. B. Mohr [Paul Siebeck], 1926), 288, and H. Lietzmann, *An die Korinter I-II,* 4th ed. (Tübingen: J. C. B. Mohr [Paul Siebeck], 1949), 81, who both argue that the reign of Christ begins at the Parousia.

The customary way to account for this lack of *basileia*-language is to subsume the function and title of the king under the common New Testament title *kyrios* (e.g., O. Cullmann, *Christology of the New Testament,* rev. ed. [Philadelphia: Westminster, 1963], 221). However, the reason for such a takeover is still a conundrum to many for several reasons: (1) No political advantage is achieved by the exchange; *Lord* Jesus is just as offensive as *King* Jesus in the Roman context. Klappert observes that "the effect of the confession *kyrios Iesous* . . . was to destroy this vital ideology of the Roman imperium, and the reaction to it called forth was the persecution of Christians during the first three centuries" (B. Klappert, "Lord," in *NIDNTT,* 2:373; cf. also I. Howard Marshall, *Jesus the Saviour,* 209). The Christian confession of 1 Corinthians 8:6 that there is "one *kyrios,* Jesus Christ" was in fact very subversive in the first century. Also the title of king does frequent the pages of the church's writings during this period in the Synoptic Gospels and Revelation. (2) Such a substitution also assumes that *basileus* was a particularly offensive title to the Romans, but this assumption also is not borne out by Pilate's reaction to Jesus "kingship" and the Romans'

fact that Christ is seldom or never portrayed as a king in the art of the pre-Constantinian Christianity.[48] (2) Psalm 110, the most important passage through which early Christians came to view the status and function of the risen Christ, while capable of justifying a present reign for Christ (110:2: "Rule in the midst of your enemies"), is never used that way in the New

---

own practice of granting the title of king to their vassal rulers (cf. Josephus's accounts of Herod the Great acquiring the title "king" [*Jewish Wars* 1.14.4. 284-85] and Archelaus's attempt to acquire it [*Antiquities* 17.9.1-3.208-22]. (3) Such an equation of Lord and King fails to appreciate any real distinctions between the two terms. Marshall brings out an important difference for the New Testament when he says, "Lord tends to have a passive meaning; it signifies someone who is to be obeyed and treated with honor and it perhaps does not bring out sufficiently the active element of the exercise of kingship and dominion and indeed of granting salvation" (*Jesus the Saviour*, 209).

Darrell Bock has recently suggested that the *christos* title subsumes *basileus* because: (1) *Messiah* includes the regal dimension, so that when the New Testament calls Jesus "Messiah" it is calling him "king," and (2) the writers of the early church needed to discourage "an over-realized eschatology that portrayed the kingdom as having already fully arrived (cf. 1 Cor 4:8-13) so there was hesitation to use the more blatant *basileia*-language (Darrell L. Bock, "Current Messianic Activity and OT Davidic Promise: Dispensationalism, Hermeneutics, and NT Fulfillment," *TrinJ* 15NS [1994]: 65-66).

These suggestions also need closer scrutiny. First, it is very doubtful that an overrealized eschatology could be countered with the term *Messiah*, particularly for Jews. If *Messiah* means "king," as Bock suggests, then in fact it is not an appropriate tool to dampen overly realized eschatological hopes. He cannot argue both ways. Second, such a substitution still cannot explain adequately the coming and going of the *basileia*-language in the New Testament. That is, why would a church concerned about overrealized eschatology produce documents like the Synoptic Gospels with all their Kingdom-of-God-language (compared to John's Gospel), let alone reintroduce that Kingdom-language later in Revelation? Furthermore, as Marshall again suggests, *christos* in the New Testament ended up more with the connotations of Redeemer and Savior and may therefore have come to prominence for other reasons than downplaying Christ's realized reign (Marshall, *Jesus the Saviour*, 209-10).

My point here is not to deny kingship (as in authority or status) to the exalted Christ, only to raise questions about his exercise of that kingship in the present era and, therefore, whether it is appropriate to assume his reign. I have pursued this possibility further in "Exaltation Christology in Hebrews: What Kind of Reign?" *TrinJ* NS 14 (1993): 41-62.

[48] P. Beskow notes that "on Roman sarcophagi or in the catacomb paintings; what we find instead [of Christ as king] is Christ, the Good Shepherd, Christ the miracle-worker or Christ the Philosopher in conversation with his disciples" (*Rex Gloriae: The Kingship of Christ in the Early Church* [Uppsala: Almquist & Wiksells, 1962], 12).

Testament.[49] Christ's role as intercessory priest seems to be the consistent New Testament picture of his present function (cf. Acts 7:55–56; Rom. 8:34; Heb. 8:1; 10:12), rather than reigning king. (3) Christ's present posture towards his enemies does not appear to correspond to that of a ruling king. In ancient Israel and her surrounding environs, one of the dominant roles of the monarch was chief of the army. As such the king vanquished all threatening enemies, both external and internal, so they constituted no

---

[49] The importance of Psalm 110:1b ("Sit at my right hand, until I make your enemies a footstool for your feet") to the earliest Christologies is evident from the sheer number of New Testament citations (5) and allusions (14). Psalm 110 (primarily vv. 1 and 4) is cited and alluded to more than any other Psalm in the New Testament. Only the Johannine corpus fails to make use of it. Despite Psalm 110's original status as a royal Psalm and the clear statement in 110:2: "Rule in the midst of your enemies" (which is significantly a part of the Psalm never cited by New Testament authors), the New Testament does not use it to show the exercise of a reign by the exalted Christ. In Hebrews, which cites Psalm 110 more than any other New Testament book and which expresses the typical New Testament use of the Psalm, the picture of the exalted Christ is one notably more passive than active, priestly than kingly. See the conclusions of D. M. Hay, who states that early Christians used Psalm 110 for one basic purpose: "to articulate the supreme glory, the divine transcendence of Jesus through whom salvation is mediated," and that "it is a serious mistake to claim that early Christian references to Psalm 110:1b regularly express convictions about Christ reigning as a royal lord in the present era" (D. M. Hay, *Glory at the Right Hand: Psalm 110 in Early Christianity*, SBL Monograph Series 18 [New York: Abingdon, 1973], 155 and 91, respectively). In light of both of these statements it is a serious misapplication by Bock to commandeer Hay's statement elsewhere that "a number of citations [of Psalm 110] do imply Christ's present role as lord of church and cosmos" as intending a particularly active expression of that Lordship (Bock, "Current Messianic Activity," 63, n. 15). Similarly Hay's statement to the effect that Jesus' Session energizes the church and its preaching "as an event visible to all who would use their eyes rightly" (Hay, *Glory at the Right Hand*, 92) does not assert, as Bock suggests, any activity of the Session itself (Bock, "Current Messianic Activity," 63, n. 15). The fact that the Session is true and visible to those with eyes to see it is what energizes the church and its preaching according to this statement, not that there is necessarily any activity done by Jesus producing these results.

On the priority of Psalm 110 in New Testament Christology and its use in the New Testament see G. Dautzenberg, "Psalm 110 im Neuen Testament," in *Liturgie und Dichtung. Ein interdisziplinäres Kompendium I*, ed. H. Becker and R. Kaczynski, 2 vols. (St. Ottilien: Eos, 1983), 1:141-71; J. Daniélou, "La Session à la droite du Pere," *Studia Evangelia* (Berlin: Akademie Verlag, 1959); J. Dupont, " Assis à la droite de Dieu: L'interprétation du Ps 110, 1 dans le Nouveau Testament," *Nouvelles études sur les Actes des Apôtres*, Lectio Divina 118 (Paris: Cerf, 1984); M. Gourges, *À la droite de Dieu: Résurrection de Jésus et actualisation du Psaum 110:1 dans le Nouveau Testament* (Paris: Libraire Lecoffre, 1978); J. H. Hayes, "The Resurrection as Enthronement and the Earliest Church Christology," *Interp* 22 (1968): 333-45; W. R. G. Loader, "Christ at the Right Hand—Ps. CX.1 in the New Testament," *NTS* 24 (1978): 199-217.

threat to national security.[50] This is clearly the picture of Yahweh's anointed representative in the Old Testament and apocalyptic hope, but it must be added that the hope included the notion that the eschatological King's *historical* conquest and rule over his enemies was supposed to extend beyond the boundaries of Israel and encompass the whole world. When we come to the New Testament it needs to be asked if this is the view of Christ during the present era. Even if the enemy is spiritualized as Satan (Merklein), does Christ's decisive action towards him constitute or even inaugurate this kind of rule over him in history? It can be plausibly argued that this kind of kingly function did not commence with the resurrection/ ascension event and that Christ's present dealings with the enemy comports better with a priestly function than a kingly one.[51]

---

[50] Gerhard Delling, *hypotasso*, *TDNT*, 8:42; Ludwig Schmidt, *"Königtum," TRE*, 19:328; and H. Lesétre, "Roi," in *Dictionnaire de la Bible*, ed. F. Vigouroux (Paris: Letouzy & Ané, 1912), 5/1: col. 1122. Beskow summarizes the functions normally associated with the concept *king* as exalted judge, ruler, and conqueror (Beskow, *Rex Gloriae*, 38). In the Greco-Roman period *basileia* was an inherently political term: "*Basileia* is what kings and rulers had: sovereignty, majesty, dominion, power, domain" (Burton L. Mack, "The Kingdom Sayings in Mark," *Forum* 3, no. 1 [1987]: 11). Semitic kingship was no different. See A. R. Johnson, who cites the king's duty to maintain his domain (i.e., "safeguard the liberty of the state") as the first of the Hebrew king's functions ("Hebrew Conceptions of Kingship," in *Myth, Ritual, and Kingship: Essays on the Theory and Practice of Kingship in the Ancient Near East and in Israel*, ed. S. H. Hooke [Oxford: Clarendon, 1958], 205). See also G. von Rad, *basileus*, *TDNT*, 1:570; J. Gray, "Hebrew Conception of the Kingship of God," *VT* 6 (1956): 268-85; E. R. Goodenough, "Kingship in Early Israel," *JBL* 48 (1929): 169-205; and Dale Patrick, "The Kingdom of God in the Old Testament," in *Kingdom in Twentieth-Century Interpretation*, 67-79.

[51] It is noteworthy that in the New Testament, in contradistinction to the universal hope of the Old Testament, Apocrypha, and Pseudepigrapha, in the present era only Christ's people are the object of the exalted Christ's dealings with Satan, and theodicy is still a live concern. That is, Christ's posture towards Satan is to control his influence over the righteous and will never, even progressively, effect Satan's personal demise or eradicate his work during this age. Evil is still present and useful to the exalted Christ in the same way it was used by Yahweh in the Old Testament. This New Testament picture of Christ in the present is, however, a very different state of affairs than envisioned in the eschatological hope for the Kingdom age, where evil is no longer useful, its perpetrators are ruled completely, and the problem of evil is settled. An example of the present situation is the epistle to the Ephesians. Ephesians 1:20-22 declares Christ's headship over all cosmic enemies because of his exaltation to the right hand, but only verses later in Ephesians 2:2 the enemy is said to still be working in the sons of disobedience. In the final chapter Christians are called upon to arm themselves for spiritual conflict. The same idea is present in all of the other passages about Christ's subjection of the celestial enemies (Col. 2:15; Heb. 2:14; 1 Pet. 3:22) as well as the demonic protest of Christ's action against them "before the

Jean Carmignac also considers the Kingdom in Jesus' teaching from the perspective of God's salvific rule *in actu*. His journey towards this conclusion began almost forty years ago in the context of his work on the Qumran scrolls.[52] In the preface to *Le mirage de l'eschatologie*[53] he writes of the experience he had in composing an article on the Qumran manuscripts in 1955. He says,

> I had written spontaneously: ". . . the Kingdom *[Royaume]* of God, which has such a place in the thought of Qumran. . . ." I had wanted to support this statement with some references, and I ascertained, to my great astonishment, that the Kingdom of God was not mentioned. Hence the question: "Under what influence had I thus projected an imaginary theology on the the the Qumran texts?"[54]

---

time" (Matt. 8:29), and biblical injunctions for Christians to be alert for spiritual warfare (e.g., 1 Pet. 5:8). See also the disjunction of sovereignty over enemies implied in the petition of the Lord's Prayer, "Your will be done on earth as it is in heaven" (Matt. 6:10), which represents the present age as more parallel to the *kingless* period of Israel ("In those days there was no king in Israel: every man did what was right in his own eyes" [Judges 17:6; 21:25]) than it does to the reign of the Lord's anointed anticipated in the prophetic hope. Thus, Percy's statement, "where Satan is driven back, the rule of God begins" (cited with approval by G. R. Beasley-Murray, "Matt 6:33: The Kingdom of God and the Ethics of Jesus," in *Neues Testament und Ethik,* ed. Helmut Merklein [Freiburg/Basel/Vienna: Herder, 1989], 87) is true to a point but cannot be used to establish a comparable link with the "rule" of God that Jesus inaugurated and the rule anticipated within the eschatological hope of the Old Testament. As critical and decisive as Jesus' defeat of Satan was at the cross, the application of that defeat during the present era only extends to the righteous and will never constitute a complete and personal rule of Satan and evil before Christ's return, and therefore does not comport well with the hope of the Old Testament for the rule of God over his enemies within history.

[52] Including Jean Carmignac, "Conjectures sur les écrits de Qumrân," in *Revue des sciences religieuses* 31 (April 1957), 140-68; *La Règle de la Guerre. Texte restauré, traduit, commenté* (Paris: Letouzey et Ané, 1958); *Les textes de Qumrân traduits et annotés,* 2 vols. (Paris: Letouzey et Ané, 1961, 1963); "La notion d'eschatologie dans la Bible et à Qumrân," *RQum* 7 (December 1969): 17-31; "Règne de Dieu. II. Qumran," *Dictionnaire de la Bible. Supplement* (Paris: Letouzey & Ané, 1985), 10: cols. 58-61; and "Roi, royauté et royaume dans la Liturgie Angélique," *RQum* 47 (1986), 178-86.

[53] Jean Carmignac, *Le mirage de l'eschatologie* (Paris: Letouzey et Ané, 1979).

[54] Ibid., 7 (author's translation).

As he continued his studies on the Qumran texts, Carmignac came to the conclusion that many of his colleagues had likewise been taken in by a biblically unfounded mirage: the mirage of eschatology.[55] The root of the mirage stems ultimately from a careless mixing of the two ideas "reign of God" and "Kingdom of God."

Carmignac's subsequent discussion uncovers the major reason for this conflation in the influence of Aramaic on the three Hebrew substantives derived from "king." Whereas in Hebrew three distinct words are used for "royalty," "reign," and "kingdom," Aramaic subsumes them all under the one term related most closely to the Hebrew word for "reign."[56] Thus,

> under the influence of Aramaic . . . the inclination is more and more to group the three ideas under the sole term ["reign"]: this tendency, which begins to manifest itself in the last books of the OT, is developed in the Hebrew of Qumran and triumphs in the Hebrew of the Mishnah, which has completely eliminated the two other terms.[57]

On the basis of the discoveries at Qumran, Carmignac observes that it is clear that Hebrew was known and used throughout first-century Palestine. There is, therefore, little doubt that Jesus also knew Hebrew, though he probably spoke Aramaic. The Gospels, written in Greek, which also have only one term for the three Hebrew words (i.e., *basileia*) relate most closely to the Aramaic Jesus spoke. Consequently,

> we are invited not to mechanically translate the Greek "basileia" with "royalty," with "reign," or with "kingdom," but to choose each

---

[55] Ibid., 7. By "eschatology" Carmignac means the apocalyptic, cosmic cataclysm that ends the world completely (as in Schweitzer) or the cataclysm that establishes the final age of history (as in Reimarus).

[56] The three Hebrew terms are *melukah* ("royalty"), *malkuth* ("reign"), and *mamlakah* ("kingdom"). The Aramaic word that can encompass all of these meanings is *malkuth*. As Carmignac understands them, " 'royalty' designates the dignity of the king; it is an abstract term expressing everything that distinguishes the king from every other person. 'Reign' designates the exercise of the royal power, including the temporal aspect. 'Kingdom' designates the territories or people over which the king exercises his authority, and thus this term evokes a spatial connotation" (Carmignac, *Mirage de l'eschatologie*, 13).

[57] Ibid., 21.

time the word that corresponds the best to the actual thought of the author, just as the Aramaic, also impoverished like the Greek at this point, does not facilitate this distinction perceived better in the Hebrew and French.[58]

The bulk of the first half of *Le mirage de l'eschatologie* is Carmignac's attempt to assign every Kingdom-logia of the New Testament one of the three meanings. In many cases the attempt is futile, as Carmignac himself is unable to judge between "reign" or "kingdom" (for example, Mark 1:15; Matt. 4:17; 9:35; 1 Cor. 6:9–10; 1 Cor. 15:22–27), but he does claim a certain measure of success for the remainder. Subsequent analysis of the results yields three main conclusions about the *basileia* of the New Testament. First, the New Testament makes only rare use of the *basileia* in the sense of "royalty." This is in marked contrast to the Old Testament, where the royalty of God's kingship is predominant.[59] Second, the verbal notion of the "reign" is clearly the dominant idea in the New Testament, and it corresponds directly to the saving act of justification.[60] Finally, Carmignac sees the territorial aspect of "kingdom" in the New Testament as descriptive of the church, though he guards himself from older associations by distinguishing the church in essence from the church as organization.[61] From this perspective, Carmignac sees a certain breadth to the *basileia*, as it may include sinners within its membership or it may not.

Whether one can fall in line with all of Carmignac's exegesis[62] or his

---

[58] Ibid., 21.

[59] Ibid., 94.

[60] Ibid., 120-29.

[61] Ibid., 98-102.

[62] Several points may be raised here. First, unlike Merklein, Carmignac spurns any critical attempts to reduce the number of authentic Kingdom-sayings (ibid., 90-91). Second, Carmignac's treatment of only the *basileia*-sayings allows him to avoid apparent Jewish elements of the future Kingdom from other sayings (e.g., Matt. 19:28). Third, Carmignac's inability to decide about "reign" or "kingdom" for verses of the apocalyptic view of the Kingdom, tends to more easily facilitate his own view (e.g., Matt. 12:43, *Mirage de l'eschatologie*, 53). Fourth, in other passages where Carmignac does claim a verdict, the decision rests on questionable premises. For example, since the poor and the persecuted (Matt. 5:3, 10) can receive their blessings in the present, the Kingdom *(royaume)* is present. For those who do not receive their blessing now, like the meek

pervasive ecclesiology,[63] the outcome of his work on the Kingdom results in a decidedly nonapocalyptic and noneschatological Jesus. The Kingdom of Jesus' proclamation was about being personally justified and being in relationship to a community of other justified ones.[64] As with Merklein, notions of the end of the world are not to be eliminated entirely from the picture, but they certainly do not comprise the main backdrop for Jesus' ministry.[65] Of course, such a view does give good hearing to the "dynamic/ active" aspect of *basileia*, popular since Dalman, but too heavy of an emphasis on the "dynamic/active" terminology for the Kingdom has given cause for even some who, like our next scholar, are generally in agreement with Merklein and Carmignac, to question whether the concept of a realm should be discarded altogether from *basileia*. Hermann Ridderbos notes that "in the nature of the case a dominion to be effective must create or maintain a territory where it can operate. So the absence of any idea of a spatial Kingdom would be very strange."[66] Some scholars, therefore, even

---

(Matt. 5:5), the blessings come after death in the future Kingdom (*Mirage de l'eschatologie*, 37). Similar misgivings arise from Carmignac's treatment of Matthew 6:10 (*Mirage de l'eschatologie*, 38). For other exegetical points see Schnackenburg's review of *Mirage de l'eschatologie* in *BZ* NS 24 (1980): 279-82.

[63] The identification of the Kingdom with the church depends heavily on the possibility of sinners within the Kingdom's membership. For this Carmignac takes up the historical Roman position founded on the parable of the wheat and the tares (Matt. 13:24-30) and then adduces the parables of the dragnet (Matt. 13:47-50) and the ten virgins (Matt. 25:1-10; *Mirage de l'eschatologie*, 97). But this will not persuade those who see the locus of the Kingdom in the parable of the wheat and tares not with the field but with the sons of the Kingdom, in accordance with Matthew 13:38.

[64] Carmignac rephrases the famous dictum "outside of the church, no salvation" to "outside of the reign (i.e., justification), no salvation" (Carmignac, *Mirage de l'eschatologie*, 127-29).

[65] The second and last part of *Mirage de l'eschatologie* is Carmignac's account of the rise of the eschatological error from Reimarus to Karl Barth, and includes a great part of his earlier essay, "Les dangers de l'eschatologie," *NTS* 17 (July 1971): 365-90. See also his more recent "Rectification d'une erreur concernant l'eschatologie," *NTS* 26 (1980): 252-58.

[66] Hermann Ridderbos, *The Coming of the Kingdom*, trans. H. de Jongste, ed. Raymond O. Zorn (Philadelphia: Presbyterian and Reformed, 1962), 26. See the similar concerns of Klaus Koch, *The Rediscovery of Apocalyptic*, Studies in Biblical Theology, 2d series 22 (London: SCM, 1972), 70.

contend that "realm" is a better translation of *basileia* than "reign," though such a realm is still spiritualized.[67]

WITHERINGTON: POSSIBLE IMMINENCE

As we saw earlier with Merklein particularly, one way scholars have attempted to deeschatologize Jesus' message of the Kingdom is by means of critical methodologies. Assuming that the New Testament contains different eschatologies,[68] understanding the eschatology of Jesus becomes a matter of first critically excising the early Church's language of imminence or near-expectation *(Naherwartung)* from the Gospel record. For those not inclined to either the methodologies or the assumption of divergent eschatologies, the argument has been made exegetically that Jesus considered imminence a possibility but not a necessity. Ben Witherington's *Jesus, Paul and the End of the World*[69] is a recent example of this argument within our nonapocalyptic category to which several others could easily be added.[70]

---

[67] Charlesworth states, "As the best scholars have seen, and as Schweizer advises, 'the kingdom is more like an area or a sphere of authority into which one can enter, so "realm" would be a better translation'" ("The Historical Jesus," 464, citing E. Schweizer *The Good News According to Mark* [Richmond: John Knox, 1970], 45-46). I. Howard Marshall agrees, saying, "While it has been emphasized almost *ad nauseam* that the primary concept is that of the sovereignty or kingship or actual rule of God and not of a territory ruled by a king, it must be also emphasized that kingship cannot be exercised in the abstract but only over a people" ("Church," in *Dictionary of Christ and the Gospels*, ed. Joel B. Green, I. Howard Marshall, and Scot McKnight [Downers Grove, Ill.: InterVarsity Press, 1992], 123). See also the similar observation by J. Ramsey Michaels, who agrees that the first meaning of Kingdom is abstract but that the abstract of necessity requires the concrete ("The Kingdom of God and the Historical Jesus," in *The Kingdom of God in Twentieth-Century Interpretation*, ed. Wendell Willis [Peabody, Mass.: Hendrickson, 1987], 114).

[68] Many like C. K. Barrett advocate three eschatologies: (1) the eschatology of Jesus; (2) the eschatology of the primitive church propelled by Jesus' ministry in his death and resurrection and the continuing life and existence of the disciples; and (3) a second eschatology of the church in light of the church's existence beyond its first generation, also known as the delay of the Parousia eschatology (C. K. Barrett, *Jesus and the Gospel Tradition* [Philadelphia: Fortress, 1968], 13, n. 26; cf. also John Gray, *The Biblical Doctrine of the Reign of God* [Edinburgh: T & T Clark, 1979], 358ff.).

[69] Ben Witherington, *Jesus, Paul and the End of the World: A Comparative Study of New Testament Eschatology* (Downers Grove, Ill.: InterVarsity Press, 1992).

[70] For example, C. E. B. Cranfield, "Thoughts on New Testament Eschatology," *ScotJT* 35 (1982): 497-512.

Witherington advocates clearly the Kingdom in the Gospels as the inauguration of the *regnum Christi*. He argues at some length that *basileia* has more than one nuance in the Gospels, depending on the context— "sometimes referring to God's present saving activity breaking into human history, sometimes referring to a future realm that one may enter as a result of that activity of God."[71] To be sure, the present saving activity Jesus announced was nonapocalyptic, that is, cosmic and catastrophic in character, but this was not the case for the future Kingdom. The coming of this future Kingdom would mean the apocalyptic return of Jesus, the Son of Man, the resurrection of the dead, and final judgment. Its realm would be the final earthly destiny of the righteous.[72]

Witherington considers "improbable" the contention of numerous scholars since Schweitzer that Jesus considered the future Kingdom as necessarily imminent. In the first place, if the authenticity of Mark 13:32 can be maintained, which Witherington argues in *The Christology of Jesus*,[73] the whole question of the Kingdom's timing is somewhat moot. Not even Jesus knew for sure. So it is not out of order to qualify all his "imminent" predictions as only showing that he "considered those events as *possibly* imminent."[74]

Beyond the cushion of Mark 13:32, it is by no means certain that the classic passages often cited for imminence are unambiguous. Mark 9:1 and parallels can just as likely refer to an event that manifests the power of the Kingdom, including miracles and exorcisms, possibly even the Transfiguration.[75] Matthew 10:23, the compelling passage for Schweitzer's

---

[71] Witherington, *Jesus, Paul and the End of the World*, 60. Witherington's detailed treatment of *basileia* is in his *The Christology of Jesus* (Minneapolis: Fortress, 1990), 192-98.

In contrast to many with his general view who lean heavily on the Kingdom's dynamic quality from the work of Dalman (e.g., Merklein, and J. Marcus, "Entering into the Kingly Power of God," *JBL* 107 [1988]: 663-75), Witherington maintains a real localized realm within the meaning of *basileia*. The future *basileia* is an earthly realm that can be entered (*Jesus, Paul and the End of the World*, 67). Witherington also sees a certain Jewish element to this future Kingdom (*Jesus, Paul and the End of the World*, 129-43).

[72] Witherington, *Jesus, Paul and the End of the World*, 225-31.

[73] Witherington, *Christology of Jesus*, 228-33.

[74] Witherington, *Jesus, Paul and the End of the World*, 36 (emphasis his).

[75] Ibid., 37-39.

consistent eschatology, could be referring to the greatness of the task or the abundance of places the disciples could minister before the return of the Son of Man. If the verse is out of its original context, as is argued by many, then it may not have the Parousia in view at all. It could mean simply the disciples would not finish the work of this particular mission before Jesus rejoined them later. If the saying is about the Parousia, the imminent language could function to simply inculcate courage and perseverance in the disciples more than establish an eschatological calendar. In this way it could also have been more eschatologically focused than missiologically.[76] Thus, Matthew 10:23, like many of the other so-called imminent passages (e.g., Mark 13:30) could also have as its referent that generation for whom the return of the Son of Man is imminent, and not necessarily that generation of Jesus' day.[77]

The subversion of the necessarily imminent, end-of-the-world Jesus of Schweitzer so characteristic of Witherington's view needs to be well-taken, especially considering the Gospel record. Certainly, at least toward the beginning of his ministry, there is substantial evidence in the Gospels that Jesus considered the Kingdom, or at least some aspect of the Kingdom, to be present, and that the Kingdom's presence did not require an imminent end of the world or of history. Indeed, there is a ring of truth to Ridderbos's observation that in the beginning of Jesus' ministry the issue of the Kingdom is one of presence and fulfillment, but at the end the Kingdom is distant, almost as if it had not yet come.[78] Witherington's discussion in terms of *possible* imminence instead of *necessary* imminence is a good mediation of the issue, allowing the language of imminence to have meaning but not be overwhelming and all-determining as it is in the case of Schweitzer.

---

[76] Witherington (ibid., 41) cites Scot McKnight, who contends the original context for Matthew 10:23 was more like the eschatological context of Mark 13:9-13. The placement of verse 23 in conjunction with 10:17-22 thus means, "When they persecute you in one place (as part of the final intense persecution associated with the Parousia), flee to the next (and so on). I tell you the truth you will not have finished fleeing through the cities of Israel (as cities of refuge) before the Son of Man comes" (Scot McKnight, "Jesus and the Endtime: Matthew 10.23," *SBL Seminar Papers 1986* [Atlanta: Scholars, 1986], 516-17).

[77] Witherington, *Jesus, Paul and the End of the World,* 37-44.

[78] Ridderbos, *Coming of the Kingdom,* 469.

WRIGHT: APOCALYPTIC LANGUAGE

Another means various interpreters have used to understand Jesus' doctrine of the Kingdom noneschatologically or nonapocalyptically focuses on the hermeneutics of apocalyptic language. Although his project is larger than the Kingdom theme specifically, the first volume of N. T. Wright's *Christian Origins and the Question of God* will serve as a recent example of this view.[79]

Wright's discussion of the Kingdom begins with a portrait of the hope of Israel in the time immediately preceding Jesus. Attention is turned to the subject of "apocalyptic" language, the vehicle ancient Jews used to express their hope. Wright notes that apocalyptic language has different layers of meaning underneath what a surface or literal reading may indicate.[80] In the apocalyptic language of Israel, the fundamental layer of meaning is theological: when the God of the Covenant acts, it will be an event of cosmic significance.[81] This, of course, is not the same as a "cosmic" event, which connotes otherworldly dualisms, for that was not the intention of the apocalyptics. Rather, their hope was entirely this-worldly, bound within the notion of the change of ages, having little to do with a catastrophic end of the world.

> Far more important to the first-century Jew than questions of space, time and literal cosmology were the key issues of Temple, Land, and Torah, of race, economy and justice. When Israel's god acted, Jews would be restored to their ancestral rights and would practice their ancestral religion, with the rest of the world looking on in awe, and/or making pilgrimages to Zion, and/or being ground to powder under Jewish feet.[82]

These conditions described Israel's hopes for ultimate shalom and salvation. They were very this-worldly, but not of this age. Israel's salvation, the Kingdom of God, was of a coming age when, "Israel's god would

---

[79] N. T. Wright, *The New Testament and the People of God* (Minneapolis: Fortress, 1992). See also George B. Caird, *The Language and Imagery of the Bible* (London: Duckworth, 1980).

[80] Wright, *People of God*, 282.

[81] Ibid., 283.

[82] Ibid., 285, where Wright also contends that the cataclysmic end of the world was a Stoic idea, not a Jewish one.

become in reality what he was already believed to be. He would be King of the whole world."[83]

When the prophetic and apocalyptic writers of ancient Israel conceived of this Kingdom in terms of socio-political events, Wright says the modern interpreter must watch for the *theological* significance of their language. Commenting on the Kingdom of Yahweh in *Testament of Moses* 10:1–10, Wright says,

> The language and imagery of the poem is designed to *denote* future socio-political events, and to *invest* those events with their full "theological" significance. Israel is to defeat her foes, under the leadership of an appointed "messenger," perhaps a priest; and *that means* that Israel's god is to become King.[84]

This does not mean for Wright that the socio-political scheme was a secondary hope for Israel, just some metaphor they all knew. To the contrary, it would be an unwarranted Hellenization of second-temple Judaism to separate the sacred from the secular.[85] In the main, Jews looked for a renewed nation, world, and people as eschatological expressions of their monotheism and covenantal theology. A *historical* expression of Israel's hope was an essential component of their worldview.[86]

When we come to early Christianity as represented in the Gospels, we see the theological meaning of the Kingdom is retained. Jewish writers are still telling the story of the revelation of Israel's God as king in history, but the story is told differently now. Matthew, Mark, Luke, and all the other writers of the New Testament affirm that Israel's God is truly the King of the world and that he has restored his Kingdom for his people within history; only the story is transformed and told in terms of Jesus. *Jesus* is the

---

[83] Ibid., 301.

[84] Ibid., 306 (emphasis his).

[85] Ibid., 320.

[86] Ibid., 306. Wright intends also to be a hedge against reading too much into the variety of "Judaisms" of the second-temple period, especially where eschatology is concerned. He summarizes his chapter on Israel's hope by saying, "I have tried to show above all that, despite the wide variety of emphasis, praxis and literature for which we have ample evidence, which indeed justify us in speaking of 'Judaisms' in relation to this period, we can trace the outlines of a worldview, and a belief-system, which can properly be thought of as 'mainline,' and which were shared by a large number of Jews at the time" (338).

climactic end of Israel's story. *His* story is Israel's story; from creation, the Exodus, the giving of the law, exile, and restoration, Jesus' life as told by the Evangelists is more Jewish story-telling about Israel and Israel's God.[87] As with the prophets and the apocalyptics, the cosmic language in the Gospels continues to function as "a lens through which historical events can be seen as bearing the full meaning that the community believed them to possess."[88] Thus, as with the older stories, the theological significance of the coming of God's kingship in the story of Jesus is what we should take from their message. Israel has been redeemed, the time of the Gentiles had come, the spirit had been poured out; "all the God-given promises find their 'yes' in Christ" (2 Cor. 1:20). This was the early Christian story.[89]

Wright's work does a great service in reminding us of the historical nature of the so-called apocalyptic hope in ancient Israel. As Christopher Rowland's thorough study of Christian origins and Jewish apocalyptic literature concludes: "God's rule and authority were ultimately to be manifested in the physical world. Salvation for a Jew was not primarily some mystical deliverance for the spirit to enter a private communion with God in the world beyond, but the manifestation on earth of God's authority over the universe and the setting right of all that was wrong."[90] The depiction of the hope of Israel as a historical phenomenon is (rightly) gaining more and more adherents in the New Testament academy.[91]

What Wright and the others of the *regnum Christi* view gain in their

---

[87] Wright cites the case of Matthew: "The gospels are therefore the story of Jesus *told as the history of Israel in miniature:* the 'typology' which is observed here and there by critics is simply a function of this larger purpose of the evangelists. Matthew gives us, in his first five chapters, a Genesis (1.1), an Exodus (2.15), and a Deuteronomy (5-7); he then gives us a royal and prophetic ministry, and finally an exile (the cross) and restoration (the resurrection). What more could we want?" (ibid., 402).

[88] Ibid., 425. This comports well with the second of Caird's three theses: "[biblical writers] regularly used end-of-the-world language metaphorically to refer to that which they well knew was not the end of the world" (Caird, *Language and Imagery of the Bible,* 256).

[89] Wright, *People of God,* 459.

[90] Christopher Rowland, *Christian Origins: From Messianic Movement to Christian Religion* (Minneapolis: Augsburg, 1985), 135.

[91] Wright, *People of God,* 333-34, cites the recent work of J. J. Collins in this regard. See also the conclusions of Klaus Koch, who denies the radical dualism often attributed to the apocalyptic visions ("What Is Apocalyptic? An Attempt at a Preliminary Definition," in *Visionaries and Apocalypses,* ed. Paul D. Hanson [Philadelphia: Fortress, 1983], 27) and notes the suggestion of many that the apocalyptic writers remythologized the Old Testament religion (*The Rediscovery of Apocalyptic,* 27).

historiography is brought into question by their desire to spiritualize a previously literal concept once they come into the New Testament.[92] That is, ancient Judaism believed in the literal fulfillment of their eschatological hope, but Jesus refigures his ancestral hope only in spiritual terms of personal salvation, making the national question supposedly null and void. But at what point does the process of spiritualizing the Old Testament hope stop? If Wright can argue the nature of apocalyptic language justifies reducing the Kingdom in the New Testament to its "theological significance," what is the real justification for retaining the Kingdom's theological significance as a *historical* phenomenon but not as a national and ethnic one? Similarly, if the real meaning of apocalyptic is to be found at deeper theological levels, on what grounds should other "apocalyptic" concepts like angels, demons, Satan, and miracles not be spiritualized according to their deeper theological meaning? Of course the fact that Jesus' miracles are presented in the canonical Gospels as *literal* fulfillment of the Old Testament hopes for the new age does argue against spiritualizing in some of these cases, but what about the others?[93] Is there any ground in the New Testament to say angels are real, or demons, or Satan? One would think

---

[92] The term "spiritualized" is admittedly not the best, but it is still the term accepted (Glasson, "Schweitzer's Influence—Blessing or Bane?" 290) and used by members of this view. See Gray's comment about the fulfillment of the blessings of Deuteronomy 28:1-14: "In the new commonwealth, . . . the Kingdom of God, the old blessings of possessing the land and being filled are symbolical and the others [i.e., other blessings] are spiritualized" (Gray, *The Biblical Doctrine of the Reign of God,* 329).

[93] Otto Betz and Werner Grimm understand the specific mention of healing the lame, deaf, and blind, and raising the dead in Matthew 11:5 as typical of Gospel miracle accounts that clearly draw from the new age promises in Isaiah (26:19; 29:18; 35:4ff.; 42:18; and 61:1-2) (*Wesen und Wirklichkeit der Wunder Jesu* [Frankfurt: Peter Lang, 1977], 31; cf. also A. E. Harvey, *Jesus and the Constraints of History* [Philadelphia: Westminster, 1982], 115). Blomberg sees Mark's account of the healing of the deaf mute as tied to Isaiah 35 through the reappearance of the hapax legomenon *(mogilalon)* of Mark 7:32 in the LXX of Isaiah 35:6b (Craig Blomberg, "Healing," in *Dictionary of Jesus and the Gospels,* 302). Moreover, the release of the deaf mute's tongue from its "bond" *(desmos)* (Mark 7:35) is prefigured by the release of the oppressive bands predicted in Isaiah 58:6 (Betz and Grimm, *Wesen und Wirklichkeit,* 31, n. 39). Grimm notes from *MekEx* 15:1 that the healings of Isaiah 35:5 (Matt. 11:5) were a messianic expectation of the rabbis that included healing of spiritual blindness and deafness as well (Grimm, *Weil Ich dich liebe,* 127-28, n. 304). On the rabbinic view of miracles in the new age see Str-B, 1:593-95.

According to the prophetic hope of the Old Testament, the eschatological Kingdom of the new age necessitated the destruction of all forces opposed to the divine order (Is. 29:20; 35:14; 61:2). W. Grimm in particular has understood Isaiah 49:24-25 (where the liberation of the captives is

that Jesus' literal fulfillment of the Old Testament hopes of a miraculous new age, especially considering that such prophecies were not completely fulfilled in Jesus,[94] would argue for the literal fulfillment of the physical

---

tied to prior submission of the mighty man and Yahweh "contends with the one who contends with you") to delineate and anticipate the spiritual warfare of the Kingdom (Grimm, *Weil Ich dich liebe. Die Verkündigung Jesu und Deuterojesaja* [Frankfurt: Peter Lang, 1976], 88-93). Regardless of whether or not spiritual warfare was a component of the Old Testament anticipation for the new age, the Gospel writers may attempt a latent connection in the link of Satan to sickness. The sick woman of Luke 13:10ff. was one "whom Satan has bound for eighteen years" (Luke 13:16). Kallas has argued a similar case for Mark 3:10; 5:29, 34, and Luke 7:21, where the Greek word for disease, *mastix*, also means "whip" or "scourge." He puts this forth as a possible link between physical sickness and the devil's oppression of his subjects (James Kallas, *The Significance of Synoptic Miracles* [London: SPCK, 1961], 79). In Matthew the lines between disease and demons blur as *therapeuo*("to heal") is used for both healing diseases and casting out demons (8:16; 10:8). In the so-called nature miracles, Jesus' rebuke *(epitimao)*of the storm (Mark 4:37-41) is the same as his rebuke of demons (Mark 1:25), which is the same as his rebuke of illness (Luke 4:39). On spiritual warfare in the Pseudepigrapha see *1 Enoch* 10:11-15, 54-55; *Testament of Levi* 18:12; *Assumption of Moses* 10:1-2; *Testament of Asher* 7:3. On miracles, see *1 Enoch* 96:3; *Sibylline Oracles* 1:351.

[94] In addition to the *prima facie* evidence of the New Testament for the future Kingdom, the provisional and signatory nature of Jesus' miracles cannot be neglected as indicators of a future event of the Kingdom. Though it is common to see Jesus' miracles as a fulfillment of the Old Testament hope and therefore the presence of the Kingdom (e.g., Hengel and Schwemer, foreword to *Königsherrschaft Gottes*, 10, and Beasley-Murray, "Jesus and the Kingdom of God," 146), many have warned against making too much of the miracles (including exorcisms) for the Kingdom in Jesus' ministry. The nature of miracles as "signs" (John 20:30, 31) means they point to something else. Ridderbos makes the point well: "[Miracles] indicate the coming of the kingdom and point to the cosmic palingenesis. . . . But they are not the beginning of this palingenesis, as if the latter were the completion of the miracles. For this palingenesis is something of the future world aeon" (Ridderbos, *The Coming of the Kingdom*, 119-20). Buchanan has also argued the point from an Exodus typology for the miracles of Jesus through the "finger of God" sayings in Jesus (Matt. 12:28) and the Exodus (Exod. 8:12-15). Just as the miracles done by the "finger of God" marked the beginning of the end for the Egyptian captivity and signaled the near establishment of God's kingdom of Israel, so Jesus' miracles are not the Kingdom, but serve to announce the near establishment of the Kingdom announced in Mark 1:14-15 (G. W. Buchanan, *Jesus the King and His Kingdom* [Macon, Ga.: Mercer University Press, 1984], 30-33).

In light of the future called for in Jesus' fulfillment of miracles and spiritual warfare, it would seem unwarranted to close the door in the first century to the possibility of the future fulfillment within history of the rest of the Jewish hope. See especially Isaiah 35 and its use by the Gospel writers (e.g., Matt. 11:5 = Is. 35:5-6). Isaiah 35:5-10 shows the hope of physical renewal (healing, vv. 5-6) is part of the restoration of the exiles to the land (v. 10). See also Zacharias's prophecy in Luke 1:71ff., which also seems to hold the national renewal (v. 71: "Salvation from our enemies") together with the spiritual (v. 77: "To give to his people the knowledge of salvation by the forgiveness of their sins"). The question needs to be asked if it is necessary to see one part of the hope fulfilled literally and the other fulfilled spiritually within Jesus' ministry.

and national dimensions of the hope as well. Furthermore, what place does the final resurrection and judgment have as part of the New Testament message since they also are notably "apocalyptic"? If Wright is correct in arguing the apocalyptic writers' "cosmic events" meant at the theological level "events of cosmic *significance,*" what is done to the New Testament apocalyptic event of the return of Christ? Is it a cosmic event or an event of cosmic significance, or both?[95]

BEASLEY-MURRAY: THE COMING OF GOD

The coming of God's Kingdom is the paradigm which G. R. Beasley-Murray contends has been much-neglected in the modern discussion of Jesus' identity.[96] That modern scholars like F. Young can suggest that "we do not have the evidence available now to speculate realistically about Jesus' so-called messianic consciousness,"[97] betrays a failure to attend closely enough to the one assured feature of the historical Jesus: his proclamation of the Kingdom of God. In an attempt to fill this lack for its christological benefit, Beasley-Murray's *Jesus and the Kingdom of God* (1986) is the first full-scale exegesis of the Kingdom sayings of Jesus since Norman Perrin's *Rediscovering the Teaching of Jesus* (1967).

---

[95] A related point can be made to Wright's contention that the story of Jesus was intended by the Gospel writers to be the story of Israel, including the parallel of Israel's restoration in Jesus' own resurrection/ascension/exaltation. What is missing seems to be an account of the remainder of Jesus' story, that is, his Parousia, and its parallel to Israel's story. Since the story of Jesus does not end at the exaltation, is there more for Israel, too?

[96] G. R. Beasley-Murray, *Jesus and the Kingdom of God* (Grand Rapids: Eerdmans, 1986). Beasley-Murray's writings on New Testament eschatology span nearly four decades, beginning with his Ph.D. dissertation, *Jesus and the Future: An Examination of the Criticism of the Eschatological Discourse, Mark 13, with Special Reference to the Little Apocalypse Theory* (London: Macmillan, 1954). See also *A Commentary on Mark Thirteen* (London: Macmillan, 1957); *Revelation,* New Century Bible Commentary (Grand Rapids: Eerdmans, 1978); "Jesus and the Kingdom of God," *BaptQ* 32 (1987): 141-46; "Matthew 6:33: The Kingdom of God and the Ethics of Jesus," *Neues Testament und Ethik,* ed. Helmut Merklein (Freiburg/Basel/Vienna: Herder, 1989), 84-98; "The Vision on the Mount," *Ex Auditu* 6 (1990): 39-52; "The Kingdom of God in the Teaching of Jesus," *JEvTS* 35, no. 1 (1992): 19-30. Beasley-Murray has rewritten *Jesus and the Future,* revising it at a number of points. See *Jesus and the Last Days: The Interpretation of the Olivet Discourse* (Peabody, Mass.: Hendrickson, 1993).

[97] F. Young, "A Cloud of Witnesses," in *The Myth of God Incarnate,* ed. J. Hick (London: SCM, 1977), 18, cited by Beasley-Murray, *Jesus and the Kingdom,* x.

Jesus' announcement of the Kingdom is prefaced by the coming of God in the Old Testament and early Judaism. In the Old Testament God's coming is his personal revelation to Israel in redemption. Often the Old Testament depicts God's redemptive interventions coming from the North (Ezek. 1:4), from Jerusalem (Amos 1:2), from Seir (Deut. 33:2), "but fundamentally the Israelite looked for God to come for his interventions on earth from heaven."[98] While the hope of redemption was earthly, it was not for Israel alone; the whole world would ultimately receive the salvation of Israel's God.[99] This hope continued into early Judaism, albeit with more dualistic, symbolic, and messianic flavor. In some cases, Beasley-Murray argues, the apocalyptic writers expanded on themes already present in the prophets, for example, the new creation of Isaiah 65–66; in other cases they advance positively to reflect the teaching of Jesus, that is, the juxtaposition of the realized and the future eschatology of the Qumran community.[100]

In Jesus the future hope of Israel is both present and future. His message and ministry demonstrate the salvific intervention of God has begun. It is as near as faith for those who would believe.[101] For those who do, the Kingdom is present, as Matthew 12:28, Luke 17:20–21, and the parables clearly say. The placement of his own ministry against the backdrop of the Old Testament prophecies about the transformed world of the exile's return (Matt. 11:5 = Isa. 35; cf. Luke 4:18–21 = Isa. 61:1–3) shows Jesus considered them already fulfilled in himself. So also the feasting and celebrating with restored sinners and tax gatherers of Galilee and Judea (Matt. 9:9–10; Mark 2:19) satisfies the hopes of Isaiah 25:6–9. Thus, while it is too narrow to say that the Kingdom of God is restricted to an individual experience of salvation, it should not be couched in the context of any sort of literal, national, Jewish hope either.[102]

---

[98] Beasley-Murray, *Jesus and the Kingdom*, 6.

[99] "When Yahweh comes to bring his kingdom, it is to this world that he comes and in this world that he establishes his reign. The hope of Israel is not for a home in heaven, but for the revelation of the glory of God in this world" (Beasley-Murray, *Jesus and the Kingdom*, 25).

[100] See chapters 5–8 of *Jesus and the Kingdom*. On Qumran, see especially 49–51.

[101] The statement in Mark 1:14-15 of the Kingdom's nearness is to be taken this way (Beasley-Murray, *Jesus and the Kingdom*, 71-72. The fact that "the time is fulfilled" and the summary nature of the announcement here also indicates the new time of the Kingdom is now beginning (Beasley-Murray, "Matthew 6:33," 86-87).

[102] Beasley-Murray, "Jesus and the Kingdom of God," 146; "Matthew 6:33," 87-88.

As the sayings about the coming Son of Man indicate, in Jesus' mind the Kingdom still awaits a future consummation at the Parousia.[103] The New Testament's near-expectation of the Parousia, seen by many as annulling the authenticity of the Parousia altogether, Beasley-Murray understands as an element essential to hope itself. He quotes Bultmann for the Old Testament and Althaus for the New Testament to say in effect that in view of the almighty sovereignty of God, the designs of his eternal plan, and personal incorporation into Christ, temporal distance shrinks to matters of inconsequence.[104] Like Witherington, Beasley-Murray understands Mark 13:32 to indicate the Parousia as a hope, not a doctrine, of the New Testament authors.[105]

In the end, the Kingdom of God for Beasley-Murray is the "saving sovereignty of God," a synonym for salvation in its broadest sense.[106] It is only a confusion of the issue to see it as another term for Christianity or any organization of society on Christian principles; the Kingdom of God denotes divine saving activity, the reign of God.[107] Its full dynamic quality

---

[103] Beasley-Murray's chapter on the Son of Man (*Jesus and the Kingdom*, 219-312) maintains a running debate with P. Vielhauer, who had argued that the Son of Man and Kingdom of God sayings were separate traditions having nothing to do with one another (P. Vielhauer, "Gottesreich und Menschensohn in der Verkündigung Jesu," in *Aufsätze zum Neuen Testament* [Munich: Christian Kaiser, 1965], 55-91). Beasley-Murray argues this hypothesis is needless in light of (1) the centrality of the Kingdom in Jesus' own ministry; (2) the inherent connection of the Kingdom of God to the Son of Man in Daniel 7:13-14; (3) the link between suffering and the Kingdom in early Judaism, along with Jesus' own choice of suffering in his vocation of the Kingdom; (4) the unified domain of the Son of Man in his lowly service, his suffering death, resurrection, and Parousia; (5) the critical confession of Jesus before the Sanhedrin in Mark 14:62.

[104] Althaus, for example, says of the near-expectation in Romans 13:11 ff.: "This end, whether it be temporally 'near' or 'far,' is essentially near to everybody. For it is one with Christ, the Crucified and Risen Lord. It is there, where Christ is. The temporal end signifies only the redemption of the essential end, which is Christ, inasmuch as he is the Crucified and Risen One, and as the risen One heading for his coming, is for the world and history the Hidden One. To this extent all of us, all generations of the church, live at the same hour, in the one last hour, in a world and time that is destined to pass away—thus as in the twilight shortly before the sunrise" (Paul Althaus, *Der Brief an die Römer,* Das Neue Testament Deutsch [Göttingen: Vandenhoeck & Ruprecht, 1966], ad loc.; cited by Beasley-Murray, *Jesus and the Kingdom,* 344).

[105] Beasley-Murray, *Jesus and the Kingdom,* 343.

[106] Beasley-Murray, "Jesus and the Kingdom of God," 142.

[107] Beasley-Murray parts company with Carmignac, Schnackenburg, et al. when he understands "kingdom" in English to denote primarily a reign, not a realm. See Beasley-Murray, "Jesus and the Kingdom of God," 141; "Matthew 6:33," 92.

is realized in the New Testament terminology of "resurrection life," that is, life from God that conquers death. It is also a dynamic that ultimately includes the whole creation:

> when Yahweh comes to bring his kingdom, it is to this world that he comes and in this world that he establishes his reign. The hope of Israel is not for a home in heaven but for the revelation of the glory of God in this world, when "the earth shall be full of the knowledge and glory of the Lord as the waters fill the sea" (Hab. 2:14).[108]

Within the ministry of Jesus, this Kingdom must be understood both as having come and yet to come, both as spiritual and physical.[109]

In contrast to the nonapocalyptic Kingdom of the newer literary criticism, the approach of the writers of the *regnum Christi* position like Beasley-Murray stands on firmer historical ground. Whether it be the nature of apocalyptic language, the kingship of God in the cult of Israel, or the Kingdom's place in the other extant documents of the second-temple period, this Jesus and the Kingdom he preached is more comfortably situated in first-century Palestine. However, as was noted for Wright, when the historical hope of Yahweh's kingship in Israel is spiritualized in Jesus' teaching as simply the "Coming of God" (Beasley-Murray) or "God in Strength" (Chilton), the door is opened to the possibility for an unbridled

---

[108] Beasley-Murray, *Jesus and the Kingdom*, 25. The coming of the Kingdom at the Parousia is not the end of the creation. Concerning the "cosmic signs" of the Parousia in Mark 13:24-26, Beasley-Murray states that they do not "mean that at the Lord's appearing the earth is destroyed or the universe collapses. It is the familiar and time-honored language of theophany, going back to ancient representations that when God steps forth for action in the world all creation is in confusion and dread before his appearing" (Beasley-Murray, "The Kingdom of God in the Teaching of Jesus," 29).

[109] On the coming of the Kingdom, see Beasley-Murray's recent solution to the problem of the chronology of Mark 13. He says now that the discourse is Mark's compilation of four groups of sayings from the Christian catechesis and functions as "paranetic eschatology" to "inspire faith, endurance and hope in the face of the sufferings of the Church and the Jewish nation" and to "warn Christians against false teaching concerning the End" (Beasley-Murray, "The Vision on the Mount," 45-46; Beasley-Murray, *Jesus and the Last Days*, 355-62). With this textual history, Beasley-Murray sees that Mark 13 reflects Jesus' teaching on numerous issues, including the coming of the Kingdom at the Parousia of the Son of Man, the disciples' request for information about the destruction of the temple, the tribulation of Israel that comes as a consequence for rejection, and the danger of the times because of pseudoprophets and pseudomessiahs (Beasley-Murray, "The Kingdom of God in the Teaching of Jesus," 28-29).

subjectivity in what is spiritualized and what is not, what of the hope is to be received as historical and what is not. For example, if the Kingdom is simply the "Coming of God" or the manifestation of God's "strength," it could be argued that this Kingdom was effectively established at the first advent, leaving the question open for the need of the Kingdom's consummation. That is, if it is to be admitted that we are to look with the New Testament for a further "coming" of God or future manifestations of his strength, the *regnum Christi* view could leave us with surprising little of substance to talk about.[110] Indeed this may be the way such matters of the future should be handled, but as we have already seen, Glasson is able to ride this view to the extreme and give us nothing at all to talk about for the Parousia because in his view the historical Jesus never even talked about it. The Parousia doctrine of the Kingdom's advent came from the early church.

HENGEL AND SCHWEMER

The worship of the community at Qumran is the vantage point from which Martin Hengel and Anna Maria Schwemer emphasize the realized quality of the Kingdom in Jesus' ministry. Under the impetus of Camponovo's study of the Kingdom in the literature of early Judaism and the more recently published critical edition of the *Sabbath Songs of Qumran* (4Q 400–407; 11Q *Shir Shabb; Masada Shir Shabb*), Hengel and Schwemer propose that the eternal, heavenly kingship of God, as seen also in the Old Testament, cannot be neglected when interpreting Jesus' message and the rest of the New Testament.[111]

---

[110] However, note Beasley-Murray's and Witherington's explication of the coming of the Kingdom at the Parousia (Beasley-Murray, "The Kingdom of God in the Teaching of Jesus," 28-29; "The Vision on the Mount," 47-50; Witherington, *Jesus, Paul and the End of the World*, 170-77).

[111] Foreword to *Königsherrschaft Gottes und himmlischer Kult im Judentum, Urchristentum, und in der hellenistischen Welt*, ed. Martin Hengel and Anna Maria Schwemer (Tübingen: J. C. B. Mohr [Paul Siebeck], 1991). The origin of this volume was an Oberseminar of the winter quarter 1986/87 at Tübingen, "New Hymnic Texts of Ancient Judaism and Early Christianity." Camponovo's *Königtum, Königsherrschaft und Reich Gottes in den frühjüdischen Schriften* is brought up short for not considering Philo, early rabbinic literature, the role of Israel's cult at Jerusalem, the semantic domain of "kingdom" (e.g., royal imagery including thrones, scepters, crowns, etc.), and early Jewish prayers such as those found at Qumran, the critical edition of which appeared after Camponovo wrote (Carol A. Newsom, *Songs of Sabbath Sacrifice: A Critical Edition*, Harvard

The kingship of Yahweh in the ancient cult of Israel has, of course, long been recognized and studied in the Psalms of Enthronement (Pss. 47, 93, 95, 96–99). The picture of these Psalms is of Yahweh as king in a universal sense. He is the everlasting ruler of the nations and the world as their Creator and Lord. This understanding of Yahweh's rulership is particularly germane to the worship of Israel and is in tension with the two other ways the Old Testament speaks of the kingship of God, that is, God's kingship expressed in the land and people of Israel and the eschatological reign that would one day come and bring God's salvation to the whole world.[112] In other words, within the cult, the kingship of Yahweh was always realized, despite the plight of Israel and the world under domination of evil usurpers.[113]

As the Sabbath Songs show, the situation at Qumran was fundamentally the same as ancient Israel. In worship, God is recognized upon his heavenly throne as king of the universe, but there is still need for patience until such times as his kingship will be visibly, socially, and politically realized over all the earth.[114] Nevertheless, it is the universal kingship that guarantees the eventuality of the eschatological kingship and undergirds it. Thus, it is important not to make too much of the tension of the different views of kingship. The present universal kingship and the future reign

---

Semitic Studies 27 [Cambridge, Mass.: Harvard University, 1985]). The Sabbath prayers at Qumran are striking in their repetition of "God is king" (55 times) and God's association with his *malkuth* (21 times). See Hengel and Schwemer, foreword to *Königsherrschaft Gottes*, 1-2, 5, and Schwemer's essay, "Gott also König und seine Königsherrschaft in den Sabbatliedern aus Qumran," 45-118.

[112] Hengel delineated these three senses of God's kingship in *The Zealots: Investigations into the Jewish Freedom Movement in the Period from Herod I Until 70 A.D.*, trans. David Smith (Edinburgh: T & T Clark, 1989), 91-93.

[113] "In heaven is eternally present what is expected for the earth in the future salvation" (Schwemer, "Gott als König und seine Königsherrschaft," 117; author's translation). Hengel and Schwemer contend that as Israel continued to languish under foreign domination the political tone of kingship rhetoric increased. This happens in Daniel and Qumran (foreword to *Königsherrschaft Gottes*, 4).

[114] This tension between God's kingship and the manifestation of that kingship is thus visible as an unbroken tradition extending from ancient Judaism through the New Testament era into the rabbinic literature. Hengel and Schwemer, foreword to *Königsherrschaft Gottes*, 3, quote the liturgical form of *m. Joma* 4, 1-3; 6, 2: "Praised be the name of the lordship *(herrlichkeit)* of his dominion *(Königsherrschaft)* for ever and ever."

are inherently and organically related—something not noticed enough in modern scholarship. Hengel and Schwemer assert that

> In our opinion it is a misleading feature of modern reflection that the contrast between the eternally-present rule of God and the future rule is highly stylized as a "fundamental difference." In reality in the Judaism of the Hellenistic-Roman period, the eternal kingship and dominion of God is the *foundation and presupposition* of the readily termed "apocalyptic" forms of speech for the future reality. One could also say: The future kingdom of God *[Gottesreich]* is only a more defined—for the people of God suffering under evil in history certainly more essential—aspect of the eternal dominion of God.[115]

It is the ever-present, universal reign of God expressed in the cult of Qumran that also informs Jesus' proclamation of the Kingdom. The worship of God as king regardless of what was happening to Israel on earth means his reign is present. It is not a future, apocalyptic venture only, though this aspect is not to be denied. The presence of the Kingdom is why Jesus can say, "the Kingdom is in your midst," that it is "upon you,"[116] that it is possible to "enter" the Kingdom, that the Kingdom now "suffers violence," that John's ministry marks the turn of the ages, and that the Kingdom's seeds are sown now.[117] Even the request for the Kingdom's coming in the Lord's Prayer is to be seen in light of the reality of God's universal kingship as not exclusively a petition for the future.[118]

---

[115] Ibid., 8 (author's translation; their emphasis).

[116] Hengel and Schwemer argue that the *engiken* of Mark 1:15, Luke 10:9/Matthew 10:7 and see 21:8 cannot be unconditionally translated "near at hand" *(nahegekommen)*, but is more like the *ephthasen eph humas* of Luke 11:20/Matthew 12:28 (ibid., 11).

[117] Ibid., 10–11.

[118] The connection of the submission to God's name and the coming of the Kingdom in the first two petitions of the Lord's Prayer shows that for Jesus the rabbinic idea of taking the "yoke of the Kingdom" upon oneself (*SLev* 18:6; *MekhEx* 20:2) is a manifestation of the Kingdom possible in the present. Here Hengel and Schwemer follow Billerbeck (H. Strack and P. Billerbeck, *Kommentar zum Neuen Testament aus Talmud und Midrasch* [Munich: Beck, 1922-1928], 1:172 ff.). On this see also Martin Hengel, "Zur matthäischen Bergpredigt und ihrem jüdischen Hintergrund," *TRu* 52 (1987): 384.

Jesus' message of the Kingdom also picks up another line of the tradition of Qumran that has roots as far back as the book of Daniel, namely, that the reign of God and the works of that reign are conjoined to an authoritative, anointed figure. In the case of Qumran this figure was Michael and Melchizedek; for Daniel it was one like a Son of man; in the Pharisaic *Psalms of Solomon* and post-Christian Judaism, it was the Messiah.[119] The same shows true for Jesus and early Christology. The facts of his authoritative proclamation, his forgiveness of sins, his many healings and exorcisms, and his fellowship at table with sinners all place him within this conception of his times.[120]

The great exception of Jesus relative to Judaism, of course, was the presentation of himself as the inaugurator of the manifestation of God's universal kingship. All the more striking in this case is the fact that Jesus (and the early church) rarely spoke of God or himself as "king." God was "Father," and Jesus, Hengel and Schwemer argue, received the kingly title from the primitive church, primarily from the crucifixion epithet: King of the Jews. The Christology of the first Christians therefore maintained that "the reign *(Königsherrschaft)* of Christ proceeds forth from the cross."[121] This being the case, it is important for modern interpreters to understand the coincidence of Jesus' kingship and the universal kingship of God celebrated in the cult of ancient Israel and Qumran. Jesus' reign is the universal reign of God.[122]

When seen in light of cultic worship, as at Qumran, the Kingdom Jesus announced is organically united with its Old Testament roots. The present submission of the King's subjects to his reign, along with their reception of his salvation as realized in the cult, began with the appearance of Jesus as God's anointed representative on the earth. In Jesus' earthly and now heavenly ministry, that is, reign, the universal kingship of God is now manifested as a the dynamic process of salvation continuing through history towards consummation.

---

[119] Hengel and Schwemer, foreword to *Königsherrschaft Gottes*, 8-9.

[120] Ibid., 10.

[121] Ibid., 12-13.

[122] See also Hengel's "Reich Christi, Reich Gottes und Weltreich im 4. Evangelium," in *Königsherrschaft Gottes*, 163-84.

Hengel and Schwemer's work on the cultic worship of the Qumran community should be credited for rightly bringing into focus the inherent relationship of the messianic kingdom and the eternal, universal kingdom of God. The messianic kingdom is the earthly manifestation of the universal sovereignty of God worshiped in the cult of Israel and the Christian church. Care needs to be taken, however, that this common touchstone in God's universal sovereignty does not serve to define down or blur the picture of what really constituted the Jewish hope of the first century, so that if Jesus only touches the "core" issue of divine sovereignty or care, he has *ipso facto* fulfilled the Old Testament hope. As noted earlier by Wright, the mainline anticipation of the Jewish people was for the sovereignty of God to be expressed in specific ways relative to the Land, the Torah, the temple, the race, and so on. The fact that Jesus also emphasizes God's sovereignty in his divine fatherhood does not in itself mean the other specific forms of the Jewish hope must have all been fulfilled at the first advent and that those hopes need to be taken symbolically. As I have suggested earlier with the question of his reign, his relationship to the enemies of his reign, and the provisional nature of his earthly ministry, there exists great differences between what Jesus inaugurated of the Kingdom and the Jewish hope, even if that hope is understood symbolically.

Each of the scholars we have considered in this chapter so far have employed a rigorous and compelling historical method. Each scholar has also used that method to apprehend a fundamental proposition from the eschatology of the Old Testament and the second-temple Judaism. Whether it is God's dynamic activity (Merklein and Carmignac), his coming (Beasley-Murray), his coming in strength (Chilton), his becoming king (Wright), or the expression of his divine sovereignty (Hengel and Schwemer), all have also proposed to find the original proposition renewed in Jesus' announcement of the Kingdom as a present, redemptive activity. If this is to be the preferred interpretation of the Kingdom, the issue will not be, as I see it, a question primarily of historical method, nor of Jesus' affinity with the eschatology of the Old Testament. It will be a question about whether the salvation Jesus inaugurated in fulfillment of this global concept latent in the Old Testament hope must necessarily mean the denial (that is, spiritualization) of all the other features of the hope as well.

CHAPTER FOUR

The Social-Economic Kingdom of the Third Quest

In contrast to the Jesus whose Kingdom meant personal, spiritual redemption in the *regnum Christi* comes the Jesus and his Kingdom of the Third Quest. This Jesus, as we shall see, is hewn from the social, economic, and political constructs of his day. His Kingdom is more earthly and socially concerned. It is broader than individuals in its concerns, affecting social structures and entire classes of people. In terms of methodology, practitioners of the Third Quest follow the verdict of Sanders, who wrote in 1980, "I think that the day is over when people could think that piously counting Aramaisms, or diligently seeking the earliest source, or fervently doing the history of individual pericopes, would tell us what we want to know about Jesus—his character and his intent."[1] This retrenchment from purely literary approaches to understanding Jesus in the Gospels has issued forth in new interdisciplinary approaches of the Third Quest. Jesus and his Kingdom are being sought in the kinds of paradigms available in the social sciences, particularly sociology and anthropology. His identification with known social types of the first century and his place within the dynamic of Palestinian class structures are said to be the keys to understanding him and his Kingdom.[2]

---

[1] E. P. Sanders, "New Testament Studies Today," in *Colloquy on New Testament Studies*, ed. Bruce Corley (Macon, Ga.: Mercer University Press, 1980), 15.

[2] See the early reviews of the role of the social sciences in biblical interpretation in Robin Scroggs, "The Sociological Interpretation of the New Testament: The Present State of Research," *NTS* 26 (1980): 164-79; Bruce J. Malina, "The Social Sciences and Biblical Interpretation," *Interp* 32 (July 1982): 229-42; Eileen Stevenson, "Some Insights from the Sociology of Religion in the Origin and Development of the Early Christian Church," *ExpTim* 90 (1979): 300-5; D. J. Harrington, "Sociological Concepts and the Early Church: A Decade of Research," *TS* 41 (1980): 181-90; Paul W. Hollenbach, "Recent Historical Jesus Studies and the Social Sciences," *Society of Biblical Literature 1983 Seminar Papers*, ed. Kent Harold Richards (Chico, Calif.: Scholars, 1983), 61-78.

MACK: SAPIENTIAL KINGDOM OF THE CYNIC SAGE

The Hellenistic Cynic sage is the paradigm for Jesus and his Kingdom offered in Burton Mack's picture of Christian origins.[3] Employing a methodology reminiscent of Bultmannian form criticism, Mack's reconstruction of early Christianity assumes considerable augmentation of the story of Jesus by the early Christians and suggests that their creations were driven by issues of social formation within the Christian communities.[4] According to Mack's scenario, four formative stages yield the type of language about the Kingdom we see in the Gospel of Mark. Stage one represents the ministry of the historical Jesus, witnessed by many of the earliest Christian movements.[5] Stage two is an optimistic time for the community as it is still fresh with the significance of Jesus' ministry. Stage three marks a period of failure for the community; it has been persecuted or disappointed in some way. The fourth and final stage is a period of "polemic and compensatory reaction." It completes the process begun in stage three and ultimately yields the finished document that has been traditionally received.[6]

Within this account of social history, the Kingdom theme can take any number of new meanings. Mack posits this has happened in Mark's Gospel, where the end product, the result of stages three and four, has clearly become apocalyptic. For the Kingdom in the Gospel as we now have it,

---

[3] Burton L. Mack, *The Lost Gospel: The Book of Q and Christian Origins* (San Francisco: Harper, 1993); *A Myth of Innocence: Mark and Christian Origins* (Philadelphia: Fortress, 1988); and "The Kingdom That Didn't Come," *SBL 1988 Seminar Papers*, ed. David J. Lull (Atlanta: Scholars, 1988), 608-35. Mack's detailed discussion of Jesus' teaching about the Kingdom appeared as an essay entitled "The Kingdom Sayings in Mark," *Forum* 3, no. 1 (1987): 3-47.

Mack's portrait of Jesus as a Cynic sage follows the similar view of F. G. Downing in *Jesus and the Threat of Freedom* (London: SCM, 1987) and *The Christ and the Cynics* (Sheffield: Sheffield Academic, 1988). Mack cites others who note similarities between the Jesus-tradition and the Cynics in *Myth of Innocence*, 69, n. 11. These, however, do not follow Mack in painting Jesus as a Cynic.

[4] One of Mack's conclusions in "The Kingdom Sayings in Mark" is that "none of the kingdom sayings in Mark is to be judged authentic" (44).

[5] Mack sees the Gospel of Thomas, Q, and the Gospel of Mark as representative of three of the early communities (Mack, "Kingdom Sayings," 19, 20).

[6] Mack, *Myth of Innocence*, 125.

"the overall impression is apocalyptic, that of a dominion as domain to be actualized when manifest in the future."[7] This apocalyptic Kingdom, however, is the result of the social formation of the Markan community. When the stages of this formation are appropriately retraced, Mack contends that the apocalyptic notions invaded the tradition at stages three and four, the stages of failure and polemic reaction. As he puts it,

> Living in the shadow of the Jewish War, smarting from a recent separation from the synagogue, and troubled by confusions, dissensions, and desertions from within, the author of the gospel is a much more likely candidate for thinking of the kingdom apocalyptically than Jesus.[8]

In the layers of tradition underneath the apocalyptic, Jesus measures up better as a nonapocalyptic, Cynic teacher such as would have been familiar to the Hellenized cities of Palestine, notably those of Galilee. The Cynic's own body of *basileia*-language could metaphorically understand as "king" any person manifesting their own "kingdom" of intractable freedom, independent bearing, confidence, and wisdom. The metaphorical kingship of the Cynic was thus not a political category of Hellenism, but, in fact, grew out of political discourse. Mack explains that within Cynicism

> the abstract models [i.e., sovereignty, kingship] constructed in order to imagine the practical issues inherent in the political structures of society could be used as well to think through basic questions about social ethos in general and how even the individual might be understood to relate best to the constraints and invitations of a very interesting but complex and sometimes dangerous world. . . . Thus, the kingship paradigm could serve as the imaginative model both for working out social critique and for constructive proposals for both a just society and a virtuous life at one and the same time.[9]

Jesus, Mack suggests, fits this paradigm. His aphoristic style, his audiences with small groups in homes, his clever poking and prodding of the "establishment" to which people had sold out, all point in this direction. In

---

[7] Mack, "Kingdom Sayings," 18.

[8] Ibid., 19.

[9] Ibid., 11-12.

this context Jesus offers no reform, no renewal, and no mission with Judaism; his concern is only for individuals, that they be "kings" like him.[10]

In contrast to most of those who follow in our survey as well as to the bulk of contemporary Jesus-research, Mack's project reflects a cynicism all its own. Rather than looking to Judaism for his social paradigms, Mack's Jesus comes from a world that is thoroughly Hellenized. Jesus stands on the edge of Judaism, distant from its hopes and critical of its institutions. To make this edifice stand, Mack must build on preexisting foundations that will not satisfy many.[11] His work does, however, open the door a little more to one aspect of life in first-century Palestine and typifies the kinds of results possible through an interdisciplinary hermeneutic.

RICHES: KINGDOM AS SOCIAL AND ETHICAL WHOLENESS

The social anthropology of Mary Douglas provides the theoretical basis of John Riches's thesis about Jesus and his proclamation of the Kingdom.[12] Taking as his task first the question of Jesus' purpose and second the question of how Jesus' theological language "related to the broad range of social and political questions which concerned Jews of the first century,"[13] Riches employs Douglas's understanding of how religious beliefs displayed in language relate to a broader context of social realities. In

---

[10] "The invitation would have been to something like the Cynic's 'kingdom,' that is, to assume the Cynic's stance of confidence in the midst of confused and contrary social circumstances. Simply translated, Jesus' 'message' seems to have been, 'See how it's done? You can do it too'" (Mack, *Myth of Innocence*, 73).

[11] As Marcus Borg and N. T. Wright have observed, Mack's thesis, in a way typical of form criticism, depends on very questionable assumptions about the social formation of communities. First, Mack must have a lot of development in an inordinately short time. Second, he assumes communities could not retain more than one tradition at a time. Third, he assumes the unlikely proposition that groups which began in a decidedly Hellenistic mode would revert to a Jewish one after the events of A.D. 70 (Marcus Borg, "Portraits of Jesus in Contemporary North American Scholarship," *HarTR* 84 [1991]: 8; N. T. Wright, *The New Testament and the People of God* [Minneapolis: Fortress, 1992], 428, 430). On the assessment of the first-century data for the Cynics see the comments addressed later to John Dominic Crossan.

[12] John Riches, *Jesus and the Transformation of Judaism* (New York: Seabury, 1983). See also John Riches and Alan Millar, "Conceptual Change in the Synoptic Tradition," in *Alternative Approaches to New Testament Study*, ed. A. E. Harvey (London: SPCK, 1985).

[13] Riches, *Transformation*, ix.

essence Douglas says that we know the meaning of one's words when "we know what other sentences he would accept or reject,"[14] meaning that it is the whole social behavior of an individual that deciphers that individual's religious language. Thus, in order to understand Jesus on the Kingdom an attempt must be made to place his proclamation against the background of other aspects of his teaching and to see how he related to the existing religious conventions of his day.

Riches begins by discussing the main groups that would have provided Jesus' religious background. In the process of describing the political and sociological dimensions of Palestine and how the Essenes, Pharisees, and Zealots interacted within those dimensions, Riches sees another socio-logical principle at work in the first century, "anomie." This is a term taken from G. Theissen's sociological analyses and "refers to a state in which individuals are no longer in a position to behave in a manner conformable to the norms of their group."[15] Riches contends that each of these groups of the first century presented detailed programs of resistance to political and social Hellenization. These programs were examples of anomie in that they each intensified and radicalized the "core" Jewish understanding of the Kingdom in one way or another. This core meaning of kingship Riches understands as the "power, sovereignty, supremacy, right" through which justice and mercy are transmitted.[16] For the Pharisees and Essenes the radicalization of this concept concerned matters of ritual purity and fel-lowship; for the Zealots the issue was militaristic nationalism.[17]

As Riches sees it, Jesus' intention with respect to the Kingdom was to rework and renew the slanted views of Yahweh's kingship dominating the social scene while still retaining the core belief of God establishing his rule over humanity and satisfying their deepest needs. Jesus accomplished this feat by means of his specific sayings about the Kingdom, but more impor-tantly, by the particular *contexts* of his remarks. For example, to correct the

---

[14] Ibid., 36. See Mary Douglas, *Purity and Danger: An Analysis of the Concepts of Pollution and Taboo* (London: Routledge & Kegan Paul, 1978).

[15] Riches, *Transformation*, 208, n. 92. See Gerd Theissen, "Wir haben alles verlassen" (MC. X.28), Nachfolge und soziale Entwurzelung in der jüdisch-palästinischen Gesellschaft des 1. Jahrhunderts n. Chr., *NovT* 19 (1977): 161-96, esp. 188-96.

[16] Riches, *Transformation*, 91-92.

[17] Ibid., 62-86.

nationalized notions of the Zealots, Jesus reveals the Kingdom as established in the healing of the sick and the forgiveness of sins.[18] To tone down Pharisaic and Qumranic exclusionary righteousness, Jesus preaches the Kingdom in the fellowship of outcasts, paupers, sinners, and tax-collectors.[19] Jesus' Kingdom message was also given in the context of collecting a group of disciples to his "vagrant and mendicant" lifestyle, again denying the need of a militaristic holy war in the name of the Kingdom.[20]

In the end Jesus delivers the core of the Kingship of God in terms of its social and ethical implications. The discourses about purity and God make some of those social implications evident. With regards to purity Jesus makes us understand the crucial issue of exchanging one definition of sacredness for another. The Kingdom is not about ritual purity but about social wholeness.[21] The question about God concerns theodicy: "How can God be said to rule while his people are oppressed?"[22] Though Jesus acknowledges the apocalyptic end and its near arrival, his discussion of rewards and punishments still shifts the emphasis from the end time to the present. In his own healing and forgiving ministry God is already manifested as victorious over Satan. The Kingdom then may have an apocalyptic future, but Jesus' purpose with respect to it, in answer to Riches's first task, was to translate the "fundamental apprehensions about God, man, and the world into social terms."[23]

HORSLEY: KINGDOM AS SOCIAL REVOLUTION

Richard Horsley's study of first-century Palestine considers the sociology of protest among oppressed peoples.[24] Noting the "spiral of violence"

---

[18] Ibid., 103.

[19] Ibid., 106.

[20] Ibid., 106.

[21] Jesus' emphasis was on the law's demand that we love our enemies (ibid., 142).

[22] Ibid., 154.

[23] Ibid., 185.

[24] Richard A. Horsley, *Jesus and the Spiral of Violence: Popular Jewish Resistance in Roman Palestine* (San Francisco: Harper & Row, 1987); see also Horsley's other works concerning the political

inherent to oppressive social situations that has been enunciated by Dom Helder Camara, archbishop of Recife in northern Brazil,[25] Horsley contends that the psychology of colonized peoples has much to say about the context and message of the historical Jesus.

Horsley begins by stating the "spiral of violence" he believes governs the Jewish situation under Roman hegemony.[26] The first stage was the violence of the *oppression* the Jews suffered through Roman taxation and the violation of their religion. Stage two was mass *protest and resistance* to this violence. Horsley observes this stage is done *en masse* among those of the lowest economic levels, and it is characteristically nonviolent. The third stage is the violent *repression* of the protest, though many occasions are noted when the Roman leaders compromised or conceded to the demands of the protest. Finally, stage four is violent *revolt*—the inevitable result of repeated provocation to the collective psyche of the colonized people. Most significant for Horsley's thesis about Jesus is his contention that Palestine under Rome was less violent, far less than commonly assumed, in its reaction to the Roman overlords, and that provocations were primarily religious in nature. Though it is true Palestine did not rest in peace, it was not the hotbed of violent revolution scholarship had often

---

and social aspects of Palestine: "Josephus and the Bandits," *JStJud* 10 (1979): 37-63; "The Sicarii: Ancient Jewish Terrorists," *JRel* 59 (1979): 435-58; "Ancient Jewish Banditry and the Revolt Against Rome, A.D. 66-70," *CBQ* 43 (1981): 409-32; "Popular Messianic Movements Around the Time of Jesus," *CBQ* 46 (1984), 471-93; "Like One of the Prophets of Old: Two Types of Popular Prophets at the Time of Jesus," *CBQ* 47 (1985): 435-63; "High Priests and the Politics of Roman Palestine: A Contextual Analysis of the Evidence in Josephus," *JStJud* 17 (1986): 23-55; "The Zealots, Their Origin, Relationships and Importance in the Jewish Revolt," *NovT* 28 (1986): 159-92; "Popular Prophetic Movements at the Time of Jesus, Their Principle Features and Social Origins," *JStNT* 26 (1986): 3-27; "Bandits, Messiahs, and Longshoremen: Popular Unrest in Galilee Around the Time of Jesus," *SBL Seminar Papers 1988*, ed. David J. Lull (Atlanta: Scholars, 1988); *Sociology and the Jesus Movement* (New York: Crossroad, 1989); Richard A. Horsley and John S. Hanson, *Bandits, Prophets, and Messiahs: Popular Movements at the Time of Jesus* (San Francisco: Harper & Row, 1985).

[25] Camara's spiral has three stages: (1) the violence of an unjust system; (2) the revolt against that system; and (3) the violent suppression of the revolt (Horsley, *Spiral of Violence*, 22-23).

[26] Ibid., 24-58.

made it out to be either.[27] Rarely did the spiral descend to stage four, that of open, violent revolt, and rarely were the religious leaders leading the charge.[28]

This sociological and historical context leads Horsley to question two common assumptions about Jesus. First, Horsley says that we cannot assume that Jesus was the pacifistic preacher of nonresistance whose common foil was the violent elements of the Jewish response. These elements, that is, the Zealots, simply did not exist in his day, and while the pattern of the day seemed to be resistance and protest, it was a nonviolent resistance and protest. Many elements of Jesus' ministry offered challenge and protest to the old order of things in this nonviolent mode. Exorcisms, for example, only indirectly addressed the Roman government as Jesus attacked the root of Rome's demonic power. The Kingdom renews individual and social life starting at the very base of power.[29] The good news to the poor was also a gauntlet to the powers and institutions that had impoverished them. Lastly, the announcement of the *Kingdom* of God, a political symbol, challenged all lesser political kingdoms.[30] Jesus announced the beginnings of what would ultimately terminate the old order, but that termination would not be the result of violent insurrection.

Second, Horsley says that it cannot be assumed that Jesus' message was only religiously oriented, as if religious matters could be completely separated from social and political ones. Jesus' goal of terminating the old order meant that his message went beyond the individual and was intended to touch the whole of society itself.

---

[27] The main issue here is the status of the Zealots and their relationship to Josephus's Fourth Philosophy. Horsley argues vigorously against the scholarly consensus (typified for example in Hengel's *The Zealots)* that the Zealots were a viable force in Palestine prior to A.D. 66. In his mind, Hengel, as representative of the consensus, has "lumped together, under the modern concept of the Zealot movement, a number of disparate incidents and the activities of quite different groups, such as brigand bands and the terrorist Sicarii" (Horsley, *Spiral of Violence,* 78). Josephus's Fourth Philosophy of 6 C.E. is to be associated not with the Zealots but with a "nonviolent, non-revolutionary resistance to enrolling for the Roman tribute" (*Spiral of Violence,* 89).

[28] The lack of prominence of the religious leaders of Israel in the protests of the first century demonstrate that the provocations were of another sort, namely economic and political (Horsley, *Spiral of Violence,* 116-20).

[29] Ibid., 157, 160.

[30] Ibid., 153.

There is no reason to believe, no evidence that Jesus and his followers or the gospel tradition were only or even primarily "religious" in their concerns. The evidence in the gospel tradition—e.g., the political symbol of "the kingdom of God" as his central message, the healing of bodies as well as souls as the activity for which he was most renowned—rather confirms the opposite: that Jesus was concerned with the whole life, in all its dimensions.[31]

Jesus' preaching about the Kingdom intended nothing less than the complete, historical restoration of Israel, religiously, socially, and politically. This restoration, Horsley believes, was not intended to be an all-transforming act in Jesus' lifetime; nor does it define the Kingdom spatially as a "realm" or "sphere." Rather, the Kingdom of God here is more of the process of restoration than the result. The Kingdom of God "means the use of power, in 'mighty deeds,' "to liberate, establish, or protect people in difficult historical circumstances."[32]

The transformation of society Jesus sought was to be carried out in the participation of people in the initiating action of God. His was a social movement of egalitarian associations, alleviation of poverty, forgiveness of debts, love of enemies, and personal reconciliation and cooperation, all of which he himself both mandated and demonstrated.[33] However, Jesus knew his social movement was just the precursor to the final Kingdom rule that would eventually be achieved within history. What begins now as a social movement will finally and nonviolently become a political movement as God's liberating power is realized throughout the earth.

> Jesus would appear to have believed that God had already begun, as it were, to implement the political revolution, even though it was hardly very far along. But in the confidence that it was under way, it was his calling to proceed with the social revolution thus made possible by God's rule, to begin the transformation of social relations in anticipation of the completion of the political revolution.[34]

---

[31] Ibid., 153.
[32] Ibid., 167-68.
[33] Ibid., 209-85.
[34] Ibid., 325.

Four main conclusions come from Horsley's consideration of Jesus and the Kingdom: (1) there was no violent, sustained resistance to Roman rule in first-century Palestine; (2) Jesus did not advocate violent acts against Rome; (3) Jesus definitely was a social agitator against the establishment, but his intentions were only social, not political; and (4) Jesus anticipated political consequences of his social movement, but they were the eventual results of what he started socially.[35]

BORG: KINGDOM AS MYSTICAL EXPERIENCE OF GOD

The work of Marcus Borg has remarkable points in common with the conclusions of Bruce Chilton. As I mentioned earlier in chapter three, Chilton's conclusions about the Targums have in turn significant similarity to Norman Perrin's plurisignificant understanding of the Kingdom as tensive symbol, and Chilton, in concert with Camponovo, used Perrin to great effect in the critical study of ancient documents. Once again in Borg's portrait of the historical Jesus, Perrin's symbolic Kingdom finds a home in the Third Quest. [36]

The vehicle for Borg to unveil Jesus' meaning of the Kingdom is the conflict dynamic of the first century and Jesus' performance within that context as a holy man, a prophet, and a sage.[37] In Borg's presentation, conflict had two foci for the Jews under Roman rule and a complete picture of Jesus should locate his position *vis-à-vis* both of them.[38] On the macrolevel

---

[35] Ibid., 318-19. See also the similar views of R. David Kaylor, *Jesus the Prophet: His Vision of the Kingdom on Earth* (Louisville, Ky.: Westminster/John Knox, 1994), 89.

[36] Borg's pertinent works here include *Conflict, Holiness & Politics in the Teachings of Jesus*, Studies in Bible and Early Christianity 5 (New York: Edwin Mellen, 1984); "A Temperate Case for a Non-Eschatological Jesus," *Forum* 2 (September 1986): 81-102; "An Orthodoxy Reconsidered: The 'End-of-the-World Jesus,'" in *The Glory of Christ in the New Testament*, ed. L. D. Hurst and N. T. Wright (Oxford: Clarendon, 1987), 207-17; *Jesus: A New Vision* (San Francisco: Harper & Row, 1989). Perrin's appearance in Borg's remarks about the Kingdom in *Conflict*, 248-65, reiterates the influence of Perrin's tensive symbol idea and the ease with which it accommodated more than one discipline of New Testament studies.

[37] This was the subject of Borg's 1972 Ph.D. dissertation at Oxford: *Conflict as a Context for Interpreting the Teaching of Jesus*.

[38] Ibid., 27-49.

was Israel's conflict with her Roman overlords. A people who were promised their own sovereignty now find themselves under the boot of a ruthless world power with its own claim to universal sovereignty. How should Israel respond to this situation? History reveals different responses were forthcoming from different Jewish renewal movements of the first century. Responses ranged from the withdrawal of the Essenes to the violent revolts of the Freedom Fighters, but all were aimed at defining the people of God in that Roman colonial setting and garnering the most popular sympathy for their cause.

The macrolevel oppression of Rome not only forced an answer where Rome was concerned but the differing Jewish answers to Rome demanded answers on the microlevel to their rivals for Israel's sympathies. That is, as each group had defined Israel's proper response to the Roman situation, to win the day they necessarily had to define their own uniqueness relative to the contradicting responses of the other groups. The common denominator upon which these internecine conflicts would be waged centered on holiness, particularly as it pertained to the two cultural benchmarks of Israel: the Torah and the temple.[39] Each major renewal group, the Pharisees, the Essenes, and the Freedom Fighters, maintained a distinct position on Torah and temple, arguing against the others the holiness of their position. It is against the background of this two-tiered conflict that Jesus appeared and established his own renewal movement. His posture toward the conflict with Rome and the conflict with the other groups *vis-à-vis* the Torah and the temple would confirm the uniqueness and viability of his movement.

Jesus' presentation of himself as a "holy man" established his credentials in the Jewish macroconflict with Rome, but his understanding of an inclusive holiness separated his movement from the others on the microlevel. Whereas the others had used holiness to exclude those not deemed worthy, Jesus' holiness did not preclude his taking meals with sinners.[40] It did not keep him from reaching out to those considered lost, outcast, or unclean. It did not preclude his ignoring ritual washings of hands or artificial

---

[39] Ibid., 51-72.
[40] Ibid., 81ff.

approbations regarding the Sabbath. In the place of a negative holiness which functioned to separate, Jesus posited the *imitatio Dei* in terms of mercy. Mercy is the true content of holiness (Matt. 9:13; 12:27) on all levels of conflict—toward the hated Romans and wrongheaded fellow Jews.[41] In Jesus' movement, it was holiness that was "contagious," not uncleanness.[42]

The second benchmark of Palestinian Judaism, the temple, intersects Jesus' movement in his role as a prophet. Borg sees Jesus as particularly prophetic through his threats and warnings delivered to the temple establishment. As the locus of civil as well as religious power, the temple ideology in Israel was the mandate of Hebrew sovereignty. However, in Jesus' day it had become a symbol for a holiness of separation from the nations and the flashpoint of Israel's collision course with Rome. Jesus' prophetic actions and threats against the temple were designed to avert a collision that Jesus knew would mean destruction for his people. He urged the people to follow him in a peaceful social movement for which the temple would be a symbol of inclusion and mercy.[43]

The Kingdom theme in Jesus' proclamation comes into Borg's discussion under Jesus' performance of the "sage."[44] Empowered by his own mystical experience and communion with God, Jesus the sage defined his movement in terms of holiness of the heart. An interior mystical dynamic framed in the language of repentance rather than external ordinance was the center of holiness and identity for Jesus' movement. The Kingdom was Jesus' unique term for this mystical experience of communion with God, and Perrin's understanding of the Kingdom as a symbol is easily commandeered by Borg for these purposes.

> The phrase Kingdom of God is thus a symbol for the presence and power of God as known in mystical experience. It is Jesus' name for what is experienced in the primordial religious experience, and his

---

[41] Ibid., 126. Borg argues for the political implications of "Love your enemy." In its original context of conflict, Jesus' call was for mercy toward Gentiles (130).

[42] Jesus' "contagious" holiness in Borg's description has similarities to the "offensive holiness" discussed by Klaus Berger, "Jesus als Pharisäer und frühe Christen als Pharisäer," *NovT* 30 (1988): 231-62.

[43] Borg, *Conflict*, 199.

[44] Ibid., 237ff.

name for the power from that realm which flows through him as a holy man. Thus one may say that Jesus as a holy man experienced the Kingdom of God, a reality which, because it is ineffable, can only be spoken of in the language of symbols.[45]

Though Jesus' phraseology had certain historic associations with the apocalyptic Kingdom, Borg sees the Kingdom in Jesus much more existentially: "Jesus' use of the phrase did not point to the temporal end of the visible world, but to the end of the world of ordinary experience, as well as the end of the world as one's center and security."[46] The Kingdom that demanded the death of self for entrance (Matt. 5:20) and the Kingdom that could be realized as a present possession (Matt. 5:10) was the mainstay of Jesus' announcement and movement. There are no unambiguous, authentic sayings about the Kingdom in the Gospels that point to a temporally conceived future.[47]

Borg's Jesus and his Kingdom is intricately connected to the cultural and political issues of his day in a way that is different from the thoroughly individualized and existential Kingdom that Perrin had difficulty avoiding. In some ways, however, this is only a cosmetic connection. When the Kingdom is relegated to an inward matter of the heart, that is, the mystical experience of the power of God, the outward political thrust is compromised. It is true Jesus may have had political intentions with the call for a holiness based on inclusion and mercy, but the final result for the Kingdom still ends up little different from that of those who use the Kingdom theme solely for an indi-

---

[45] Ibid., 254. Borg would also allow the Kingdom to designate "a community created by that power, or in which that power is known" ("The End-of-the-World Jesus," 216).

[46] Borg, *Conflict*, 255.

[47] Ibid., 257ff. Borg cites Hengel (*Judaism and Hellenism* [Philadelphia: Fortress, 1974], 1:253) to assert that the temporal imagery of the apocalyptics must be allowed to also denote a nontemporal reality. This is the option Borg takes with Mark 1:14-15 and the second petition of the Lord's Prayer: "The petition *may* refer to a temporally future consummation visible in the external world, or it may be a petition for the internal experience of entering God's presence, of having God's presence come upon one. In fact, it could refer to both" (Borg, *Conflict*, 258). A large part of Borg's deeschatologizing Jesus is his consignment of the coming Son of Man sayings to the post-Easter church (*Conflict*, 221ff.; "A Temperate Case," 95-96; "End-of-the-World Jesus," 211-12). The remaining futuristic Kingdom sayings do not *in se* mandate temporality as in an imminent expectation (e.g., Matt. 8:11-12; see *Conflict*, 259).

vidual experience of God. The question then becomes, as we have already seen in chapter two, how well does this inward Kingdom fit with the cosmology and eschatology of the first century, a milieu that Charlesworth notes as "charged with expectations that the end of the world was about to occur"?[48] While Borg is likely correct in his attack on the imminent eschatological Kingdom and the Jesus whose every word was tinged with eschatology, the noneschatological Jesus, the holy man/sage, takes us too far the other way.

Craig A. Evans partially frames my own observations for Borg and the others of the Third Quest when he asks, "What has the scholarship of the last two decades discovered? Not the historical Jesus, it would appear, but what has been discovered is the background and environment against which he must be sought."[49] Borg's work certainly typifies the positive side of Evans's assessment, as his and also the other studies reviewed here have yielded fascinating results as far as the historical situation of first-century Palestine. From the Hellenistic influence on the Galilean pugnacious temperament through Sepphoris (Mack and Crossan), to the cultural significance of purity (holiness) and the temple in a setting of conflict (Riches, Horsley, and Borg), insights into the context of the historical Jesus certainly offer improved prospects for his apprehension, and beyond him the apprehension of his earliest followers. Also significant are the insights of Horsley and the others who want to make Jesus' message more inherently earthly, historical, and social/political than the other supermundane views of the Kingdom we have seen.[50]

Significant as these contributions may be, our survey seems to confirm Evans's pessimism about the array of "gestalts" being claimed for the historical Jesus. The variety of Jesuses that the Gospels seem to be capable of producing in the various interdisciplinary approaches brings up the query made of the Old Quest of the last century: Is this the historical Jesus, or a Jesus made in our own image? The fact that little unanimity is forthcoming

---

[48] James H. Charlesworth, "Jesus Research Expands with Chaotic Creativity," in *Images of Jesus Today*, ed. James H. Charlesworth and Walter P. Weaver, Faith and Scholarship Colloquies 3, Florida Southern College, 1-41 (Valley Forge, Pa.: Trinity Press International, 1994), 22.

[49] Craig A. Evans, "Jesus of Nazareth: Who Do Scholars Say That He Is? A Review Article," *Crux* 23/24 (1987): 18.

[50] The difference between the social and political aspects of the Kingdom is not always clear in our authors. Horsley and Borg paint Jesus as quite political, while Crossan, for example, seems unwilling to extend the consequences of his social movement to the political realm.

from the scholars surveyed thus far would appear to be *prima facie* evidence for the latter, but why should it? Is there something inherent to a nonapocalyptic Jesus that produces such variety? Borg himself illuminated the confusion relative to the Kingdom of God in a recent review of historical Jesus research in North America. He notes that

> when the eschatological consensus was intact, the [kingdom of God] had a clear meaning: it referred to the coming messianic kingdom, and/or the power (reign) of God by which that kingdom would be established. With the collapse of the imminent eschatological consensus, there is no longer a clear framework for locating the meaning of the kingdom of God. If Jesus' use of kingdom language did not pertain to the imminent end of the world, how are we to understand it?[51]

Borg's question here strikes at the very underpinnings of the answers he and the others with the Third Quest have given to it. That is, Borg's own portrait of the historical Jesus as well as the others here is based on dismissing the authenticity of the Son of Man sayings or else applying them to someone other than the historical Jesus.[52] Two factors, however, complicate any possibilities that such an approach has for wide appeal; first, the Son of Man debate has hardly delivered a consensus,[53] and second, the case

---

[51] Borg, "Portraits of Jesus," 20.

[52] The center place the unauthenticity of the coming Son of Man sayings has for these views is highlighted by Borg, who lists it as the first of the reasons he turned from the eschatological Jesus (Borg, "A Temperate Case," 86).

[53] Charlesworth is just one example of those who cannot follow the nonapocalyptic Quest here. He writes, "I am convinced that *all* three classes of Jesus' Son of Man sayings—those that depict the Son of Man's authority, future coming, and present suffering—were *not* invented by the *Church* (pace Vielhauer and Conzelmann)" (James H. Charlesworth, in *Jesus Within Judaism: New Light from Exciting Archaeological Discoveries*, Anchor Bible Reference Library [New York: Doubleday, 1988], 42 [emphasis his]). Along with other experts of the Old Testament Pseudepigrapha, he sees an apocalyptic titular use of Son of Man available to pre-A.D. 70 Palestine through *1 Enoch* 62-63, 69 (Charlesworth, *Jesus Within Judaism*, 42, 235). For a recent appraisal of the Son of Man discussion, see de Jonge, "The Christological Significance of Jesus' Preaching," 3-17. See also the other recent works by W. G. Kümmel, *Jesus der Menschensohn* (Stuttgart: Steiner, 1983), 41-46; Barnabas Lindars, *Jesus, Son of Man: A Fresh Examination of the Son of Man Sayings in the Gospels in the Light of Recent Research* (Grand Rapids: Eerdmans, 1984); W. O. Walker, "The Son of Man: Some Recent Developments," *CBQ* 45 (1983): 584-607; J. R. Donahue, "Recent Studies on the Origin of 'Son of Man' in the Gospels," *CBQ* 48 (1986): 484-98; and A. Y. Collins, "The Origin of the Designation of Jesus as 'Son of Man,'" *HarTR* 80 (1987): 391-407.

for apocalyptic is not really to be won or lost over the Son of Man issue anyway.[54] This lack of appeal will also be exacerbated all the more as the differing pictures of Jesus continue to surface in the studies of the Third Quest. Cut loose from his New Testament moorings as the Son of Man who predicted his return in judgment, it is indeed much less likely that Jesus saw himself different from a rabbi, a social critic, or social reformer of one kind or another. It is also easier to limit the Kingdom to the social and moral realms pertinent to the sayings of the Kingdom's presence. Without appropriate textual moorings in the New Testament, the nagging problem for the Third Quest will continue to be that the more the gestalts of Jesus multiply, the harder it will be for any one gestalt to persuade. In this case the political dictum holds true: the stature of any one candidate is diminished by the size of the field.

CROSSAN: THE BROKERLESS KINGDOM

John Dominic Crossan's most recent contribution to the debate, *The Historical Jesus: The Life of a Mediterranean Jewish Peasant* (1991),[55] is perhaps the most wide-ranging example of the interdisciplinary methodology of the Third Quest to date. Thoroughly indebted to the anthropological models of Lenski (*Power and Privilege: A Theory of Social Stratification* [1966]), Gurr (*Why Men Rebel* [1970]), Bryan Wilson (*Magic and the Millennium: A Sociological Study of Religious Movements of Protest Among Tribal and Third-World Peoples* [1973]), and others, Crossan rounds out his method with equal input from Greco-Roman history and a rigorous criticism of the Gospel documents.[56] The portrait of Jesus and his Kingdom

---

[54] The case for the apocalyptic Kingdom in Jesus' teaching according to the influential work of Meier, for example, is established entirely apart from the tangle of the Son of Man question. He examines the Kingdom teaching of the Lord's Prayer (Matt. 6:10), the Last Supper (Mark 14:25), the Gentiles at the last banquet (Matt. 8:11-12), and the Beatitudes of the Sermon on the Mount (Matt. 5:3-12). See John P. Meier, *A Marginal Jew: Rethinking the Historical Jesus*, vol. 2, *Mentor, Message and Miracle* (New York, N.Y.: Doubleday, 1994), 289-397.

[55] John Dominic Crossan, *The Historical Jesus: The Life of a Mediterranean Jewish Peasant* (San Francisco: HarperSanFrancisco, 1991).

[56] Crossan's view of authenticity (though he dislikes this term, see xxxi), involves historical stratification, external testimony, and plurality of testimony available for individual pericopes. His methodology on this is explained on pages xxxi-xxxii. See also appendix 1, 427ff.

that results is a striking blend of Mack's Cynic sage and Horsley's social agitator, with some key differences.

Given the genres of social stratifications and social types available in the Mediterranean world of the first century, Crossan takes the three social categories of peasant, magician, and Cynic as particularly applicable to the historical Jesus. Peasants, according to Crossan's rendering of anthropologist A. L. Kroeber, were the "structured inferiors" of the agrarian society. They are

> definitely rural, yet live in relation to market towns; they form a class segment of a larger population which usually contains also urban centers, sometimes metropolitan capitals. They constitute part-societies with part-cultures. They lack the isolation, the political autonomy, and the self-sufficiency of tribal populations; but their local units retain much of their old identity, integration, and attachment to soil and cults.[57]

History (i.e., the accounts of Josephus as interpreted by Horsley) reveals how the peasant masses of Palestine chafed under the colonizing and imperial conditions of Roman occupation. Mass protests of one kind or another punctuated the whole era of Jesus' life. Their role in this churning protean bed of social disruption demonstrates to Crossan that the peasants were the "performers" of a protest-drama about which the higher and more elite classes only wrote in their apocalyptic literature. None but the upper class collaborators with Rome liked the oppressive social situation, but the only avenue for protest open to the peasants was public social disruption. It was in this milieu and to this class of society that Jesus primarily ministered, meaning his message was also "performed."

The Magician was a chief role through which Jesus' protest-performance came.[58] As one who could make divine power present through personal miracle, Jesus fit the category of *religious* protester.[59] Against the communally

---

[57] A. L. Kroeber, *Anthropology: Race, Language, Culture, Psychology, Prehistory* (New York: Harcourt, Brace, 1948), 284 (cited by Crossan, *Historical Jesus*, 125).

[58] The role of the magician within Hellenism is explained by John Hull, *Hellenistic Magic and the Synoptic Tradition* SBT 2/28 (Naperville, Ill.: Alec R. Allenson, 1974) and Morton Smith, *Jesus the Magician* (New York: Harper & Row, 1978). Crossan leans on both of these studies.

[59] "Magic" for Crossan is not a pejorative term but simply signifies "personal and individual rather than communal and institutional access to, monopoly of, or control over divine power" (ibid., 138).

and institutionally "brokered" divine power of the religious leaders, Jesus achieved even greater feats of power on his own. As such he effectively challenged those with religious power. In the face of Jesus' miracles, they could not claim sole right as the broker of divine power to the lower classes.[60] Jesus' miracles also served as the primary vehicle of the social movement he was attempting to inaugurate among the peasants of Palestine. This fact is most clearly visible from the recorded instances of Jesus sending out his disciples (*GThom* 14:2; *Sayings Gospel* Q [1Q =Luke 10:1, 4–11 par.]; Mark 6:7–13). Crossan notes that Jesus sent them to perform miracles of healing and exorcism and to receive in turn commensuality of table fellowship. This "shared egalitarianism of spiritual and material resources" was the heart of Jesus' ministry and message of the Kingdom.[61]

The Hellenistic Cynic figure is the character through which Jesus' meaning of the Kingdom is most visible within his egalitarian peasant movement. Following Mack's delineations, Crossan opts for the sapiential Kingdom of the Cynics as the meaning of Jesus' message. The Kingdom Jesus proclaims is the manifestation of the highest ethical excellence, freedom, and confidence.[62] Two factors indicate this conclusion. First, the other option for Jesus, that of the apocalyptic Kingdom, did not interface well with Jesus' peasant context, a context of performance. The apocalyptic Kingdom came from the literature of society's elite. Second, the sapiential Kingdom is most prominent in the twelve sayings of the Kingdom having the highest plural and external attestation.[63] The specifics of

---

[60] According to Crossan, Magic as a religious protest stands contrary to banditry, which in the first century was *political* protest (ibid., 158). Crossan parts company with Horsley in this respect. Though Horsley does not see Jesus in a bandit's role, his Jesus is notably more political than Crossan's. It is by the means of Jesus' ministry of "magic" that Crossan tries to escape the political element in favor of the religious. The ministry of miracle/magic is more organically tied to Crossan's version of Jesus' mission than Horsley's. See *Historical Jesus*, chap. 13, "Magic and Meal."

[61] Ibid., 341, 344. The unusual success of Jesus' mission was due, in Crossan's mind, to the way his miracles and those of his followers went beyond disease into the realms of illness and sickness, which are all differentiated by anthropology (see the discussion on p. 337).

[62] Crossan, *Historical Jesus*, 287, quotes extensively from Mack's *Myth of Innocence*.

[63] Crossan, *Historical Jesus*, 265ff. Crossan does not count the apocalyptic Son of Man sayings in the Gospels as authentic. If Jesus did use "son of man" he meant simply "like a human" (243). The titular Son of Man is a Christian creation in all likelihood stemming from Jesus' own usage of "son of man" (247, 255, 258).

these passages describe the Kingdom with reference to children and the poor, leading Crossan to the conclusion that Jesus' Kingdom was a Kingdom of "Nobodies" and it is a Kingdom of the here and now.[64]

> My proposal is that when we cross apocalyptic and sapiential with scribes and peasants, it becomes necessary to locate Jesus in the quadrant formed by sapiential and peasant. What was described by his parables and aphorisms as a here and now Kingdom of nobodies and the destitute, of mustard, darnel, and leaven, is precisely a Kingdom performed rather than just proclaimed.[65]

When all the paradigms of Peasant, Magician, and Cynic are brought to the historical Jesus and his Kingdom, Crossan's picture looks like this:

> [Jesus'] strategy for himself and explicitly for his followers, was the combination of *free healing and common eating*, a religious and economic egalitarianism that negated alike and at once the hierarchical and patronal normalcies of Jewish religion and Roman power. And, lest he himself be interpreted as simply the new broker of a new God, he moved on constantly, settling down neither at Nazareth nor Capernaum. He was neither broker nor mediator, but, somewhat paradoxically, the announcer that neither should exist between humanity and divinity or between humanity and itself. Miracle and parable, healing and eating were calculated to force individuals into unmediated physical and spiritual contact with God and unmediated physical and spiritual contact with one another. He announced, in other words, the brokerless kingdom of God.[66]

The inclusive Jesus, the Jesus of Mack and Crossan, is one whose Judaism is inherently open to the world beyond Judaism. He derives the content of his teaching and his social models from the world of Hellenism. The Cynic sage and the sapiential Kingdom explain his actions

---

[64] Ibid., 266, 268.

[65] Ibid., 292. It is Jesus' presence among the peasantry that also distinguishes him from the Cynic of Hellenism. The Cynic "concentrated primarily on the marketplace rather than the farm, on the city dweller rather than the peasant" (421).

[66] Ibid., 422.

and intentions. Perhaps the greatest hurdle for this Jesus revolves around the question of the data. This point is made by Robin Scroggs, who cautions that

> most sociologists . . . would probably be aghast when they learned how little in the way of data was available for the sociological analysis of the New Testament. Furthermore, what we do have is not directly sociologically accessible. That is, most texts are speaking about theological verities, not sociological conditions. The sociologist must read the text as if it were palimpsest.[67]

When seen in this light, it is apparent how dependent the Hellenistic Jesus is on the thinnest of evidence. It would seem that Mack and Crossan require a great deal of Cynic activity in Palestine, a great deal more than they can account for, in order for the Cynic to have been a viable option for Jesus over and against the typical Jewish models of prophet or divine agent.[68] The same goes for the sapiential Kingdom. How likely is it that Jesus'

---

[67] Scroggs, "Sociological Interpretation Today," 166.

[68] Downing's collection of Cynic-sayings shows that the Kingdom was evidently not a prominent feature of Cynic discourse. See Downing, *Christ and the Cynics*, 50, 87. Similar conclusions about the lack of evidence for the Cynic thesis are expressed by C. M. Tuckett, "A Cynic Q," *Biblica* 70 (1989): 349-76; Richard Horsley, "Jesus, Itinerant Cynic or Israelite Prophet?" in *Images of Jesus Today*, 68-97; Bruce Chilton, "The Kingdom of God in Recent Discussion," in *Studying the Historical Jesus: Evaluations of the State of Current Research*, ed. Bruce Chilton and Craig A. Evans (Leiden/New York/Cologne: E. J. Brill, 1994), 269; and James H. Charlesworth, "Jesus Research Expands with Chaotic Creativity," 16-19. In Downing's mind, Mack and Crossan "risk spoiling the case by assuming it can stand without much argument" (Downing, *Cynics and Christian Origins*, 146, n. 7). Downing himself is more cautious, noting that the apparent parallels between the Jesus tradition and popular Cynicism argue only that "some kind of Cynic influence may have been accepted by Jesus of Nazareth himself" (31).

The Jewish notion of the agent has an important paradigmatic significance for the gestalt of Jesus which Crossan and Mack neglect. The rabbis' use of the term *shaliach* for the commissioned agent established the paradigm that "the one sent by a man is as the man himself" (*Ber* 5:5; cf. also *MekEx* 12:3; 12:6; *Men* 93b; *SNum* 12:9). The agent was to be considered as the sender in everything he would say and do in the fulfillment of his commission. The rabbinic understanding of the *shaliach* is most closely parallel to the New Testament *apostolos*. The fourth Gospel in particular maintains Jesus' role as the sent one of God who similarly commissioned the disciples as his own agents (John 20:21). Contrary to Crossan, who saw Jesus implementing a "brokerless" Kingdom, the concept of the agent affirms just the opposite: Jesus, the sent one, is in fact God's broker in the Kingdom (Colin Brown, "The Doctrine of the Trinity and the Shape of the

basileia-language would have come from the Cynics and not from Judaism, particularly considering the subject of the "rule"? As Mack demonstrated, the sapiential concept of *basileia* in Hellenism grew out of Greek discussions of political philosophy relative to *tyrants*.[69] Creation of the novel sapiential Kingdom was a means of criticizing the rule of unworthy despots. They were not real kings because they were not wise. In a Jewish context which has no such sapiential tradition relative to its understanding of kingship,[70] let alone the kingship of Yahweh, how successful is Jesus likely to be? As I have already noted, there is historical evidence indicating a definite appreciation in Palestine for the hope of a literal and historical manifestation of the rule of God. For Jews Yahweh's kingship was hardly that of a tyrant, so on what grounds could the Hellenistically inclined Jesus argue to them that Yahweh's true kingship should not extend to the realm of politics?

Finally, brief mention needs to be made of the ramifications of the Kingdom's presence as a social movement for human participation in the Kingdom. Departing from other nonapocalyptic views, which tend to

---

Christological Question," unpublished paper, Pasadena, Calif. [Jan. 1994], 47, n. 107). For a more detailed consideration of Crossan's Jesus see Jeffrey Carlson and Robert A. Ludwig, eds. *Jesus and Faith: A Conversation on the Work of John Dominic Crossan* (Maryknoll, N.Y.: Orbis, 1994). On the Jewish and biblical concept of agency, see K. H. Rengstorf, *TDNT*, 1:403-5, 413-24, 430-37; Peter Borgen, "God's Agent in the Fourth Gospel," in *Religions in Antiquity*, ed. J. Neusner (Leiden: E. J. Brill, 1968); Anthony Harvey, "Christ as Agent," in *Glory of Christ in the New Testament*, 239-50; Howard Clark Kee, *What Can We Know About Jesus?* (Cambridge: Cambridge University Press, 1990), 104-10; Colin Brown, "The Unjust Steward: A New Twist?" in *Worship, Theology and Ministry in the Early Church: Essays in Honor of Ralph P. Martin*, ed. Michael J. Wilkens and Terence Paige, JSNTSS 87 (Sheffield: Sheffield Academic Press, 1992), 121-45; John Ashton, *Understanding the Fourth Gospel* (Oxford: Clarendon, 1991), 312-17; Calvin Mercer, *"APOSTELLEIN* and *PEMPEIN* in John," *NTS* 36 (1990): 619-24.

[69] Mack, "Kingdom Sayings," 11-12.

[70] Hebrew conceptions of kingship expected the king to be wise in the administration of justice, but there is no tradition where the kingship paradigm could serve as an "imaginative model both for working out social critique and for constructive proposals for both a just society and a virtuous life all at the same time" (Mack, "Kingdom Sayings," 12). According to A. R. Johnson, three functions define the Hebrew king: (1) safeguarding the political integrity of the state through his role as head of the army; (2) administration of justice as judge in the realm; and (3) representative of the nation to Yahweh (A. R. Johnson, "Hebrew Conceptions of Kingship," *Myth, Ritual, and Kingship: Essays on the Theory and Practice of Kingship in the Ancient Near East and Israel*, ed. S. H. Hooke [Oxford: Clarendon, 1958], 205ff.).

emphasize the Kingdom's presence in spiritual salvation, the Kingdom of the New Quest is primarily intended as the reordering of society's institutions, moving ultimately to the conquest (nonviolently) of even the "realm of Caesar" in the present era. The practice of egalitarian love, inclusive holiness, and justice by Christ's disciples expands the Kingdom's domain in ways reminiscent of the ethical Kingdom of Ritschlian liberalism in the nineteenth century. Though more sophisticated in presentation, the Third Quest here legitimately inherits the same charges that were brought against Ritschl's moral Kingdom of the nineteenth century: (1) unwarranted critical reduction of the apocalyptic element of the New Testament; (2) the Kingdom's establishment requires a divine act, specifically the return of the divine Son, not lesser human acts; (3) the Kingdom is intricately tied to *personal* reform through repentance before it can be otherwise realized.[71]

VERMES: KINGDOM AS THE YOKE OF THE TORAH

Geza Vermes's trilogy about the historical Jesus represents a number of scholars interpreting Jesus and his Kingdom from the perspective of Pharisaic Judaism.[72] Considering Pharisaism "as a many-sided movement, able to include within itself a wide range of outlook: lawyers and scholars, politicians and saints, militants and pacifists,"[73] these views sometimes differ

---

[71] Crossan's Jesus, for example, has precious little to do with the call to repentance. The call to repent is often lost to Jesus in the process of separating him from John. See Crossan's discussion in *Historical Jesus*, 234-38.

[72] Vermes's trilogy began with *Jesus the Jew: A Historian's Reading of the Gospels*, rev. ed. (Philadelphia: Fortress, 1981), then continued with publication of several of his important lectures and essays in *Jesus and the World of Judaism* (Philadelphia: Fortress, 1983), concluding with *The Religion of Jesus the Jew* (London: SCM; Philadelphia: Fortress, 1993). Other works that could be mentioned from the last thirty years are David Flusser, *Jesus*, trans. Ronald Walls (New York: Herder and Herder, 1969); Max Wilcox, "Jesus in the Light of His Jewish Environment," *ANRW* 25:1:131-95; Harvey Falk, *Jesus the Pharisee: A New Look at the Jewishness of Jesus* (New York: Paulist, 1985); W. E. Phipps, "Jesus, The Prophetic Pharisee," *JEcuSt* 14 (1977): 17-31. For the perspective of Jewish scholarship, which has tended to see Jesus in these terms, see Donald A. Hagner, *The Jewish Reclamation of Jesus: An Analysis and Critique of Modern Jewish Study of Jesus* (Grand Rapids: Zondervan, 1984).

[73] Wilcox, "Jesus," 181. On the breadth of Pharisaism see also John Bowker, *Jesus and the Pharisees* (New York: Cambridge University Press, 1973).

on the exact social type Jesus represents, yet the Kingdom of Jesus the Pharisee is always eschatological, personal, and individual.[74]

Vermes's methodology for treating the Kingdom theme in Jesus involves a study of the Kingdom's long history from the Old Testament to the first century.[75] From his study he finds the Kingdom formulated in four ways throughout this period. At the root of all of them is the concept of God's reign (as opposed to a realm) as an issue of divine sovereignty. The first formulation begins with the monarchy, where the sovereign rule of the eternal God became especially associated with the earthly king. With the loss of Israel's sovereignty at the exile, God's kingship then became formulated in terms of the hope for a returning Davidic ruler who would reestablish God's visible rule over all peoples. "Extremist dreamers" during the apocalyptic milieu of the intertestamental period took the royal vision of the messianic kingdom and made it cosmic. This third formulation of the Kingdom would irrupt from heaven, cataclysmically overpowering all obstacles and dominating all creation, including the world of spirits. The fourth formulation of the Kingdom Vermes sees as having roots back in the sixth century B.C., where word of God's rule is not accompanied by any mention of violence or war (e.g., Isa. 60:1–6). In this case "a pure and sanctified Israel was to draw the Gentiles to God. The manifestation of God's sovereignty over his own was to serve as a magnet to the rest."[76] The rabbis of the postbiblical era took up this idea, positing God's sovereignty as manifested through personal obedience of the Torah, one's acceptance of the "yoke of the Torah" (*mAb.* 3:5).

---

[74] It is again a question of emphasis as to why a Pharisaic view of the Kingdom is categorized in this chapter as "nonapocalyptic." Certainly, as Wilcox notes, "the expectation of an end to 'this age,' a coming of Messiah, and the advent of 'the age to come' runs like a silver thread through Pharisaic-Rabbinic faith" ("Jesus," 183; see n. 277 for the original source data). Yet as we shall see with Vermes, Jesus the Pharisee is not concerned primarily with the *what* of the Kingdom, as in the apocalyptic vision, but the *when* and *how*. "In the mind of Jesus the *nature* of the Kingdom comes second to the *role* to be played by the actors of the drama, himself and his adepts, in ushering it in" (Vermes, *Religion of Jesus*, 146). Other scholars who note the Jewishness of Jesus but dispute this emphasis of Vermes will be considered in the next chapter.

[75] Vermes, *World of Judaism.* 33-35; cf. also *Religion of Jesus*, 121-35.

[76] Vermes, *World of Judaism*, 35.

Vermes sees only the last one of these four formulations of the Kingdom as consistently reflecting the historical Jesus.[77] Like the rabbis after him, Jesus evidently assumed there would be a certain eschatological nature to the Kingdom, and like some of them he had mistakenly expected the Kingdom imminently, but his primary purpose was more practical and responsive to the present situation of his countrymen. "Jesus, the existential teacher, was more concerned with man's attitude and behaviour towards the Kingdom than with its essence or structure."[78] Thus, "what he strove to emphasize was inward piety for the individual devotee of the Kingdom of heaven. In brief, he adopted, intensified and sought boldly to inject into the Judaism of ordinary people the magnificent prophetic teaching of the religion of the heart."[79]

The religion of the heart that Jesus sought to enhance is coincidental to the two Jewish ideas of *teshuvah* (repentance) and *emunah* (faith). Both of these notions permeate Jesus' presentation of the Kingdom in his parables, his prophetic proclamations, and his other sayings and commands. From the beginning with his baptism under John, Jesus was driven by the Baptist's demand that Israel repent. He believed that his was an end-time demand for irrevocable *teshuvah* that required a new way of life for his followers.[80] The Kingdom was present, or at the very worst, "just round the corner" awaiting personal repentance (Mark 1:14-15; Luke 17:20-21) and necessitating human collaboration[81] (e.g., the characters of the parables).[82] Jesus' "eschatological Judaism" thus differs from the later

---

[77] The "kingly" formulation is nullified because kingly language is rarely used by Jesus even for God. The royal messianic formulation does not correspond to Jesus' seeming lack of interest in royal metaphors. The apocalyptic vision was too cosmic, fanciful, and futuristic in comparison to Jesus' own outlook (ibid., 35-36).

[78] Vermes, *Religion of Jesus*, 137.

[79] Ibid, 194.

[80] Ibid., 138.

[81] "The seed must be sown and the leaven mixed by men and women" (ibid., 137-38).

[82] Vermes dismisses all accounts of the eschatologically distinct Kingdom as secondary (ibid., 140-42). The Parousia reflects the church on "methodological principles" (Vermes, *World of Judaism*, 37; cf. also *Jesus the Jew*, 183ff.), and the Son of Man title is of Aramaic derivation and functions as a circumlocution for the first personal pronoun in all of the genuine logia (Vermes, *Jesus the Jew*, 160-91).

rabbinic versions in its probing of the root causes and inward aspects of God's rule over his people.[83]

In the end, Jesus' message of the Kingdom in some ways continues and in some ways deviates from the lineage that proceeded and followed him in Judaism. Though his own perspective is much closer to the Tannaitic rabbis in the way he reduced the cosmic view of reality to a "more manageable, individual size," and the way he understood the individual's need to appropriate the divine sovereignty through his or her own acceptance of the Kingdom's yoke with repentance and faith, Jesus' eschatological unction and radical focus on the individual made him unique and influential in his day—so influential that he was ultimately given up for crucifixion because of the *potential* for social disorder within his ministry.[84]

If the issue for the inclusive Jesus of Mack and Crossan is over enthusiasm for Jesus' differences with Judaism, the critical issue for the exclusive Jesus of Vermes is just the opposite. Jesus the Jew is less open to non-Jewish social models and non-Jewish teachings. In Vermes's case this Jesus preaches the same rule of God as the rabbis before and after him: an individual submission to God apprehended by repentance and faith. For this Jesus the question now becomes not one of straying too far from Judaism so as to doubt his authenticity but one of not going far enough away to credibly found the renewal movement that bears his name.[85] On the Kingdom theme alone, if Jesus' proclamation was the same as the rabbis, why all the stir?[86] In short, the exclusive Jesus labors to deliver a justification for his crucifixion, as well as justification for why

---

[83] Vermes, *Religion of Jesus*, 195. "Unlike the religious vision which takes the future for granted and envisages life in a solidly established group context, eschatological ardour demands a complete break with the past, exclusively concentrates on the present moment, and does so not from a communal but from a personal perspective" (191).

[84] Vermes sees the story of Jesus son of Ananias related by Josephus in *Jewish Wars* VI: 300-5 as parallel to Jesus. In the former's case, the Jews handed him over to punishment as a precautionary measure to protect social order (Vermes, *World of Judaism*, viii-ix).

[85] Vermes ultimately concludes in *The Religion of Jesus the Jew* (214) that Christianity is in fact the work of Paul and those who came after him, not Jesus.

[86] This is the observation of Hagner, *The Jewish Reclamation of Jesus*, 136.

his followers did not assimilate back into Judaism after his death.[87] Much more likely on this point is that Jesus saw his own person as significant to the Kingdom's realization (as the Gospels indicate), that Christology does in fact begin with him, and that his followers continued the work he began, being willing themselves to die for his uniqueness.[88]

---

[87] Vermes' account of the crucifixion as parallel to the case of Jesus son of Ananias is not convincing on two counts. First, the censure of Jesus son of Ananias did not involve capital punishment. Second, even the possibility for social unrest must derive from aberrant doctrine. If Jesus' teaching was not at odds with "establishment" teaching, he would have in fact made no commotion. Vermes also argues that Jesus himself had no intention of founding an organization that would survive him, but why then choose disciples?

[88] Reminiscent of the Old Quest of the nineteenth century, Christology is discussed very little in reference to the historical Jesus of the Third Quest. For the error in such an approach, see, for example, Marinus de Jonge, "The Christological Significance of Jesus' Preaching of the Kingdom of God," in *The Future of Christology: Essays in Honor of Leander E. Keck,* ed. Abraham J. Malherbe and Wayne A. Meeks (Minneapolis: Fortress, 1993), 3-17; G. R. Beasley-Murray, *Jesus and the Kingdom of God* (Grand Rapids: Eerdmans, 1986), 224-29; R. E. Brown, "How Much Did Jesus Know?—A Survey of the Biblical Evidence," *CBQ* 29 (1967): 315-45; and Benjamin Witherington, *The Christology of Jesus* (Minneapolis: Fortress, 1990).

CHAPTER FIVE

The Apocalyptic Kingdom

Our survey of the Kingdom in New Testament studies concludes in this chapter by revisiting the apocalyptic Kingdom popularized earlier this century by Weiss and Schweitzer. As the previous chapters have demonstrated, this vision of the Kingdom is not without its assailants, some going so far as to proffer its obituary, but in this chapter we will take a look at some of the recent bearers of the apocalyptic tradition. According to Marcus Borg's analysis that the abandonment of the apocalyptic Kingdom has also meant a loss of control over the historical Jesus, or better, a loss of control for the scholars researching him, the portraits of Jesus and his Kingdom offered here will be more unified. In general the Kingdom here will be defined as a future event, in most cases an immediately future event. This Kingdom will also closely reflect the Jewish hope of a spatial, territorial Kingdom, though some will qualify this Kingdom differently according to its temporality. Differences will also be evident in the role human beings have in this Kingdom's inauguration. The pictures of Jesus will also shade away from each other. At one extreme Jesus was a revolutionary every bit as nationalistic and militaristic as the Zealots; at the other, he is the pacifistic preacher of love urging his followers to prepare the way spiritually for the historical irruption of the divine world order.

ABSOLUTE APOCALYPTIC: HIERS AND SULLIVAN

The works of Richard H. Hiers and Clayton Sullivan lead off our survey of the apocalyptic Kingdom because they represent the endurance of

Schweitzer's *Konsequent Eschatologie* in its purest form.[1] Standing against the recent tide of those who would deemphasize or annihilate altogether the eschatological Kingdom, Hiers and Sullivan do not even admit the mediating consensus forged since the New Quest that allowed for the Kingdom to be both present and future. Though the Kingdom was near, for the Jesus of Hiers and Sullivan it had not yet come.

The case for the eschatological Kingdom for Hiers begins with the *via negativa* argument in *The Kingdom of God in the Synoptic Tradition* (1970). Recognizing the iconoclastic nature of his position relative to the prevailing consensus about the already/not yet Kingdom, let alone the completely present Kingdom of realized eschatology, Hiers's aim is to scrutinize the exegetical pillars that are said to support the Kingdom as a present reality. The first is Luke 17:20–21, where Jesus says to the Pharisees: "The Kingdom of God is not coming with signs to be observed; nor will they say, 'Lo here it is!' or 'There!' for behold the Kingdom of God is in the midst of you *[entos hymē estin].*" Hiers criticizes the "liberal and/or Platonizing interpreters,"[2] who think the *entos hymē estin* means the Kingdom is "in your hearts," and raises the question of why Jesus would say such a thing to the Pharisees, his constant adversaries. Surely the meaning should follow the usual translation of "in your midst" or "among you." The decisive question then becomes "whether Jesus meant that the Kingdom was already in the midst of his hearers or that at some future point it would be in their midst."[3]

Hiers argues for the futurity of the statement primarily from the verb tenses of the context (21a, "they will say") and the parallelism in verse 23. Similar language ("They will say to you, 'Lo there!' or 'Lo, here!'"—23a)

[1] Hiers reviewed Schweitzer's conception of Jesus and his significance in *Jesus and Ethics* (Philadelphia: Westminster, 1968) and "Interim Ethics," *Theology and Life* 9 (1966): 220-33. For the Kingdom theme specifically, see Hiers, *The Kingdom of God in the Synoptic Tradition*, University of Florida Humanities Monograph 33 (Gainesville: University of Florida, 1970); *The Historical Jesus and the Kingdom of God: Present and Future in the Message and Ministry of Jesus* (Gainesville: University of Florida Press, 1973); *Jesus and the Future: Unresolved Questions for Understanding and Faith* (Atlanta: John Knox, 1981); see also Hiers's contribution to the English translation of Johannes Weiss, *Die Predigt Jesu vom Reich Gottes, Jesus' Proclamation of the Kingdom of God,* trans. and ed. Richard H. Hiers and David L. Holland (Philadelphia: Fortress, 1971); Clayton Sullivan, *Rethinking Realized Eschatology* (Macon, Ga.: Mercer University Press, 1988).

[2] In this category are those like Harnack and Dodd (Hiers, *Kingdom of God,* 23).

[3] Ibid., 23.

shows that the issue of verse twenty-one is not the Kingdom's apocalypticism, but the fact that when the Kingdom comes it will be plain to all.

> The reason it is pointless to look for signs is not that the coming of the Kingdom of God and the Son of man will be invisible, but that, on the contrary, it will be universally and unmistakably visible, 'as the lightning flashes, and lights up the sky from one side to the other,' That is why, *then* the bystanders will not say, 'Lo, here!' or 'There!' And that is also why those who *in the meantime* say 'Lo, there!' or 'Here!' are to be ignored.[4]

Hiers sees in Luke 17:20–21 a situation similar to what was going on in the question put to Jesus in Matthew 24:3/Mark 13:4. The Pharisees here, like the disciples in the other passages, ask when the Kingdom of God is coming, which Jesus answers in terms of the implied question, "When the time comes, how will men know that the Kingdom of God is here?" To this question Jesus answers plainly, "When the Son of man comes, it will not be accompanied by a sign (Luke 17:21) for there will be no mistake about it" (Luke 17:23).[5]

This means that the "Kingdom among you" is a description not of the present circumstances of the questioners standing before Jesus, but the condition of those present *when the time for the Kingdom comes.*

The next pillar of the realized Kingdom to be attacked by Hiers is Matthew 12:28/Luke 11:20: "But if it is by the Spirit of God that I cast out demons, then the Kingdom of God has come upon you *[ephthasen eph hymas]*." While Hiers notes there is a definite relationship between exorcism of demons and the coming of the Kingdom, the major issue is what kind of relationship it is. Usually these verses are cited to show the presence of the power of the Kingdom, or as some have put it: the Kingdom was *breaking in,* or *dawning,* or *proleptically* present. Hiers, however, noting the non-Synoptic nature of these terms, contends that exorcisms are

---

[4] Ibid., 28.

[5] That Jesus' answer is about signs when the Pharisees had not asked about them is significant for Hiers's contention about what question Jesus is actually answering. The issue is not the apocalyptic nature of the Kingdom, but identifying the authentic Kingdom. See ibid., 26.

in fact preparatory to the Kingdom's actual coming. They do not signal the Kingdom's actual presence.[6] To accomplish this Hiers must deny the equation of the Kingdom of God and the power of the Spirit[7] and at the same time he must assert the eschatological significance of exorcism. On this count, Hiers observes that in the age to come, which clearly was not a present reality in Jesus' context (cf. Matt. 12:31–32), demonic activity would no longer have a place on the earth. God would rule the earth and Satan would be out. Jesus' exorcisms, though they were directed toward Satan's kingdom, were nonetheless only provisional in their effect toward Satan and therefore not descriptive of the age of the Kingdom, that is, the age to come. Exorcisms did not change the fundamental condition of the present age relative to Satan, as he still posed a perilous threat to the creation. Exorcisms did show that Satan's doom was certain, and that his doom was near.[8]

Of final interest for Hiers's *via negativa* is his position relative to the parables. As Dodd made great use of the parables for his realized eschatology, so Hiers must meet their challenge if his project is to succeed. The tone of Hiers's approach to the parables comes early in the chapter: "[The parables] do not describe the Kingdom of God as such, but suggest some analogy between the action of one (or more) of the figures in the story and the kind of response Jesus' hearers should make in view of the prospective events."[9] These "prospective events" are the future coming of the Kingdom of God as the Son of Man in judgment, which is the clear reference of many parables (e.g., the parables of the hidden treasure, the pearl, and the ten maidens). Parables that concentrate on the kind of behavior necessary to be a part of this Kingdom (e.g.,

---

[6] Ibid., 32.

[7] "The presence of the power of God or his Spirit, however, is not the same as the presence of the Kingdom of God" (ibid., 33).

[8] Ibid., 33. The other Synoptic passages about Satanic conflict are treated in the same manner. In chapters 4-6 of *Kingdom of God*, Hiers considers the binding of the strong man (Mark 3:27), Satan's fall from heaven (Luke 10:17-18), and violence toward the Kingdom (Matt. 11:12) as only provisional and signatory for the Kingdom. The Kingdom of God *ephthasen eph hymas* of Matthew 12:28, therefore, is parallel in meaning to the other Synoptic passages which announced the nearness of the Kingdom (Mark 1:15; Matt. 4:17; 10:7; Luke 10:9, 11; see *Kingdom of God*, 35).

[9] Ibid., 72.

the parables of the talents, the pounds, and the good Samaritan) likewise assume the futurity of the Kingdom. In the three parables particularly highlighted by Dodd where the Kingdom appears to be a presently growing entity (the parables of the mustard seed, the leaven, and the seed growing secretly), Hiers questions the analogue. Is the Kingdom to be likened to its own growth or the miraculous result? Since it is doubtful that "Jesus or the evangelists thought in terms of modern theories of evolution," Hiers argues the option of the miraculous result makes best sense of the passage.[10]

A few years after *The Kingdom of God in the Synoptic Tradition*, Hiers published *The Kingdom of God and the Historical Jesus* (1973) as a companion volume. Whereas the purpose of the first volume was more negative in tearing down the arguments in the secondary literature for the realized Kingdom, the purpose of *The Kingdom of God and the Historical Jesus* is to "set forth in positive terms the basic pattern of Jesus' ministry and message."[11] Hiers's thesis is simply stated:

> Jesus believed that the Present world was about to end, in fact that certain preliminary events marking the last days of the Old world had already begun to occur, and that the final and decisive events—the coming of the Son of man, the Judgment, and the Kingdom of God— would take place soon. Not only did Jesus so believe and proclaim; he also acted accordingly. Many of his actions that otherwise seem strange or incoherent are found to be entirely consistent with the structure of his beliefs and expectations.[12]

There follows a semichronological presentation of Jesus' message and ministry, detailing the eschatological core of everything Jesus said and did. From the outset, Hiers says, Jesus did not explain to his audiences what he meant by the Kingdom—he merely announced that it was near.[13] His ethical teachings were "ethics for the interim, a summons to actions in

---

[10] Hiers does admit these parables suggest Jesus or the evangelists may have possibly thought the Kingdom was already on the earth in some "hidden or incipient fashion" (ibid., 77, 96).

[11] *The Kingdom of God and the Historical Jesus*, iv.

[12] Ibid., iii.

[13] Ibid., 13.

the time that remained before it was too late, before the coming of the Kingdom and the time of Judgment."¹⁴ Jesus shared the belief of some of his contemporaries that the final age of salvation would be preceded by a period of terrible tribulation and a resurrection of the dead.¹⁵ The Judgment that would end the present age would take place before the Son of Man, whose presence in judgment would coincide with the inauguration of the Kingdom. Jesus expected the imminent revelation of the Son of Man, whom in all likelihood he considered to be himself. His disciples were to "watch" because they do not know when the time would come (Mark 13:33–37), and to take care of business because the time was short.¹⁶ Jesus taught his disciples to pray for the coming of the Kingdom and to ask for the bread of its banquet feast and the forgiveness that would precede its arrival.¹⁷

Jesus' eschatological beliefs are also obvious from the pattern of his ministry. They account for the wild success of his Galilean ministry and the reason why he should go to Jerusalem.¹⁸ The Galilean ministry is thoroughly eschatological in Jesus' presentation of John as Elijah, his preaching of repentance and judgment (the sign of Jonah), his own prophetic function by means of the Spirit, and his exorcisms of Satan.¹⁹ During this time Jesus also commissions his disciples as heralds of the Kingdom's nearness and on at least one occasion celebrated in advance the banquet feast of the messianic age, providing food for thousands of followers in the

---

¹⁴ Ibid., 19.

¹⁵ Ibid., 25. Hiers notes that this belief of Jesus does not make it unlikely that Jesus eventually came to see his own death as his participation in the tribulation that must precede the Kingdom's establishment (28, 45).

¹⁶ Hiers sees the admonition of the Matthew 5:25 parallels ("Make friends quickly with your opponent at law. . .") as a typical example of interim ethics that "was not intended as a moral maxim for his followers in the centuries to come" (ibid., 29-30).

¹⁷ Hiers suggests the redundancy of "give us this day our daily bread" is solved by a new translation: "Give us this day our bread for tomorrow." The new reading makes best sense in the context of the anticipated banquet table of the messianic Kingdom (ibid., 35).

¹⁸ Hiers notes these are two situations either denied or unexplained by the noneschatological Jesus of contemporary scholarship (ibid., 47).

¹⁹ Ibid., 47-64.

wilderness.[20] The final journey to Jerusalem is steeped with eschatological significance in its associations with Zion, the Mount of Olives, the foal of the donkey, and the temple.[21] The eschatological significance is clearly understood by the crowds as well as by the disciples. The crowds of Jerusalem receive and hail Jesus as the messianic deliverer, and the disciples argue over their own priority in the Kingdom (Mark 10:35–45).[22] Right up to and including his death, Jesus' final actions are driven by his eschatological hopes of the Kingdom's soon advent.[23] Gradually, however, Jesus reckons with the fact that the Kingdom's arrival will mean his death, but even then he thought his resurrection was imminent in the Kingdom and said to the thief crucified next to him, "This day you will be with me in paradise" (Luke 23:63).

Clayton Sullivan's *Rethinking Realized Eschatology* (1988) is another recent reiteration of the consistent eschatology enunciated by Weiss and Schweitzer. Although polemical like Hiers's *The Kingdom of God in the Synoptic Tradition* and presenting many of the same arguments,[24] Sullivan's noteworthiness comes in his analysis of the works of C. H. Dodd, the

---

[20] Hiers suggests there is a "sacramental character" to Jesus' gathering the throngs to the wilderness and feeding them. In Mark's account (6:33) the people followed the disciples because "they recognized them"—no doubt as Jesus' heralds of the coming Kingdom. According to Hiers, Jesus is either proleptically celebrating the messianic feast or attempting to hasten its coming (ibid., 67).

[21] Ibid., 77–94.

[22] The shout of "Hosanna," which Hiers suggests is an allusion to Psalm 118:25, "Blessed be the one who comes in the name of the Lord," and the recognition of the meaning of Jesus' name, "salvation" (Isa. 62:11b: "Lo, your salvation *[yeshuah]* comes"), are both eschatologically significant (*Historical Jesus*, 80–81). For the two disciples, Hiers notes that "Jesus does not take issue with the brothers' assumption that there would be special seats of honor and office in the coming Kingdom. He says only that he does not have authority to grant these distinctions (Mark 10:40)" (75).

[23] Hiers sees eschatological significance in the cursing of the fig tree (Mark 11:12-14), the predictions of the temple's destruction (Mark 13:1-2), the anointing at Bethany (Mark 14:3-9), the last supper (Mark 14:12-26), the prayer at Gethsemane (Mark 14:32-40), and Jesus' confession before the high priest (Mark 14:62) (ibid., 83-105).

[24] Sullivan's discussions of Matthew 11:11; 12:28; Mark 1:14-15; and the Kingdom parables are parallel to those of Hiers (Sullivan, *Rethinking*, 74-96).

father of realized eschatology.[25] Sullivan is critical of Dodd's conclusions about the Kingdom for two reasons: (1) Dodd's heavy-handed reliance on the two-source documentary theory of the Synoptic Gospels, and (2) Dodd's "slippery" use of Kingdom-language.[26] Examination of the two-source hypothesis is especially important for Sullivan because it was on the basis of this theory that Dodd had excluded as secondary many significant passages about an eschatological Kingdom.[27] In a section entitled "The Dethroning of the Two-Document Hypothesis," Sullivan argues from the recent studies of W. R. Farmer, Hans-Herbert Stoldt, and others that the Mark-Q hypothesis can no longer be used as the assured hermeneutical tool it was in Dodd's day.[28] Sullivan has no new theory to propose, but he does contend that Synoptic data on the Kingdom cannot not be excluded out of hand simply because it is not in Mark or Q.[29] The result of this is that Sullivan is postured anew to explore Jesus' conception of the

---

[25] Dodd's realized eschatology is "an ideological shovel with which Christian apologists keep Johannes Weiss and Albert Schweitzer in their graves" (ibid., 115).

[26] Ibid., 37. On Dodd's "slippery use of language," Sullivan notes, "Numerous readings of *The Parables of the Kingdom* have convinced me that Dodd (in a subtle, almost imperceptible way) engages in paraphrasing eisegesis and gave *basileia* unwarranted extensions of meaning wherein it became a *term inclusive of historical events*. . . . I have in mind Professor Dodd's use of *basileia* as an encompassing terms to include, on one hand, *the series of events that constituted Jesus' ministry* and, on the other hand, *the experiences of Jesus' early followers*. Moreover, there is still another extension of meaning wherein the Kingdom was presented by Dodd as a *potentiality or possibility for people of all time*" (Sullivan, *Rethinking*, 40; [emphasis his]). This is not a major portion of Sullivan's overall study, but it does, in his mind, serve to weaken Dodd's credibility as a theologian (Sullivan, *Rethinking*, 37).

[27] Sullivan notes that passages speaking of "entering the Kingdom" (Matt. 5:19-20; 7:21), being "in" the Kingdom (Matt. 18:4), the Kingdom being "near" (Luke 21:31), or future (Luke 22:15-16) are not dealt with by Dodd in *The Parables of the Kingdom* for this reason. Sullivan adds, "*Practically all synoptic evidence presenting the Kingdom in concrete details as a place occurs outside of Mark and Q*" (*Rethinking*, 34 [emphasis his]).

[28] See W. R. Farmer, *Jesus and the Gospel: Tradition, Scripture, and Canon* (Philadelphia: Fortress, 1982); *The Synoptic Problem* (1964; corrected reprint, Dillsboro, N.C.: Western North Carolina, 1976); Hans-Herbert Stoldt, *History and Criticism of the Marcan Hypothesis*, trans. and ed. Donald Niewyk (Macon, Ga.: Mercer University Press, 1980). Other important references are listed in Sullivan, *Rethinking*, 20-21.

[29] Sullivan concludes, "Perhaps the sensible posture to assume at the present time toward synoptic source analysis is, to use Austin Farrer's expression, a 'decent agnosticism'" (Sullivan, *Rethinking*, 33).

Kingdom *as a place* soon to be realized, rather than a presently operating *power* as seen by Dodd.[30]

The position of Hiers and now Sullivan elicits a question about Christian faith that has dogged the Jesus of consistent eschatology since the days of Weiss and Schweitzer. That is, how useful for Christian faith is a Jesus who was driven by such mistaken notions? The Kingdom did not come, and Jesus' death was a tragic, even foolhardy, attempt to hasten it. For Sullivan and Hiers the fact that Jesus experienced historical relativism like everyone else does not preclude his being "transformed by the power of God into the Risen Lord of Christian devotion—the One who lives in the *kerygma* and worship of the Church."[31] Indeed the fact that God would raise Jesus, the "mistaken proclaimer of the Kingdom of God," has a comforting implication to Sullivan's mind, namely that *"belief accuracy or doctrinal rectitude is not a prerequisite for divine approval."*[32]

Hiers himself sees several appropriate implications in Jesus' eschatological message even though, "so far as we can tell, [Jesus] was not thinking of us or our time" when he spoke.[33] First, when Jesus preached the Kingdom as near he was affirming that God "intended and was able to make things right on earth."[34] Second, Jesus' proclamation of Judgment also entailed a realistic appraisal of human corruption, oppression, and all around general need of God's Kingdom. There was indeed a great gulf between human self-serving love and the love of God for righteousness.[35] Third, Jesus' call to repentance affirms the free will of human beings against the social determinists of the modern day.[36] Fourth, Jesus' message showed he believed all history was in God's hands—a source of liberation and confidence. Finally, "Jesus' expectation that the righteous would eat and drink together in the Kingdom of God indicates that he affirmed the

---

[30] He does this in *Rethinking*, 48-64, recapitulating many of the points already made by Hiers, though he does not appear to be aware of Hiers's *The Historical Jesus and the Kingdom of God.*

[31] Sullivan, *Rethinking*, 118.

[32] Ibid., 118.

[33] Hiers, *Jesus and the Future*, 102.

[34] Ibid., 104.

[35] Ibid., 104-5.

[36] Ibid., 106.

goodness of physical life in the material world."[37] All these things considered, Hiers's Jesus is not important in himself, but he is important for whom he proclaimed:

> Jesus expected that God's justice and love would soon be revealed in the Judgment and the establishment of his rule on earth in the peaceable Kingdom. This expectation was not fulfilled. But if the God in whom we trust is the same as the One proclaimed by Jesus, we too may experience the eager longing and confidence that he will, in his own way and time, make things right. In the meantime, we live in the presence of our neighbors and other companions in being for whom, we believe, he cares, and for whom, in the miracle of grace that frees us from concern only for ourselves, we find that we can come to care as well. We do not thereby establish the Kingdom of God on earth. But we may be so bold as to trust that he can use even our small acts of obedience, justice, and love for his own purposes, which surely encompass, but far surpass our best human hopes and understanding.[38]

As the efforts of Hiers evidence, justifying the Christian movement that follows the historical Jesus remains an important problem for those who believe that Jesus preached an apocalyptic Kingdom but was mistaken on the issue of the Kingdom's imminence. Strained as the salvage operations of Hiers and Sullivan, credibility is strained even further when it comes to justifying the existence of the early church as an entity separate from Judaism. Hiers says the doomsday Jesus is important for modern believers because in him we see that God intends and is able to make things right on earth, that there is a great gulf between human depravity and the righteousness of God's Kingdom, that Jesus affirms the free will of human beings, that all history is in God's hands, and that life in the material world is a good thing, not a negative one. The question is, however, are these affirmations so unique in human religious experience that they would compel Jews (or members of any other faith) to embrace Christianity? Does Hiers's mistaken Jesus really offer anything substantially different to

---

[37] Ibid., 108.
[38] Ibid., 110.

his followers from what Abraham and Moses offered theirs? In fact, Jesus, the false prophet, should not have attracted anything but negative attention from Jews who would know the verdict of the law: "If what the prophet says does not happen, you need not fear that prophet" (Deut. 18:22). So, if Jesus was mistaken in so much of the things he said, why did so many Jews follow the false prophet?

As the high Christology of the early Christian writings clearly shows, the early Christians based their belief of the uniqueness of Jesus on more than his ethical teachings. They believed his death and resurrection to be a complex of events without parallel in all human history, and beyond that, they believed them to be actions appropriate only of God himself! The difficulty of correlating a tragically mistaken historical Jesus with the risen Lord and God of the early church strains all attempts to explain the existence of the Christian movement. How would such a Jesus have even survived in the early Christians' writings, let alone commanded their worship and even their dramatic abandonment of Judaism? As problematic as the apparently imminent Kingdom may be, the beliefs and the successes of the early Jewish church point us in directions other than those offered in a mistaken Jesus. Later Jewish Christians evidently did not stumble over Jesus' pronouncements, so other options still appear open within the prophetic motif. As we have already seen, Ben Witherington's argument for the Kingdom's possible but not necessary imminence in the teaching of Jesus offers a viable explanation of later Christian worship of him.[39] George Ladd also offers a similar vision of the imminent language in Jesus' teaching from the temporal tension characteristic of the prophetic perspective.[40]

The question also remains as to whether Jesus saw any presence of the future Kingdom in his ministry. Was the Kingdom a purely futuristic hope? Much as Hiers and Sullivan would want to maintain that the Kingdom

---

[39] Benjamin Witherington, *Jesus, Paul and the End of the World: A Comparative Study of New Testament Eschatology* (Downers Grove, Ill.: InterVarsity Press, 1992), 36-44.

[40] George Eldon Ladd, *The Presence of the Future: The Eschatology of Biblical Realism*, a revised and updated version of *Jesus and the Future* [Grand Rapids: Eerdmans, 1974], 309-28. See also Meyer's discussion of imminence as a standard feature of Israel's prophetic tradition (Ben F. Meyer, "Jesus's Scenario of the Future," *DRev* 109 [1991]: 1-15).

had a single, future referent,[41] they have difficulty being consistent or totally convincing at this point. It is certainly true that some of the passages of the present Kingdom, like Matthew 12:28 and Luke 17:20, 21, are capable of reasonable futuristic interpretation, that realized eschatology leans too heavily on the meaning of one Greek verb, and that the exegetical evidence for the realized Kingdom is much more scanty, but the Kingdom of the parables still presents problems for the purely futuristic view. On the growth parables (the seed growing [Mark 4:26–29]; mustard seed [Mark 4:30–32]; and leaven [Matt. 13:33]), while arguing that they were intended as encouragements to Jesus' companions engaged in urgent mission, Hiers nonetheless has to admit the possibility that "[Jesus], or [the evangelists], may have thought the Kingdom present on earth in some hidden or incipient fashion."[42] If that in fact is so, then Hiers has admitted a huge deviation from the paradigm of consistent eschatology. Sullivan is less open to such compromise but is therefore forced into the uneasy place of arguing that these

> parables are of no help in determining whether the evangelists conceived of the Kingdom in abstract or spatial terms. The Kingdom parables do not define the Kingdom; rather, they speak of what the Kingdom is *like*. An exegete in dealing with non-interpreted Kingdom parables is confronted with the hermeneutical problem: *it is impossible to argue with certainty from a comparison.*[43]

EXISTENTIAL APOCALYPTIC: KLEIN AND BRAUN

As the eschatological views of Schweitzer and Weiss received a modern voice in the writings of Hiers and Sullivan, so the existential/apocalyptic view of Rudolf Bultmann also thrived in the decade after 1960. These were particularly turbulent days for the Bultmannian hypothesis outside of the New Hermeneutic as political theologians were starting to argue

---

[41] See Sullivan's criticism of the double referents given the Kingdom by the mediating scholars like Ladd. He argues the Kingdom cannot be both a curative power and a place (Sullivan, *Rethinking*, 46-47). Hiers refers to the meditating positions of Ladd and Jeremias as "thoroughly confusing" and full of terminology not found in the synoptic tradition (Hiers, *Kingdom of God*, 94).

[42] Hiers, *Kingdom of God*, 77, 96.

[43] Sullivan, *Rethinking*, 95 (emphasis his).

for the Kingdom's liberation from the ghetto of individualized, existential theology. Yet Bultmann had his defenders, two of whom will be briefly considered here.

Günther Klein's influential essay, "The Biblical Understanding of the 'Kingdom of God'" was originally written as a response to those seeking to use the Kingdom as a banner for human activism.[44] Klein begins by denoting what he considers to be the three main paradigms for the Kingdom currently present on the theological scene. First is the view of "orthodoxy," which Klein says is characterized by the otherworldliness and temporal remoteness of the Kingdom. "According to [orthodoxy], the Kingdom of God refers to nothing other than the end of the temporal world followed by its continuation on a supernatural plane."[45] This Kingdom is not here now, but it will definitely appear later, with cataclysmic suddenness. The second view is the one Klein would have taken for himself had the scope of his essay stopped at the historical Jesus. This is the existentialism of Herbert Braun and Bultmann; its chief characteristics of the Kingdom are this-worldliness and temporal presence. That is, Jesus' mistaken calculations about the end have existential significance for the modern person, not as instruction about the imminent end but as summons to be true to themselves. "The Kingdom thus stands as a cipher warning man of this basic alternative. The cipher itself, however, is purely a product of its time."[46] The third paradigm is that one taken up in the modern political theologies whereby human beings are charged with responsibility to bring in the Kingdom of God through reformations of social structure according to the divine rules of justice and love. This Kingdom's features are its this-worldliness and its futurity.[47]

---

[44] Originally delivered as an address before a conference held in Munich on April 24, 1970, under the general theme, "Gottesreich und Menschenreich. Ihr Spannungsverhältnis in Geschichte und Gegenwart." The essay first appeared in *EvT* 30 (December 1970): 642-70. The English translation was made by Richard N. Soulen and appeared as "The Biblical Understanding of the 'Kingdom of God,'" *Interp* 26 (October 1972): 387-418.

[45] Klein, "Kingdom of God," 388.

[46] Ibid., 390.

[47] Klein says this view was formulated in a programmatic way by none other than Albert Schweitzer ("The Kingdom of God," 391, citing from Schweitzer, *The Kingdom of God and Primitive Christianity*, ed. Ulrich Neuenschwander [New York: Seabury, 1968]), showing that even though Schweitzer's biblical exegesis reached conclusions that were exactly opposite to those of Ritschl, the father to the ethical Kingdom of the nineteenth century, his theological application of that exegesis was not so different.

Following a brief history of the Kingdom from the time of the Old Testament to the time of Jesus,[48] Klein tests each of these modern paradigms against his reading of the historical Jesus' relationship to the views of the Kingdom available in his day. The first paradigm, that of "orthodoxy," is supposedly embodied in rabbinic thought of the first century. According to Klein, however, this view does not comport well with the historical Jesus. Unlike the rabbis, for whom the Kingdom was an abstraction in their notion of the "yoke of the Kingdom," Jesus fully endowed the Kingdom with the temporal and apocalyptic overtones that were "so alive and ubiquitous within Judaism."[49] For Jesus, the Kingdom was a living reality. Moreover, in Jesus the Kingdom is at the center of his proclamation, whereas for the rabbis the Kingdom is mentioned relatively infrequently.[50] The third paradigm, that of the modern political theologies, had its first century adherents in the Zealots. Klein notes that Jesus is also against this view of the Kingdom. He did not practice the radical categorization of humanity the way the Zealots did;[51] he did not think of the coming Kingdom in any way as the function of human activity; the main object of his address was the individual, not society at large; and, finally, Jesus did not "demonize" the structure of society and call for revolution.[52]

What is left for Klein and Jesus is the second paradigm of the existentialist. This Kingdom is both near (i.e., future) and present. It is future as it is the power that "bursts history asunder," but it is also present in its effects.[53] Proclamation of this Kingdom's nearness makes a difference to the audience of the present.

---

[48] Klein, "Kingdom of God," 394-400.

[49] Ibid., 400-1.

[50] Klein follows Vielhauer (*Gottesreich und Menschensohn in der Verkündigung Jesu. Aufsätze sum Neuen Testament* [Munich: Christian Kaiser, 1965], 55-91) in suggesting that because the Kingdom was an abstraction the rabbis lost it within their hope of the coming of the Messiah. The fact that the Kingdom was abstract to them is therefore the reason it is so infrequent in their literature (Klein, "Kingdom of God," 398).

[51] That is, Jesus ate and associated with members of the "establishment."

[52] Ibid., 402-4.

[53] Ibid., 405-6.

As [the Kingdom's] nearness is proclaimed it is itself already present. History will of course continue a little while longer; the world has not quite run its course. But for the one who hears there is no more time; through the person of Jesus he is immediately confronted with the end.[54]

To the modern ear this "end" is, as Braun says, a cipher for a "state of mind" about one's own authenticity. When properly deciphered, Jesus' message is not the ranting of a deluded apocalyptic visionary completely out of touch with respect to the Kingdom's imminence; rather, Jesus spoke to the greatest existential needs of humanity for all time.[55]

The work on the historical Jesus by the New Testament scholar Herbert Braun, so influential in Klein's essay, was published the year before in a popularly styled volume, *Jesus. Der Mann aus Nazareth und seine Zeit*.[56] In the spirit of the New Quest, Braun believed it possible to search the New Testament for evidence about "Jesus the true human being."[57] This Jesus, he contends, lived in a world shaped by two movements of Jewish piety,

---

[54] Ibid., 405.

[55] Ibid., 406. It needs to be noted that this is Klein's vision of the historical Jesus, not the Christ of faith preached by the church. As his essay continues, Klein ends up actually moving away from Braun's picture as far as modern application is concerned. By means of Pauline Christology, Klein describes his paradigm for the Kingdom as otherworldly and present. "It is other-worldly because it is brought about by God's action; it is present because it concretely ends genuine rebellion against God" (Klein, "Kingdom of God," 418). Klein believes the present experience of the Kingdom is first the salvation of the individual. Changes in the social structure of the world are the result of the conversion of individuals.

[56] *Themen der Theologie I* (Stuttgart: Kreuz, 1969); English translation, *Jesus of Nazareth: The Man and His Time*, trans. Everett R. Kalin (Philadelphia: Fortress, 1979). Braun's understanding of Jesus is also available in his *Qumran und das Neue Testament*, II (Tübingen: J. C. B. Mohr [Paul Siebeck], 1966).

[57] Braun, *Jesus*, 16-23. Braun takes much from form-critical dogmas in his approach to the Synoptic Gospels. He says that "the first three gospels do not enable us to know and depict the course of Jesus' life in detail" and that a considerable number of Jesus' words in the Gospels originate from charismatic Christian prophets, not the historical Jesus (Braun, *Jesus*, 19-20). Where the Gospel of John is concerned, Braun says, "in the search for the historical Jesus the fourth gospel, the Gospel of John, is of no use whatsoever. . . . The man Jesus *cannot* have spoken both like the synoptic *and* the Johannine Jesus; he did not speak like the Johannine Jesus" (Braun, *Jesus*, 17).

apocalypticism and Pharisaism, which coexisted in a peaceful tension about true observance of the law. From what may be garnered from the sources, Braun claims that Jesus clearly falls in with the apocalyptic groups (e.g., Qumran) that expected the end of the world to come in wild, cataclysmic fashion in their own generation.[58] At the heart of Jesus' proclamation about the end is the "reign of God," which Braun understands in dynamic rather than concrete terms.[59] The reign of God irrupts into history at the world's final hour. It comes suddenly and threateningly with the appearance of the apocalyptic figure called the Son of Man.[60]

As we know, these end-time apocalyptic calculations were mistaken in the first century, and in Braun's view "we do not further a true and honest understanding of Jesus if we hide from ourselves and others the fact that this imminent expectation of Jesus, which is an aspect of Jewish apocalyptic, was mistaken."[61] The solution for us, according to Braun, is to distinguish between Jesus' *information* and his *intention*. In his information, Jesus was clearly wrong, but in his intention, which was to warn against the failure of being unprepared for the end, Jesus has relevance for today. Today the "end" cannot mean the final hour as in an apocalyptic scheme, but its meaning comes from one's view of oneself: "Whether a person fails or not depends on what he is in his own eyes and how he acts on the basis of this self understanding."[62] Along with Jesus' apocalypticism, the Gospel traditions do retain some of what the historical Jesus said on the subject of not failing oneself. These are the areas about which the historical Jesus needs to be heard. Jesus' self-referential truth and relevance on topics like grace, man and woman, cultic purity, possessions, and so on, is therefore

---

[58] Ibid., 36ff.

[59] Ibid., 37. The Kingdom "does not signify the *territory* God rules but his reign, the activity as ruler which he will undertake at the end of history" (emphasis his).

[60] The suddenness and threatening nature of the return is Jesus' unique contribution to the apocalyptic message (ibid., 37). On the Son of Man theme, Jesus made use of it, but he did not see himself in the role of the coming Son of Man (38).

[61] Ibid., 41.

[62] Ibid., 43.

what constitutes his authority to demand our obedience and repentance, not his teaching about the nearness of the end.[63] A Kingdom that is ultimately interior and individualized, even when dressed in apocalyptic clothing, still inherits the genealogical weaknesses of its ancestors. That is, it is the mistake of existential apocalyptic to finally separate the spiritual from the physical and the interior from the exterior in the meaning of the Kingdom for the historical Jesus. As Buchanan, among others, clearly shows, the hope of the Jew was not that of a twentieth-century Heideggerian philosopher of true Being, but it was a grand and divine hope of the spiritual regeneration expressed throughout the entire physical world. The Kingdom means something more than the inward focus on oneself. As we shall see in part two, the disjunction of the spiritual from the material so typical to existential Christianity is a major criticism of Bultmann and his disciples made by the more earthly oriented political theologies and theologies of liberation. It is a criticism well-taken.

REVOLUTIONARY APOCALYPTIC

The next focus of our attention regarding the Kingdom is in large measure the apocalyptic equivalent of the works of Marcus Borg and Richard Horsley discussed in the last chapter where Jesus' intentions concerning the Kingdom were firmly rooted in the social and political circumstances of his day. Jesus sought to lead a movement that would have real social impact. His concerns were not just for the spiritual realm. Jesus' egalitarian Kingdom founded on love and justice would be the result of a human activation of these principles that would eventually peacefully permeate and ultimately convert the entire society. To this scenario S. G. F. Brandon and George Wesley Buchanan would give assent in all but one point. They would agree

---

[63] Ibid., 43. See also Braun's explanation of the nature of Jesus' authority as "an authority with a choice." Jesus is authoritative to us in the areas of our choosing, that is, true authority is that which is not coerced but given free assent (117). "Precisely when we are speaking of real authority, that is, one that includes positive assent, the hearer's yes to Jesus' authority cannot be a blank check on which any word of Jesus whatsoever may be written. Precisely when it is a question of true authority, it remains an authority in dialog, an authority with a choice" (118).

that Jesus' Kingdom was a Kingdom of this earth, that it was a Kingdom with political ramifications, and that it was a Kingdom that was inaugurated in human struggle against adversarial forces. All similarity ends there however, as Brandon and Buchanan make the apocalyptic in-breaking of the divine the foremost ingredient in understanding Jesus' message and ministry. To their mind, Jesus is closer to the revolutionary Zealot party of the first century than to anyone else.

Brandon

S. G. F. Brandon's *Jesus and the Zealots: A Study of the Political Factor in Primitive Christianity*[64] carries on the argument of his earlier *The Fall of Jerusalem and the Christian Church*[65] that apologetic purposes profoundly determined the New Testament picture of Jesus. Brandon applies Tendency Criticism *(Tendenzkritik)* to the Gospel of Mark, attempting to demonstrate the author's portrayal of the pacifistic Jesus is driven by his own "life-setting" to cover up the fact that the historical Jesus was quite a political agitator.[66] Brandon postulates that the Gospel of Mark was composed for use in Rome after the Flavian conquest of insurgent Judea in A.D. 71. The Gospel is written because this triumph had a disturbing effect on the Roman Christians; they had to face the fact that

---

[64] S. G. F. Brandon, *Jesus and the Zealots: A Study of the Political Factor in Primitive Christianity* (Manchester: Manchester University Press, 1967).

[65] S. G. F. Brandon, *The Fall of Jerusalem and the Christian Church* (London: SPCK, 1951). The so-called Revolution Theory has a long history in critical scholarship. See E. Bammel's review and critique, "The Revolution Theory from Reimarus to Brandon," in *Jesus and the Politics of His Day*, ed. E. Bammel and C. F. D. Moule (Cambridge: Cambridge University Press, 1984), 11-68. In *Fall of Jerusalem and the Christian Church* (x-xi) Brandon is most immediately indebted to the works of Robert Eisler, for example, IHSOUS BASILEUS OU BASILEUSAS *(Die messianische Unabhängigkeitsbewegung vom Auftreten Johannes des Täufers bis zum Untergang Jakobs des Gerechten. Nach der neuerschlossenen Eroberung von Jerusalem des Flavius Josephus und den christlichen Quellen)*, 2 vols. (Heidelberg: 1929-1930). English edition: *The Messiah Jesus and John the Baptist (According to Flavius Josephus' recently discovered 'Capture of Jerusalem' and other Jewish and Christian sources)*, trans. A. H. Krappe (London: Methuen, 1931).

[66] Tendency criticism is the critical tool of historical research made famous in the last century by F. C. Bauer, A. Swegler and others of the "Tübingen School"; it enjoyed a hearty approval in Brandon's work. See his "Tübingen Vindicated?" *HibbJ* 49 (1951): 41ff.

their faith stemmed from this Jewish people who had so fiercely revolted against Roman rule, and it faced them also with the serious possibility that they might be regarded by their pagan neighbours and the Roman authorities as being themselves infected with Jewish revolutionary ideas.[67]

The writer of Mark was also keenly aware of Jesus' own execution by the Romans, so with his Gospel he sought to allay the embarrassment of his readers and the suspicions of his overlords.

The primary evidence of Mark's character as an *apologia* to disguise the political activities of Jesus is revealed when his version is compared to the other Gospels, which do not have quite the same ax to grind. A most telling discrepancy occurs at Mark 3:18, where Mark has delicately masked the fact that one of Jesus' own disciples was a Zealot by the mention of "Simon the Kananaios *[ton Kananaion]*." Whereas Luke elsewhere lists this individual as "Simon the Zealot" (Luke 6:15; Acts 1:13), Mark has cleverly hidden his identity with the Greek transliteration of the Aramaic *qanana,* meaning "Zealot." Also suspicious about the entry here is the fact that Mark's habit of explaining to his readers Hebrew or Aramaic words as well as Jewish customs is completely lacking. At every other point he is concerned that his non-Jewish readers understand the meaning of foreign words or concepts, but at 3:18 the title that would divulge the true identity of one of Jesus' closest followers is strangely not explained.[68]

Brandon also sees Mark's treatment of Jesus' trial as tendentious in its incredibility and plain illogicality. In his *apologia* Mark would have his somewhat bumbling readers[69] believe first that Pilate, "a remarkably tough character," could so easily be influenced by the Jewish leaders he despised; second, that though he was convinced of his prisoner's innocence, Pilate resorted to a previously unheard-of custom of releasing prisoners; third, that crowds could be instantaneously turned even though only a week prior

---

[67] Brandon, *Jesus and the Zealots,* 242-43.

[68] Ibid., 243-44.

[69] "The story, it is important to remember, was written for humble and poorly educated people, living in Rome" (ibid., 258).

they had greeted Jesus with the highest praise; fourth, that Pilate would actually go ahead and release a known enemy of Rome and execute someone he knew was innocent of the sedition charge.[70] In actuality, to Brandon's mind this elaborate tale is just a cover-up for what Mark knew to be the truth: Jesus was a convicted revolutionary executed by Pontius Pilate for subversion of the state.[71]

Though Brandon comes short of finally listing Jesus as a member of the Zealot party,[72] this does not mean he believes that Jesus was less active or violent than the actual members of this group. So strong is this violent stratum in the received tradition that even Mark cannot hide the fact that Jesus moved about in a society troubled by political issues, that Jesus never publicly condemned the Zealot party (though he did contend with the Pharisees, Sadducees, and the Herodians), that armed resistance was offered to Jesus' arrest in Gethsemane, that Jesus armed and inspected the weapons of his "troops," that he violently attacked the temple, and that he was finally executed between two Zealots.[73] To the discerning modern reader, these and other clues leach through the Gospel cover-up, betraying the ultimate intentions of the Evangelists to present a falsely pacifistic Jesus.[74]

For all the similarities Jesus shared with the Zealots and those like them, the showcase for Jesus' fundamental difference with the Zealots and his understanding of the Kingdom of God was the "attack" on the temple. From the beginning of his ministry Jesus had proclaimed the nearness of

---

[70] Ibid., 256-62.

[71] Brandon is careful to maintain that Jesus' threat to the Roman state was not a direct one. Rather, Jesus' main object was the corrupt sacerdotal aristocracy ensconced in the temple complex. Because the Roman government needed the stabilizing influence of the collaborating classes leading the temple system, any attack on their position would have indirectly threatened Pilate's hold on the situation (ibid., 336).

[72] Ibid., 355.

[73] On Jesus' arming of the disciples see ibid., 340-42; for his resistance in Gethsemane, 306-8; for his attack on the temple, 350-58; for his crucifixion between two Zealots, 356, 358.

[74] Brandon argues that Mark's scenario was taken up by the other evangelists to meet the particular needs of their own context. Sometimes, however, their versions are less circumspect in masking the revolutionary aims of Jesus. See ibid., 283-321.

the Kingdom of God, and although the Kingdom is undefined by Jesus, Brandon notes the authentic ring of Mark 1:15 ("The time is fulfilled, and the kingdom of God is at hand; repent and believe in the gospel") in light of Jewish apocalyptic:

> If the saying was indeed addressed by Jesus to a Jewish audience, it must have involved the destiny of Israel. In other words, the coming of the kingdom of God must have meant the achievement of the prophetic tradition of Israel as the Holy People of Yahweh, vindicated for its faithfulness before the nations of the world, and freed from all mundane hindrance to devote itself wholly to the service of its God.[75]

Jesus corroborates the apocalyptic meaning of the Kingdom in his call to repentance. According to a common apocalyptic belief of the day, Israel's servitude was the result of her sin, and national repentance was a necessary precedent to the nation's restoration. Jesus therefore knew that the repentance he had urged on his followers from the start also had to permeate the highest reaches of Israel's cult. Thus, his mandate to prepare Israel for the Kingdom brought him necessarily into confrontation with the corrupt temple establishment, unlike his Zealot counterparts, whose main opponent, at least initially, was Rome.[76]

In the end, Brandon's Jesus only prepares the way for the Kingdom. His own significance stopped far short of bringing in that Kingdom, despite the possibility that he may have given way to the exaggerated hopes of his followers and fashioned himself in a messianic mode. On these topics Brandon says we can only speculate, but there is no doubt the historical Jesus intended an apocalyptic Kingdom.[77]

Brandon's account of this apocalyptic, militaristic Kingdom ushered in at the hands of its human accomplices provoked no little scholarly

---

[75] Ibid., 337. Brandon is unsure whether Jesus understood the Kingdom to be located in this world or in one following a cosmic cataclysm.

[76] Brandon notes that Jesus' actions toward the temple *anticipate* the Zealots, because Zealot activity did eventually come against these Jewish collaborators (ibid., 338).

[77] Ibid., 337ff.

scrutiny and suffered much because of it.[78] E. Bammel, for example, has shown the many hypothetical propositions that creak and groan trying to prop up Brandon's view. For example, can we assume that Mark was written after A.D. 70? Can we rely on Brandon's perspective of the historical changes effected by the events of A.D. 70? If the Evangelists were so bent on hiding Jesus beneath pacifism, why do they not then go ahead and make Jesus openly condemn the Zealots, or at least erase the evidence of his militarism completely? How hard can we lean on *absent* evidence, that is, that early Christianity was just as militaristic as Jesus, but we do not know about it because the Romans obliterated the Jerusalem church in A.D. 66–70? These are only some of the issues that make Brandon's thesis "merely a *Luftgebäude*" (castle in the air), in Bammel's judgment.[79]

Buchanan

The apocalyptic Kingdom continues in a revolutionary tone throughout the twenty-five years of George Wesley Buchanan's investigation of the historical Jesus. Two of his many writings are especially relevant to the subject of the Kingdom. The first one, *The Consequences of the Covenant*, published in 1970,[80] seeks to lay a solid foundation within the Jewish worldview for a Jesus who envisioned a purely nationalistic Kingdom. That Jesus appears in full revolutionary garb in *Jesus: The King and His Kingdom* almost fifteen years later.[81]

The sabbatical eschatology of ancient Israel is the first of two foci undergirding Buchanan's understanding of Jesus' nationalistic aims for the Kingdom. In *Consequences of the Covenant*, Buchanan begins by noting the importance of the concepts of the Sabbath and Jubilee for Israel's

---

[78] See for example the works of Martin Hengel, *Was Jesus a Revolutionist?* trans. William Klassen (Philadelphia: Fortress, 1971); Oscar Cullmann, *Jesus and the Revolutionaries*, trans. G. Putnam (New York: Harper & Row, 1970); and the various contributors to *Jesus and the Politics of His Day*, ed. E. Bammel.

[79] E. Bammel, "The Revolution Theory from Reimarus to Brandon," 38–41.

[80] George Wesley Buchanan, *The Consequences of the Covenant* (Leiden: E. J. Brill, 1970).

[81] George Wesley Buchanan, *Jesus: The King and His Kingdom* (Macon, Ga.: Mercer University Press, 1984).

eschatology. At the time of the giving of the law, periods of Sabbath and Jubilee were mandated for all Israelites. In times of national despair because of foreign domination, hopes for the future were put in the language of the Sabbath and the Jubilee. The restoration of national sovereignty was thus anticipated in these times as the period of the national Jubilee.[82] The significance of this is to establish an inexorable link between Israel's sabbatical eschatology and issues of her politics. In other words, Israel's future hopes were national hopes tied to their sovereignty over the land of Palestine. Eschatology is clearly the provenance of a "conquest theology."[83]

Within Israel's theology of conquest operated two ethical schemes, one active and one passive. Active ethics are the ethics of holy war. When Israel was free from sin the Lord fought on their side and they were victorious. Passive ethics stem from the opposite situation. That is, when Israel was in sin, Yahweh withdrew, and Israel went to battle without his help and suffered ignominious defeat. Conquest of the land was not feasible in the face of sin, as the account of Ai attests. Moreover, sin in Israel incurred a national debt, which Yahweh justly extracted not only through Israel's failure to conquer, but, more seriously, through her inability to resist foreign domination. Foreign domination and even exile, therefore, were the prophetically revealed means of beginning the payment plan to settle the national debt. When the debt was paid Yahweh would again be on Israel's side, and she would throw off her oppressors with a glorious reassertion of autonomy; active ethics would again apply. Until such time as the debt was paid, however, Israel waited and suffered passively, building up credit that would eventually bring an end to her enemies and their cruel domination.

---

[82] For example, Jeremiah reveals the abuse of the Jubilee year as the cause for the nation's exile, and in Isaiah 27:13 the return of the exiles is heralded with the blast of the trumpet as at Jubilee (Buchanan, *Consequences of the Covenant*, 9-11).

[83] Israel's conquest theology is rooted in the covenants made with Abraham and demonstrated through Moses. In these events Yahweh had revealed himself to be "the God who directed the affairs and destiny of his chosen people. He was the God of armies who decisively disclosed his character and intention at the Reed Sea when he delivered his chosen people from the hand of Pharaoh and set them free to return to the land which he had promised them as an inheritance by a covenant previously made with their father Abraham" (ibid., 1-2).

Both active and passive ethics were, therefore, aimed at Israel's possession of the land.[84]

Buchanan argues that Israel's theology of conquest, driven by both active and passive ethics, was a live concern on into the first century and forms the backdrop for the message and ministry of Jesus.[85] Through some calculation of his own, Jesus had apparently reckoned the time of Israel's passive suffering to be at an end and, therefore, appears on the scene operating with an active ethic. Numerous evidences in the Gospels point to Jesus' active ethic and his preparations to wage a holy war against Rome the moment Yahweh signaled the time was at hand. Jesus proclaims without qualification the Kingdom of God—a clearly political gesture in light of the Kingdom's reference to the land of the Davidic Kingdom.[86] Jesus is associated with politics by the titles associated with him: Messiah, Son of God, and Son of Man.[87] Jesus' interpretation of his miracles in an Exodus

---

[84] Buchanan demonstrates from the Old Testament that the inherent nexus the land of Palestine had to all aspects of Israelite life. Life itself was defined by possession of the land, and death was the consequence of losing the land (e.g., Ezra 9:8; Consequences of the Covenant, 123-31). The life of the future, that is, eternal life in the Kingdom, was thus also related to the land. For both Jews and Christians Buchanan argues that the emphasis of resurrection and eternal life "was not on physical resuscitation of bodies or endless physical existence, but rather the fulfillment of the promise of eternal life in the covenant community on the land of life" (145; cf. the discussion of "Life in the Future," 136-49).

[85] The eschatology of the Apocrypha, the pseudepigraphal writings, the Targums, and the rabbinic literature is discussed in Consequences of the Covenant, 56-89, and Jesus, 17-24. Buchanan concludes that all anticipated a historical, political restoration of Israel to the land of Palestine. Even Qumran did not expect the imminent end of the world of space/time history. Buchanan cites M. Black's statement that "so far as Qumran eschatology is concerned it seems to be fairly generally assumed that the Qumran sectarians shared the general eschatological outlook of the NT period. Their eschatology was of the apocalyptic order. But the view that it was dominated by the belief in the imminent end of the world and its destruction by fire does not seem to me to be very convincingly borne out by the evidence" (M. Black, "The Gospel and the Scrolls," in Studia Evangelica III, ed. K. Aland et al. [Berlin: Akademie Verlag, 1964], 575; cited in Buchanan, Consequences of the Covenant, 14, n. 1).

Buchanan also challenges the supposed abstract nature of the Kingdom in the rabbinic literature from the statements calling for taking upon oneself the "yoke of the Kingdom." He sees statements of this nature as oaths of allegiance made to the national, temporal, and earthly Kingdom that was coming in the future (Jesus, 23-24).

[86] "Kingdom of heaven" was another way of talking about the Davidic Kingdom in the land of Palestine (Buchanan, Jesus, 17-18).

[87] Buchanan, Jesus, 12.

motif shows that he thought the restoration of Israel to be near.[88] Jesus actively recruited followers to his movement.[89] He associated with businessmen and other people of wealth that they might financially underwrite his movement.[90] Jesus utilized an elaborate code system to communicate his message to his people and confound any Roman sympathizers in his audience.[91] His statements about the Kingdom being "among you" were cloaked references to clandestine preparations being made throughout the land by his guerilla forces.[92] Admonitions about "heavenly treasure" were aimed at retiring Israel's "national debt" in accordance with the theology of conquest.[93]

Things did not turn out as Jesus had figured in his pursuit of the active ethic. His movement faced some opposition, most notably seen through the beheading of John the Baptist. Buchanan guesses this opposition gave Jesus cause to question his mission of war on Rome.[94] Perhaps his new call

---

[88] Ibid., 30–31.

[89] Ibid., 127.

[90] Ibid., 169.

[91] For example, Jesus' answer to the query of John the Baptist's disciples in Matthew 11:1-6 was based on Isaiah 29:18-21 (not Isa. 61:1), which speaks of the end of the ruthless and the scorner and the cutting off of the wicked (*Jesus*, 218-19). The greatest source of Jesus' codes were the parables of the Kingdom that dealt with the "mysteries" of the Kingdom. The hiddenness of the leaven, the double reference of leaven to political organizations, and the mention of the sickle at the harvest (Mark 4:26-29 in reference to Joel 4:13) are just some of the ways Jesus consistently conveyed three coded messages about the Kingdom based on Daniel: (1) the coming Kingdom is in the extent of its dominion like the Kingdom of Daniel 4:22; (2) the sovereign God gives the Kingdom according to his will; no force on earth can resist him (Dan. 4:17, 37); (3) the Kingdom will one day be taken from the Gentiles and given to Israel (Dan. 7:13). Jesus' discussion of the binding the strong man was a reference to throwing off Roman oppression. "Satan" was also probably a code word for Rome (*Jesus*, 208-15).

[92] Ibid., 217-18.

[93] Ibid., 225.

[94] Buchanan says, "Jesus and John may at one time have been confident that God wanted them to lead an open conflict against Rome as the two anticipated messiahs. That plan was partially frustrated, however, by the death of John the Baptist. This may have given Jesus an opportunity to rethink his role. It was at that time that he began to reorganize his program to include wealthy, Jewish businessmen and tax collectors. He expanded his program in size and financial support to be prepared for a war with Rome, if that seemed to be the will of God. He may also have reconsidered, at that same time, whether or not God willed an open war at that time. The death of John may have been understood as a sign to the contrary. There are some indications that Jesus struggled with this issue seriously" (ibid., 250).

to an active ethic was premature and Yahweh was not behind Israel's liberation from Rome at this time. Buchanan thinks that this kind of soul-searching eventually effected a shift of emphasis in Jesus' teaching away from the active ethics of revolution to the passive ethics of meekness, suffering, and even martyrdom. And Jesus' life ends in the manner of passive ethics. Caught by the Romans and convicted for his ill-timed revolutionary activities, Jesus, now convinced of the need for more meritorious suffering, submits meekly to torture and death.

> Jesus was a religious leader not just a secular militarist. He was apparently ready to fight or die to bring in the Kingdom of Heaven. When the Romans came to capture him, he did not try to force God's hand, utilizing the forces at his command, and expect God to defeat the enemy. This may have been understood as a sign from God that he was expected to respond passively, assuming that God would use Jesus' suffering as payment against the indebtedness of sin still held against Israel.[95]

The transformation from active to passive ethics in Jesus allows Buchanan to avoid the need for the tendency criticism of Brandon in dealing with Jesus' more pacifistic statements in the Gospels and the subsequent pacifism of the early church. Both active and passive types of activity simply need to be correlated with their respective periods of Jesus' life.[96] Since Jesus' life ended following the ethics of pacifism, the movement that followed under the leadership of his disciples continued on in that same vein. Buchanan still wants it to be remembered, however, that this does not mean that Christian pacifism was more loving and warm to its enemies than active militarism. Within the theology of conquest, pacifism

---

[95] Ibid., 251.

[96] See Buchanan's discussion of the Beatitudes in terms of passive ethics in "Matthean Beatitudes and Traditional Promises," in *New Synoptic Studies: The Cambridge Gospel Conference and Beyond*, ed. William R. Farmer (Macon, Ga.: Mercer University Press, 1983), 161-84.

and militarism were only different tactics aimed at the same end. "Jewish and Christian pacifism was no more human or kind than militarism. Both were designed to destroy Rome and establish the kingdom of Heaven on the promised land. The difference was purely tactical."[97] Whether pursued actively or passively, Jesus' intentions were ruthless towards Israel's enemies.[98]

Besides distancing himself from Brandon's methodology and also avoiding many of the criticisms Brandon received, Buchanan's proposal of passive and active ethics in the teaching of Jesus has other virtues. First, active and passive ethics allow Buchanan to draw the meaning of the Kingdom from as many of the Gospel's pericopes as possible. Less needful to such a view is the suspicious sloughing off of any particular group of Kingdom sayings as both spiritual and literal hope are given full meaning at different times.[99] Second, such a theory of development is visible in the Gospel record itself when the Gospels are allowed to speak as complete narratives. When read as a narrative unit, the Gospel of Matthew, for

---

[97] Buchanan, *Jesus*, 250.

[98] Jesus' command to love one's enemy (Matt. 5:44) is another expression of Paul's command to leave revenge for the Lord in Romans 12:18-20 (*Jesus*, 249-50).

[99] This may partially explain why many scholars of past years have also held to some development theory in Jesus' ministry. Before sophisticated critical tools were developed that made textual dissection easier, more of the Gospel data was allowed a hearing. Schweitzer notes that the idea of two different periods in Jesus' life was the prevailing method of the nineteenth-century Old Quest to account for the apocalyptic and the religious statements of Jesus. He cites as especially influential the works of Oskar Holtzmann (*Das Leben Jesu* [1901]), Theodor Keim (*Die Geschichte Jesu von Nazara* [1867-1872]), and Karl August von Hase (*Das Leben Jesu* [1829]; and *Geschichte Jesu* [1876]) (Albert Schweitzer, *The Quest of the Historical Jesus: A Critical Study of Its Progress from Reimarus to Wrede*, trans. W. Montgomery [New York: Macmillan, 1968], 61, 215). A two-phase theory was also put forth in this century by T. W. Manson. Early in his career Jesus thought of the Kingdom as future, but after his identification at Caesarea Philippi as the Christ he changed the concept of the Kingdom to be the personal realm of salvation (T. W. Manson, *The Teaching of Jesus* [Cambridge: Cambridge University Press, 1931], 124-29, 135; cited by Hiers, *Kingdom of God*, 17). These theories differ of course from Buchanan, who sees no fundamental change in the Kingdom per se. The locus of the change is Jesus' means of achieving the eschatological Kingdom.

example, readily reveals a development in Jesus' ministry and his meaning of the Kingdom.[100] For all its virtues, Buchanan's presentation still only grasps for credibility in some of the details. First, there is Jesus' alleged obsession with Rome. In light of the Old Testament hope, is it likely that Satan and the strong man were Jesus' codewords for Rome, that all discussion of spiritual warfare is aimed at Rome, and that the parables are only to be understood in a militaristic context because they are secret instructions for sabotaging Roman rule?[101] Second, Buchanan struggles to explain the church's politically passivity. How can we account for the movement that followed Jesus being so different from the fundamental thrust of his life? Can Jesus' passive surrender to arrest, trial, and crucifixion alone account for the divergent path Christianity followed when compared to the rival Jewish sects

---

[100] Matthew's presentation of the Kingdom in Jesus' ministry is notably different before and after the conflict and rejection in chapters 11-12. Before the rejection the Kingdom is in every way reminiscent of the rule of Yahweh called for in the Old Testament prophetic hope. Jesus sees no need to define the Kingdom; he claims prophetic fulfillment for himself in his words and miracles (e.g., Matt. 11:1-5); spiritual Elijah had come (Matt. 11:14); Jesus calls for repentance and is described as openly "preaching" (*kēryssō*) the "gospel of the Kingdom" *(euangelion tēs basileias)* hearkening back to Isaiah 52:7; 61:1; 40:9; and 41:27 (Matt. 4:23; 9:35); and the Kingdom is "at hand" (*ēngiken;* Matt. 4:17). Beginning in chapter 13, however, the Kingdom is revealed only to the spiritually receptive and then only in terms of parables *(en parabolais)* and mysteries *(ta mystēria)* which confound those "outside" (Matt. 13:3, 11ff.). The Kingdom of the parables is different from the Kingdom of the Old Testament hope. It is presently growing, but secretive and hidden (Matt. 13). After chapter 13 Jesus no longer openly "preaches" (*kēryssō*) the "gospel of the Kingdom" *(euangelion tēs basileias);* the only "Kingdom" information understood by the unbelieving crowds and religious authorities is negative, that is, that the Kingdom is taken away from them and they will not enter it (Matt. 21:43); and the Kingdom is no longer near *(ēngiken)* but seems distant (Matt. 24-25). The turning point of Jesus' rejection in chapter 13 also means the Kingdom will be associated with the *ekklēsia* which will have charge of the "keys of the Kingdom" (Matt. 16:18-19) and which will not be identified by its Jewish ethnicity. Jesus' own career turns at the rejection. Before it Matthew summarizes Jesus' career as that of the herald of the coming Kingdom (Matt. 4:23; 9:35). After the rejection Matthew says that Jesus began to show his disciples his Passion (Matt. 16:21). The point of all this against Buchanan is that if Jesus changed at any time in his ministry, Matthew presents the turning point as being long before the events of Gethsemane and the execution that followed. See Mark Saucy, "The Kingdom-of-God Sayings in Matthew," *BS* 151/602 (1994), 175-97.

[101] Buchanan, *Jesus,* 200-15; *Consequences of the Covenant,* 83-84.

Buchanan sees as so parallel to it?[102] Jesus the prophet who calls Israel to the spiritual requirements of the physical and glorious Kingdom, as in the view of Ladd, still seems more comfortably situated in the Gospels than Jesus the guerilla-terrorist—although the ultimate nature of the Kingdom remains the same in each case. Finally, Buchanan cannot consistently sustain the literal, only future, apocalyptic Kingdom with the Gospel data. Like Hiers, the Kingdom of the parables ultimately forces him to admit the possibility of another meaning for the Kingdom that would allow for the Kingdom's presence in this age. Credibility is again stretched when Buchanan describes the Kingdom of the parables as a political resistance movement "that was quietly, infectiously, working its way through the land."[103]

Mediating Apocalyptic: Ladd and Meier

George Eldon Ladd's work on the Kingdom in Jesus' teaching represents one of the early voices of our period in favor of an "Already but Not Yet" Kingdom. Ladd's vision of the Kingdom as both present and future has had an important impact within conservative scholarly circles.[104]

---

[102] On this question, see further E. Bammel, "The Revolution Theory from Reimarus to Brandon," 53.

[103] Buchanan, *Jesus*, 214.

[104] One can see the emergence of the Already/Not Yet consensus in Ladd's works. In 1952 Ladd claimed no one view of the Kingdom had established universal recognition within scholarly circles (*Crucial Questions About the Kingdom of God* [Grand Rapids: Eerdmans, 1952], 39). By 1964 the Kingdom as present and future was an "emerging consensus" (*Presence of the Future*, 188; *Jesus and the Future: The Eschatology of Biblical Realism* [New York: Harper & Row, 1964]) and, as our survey has shown, it remains the dominant view.

In addition to these three monographs, Ladd's important writings on the Kingdom include "The Kingdom of God: Reign or Realm?" *JBL* 81 (1962): 230-38; "The Life Setting of the Parables of the Kingdom," *JBiRel* 31 (1963): 193-99; "The Place of Apocalyptic in Biblical Religion," *EvQ* 29 (1957): 94-100; "Why Not Prophetic-Apocalyptic?" *JBL* 76 (1957): 192-200; *The Pattern of New Testament Truth* (Grand Rapids: Eerdmans, 1968), chap. 2, "The Synoptic Pattern: The Kingdom of God."

In the 1960s Ladd's conservative approach to critical methodologies (see remarks in the preface to *Presence of the Future*) hindered the acceptance of his work outside of conservative circles. Though it was Ladd's very great desire to be respected beyond his immediate sphere of influence, a scathing review of *Jesus and the Kingdom* by Norman Perrin ("Against the Current," *Interp* 19 [1965]: 228-31) showed it was not be as he wanted. History will doubtless be kinder to Ladd than Perrin was!

Ladd described his own view of Kingdom as "historic premillennialism," and he diverged from

Fulfillment and consummation are the two defining terms of Ladd's understanding of the Kingdom in Jesus' teaching. They figure prominently in the stated thesis of *The Presence of the Future* that

> the Kingdom of God is the redemptive reign of God dynamically active to establish his rule among men, and that this Kingdom, which will appear as an apocalyptic act at the end of the age, has already come into human history in the person and mission of Jesus to overcome evil, to deliver men from its power, and to bring them into the blessings of God's reign. The Kingdom of God involves two great moments: fulfillment within history, and consummation at the end of history.[105]

The notion of the Kingdom as the fulfillment within history of the reign of God directs attention back to the Old Testament hope of Israel. Here Ladd means to clarify obfuscations of terminology that have occluded the Old Testament and pseudepigraphal eschatological picture in the scholarly literature. In his own discussion of the Old Testament hope as an eschatological hope, an earthly hope, and an ethical hope, Ladd offers several noteworthy conclusions pertinent to the study of the Kingdom in Jesus' teaching. First, there is no radical cleavage in the Old Testament hope between history and eschatology. Eschatological hopes were hopes for history and the earth set in motion by suprahistorical forces.[106] Second, despite the fact that biblical redemption is always earthly, it is the ethical nature of the hope that takes precedence in the prophetic proclamation.

---

his dispensational background particularly at the place of the future of Israel. This move caught Ladd in a crossfire between his former friends in fundamentalism and those more liberal like Perrin. The conflict exacted a heavy personal toll. See the discussion of Ladd in George Marsden, *Reforming Fundamentalism: Fuller Seminary and the New Evangelicalism* (Grand Rapids: Eerdmans, 1987), 248-50. For Ladd's presentation of historic premillennialism, see "Historic Premillennialism," in *The Meaning of the Millennium: Four Views*, ed. Robert G. Clouse (Downers Grove, Ill.: InterVarsity Press, 1977), 17-40.

[105] Ladd, *Presence of the Future*, 218.

[106] Ibid., 59. As to the question of the timing of the Kingdom, Ladd notes that "the Hebrews did not have an abstract idea of time or eternity." Consequently, "the question of whether the consummation takes place in time or in eternity is foreign to the Old Testament" (Ladd, *Pattern of New Testament Truth*, 51).

The language of imminence (e.g., Isa. 13:9; Zeph. 1:7; Joel 1:15; 3:14; Obad. 15) is primarily the means of putting force to the ethical demands of repentance and should not be taken as strict statements about chronology. The Day of the Lord could come at any time.[107] Third, the historical conditioning of the later apocalyptic literature meant a sharpening of the Old Testament dualism between history and eschatology as well as a loss of hope for the present history. The result was a hope "reposed only in the future."[108]

In contrast to this post-Old Testament development, Jesus comes announcing the presence of the Old Testament salvation. Side by side with the apocalyptic Kingdom that would consummate history in an earthly, glorious Kingdom was the clear herald's announcement that the eschatological salvation is now being fulfilled.[109] Claims to the present as the time of "fulfillment" abound in Jesus' explicit declarations in Mark 1:15 and Luke 4:21, as well as in his allusions to the presence of the bridegroom (Mark 2:19), the blessing of those who witness his ministry (Luke 10:23–24), and the prophetic credentials of his ministry (Matt. 11:4–5; Isa. 35:5–6).[110] But how is this to be understood? How can the future Kingdom of God that was to be the final victory over Satan be a present event?

Ladd finds the answer in his understanding of the Kingdom as the dynamic power of salvation. Following the prevailing view of the Kingdom

---

[107] The ethical focus of Old Testament hope means for Ladd the denationalization of the hope. "The redeemed of the future will experience the eschatological salvation not because they are Israelites but because they are faithful, holy, righteous." Thus, "the Israel which will experience salvation is the 'church' rather than the nation, the spiritual rather than the physical Israel. The national and physical elements are not sloughed off, but they are subordinated to the spiritual forces" (Ladd, *Presence of the Future*, 73–74).

[108] Ibid., 101. This third point is also the subject of Ladd's essay "Why not Prophetic-Apocalyptic?" which argues it is mistaken to radically separate the prophetic hope of the Old Testament from the so-called apocalyptic hope of the Apocrypha and Pseudepigrapha, as is often done in scholarly literature. Both hopes were earthly, temporal, and cataclysmic.

[109] Ladd's view of the consummated Kingdom is what differentiates him from those of the *regnum Christi* view discussed earlier. Whereas both Ladd and these others strongly emphasize the dynamic presence of the Kingdom in Jesus' ministry and message, for Ladd this concept is something Jesus *adds* to the prophetic hope and not the means of *transforming* the prophetic hope. See his discussion of the nature of the consummated Kingdom in *Presence of the Future*, 307–28.

[110] Ibid., 105–20.

as the abstract dynamic rule or reign of God in the realm of salvation,[111] Ladd strips Jesus of all militaristic intentions (contra Buchanan and Brandon) and makes him a proclaimer of the Kingdom's "mysteries" of the spiritual salvation of the present age.[112] God's reign has become dynamically, that is, redemptively, active in Jesus' person and ministry. He breaks the power of evil, speaks with unheard of authority, and preaches the dynamic activity of God.[113] A new age of salvation breaks forth in which the blessings of the coming age can be enjoyed now. Eternal life, resurrection life, the possession of immortality, the joy of the Lord, fellowship with God and man, forgiveness of sins, physical healing, and absolution of guilt are all attained from entering into the realm of the Kingdom's dynamic activity.[114]

The remainder of Ladd's project is to lay out the ramifications of this divine activity of the Kingdom for the church that followed after Jesus. As the fellowship of those having experienced the rule of God, the church is to work as the Kingdom's instruments in the world. The personal ethics of the inner life of each believer will issue forth not only in proclamation of the word of the Kingdom, but in deeds of the Kingdom as well. In social activity "the world [is] to feel the influence of God's Kingdom."[115]

---

[111] See ibid., 122-35.

[112] Militarism is discarded as Jesus reinterprets the prophetic hope in spiritual terms. The ultimate enemy is Satan; the eschatological salvation is aimed primarily at his demise, not Rome's (ibid., 150). The mysteries of the Kingdom in Matthew 13 and Mark 4 are Jesus' disclosure "that the Kingdom which is to come finally in apocalyptic power, as foreseen in Daniel, has in fact entered into the world in advance in a hidden form to work secretly within and among men" (225).

[113] Ladd argues that Jesus' theology is part of the case for God's Kingdom being dynamic. Jesus preaches God as the seeking, inviting, fathering, and judging God (ibid., 171-88).

[114] See the discussion of these features of the present Kingdom in ibid., 195-217. The "realm" of salvation is as far as Ladd goes with his understanding of the Kingdom as the abstract rule of God. The sayings of entering the Kingdom (e.g., Mark 9:47; 10:15; Matt. 18:3) force this retraction, although Ladd does note that Jesus could speak of entering the Kingdom or the Age to Come as synonymous with eternal life in Mark 10:17-30, making it still abstract in essence (196).

[115] Ibid., 303. Ladd's presentation stops short of a full manifesto for Kingdom social action. He says he has implied a "social gospel" but has left to others the task of working out the details (304).

John P. Meier's recent and influential portrait of the historical Jesus, the "marginal Jew," also powerfully articulates a Kingdom that was eschatologically future and at the same time partially present.[116] Writing partially in response to the trends of the last ten years that have deeschatologized Jesus' proclamation, Meier's rigorous source and tradition criticism of the Gospel data aims the weapons of those like the members of the Jesus Seminar back upon them. It is only by means of contorted and convoluted exegesis, says Meier, that the historical Jesus can be made into the wandering charismatic-cynic-philosopher who urged people to find God and/or ultimate meaning in the present moment.[117] Meier's quest of the historical Jesus' meaning of the Kingdom begins in the historical milieu of first-century Judaism, and rightly so. Starting with the Old Testament, all of the pertinent extant documents of Judaism are examined on the question of God's Kingdom and are found to make at least three crucial contributions to understanding the context of Jesus' teaching. First, with most of modern scholarship, the Kingdom should be seen primarily as a dynamic, not a static, entity. It describes the expression of Yahweh's kingly rule over all of his creation and especially over his covenant people Israel. The Kingdom is not a strictly defined concept, but, in words reminiscent of Perrin, multilayered, multivalent, and "tensive." "The kingdom of God does not have a definition; it tells a story."[118] Second,

---

[116] John P. Meier, *A Marginal Jew: Rethinking the Historical Jesus*, vol. 2, Anchor Bible Reference Library (New York, N.Y.: Doubleday, 1994). A third volume is promised that will consider the teaching of Jesus relative to the Jewish groups of his day and also take in detailed study of the parables. References to *Marginal Jew* that follow will be to the second volume, where Meier takes up the themes of "Mentor, Message and Miracles."

[117] "A completely un-eschatological Jesus, a Jesus totally shorn of all apocalyptic traits, is simply not the historical Jesus, however compatible he might be to modern tastes, at least in middle-class American academia" (ibid., 317; cf. 291; 352, n. 4; 1045).

[118] Ibid., 241. Though he retains Perrin's terminology, Meier, like others, fills the meaning of "tensive" with things Perrin himself would not have tolerated. Challenging Perrin's assertion that tensive symbols are not concepts or ideas, Meier asks why this must be so. He conceives of his own use of the Kingdom as a tensive symbol that is both multilayered *and* conceptual (242). Therefore the Kingdom of God known to Judaism and Jesus need not exclude temporality or reference to a domain or concrete reality that is ruled (240-42).

while the terminology of God's Kingdom is present, it was central neither to the Old Testament nor to intertestamental traditions of Judaism. Where it does appear, the symbol of the Kingdom conjures up Israel's eschatological hope for a definitive salvation in the future—a salvation that concerned the restoration of all Israel gathered around Mount Zion or Jerusalem.[119] Finally, if Jesus were to teach a Kingdom that was at the same time present and future, he would have precedent from at least two sources available to Judaism in the first century. Both the canonical book of Daniel and the extracanonical book of the Wisdom of Solomon, claims Meier, paradoxically combine eschatologies of the Kingdom's presence and futurity.[120]

With the beliefs of first-century Judaism as his foundation, Meier launches into the Gospel data of Jesus' teaching about the Kingdom of God. The tools of form, source, and tradition criticism yield no doubt that for Jesus the Kingdom of God was both a future eschatological concept and a present reality.[121] Historical critical judgments about the petition "your kingdom come" of the Lord's Prayer (Matt. 6:10; Luke 11:2), the Last Supper tradition that Jesus would no longer drink wine until the banquet in the kingdom (Mark 14:25), the place of the Gentiles at the banquet in the Kingdom (Matt. 8:11–12; Luke 13:28–29), and the Beatitudes of the Sermon on the Mount (Matt. 5:3–12; Luke 6:20–23) reveal that Jesus believed

---

[119] Ibid., 264, 269.

[120] Ibid., 250.

[121] Meier lists five criteria that "have proved especially useful" for the quest of the historical Jesus: (1) the criterion of embarrassment, that is, the early church would be less likely to add material that would be embarrassing to it; (2) the criterion of discontinuity, that is, discontinuous with Judaism and Christianity; (3) the criterion of multiple attestation focuses on the sayings or deeds of Jesus that are attested in more than one literary genre; (4) the criterion of coherence, that is, how well material fits with the previously tested "data base" of material; (5) the criterion of Jesus' rejection and crucifixion; in a way similar to the criterion of coherence this considers how a saying fits with the fact of Jesus' rejection and ultimate crucifixion (ibid., 5-6). Meier's first volume addresses questions of introduction and method more extensively; see *Marginal Jew*, 1:167-95. Among the other conclusions about method propounded by Meier is the contribution of form criticism that "dissolve[s] the chronological frameworks of the public ministry as found in the Four Gospels" (Meier, *Marginal Jew*, 2:1048, n. 3; cf. 1:406-9).

in an imminent, future coming of God to rule as king that would not reform the world; it would end the world.[122] The timetable of this end Jesus himself did not set, but, along with the Old Testament prophetic voice, he emphasized the potential imminence of the Kingdom's arrival.[123]

The Kingdom already present is a theme that is also established upon logia with the highest claim to authenticity. Interestingly enough, in making his case for the presence of the Kingdom, Meier does not consider the parables.[124] It is Jesus' answers to the inquiries of John the Baptist (Matt. 11:2–19), his statements to the Pharisees about his exorcisms being proof that the Kingdom is among you (Luke 11:20; Matt. 12:28), and the cryptic claim of Luke 17:21, "the Kingdom of God is in your midst," that all form the surest evidence that Jesus understood the Kingdom to be at least partially present. Not to be left out, but somewhat less helpful, is Mark 1:15 and the Beatitudes congratulating those who see what the disciples see (Luke 10:23–24) and Jesus' rejection of voluntary fasting (Mark 2:18–20). This block of material also shows that Jesus thought that his exorcisms were a partial realization of that rule of God that would soon be fully displayed.[125]

---

[122] The logion about Gentiles joining the long-dead patriarchs at the banquet in the Kingdom shows the Kingdom to be discontinuous with this world—contra the scenarios of other in the apocalyptic camp like Brandon, Buchanan, and Reimarus (Meier, *Marginal Jew*, 2:317; cf. 375, n. 100).

[123] Meier follows Ben Meyer who notes that "the tradition of prophecy in Israel *always* strikes the note of imminence. There is no prophecy of the distant future . . . his [Jesus'] prophecy—if, as a history-of-religion phenomenon, it was in any sense significantly aligned with that of the prophets of Israel—bore on the immediate future" (Meyer, "Jesus's Scenario of the Future," 6; cited by Meier, *Marginal Jew*, 2:377, n. 111).

[124] Meier's hesitation on the parables stems from the last generation of literary critical study that "has reminded us how open is each parable to multiple interpretations—at least if taken by itself, in isolation from the rest of Jesus' message and praxis" (Meier, *Marginal Jew*, 2:290). He proposes to investigate the parables only after a contextual foundation is established by other means. This investigation will presumably be part of the forthcoming third volume.

[125] Meier goes against the flow of the way historical criticism is usually practiced and asserts that the sayings as well as actions of Jesus should be allowed to reveal the beliefs of the historical Jesus (ibid., 451). The miracle-traditions, argues Meier, have unique contributions to make to the quest because of their impact on at least some Jews of the first century and their broad attestation in every layer of Jesus tradition in the Gospels (3).

But how are modern exegetes to reconcile this conundrum of a Kingdom that is at once imminent and present, both near and realized? Meier's answer, in short, is that we are not. Jesus evidently used the Kingdom of God as a particular tensive symbol that was broad enough to include both the already and the not yet. The modern preference for noncontradiction was not the rule in Jesus' day, especially with prophetic discourse. Such a diverse mode of expression was the stated function of symbols like the Kingdom of God that "tell stories" and did not call for precise definition.[126] In the end the Kingdom simply means God coming in power to rule his people Israel in the end time. At times this symbol can suggest the substance of the ancient Jewish hope of restored sovereignty in their land, at other times it can mean the end-time power that can heal and exorcise.[127]

Although to my mind he has admirably taken up the cause of the apocalyptic Jesus in the face of recent contrary trends, in some ways Meier's conclusions resemble those of Chilton (God in Strength) and Perrin (nonapocalyptic tensive symbol) some ten and twenty years ago. Using the same methods and criteria as Chilton and Perrin, albeit with different results, one still senses in Meier a certain "boiling down" of Jesus' proclamation to an amorphous, vague, common-denominator kind of Kingdom.[128] Was "God coming in power to rule his people" all that Jesus meant when he mounted the Gospel stage in Mark 1:14-15 and Matthew 4:17 and proclaimed without definition the nearness of the Kingdom? Surely this was what first-century Jews believed, but it was also much more, and with much more defined beliefs as well. God's coming rule was political, national, and sovereign. But how does such a Kingdom compare with the mysterious Kingdom of the parables—one that was small, growing, and invisible? When all logia are extracted from their narrative context and made to stand the trial of the criteria on their own, a trial where the standards always change,[129]

---

[126] Ibid., 452, cf. 453, and 506, n. 230.

[127] Ibid., 452.

[128] Some benefit of the doubt should be accorded Meier in view of the fact that his final volume has not been released. He admits his results to this point are somewhat sketchy (ibid., 1044-47).

[129] For yet another recent attempt at redefining the criteria of authenticity see Gerd Theissen, "Historical Scepticism and the Criteria of Jesus Research *or* My Attempt to Leap Across Lessing's Yawning Gulf," *ScotJT* 49, no. 2 (1996): 147-76.

one is invariably forced into this bland kind of definition of the Kingdom. One's definition must be able to handle a Kingdom that is powerful yet suffering, visible yet secret, universal yet growing, full of resurrected patriarchs yet present. Such a procedure also demands a monolithic Jesus who is not allowed to develop in his preaching and ministry of the Kingdom. Granted, Meier, somewhat instinctively, believes that Jesus did develop in his ministry, but the commitment to the canons of historical criticism, and notably the form critical denial of even a basic chronology to the Gospels, has made him powerless to articulate beyond his instincts.[130]

APOCALYPTIC KINGDOM OF THE THIRD QUEST: MEYER, HARVEY, AND SANDERS

The final subjects of our survey of the apocalyptic Kingdom come from the domain of the Third Quest. The Third Quest is the nomenclature that has been given to investigations of the historical Jesus over the last fifteen years that typically begin study of Jesus from the larger cultural frame of reference rather than from the literary history of his sayings. At center place for these studies are the tools of cultural anthropology, sociology, and economics, rather than the tools of literary criticism. As we shall see, the conclusions for the Kingdom from these scholars of the Third Quest closely parallel those of Hiers who works in more of the literary mode; consequently the reason for their separate mention primarily reflects a difference in methodology.

Ben F. Meyer's 1979 study of *The Aims of Jesus*[131] begins our look at the apocalyptic Kingdom establishing the case for a Third Quest. Early on in *Aims* he affirms the goal pursued in the New Quest, Jesus' inner world of aims and intentions, but he repudiates the means adopted to achieve that goal. History is more than "minute examination of gospel data with a view to passing judgments on them. It is reconstruction through hypothesis

---

[130] "*That* Jesus changed and developed his ideas and practice during the public ministry is highly probable; *what* exactly that change was and how it took place is unknowable to us today" (ibid., 1048, n. 3; italics his).

[131] Ben F. Meyer, *The Aims of Jesus* (London: SCM, 1979).

and verification. Its topic is 'aims and consequences.'"[132] Part one of his work functions therefore as an inquiry into issues of hermeneutics, philosophy, and historiography that sets the stage for the discussion of Jesus and his Kingdom that follows in part two.[133]

The topic of eschatology best satisfies Meyer's conditions for establishing the aims of the historical Jesus. First, from the time he embraced the prophetic scheme of the Baptist to his crucifixion on a Roman cross, there is no doubt that Jesus' public and private words and actions were keyed to the eschatological concept of the Kingdom.[134] Second, Jesus' ministry as centered around the theme of the Reign of God best accounts for the *de facto* existence of the Christian church, as well as its departure from Judaism. For Jesus God's reign ultimately referred to the realization of God's will for the restoration of Israel and the nations.[135] In contrast to the Baptist's announcement of the Kingdom as the "wrath of God," Jesus' version was primarily a positive message that came to be known as "gospel," the good news of salvation.[136] Jesus understood God's reign as "an approaching order

---

[132] Ibid., 19.

[133] Part one (23-110) is an account of the historical "quests" for Jesus since Reimarus. It argues against them in favor of "a hermeneutic open to human action's social and historical impact as well as to its illumination of possibilities of human existence" (20). Under the guidance of Lonergan's cognitional theory (B. J. F. Lonergan, *Insight: A Study of Human Understanding* [London: Longmans, 1958]) and Collingwood's philosophy of history (R. G. Collingwood, *The Idea of History* [Oxford: Oxford University Press, 1946]), Meyer lays the foundation for his own historical reconstruction of Jesus' intentions. This foundation includes Meyer's beliefs that Jesus' intentions can be known from the "coming to be of the Christian *ekklesia*" and the "historically definitive break between Jesus and Judaism" (20), that the Gospels do "intend the past" and supply data on Jesus (72), and that questions of historicity are not settled when "indices of historicity" (i.e., discontinuity, originality, personal idiom, resistive form, multiple attestation, multiform attestation, Aramaic substratum) are lacking for the Gospel data (87).

[134] Summaries of the key role of the Kingdom theme appear throughout *Aims*. See for example, page 221: "The reign of God was the focal point . . . once the theme of the national restoration in its full eschatological sweep is grasped as the concrete meaning of the reign of God, Jesus' career begins to become intelligible as a unity."

[135] Isaiah 52:7-9 provides the three features of the reign of God that circumscribe the hopes of all Jews from the exile onward: the herald of salvation, the reign of God, and the restoration of Israel. In Meyer's mind, "dissociation of 'the reign of God' and its proclamation from 'the restoration of Israel' is *a priori* implausible" (Meyer, *Aims*, 133). "Israel" is understood by Meyer to mean the nation (see 133-35), though he does see Jesus' intentions as primarily religious.

[136] Meyer, *Aims*, 129-30.

of things" that comes as a gratuity to the unworthy of Israel. "Kingdom of God" had a periphrastic function for the nearness of God himself with his intentions to lavish the blessings of the eschaton on the poor, the sick, and the hungry.[137] In terms of temporality, seeing the reign in terms of the fulfillment of God's will allows for great flexibility. For Meyer, the Kingdom is present when Jesus announces God's will for Israel to repent[138] and when he begins to "restore" Israel religiously;[139] it is future in the imminent and final act of the history and the posthistorical restoration of all humanity.[140]

Jesus' self-understanding must also be defined by the inexorable

---

[137] Ibid., 136.

[138] Jesus' proclamation of the gratuity of the Kingdom, along with demonstrations of its present operation (as in Matt. 12:28), was an explosive power in his audience the magnitude of which is impossible to exaggerate. In this capacity the proclamation produced what it proclaimed and was operational in the present (ibid., 131, 135).

[139] "[T]he reign of God as already overtaking Israel in Jesus' words and acts meant that Israel was already in process of being restored. His teaching was Torah appropriate to restored Israel and requisite to perfect restoration. His wonder-working signified the restoration of Israel and effected it by restoring the afflicted to their heritage as children of Abraham. The appeal to 'the sinners' likewise belonged to this context. Offering forgiveness and eliciting conversion, it was designed to restore the outcasts to Israel. This is confirmed by Jesus' repeated efforts to reconcile the righteous to this move toward socio-religious integration" (ibid., 221; cf. 173).

[140] The Kingdom as the "consummation of history" (ibid., 134) still allows for a historical restoration of the nation of Israel. Meyer writes, "The post-historical restoration of mankind would hinge on the historically rooted restoration of Israel" (137).

On the question of Jesus' language of imminence, Meyer argues that Jesus' temporal language of the Kingdom should be taken symbolically (241-49). In his symbolic announcement of the Kingdom, Jesus himself did not have "determinate knowledge" of the meaning intended by God. His prophetic utterances utilized the "characteristic symbolic idiom" which only the "eye of faith" can correlate to actual historical events because it alone is intimately aware of the ever-progressing movement of salvation history. For example, Jesus' prophecy that many would come from east and west to banquet with Abraham in the Kingdom (Matt. 8:11) was fulfilled in the eye of the believers through the missionary thrust of the church to the Gentiles. Thus, "to the cold eye of the unbeliever Jesus' vision of things may seem like an exotic hallucination; to the believer it stands in profound and creative continuity with an ongoing history of salvation yet to find its final culmination" (247). See also Meyer's "Jesus's Scenario of the Future," *DRev* 109 (1991): 6, where Meyer notes that Jesus' language of imminence coheres well with the prophetic tradition of Israel's past: "the tradition of prophecy in Israel *always* strikes the note of imminence. There is no prophecy of the distant future. . . . [Jesus'] prophecy—if, as a history of religion phenomenon, it was in any sense significantly aligned with that of the prophets of Israel—bore on the immediate future."

eschatological drama that was unfolding in his ministry. In Meyer's mind it is through the lens of the temple that Jesus' claims for himself most clearly emerge.[141] Jesus' own sayings, the accusations at the trial and his actions towards the temple converge with the historically indisputable facts of the *titulus* ("The King of the Jews") and the Christology of the postresurrection church to verify that Jesus offered a messianic performance.[142] He thought he was building the house of God like the son of David described in Nathan's oracle (2 Sam. 7:12–14a). Moreover, his startling announcement and demonstration of the Reign of God was a divisive factor by which he separated the messianic remnant out from Israel.[143]

A. E. Harvey's approach to the historical Jesus is also conceived more globally than investigation of the sayings. His thesis is simply deduced from the premise that:

> No individual, if he wishes to influence others, is totally free to choose his own style of action and persuasion: he is subject of constraints imposed by the culture in which he finds himself. If communication is to take place, there must be constraints which are recognized by both the speaker and his listeners, the artist and his public, the leader and his followers.[144]

Given what is known of the historical Jesus plus the environmental constraints of politics and religious and eschatological beliefs at work in the first century, Harvey sees only limited options for Jesus' identity. This identity, Harvey eventually concludes, was essentially that of a prophet who preached the urgency of the hour, referred to himself as "Anointed," performed miracles, and related to God the Father as an obedient son.[145]

Responding to the deepest longings of the people for the kingship of

---

[141] Meyer, *Aims*, 178-202.

[142] Meyer states: "The entry into Jerusalem and the cleansing of the temple constituted a messianic demonstration, a messianic critique, a messianic fulfillment event, and a sign of the messianic restoration of Israel (*Aims*, 199).

[143] Ibid., 210-19.

[144] A. E. Harvey, *Jesus and the Constraints of History* (Philadelphia: Westminster, 1982), 6.

[145] On the fundamental gestalt of Jesus, Harvey states, "We can say of him without incongruity of any kind that he was the first and only Jewish teacher to have combined in a single style of teaching the roles of legal expert and prophet, with perhaps a touch of the esoteric seer thrown in" (Harvey, *Constraints*, 59). Regarding Jesus' miracles Harvey admits, however, that "Jesus conforms to no known pattern" (113).

God was critical to Jesus' prophetic ministry. All Jews knew the timeless truth that God is always king, but Jesus' announcement of the final manifestation of his kingship and a new age was the unprecedented backdrop to his prophetic role.[146] Harvey thinks the first-century beliefs about the Kingdom had given Jesus wide latitude for interpretation within the boundaries of the basic earthly hope: God's kingship might be exercised over Israel or it might be universal; it might be exercised directly by God himself or it might be delegated out to an earthly king ruling in God's stead.[147] Jesus evidently seized the opening given to him and chose to slant the Kingdom theme in the direction of the imminent revelation of God himself. "His concept and understanding of the kingdom is nothing less than a radical and unprecedented reinterpretation of the whole notion of God's influence upon the ways of men."[148] As proclaimer of the Kingdom Jesus was the unique revealer of God according to the hopes for the new age.[149]

E. P. Sanders's impressive portrait of Jesus also describes a prophetic figure who preaches Jewish restoration theology.[150] Within these paradigms, Sanders understands the Kingdom proclamation to intend

> a new order, created by a mighty act of God. In the new order the twelve tribes would be reassembled, there would be a new temple,

---

[146] God's eternal kingship is the context for Harvey's discussion of the presence of the Kingdom in the already/not yet paradigm (ibid., 91). He describes Jesus' miracles as tokens of assurance for the authenticity of the hope for the new age (117).

[147] Ibid., 144.

[148] Ibid., 144. Harvey also notes suddenness as a key factor in Jesus' revelation of the Kingdom (87).

[149] "By the time of Christ . . . the expectation that an individual revealer would be a factor in the coming new age was expressed with a considerable richness of content. This individual would be like Moses, who saw God face to face and was the mediator of the fundamental historic revelation; he would be a prophet, with the authority at the very least to arbitrate in matters affecting the temple, but also anointed to proclaim and even bring about the conditions of the new age; and he would be the wise man *par excellence*, possessing and imparting final and authoritative knowledge about God" (ibid., 147).

[150] E. P. Sanders, *Jesus and Judaism* (Philadelphia: Fortress, 1985), 222, passim. See also Sanders, "Jesus and the Kingdom: The Restoration of Israel and the New People of God," in *Jesus, the Gospels, and the Church: Essays in Honor of William R. Farmer,* ed. E. P. Sanders (Macon, Ga.: Mercer University Press, 1987), 225-39. Craig Evans in 1987 considered that *Jesus and Judaism* "may be the most important book on the historical Jesus in fifteen or twenty years" (Craig A. Evans, "Jesus of Nazareth: Who Do Scholars Say that He Is?" *Crux* 3/24 [1987]: 17). Other important reviews of *Jesus and Judaism* are by A. J. Droge in *Criterion* 26 (1987): 15-18; and D. M. Smith, "A Review of Marcus J. Borg, *Jesus: A New Vision,"* *Forum* 5, no. 4 (1989): 71-82.

force of arms would not be needed, divorce would be neither necessary nor permitted, outcasts—even the wicked—would have a place,
and Jesus and his disciples—the poor, meek and lowly—would have
the leading role.[151]

Like Meyer and Harvey before him, Sanders demotes the impact of the
sayings-data for his conclusions and works primarily from what he calls the
"almost indisputable facts" about Jesus.[152] Central to these facts was Jesus'
controversy about the temple, and it is here that Sanders believes Jesus' restoration theology is most plainly evident. Taking the so-called cleansing of
the temple as having to do more with prophetic symbolism than with purification,[153] Sanders links Jesus' actions towards the temple with his predictions of the destruction of the temple. The fact that Jesus predicts the
destruction of the temple (Matt. 24:1; Mark 13:1–2; Luke 21:5) points to Jewish restoration as the ultimate point of his ministry.

Jesus predicted (or threatened) the destruction of the temple and carried out an action symbolic of its destruction by demonstrating against
the performance of the sacrifices. He did not wish to purify the temple,

---

[151] Sanders, *Jesus and Judaism*, 319.

[152] See Sanders's discussion of the scholarly treatment of the sayings of the Kingdom in the
Gospels. It is a telling reflection of the point that making the right selection of sayings will
determine the historical Jesus in innumerable ways (ibid., 123-56). For this reason Sanders hesi-
tates to depend on the sayings excised from the events of Jesus' life. Adding the facts of Jesus' life
to the sayings, which are notably more "individualistic," especially on repentance, produces a
more responsible picture of the historical Jesus (Sanders, "Jesus and the Kingdom," 238; *Jesus and
Judaism*, 116-19).

Sanders's "indisputable facts" are (1) Jesus was baptized by John the Baptist; (2) Jesus was a
Galilean who preached and healed; (3) Jesus called disciples and spoke of there being twelve; (4)
Jesus confined his activity to Israel; (5) Jesus engaged in a controversy about the temple; (6) Jesus
was crucified outside Jerusalem by the Roman authorities; (7) after his death Jesus' followers
continued as an identifiable movement; (8) at least some Jews persecuted at least parts of the
new movement, and it appears that his persecution endured at least to a time near the end of
Paul's career (Sanders, *Jesus and Judaism*, 11).

[153] Mark 11:17 and parallels are secondary explanations not reflecting Jesus' own reasons for his
actions (Sanders, *Jesus and Judaism*, 66-67). For a critique of Sanders's interpretation of this event
see Craig A. Evans, "Jesus' Action in the Temple: Cleansing or Portent of Destruction?" *CBQ* 51
(1989): 237-70.

either of dishonest trading or of trading in contrast to "pure" worship. Nor was he opposed to the temple sacrifices which God commanded to Israel. He intended, rather, to indicate that the end was at hand and that the temple would be destroyed, so that the new and perfect temple might arise.[154]

Sanders finds corroborating evidence for this thesis in Jesus' association with John the Baptist, his inauguration of the inclusion of Gentiles, his posture towards the twelve tribes of Israel through the twelve disciples, his demand for repentance, and his announcement of judgment.[155] Considering evidences like these, Sanders believes the nature of the Kingdom emerges as being primarily *earthly*, as in a new social order centered on the nation of Israel,[156] and *otherworldly*, in the sense that the transformation of the world would be a miraculous event not necessitating the use of weapons.[157] This Kingdom, Jesus believed, was "immediately future," though

---

[154] Sanders, *Jesus and Judaism*, 75.

[155] Ibid., 92-119. Sanders also adduces for his argument the behavior of the disciples after the ascension of Jesus. At many points it is evident they continued the restoration theology of Jesus. They continued to expect the restoration of Israel; they continued to look for the inauguration of a new age; they continued to see Jesus as occupying a central place in the Kingdom; they continued to look for an otherworldly kingdom to be established by a miracle (334).

[156] The focus of Jesus' ministry is the nation of Israel, not the people of Israel, as some like W. D. Davies, *The Gospel and the Land* (Berkeley: University of California Press, 1974), 336-54, have tried to argue (Sanders, "Jesus and the Kingdom," 239; *Jesus and Judaism*, 116-19).

[157] An important qualifier in Sanders's earthly and otherworldly thesis is Jesus' discussion of the divorce question (Matt. 5:31-32; 19:1-9). Jesus' views here show the recapitulative nature of the Kingdom. Humanity's end is like the beginning (Sanders, *Jesus and Judaism*, 230; 256-60). It is important to note that Sander's use of "otherworldly" is different from the way Schweitzer and Weiss would have used it. The latter two thought of the otherworldly Kingdom as the end of the world. Sanders, Meyers, and Harvey use the term to describe the nature of the advent of a *historical* Kingdom. On this count they are similar to many we have labeled as "nonapocalyptic" (e.g., the *regnum Christi* view) except they do not see Jesus transforming the *physical* nature of the Kingdom's presence in history.

The otherworldly, or miraculous, nature of the Kingdom denies that Jesus had any political or military intentions. "It is now virtually universally recognized that there is not a shred of evidence which would allow us to think that Jesus had military/political ambitions . . . and the same applies to the disciples" (Sanders, *Jesus and Judaism*, 231).

some allowance should be made in his language for the presence of the Kingdom's power in his ministry.[158] With these conclusions Sanders thinks all of the other groups of sayings of Jesus "blend happily enough."[159] Though he is more hesitant on the subject of Jesus' own identity and role in the Kingdom,[160] Jesus' miracles, his relationship to the law, his welcoming sinners, his posture towards his opponents, and his death all contribute to the notion of the eschatological Kingdom Jesus thought was imminent. Jesus, thus, was leader of a "charismatic-prophetic movement of an eschatological stamp."[161]

The greatest advantage of the view that Jesus' Kingdom was apocalyptic is the continuity this maintains with first-century Judaism. This was the point Weiss had made against Ritschl. As more and more scholars come to perceive the historical Jewish hope as consistently earthly and ethnic in spite of some abstract language, the apocalyptic Kingdom in Jesus' preaching stands out in bolder relief. Christopher Rowland has noted this continuity, saying,

> We must not misrepresent the understanding of God's reign in the preaching of Jesus by stressing an individual, otherworldly experience

---

[158] This is Sanders's reading on the Kingdom-as-present passages like Matthew 12:28 and Luke 17:20, 21. In his extensive analysis he believes Greek verbs like *ephthasen* ("has come") in Matthew 12:28 have been forced to carry too much weight for the Kingdom itself being present and that such passages do not reveal "the particular and decisive character" of Jesus' preaching of the Kingdom (Sanders, *Jesus and Judaism*, 129-41; 150-52). Sanders sees the need for some manifestation of the Kingdom to be present, contrary to consistent eschatology, but he does not want to say this constituted the fundamental nature of the Kingdom for Jesus as is the case in realized eschatology. On the diversity of the Gospel statements about the Kingdom Sanders writes, "One need realize only that 'kingdom' does not always carry precisely the same meaning. The kingdom in the full eschatological sense could not be present, nor could it be entered into by individuals, but the meaning of the word can be stretched so that one can talk of the kingdom, in the sense of God's power, as present and extended to individuals in the present" (237).

[159] Sanders, *Jesus and Judaism*, 236.

[160] "I have proposed as a strong inference that Jesus thought of himself as 'king' (whether or not he directly used the title), but beyond that everything gets murky. Did he identify himself with the suffering servant? Did he ever call himself 'Messiah'? What are we to make of the enigmatic Son of man? I have no answers to any of these questions" (ibid., 324).

[161] Ibid., 237-38. The description is Hengel's (*The Charismatic Leader and His Followers*, trans. J. Greig [Edinburgh: T & T Clark, 1981], 20-21).

at the expense of the restoration of the community and physical order. To this extent, the Matthaean version of the Lord's Prayer, with its petition that God's kingdom would come and his will be done on earth as in heaven (Matt. 6.10), is an accurate exposition of the essential features of the Jewish (and Jesus') belief concerning the eschatological and this-worldly character of the kingdom.[162]

Thus, in contrast to other views demanding a transformation of the Jewish hope, the apocalyptic Kingdom still plausibly explains, as Reimarus observed two hundred years ago, why Jesus does not need to define his use of the Kingdom at the outset of his ministry (Mark 1:15). It also seems to handle more easily the persistence of the nationalized hopes of the disciples at the end of his ministry as well as their own early preaching (Acts 1:6–8; cf. also 3:21).

Furthermore, as all of the present writers demonstrate, the apocalyptic Kingdom is not antithetical to the tenor of Jesus' religious and spiritual proclamations. If anything, the apocalyptic Kingdom demonstrates well the organic unity of physical and spiritual in the Jewish belief-system of the first century. The physical/earthly cannot be disjoined from the spiritual/religious as easily as some who would reduce the Kingdom to a spiritual cipher might wish. To the contrary, a Kingdom rooted in love, forgiveness, mercy, inclusion, and conversion (repentance) before God is completely coherent within a theology of Jewish restoration. Hence, suspicious explaining away of contradictory passages is less necessary. The apocalyptic Kingdom can embrace both the coming Son of Man and the golden rule. Sense can be made of both these elements in Jesus' proclamation without removing Jesus from his Jewish roots.

Preferable, therefore, is the option of the mediating positions on the Kingdom's presence and future taken by Ladd, Meier, Meyer, and Sanders. In these scholars' writings the semantic domain of *basileia* retains its

---

[162] Christopher Rowland, *Christian Origins: From Messianic Movement to Christian Religion* (Minneapolis: Augsburg, 1985); see also the more recent works of Brian Rice McCarthy, "Jesus, the Kingdom, and Theopolitics," Society of Biblical Literature Seminar Papers Series 29, 1990, ed. David J. Lull (Atlanta: Scholars, 1991), 311-21; Maurice Casey, *From Jewish Prophet to Gentile God: The Origin and Development of New Testament Christology* (Louisville: Westminster/John Knox, 1991).

spatial and temporal eschatological focus, but it is also broad enough to include the concept of overt power in the present. In other words, the complete manifestation of the Kingdom's world-changing glory need not exclude the possibility of some portion of that Kingdom, namely its power, being present. Both power and domain can be the referent of *basileia* and can separately occupy the temporal dimensions of the present and future. Strong warrant for such an option comes not only from the function of the Holy Spirit with the Kingdom in Matthew 12:28, but also from the reference in Hebrews 6:5 to the presence in this age of the "powers *(dynameis)* of the age to come" in and the biblical nexus of the Holy Spirit, power *(dynamis)*, and the Kingdom of the Age to Come.[163]

The apocalyptic Kingdom now marks the conclusion of our survey and

---

[163] The argument of Hiers and Sullivan that "the presence of the power of God or his Spirit . . . is not the same as the presence of the Kingdom of God" (Hiers, *Kingdom of God*, 33; cf. Sullivan, *Rethinking*, 74-79) fails to see the interdependence of the relationship between God's power by his Spirit and the manifestation of God's glory in the Kingdom. In the Old Testament the Spirit is presented as "the medium through which God's presence in the midst of his people becomes a reality" (Walther Eichrodt, *Theology of the Old Testament*, trans. J. A. Baker [Philadelphia: Westminster, 1961], 2:61). Consequently, it was through the Spirit that God's people realized all divine powers and gifts recorded in Scripture (*Theology of the Old Testament*, 2:61). The future age of Yahweh's New Covenant (the age to come, the Kingdom of God) would mean greater participation of the individual in the realm of the Spirit (Jer. 31:33-34; Ezek. 36:26-27). The Spirit would be poured out in the end time as the cleanser and renewer who would establish righteousness (Isa. 32:15; 44:3; Ezek. 18:31; 36:25ff.; 37:14; 39:29; Joel 2:28-32). The inaugurator of the future messianic rule, the Lord's servant, would be one specifically anointed by the Spirit for the accomplishment of this task (Isa. 11:2; 42:1; 48:16; 59:19-21; 61:1). The overall character of the future age in the prophetic hope of the Old Testament is thus wholly Spirit-conditioned in comparison to the present age, as Eichrodt notes: "there is an advance from a picture of power working externally to one involving the innermost foundation of the personal life; man's relationship with God is no longer left to his own efforts, but is given him by the spirit. Because, however, all this is seen as the central miracle of the new age, the spirit as the living power of the new creation finds its proper place in eschatology" (*Theology of the Old Testament*, 2:59). In the New Testament, the writer of Acts makes it clear that the early church considered itself and Jesus uniquely anointed in the present with the *dynamis* of the Holy Spirit and the coming age (Acts 1:8; 2:14:21; 10:38). On the Holy Spirit's relationship to the final age and the Kingdom of God see James D. G. Dunn, "Spirit and Kingdom," *ExpTim* 82 (1970-1971): 36-40; D. Wilhelm Michaelis, *Reich Gottes und Geist Gottes nach dem Neuen Testament* (Basel: Friedrich Reinhardt, n. d.), 3-6; Erik Sjöberg, *pneuma, TDNT,* 6:384-86; Eberhard Kamlah, "Spirit," *NIDNTT,* 3:692; and Max Turner, "The Spirit and the Power of Jesus' Miracles in the Lucan Conception," *NovT* 33, no. 2 (1991): 124-52.

analysis of the Kingdom from its major voices in New Testament scholarship since 1960. Since Perrin and Lundström wrote, the Kingdom has been presented as ultimate self-understanding (the New Hermeneutic), virtually any experience of the divine (the Newer Literary Criticism), and as God-willed but humanly enacted social and economic structures (parts of the Third Quest) along with persistent re-presentations of older views (*regnum Christi* and the apocalyptic Kingdom). To my way of thinking, when all is said and done, the apocalyptic Jesus still has much to commend him from a consistent reading of the biblical record. So far as "apocalyptic" defines the Kingdom of God (1) according to the earthly, historical, and otherworldly (in the sense of divine inauguration and presence of resurrected patriarchs) hope of Judaism, (2) with possible but not necessary imminence, and (3) broadly enough to encompass the manifestation of dynamic Kingdom power through the Holy Spirit in the present age, then it has the advantages of (1) maintaining realistic points of contact with the first century (viz., the pervasive Jewish hope for the restoration of Israel), (2) being able to account for the full complex of human life represented in Jesus' teaching (i.e., spiritual to political and social elements), (3) not having to selectively excise contradicting Gospel data, and (4) being able to best account for the form of the Christian movement that followed.

PART THREE

*Systematic Presentation
of the Kingdom Since 1960*

CHAPTER SIX

The Political Theology
of the Kingdom in Jürgen Moltmann

The early 1960s were a time of theological transition. Dissatisfaction with the earlier anthropocentric and humanistic theology, driven by shame for the church's complicity with the "Beast" during World War II, pushed continental scholars anew to search for the immanence of God and his rule in the modern world. The works of a World War II martyr, Dietrich Bonhoeffer, struck a particularly resonating chord, with his calls for Christian loyalty to the earth in a "world come of age." Human beings, he said, were the partners of God in fulfilling his will in shaping the world.[1] Further reflection in this vein by Bonhoeffer's theological and cultural heirs of the 1960s produced a genre of theologies that were notably practical, public (in contrast to privatized faith), critical (of institutions and ideologies), and above all political.[2] Methodologically, these theologians read Scripture in a manner sensitive to the interpreter's own social and political context as a means of bringing biblical truths about the fundamental character of human existence to bear on the contemporary world.[3] They understand politics to be the most appropriate medium for their theology, or any truly

---

[1] See especially Bonhoeffer's "Thy Kingdom Come," in John D. Godsey, *Preface to Bonhoeffer* (Philadelphia: Fortress, 1965); and *Letters and Papers from Prison* (London: Fontana, 1963), 88-125. On the influence of Bonhoeffer in the political theologies of the 1960s, see Stanley J. Grenz and Roger E. Olson, *Twentieth-Century Theology: God & the World in a Transitional Age* (Downers Grove, Ill.: InterVarsity Press, 1992), 146ff.

[2] These are the essential features of political theology according to Alfredo Fierro, *The Militant Gospel: A Critical Introduction to Political Theologies,* trans. John Drury (Maryknoll, N.Y.: Orbis, 1977), 33.

[3] On the hermeneutics of political theology in general, see the review essay by Douglas Sturm, "Praxis and Promise: On the Ethics of Political Theology," *Ethics* 92 (July 1992): 733-50.

Christian theology for that matter, as it is the primary sphere in which the way human beings live together on the earth is structured.

Different labels for these politically oriented theologies have evolved over the recent decades into the main categories of political and liberation theology. The distinction in nomenclature comes partially from the presumed method of political theology wherein the interpreter's social and political context is critical to the shape of his or her theology. Accordingly, theologies labeled "political" originate in nonoppressive political situations, usually in North America or Western Europe. Indeed, liberation theologians often claim that practitioners of political theology speak as members of the oppressing structures,[4] whereas theologies of "liberation" are the theological reflections of the oppressed. They represent the on-site applications of the theories expressed in political theology, but their Third-World context gives them unique theological authority and identity.

The approach for the function of the Kingdom in these two brands of political theology will be through the most influential writer and an influential movement. This chapter will consider the Kingdom of God in the thought of Jürgen Moltmann, who will represent political theology. The Kingdom of the liberation theologies will follow in the next chapter and will be represented by their earliest and most prolifically published member: Latin American liberation theology.[5]

THE KINGDOM AND HOPE

It almost goes without saying that any theology which calls itself "eschatological" and "messianic," and which is avowedly driven by hope will

---

[4] This is one of the reasons liberation theologians seek to distance themselves from their North Atlantic brethren. See Michael L. Cook, "Jesus from the Other Side: Christology in Latin America," *TS* 44 (June 1983): 260, n. 5, 6; and Deane William Ferm, *Third World Liberation Theologies: An Introductory Survey* (Maryknoll, N.Y.: Orbis, 1986), 43.

[5] An added rationale for the place of Moltmann and Latin American liberation theology in our survey is that both Moltmann as an individual and Latin American liberation theology as a movement have produced theological works spanning from the birth of their respective movements to the present. They allow a rare generation-long view of their understanding of the Kingdom.

have much to say about the Kingdom of God.[6] For Jürgen Moltmann this assumption is certainly true, but to consider the Kingdom as merely a component of his theological reflection is to fail in the most profound way to understand his total program. Driven by his personal pilgrimage as a prisoner of war after World War II,[7] the "secular theology" of Dietrich Bonhoeffer,[8]

---

[6] Jürgen Moltmann says of his theological endeavor: "My whole theological work is aimed at overcoming the false alternative between an unreal God and a godless reality, between faith without hope and a hope without faith ("Politics and the Practice of Hope," *The Christian Century* [March 11, 1970], 290).

[7] For the personal theological pilgrimage of Moltmann see Meeks, *Origins;* Richard Bauckham, *Moltmann: Messianic Theology in the Making* (Basingstoke, U.K.: Marshall Pickering, 1987); Walter H. Capps, *Time Invades the Cathedral: Tensions in the School of Hope* (Philadelphia: Fortress, 1972); Christopher Morse, *The Logic of Promise in Moltmann's Theology* (Philadelphia: Fortress, 1979); and Moltmann, "Politics and the Practice of Hope," passim.

[8] Moltmann's debt to Bonhoeffer is such that one of Moltmann's reviewers says, "Moltmann (more than anyone else, in my opinion) has taken up and advanced the concerns of Bonhoeffer in theology today" (George Hunsinger, "The Crucified God and Political Theology of Violence: A Critical Survey of Jürgen Moltmann's Recent Thought, II," *HeythJ* 14, no. 4 [1973]: 392). Regarding the Kingdom, one of Moltmann's early writings (1959) was a study of Bonhoeffer's sociology entitled *The Lordship of Christ in Human Society* (in *Two Studies in the Theology of Bonhoeffer*, by Jürgen Moltmann and Jürgen Weissbach, trans. Reginald H. Fuller and Ilse Fuller [New York: Scribner's, 1967], 19-94), where Moltmann encounters Bonhoeffer's critique of the hierarchical church/state conjunction, the actional rather than ontological categories of "Being for Others" *(Dasein-für Andere)* (from Bonhoeffer's "Act and Being"), and Luther's notion of the church as the "larvae" of the Kingdom (Moltmann, *Two Studies in the Theology of Bonhoeffer,* 71-94). In *The Church in the Power of the Spirit: A Contribution to Messianic Ecclesiology* (trans. Margaret Kohl [New York: Harper and Row, 1977], 378, n. 2), Moltmann sees the horizontal concerns of the Kingdom in *Sanctorum communio* (Eng. trans., *The Communion of the Saints* [New York: Harper and Row, 1963]), where Bonhoeffer says, "The concept of the Kingdom of God does indeed embrace not only the consummation of the Church but also the problem of the 'new world,' that is, the eschatology of civilization and nature." On this last point see also Moltmann's discussion of this theme in Bonhoeffer in "Das Reich Gottes und die Treue zur Erde," 13-14; *The Crucified God: The Cross of Christ as the Foundation and Criticism of Christian Theology,* trans. R. A. Wilson and John Bowden (London: SCM, 1974), 313; *Church in the Power of the Spirit,* 283-84; *The Passion for Life: A Messianic Lifestyle,* trans. M. Douglas Meeks (Philadelphia: Fortress, 1978), 41-43; *The Future of Creation: Collected Essays,* trans. Margaret Kohl (Philadelphia: Fortress, 1979), 74, n. 9. For more on the tie of Bonhoeffer to Moltmann see Walter H. Capps, "Mapping the Hope Movement," in *The Future of Hope,* ed. Walter H. Capps (Philadelphia: Fortress, 1970), 24; Capps, *Time Invades the Cathedral,* 55; G. C. Chapman, "Hope and the Ethics of Formation: Moltmann as an Interpreter of Bonhoeffer," *SR* 12 (1983): 449-60; and Meeks, *Origins,* 44-47.

the biblical theology of Ernst Käsemann,[9] and the utopian hope of Marxist Ernst Bloch,[10] Moltmann understands the theme of the Kingdom to press deeply to the heart of all theology. This means, however, that theology does not begin in the past with the incarnation, but in the future with the coming of God. True theology is eschatology in that its main concerns are how the future affects the present.[11] In this way theology must be practical and horizontal, that is, aimed at the earth, not heaven, as Moltmann detailed in his essay, "Das Reich Gottes und die Treue zur Erde."[12] The Kingdom of God is

---

[9] Käsemann influenced Moltmann concerning the apocalyptic hope of the early church. In Moltmann's view, Käsemann had demonstrated that the Hellenization of early Jewish Christian hopes was the beginning of the triumph of the transcendent over the earthly, the triumph of heaven over earth, in subsequent Christian theology. See Moltmann "Hope and History," *TToday* 25, no. 3 (1968): 374-75; *Theology of Hope: On the Ground and the Implications of a Christian Eschatology*, trans. James W. Leitch (New York: Harper and Row, 1967), 155ff.; *The Way of Jesus Christ: Christology in Messianic Dimensions*, trans. Margaret Kohl (San Francisco: Harper, 1990), 379, n. 3; and Morse, *Logic of Promise*, 8. The Old Testament scholar Gerhard von Rad was part of the biblical theology movement along with Käsemann, and he influenced Moltmann with his theme of promise in the Old Testament (Capps, *Time Invades the Cathedral*, 92). For Moltmann's debt to von Rad see his "Theology in Germany Today," in *Observations on the "Spiritual Situation of the Age": Contemporary German Perspectives*, ed. J. Habermas, trans. A. Buchwalter (Cambridge, Mass.: MIT Press, 1984), 202.

[10] Personal encounters between the two began in 1960 and continued throughout the 1960s and 1970s after Bloch accepted a professorship at Tübingen, the year the Berlin wall was built (1961). Bloch's interest in social utopia led him to the biblical category of the Kingdom of God. His writings trace the Kingdom as an earthly and historical reality through the Old Testament prophets, Jesus, and select figures in church history, including Joachim of Fiore. See Bloch's discussion of "Christian Social Utopias" in *Das Prinzip Hoffnung* (1959) which is reprinted in the collection of Bloch's essays in *Man on His Own: Essays in the Philosophy of Religion*, trans. E. B. Ashton (New York: Herder and Herder, 1970), 118-41. On Moltmann's conversation with Bloch, see Moltmann, *Im Gespräch mit Ernst Bloch: Eine theologische Wegbegleitung* (Munich: Christian Kaiser, 1976); G. Clarke Chapman Jr., "Jürgen Moltmann and the Christian Dialogue with Marxism," *JEcuSt* 18 (summer 1981): 435-50; and James M. Childs Jr., "Marxist Humanism and the Hope of the Gospel," in *Christians and the Many Faces of Marxism*, ed. Wayne Stumme (Minneapolis: Augsburg, 1984), 110-22.

[11] Moltmann, *Theology of Hope*, 26-32.

[12] *Das Gespräch* 49 (1963): 3-23. This essay, published the year before the monumental *Theology of Hope*, anticipates the essence of main argument of *Theology of Hope*. For a presentation and analysis of the new "horizontal" dimension adduced to theology in Moltmann and others of this time, see Walter H. Capps, "Vertical v. Horizontal Theology: Bloch-Dewart-Irenaeus," *Continuum* 5 (winter 1968): 616-33. Moltmann's work on the Kingdom proper began early in his career with

the natural foundation of theology because "Theology is never concerned with the actual *existence* of God. It is interested solely in the *rule* of God in heaven and earth."[13]

Writing of his theological method, Moltmann says that his is a "daring," "dialogical," and "experimental" venture which seeks to describe the whole of theology in one focal point.[14] For him that focal point is the doctrine of hope, which means that the whole of theology is cast in the light of eschatology. "Eschatology is the *doctrine of hope*, the doctrine of the future for which we can hope, *and* simultaneously the doctrine of the action of hope which brings the hoped for future into the suffering of the present age."[15] Eschatology is thus all-encompassing, addressing all life, religions, social systems, and nature. Very importantly, the doctrine of hope is also to be realized in actional categories. Moltmann asserts:

> If one hopes for the sake of Christ in the future of God and the ultimate liberation of the world, he cannot passively wait for this future, and, like the apocalyptic believer, withdraw from the world. Rather he must seek the future, strive for it, and already here be in correspondence to it in the active renewal of life and of the conditions of life, and therefore realize it already here according to the measures of possibilities.[16]

These actional categories are facilitated by hermeneutics that must include "exposition of the meaning of our experience" and "presentation of the eschatological meaning of a text for that hope that drives men on to

---

an article on the Kingdom jointly written with H. Kremers and L. Goppelt in *Evangelisches Kirchenlexikon* (Göttingen: Vandenhoeck & Ruprecht, 1955). See under "Reich Gottes." Moltmann contributed the discussions of the history of the doctrine and its theological implications. A more recent statement of the Kingdom's profound role in his work is revealed in the title of "God's Kingdom as the Meaning of Life and of the World" (*Concilium*, 108 [1978]: 97-103).

[13] *The Trinity and the Kingdom: The Doctrine of God*, trans. Margaret Kohl (San Francisco: Harper and Row, 1981), 191 (italics his).

[14] Moltmann, foreword to Bauckham, *Moltmann*, viii, ix.

[15] Moltmann, "History and Hope," 371 (emphasis his). Note also the subtitle of the *Theology of Hope: On the Ground and the Implications of a Christian Eschatology*.

[16] Moltmann, "Hope and History," 369. See also Moltmann, *Theology of Hope*, 335-36.

new actions and experiences."[17] In this way hermeneutics bridges the past of the text to the future of the interpreter. For Moltmann it is the future with its full identity of the coming God which dominates all other readings of the Bible.[18]

The theme of the Kingdom of God naturally interfaces with Moltmann's emphasis on the future, as God's Kingdom is nothing other than the coming manifestation on the earth of his full identity, in other words "the future of God."[19] With Hans Küng and others, Moltmann sees the Kingdom of God in the Bible as an eschatological reality different from God's universal "reign" which is now exercised in creation and providence.[20] Within history the Kingdom will be the eschatological fulfillment of God's liberating lordship and is, therefore, the "messianic" face of the Kingdom,[21] but beyond history the Kingdom is the final revelation of the God who makes all things new. History and the messianic Kingdom of God will ultimately transition and merge into the Kingdom where "God may be all in all" and

---

[17] Moltmann, *The Experiment Hope*, ed., trans. M. Douglas Meeks (Philadelphia: Fortress, 1975), 9; cf. Moltmann, "Toward a Political Hermeneutics of the Gospel," *USemQR* 23 (1968): 303-23. See also the discussion of Moltmann's hermeneutics in Ben Wiebe, "Interpretation and Historical Criticism: Jürgen Moltmann," *RestQ* 24 (1981): 155-66; and Daniel L. Migliore, "Biblical Eschatology and Political Hermeneutics," *TToday* 26 (1969-1970): 116-32.

[18] Moltmann, *Theology of Hope*, 224.

[19] Moltmann, "Hope and History," 376.

[20] Moltmann cites Küng's *The Church* (trans. Ray and Rosaleen Ockenden [New York: Sheed and Ward, 1967], 47), in *Church in the Power of the Spirit*, 99-100.

[21] Moltmann posits a "messianic understanding of reality" derived from the conjunction of the idea of a creating God and the idea of the future. The result is s future which assumes a creative character for time and history (Moltmann, "Hope and History," 382). The term "messianic" as Moltmann applies it to his work speaks to this historical face of the eschatologically future Kingdom as it reaches into and determines the present historical order (Moltmann, *Church in the Power of the Spirit*, 192). The messianic Kingdom, therefore, is an earthly Kingdom which, in fulfillment of the promised Sabbath of the Old Testament, reconciles and recreates the suffering earth (Moltmann, *The Way of Jesus Christ*, 121). The New Testament (Col. 1:15, 20) mediates the earthy dimensions of the messianic hope through the idea of the Cosmic Christ who not only suffered for the creation but rose as the firstborn of all creation (Moltmann, *The Way of Jesus Christ*, 255).

the coming eschatological Kingdom will be joined to the creative and providential lordship of God forever.[22]

THE KINGDOM AND THE TRINITY

In *The Trinity and the Kingdom: The Doctrine of God* (1981), Moltmann elaborates the manner of God's liberating and creative rule over his creation by way of the Kingdom's interaction with each person of the Holy Trinity in what he calls the "trinitarian history of God."[23] In the final section of the book Moltmann, taking his cue from a thirteenth-century kindred spirit, Joachim of Fiore,[24] attempts to answer Bloch's criticism of God's Kingdom defiling human liberty. It is in this context that Moltmann explains his understanding of the three kingdoms of the Father, Son, and Holy Spirit.

---

[22] Heavenly/eternal categories blur readily with the earthly/temporal in Moltmann: the notion of the *novum* for the Kingdom of God (employed by Bloch) is taken up by Moltmann on the basis of Revelation 21:1-5—"Behold I make all things new." In *The Way of Jesus Christ*, 98, Moltmann proposes to translate "the kingdom of God" by "new creation." See also Moltmann, *Church in the Power of the Spirit*, 100, 190; and "God's Kingdom as the Meaning of Life and of the World," 102.

[23] See also Moltmann's article, "The Trinitarian History of God," *Theology* 78 (December 1975): 632-46.

[24] Many of the same themes of Moltmann appear in Joachim of Fiore's works as well; for example, Joachim had a problem with the church's strong distinction between nature and grace because of which the church dealt with converting sinners but neglected other societal issues; Joachim was interested in the historical presence of the Kingdom in contradistinction to the allegorized spiritual Kingdom popularized by Augustine in *Civitate dei* (20:6-7); Joachim rejected the corruption of the Kingdom mandate that ensued when the church became party to the political state. See M. Bloomfield, "Joachim of Flora: A Critical Survey of his Canon, Teachings, Sources, Biography, and Influence," in *Joachim of Fiore in Christian Thought*, ed. Delno C. West (New York: Burt Franklin, 1975), 1:29-92. Bloomfield (41 n. 57) quotes Etienne Gilson *(L'esprit de la philosophie médiévale*, 2d ed. [Paris, 1944], 367-68), whose statement of Joachim could very well have been made of Moltmann: "[for Joachim] in announcing the good news, the Gospel had not only promised to the faithful a kind of individual blessing, it had announced to them the entrance into a Kingdom, that is to say, into a society of faithful, united by the bonds of their common blessing." For a helpful discussion of the influence of Joachim in recent theology, including that of Moltmann, see A. J. Conyers, "The Revival of Joachite Apocalyptic Speculation in Contemporary Theology," *PerspRelSt* 12 (fall 1985): 197-211.

Like Joachim of Fiore before him, Moltmann posits separate and over-lapping kingdoms for each member of the Trinity.[25] The Father's kingdom is manifested in his creation and preservation of a world open to the fu-ture, that is, the future directed towards the goal of the glory of the Triune God. The Son's kingdom consists "of the liberating lordship of the cruci-fied one and the fellowship with the first born of many brothers and sis-ters."[26] Through his suffering love the Son liberates men and women from sin which withdraws them into themselves *(homo incurvatus se)* and closes them from God and from the future God intended for his creation in the image of God *(imago Dei)*.[27] The Son's Kingdom, like the Father's, is fu-ture-oriented and filled with hope as the Son's own demonstration of open-ness to the future is humanity's model. The Spirit's kingdom, though still historical, is actually the dawn of the final kingdom of glory where God is all in all. The Spirit is the gift experienced in power and energy by those who have been liberated by the Son. Through sharing in the Spirit's gift people become God's dwelling and participate in a new creation filled with liberty, blessing, and infinite hope. In the Spirit's kingdom all creation

---

[25] Joachim of Fiore's theology of history is a complex of allegorical and typological hermeneutics. Despite these difficulties it is clear that two intertwined elements comprised his theology of history: (1) Augustine's seven day-ages of history, where according to the creation paradigm seven ages will complete history (Augustine *Enarratio in Psalmum XCII* [*MPL* 37.1182], *De diversis quaestionibus LXXXIII liber unus* [*MPL* 40.43-44], *De catechizandis rudibus liber unus* [*MPL* 40.338], *De Trinitate libri XV* [*MPL* 42.892]); and (2) the Cappodocian fathers' and the Montanists' distinct kingdoms of the Father, Son, and Holy Spirit which rule sequentially through-out history (for example, see Tertullian *De exhortatione castitatis* 4 [*MPL* 2.969] and *De jejuniis* [*MPL* 2.1020-23]). The result in Joachim de Fiore was a scheme where all history would be fulfilled in seven ages (Adam; Noah; Abraham; David; Babylonian exile; Jesus; St. Benedict [13th century]; the end) the last of which would coincide with the Kingdom of the Spirit. His scheme is notable in its speculation of a radical change in earthly order *before* the close of history, not after. His discussion of these seven ages is found most completely in his *Liber concordie novi ac Veteris Testamenti* (Venice, 1519), book five, part one. The thought of Joachim fueled major upheavals in the Roman church as Franciscan preachers proclaimed the ultimate historical eman-cipation from all institutions, the Roman Church and the pope included! The Catholic response to Joachim was given by Aquinas in *Summa theologica* Ia2æ. 106 a4. See further Bernard McGinn, *The Calabrian Abbot: Joachim of Fiore in the History of Western Thought* (New York: Macmillan, 1985), and Delno C. West and Sandra Zimdars-Schwartz, *Joachim of Fiore* (Bloomington, Ind.: Indiana University Press, 1983).

[26] Moltmann, *Trinity and Kingdom*, 210.

[27] Ibid., 212.

begins to lay hold of the freedom for which it was originally made in the Father's kingdom. The Spirit's kingdom looks forward to the final "eschatological kingdom of glory in which people will finally, wholly and completely be gathered into the eternal life of the triune God and—as the early church put it—be deified *(theōsis)*.[28]

JESUS AND THE KINGDOM

Given the liberating role of the Son's kingdom within its trinitarian context, the historical Jesus marks a key transition in making the future of God immanent. Through his liberating proclamation, ministry, death, and resurrection, Jesus is the great *Anticipator Dei.* In the hope his message, ministry, and passion engender he brings the coming reign close to the present.[29]

In his proclamation of the Kingdom Jesus essentially continues the content of the prophetic hope offered to Israel in the Old Testament. Jesus' recitation of Isaiah 61 in answer to the disciples of John's query about Jesus' identity proves this.[30] A significant development Jesus effects in this hope comes from his own unique filial relationship with the Father. In contrast to John, who preached the kingdom in the light of God's wrathful judgment on the sin and human readiness through repentance, Jesus uniquely reveals the Father's kingdom as one of particular intimacy, grace, mercy,

---

[28] Ibid., 213. Besides the valid charge that Moltmann's Trinitarian interpretation of the Kingdom lacks in terminologic justification from the Bible for the Kingdom of the Spirit that is on the same order as the Kingdoms of the Son and the Father, it should be noted that Moltmann denies the charge of modalism and tritheism which are leveled at him. He sees the three historical Kingdoms each as "continually present strata" and transitions of the Kingdom of God in history (*Trinity and Kingdom,* 209). His emphasis, therefore is on the *quality* of the different Kingdoms over their *chronology* (Conyers, "Joachite Apocalyptic," 204).

[29] Technically Moltmann does not see the future coming Kingdom "present" in Jesus except in "signs," "anticipations," and power of the Spirit. Note his translation of the *engys*-language of the Kingdom (e.g., Matt. 4:17) as "at hand" or "near," not "present" (Moltmann, *The Way of Jesus Christ,* 97).

[30] In "Das Reich Gottes und die Treue zur Erde," 4, Moltmann states, "The inconceivable, blessed and at the same time provocative New in Jesus of Nazareth was not in that he announced another future from what was promised in the prophets, but that he promised to be the presence of this future with his deeds and his whole existence" (author's translation).

and forgiveness. God is now "Abba" and the *basileia* exists only in the context of God's fatherhood.[31] The Kingdom is near (Mark 1:15) in the sense that the intimacy of Abba is near.

The Kingdom that Jesus announces is also cleansed of the crassly temporal hope of apocalypticism that polluted the Old Testament prophetic message of his day. On the order of Bultmannian existentialism, Moltmann says that Jesus, in his talk of the nearness, entry, and inheritance of the Kingdom, announces the meaning of the Kingdom for existence, that is, the need for decision for God and practice of Kingdom ethics.[32] Jesus could not have intended the "end of the world" with his proclamation, because

> Anyone who expects "the end of the world" is denying the world's Creator, whatever may prompt his apocalyptic anxiety. Faith in God the Creator cannot be reconciled with the apocalyptic expectation of total *annihilatio mundi*. What accords with this faith is the expectation and active anticipation of the *transformatio mundi*.[33]

Similarly, the Gospel's apocalyptic Son of Man does not come from Jesus' own self-understanding but is an early Christian mnemonic device to recall Jesus' meaning for them after the Easter-event.[34]

---

[31] Moltmann, *Trinity and Kingdom*, 69-70; Moltmann, *The Way of Jesus Christ*, 90.

[32] Moltmann (*Theology of Hope*, 218) cites Conzelmann's famous article "Reich Gottes" in *RGG* (5 col. 915) and Bultmann's *New Testament Theology* on how Jesus surmounted the apocalyptic question of times and historic circumstances in his day. Bultmann said, "The eschatological proclamation and the ethical demand both point men to the fact that he is brought before God and that God is at hand; both point him to his Now as the hour of decision for God."

[33] Jürgen Moltmann, *God in Creation: A New Theology of Creation and the Spirit of God* (San Francisco: Harper & Row, 1985), 93.

[34] Moltmann, *Theology of Hope*, 218-20. In the twenty-five intervening years since *Theology of Hope* Moltmann appears to have softened in his assessment of the early Christian revisions of the historical Jesus. In his recent *The Way of Jesus Christ*, 137, Moltmann now says that he is starting from the "historical assumption that Jesus of Nazareth did in fact talk and act messianically; that he put himself in an identifying relationship to the messiah and the Son of man . . . and that the account of Jesus' messianic history is therefore not a projection by the Christian community after Easter on to a human life which in itself provided no grounds for this. Historically speaking, it is inadmissible to assume that on the basis of its experience with the risen and present Christ the Christian community projected anything into the history of Jesus which was inconsistent with the remembrance of him as he was during his lifetime."

In his restorative ministry to the poor, sick, demonized, lame, blind, and deaf, Jesus shows that the power and energy of the coming Kingdom are present in him through the Holy Spirit. The abiding presence of the Spirit in Jesus demonstrates that he is the true anticipatory beginning of the coming eschatological Kingdom of the new creation in history.[35] In his words and deeds, he "shared with other persons, what, according to the Old Testament expectancy, can only happen on the last day. He does already today what is supposed to come tomorrow. He lives entirely from the nearness of God's future."[36] His care for the marginalized of society also manifested the Fatherly nature of the Kingdom (Matt. 11:28). When the Kingdom comes to the poor, the wretched, and the sick, it restores them by relieving their humiliation and returning their dignity.[37]

Finally, in his passion Jesus also demonstrates the yet-to-be-realized nature of the Kingdom. The cross of Jesus shows his solidarity with the earth in its sufferings as well as the current hiddenness of the Kingdom in this age.[38] With the Reformers the Kingdom now is *tectum sub cruce et sub contrario.*[39] In his resurrection, Jesus heralded the dawn of the eschatological event of the Kingdom in such a way that he veritably ended history.

> The cross and the resurrection stand in the same relation to one another as death and eternal life. Since death makes every life historical, death has to be seen as the power of history. Since resurrection brings the dead into eternal life and means annihilation of death, it breaks the power of history and is itself the end of history. . . . That is why we are talking about "the eschatological resurrection of Christ."[40]

---

[35] Moltmann's Spirit Christology is important in understanding the Kingdom focus of Jesus' ministry here. See Moltmann, *The Way of Jesus Christ,* 92, 98-99.

[36] Moltmann, *The Experiment Hope,* 54.

[37] The objects of the Kingdom's restoration are the economically, socially, physically, psychologically, morally, and religiously poor. They are those who are at the mercy of others and therefore must endure injustice and violence (Moltmann, *Church in the Power of the Spirit,* 79).

[38] Moltmann, "Das Reich Gottes und die Treue zur Erde," 15.

[39] Moltmann, *Church in the Power of the Spirit,* 82-83. See also Moltmann, *Theology of Hope,* 223, and *The Way of Jesus Christ,* 151-210.

[40] Moltmann, *The Way of Jesus Christ,* 214. Whereas Bultmann makes much more of the cross for the existential issue of the Kingdom, for Moltmann the empty tomb is especially paradigmatic for the Kingdom hope. See Moltmann, *Theology of Hope,* 218-20.

As it is again by the Spirit's power that Jesus went to the cross and was raised from the dead, so these events proclaim the arrival of the age of the Spirit in hope of the coming final eschatological Kingdom of life and peace.

THE CHURCH AND THE KINGDOM

Just as Jesus anticipated the future Kingdom of God in his own signatory manifestations of the messianic era, so also the church is the vehicle which anticipates in the present age the final dominion of the Lord. The life-giving Spirit dwells in the church and leads the church in its main function of challenging the status quo to relieve the alienated so that all life can be kept open to the future.[41]

Several facets of the church's anticipation are important to note. First, in its anticipations of hope the church may not withdraw from the world into a privatized, otherworldly hope.[42] Second, the church encounters the world through the proclamation of the Word and makes known the path by which God's future promises are realized.[43] Third, because of the social and collective nature of the coming rule of God, the church must also reach out socially to the collective groups of marginalized who are not yet suited for the coming final kingdom. Fourth, on behalf of all these groups the church must act economically, politically, and religiously.[44]

---

[41] Moltmann, *Religion, Revolution, and the Future*, 104, 106; Moltmann, *Church in the Power of the Spirit*, 190-93, 206-7; *Theology of Hope*, 304-38.

[42] Moltmann speaks of the church as responsible to "seek" the Kingdom as the "construction workers" of the future. The hope of Christianity in history is a militant and earthly hope (Moltmann, "History and Hope," 383-84).

[43] In the proclamation of the Word people are made free to repent and free themselves from the world of oppression and experience life of the future (Moltmann, *Church in the Power of the Spirit*, 80). The church's mission is not just moralism (Moltmann, *Church in the Power of the Spirit*, 190).

[44] In the spheres of economics and politics Moltmann advocates the church's involvement in the cause of *power* (the just use of force), but not violence (the unjust use of force). Power should be exercised according to law (Moltmann, *The Way of Jesus Christ*, 129-31; cf. *Creating a Just Future* [Philadelphia: Trinity Press International, 1989], 44-45). Hope is an act of perseverance (Moltmann, "Politics and the Practice of Hope," 291). The distinction between violence and nonviolence is not as well defined in some of Moltmann's early writings. For example, in *Religion, Revolution, and the Future*, 143, Moltmann calls the problem of violence and nonviolence illusory, and says that the only real question is the use of justified or unjustified force.

Economically, Moltmann calls the church to an ethic of *Symbiosis*.[45] Politically the church is to seek human rights.[46] Religiously, the church must engage in dialogue with other world religions.[47] Fifth, the universal nature of God's coming Kingdom means that the church must in hope demonstrate restorative care for the earth and all its creatures.[48] As the church fulfills its messianic mission through these anticipatory prefigurations, then God and his kingdom are present, because God's future has taken control over the present.[49]

According to Moltmann the church has failed in this mission to anticipate the Kingdom because early on it lost its courage and its identity.[50] Beginning with the transformation of the earthly to a heavenly hope begun in its contact with Hellenism and then in the face of the mighty Roman Empire the church gave up its horizontal mandate. Rather than call the state to account politically and economically, the church capitulated and settled in. Theologically the church's resolve was also weakened in the controversy with Marcion, who in radical pursuit of the apocalyptic *Novum* of the New Testament went too far and denied the Old Testament entirely. His condemnation served to distance the church further from its true apocalyptic roots.[51] The compromise was exacerbated when Christianity conquered the state through the conversion of Constantine. This allowed the Kingdom of God to be identified with the church as the *pax Christi* was obtained through the *pax Romana*. Christianity became institutionalized on the same order as the state and thereafter sought and used

---

[45] "Symbiosis" in economics means interdependence. The church must call and influence economic systems to resist trends which separate and divide groups. All the earth's people must have a chance of survival through the just distribution of social justice (Moltmann, *Church in the Power of the Spirit*, 168-79).

[46] Ibid., 176-82.

[47] See ibid., 150-64, for his understanding of how this dialogue ought to be engaged.

[48] This is a prominent theme in *The Way of Jesus Christ*, 270-74; 305-13.

[49] Moltmann, "History and Hope," 376; *Church in the Power of the Spirit*, 190.

[50] This is a prominent theme in Moltmann's writings. See for examples Moltmann, *Church in the Power of the Spirit*, 135-36; *The Way of Jesus Christ*, 29-37, 135; *Religion, Revolution and the Future*, 13-15, 120; and "History and Hope," 379.

[51] Moltmann, *Religion, Revolution and the Future*, 13-15.

power for its own earthly benefit and not the Kingdom's. Triumphalism ensued and with it Christian anti-Semitism.[52]

Though Moltmann's account of the early church's apostasy is not the usual route taken by most (the delay of the Parousia),[53] his explanation still struggles for credibility in light of the phenomenon of the New Testament. That is, how likely is it that an early church that was not politically driven, and that even appears at times to be politically passive (e.g., Rom. 13:1–8), would produce documents portraying their beloved leader as something other than they? If Jesus was as "horizontally" (i.e., politically) driven, as Moltmann indicates, and if the Gospels are an accurate record of this fact, we must not forget who it is that gave us the Gospels. As we shall see later, Moltmann is forced here to grapple with the same paradox as all political and liberation theologies. Like these others, he can find easy justification for a "horizontal" theology in the proclamation of the Old Testament prophets and Jesus, but he must admit the paradox of an early church that was not oriented this way. The fact that the early Christians claimed to have been instructed specifically about the Kingdom by the resurrected Jesus (Acts 1:3) casts doubt on the hypothesis of Moltmann and political theologies in general. Instead of sloughing off the early church as apostate

---

[52] Moltmann (Church in the Power of the Spirit, 136) cites the fourth Lateran Council's passage of anti-Jewish measures (in 1215) that superseded those of the pagan state under the emperors Justinian and Theodosius. Anti-Semitism reached its zenith under the church/state league of the Third Reich and the "final solution" of the Holocaust (Moltmann, The Way of Jesus Christ, 31).

[53] Against Moltmann many of the major theologians of Latin American liberation theology see the delayed hopes of the imminent end as responsible for the early church's divergence from Jesus. See, for example, Juan Luis Segundo, The Historical Jesus of the Synoptics, trans. John Drury (Maryknoll, N.Y.: Orbis, 1985), 182-88; and George V. Pixley, God's Kingdom: A Guide to Biblical Study, trans. Donald D. Walsh (Maryknoll, N.Y.: Orbis, 1981), 89. Moltmann also does not see the Gospels primarily as creative projections of the early Christians (Moltmann, The Way of Jesus Christ, 137). The whole discussion of the near expectation (Nah-erwartung) of the Parousia critical to the "delay of the Parousia" theory has been challenged as misrepresenting much of the biblical material concerning the parables, the role of Satan, the delay of Judgment, the mission of seeking the lost, and so on, which all suggest that Jesus did not expect an immediately imminent Kingdom. See Herman Ridderbos, The Coming of the Kingdom, trans. H. de Jongste, ed. Raymond O. Zorn (Philadelphia: Presbyterian and Reformed, 1962), 444-55; and C. E. B. Cranfield, "Thoughts on New Testament Eschatology," ScotJT 35 (1982): 497-512.

from the pure message of Jesus, perhaps it is the supposed politically aggressive notions of Jesus that need another look.

All the same, Jürgen Moltmann's concern to write a theology that would be "daring, dialogical and experimental" through its eschatological orientation and its call to Christian praxis has its strengths. Certainly welcome to the subject of Kingdom ethics is the repudiation of a hope that retreats from the world around it into the sphere of the individual or the otherworldly. This is the advantage of political theologies in general, which serve as reminders to all Christians that the future coming Kingdom does "cast its shadow" in our midst and establishes New Testament Christianity in the pursuit of justice and care for the poor. Of course Moltmann's emphasis on the collective and social side of the Kingdom's praxis in these areas often draws the charge of neglecting the individual and personal aspect of the Kingdom's salvation.[54] Some imbalance on this count is to be expected given Moltmann's context within individualized and otherworldly religion of postwar Germany, but he still appears to give only the barest lip service to the need of an individual, personal relationship to the King as the source of power to enact justice and care for the disenfranchised. On this issue Moltmann can sound very much like his Social Gospel cousin, Walter Rauschenbusch. Like Moltmann, Rauschenbusch refused to just "decorate the inside of the prison" through good works.[55]

THE KINGDOM AND ISRAEL

The messianic dimensions from which Moltmann fashions his concept of the Kingdom draw him inevitably into discussion with those whose most significant contribution to the world was the Messiah—the people

---

[54] For Moltmann's critics here, see Capps, *Time Invades the Cathedral*, 115-116, 130.

[55] Moltmann, *Religion, Revolution, and the Future*, 105-6, cites *Christianity and the Social Crisis*, 47-48, where Rauschenbusch says, "No comprehension of Jesus is even approximately true which fails to understand that the heart of his heart was religion. No man is a follower of Jesus in the full sense who has not through him entered into the same life with God. But on the other hand no man shares his life with God whose religion does not flow out, naturally and without effort into all relations of his life and reconstructs everything that it touches. Whoever uncouples the religious and the social life has not understood Jesus."

of Israel. In *The Way of Jesus Christ* Moltmann engages in a lengthy discussion of his perception of the current Jewish-Christian dialogue.[56] In this context he notes that a wrong-headed antichiliastic path was followed by Christians in the fourth century that, led by Augustine and Tyconius, squeezed the Jews from their own hope. In its antichiliasm and institutional triumphalism the church saw itself as taking over the Old Testament promises to the nation of Israel and applying them in spiritual or heavenly terms. Moltmann resists these developments at all points. In light of his study of messianic categories from the Old Testament, he sides with the Jews in their rejection of a Christianity that claims redemption without Israel's future or a future for the earth *in history*.[57] In the New Testament (Rom. 11:29) Moltmann is equally adamant that it is wrong to join Israel and the church. "Israel's promises remain Israel's promises. They have not been transferred to the Church."[58]

It is a strength of Moltmann's view of the Kingdom that he expends great energy to place the historical Jesus firmly within the messianic categories of his day. The intention to develop "christology out of the Jewish contours of the messianic promise" situates Moltmann's Jesus and his Kingdom message squarely on the Old Testament.[59] For Moltmann Jesus comes forward as Israel's Messiah proclaiming the Kingdom from the horizontal and vertical categories his hearers would have understood as political, social, and spiritual.[60] Moreover, the chiliastic hopes of Jews and the early church are given important exposure in Moltmann's critique of Christian

---

[56] Moltmann, *The Way of Jesus Christ*, 8, 12, 28-37. See also *Church in the Power of the Spirit*, 148-49. Moltmann's own efforts in Jewish-Christian dialogue are the subject of his *Jewish Monotheism and Christian Trinitarian Theology* (Philadelphia: Fortress, 1981) and represent conversation with his friend the Jewish theologian Pinchas Lapide.

[57] In response to Martin Buber who wishes to relegate the messianic Kingdom to an "absolute future" beyond history, Moltmann argues such an ethereal hope cannot engender prefiguring anticipations of itself in this world (Moltmann, *The Way of Jesus Christ*, 12).

[58] Moltmann, *The Way of Jesus Christ*, 35; *Church in the Power of the Spirit*, 148.

[59] Moltmann, *The Way of Jesus Christ*, 74.

[60] The historical conclusion is obvious, Moltmann says, "that Jesus must have come forward as Israel's messiah, that the title on the cross is correct, and that the Christian church is the community of the disciples of Israel's crucified messiah" (Moltmann, *The Way of Jesus Christ*, 141).

triumphalism and anti-Semitism. A feature of the early church too often neglected by much post-Reformation eschatology is the earliest Christian chiliasm. Many important fathers of the first three centuries adhered to this view of a messianic interregnum on earth before the eternal state.[61] There is also some merit to Moltmann's contention that early Christian chiliasm was initially questioned because of its abusers and not its users.[62]

THE KINGDOM AND TIME

Central to comprehending the relationship of the Kingdom of God to time and history is Moltmann's understanding of the traditions of Parousia

---

[61] While this is not the place for a complete investigation of early Christian millennialism, a couple of issues do seem to be clearly established on the subject. (1) The millennialism of the New Testament (Rev. 20) is fully in line with the Jewish beliefs of the first century (Str-B, 3:823-827; J. W. Bailey, "The Temporary Messianic Reign in the Literature of Early Judaism," *JBL* 53 [1934]: 170-87). (2) The majority of church fathers of the first three centuries were chiliasts, including Papias, Irenaeus, Lactantius, Justin Martyr, and Tertullian. See Hans Bietenhard, "The Millennial Hope in the Early Church," *ScotJT* 6 (March 1953): 12-30; Georg Günter Blum, "Chiliasmus II: Alte Kirche," *TRE*, 7:729-33; Norman Cohn, "Medieval Millenarism: Its Bearing on the Comparative Study of Millenarian Movements," in *Millennial Dreams In Action: Essays in Comparative Study*, ed. Sylvia L. Thrupp (The Hague: Mouton, 1962), 33; Norman L. Geisler, "A Premillennial View of Law and Government," *BS* 142 (July-Sept., 1985): 250-52; D. H. Kromminga, *The Millennium in the Church* (Grand Rapids: Eerdmans, 1945), 29-99; Bernard McGinn, *The Calabrian Abbott*, 59-63; Jean Daniélou, *The Development of Christian Doctrine Before the Council of Nicea*, vol. 1, *The Theology of Jewish Christianity*, trans. and ed. John A. Baker (London: Darton, Longman and Todd, 1964), 377-404.

[62] The church's struggle against Montanism hurt the chiliast cause because millennialism was a feature of Montanism (see Bietenhard, "The Millennial Hope in the Early Church," 17). In the East chiliasm became an issue of hermeneutics when Origen waged war on millennialism on the basis of its fleshly literalism (Bietenhard, "The Millennial Hope in the Early Church," 20-21). In the West, Augustine, who once embraced the idea of a millennial Sabbath rest before the end of history, finally rejected it because of the wild exaggerations and crude depictions of the chiliast's millennium (*Civitate Dei*, 20.7, Eng. ed., Loeb, *City of God*, 6: 285). The idea of the chiliast's *usus* perishing with its *abusus* has also been noted by several nineteenth-century Lutherans that Moltmann cites (Moltmann, *Church in the Power of the Spirit*, 379 n. 14). F. Delitzsch, J. C. K. von Hofmann, and C. C. Luthardt all noted that the early church's rejection of the "chiliasmus crassus" but not the "chiliasmus subtilis." Historically, however, the strong rejection of the former also ended up in damaging the latter (cf. Geisler, "Premillennial View of Law and Government," 251).

and aeon.[63] Whereas the New Testament church (and almost everyone since then except existentialists) had understood the Parousia of Christ to be a temporal expectation within the "general flow of time," Moltmann works with the meaning of the word directly to go beyond a time-conditioned understanding. Translated literally *parousia* means "coming" or "presence"[64] so that when applied to the future of Christ it only speaks in broad categories about the coming presence of Christ, that is, the full identity of God and his Kingdom.[65] About this coming presence which Moltmann calls the "eschatological moment" we can really know very little except what is revealed in the present Kingdom anticipations of the Holy Spirit in our midst.[66] We can know that the Parousia does mark the end of history and the beginning of the "Kingdom that has no end." It is the fulfillment of the whole history of Christ, the fulfillment of the promises

---

[63] Moltmann's understanding of temporal categories also takes place in terms of the differences between *Futurum* and *Zukunft*. See Moltmann's *The Future of Creation*, 29-31, and especially "Verschränkte Zeiten der Geschichte: Notwendige Differenzierungen und Begrenzungen des Geschichtsbegriffs," *EvT* 44 (1984): 213-27. See also Randall E. Otto's discussion of Moltmann's eschatology: "The Eschatological Nature of Moltmann's Theology," *WestTJ* 54 (1992): 115-33; and *The God of Hope: The Trinitarian Vision of Jürgen Moltmann* (Lanham, Md.: University Press of America, 1991), chaps. 2 and 3. Any discussion on Moltmann's understanding of time is necessarily contingent upon his forthcoming treatise on eschatology per se (Moltmann, *The Way of Jesus Christ*, 321). Clearly there will have to be more said about the time of the Kingdom of God where Moltmann is concerned.

[64] Albrecht Oepke, *parousia*, *TDNT*, 5:863, supports Moltmann's lexical conclusions (Moltmann, *The Way of Jesus Christ*, 379, n. 10). For the biblical writers, temporalized and detailed expressions of the "coming Son of Man" were literary tools which served to provoke people's memory of the Christ's history, the experience of his presence in the Spirit, and their understanding of world history (Moltmann, *Church in the Power of the Spirit*, 131).

[65] See Moltmann, *The Way of Jesus Christ*, 317-18. Determinative for Moltmann of the interplay of Christ's presence and coming is the paradigmatic description of God in Revelation 1:4 as being the One "who was, who is, and who is to come" (Moltmann, "Verschränkte Zeiten der Geschichte," 221).

[66] Moltmann, *Church in the Power of the Spirit*, 131. The "eschatological moment" cannot be dogmatized (Moltmann, "Verschränkte Zeiten der Geschichte," 223), and our vision of what the presence of God will be like when it enters time is bound by our own captivity to the process of growth and decay in the Kingdom's present anticipations. The coming God impregnates the present through the church's realization of its future freedom through its own historical "anticipations" (Moltmann, *The Experiment Hope*, 54ff.)

of redemption to Israel, the transition from the Spirit's Kingdom to the Kingdom of glory, and the occasion when this unredeemed world is created anew.[67] Just the opposite of the "primordial moment" when God "restricted himself" in the act of creation, the eschatological moment means the "derestricting" of God and the manifestation of his glory so that in the transfigured creation he may be all in all. "The created spaces will be dissolved and 'the space of creation' passes away. Heaven and earth find their final, transfigured form in God's unrestricted omnipresence itself."[68]

The new time in which the fully identified and present Kingdom will function is eternity. Here Moltmann takes up the patristic term "aeon" to speak of what he calls a "relative eternity" fit for created beings. Eternity in this sense is not the absolute eternity of God but a participation of sorts in his essential eternity. Its meaning is not found primarily in the notion of life of endless time as in "everlasting life" but in a divine quality of life: life in depth over life in length.[69] This is the life that has begun now for those who have been set free by the Son, who have received the eschatological gift of the Spirit, and who have ventured into the openness of the future for which they were made. The "aeonic" concept of time therefore does not concern an historical demarcation as to when "this age" becomes "the age to come." Rather, since the resurrection the two ages are mixing through Christian anticipatory actions of the Kingdom in this present closed-to-the-future world, like the overlapping and blending of the edges of two conjoining clouds.[70] Time, in Moltmann's understanding, is ultimately not linear, but is rather this complex interplay of the historical process and the

---

[67] The transformation of the old earth into the newly created one is only vaguely alluded to by Moltmann. From the idea of the "Day of the Lord" he speaks of time as the dissipated darkness of night as it is permeated by the first rays of dawn. In the Holy Spirit's anticipations through Jesus and his church the dawn of the eternal day has already broken, and "this transitory time does not end in the night of the eclipse of God. There is no 'end of the world' in which the world will go down into nothingness. What is to come is a 'day' without any evening, the eternal light, the day of the new creation" (Moltmann, *The Way of Jesus Christ*, 327).

[68] Ibid., 329.

[69] Ibid., 330-31.

[70] Moltmann, *Church in the Power of the Spirit*, 192.

constant in-breakings of the eternal, that is, the "aeonic," through the obedient acts of the church.[71]

The subject of the Kingdom's timing is an especially intriguing and at the same time confusing part of Moltmann's scheme. Positively, we may say that Moltmann's advancement of the "aeonic" concept of time does put the Kingdom as a present reality in appropriate conjunction to "eternal life" *(aiōnios zōē)* so common in the Johannine corpus.[72] Johannine scholars have long put forth the notion of "eternal" life speaking more to a kind or quality of life (life appropriate to the age to come) rather than to life of endless duration, as in a linear concept of time.[73] In light of John, for whom eternal life is the future quality of life that may be experienced in the present, Moltmann's aeonic understanding of the Kingdom is justified.

What remains confusing, however, in Moltmann is his need to detemporalize so much of the New Testament, particularly the Parousia event,[74] and the subsequent explanation given about the nature of the interplay between processive history and the in-breaking of aeonic time of the Kingdom. Several points may be made. First, though Moltmann says that neither the temporalization nor the eternalization of the Parousia expectation meets the eschatological orientation of early Christian faith adequately, he is vulnerable to the charge that one cannot simply excise so

---

[71] *"Linear time* only grasps the simple course of events. But the course of events stands in a network of correlations and multiple effects; one thus must develop *time networks* in which linear and cyclical concepts of time can be combined" (Moltmann, "Verschränkte Zeiten der Geschichte," 217 [author's translation]).

[72] Many have noted the correlation of the Kingdom of God to eternal life in John. See, for example, R. H. Charles, *Eschatology* (New York: Schocken, 1963), 368; C. K. Barrett, *The Gospel According to St. John,* 2d ed. (Philadelphia: Westminster, 1978), 214-15; and U. E. Simon, "Eternal Life in the Fourth Gospel," in *Studies in the Fourth Gospel,* ed. F. L. Cross (London: A. R. Mowbray, 1957), 97-98.

[73] Translating *aiōnios zōē* as "everlasting life" slants the meaning unwarrantedly towards linear modes of time. "Eternal life" offers better potential for apprehending the nuances of aeonic time. See the conclusions of Richard W. Thomas, "The Meaning of the Terms 'Life' and 'Death' in the Fourth Gospel and in Paul," *ScotJT* 21 (1968): 204; C. H. Dodd, *The Interpretation of the Fourth Gospel* (Cambridge: Cambridge University Press, 1954), 149; David Edward Aune, *The Cultic Setting of Realized Eschatology in Early Christianity,* Supplements to Novum Testamentum 28 (Leiden: E. J. Brill, 1972), 105; and Rudolf Schnackenburg, *The Gospel According to St. John* (New York: Seabury, 1980), 1:389.

[74] See Moltmann, *The Way of Jesus Christ,* 316-17.

much of New Testament temporality without violating the Kingdom he wishes to establish. In the New Testament the Kingdom is preached as the fulfillment of God's design for history ("The time is fulfilled, and the kingdom of God is at hand," Mark 1:15, cf. also Matt. 17:10; 24:6; Luke 24:44; Rev. 1:1), and it is preached as the further revelation of the God who has bound himself to history (i.e., time) to reassert his right to be glorified in all his creation (Matt. 22:31, 32 speaks of the living God who has bound himself to the historical agreement with Abraham).[75] For one so intent on the future of the earth in history, Moltmann's backtracking from temporalization of the Kingdom at this point seems incongruous.

Second, the confusing combination of linear and nonlinear concepts of time raises questions for his understanding of the mission of the church in this age. If the Day of the Lord has already dawned in the resurrected life of the new aeon and these dawning rays of light are the same eternal light which never dims but ever increases into the eternal Kingdom of God,[76] how does the church escape from the triumphalism Moltmann so vehemently repudiates? That is, as the church continually anticipates in economic and political deeds the coming Kingdom and thereby the Kingdom's future becomes increasingly manifested in the present, does not the church become eventual victor, with the Kingdom of God reigning over politics and economics and coercing behavior in its subjects through law?[77]

Third, the interplay between the process of history and aeonic time obfuscates Moltmann's terminologic distinction between the Kingdom of Christ and the Kingdom of God. On one level Moltmann is very careful to separate the messianic Kingdom of Christ (which is prophetic, earthly, and historical) from the Kingdom of God (which is apocalyptic and universal): "The Messianic Kingdom will be set up in 'the last days' of this aeon, but the Kingdom of God will be established in the eternity of an aeon that is new."[78] On another level this very clear demarcation becomes

---

[75] Ridderbos, *Coming of the Kingdom,* 44-47.

[76] Moltmann, *The Way of Jesus Christ,* 327.

[77] Dale Vree has noted the postmillennial rhetoric occasionally coming from Moltmann, but finally, and somewhat tentatively, classifies Moltmann's views as more premillennial (Dale Vree, *On Synthesizing Marxism and Christianity* [New York: John Wiley, 1976], 37-44).

[78] Moltmann, *The Way of Jesus Christ,* 21.

blurred when Moltmann says that Christ will set up his Kingdom and reign in history (the last days of this aeon), but in the "eschatological moment" of his Parousia the Christ ends time and history on the apocalyptic order of the Kingdom of God.[79]

Further blurring occurs when Moltmann brings the notion of God's reign and lordship into conjunction with that of Christ. Following Buber (*Königtum Gottes* [1936]), Moltmann believes the Kingdom of God began historically when God exercised his lordship over the nomadic tribes of Israel.[80] But when the New Testament affirms Christ's *present* lordship of all (Acts 2:36; Eph. 1:22), Moltmann has a hard time (1) separating Christ's reign from God's and (2) justifying a future messianic reign which culminates in the final Kingdom of God (1 Cor. 15:28). He retreats to saying the two New Testament strata of the Christ who is yet to reign in his Kingdom and subject all things under his feet and then give the Kingdom to the Father (1 Cor. 15:23–24, 28), and the Christ who already rules as the Cosmic Lord (Ephesians and Colossians), are unharmonizable in their contradictory representations of the presence of the Kingdom of God.[81] In lieu of the problem being "unharmonizable," Moltmann's dilemma points to the need to further investigate the initial premise that simply equated the language of Lord/lordship to the language of King/kingship/Kingdom in the New Testament. In other words, the New Testament affirms Christ as present Lord, but this may not mean he is presently the *reigning* King of his Kingdom as well.[82]

---

[79] Ibid., 317-18.

[80] Moltmann, *Theology of Hope*, 216. On this Moltmann is in great company, since Dalman's *The Words of Jesus* set the agenda for much subsequent scholarship in saying the Kingdom of God language of the Bible referred to the kingly activity of God and not a spatio-temporal realm, despite the lexical fact that *malkuth* originally was used only in reference to a "concrete sphere of power" and that Yahweh is never called "king" prior to the monarchy (Gerhard von Rad, *basileus*, *TDNT*, 1:570).

[81] Moltmann, *The Way of Jesus Christ*, 285-86.

[82] The negative possibilities here are highlighted by the inability of Lord/lording language to account for the dearth of King/reigning language for the present status of the risen Christ in the New Testament, and by the fact that Christ as King is not a feature of the earliest Christian art. Three observations deserve consideration when attempting to substitute "Lord" for "King" in the New Testament. (1) As I have already noted elsewhere, there is no political advantage in the switch; "Lord Jesus" is just as offensive to the Roman cult as "King Jesus," so courage is not the

Fourth, when Moltmann maintains that the promises to Israel and the earth are fulfilled in the "eschatological moment" of the universal Kingdom of God, that is, the nontemporal Parousia,[83] in what sense does their fulfillment correlate to the Old Testament Messianic hope which was earthly and historical? Moltmann appears to exhibit the same "confusing lack of system" typical of the way the Old Testament hope sometimes expressed the interface of the coming messianic Kingdom and the eternal state. For example, in Isaiah 65:17 and 66:22, along with Jeremiah 33:14–16, the earthly messianic kingdom is given some rather unearthly quality of eternal duration.[84] The New Testament sheds light on the consummation of the age with the mention of the burning of the elements by fire (2 Pet. 3), but Moltmann unfortunately offers no comment at this point and thereby remains to us as enigmatic as the prophets.[85]

With a more complete statement on eschatology still in the works, at this point Moltmann's concept of the Kingdom of God appears to defy easy labeling by usual categories. On one hand the messianic dimensions of his Kingdom theology, the strong statements of a historical redemption

---

issue. (2) "King" was a title the Romans granted to their vassal rulers as in Herod's case (Josephus, *Jewish Wars* 1.14.1 §284-285 [Eng. ed., Loeb, *Jewish Wars* 2:105]). It was not inherently offensive to have other kings in the empire. (3) The early church does return the title of King to Christ at the Second Advent (Rev. 19:11ff.) when he forcibly puts down his enemies. I. Howard Marshall has noted a difference in the New Testament use of the two concepts of king and lord that may indicate they are not simply equated and that Jesus may be Lord and King, but not presently reigning in his kingship: "Lord tends to have a passive meaning; it signifies someone who is to be obeyed and treated with honor and it perhaps does not bring out sufficiently the active element of the exercise of kingship and dominion and indeed of granting salvation" (*Jesus the Saviour* [Downers Grove, Ill.: InterVarsity Press, 1990], 209). The possibility seems open that, contra Moltmann, Christ may be presently the Lord but not presently reigning.

[83] "Christ's parousia therefore does not merely unveil the salvific meaning of Christ's death. It also, and much more, brings the *fulfillment* of the whole history of Christ, with all that it promises; for it is only with Christ's parousia that the 'kingdom that shall have no end' begins. It is only in Christ's parousia that 'all tears will be wiped away.' It is only in the parousia that Israel will be redeemed, and this 'unredeemed world' created anew" (Moltmann, *The Way of Jesus Christ*, 318).

[84] Sigmund Mowinckel, *He That Cometh* (New York: Abingdon, 1954), 268. On this phenomenon in the prophets see also Dirk H. Odendaal, *The Eschatological Expectation of Isaiah 40-66 with Special Reference to Israel and the Nations* (Philadelphia: Presbyterian and Reformed, 1970), 126.

[85] Moltmann may put 2 Peter 3 together with all the other apocalyptic images of the New Testament as serving as a literary tool to stir the memory of the early Christians.

of Israel and the earth, the challenge brought to the spiritualizing herme-neutic of Augustine, and the challenge to the historically antichiliastic path of the church, all give appeal to the millennialists in his audience. On the other hand, the broad detemporalized strokes with which he paints that endtime dispensation and the Kingdom's increased presence in the Church's mission give appeal to nonmillennial interpretations. This leaves Moltmann's Kingdom, I believe, initially attractive and interesting to many but finally really satisfying to few. This conclusion may be considered Moltmann's great strength in challenging us to new lines of thinking, but it may also be a greater weakness in simply necessitating more unnatural biblical exegesis or outright resignation towards supposedly unharmonizable material in the Scriptures.

CHAPTER SEVEN

The Kingdom of God
in Latin American Liberation Theology

The Kingdom theme within Latin American liberation theology (henceforth liberation theology) involves a change in theological climate from that of Moltmann. Whereas Moltmann tended to discuss the Kingdom in terms of his overall eschatologically centered program, the Kingdom in liberation theology finds its place more in the context of Christology.[1] Consequently, it is from the major christological writings of liberation theologians that our consideration of the Kingdom of God will come.[2]

---

[1] See Roger Haight, *An Alternate Vision: An Interpretation of Theology* (Mahwah, N.J.: Paulist Press, 1985), 107, for the rationale of this phenomenon. Arthur F. McGovern also notes the connection between the Kingdom and Christology in liberation theology because of liberation theology's concern for the poor. Jesus' message of the Kingdom was directed to the poor (Arthur F. McGovern, *Liberation Theology and Its Critics: Toward An Assessment* [Maryknoll, N.Y.: Orbis, 1989], 76).

[2] For example, Leonardo Boff, *Jesus Christ Liberator,* trans. Patrick Hughes (Maryknoll, N.Y.: Orbis, 1978); Boff, "Salvation in Jesus Christ and the Process of Liberation," *Concilium* 96 (1974): 78-91; Jon Sobrino, *Christology at the Crossroads,* trans. John Drury (Maryknoll, N.Y.: Orbis, 1978); Sobrino, "La centralidad del 'Reino de Dios' en la teología de la liberación," *Revista Latinamericana de Teología* (San Salvador) (September-December 1986): 248-65; and Juan Luis Segundo, *Jesus of Nazareth Yesterday and Today,* vol. 2, *The Historical Jesus of the Synoptics,* trans. John Drury (Maryknoll, N.Y.: Orbis, 1985). Other important works for the Kingdom of God in Latin American Liberation Theology include Gustavo Gutiérrez, *A Theology of Liberation,* trans. Caridad Inda and John Eagleson (Maryknoll, N.Y.: Orbis, 1973); George V. Pixley, *God's Kingdom: A Guide to Biblical Study,* trans. Donald D. Walsh (Maryknoll, N.Y.: Orbis, 1981); and Pixley, "The Key: The Kingdom of God," in Claus Bussmann, *Who Do You Say? Jesus Christ in Latin American Theology,* trans. Robert R. Barr (Maryknoll, N.Y.: Orbis, 1985).

ANTECEDENTS OF LATIN AMERICAN LIBERATION THEOLOGY

To understand how the Kingdom of God functions within liberation theology it is important to be familiar with two contextual moorings of liberation theology: Roman Catholicism and European political theology.

Origins and Dialogue within Roman Catholicism

The Latin American Bishops Conference held at Medellín, Columbia, in 1968 (CELAM II) was the occasion that marked the birth of liberation theology.[3] Responding to the pronouncements of the recently concluded Second Vatican Council (1962–1965), which only slightly softened the traditional equation of the church and the Kingdom in Roman theology, the Latin American bishops agitated for real involvement of the church in the plight of the oppressed masses in their parishes. In their opinion, the traditional equation of church and Kingdom resulted in a triumphalism that meant that while the world needed a serving church, it had received primarily a reigning one.[4] At the conference the biblico-theological concept of liberation was given a sociopolitical sense: God acted in history to rescue people from every form of bondage—spiritual, social, economic, and political. The church as the people of God had a responsibility to support the oppressed classes in resisting the economic dependence of the Third World on the First and Second Worlds and in denouncing the "institutional violence" of unjust economic systems.[5]

---

[3] For a history of the important events and people associated with liberation theology, see Deane William Ferm, *Third World Liberation Theologies: An Introductory Survey* (Maryknoll, N.Y.: Orbis, 1986); McGovern, *Liberation Theology and Its Critics*, 1–19; Phillip Berryman, *Liberation Theology* (Philadelphia: Temple University Press, 1987); Edward L. Cleary, *Crisis and Change: The Church in Latin America Today* (Maryknoll, N.Y.: Orbis, 1985); and Leonardo Boff and Clodovis Boff, *Introducing Liberation Theology*, trans. Paul Burns (Maryknoll, N.Y.: Orbis, 1986).

[4] John C. Haughey, "Church and Kingdom: Ecclesiology in the Light of Eschatology," *TS* 29 (1968): 85. The traditional Catholic approach to the Kingdom in terms of ecclesiology had also resulted in little discussion in the magisterium of the Kingdom's praxis. Shortly after Vatican II, Catholic theologian Avery Dulles noted that the relationship between ecclesiology and eschatology in Roman Catholic teaching "occupied an extremely restricted place . . . none at all in scholarly theology, at least in the manuals" ("The Church as Eschatological Community," in *The Eschaton: A Community of Love*, ed. Joseph Papin [Villanova, Pa.: Villanova University Press, 1971], 69).

[5] See the documents of CELAM II in Joséph Gremillion, ed., *The Gospel of Justice and Peace* (Maryknoll, N.Y.: Orbis, 1976), especially "Peace," nos. 3, 9, 16-19, and "Poverty of the Church," no. 7.

In 1979 the Latin American Bishops Conference convened in Puebla, Mexico, (CELAM III) amid great fear of a papal backlash against the liberation agenda begun in Medellín. Liberation theologians were conspicuously uninvited, and delegates were selected in hopes of clamping down on the liberation movement. The expected rebuff, however, did not happen on the scale anticipated, and in many commentators' opinions John Paul II's message at Puebla represented a careful toning down of some of the themes of earlier liberation theology rather than a repudiation of them. The final document itself was something of a compromise, allowing both the radical-progressives and the reactionary-conservatives to take something home.[6] Liberationists got a statement of "preferential option for the poor" and an encouragement of base communities, as well as discussion of "integral liberation" that included the political, spiritual, and economic realms of life.[7] Conservatives took heart in the pope's denial of a political Christ[8] and his denouncement of those who would empty the Kingdom of its spiritual content by equating its coming with "structural change and socio-political involvement."[9]

---

[6] See John Eagleson and Philip Scharper, eds., *Puebla and Beyond: Documents and Commentary*, trans. John Drury (Maryknoll, N.Y.: Orbis, 1979); Quentin L. Quade, ed., *The Pope and Revolution: John Paul II Confronts Liberation Theology* (Washington, D.C.: Ethics and Public Policy Center, 1982) and Hans-Jürgen Prien, ed., *Lateinamerika: Gesellschaft, Kirche, Theologie* (Göttingen: Vandenhoeck & Ruprecht, 1981).

[7] McGovern's account typifies the liberationists' reading of Puebla (McGovern, *Liberation Theology and Its Critics*, 14-15).

[8] The pope's opening address stated: "This conception of Christ as a political figure, a revolutionary, as the subversive from Nazareth, does not tally with the church's catechesis" ("Opening Address at Puebla," in *The Pope and Revolution*, ed. Quade, 54). For the conservative interpretation of Puebla, see Ronald H. Nash and Huberto Belli, *Beyond Liberation Theology* (Grand Rapids: Baker, 1992), 181-83. For a treatment of Puebla more sympathetic to traditional liberation themes, see *Born of the Poor: The Latin American Church since Medellín*, ed. Edward L. Cleary (Notre Dame, Ind.: University of Notre Dame Press, 1990). On the debate about liberation theology in general, see Rosino Gibellini, *The Liberation Theology Debate* (Maryknoll, N.Y.: Orbis, 1988), 43-60; and Reinhard Freiling, *Befreiungstheologien* (Göttingen: Vandenhoeck & Ruprecht, 1984), 14-17.

[9] This statement was consistent with Pope Paul VI's declaration in the 1975 Apostolic Exhortation *Evangelii Nuntiandi* subordinating economic and political oppression to spiritual oppression. Jesus' own evangelization, the pope said, consists of everything that frees oppressed man, "but is above all liberation from sin and the Evil One" (cited by Richard P. McBrien, *Catholicism* [Minneapolis: Winston, 1981], 1134). For the relevance of Puebla to the Kingdom in liberation theology see especially Prien, ed., *Lateinamerika: Gesellschaft, Kirche, Theologie*, vol. 2, *Der Streit um die Theologie der Befreiung*, 91-95.

The Vatican's most pointed response to liberation theology appeared five years after Puebla in the *Instruction on Certain Aspects of the Theology of Liberation* issued by the Congregation for the Doctrine of the Faith.[10] In it liberation theology was strongly criticized for its "uncritically borrowed Marxist ideology" (VII: 7, 8). This Marxist "theology of class" was accused of bringing forth a dangerous new hermeneutic that colors all reality in terms of the class struggle (X) and reduces the Bible to politics (X:5), so that sin becomes economic and worldly oppression and is only secondarily cosmic evil (IV:2). The *Instruction on Certain Aspects of Liberation Theology* is further critical of liberation theology for tending to identify the Kingdom of God and its growth with human liberation movements almost to the point of a self-redemption of man by means of the class struggle (IX:3).[11]

---

[10] The full text of the document is available in the appendix of Juan Luis Segundo's *Theology and the Church: A Response to Cardinal Ratzinger and a Warning to the Whole Church* (New York: Winston, 1985).

[11] Many of the points contained in the *Instruction* reiterate points made earlier in *Human Development and Christian Salvation*, a document of the International Theological Commission issued in 1976 (*International Theological Commission: Texts and Documents 1969-1985*, ed. Michael Sharkey [San Francisco: Ignatius, 1989], 145-62). This document rejects the tendency of liberation theology to efface the difference between world history and salvation history ("faith's praxis is not reducible to changing the conditions of human society" [148]). The church should remind its people that politics does not have ultimate value (160). Yahweh is the ultimate agent of change, not man (150, 154). True social change is only that which is preceded by interior conversion and justice (151). The New Testament is still "not primarily concerned with the social sphere and human togetherness" (152). The chief category of human liberation is a function of "being," not "having" (154). "Institutional sin" is a dubious concept since the Bible speaks of sin in the first instance of an explicit, personal decision that stems from human freedom (155). Human participation in transforming the world is an integral not an essential part of preaching the gospel (156). There is a harmony between the eschatological salvation and the human efforts to build a better world, but the church as a whole must act prophetically offering its critique of the social order (159).

Not long after the *Instruction on Certain Aspects of Liberation Theology* appeared, the Pontifical Biblical Commission also issued a document touching on certain aspects of liberation theology (Joseph A. Fitzmyer, *Scripture and Christology: A Statement of a Biblical Commission with a Commentary* [New York: Paulist, 1986], 14-16, 28-29; cf. also Colin Brown, "Scripture and Christology: A Protestant Look at the Work of the Pontifical Biblical Commission," in *Perspectives on Christology: Essays in Honor of Paul K. Jewett*, ed. Marguerite Shuster and Richard Muller [Grand Rapids: Zondervan, 1991], 62-65). The commission agreed with liberation theology in reiterating that salvation is not only a spiritual issue (28), but it was wary of the atheistic theoretical base of Marxist social analysis "falsifying the very nature of God, the correct interpretation of Christ, and in the long run even the understanding and comprehension of humanity itself" (29). The

Reeling from their strongest denunciation to date, some liberationists responded to the *Instruction* with conciliatory tones and some with antagonism.[12] Both groups gained renewed hope from the companion document that appeared eighteen months later, the *Instruction on Christian Freedom and Liberation*.[13] While not taking up liberation theology directly, the new *Instruction* still stressed true human freedom in terms of personal and spiritual issues over sociopolitical ones, but it did recognize liberation as an important issue in Christian theology and left application to local churches (n. 3). It affirmed base communities as a "treasure for the whole church" (n. 69) and in at least one place asserted that as a last resort the poor were justified in taking armed action against oppression (nn. 75, 79). To no one's great surprise this *Instruction* received high praise from prominent liberationists.[14]

---

commission cautioned the tendency of liberation Christologies to follow liberal Protestant models more inclined to separate the Christ of faith from the Jesus of history. As the Jesus of history is the supreme model for liberating praxis, the danger was that liberation theology would see Jesus only as a model and thereby reduce Christology to anthropology (29).

[12] See for example, the Boffs' conciliatory and positive tone toward the *Instruction* of 1984 in *Introduction to Liberation Theology*, 75-77. Less positive is Segundo's *Theology and the Church* and "Capitalism-Socialism: A Theological Crux," *Concilium* 96 (1974): 113-14, which charge the *Instruction* with retreating into Luther's two-kingdom doctrine so that the Kingdom is God's work alone and is only tangentially concerned with the kingdoms of humankind on earth. Luther had rejected the union of the Kingdom of God and the secular state. God's Kingdom was invisible and spiritual and not involved in politics. The proper sphere of the Kingdom was piety and preaching the gospel. Law was the realm of the secular kingdoms of man responsible for peace and punishing evil (Richard P. McBrien, *Catholicism* [Minneapolis: Winston, 1981], 1115). Freiling and Segundo both observe this movement toward Lutheranism as a trend of Roman Catholicism since Vatican II, seen particularly in the conciliar document *Man's Activity Throughout the World.* See especially the subsection "The Rightful Independence of Earthly Affairs" (in *The Documents of Vatican II*, ed. Walter M. Abbott [New York: America, 1966], 233-35; see Freiling, *Befreiungstheologien*, 16; and Segundo, "Capitalism-Socialism," 113-14).

[13] Congregation for the Doctrine of the Faith (Cardinal Ratzinger), *Instruction on Christian Freedom and Liberation* (Vatican City: Libreria Editrice Vaticana, 1986). This *Instruction* followed the *Instruction on Certain Aspects of the Theology of Liberation* by eighteen months, but it was intended to be in "organic relationship" with the former document. On this document see Gibellini, *Liberation Theology Debate*, 52; McGovern, *Liberation Theology and Its Critics*, 17-18; Belli and Nash, *Beyond Liberation Theology*, 48.

[14] See McGovern, *Liberation Theology and Its Critics*, 245, n. 42, for the positive reactions of Leonardo Boff, Gustavo Gutiérrez, Jon Sobrino, and Ignacio Ellacuría, recorded in *Latinamerica Press*, May 1, 1986.

Also consoling to the liberationists was the pope's letter to the Brazilian Bishops that same year (April 9, 1986) as the second *Instruction*.[15] The letter praised the bishops for their solidarity with the people and affirmed their development of a theology of liberation that would be faithful to church doctrine. As long as this is done, the pope said, "the theology of liberation is not only opportune, but useful and necessary." Accordingly, he called for a "new stage" in liberation theology that would unite with the social doctrine of the church.[16]

The encyclical *Sollicitudo Rei Socialis [Social Concerns]* of 1988 addressed several issues of the liberation debate in a way that was again capable of different interpretations.[17] Liberationists looked to the encyclical's endorsement of the socialist's caricature of runaway capitalism and its comments that harmonized with their own "moral equivalence" theories about the U.S.A. and the U.S.S.R. Conservatives saw the encyclical as further evidence of the Vatican trying to walk the tightrope between wanting to distance itself from the radicals but still retain a hearing for the Gospel in Marxist countries. In their mind the effort was fraught with inconsistencies, however, they could rally behind the perceived development the encyclical meant toward a new liberation theology that would be free of Marxist and socialist class analysis.[18]

---

[15] The letter is published in part in the *National Catholic Reporter*, May 9, 1986 (see McGovern, *Liberation Theology and Its Critics*, 245, n. 43).

[16] The two sides of the liberation debate give the pope's letter different slants. The liberationists see the letter as a ringing endorsement of their program, emphasizing the pope's description of liberation theology as "useful and necessary." They also note what the letter did not do by way of sanctioning any previous liberation theologian or writing. The "new stage" of liberation theology they interpret as referring to a development of Latin America's own theology. See McGovern, *Liberation Theology and Its Critics*, 18. The other side emphasizes the conditional qualification that *as long as* liberation theology was in accord with church doctrine it was "useful and necessary." They also see the call for a new stage as a call for a new direction to come eventually from the Vatican itself. See Belli and Nash, *Beyond Liberation Theology*, 177-78.

[17] The full text of the encyclical is reprinted in *Aspiring to Freedom: Commentaries on John Paul II's encyclical "Social Concerns,"* ed. Kenneth A. Myers (Grand Rapids: Eerdmans, 1988), 3-63.

[18] One of the pope's close associates confirmed the intention of *Sollicitudo Rei Socialis* to be the initial installment of a truly new liberation theology from the Vatican. Robert Suro cites Rocco Buttiglione to say of *Sollicitudo Rei Socialis*, "This encyclical offers a new Liberation Theology. . . . It is a new Liberation Theology that surpasses the limits of the old one that is so thoroughly grounded in the Latin American experience and it is a theology that knows Communists" (Robert Suro, "The Writing of an Encyclical," in *Aspiring to Freedom*, ed. Myers, 162-63). See Belli and Nash, *Beyond Liberation Theology*, 49-53.

That direction seemed confirmed in the advent of the encyclical *Centesimus Annus* in 1991. Issued in honor of the hundredth anniversary of *Rerum Novarum*, Pope Leo XIII's encyclical of 1891, *Centesimus Annus* was the strongest Vatican endorsement of capitalism in history.[19] Stunned with the rest of the world by the recent dismantling of the socialist governments of Eastern Europe and Nicaragua, *Centesimus Annus* was indeed a bitter pill for the socialist liberationists to swallow. Section 48 is most affrontive:

> Economic activity, especially the activity of a market economy, cannot be conducted in an institutional, juridical or political vacuum. On the contrary, it presupposes sure guarantees of individual freedom and private property as well as a stable currency and efficient public services. Hence the principal task of the state is to guarantee this security so that those who work and produce can enjoy the fruits of their labors and thus feel encouraged to work efficiently and honestly. The absence of stability, together with the corruption of public officials and the spread of improper sources of growing rich and of easy profits deriving from illegal or purely speculative activities constitutes one of the chief obstacles to development and to economic order.

Clearly the Roman Catholic Church's call for a "new stage" of liberation theology intends, in addition to true spiritual liberation, liberation from "coercive institutions, private or public, that stifle the lives and entrepreneurship of the poor while further impoverishing them and society."[20] It intends the preferential "option" for the poor to mean advocacy on behalf of the poor for their freedom as economic actors in a properly regulated market.[21] It also understands the need to recast dependency theory to include exploration of the role dependency on the state has played in perpetuating poverty.[22]

The Vatican's increasing retrenchment against the Marxist rhetoric prominent in the early days of liberation theology has paralleled a similar

---

[19] See the text of *Centesimus Annus* in *Origins*, CNS Documentary Series, May 16, 1991.

[20] Belli and Nash, *Beyond Liberation Theology*, 144.

[21] George Weigel, "The New, New Things: Pope John Paul II on Human Freedom," *American Purpose* (May-June 1991): 33; cited by Belli and Nash, *Beyond Liberation Theology*, 54.

[22] Belli and Nash, *Beyond Liberation Theology*, 144.

softening of that rhetoric by liberationists in the 1980s. Other forms of social analysis were also becoming viable options. In *We Drink from Our Own Wells: The Spiritual Journey of a People*, Gustavo Gutiérrez advocates a continuing critical analysis of poverty by the social sciences that would be open to review.[23] One recent investigation of poverty in Latin America by a Peruvian, Hernando de Soto, accounts for the impoverished situation in terms of moral and cultural values, rather than the dependency theory popularized in the 1970s brand of liberation theology.[24]

European Political Theologies

In 1965 and 1966 a confluence of several vibrant streams, including the response to Vatican II, the World Council of Churches' Geneva meetings (1966), Harvey Cox's *The Secular City*, Jürgen Moltmann's *Theology of Hope*, and various European Marxist/Christian dialogues all made talk of God suddenly a political issue.[25] United as a reaction to the earlier anthropocentric and humanistic theology which had overlooked the concrete situation of man, political theologies of both the Protestant and Catholic variety sought theological answers to the social and economic conditions of the world. In this quest European political theology espoused major themes which occurred later in liberation theology giving rise to the charge (largely by critics) that liberation theology is nothing more than the stepchild of Europe.[26]

[23] Gustavo Gutiérrez, *We Drink from Our Own Wells: The Spiritual Journey of a People*, trans. Matthew J. O'Connell (Maryknoll, N.Y.: Orbis, 1984).

[24] Hernando de Soto, *The Other Path: The Invisible Revolution in the Third World*, trans. June Abbott (New York: Harper and Row, 1989).

[25] The rise of European political theologies is chronicled by Alfredo Fierro, *The Militant Gospel: A Critical Introduction to Political Theologies*, trans. John Drury (Maryknoll, N.Y.: Orbis, 1977).

[26] Fierro notes the similar themes as (1) theology must be practical, (2) it must be public (as opposed to a privatized faith), (3) it must be critical (of institutions and ideologies), and (4) it should utilize politics in the mediating role of all (Fierro, *Militant Gospel*, 33). Those suggesting liberation theology is dependent on European political theology include Haight, *An Alternate Vision*, 296, n. 8; Alan Preston Neely, "Protestant Antecedents of Latin American Theology of Liberation" (Ph.D. diss., American University, 1977), 209-312; Robert C. Walton, "Jürgen Moltmann's Theology of Hope," in *Liberation Theology*, ed. Ronald H. Nash (Milford, Mich.: Mott Media, 1984), 143.

Though many within liberation theology deny the stepchild relationship with Europe,[27] a good case can be made that much of liberation theology, including its thoughts related to the Kingdom of God, has an antecedent in Europe. First, while liberation theologians are critical of the way Europe has failed to apply political theology to the masses,[28] this should not be taken to mean that at the deepest theoretical levels there is not approval, alliance, and even dependence on Europe. At these levels some liberation theologians even admit dependence.[29] Second, history itself seems to point to the originator and the imitator. For example, it is well known that the leading liberation theologians were educated in Europe. Moreover, the European works appeared first, and the Latin American writers quote the European, not vice versa.

Several features of European political theology have similar emphasis on the Kingdom of God as it appears in liberation theology. First, in reaction to the privatized Kingdom of personal faith that came from existential exegesis, the Kingdom of God is to be given a collective and social understanding.[30] Second, the emphasis that the future eschatological Kingdom has impact in the present dimension through the praxis of the faith of the church is also a feature common to liberation and political

---

[27] Ferm, *Third World Liberation Theologies*, 23, denies the relationship, as does Claude Geffre, "A Prophetic Theology," *Concilium* 96 (1974): 7-16, and Gutiérrez, *Theology of Liberation*, 225. In their *Introduction to Liberation Theology*, 75-77, Clodovis and Leonardo Boff do not allude to any European movements in their summary of the antecedents to liberation theology.

[28] Jon Sobrino (cited by Ferm, *Third World Liberation Theologies*, 43) and Enrique Dussel (cited by Michael L. Cook, "Jesus from the Other Side: Christology in Latin America," *TS* 44, no. 2 [June 1983]: 260, n. 5, 6) wish to be considered separate from European theology because of its inherent center in the oppressing First World and because in Europe political theology is only an academic and intraecclesial activity, not a mass movement.

[29] José Bonino claims dependence on Moltmann (Bonino, *Doing Theology in a Revolutionary Situation* [Philadelphia: Fortress, 1975], 144). Gutiérrez refers to Moltmann's theology as "undoubtedly one of the most important in contemporary theology" (Gutiérrez, *Theology of Liberation*, 218). Hugo Assmann, for all his criticism of Moltmann, is still obviously indebted to him. See Hugo Assmann, *Theology for A Nomad Church* (Maryknoll, N.Y.: Orbis, 1976), 94. Neely, "Protestant Antecedents," 209-45, has convincingly argued for a dependence of Gutiérrez on the theological precepts of Bonhoeffer, Moltmann, Pannenberg, and von Rad.

[30] Fierro, *Militant Gospel*, 224-27.

theologies.[31] Third, there is a common appeal to the Old Testament for understanding the nature of the Kingdom—not only to the Exodus event but to the prophetic proclamations.[32] Finally, the Kingdom proclamation of the historical Jesus becomes critically significant in the light of his political and social intentions.[33]

METHODOLOGICAL ISSUES IN LIBERATION THEOLOGY

Gustavo Gutiérrez speaks for every liberation theologian when he says his work is a "new way to do theology."[34] In discussing the theme of the Kingdom in liberation theology, it is important to understand the liberation theologians' theological method, as it is what determines their selection and interpretation of the biblical data. The three-part synthesis of Leonardo and Clodovis Boff of the method of liberation theology provides a helpful framework from which to begin.[35]

---

[31] Bonino, for example, notes that "it is in recent theology where a systematic attempt has been made to overcome dualism, as in Moltmann and Metz, by stressing the historical significance of the eschatological expectation as critical questioning and, in our theology, the eschatological value of present historical praxis of liberation. God builds his Kingdom from and within human history in its entirety" (Bonino, *Doing Theology in a Revolutionary Setting*, 137-38).

[32] Ernst Bloch, who influenced Moltmann, observes how the Old Testament prophets are much used by Christian revolutionaries because they are so critical towards the prevailing social order. See Ernst Bloch, *Thomas Münzer als Theologe der Revolution* (Frankfurt: Suhrkamp, 1960), 47; cited by Fierro, *Militant Gospel*, 151.

[33] Speaking as a political theologian, Dorothee Sölle states: "it is not a matter of compiling in a biblicistic sense materials pertaining to the political activity of Jesus and using them to establish whether or not he was a revolutionary. The main thing is not to describe his concrete behavior and initiate, but rather to discern the intention or tendency of that behavior and realize anew his goals in our world" (Dorothee Sölle, *Political Theology* [Philadelphia: Fortress, 1974], 64).

[34] Gutiérrez, *Theology of Liberation*, 15.

[35] Boff and Boff, *Introducing Liberation Theology*, 22-42. The Boff's three-part scheme is a simplification of what is often appears as a more complex method in the writings of other liberation theologians. For example, Juan Luis Segundo's method in *The Liberation of Theology* (Maryknoll, N.Y.: Orbis, 1976) includes no less than seven steps, and J. Severino Croatto's methodology is likewise complex, drawing from the philosophy of Paul Ricoeur (J. Severino Croatto, *Biblical Hermeneutics: Toward a Theory of Reading as the Production of Meaning*, trans. Robert R. Barr [Maryknoll, N.Y.: Orbis, 1987]). See also the discussions of hermeneutics by Hugo Assmann (*Theology for a Nomad Church*), J. Miguez Bonino (*Revolutionary Theology Comes of Age* [Philadelphia: Fortress, 1975]), and Clodovis Boff (*Theology and Praxis: Epistemological Foundations,*

Leonardo and Clodovis Boff describe liberation theology as a task of socio-analytical mediation, hermeneutical mediation, and practical mediation. Though the listing is not intended to imply any particular sequence of the mediations in the theological process, the three features are all-inclusive of liberation theology's method. The definitions of the different mediations Boff and Boff describe this way:

> Socio-analytical (or historico-analytical) mediation operates in the sphere of the world of the oppressed. It tries to find out why the oppressed are oppressed. Hermeneutical mediation operates in the sphere of God's world. It tries to discern what God's plan is for the poor. Practical mediation operates in the sphere of action. It tries to discover the courses of action that need to be followed so as to overcome oppression in accordance with God's plan.[36]

The first mediation, the socio-analytical, points to the poor and the oppressed as the immediate objects of liberation theology's concern. In the name of Christian charity and after the example of Jesus, the church must become active on their behalf. What the church must do, however, is determined in part by the diagnosis given to the problem. Why are the poor, poor? At this point liberation theology has typically relied on the social sciences to reject explanations of laziness or backwardness and embrace "dialectical" explanations.[37] Thus, liberation theologians have habitually attributed poverty to exploitive economic systems designed for the prosperity of the few and the exclusion of the many. Use of the Marxist paradigm at this point has drawn much fire from critics, even though liberation

---

trans. Robert R. Barr [Maryknoll, N.Y.: Orbis, 1987]). Also complicating the hermeneutics of liberation theology is its more recently realized dual nature in the exegetical practices of the base communities. What began as a theoretical exercise of professional theologians has moved into the grassroots arena of lay exegesis. See Anthony C. Thiselton, *New Horizons in Hermeneutics: The Theory and Practice of Transforming Biblical Reading* (Grand Rapids: Zondervan, 1992), 411-13; and Christopher Rowland and Mark Corner, *Liberating Exegesis: The Challenge of Liberation Theology to Biblical Studies* (Philadelphia: Fortress, 1990).

[36] Boff and Boff, *Introduction to Liberation Theology*, 24.

[37] See especially part one of Boff, *Theology and Praxis,* for a discussion of the role of the social sciences in liberation theology.

THE KINGDOM OF GOD IN THE TEACHING OF JESUS

theologians and their apologists claim Marxism is "only a tool" which offers "methodological pointers."[38]

In the second mediation theologians give their attention to what God has to say to the poor and oppressed in his Word. Two things happen here as specific biblical events and passages come into view according to their pertinence to the situation of the poor. First, the hermeneutic circle begins with the life-setting of the poor, as Segundo proclaims in *Liberation of Theology*.[39] Thus the Bible is contextualized to the situation of the poor, as it is only from their perspective that it is legitimately interpreted.[40] The second thing happening hermeneutically is an ideological critique of theologies resistant to this preferential interpretation of Scripture by and for the poor.[41] The idea is that noncontextualized theology, like that coming from North America and Europe, is theology that claims universal application but really is itself contextualized to serve a cultural ideology, namely the ideology that keeps the poor poor and the rich rich. Gutiérrez draws a key contrast between theology done in the social situation of Latin America and that done in North America and Europe:

---

[38] For example, McGovern, *Liberation Theology and Its Critics*, 36. On the role of Marxism within liberation theology, see Belli and Nash, *Beyond Liberation Theology*, 67-91; and Marc Kolden, "Marxism and Latin American Liberation Theology," in *Christians and the Many Faces of Marxism*, ed. Wayne Stumme (Minneapolis: Augsburg, 1984), 123-31.

[39] Segundo, *Liberation of Theology*, 7-8. Berryman likewise implies the hermeneutic circle of liberation theology when he says people in base communities "understand the Bible in terms of their experience and reinterpret that experience in terms of biblical symbols. . . . Interpretation moves from experience to text to experience" (*Liberation Theology*, 60).

[40] The parables are particularly fruitful territory for the exegesis of the poor. For example, the parable of the lost sheep in Matthew 18:10-14 is taken to mean that the church should not be overly concerned with "preservation" (i.e., taking care of the ninety-nine) but should reach out and serve the oppressed (the lost sheep; see Thiselton, *New Horizons*, 412). More radical examples of this exegesis can be found in Ernesto Cardenal's transcripts of Bible study groups in Nicaragua published as *Love in Practice: The Gospel in Solamentiname*, 4 vols. (Maryknoll, N.Y.: Orbis, 1977-1984). One discussion of the Magnificat (Luke 1:46-55) describes Mary as a communist because she looked for good things to happen to the poor (Cardenal, *Love in Practice*, 1:30-31). See further Rowland and Corner, *Liberating Exegesis*.

[41] See Juan Luis Segundo, *Faith and Ideologies* (Maryknoll, N.Y.: Orbis, 1984); José Porfirio Miranda, *Marx and the Bible: A Critique of the Philosophy of Oppression*, trans. John Eagleson (Maryknoll, N.Y.: Orbis, 1974); and Alfred T. Hennelly, *Theologies in Conflict: The Challenge of Juan Luis Segundo* (Maryknoll, N.Y.: Orbis, 1979).

Here faith is lived by the poor of the world. Here the theological reflection seeking self-expression has no intention of being a palliative for these sufferings and refuses integration into the dominant theologies, conservative or progressive.[42]

Implicit in this critique, as Dermot A. Lane has noted,[43] are the tenets of the "sociology of knowledge" that all knowledge (and doctrine) is shaped by a specific cultural environment. Knowledge is never neutral but embodies the social circumstances of the time. Theologies of the First World, therefore, inevitably reflect and further the oppressive cultural beliefs (ideologies) of the First World. They have no place in the realm of the oppressed other than to maintain their oppression, and liberation theologians consequently reject criticism based on these theologies.[44]

The Boffs' third mediation of praxis actually stands at the beginning of Gustavo Gutiérrez's theological program. Defining liberation theology as "a critical reflection on Christian praxis in the light of the Word,"[45] Gutiérrez brings what he considers a neglected element to Christian theology. He writes that from the twelfth century on, theology became an academic exercise confined as a science to rational categories. According to his vision liberation theology now wishes to return theology to being an activity of ortho-doxy (right thinking) and ortho-praxy (right practice). Technically, both right theory and right practice constitute the *praxis* of the liberation theologian, and both are done with an eye to change.[46]

---

[42] Gustavo Gutiérrez, *The Power of the Poor in History*, trans. Robert R. Barr (Maryknoll, N.Y.: Orbis, 1983), 186.

[43] Dermot A. Lane, *Foundations for a Social Theology: Praxis, Process and Salvation* (New York: Paulist, 1984), 76-77.

[44] Just as the "sociology of knowledge" realized its relativistic limits in the works of Karl Mannheim (*Ideology and Utopia* [New York: Harcourt, Brace and World, 1955] and *Essays on the Sociology of Knowledge* [Oxford: Oxford University Press, 1952]; see also Robert J. Schreiter, *Constructing Local Theologies* [Maryknoll, N.Y.: Orbis, 1986], 78-79), so liberation theology, as a contextualized theology, has been charged with relativism and lacking a transcendent critique. See Belli and Nash, *Beyond Liberation Theology*, 132-33; and Thiselton, *New Horizons*, 410ff.

[45] Gutiérrez, *Liberation Theology*, 13.

[46] Praxis is usually regarded only as right action or practice, but technically it includes right theory as well. McGovern says praxis connotes "transforming activity *guided* by theory and goals" (McGovern, *Liberation Theology and Its Critics*, 32).

Schreiter gives a full description of the ideas involved in praxis for liberation theology:

> Praxis is the ensemble of social relationships that include and determine
> the structures of social consciousness. Thus thought and theory are con-
> sidered sets of relations within the larger network of social relation-
> ships. . . . Theory's task is to illumine the exact nature of those social
> relationships. By so doing, theory can point to false and oppressive rela-
> tionships within the social fabric. This pointing to false and oppressive
> relationships brings them to awareness, which is the first step toward
> transforming them . . . praxis can come to be defined as a revolutionary
> or transformative praxis, aimed at the changing of those patterns.[47]

When used in this manner, it is apparent how praxis can be an appropriate summary of Gutiérrez's whole liberation program.

IMPORTANT FEATURES OF THE
KINGDOM OF GOD IN LIBERATION THEOLOGY

Having discussed these important background methodological issues, it is
now possible to investigate liberation theology's understanding of the Kingdom per se. Center stage of this query is the historical Jesus.

The Kingdom of God and the Historical Jesus

Liberation theology seeks to ground Christian understanding of the Kingdom of God in the historical Jesus.[48] The message of Jesus about the
Kingdom is not only critical to understanding the deepest verities of liberation theology,[49] it is inexorably tied to the apprehension of the true

---

[47] Schreiter, *Constructing Local Theologies*, 91. As Thiselton has observed, "praxis" is a notoriously
slippery but also technical term in the theologies of liberation (Thiselton, *New Horizons*, 380).
For more on the history of the term see Nickolas Lobkowicz, *Theory and Practice* (Notre Dame,
Ind.: University of Notre Dame Press, 1968).

[48] Jon Sobrino considers that "Liberation Theology has rehabilitated the figure of the historical
Jesus within theology" (Sobrino, *Christology at the Crossroads*, 79).

[49] Leonardo Boff, "Salvation in Jesus Christ and the Process of Liberation," 80, makes this connection, showing not only the importance of the theme of the Kingdom to liberation theology,
but specifically the Kingdom as presented by Jesus. In *Jesus Christ Liberator*, 52, Boff makes the
common observation that Jesus did not preach God, but God's Kingdom.

nature of Jesus himself. Jon Sobrino has noted that Jesus' very identity is not known apart from the Kingdom of God. His divine nature is revealed only in the context of the signs of the Kingdom.[50]

Old Testament Antecedents to Jesus

Liberation theology understands the meaning of Kingdom for the historical Jesus to come from the Old Testament. When Jesus appears in public after the arrest of John, he offers no new definition of the Kingdom in his call to "Repent and believe the gospel, the Kingdom of God is at hand" (Mark 1:15). He simply assumes his audience understands his meaning.[51] Jesus stands in the best of the prophetic tradition on the subject of the Kingdom. Therefore if one is to understand what Jesus meant by "the Kingdom of God," the Old Testament must be the starting point.

In studying the theme of the Kingdom in the Old Testament it is critical for liberation theology not simply to study the related terms in isolation from historical contexts. This is plain for Sobrino because the "Kingdom of God" is inextricably linked to the Semitic understanding of God and how he reveals himself.[52] In contrast to a more Greek ontological treatment of God's existence, the Old Testament knows the reality of God as he reveals himself through events of history. He is not known except by his acting in history. In the Old Testament the concept "God exists" is expressed "God acts or God reigns."[53] Thus to truly comprehend God or God's Kingdom one must study the historical contexts in which they appear and not treat the ideas simply as "abstractions" or "pure concepts."[54]

---

[50] Sobrino, *Christology at the Crossroads*, 49.

[51] Ibid., 42, 44. See also Segundo, *Historical Jesus of the Synoptics*, 88.

[52] Sobrino, *Christology at the Crossroads*, 44.

[53] Sobrino here claims to be following the course of Vatican II, which recognized this point in the Old Testament and moved beyond the Greek perspective of Vatican I. See Sobrino, *Christology at the Crossroads*, 76, n. 10.

[54] Pixley, demonstrating the ideological critique of liberation theologians, notes the danger of treating biblical subjects like the Kingdom as abstractions, because history has demonstrated that abstractions are easily bent into tools of oppression by First World exegetes (Pixley, *God's Kingdom*, 112).

The first significant event after the creation for understanding the Kingdom in the Old Testament is the exodus.[55] The exodus proper and the ensuing political establishment of the nation of Israel constitute for liberation theology an impressive agenda-setting manifestation of the reign of God.[56] Specifically, in the exodus event we see the liberative function of the Kingdom in that God hears the cries of the oppressed and acts on their behalf. Likewise the political function of the exodus is evident from the fact that for the nation of Israel the exodus marked freedom from a political state and Israel's constitution as a sovereign state under Yahweh. Many features of the exodus story point to the inherently political nature of the exodus. Aside from the explicit references that Israel would be a "kingdom of priests" for God, Pixley sees political and revolutionary implications in the first command of the Decalogue. He contends, for example, that, given the social context of the surrounding Canaanite states, Yahweh's demand of unique devotion was a clear reference to his political kingship over Israel.[57]

The early history of Israel in the land of Canaan continued the revolutionary project of the Kingdom of God within history. In contrast to the surrounding political environment, the tribes of Israel had distinct antimonarchial tendencies as they existed under Yahweh's reign. Several passages are used as evidence that Israel had no state but existed as a stateless group of states under the reign of God. Judges 9:7–15 and the parable of the olive tree give eloquent testimony to Israel's antimonarchial

---

[55] Gutiérrez notes that God's saving activity in history began with the first creative act. "Creation is presented in the Bible not as a stage previous to salvation but as a part of the salvific process" (*Theology of Liberation*, 154). The Kingdom of God as his "salvific reign" is first revealed biblically in Creation. For the paradigmatic significance of the Exodus, see Gutiérrez, *Theology of Liberation*, 155-57.

[56] In accord with prevailing biblical scholarship, liberation theologians generally understand the fundamental meaning of "kingdom" in dynamic terms rather than static ones. That is, the Kingdom means the reign or rule of God, as opposed to a specific realm. See for example Sobrino, *Christology at the Crossroads*, 43; and Boff, *Jesus Christ Liberator*, 55.

[57] Pixley, *God's Kingdom*, 27ff.

preferences.[58] The fact that Israel was commissioned to live this way (as twelve tribal states) in a neighborhood of highly centralized and militant Canaanite states is said to demonstrate the revolutionary character of the Kingdom of God as it is realized in history.[59]

The prophets are the last major Old Testament antecedent to Jesus' preaching and praxis of the Kingdom of God. This is because for liberation theology the motif of the Old Testament prophet most closely approximates Jesus' ministry.[60] The prophets' function as heralds of denunciation and annunciation to apostate Israel revealed important tenets of the Kingdom of God also revealed in Jesus. One of the most important concerns of the Kingdom is that of justice for the oppressed. The prophets announced the reign of Yahweh over Israel to be nothing less than an Israelite utopia (Isa. 2:4; 25:8; 45:21; 65:17).[61] But with the presence of injustice for the poor and the oppression of the marginalized, the reign of God is abrogated. The prophets assured Israel that Yahweh was still the king (Isa. 33:22) and that he would act as Judge to all those who demon-

---

[58] See also Judges 8:22-23 and 1 Samuel 8:4-5; 10-17 as examples of Israel's deliberate rejection of unified statehood. An important work on this subject for Liberation Theology is Norman K. Gottwald, *The Tribes of Yahweh: A Sociology of the Religion of Liberated Israel 1250-1050 B.C.E.* (Maryknoll, N.Y.: Orbis, 1979). For an assessment see "Theological Issues in *The Tribes of Yahweh* by N. K. Gottwald: Four Critical Reviews," in *The Bible and Liberation: Political and Social Hermeneutics*, ed. Norman K. Gottwald (Maryknoll, N.Y.: Orbis, 1983), 166-89.

[59] Pixley, *God's Kingdom*, 19-20.

[60] Though Sobrino believes Jesus combined two Old Testament traditions in his presentation of the Kingdom—sapiential and apocalyptic-prophetic—he says the apocalyptic-prophetic was most certainly predominant (Sobrino, *Christology at the Crossroads*, 356).

[61] Utopia is an important concept in all political theologies (Fierro, *Militant Gospel*, 276). Within liberation theology some writers appear hesitant to use the term because of its humanistic connections. Gutiérrez on the one hand states, "the gospel doesn't provide us with a utopia" (*Theology of Liberation*, 238); but he earlier says, "faith and political action enter a correct and fruitful relationship only through the project of creating a new type of human being in a very different sort of society—which is to say, only through utopia" (*Theology of Liberation*, 236). Boff uses the term freely in association with the Kingdom: "the kingdom of God is the realization of the fundamental utopia of the human heart" (*Jesus Christ Liberator*, 49). Sobrino also employs the term favorably (*Christology at the Crossroads*, 43).

strated ignorance of him by their practice of injustice. They taught that to know Yahweh and participate in his reign means to do justice (Jer. 22:16).[62]

As we will discuss later, liberation theology at times appears to lack balance in its exegetical treatment of the New Testament. Imbalance on several points also should be noted in its reading of the Old Testament evidence for the Kingdom. First, the exodus was indeed significant politically, but it also had a religious dimension that is all too often neglected in liberation exegesis.[63] Second, justice was not the only focus of the Old Testament prophets (cf. Micah 6:8). Third, the prophets called the wealthy to convert and did not advocate collective political action by the oppressed. Fourth, the prophets' (and Jesus') harsh denunciation of political and social leaders were largely given within God's covenant community. These were leaders whose ancestors had committed them to be Yahweh's "kingdom of priests" and "holy nation." Any abrogation of the covenant would naturally call down strong condemnation from Yahweh's messengers. Similarly, where the leaders of God's people are not under the Mosaic covenant (as in the case of the Roman political leaders of the New Testament era), the rhetoric against their actions is not the same (e.g., Rom. 13:1–8).

The Proclamation of Jesus

The Synoptic Gospels present Jesus proclaiming the Old Testament dynamic reign of God politically and socially manifested to mankind. When preaching for the first time in the synagogue, Jesus read the highly charged liberation words of Isaiah 61:1–2.

---

[62] José Miranda devotes several chapters (2-4) of *Marx and the Bible* to an examination of the prophetic proclamation. He contends that justice is the fundamental Old Testament attribute of God and its practice is not just one manifestation of the knowledge of God, it is *the* manifestation of such knowledge (Miranda, *Marx and the Bible*, 14-15).

[63] François Biot, *Théologie du politique: Foi et politique elements de reflexion* (Paris: Editions Universitaires, 1972), 130-31. It is also often noted that the exodus does not have the same paradigmatic function for the rest of the Bible as it does in liberation theology. See Arthur F. McGovern, "The Bible in Latin American Liberation Theology," in *The Bible and Liberation*, ed. Norman K. Gottwald (Maryknoll, N.Y.: Orbis, 1983), 467-71; Jon D. Levenson, "Exodus and Liberation," *HorBibT* 13 (1991): 95-174.

The Spirit of the Lord is upon me because he anointed Me to preach the Gospel to the poor. He has sent me to proclaim release to the captives, and recovery of sight to the blind, to set free those who are downtrodden, to proclaim the favorable year of the Lord.

Jesus' further comment that "today this scripture has been fulfilled in your presence" shows the programmatic nature of the Old Testament meaning of the Kingdom for his own life events and ministry.[64] For Jesus the Kingdom of God expresses "man's utopian longing for liberation from everything that alienates him, factors such as anguish, pain, hunger, injustice and death, and not only man but all creation."[65] In his sermons it is the poor, those who weep, and the hungry who are the blessed of the Kingdom.

The Kingdom Jesus preached comes against sin, which is everything that denies the full liberation of God's created order.[66] Jesus demands personal repentance and conversion (Mark 1:15) to the Kingdom's liberative purposes. Salvation is taking up the cause of the Kingdom. Followers of the Kingdom must be willing to change their thinking so as to allow sacrifice of all for the Kingdom (Matt. 13:44–46), including family, possessions, and personal well-being. Sin would mean saying no to these demands of the Kingdom. It is the force people use to secure themselves against God's Kingdom and to oppress others. The Kingdom calls all who are under the power of sin to completely trust in God who is greater than the "standing order" that has religiously, socially, politically, and economically oppressed them. In the service of the Kingdom Jesus is not just interested in pardoning sin; he must eradicate it.

The Kingdom as God's salvation is not only personal spiritual relief from the oppression of sin, it is the conversion of all society, which means

---

[64] Luke 4:16-22 is likewise programmatic for liberation theology. The message of Jesus is from the Old Testament and it is for the poor. See Boff, *Jesus Christ Liberator,* 52-54.

[65] Boff, "Salvation in Jesus Christ," 80-81.

[66] See Sobrino, *Christology at the Crossroads,* 50-61, 360 ff.; and Boff, *Jesus Christ Liberator,* 64-72.

of necessity that it is political and substantial.[67] It comes against societal structures which are the outward expression of oppression within the hearts of men (i.e., sin). Again in Matthew 11:3, 5, in Jesus the blind see, the deaf hear, the lame walk, and the poor have the good news preached to them. In this context Jesus condemns the religio-socio-politico establishment for their collective manifestations of oppression against the poor. He denounces the Pharisees for their injustice (Matt. 23:23), the lawyers for their heavy burdens (Matt. 23:4), the intelligentsia for stealing the keys of knowledge (Luke 11:52), and the rulers for governing despotically (Matt. 20:26). In contrast Jesus announces the Kingdom in reified terms. It has houses and lands (Mark 10:30), and in it the disciples will one day sit and judge the twelve tribes of Israel (Luke 22:29–30).

The Praxis of Jesus

Jesus not only proclaimed the complete revolution of the human world, he demonstrated it in liberative action. His miracles of healing and exorcism provided for the oppressed personal liberation from the Kingdom's fundamental adversary, the Devil. The Kingdom comes to plunder the Devil's house and take back his victims (Matt. 12:29) from every condition wherein they have been oppressed. Jesus confronts the power of Satan and defeats him and judges him on every level.

The action of Jesus against the kingdom of Satan shows the indisputable arrival of the Kingdom of God (Matt. 12:28: "If I cast out demons by the Spirit of God then the kingdom of God has come upon you"). The arrival of the Kingdom has physical implications for the political kingdoms

---

[67] True to the form of political theologies, politics is the critical medium for the Kingdom's revolutionary agenda in liberation theology because it is the realm that structures the way human beings live together on earth (Sobrino, *Christology at the Crossroads*, 210). See also Boff, "Salvation in Jesus Christ," 80–82; and *Jesus Christ Liberator*, 51–62. The focus on politics often has the effect in liberation theology of subverting the traditional doctrines of salvation. Salvation becomes equated primarily with the process of social and structural liberation and secondarily with personal liberation (Leonardo Boff and Clodovis Boff, *Salvation and Liberation* [Maryknoll, N.Y.: Orbis, 1984], 116). Examples of this subversion are Berryman, who is uncomfortable interpreting Jesus' death as an atoning sacrifice for sin (*Liberation Theology*, 56), and McGovern, who delights in Boff's "striking insight that much of our Christian interpretation of salvation resulted, in great measure, from the personal problems of St. Paul, Augustine, and Luther" (*Liberation Theology and Its Critics*, 158; citing Leonardo Boff, *Liberating Grace*, trans. John Drury [Maryknoll, N.Y.: Orbis, 1979], 23).

of this world according to the actions of Jesus. Especially when seen against the social and political conditions of first-century Palestine,[68] Jesus' actions against the temple and the social order supported by the temple,[69] and the circumstances surrounding his own death prove his politically revolutionary demeanor in the service of the Kingdom of God.[70]

Within his political demonstrations of the Kingdom, liberation theology is careful to separate Jesus from the messianism of the Zealot party of his day.[71] Even though Jesus did agree with their political notions of the Kingdom, God's Kingdom cannot be limited to a particular regime on the order of what they sought. At this point different writers vary in their account of the relationship between Jesus and the Zealots as well as in their explanation of Jesus' overall perspective on power and the Kingdom's establishment. Sobrino sees Jesus growing into this position from the results of his early ministry. Initially Jesus comes in the service of the Kingdom program, but with his rejection by the masses in Galilee he begins to deny the particular power-mode of the Kingdom of the Zealots. After his rejection Jesus showed that the Kingdom would come only through the triumph of love and not the worldly power of the Zealots. To do this love would have to be overcome by evil so that evil could be broken from within.[72]

Boff has Jesus commandeering the messianic and apocalyptic categories of the day to adequately communicate his message. Jesus, however, never feeds Jewish nationalism. He was appointed to preach and demonstrate the beginning of the end of the old order which God himself would shortly finish.[73]

---

[68] Pixley (*God's Kingdom*, 64-72) gives a lengthy sociological evaluation of Palestine very similar to Richard A. Horsley's in *Jesus and the Spiral of Violence* (San Francisco: Harper & Row, 1987). Horsley's presentation is much more detailed and well researched than Pixley's, but it is interesting that Pixley had taken Horsley's major thesis (except for the place of the Zealots in the first century) into the service of liberation theology six years before.

[69] Pixley notes that Jesus' real targets were not the Romans but the oppressive aristocratic class of Jews. This is where Jesus and the party of the Zealots differed (*God's Kingdom*, 79).

[70] The politically revolutionary Jesus is a constant throughout liberation theology. See also Sobrino, *Christology at the Crossroads*, 211.

[71] Cf. Gutiérrez, *Theology of Liberation*, 227-28; Boff, *Jesus Christ Liberator*, 59; Sobrino, *Christology at the Crossroads*, 210.

[72] Sobrino, *Christology at the Crossroads*, 354-59.

[73] Boff, *Jesus Christ Liberator*, 56-59.

Segundo distinguishes his view by separating the ideas of the political and the eschatological. He supposes Jesus to be political in his outlook of the Kingdom, but not eschatological in that he does not consider the Kingdom in reified terms. The Kingdom of God is a dynamic reality that has "come near" or "arrived" in Jesus. The so-called apocalyptic passages of the Gospels and those other places in Matthew that present the Kingdom as a place or a thing are explained by Segundo as either a consequence of Matthew's particular moralizing which requires some "thing" (i.e., the Kingdom) as reward for righteousness, or they speak of the *human collaboration* necessary for the full program of the Kingdom to be realized on earth. Segundo agrees with most modern exegetes in supposing that Jesus did expect the coming of the Kingdom "in power" within his own generation. But according to Jesus and the early Christians (e.g., Rom. 1:4), the Kingdom did come with power at the resurrection of Jesus.[74] What remains for its final establishment is the human collaboration with its principles. The reason that Jesus did not speak and do more of this human collaboration comes from the fact that his primary aim was to first raise the consciousness of the people to the dynamic of God's reign.[75]

Numerous positive elements come from such a presentation of the Kingdom in the ministry of the historical Jesus. First, we should note that the fundamental priority of the Kingdom of God in the method and message of liberation theology is quite appropriate. There is a wide consensus in biblical scholarship that the Kingdom of God was the overarching theme of the historical Jesus and the Bible in general. Also as the Kingdom of God does appear to encompass every aspect of God's salvific work in the Synoptics and John,[76] the idea of "liberation" bears the Kingdom's function well in this present age.[77]

---

[74] Segundo follows Pannenberg; see Segundo, *Historical Jesus of the Synoptics*, 215, n. 19.

[75] Segundo, *The Historical Jesus of the Synoptics*, 150-65; 178-88.

[76] The Kingdom of God is related to the effects of salvation in the fourth Gospel by its association to the Johannine concept of eternal life. See R. H. Charles, *Eschatology* (New York: Schocken, 1963), 368; and U. E. Simon, "Eternal Life in the Fourth Gospel," *Studies in the Fourth Gospel*, ed. F. L. Cross (London: A. R. Mowbray, 1957), 97-98.

[77] Leonardo Boff aligns his own views with Luther's dictum: "Instead of justification, we say liberation" (Leonardo Boff, *Erfahrung von Gnade. Entwurf einer Gnadenlehre* [Dusseldorf: Patmos, 1978], 221; cited by Freiling, *Befreiungstheologien*, 15).

Further, as we have seen in the works of the Third Quest, the social and political elements of the Kingdom in the teaching of the historical Jesus are finding greater audience and support in scholarly circles.[78] In the case that liberation theology holds to an "Already/Not Yet" understanding of the Kingdom, it also finds itself squarely within a major consensus of biblical studies of the last thirty years. But to the degree that it posits a political and social understanding of the Kingdom in Jesus, it moves beyond this consensus in certain positive ways. That liberation theology attempts to locate the meaning of the Kingdom solidly in the context of first-century Palestine and argues for the Kingdom's reification over its spiritualization should also be viewed positively.[79]

The Kingdom and the Poor

In liberation theology the Kingdom of God has special interest for the marginalized of society.[80] This is due in part to the hermeneutical bent of liberation theology in light of the gospel proclamation itself: "Blessed are you who are poor, for yours is the kingdom of God" (Luke 6:20). For liberation theologians it is important to define who the poor are. On this count, Puebla's definition has met with general approval. The poor are "young children, frustrated youths without a future, the native population, the Afro-Americans, peasants, laborers, under-employed, unemployed,

---

[78] We have already noted the parallel between Pixley's sociological analysis and that of Horsley. Charlesworth refers to the current consensus that Jesus must be seen against a Jewish background and that that background did not separate religion and politics (James H. Charlesworth, "Jesus Research Expands with Chaotic Creativity," *Images of Jesus Today*, ed. James H. Charlesworth and Walter P. Weaver, Faith and Scholarship Colloquies 3, Florida Southern College [Valley Forge, Pa.: Trinity Press International, 1994], 20).

[79] All the major liberation theologians, with the exception of Segundo, would agree with George Wesley Buchanan's despair over how "scholars have internalized, de-temporalized, de-historicized, cosmologized, spiritualized, allegorized, mysticized, psychologized, philosophized, and sociologized the concept of the Kingdom of God" (*The Consequences of the Covenant* [Leiden: E. J. Brill, 1970], 55).

[80] See Enrique Dussel, "The Kingdom of God and the Poor," *IntRMiss* 68/270 (April 1979): 115–30; Paul Löffler, "The Reign of God Has Come in the Suffering Christ: An Exploration of the Power of the Powerless," *IntRMiss* 68/270 (April 1979): 109–14; and Malcolm Cuthbertson, "The Kingdom and the Poor," *ScotBEv* 1/4 (spring 1986): 123–33.

aged, the human refuse of the cities."[81] The central attribute of these groups is that socio-economic factors are the cause of this poverty.

These economically deprived are the poor for whom the gospel of the Kingdom is truly good news (Luke 4:16–22). Their presence in our midst signifies the absence of the full fruit of the Kingdom.[82] The Already of the Kingdom has not become the Not Yet. The poor are those to whom God has chosen to reveal himself in the Kingdom. God is preferential to the poor because they stand to benefit most from its presence.[83] Jesus himself evangelized the poor and called them to repentance. Therefore it is the poor who really understand the Kingdom. They are the "carriers" of the Kingdom. Their knowledge and possession of its realities are brought to bear on all that which is opposed to the Kingdom in society, individually and collectively. The Kingdom comes to earth through the transforming work of the poor.[84]

Because it gives such deference to the poor in its reading of Scripture, liberation theology leaves itself open to the charge of unbalanced exegesis and unbiblical results. Such charges can be justified in two ways. First, there is good exegetical evidence to support a broadening of the concept of "the poor" beyond the parameters of those of liberation theology, that is, the materially poor. For example, from a study of the followers of Jesus as identified by Jesus himself, Jeremias concludes: " 'Poor' not only means economically poor, but widens when we consider the designations Jesus gives them. He calls them the hungry, those who weep, the sick, those who labor, those who bear burdens, the lost, the simple, the last, the sinners."[85]

Jeremias also notes that from Luke's perspective, the poor are the disciples of the early church who suffer poverty and persecution for the name of Jesus.[86] Such evidence also calls into question some unguarded state-

---

[81] Cited by Pieter De Villiers, "The Gospel and the Poor: Let Us Read Luke 4," in *Liberation Theology and the Bible*, ed. Pieter G. R. De Villiers (Pretoria: University of South Africa Press, 1987), 58.

[82] Dussel, "The Kingdom and the Poor," 115, 121.

[83] See Segundo Galilea, *The Beatitudes: To Evangelize As Jesus Did* (Maryknoll, N.Y.: Orbis, 1984), 16-19.

[84] Dussel, "The Kingdom and the Poor," 125.

[85] Joachim Jeremias, *New Testament Theology*, trans. John Bowden (London: SCM, 1971) 112-13.

[86] Ibid., 112.

ments of liberation theologians that the economically poor are the "elect" of God and sole heirs of the Kingdom.[87] Traditional orthodoxy will reject these kinds of statements, along with those that mitigate the doctrines of justification with political activism.[88]

Second, because of its deference to the poor in its reading of Scripture, the doctrine of the Kingdom in liberation theology is developed primarily from the exodus event, the prophets, and the Gospels, leaving out the data from the epistles.[89] This literature is notably more passive and obedient relative to the existing political and social orders[90] and admittedly contrary to the political agenda of liberation theology.[91] Couple this also with the fact that Jesus, for all his political machinations, did not join the Zealot movement of his day, the obvious parallel to liberation theology.[92] All of this points to liberation theology's myopic view of the Scriptures and hence its view of the Kingdom. To the degree liberationists are tempted to counter this objection by citing their right to this reading of the biblical data under the guise of the sociology of knowledge, they relativize their own ability to convince anyone of their exegesis outside of their own group.

---

[87] Pixley, for instance, states, "in its original biblical expression, God's Kingdom was for the poor and not for believers" (Pixley, *God's Kingdom*, 104).

[88] Recall, for example, Boff's attributing much of the traditional doctrine of justification to the personal problems of St. Paul, Augustine, and Luther (Boff, *Liberating Grace*, 23).

[89] It would be in error to say that liberation theology is completely silent about the epistles. Costas comments on the political nature of the Kingdom from Romans 15:18-19 (Orlando Costas, *Christ Outside the Gate: Mission Beyond Christendom* (Maryknoll, N.Y.: Orbis, 1982), 91) and several non-Latin Americans sympathetic to liberation themes have commented on political ramifications of Colossians 2:15 and Revelation 14:8 and 18:2 (e.g., Ernst Käsemann, "The Eschatological Royal Reign of God," in *Your Kingdom Come: Mission Perspectives Report on the World Conference on Mission and Evangelism: Melbourne Australia, 12-15 May, 1980* [Geneva: World Council of Churches, 1980], 67).

[90] Note particularly the history of the early church in Acts. It is not political *and* it has shouldered the cause of the poor and sinners. On this see for example Edmund P. Clowney, "The Politics of the Kingdom," *WestTJ* 61, no. 2 (1979): 291-310, whose study from the New Testament concludes: "The politics of the kingdom of heaven is the politics of faith, hope and love. . . . The Christian will be charged with other-worldliness, aloofness, non-involvement. He cannot forget his heavenly citizenship to be conformed to this world. He refuses to make patriotism or revolution his religion or a socialist utopia his hope."

[91] Segundo admits the position of liberation theology on the Gospels is not shared by the apostolic literature of the church (Segundo, *Historical Jesus of the Synoptics*, 182-83).

[92] Oscar Cullmann, *Jesus and Revolutionaries* (New York: Harper & Row, 1976), vii.

The explanation usually offered by liberation theology for the nonrevolutionary phenomenon in the rest of the New Testament is that a certain social conditioning occurred after the death of Jesus. For some liberation theologians this social conditioning was due to the delay of the Parousia.[93] The imminent Kingdom which Jesus preached and believed would break in within his own generation simply did not come. The apostolic church accommodated itself to a more passive, less radical stance as time wore on and they settled in for the "long haul." The writings of this church therefore are not normative and liberation correctly calls us back to the message of Jesus.

Segundo, however, accounts for the social conditioning of the early church differently.[94] First, in the view of the early Christians, Jesus' preaching and praxis of the Kingdom did not travel well outside of Palestine. The context of the historical Jesus and the Kingdom he offered was Israel, not the entire Roman Empire. Jesus simply could not be duplicated outside his Judaic context, so the first Christians changed the message that was originally political to one that was religious and moral. Second, the events of the cross and resurrection were so astounding that they in fact shook the focus of the church from Jesus' own prepaschal agenda to Jesus himself. After the resurrection "Jesus as Messiah" becomes the apostolic focus, in lieu of the Kingdom thrust of the historical Jesus. " 'Salvation' in 'the name of Jesus' takes the place of 'the year of grace,' that is, the realization on earth of the values of the kingdom that will transform the plight of the poorest and most exploited members of Israelite society."[95]

A few observations may be offered in response to the proposed social conditioning of the early church. First, for those who posit social conditioning on the ground of widespread disappointment due to the failure of the Parousia, the exegetical footing for widespread disappointment is not exactly firm. C. E. B. Cranfield, for one, has offered interesting evidence from the New Testament suggesting that there was a general expectation of delay in both Jesus and the early church.[96] Second, if Jesus did believe in

---

[93] See Fierro, *Militant Gospel,* 212-16; and Pixley, *God's Kingdom,* 89.

[94] Segundo, *Historical Jesus of the Synoptics,* 182-88.

[95] Segundo, *Historical Jesus of the Synoptics,* 186.

[96] C. E. B. Cranfield, "Thoughts on New Testament Eschatology," *ScotJT* 35 (1982): 497-512.

the imminent arrival of the Kingdom, which much of liberation theology posits,[97] why does not his evident error call into question his particular proclamation and praxis of the Kingdom? Namely, is the Kingdom praxis which Jesus originally anticipated only for a brief interim necessarily applicable for a much longer time period? Furthermore, can anyone, liberation theologians included, seriously pattern their praxis after the pattern of one so obviously out of step with the times? Perhaps it could be argued that the epistles were a *necessary corrective* to the idealistic and deluded Jesus and provide a more appropriate praxis after all. Third, there is some inconsistency in saying some of the writings of the politically passive apostolic church are not normative (i.e., the epistles) and some are (i.e., the Gospels). It was the same church that gave us both writings.

Segundo avoids much of this critique as he believes that at the resurrection Jesus did realize the cosmic, in-breaking power he anticipated,[98] but his proposals likewise struggle for credibility. Regarding the notion that Jesus' radical agenda did not travel well beyond Palestine, we must ask if it is reasonable to believe that the early church, which itself could not (or would not) reproduce the politically enterprising Jesus of the Gospels, could not (or would not) discern and apply the *intentions* of the risen Christ, even if his exact actions and context could not be theirs? As this is exactly what liberation theologians claim to be doing, albeit with different results,[99] they shoulder the burden of proof to (1) claim more realistic and truer conclusions after nearly two thousand years; and to (2) prove that the early church would almost cavalierly accommodate itself so as to alter the message of the Lord they believed had risen from the dead.

Segundo's second proposal that the disciples lost the focus of the historical Jesus on the subject of the Kingdom appears to contradict early Christian teaching. While it is true that the early Christian preachers employ *different expressions* than Jesus in their preaching (e.g., Jesus preached the Kingdom and the disciples preached Jesus), argument can be made

---

[97] See for example Boff, *Jesus Christ Liberator,* 114; Sobrino, *Christology at the Crossroads,* 52.

[98] Segundo, *Historical Jesus of the Synoptics,* 215.

[99] Boff insists that the permanent validity of Jesus is not the "very words and deeds" *(ipsissima vox et facta)* but the "the intention" *(ipsissima intentio)* of the historical Jesus ("Salvation in Jesus Christ," 80).

that there was no difference between the two in *essential content:* (1) in numerous places in Acts the "Kingdom of God" functions as a summary statement for the essential content of the apostles' preaching (Acts 8:12, Philip's preaching in Samaria; Acts 19:8, Paul's preaching in Corinth; Acts 28:23, 31, Paul in Rome); (2) in Acts 20:24–25 Paul makes an explicit parallel between his preaching the "Kingdom" at Ephesus and his declaring the "gospel of grace" which for him was the life events and mission of Jesus (cf. 1 Cor. 15:1–4); and (3) according to Acts 1:3 the content of the postpaschal teaching of Jesus to the apostles for forty days was the Kingdom of God. They of anyone would know best its meaning and praxis. Segundo's suggestion that the apostles listened to the risen Jesus for forty days instruct them concerning the Kingdom of God and then as soon as he was gone promptly took up and preached something else is incredible.[100]

Instead of the early church being a dubious source, it is rather the indispensable source for understanding the Kingdom of God. To the degree that liberation theology admits its own variance with the apostolic writings it is therefore weakened. A balanced presentation of the Kingdom of God must fully incorporate the perspectives of both the Gospels and the epistles, without attempting to explain away one or the other. A theological system that attempts to build without this foundation will be a limited one and a relative one.

The Kingdom and Ecclesial Praxis

The necessity of historical Kingdom praxis for that which Jesus inaugurated by word and deed cannot be understated in the agenda of liberation theology. Segundo gives the rationale:

> The *totality* of Jesus' public life, in terms of what is most historically reliable, makes clear one thing: Jesus is seeking to *place historical causality* in the service of the kingdom. And not only does he invest his all as *perfectus homo* in that service; he invests his disciples' all as well.[101]

To be a member of the Kingdom, to have experienced its liberation in one's own life, carries with it the call to establish the "historical anticipations"

---

[100] Luke 24:27 may have a connection here also as during the post-resurrection period Jesus explains all things concerning *himself* to the two disciples while with them on the road to Emmaus.

[101] Segundo, *Historical Jesus of the Synoptics,* 149 (emphasis his).

of the Kingdom of God on earth.[102] The radical utopia of the Kingdom can be realized now, and those who are its citizens must work towards its establishment by standing against every notion, whether individual or structural, which opposes the Kingdom. This is the meaning of Christian faith.[103] It is the only way Jesus and God are known.[104]

How exactly the Christian community is to stand against the anti-Kingdom forces of this age is a varied matter in liberation theology. Bussmann has categorized the various approaches to Kingdom praxis in two parts: the Kingdom as prophetic motivation, and the Kingdom as political motivation.[105] In the former category the church in the tradition of the prophets announces the justice of the Kingdom, affirms the right of the poor to life, champions fair legal practices, and so on. In this mode the church also denounces injustice wherever it is found.[106] In the second category of political motivation, advocates call for the church's political involvement in the name of the Kingdom. This has included application in socialist and Marxist political movements and at times advocacy of violence against unjust institutions.[107] Whatever the particular expression of the Kingdom, both groups are unified in the fact that it is the church's responsibility to act in history on behalf of the Kingdom and to some extent aid in its establishment.[108]

---

[102] This is Boff's terminology, cited by Bussmann, *Who Do You Say?* 138.

[103] In liberation theology the doctrine of faith, like the doctrine of salvation, is closely tied to the practical expression of the Kingdom of God. Liberation theology gives priority to orthopraxy over orthodoxy (Boff, *Jesus Christ Liberator,* 46; Sobrino, *Christology at the Crossroads,* 45).

[104] God is only known by his actions. Our participation or collaboration with him brings forth true knowledge of him (Sobrino, *Christology at the Crossroads,* 27).

[105] Bussmann, *Who Do You Say?* 131-37.

[106] An advocate of these activities is Orlando Costas (*Christ Outside the Gate,* 94-97).

[107] For examples in this category particularly espousing violence see citations in Freiling, *Befreiungstheologien,* 117-18, about the work of Francisco Torres, and citations in Bussmann, *Who Do You Say?* 136-37, about Arnaldo Zenteno. See also Segundo's discussion of the possibilities for concrete action, including violence (*Liberation of Theology,* 156-75).

[108] Segundo says, "There is something common and basic for all of us [liberation theologians]— the view that men, on a political as well as individual basis, construct the Kingdom of God from within history now" ("Capitalism-Socialism," 112). See also Cook, "Jesus from the Other Side of History," 266; and Elizabeth Lord, "Human History and the Kingdom of God: Past Perspectives and Those of J. L. Segundo," *HeythJl* 30 (1989): 293-305.

The exact "extent" to which the church really establishes the Kingdom could open liberation theology to the charge of seeking only to establish a humanistic utopia in the Kingdom's name, and such is the charge of some of liberation theology's many critics.[109] This must be avoided as the major theologians all deny that human beings can finally approximate the divine nature of the Kingdom.[110] Gutiérrez, for example, notes that the Kingdom of God is of such a divine quality that a society that was merely just would not necessarily be part of the Kingdom.[111]

To its credit, liberation theology's emphasis on the orthopraxy of the Kingdom reminds us of the immanence of at least some aspect of the Kingdom in the present age. That Kingdom yet to come in full glory exerts considerable influence now, it "casts a shadow," and it brings observable effects through its citizens. Praxis of the Kingdom ethic is imperative to New Testament Christianity, and this praxis does have ramifications for the pursuit of justice and the care of the poor. To this extent liberation theology points to the Kingdom theme as establishing the justification and parameters of Christian social action.[112] Care must be taken that the praxis of the Kingdom in this age does not dominate or even eradicate the message of the eschatological Kingdom in the age to come. The Kingdom "in your midst" must not eclipse the "coming Kingdom" in the rhetoric of Kingdom orthopraxy during this age.[113]

---

[109] For critiques of liberation theology, see Ronald Nash, ed., *Liberation Theology;* Carl E. Armerding, ed., *Evangelicals and Liberation* (Nutley, N.J.: Presbyterian and Reformed, 1977); Marc H. Ellis and Otto Maduro, eds., *The Future of Liberation Theology: Essays in Honor of Gustavo Gutiérrez* (Maryknoll, N.Y.: Orbis, 1989); Ph. I Ander Vincent, "Les 'theologies de la liberation,'" *NRT* 98 (1976): 109-25; François Hubert Lepargueur, "Theologies de la liberation et theologie tout court," *NRT* 98 (1976): 126-69; McGovern, *Liberation Theology and Its Critics;* Haight, *An Alternate Vision;* Alan Neely, "Liberation Theology and the Poor: A Second Look," *Missiology* 17 (1989): 387-404; J. Ronald Blue, "Major Flaws in Liberation Theology," *BS* 147 (1990): 89-103; Michael Novak, *Will It Liberate? Questions About Liberation Theology* (Mahwah, N.J.: Paulist, 1986); Emilio A. Nunez, *Liberation Theology* (Chicago: Moody, 1985); Norman Edward, *Christianity and the World Order* (New York: Oxford University Press, 1979); James V. Schall, *Liberation Theology in Latin America* (San Francisco: Ignatius, 1982); Raymond Hundley, *Radical Liberation Theology: An Evangelical Response* (Wilmore, Ky.: Bristol, 1987).

[110] Fierro, *Militant Gospel*, 281ff.

[111] Gutiérrez, *A Theology of Liberation*, 231-32. See also Boff, *Jesus Christ Liberator*, 64.

[112] Paul Ballard explores this thesis in "The Kingdom of God and Christian Political Theory," *ModChu* NS 31, no. 4 (1990): 20-27.

[113] Cook, "Jesus from the Other Side," 276-77.

The theme of the Kingdom of God reveals the reactionary nature of liberation theology as a whole. In reaction to the impoverished conditions of the Third World, the theme of the Kingdom of God has motivated the hands of its practitioners. Liberation theology makes a valuable contribution in its "rehabilitation of the historical Jesus" and his perspective on the Kingdom as something more than a spiritualized and individualized reign. On the other hand, like most groups for whom the Kingdom has become a banner, liberation theology suffers from overstatement and sometimes heavy-handed exegesis, both of which tend to weaken even what is meritorious in its contribution.

CHAPTER EIGHT

The Kingdom in Roman Catholicism, the World Council of Churches, and Evangelicalism

As we saw in the last chapter, the great social needs of the modern world turned the attention of certain individuals and groups to the Kingdom of God as the biblical mandate for Christian social action. This attention did not stop with the political theologies, however, and the impetus to be more socially interactive was felt in many other groups. In some cases these groups were encouraged in these positions through conversation with political theologies, as, for example, the Roman Catholic Church's dialogue with Latin American liberation theology; in other cases the turbulent times were ripe for a revivification of older views advocating the Kingdom's reification in the present age as seen in the social and political work of the World Council of Churches and Theonomists. Each of these groups make significant use of the Kingdom theme in their theologies; we begin our analysis with the views of the Kingdom of the Roman Catholic Church.

THE KINGDOM IN ROMAN CATHOLICISM

The Kingdom Prior to Vatican II

The Kingdom of God has never been defined by the official magisterium of the Roman Catholic Church. Nor has the magisterium discussed the Kingdom in terms of topics relevant to the Kingdom's praxis, topics such as the relationship between the divine and human in the Kingdom, the transcendence and immanence of the Kingdom, and the spiritual and the political in the Kingdom of God.[1] In the past, eschatological subjects

---

[1] Richard P. McBrien, *Catholicism* (Minneapolis: Winston, 1981), 1132-34.

generally received only minimal treatment in the Catholic Church, and always eschatology was handled within the context of ecclesiology.[2] Given this subordination of eschatology to ecclesiology, it was not uncharacteristic that the Kingdom would simply be equated with the Catholic Church for much of that church's history. Statements identifying the church and the Kingdom appear as early as Augustine's *City of God* and the homilies of Pope Gregory the Great (A.D. 540–604).[3]

On into this century, papal encyclicals have also affirmed the subordination of eschatology to ecclesiology and the identification of church and Kingdom. In some cases the Kingdom is reduced to just one of the many scriptural images of the church. Pius IX (d. 1878), in *Amantissimus* to the bishops of the Eastern Church, states that Christ "instituted and established the Catholic Church . . . as the one kingdom of heaven."[4] The Encyclical *Mortalium Animos* of Pius XI (d. 1939) sees the illustrative function of the Kingdom for the church: the church is a "perfect society, by its very nature external and perceptible to the senses," which is why Christ "compared it to a kingdom, a household, a sheepfold, a flock."[5] Pius XII (d. 1958) declared in *Mystici Corporis* that "the Eternal Father

---

[2] Even within the confines of ecclesiology, Avery Dulles notes that the relationship between ecclesiology and eschatology in Roman Catholic teaching "occupied an extremely restricted place . . . none at all in scholarly theology, at least in the manuals" ("The Church as Eschatological Community," in *The Eschaton: A Community of Love*, ed. Joseph Papin [Villanova, Pa.: Villanova University Press, 1971], 69).

[3] In the *City of God* Augustine noted, "the Church even now is the kingdom of Christ, and the kingdom of heaven" (Augustine *City of God*, 20:9 [Loeb, Augustine *City of God*, 6:307, 309]). It should be noted that in the *City of God* the parallels between the heavenly City and the church are often inconsistent. Sometimes Augustine notes the earthly city as having two parts, one evil and one good, with the church being the visible expression of the latter (*City of God* 15:2; 15:5 [Loeb, 4:419; 4:429, 431]).

Gregory I read Luke 9:27 ("I assure you, there are some standing here who will not taste death until they see the kingdom of God") in conjunction with Matthew 13:41 and concluded that Scripture at times speaks of the church and the Kingdom as synonymous. See Homilia XXXII:6 in *MPL*, 76:1236-37.

[4] Encyclical *Amantissimus* to the bishops of the Eastern Churches; *Papal Teachings: The Church*, selected and arranged by the Benedictine monks of Solesmes, trans. E. O'Gorman (Boston, 1962), 165 (cited by John C. Haughey, "Church and Kingdom: Ecclesiology in the Light of Eschatology," *TS* 29 [1968]: 73).

[5] *Mortalium Animos*, in *AAS* 20, no. 1 (1928): 8; cf. Haughey, "Church and Kingdom," 73.

willed that the Church should be the kingdom of the Son of His love . . . a kingdom in which all believers would pay perfect homage of their intellect and their will."[6]

At least four observations may be made about the Kingdom and the church according to their identity in the Catholic Church. The first reflects the way the Kingdom and the church shape each other. That is, as the Kingdom is expressive of the final celestial state representing the fullness of God's transcendent rule over his creation, its identity with the church in turn buttresses the Catholic Church's doctrine of the heavenly destiny and existence of the church. The church in Catholic theology thus has legitimate claim as an end in itself. It is subordinate to nothing and seeks no other end.[7] On the other side, the historical presence of the church would also infer a realized eschatology for the Kingdom, though it should be noted this inference was not made within the general perspective of the Catholic Church. Second, it is exactly because of the Catholic Church's association of the church with the celestial Kingdom that little or no attention has been given to the Kingdom by the magisterium. Prior to Vatican II the institutional model of the Church inspired by the Counter-Reformation focused little on the heavenly church. Consequently the Kingdom also received little attention.[8] Third, Jesus' establishment of the church as the earthly form of the transcendent Kingdom easily inspired exalted visions of the church. The celestial transcendence of the Kingdom of God combined well with an *ecclesia triumphans* motif and helps to explain the judgment of many about the Catholic Church's history in the world of being the *ecclesia triumphans* rather than the *ecclesia militans et pressa*.[9] Fourth, the sparse treatment of the Kingdom as a subject in its own right meant little magisterial discussion of the Kingdom's praxis beyond functions of the institutional church. With the church as its own end, the Catholic Church remained trapped in its "religious perspective" of piety that was primarily mystical

---

[6] *Mystici Corporis*, in *AAS* 35, no. 7 (1943): 224; see Haughey, "Church and Kingdom," 73.

[7] See the expression of this in Avery Dulles, *The Reshaping of Catholicism: Current Challenges in the Theology of Church* (San Francisco: Harper & Row, 1988), 136-38.

[8] Avery Dulles, *Models of the Church* (Garden City, N.J.: Image Books, 1974), 116.

[9] Haughey, a Jesuit, states that "the Church is saddled with an ecclesiology of glory which makes reigning more inevitable than serving" (Haughey, "Church and Kingdom," 85).

and psychological "because the goal was only to redeem the individual soul from the clutches of this world."[10] Such a vertical perspective of mission was a chief source of discontentment for those in the Catholic Church who would later pursue more social involvement through liberation theology.

The Kingdom and Vatican II

The second Vatican Council (1963–1965) was convened by Pope John XXIII as an "update" *(aggiornamento)* and renewal of the Catholic Church so that it might better bring the gospel to the modern world. As such the documents it produced marked an important transition and point of departure for new expressions in many areas of Roman Catholic teaching, the Kingdom included. The two most critical documents of Vatican II for the discussion of the Kingdom of God are the *Dogmatic Constitution on the Church (De ecclesia)* and the *Pastoral Constitution of the Church in the Modern World (De ecclesia in mundo).*[11]

As is evident from the titles of these documents dealing with the Kingdom, Vatican II was not to be the liberation of the Kingdom of God from the confines of ecclesiology. There would be no definition or discussion of the Kingdom outside the doctrine of the church, even though there was substantial new attention to the subject of the Kingdom. This new attention is reflective of a general new awareness of eschatological themes and their implications for the church in the documents.[12] In a chapter added finally at the insistence of Pope John XXIII, *De ecclesia* asserts clearly the eschatological nature of the church and its consequent pilgrimage toward the consummation of history.

---

[10] Kristen E. Skydsgaard, "The Church as Mystery and as People of God," in *Dialogue on the Way*, ed. George A. Lindbeck (Minneapolis: Augsburg, 1965), 170.

[11] The Kingdom is also mentioned briefly in *Decree on the Church's Missionary Activity (Ad gentes)*. Citations are from the English translation, *The Documents of Vatican II*, ed. Walter M. Abbott, trans. Joseph Gallagher (New York: America, 1966), by article number of the text.

[12] The new awareness of eschatology within the Roman Catholic Church can be attributed in some part to the attention eschatology had received in Protestant biblical studies since Schweitzer. See Richard P. McBrien, *The Church in the Thought of Bishop John Robinson* (Philadelphia: Westminster, 1966), 47ff.

The Church . . . will attain her full perfection only in the glory of heaven. Then will come the time of the restoration of all things. . . . the promised restoration which we are awaiting has already begun in Christ, is carried forward in the mission of the Holy Spirit, and through Him continues in the Church. . . . The final age of the world has already come upon us. . . . The renovation of the world has been irrevocably decreed and in this age is already anticipated in some real way.[13]

In this context the theme of the Kingdom surely can move more freely, and it first appears in the opening chapter of *De ecclesia* within the Trinitarian framework of the document:

To carry out the will of the Father, Christ inaugurated the kingdom of heaven on earth and revealed to us the mystery of the Father. . . . The Church, or, in other words, the kingdom of Christ now present in mystery, grows visibly in the world through the power of God.[14]

The documents of Vatican II thus recognize the realized nature of the Kingdom, its vital connection to Christ, its relationship to the church in mystery, and the dynamic process of the Kingdom's growth.[15]

---

[13] *De ecclesia* 48. On the new eschatological tenor of Vatican II, see further Juan Alfaro, "Reflections on the Eschatology of Vatican II," in *Vatican II: Assessment and Perspectives Twenty-five Years After (1962-1987)*, ed. René Latourelle, vol. 2 (New York: Paulist, 1989), 501-13; George A. Lindbeck, *The Future of Roman Catholic Theology: Vatican II—Catalyst for Change* (Philadelphia: Fortress, 1970, 9-25; and Christopher Butler, *The Theology of Vatican II*, the Sarum Lectures, 1966 (London: Darton, Longman & Todd, 1967), 141-58. Lindbeck especially takes note of the new direction that the description of the church as the eschatological community in *De ecclesia* 48 means for the Catholic Church's view of itself and history.

[14] *De ecclesia* 3; see *De ecclesia in mundo* 39. It still should be noted that the material on the Kingdom in *Lumen gentium* was added only in the last draft of the document. For a history of this portion of the text see Herwi Rikhof, *The Concept of Church: A Methodological Inquiry into the Use of Metaphors in Ecclesiology* (London: Sheed and Ward, 1981), 30ff.

[15] Patrick F. O'Connell, "The Bishops, The Critics, and the Kingdom of God," in *Theology and the University*, ed. John Apczynski. The annual publication of the College of Theology Society, vol. 33 (Lanham, Md.: University Press of America, 1987), 91-92. Avery Dulles notes the sacramental model operant between the church and the Kingdom from this statement of *De ecclesia* 3. He states "this sacramental model correctly views the Church as the symbolic embodiment of the Kingdom" (Dulles, *Models of the Church*, 121).

While this new and initial spotlight given to the Kingdom is often argued as showing how "integral" the council makes the Kingdom in the Catholic Church's renewed theology, the greater message is conveyed by the content. Contrary to the contentions of numerous Vatican II apologists, the contents of the statement reveal only little change in the magisterium relative to the identity of church and Kingdom.[16] Here in this significant first mention of the Kingdom in *De ecclesia* the church is clearly the "kingdom of Christ now present in mystery." Later on, the identity is softened somewhat as the church "becomes the initial budding forth of that kingdom"[17] and the sacrament of the Kingdom, but there is still enough history behind these opening words to give Catholic theologian Avery Dulles cause to say, "In the documents of Vatican II, . . . the church is not simply a sign or pointer to the kingdom of God, nor is it a mere servant of the kingdom. The church is either identical with or at least central to the kingdom."[18]

The new eschatological awareness of the council also dovetailed with the council's pastoral concerns for the mission of the church, and the Kingdom finds important expression here as well. As Jesus inaugurated and manifested the Kingdom in his words and deeds,[19] so the church is charged to manifest the Kingdom by the Lord's commission.[20] The Kingdom is

---

[16] Kloppenburg says, "we must insist on this point: *The Church is not the kingdom of God and is not identifiable with the kingdom of God, but is rather its germ and beginning*" (Bonaventure Kloppenburg, *The Ecclesiology of Vatican II*, trans. Matthew J. O'Connell [Chicago: Franciscan Herald, 1974], 33 [emphasis his]). See also the denials of the church-Kingdom identity by O'Connell, "The Bishops, the Critics, and the Kingdom," 92; and Walter M. Abbott, *The Documents of Vatican II*, 17, n. 11.

[17] *De ecclesia* 5.

[18] Dulles, *Reshaping of Catholicism*, 138. Butler notes that an earlier draft of *De ecclesia* affirmed that the church is "this perfect city which holy writ calls the Kingdom of God" (Butler, *Theology of Vatican II*, 144).

[19] "The mystery of the holy Church is manifest in her very foundation, for the Lord Jesus inaugurated her by preaching the good news, that is, the coming of God's Kingdom, which, for centuries, had been promised in the Scriptures. . . . In Christ's words, in His works, and in His presence this kingdom reveals itself to men. . . . Those who hear the word with faith and become part of the little flock of Christ (Lk. 12:32) have received the kingdom itself. . . . The miracles of Jesus also confirm that the kingdom has already arrived on earth" (*De ecclesia* 5).

[20] "The Church . . . receives the mission to proclaim and to establish among all people the kingdom of Christ and of God" (*De ecclesia* 5).

ultimately the activity of God himself, but this does not weaken the church's concern and cultivation of it: "Earthly progress must be distinguished from the growth of Christ's kingdom. Nevertheless, to the extent that the former can contribute to the better ordering of human society, it is of vital concern to the Kingdom of God."[21] The descriptions in Vatican II of what is within the power of the church and its human instruments in regards to the better ordering of society in the name of the Kingdom are revealing. The council's position is that people in Christ can "spread" (*De ecclesia* 34), "proclaim" (*De ecclesia* 5), "establish" (*De ecclesia* 5, 13), "root" (*De activitate missionali* 15), "intensify" (*De ecclesia* 34), and "strengthen" (*De activitate missionali* 15) the Kingdom. The Kingdom then, as Haughey says, is "present, organic, immanent, and to some degree dependent on the Church."[22]

The Kingdom After Vatican II

The dependence of the Kingdom on the church, or, to put it another way, the relationship of the church to social transformation, has dominated the discussion of the Kingdom in Catholic theology since Vatican II. With the statements in the constitutions *De ecclesia* and *De ecclesia in mundo* not entirely unambiguous, advocates of all political views within the Catholic Church have tried to garner support for their own agenda from Vatican II. Since liberation theologians in Latin America were among the most radical, much, but not all, of the Vatican's reflection on the Kingdom since Vatican II has been made in the context of curbing the excesses of liberation theology.

One particular excess addressed by the Vatican was the perceived "broadening" of the Kingdom concept that threatened to minimize the Kingdom's concern with spiritual salvation. It was a mistake of emphasis, the pope said in the Apostolic Exhortation *Evangelii Nuntiandi* (1975), to suppose the Kingdom meant liberation from oppressive social structures, because it is "above all liberation from sin and the Evil One."[23] Likewise, the *Instruction on Certain Aspects of the Theology of Liberation* from the Congregation

---

[21] *De ecclesia in mundo* 39.
[22] Haughey, "Church and Kingdom," 85.
[23] Cited by McBrien, *Catholicism*, 1134.

for the Doctrine of the Faith was critical of liberation theology for its tendency to identify the Kingdom of God and its growth with human liberation movements almost to the point of the self-redemption of man by means of the class struggle.[24]

Another source of the Catholic Church's postconciliar reflection on the Kingdom is the International Theological Commission. Established in 1969 as a result of requests for a continuation of the scholarly and pastoral rapprochement characteristic of Vatican II, the commission's purpose was to give a continued hearing "for the common voice of theology amid all the diversities that exist."[25] In the years since its establishment the commission has produced documents on a variety of subjects, but the document most relevant to the Kingdom theme appeared in 1984 under the title "Select Themes of Ecclesiology on the Occasion of the Eighth Anniversary of the Closing of the Second Vatican Council." Constituted as a reexamination of *De ecclesia* in light of ecclesiological discussions since Vatican II, "Select Themes of Ecclesiology" does not break new ground on the Kingdom, but its elaboration of older themes does provide means of interpreting Vatican II.

On the subject of the church's relationship to the Kingdom, the commission recognizes the efforts in the last two centuries to distance the

---

[24] *Instruction on Certain Aspects of the Theology of Liberation*, IX:3. The text of the document is available in the appendix of Juan Luis Segundo, *Theology and the Church* (New York: Winston, 1985).

[25] Joseph Ratzinger, foreword in *International Theological Commission: Texts and Documents, 1969-1985*, ed. Michael Sharkey (San Francisco: Ignatius, 1989), viii. Pope Paul VI established the commission in a Consistory address, April 28, 1969 (*AAS* 61 [1969]: 431-32). The International Theological Commission is the counterpart to the Pontifical Biblical Commission, which was originally convened in 1902 and reconstituted in 1971. Both commissions are associated with the Congregation of the Doctrine of the Faith through their presiding officers. The International Theological Commission is comprised of thirty international members who serve five year terms and convene generally once a year. The commission selects its own topics for discussion but plans its program so as to serve various synods of bishops as well as the curial organisms of the church, for example, the Commission for Justice and Peace and the Pontifical Council for Culture. The history of the International Theological Commission is available in the publications of the Commissions' General Secretary, Philippe Delhaye: "Memoirs of the First Five Years of the International Theological Commission," *L'Osservatore Romano* (July 1, 1976), 1; Delhaye, "Paul VI et la Commission Théologique Internationale," *RTLv* 9 (1978): 417-23; Delhaye, "L'après Vatican II et la constitution de la Commission Théologique Internationale," *RTLv* 16 (1985): 288-315.

church from the Kingdom. It notes, however, that the separation is centered on seeing the church as a historical reality and the Kingdom as an eschatological one.[26] This distinction affirms for the commission the *sacramental* relationship of church and Kingdom taken up in *De ecclesia.*

> Sacrament is understood in its full sense of *jam praesens in mysterio*, . . . where the reality present in the sacrament is the Kingdom itself. . . . The Church is not a mere sign *(sacramentum tantum)* but a sign in which the reality signified is present *(res et sacramentum)* as the reality of the Kingdom.[27]

Within the sacramental relationship, the commission sees that in points of origin, growth, and destiny, Vatican II understands the Kingdom and the church as inseparable and perfectly synchronous. Thus, the present mode of the Kingdom that is the pilgrim church does include the wicked: "The Church is the holy Church, though including sinners among her own (*De ecclesia*, 8). The Kingdom itself, 'mysteriously present *(in mysterio)*,' is hidden in the world and history, and so not yet purified of elements that are a stranger to it (cf. Mt 13:24–30, 47–49)."[28]

Pervading the commission's work is the dynamic understanding of the Kingdom as the salvific process that culminates in the final eschatological rule of God. "The Kingdom of God," the commission says, " 'directs' history and utterly transcends all the possibilities of earthly fulfillment; it presents itself, therefore, as the action of God."[29] The saving action of the Kingdom was present in Jesus. A decision for him is a decision for the coming of the Kingdom.[30] The church, as the mystery modality of the Kingdom, operates freely in the process of universal salvation. The commission reiterates the wording of Vatican II, saying that the church "proclaims" and "establishes among all peoples the Kingdom of Christ and of

---

[26] *International Theological Commission*, ed. Sharkey, 302. The commission considers the discussion of the church as the "seed" and "beginning" of the Kingdom in *De ecclesia* 5 and 9 as expressing the Kingdom's and the church's "simultaneous unity and difference" (303).

[27] Ibid., 304.

[28] Ibid., 303.

[29] Ibid., 157.

[30] Ibid., 231.

God."[31] Moreover, it considers the church to actually "construct" the Kingdom in the present age.[32]

Application of the Catholic Church's construction of the Kingdom has been visible in the last decade in America through the pastoral letters of the U.S. bishops on the *Challenge of Peace* and *Economic Justice for All*, both of which are strongly premised on the vision of the Kingdom of God found in *De ecclesia*.[33] Their particular interest for us here is not in new dogmas about the Kingdom, but in what these documents represent of the Catholic Church's use of the Kingdom theme to address social issues. An eschatological denouement of history is evident in the letters that understand the Kingdom not just as the goal of celestial salvation but also a factor in the process towards the goal. In *The Challenge of Peace*, for example, the bishops claim as their assumption the ultimate peace of the eschatological Kingdom mediated through Christ. Peace is described as "one of the signs of the Kingdom present in the world."[34] The bishops consider that the Kingdom is capable of "progressive realization" in history and "therefore is continuing work, progressively accomplished, precariously maintained, and needing constant effort to preserve the peace achieved and expand its scope in personal and political life."[35] The church, as the "instrument of the kingdom of God in history," is uniquely called to make the peace of the Kingdom an ever greater reality.[36]

---

[31] Ibid., 303.

[32] Ibid., 280.

[33] O'Connell, "The Bishops, the Critics, and the Kingdom," 89, 94; see also Donal Dorr, *The Social Justice Agenda: Justice, Ecology, Power and the Church* (Maryknoll, N.Y.: Orbis, 1991), 52-53; Roger Haight and John Langan, "Recent Catholic Social and Ethical Teaching in Light of the Social Gospel," *JRelEth* 18 (1990): 103-28; *The Challenge of Peace: God's Promise and Our Response, A Pastoral Letter on War and Peace* (Washington, D.C.: United States Catholic Conference, 1983); *Economic Justice for All: Catholic Social Teaching and the U.S. Economy* (Washington, D.C.: United States Catholic Conference, 1986). Citations are by section number of the text.

[34] Challenge of Peace, n. 22.

[35] Ibid., n. 20.

[36] Ibid., n. 22.

Despite the many positive points in the Catholic Church's doctrine of the Kingdom, such as the view of the Kingdom as both realized and future, the dynamic action of the Kingdom in the salvific process, the general eschatological denouement of history, and the Kingdom's activity in the person and work of Jesus, two issues still loom large for the Kingdom in the Catholic Church. First, there can be little argument that the Kingdom theme is still confined to the realm of ecclesiology within the Catholic Church. Separate treatment of the Kingdom as a topic in its own right has yet to appear, and what discussion there has been on the Kingdom has always been done within documents primarily interested in the church. The situation of Vatican II is fairly typical: the Kingdom appeared most prominently in the ecclesiological documents, *De ecclesia* and *De ecclesia in mundo*. Even the International Theological Commission addressed the Kingdom only as a "select theme of ecclesiology."

The confinement of the Kingdom to the church does injustice to the biblical doctrine of the Kingdom. This is evident from the way ecclesiology has prevented the Catholic Church from seeing much need to deal with the Kingdom of God in its own right. The magisterium is yet to even define the Kingdom of God apart from the church. That this was not remedied at Vatican II has been admitted by even staunch defenders of the Catholic Church's exegesis of the Kingdom.[37] In all likelihood the reason for this situation is the enduring dominance of the traditional equation and subordination of the Kingdom to the church. While it is true that the magisterium of the Catholic Church no longer speaks of the Kingdom simply as an illustration of the church, and it no longer makes overt statements equating church and Kingdom, the evidence since Vatican II for any great change beyond this is not thoroughly convincing.[38] The impact

---

[37] Cf. O'Connell, "The Bishops, the Critics, and the Kingdom of God," 92.

[38] Certainly not convincing enough to maintain O'Connell's contention that the Kingdom was "integral" and "central" to the discussion in *Lumen gentium* of the "Mystery of the Church" (O'Connell, "The Bishops, the Critics, and the Kingdom of God," 90).

of the eschatological discussion within Protestantism during the last century has not yet been realized in the Catholic Church.[39]

That Vatican II did not set a substantially new course for the Kingdom in the Catholic Church's theology is seen in the difficulty the Kingdom had in gaining entrance to the documents in the first place. It was not until the final (i.e., third) draft that the Kingdom was added to *De ecclesia* and that mention of the Kingdom as an illustration of the church was taken out. Added to this is the ambiguous nature of the "organic" relationship Vatican II assigned the church and the Kingdom. When the church is portrayed as simply the "initial budding forth of the kingdom" or the Kingdom's earthly phase, no distinction has been made between church and Kingdom at an ontological level. At most, Vatican II and subsequent Catholic theology has separated the Kingdom and the church modally, with the church seen as the historical form of the Kingdom and the Kingdom as the eschatological form of the church. Just as Modalism was a furtive attempt to maintain the divine essence among the different members of the Trinity, so in its modalism of the Kingdom of God the Catholic Church has the church and the Kingdom partaking of the same essence. They are still really the same thing, as Skydsgaard noted shortly after Vatican II: "To state the church is not the kingdom of God in all its perfection but the beginning of it still cradles the idea of her unbroken continuity."[40] This

---

[39] In 1941 F. M. Braun noted the refusal to identify the church and Kingdom as perhaps the most significant characteristic of Protestant ecclesiology. He attributes this to the recent focus of the scholarly discussion on eschatology in which the church was seen as a messianic community looking forward to the realization of God's universal rule. With the mission of the church viewed in these terms, the church was subordinated to the Kingdom, contra the Catholic Church's paradigm (F. M. Braun, *Aspects nouveaux du problème de L'Église* [Fribourg: Librairie de l'Université, 1941], 301ff., 161-70). Typical of Protestantism's conclusions at this time was the statement of K. L. Schmidt: "The eschatological presuppositions of Jesus' self-designation as Son of Man, and of the institution of the Lord's Supper, prove that the idea of the Church also is eschatological. But this does not mean that Church and Kingdom of God are the same thing. They are not the same in the early Church, which certainly regarded itself as the *ekklēṭia* while continuing the proclamation of the Kingdom. Nor are they the same in the preaching of Jesus, for he promised the Kingdom of God to his Church, i.e., the Church which he founded. The *ekklēṭia* after Easter regarded itself as eschatological in this sense. Similarly the individual Christian may be called eschatological, because he is a justified sinner" (K. L. Schmidt, *ekklēṭia*, *TDNT*, 3:522-23).

[40] Skyksgaard, "The Church as Mystery and as People of God," 169.

context still allows for the propagation of some rather blunt statements of equation like those of Jean Carmignac,[41] Avery Dulles, cited earlier, and M. J. Cantley, in the *New Catholic Encyclopedia*, who reiterates, "The earthly phase of this glorious kingdom is the Church of Christ . . . that visible society of which Christ is the head."[42]

The simple historical/eschatological distinction of the Kingdom and the Church in the magisterium has not satisfied Protestants, or even all Catholic theologians, as doing justice to the biblical picture of the Kingdom and the church. About the time of Vatican II, Rudolf Schnackenburg, a Catholic scholar, had argued in his significant work on the Kingdom that

> God's reign is not so associated with the Church that we can speak of it as a "present form of God's kingdom," since this would suppose an amalgamation with the Church's history on earth. God's reign as such has no organization and goes through no process; it does not embrace the just and sinners, it is in no sense dependent upon earthly and human factors. It is not "built up" by men and thus brought to its goal. Yet all this can be said of the Church in its mundane form.[43]

It is evident that Schnackenburg had realized at least some of the effect of the eschatological climate pervading scholarly circles prior to Vatican II that maintained the centrality of the Kingdom to God's program and the church's subordination to it. The Kingdom subsumes the church and uses it as its instrument. It is greater than the church, absorbing all history. At the Judgment, for example, the Kingdom comprises those who were not even in the church, and it excludes some of those who were (Matt. 7:22–23;

---

[41] See the treatment of Carmignac's *Le mirage de l'eschatologie* in chapter three.

[42] M. J. Cantley, "Kingdom of God," *New Catholic Encyclopedia*, 17 vols. (New York: McGraw-Hill, 1967), 8:195. Compare this with Hugh Pope's statement nearly fifty years earlier: "The kingdom of God means, then, the ruling of God in our hearts; it means those principles which separate us off from the kingdom of the world and the devil; it means the benign sway of grace; *it means the Church as that Divine institution* whereby we may make sure of attaining the spirit of Christ and so win that ultimate kingdom of God where He reigns without end in 'the holy city, the New Jerusalem, coming down out of heaven from God'" ("Kingdom of God," in *Catholic Encyclopedia: An International Work of Reference on the Constitution, Doctrine, Disciplines, and History of the Catholic Church*, 15 vols. [New York: Encyclopedia, 1913], 8:647; author's emphasis).

[43] Rudolf Schnackenburg, *God's Rule and Kingdom*, trans. John Murray (New York: Herder and Herder, 1963), 233-34.

Luke 13:16; Matt. 13:24–30; 36–43; 47–50; and 22:11–13).[44] Though some of these ideas are occasionally to be found in Catholic theology,[45] it is still clear that the Catholic Church does not place the Kingdom at the center of its theological thinking.[46]

At the root of the Catholic Church's inability to cleanly distinguish the Kingdom from the church is the matter of the Kingdom's realization in the present era. Even the statement that the church is the earthly phase of the Kingdom needs more qualification. On this count the Catholic Church is clearly not alone. As we have seen numerous times already, exegetes of the Kingdom-as-present passages (e.g., the parables of the Kingdom and Luke 17:20–21) are habitually tempted to go beyond the Kingdom's presence in the power of the Holy Spirit (Matt. 12:28; Heb. 6:5). What was at hand in Jesus' miracles and manifested in his church was the Kingdom's power, but this power does not fulfill every dimension of the Kingdom's ultimate reality. Jesus' miracles were signs of the Kingdom that pointed to some other future reality. Ridderbos catches the sense of the Gospels:

> [Jesus'] miracles, however, are only incidental and are therefore not to be looked upon as a beginning from which the whole will gradually develop, but as signs of the coming kingdom of God. For the cures and the raisings of the dead done by Jesus only have a temporary significance. Those cured or revived might again fall ill and would eventually die. In connection with this, Jesus' miracles nowhere serve as a purpose but always as a means in his activities, and always remain subservient to the preaching of the gospel.[47]

---

[44] McBrien, *The Church in the Thought of Bishop John Robinson*, 52. See Schnackenburg, *God's Rule*, 230-32, and Kristen E. Skydsgaard, "Kingdom of God and Church," *ScotJT* 4 (1951): 383-97 for more detailed discussion of the relationship between the Kingdom and the church.

[45] Kloppenburg says that the church is only the instrument of the Kingdom's fulfillment (Kloppenburg, *Ecclesiology of Vatican II*, 32) and the International Theological Commission observed that the Kingdom directs all history (*International Theological Commission*, 157).

[46] Several voices within the Catholic Church have called for the Kingdom to occupy a more central position. See Karl Rahner, "The Church and the Parousia of Christ," *Theological Investigations*, trans. Karl-H and Boniface Kruger (Baltimore: Helicon, 1969), 6:298; Richard P. McBrien, *Do We Need the Church?* (New York: Harper & Row, 1969), 98; and Hans Küng, *The Church*, trans. Ray and Rosaleen Ockenden (New York: Sheed and Ward, 1968), 92-93.

[47] Herman Ridderbos, *The Coming of the Kingdom*, trans. H. de Jongste, ed. Raymond O. Zorn (Philadelphia: Presbyterian and Reformed, 1963), 115.

The second question of the Kingdom in Catholic theology concerns the new direction since Vatican II towards social involvement. What about the human role in the present aspect of the Kingdom? Certainly the new eschatological view of history in Catholic theology that constitutes the church as an eschatological community is to be welcomed. Unfortunately it is apparent that the failure to give central place to the Kingdom that occurs through the ontological blurring of the Kingdom and the church also tends to blur the relationship of human effort and the Kingdom. Do people really "construct" the Kingdom of God, as the International Theological Commission suggests? Do we build the Kingdom like we build the church? As we have seen from *De ecclesia* and *De activitate missionali*, Vatican II's decree on the church's missionary activity, O'Connell seems to be correct in saying that the bishops are building on the vision of Vatican II that calls for members of the church to establish, root, strengthen, and spread the Kingdom of God.[48] If it is true that the present era is the time of signatory Kingdom power, is it not better, however, to say that the Kingdom (or the Kingdom's power) now constructs the church, rather than vice versa?

Human effort is never characterized in the New Testament as "building," "constructing," "spreading," "establishing," or even "rooting" the Kingdom of God. The human actions that are associated with the Kingdom in the New Testament are of a different sort: we proclaim the Kingdom (e.g., Matt. 9:35; Luke 9:2; 9:60; Acts 28:31); we wield the keys of the Kingdom (Matt. 16:19); we inherit the Kingdom (Matt. 25:34); we enter the Kingdom (Matt. 7:21; Acts 14:22); we wait for the Kingdom (Mark 15:43); we seek the Kingdom (Matt. 6:33); and we work for the Kingdom (Col. 4:11). Admittedly the point here may be a small one semantically, but as the phenomenon of liberation theology amply demonstrates, language about "constructing" the Kingdom can easily reify the Kingdom in the present age in ways that separate it from its spiritual concerns. Utopian visions of evolutionary optimism dilute the Kingdom's spiritual message and threaten to attempt change without the necessary spiritual power. As Pope Paul VI answered liberation theology: the Kingdom's liberation

---

[48] O'Connell, "The Bishops, the Critics, and the Kingdom of God," 89. Although remember *De ecclesia in mundo* 39: "earthly progress must be carefully distinguished from the growth of Christ's kingdom."

is first and foremost a liberation from sin and the Evil One.[49] Dulles correctly notes the relationship of faith and action in expression of the Kingdom's power:

> The Kingdom of peace and justice is not simply a remote ideal for which we long. In Jesus Christ the Kingdom of God has entered into history. It is already at work, albeit germinally, transforming the world in which we live. Faith is the Christian's mode of participation in that Kingdom. Insofar as we have faith, the Kingdom takes hold of us and operates in us. This means that through faith we become instruments in the healing and reconciliation of the broken world. We become agents of justice and bearers of the power of the Kingdom.[50]

Due to its captivity to ecclesiology, the Kingdom of God in the Catholic Church still remains largely uncharted territory. From the Vatican's perspective, that does not seem likely to change without serious reconsideration of ecclesiological dogma. Until that happens, however, most use of the Kingdom will likely continue to come from the activists of the Catholic Church, as the U.S. bishops' pastoral letters and liberation theology testify.

THE KINGDOM IN THE WORLD COUNCIL OF CHURCHES

As the leading institutional venue for "ecumenical theology,"[51] the World Council of Churches (WCC) has given much attention to the theme of the Kingdom over the last thirty years. The majority of that attention has been within the context of social action on the order of the political and liberation theologies already discussed, so the parallels will not be repeated in depth. However, the doctrinal and missiological commissions of the WCC, the Commission of Faith and Order (CFO) and the Commission on World Mission and Evangelism (CWME) do provide important insights into the WCC's view on the Kingdom's theory and practice.[52]

---

[49] Pope Paul VI in the Apostolic Exhortation, *Evangelii nuntiandi,* 1975.

[50] Avery Dulles, "The Meaning of Faith Considered in Relationship to Justice," in *The Faith that Does Justice,* ed. John C. Haughey, Woodstock Studies 2 (New York: Paulist, 1977), 43. See also Dulles, *Models of the Church,* 124.

[51] Karl Hertz, "An Investigation of Ecumenical Theology," *Mid-Stream* 19 (October 1980): 404-16.

[52] The very nature of ecumenical theology requires a degree of caution when reporting on the whole movement. By design the WCC is primarily a forum for consultation, meaning it has the

God and the Nature of History

The theme of the Kingdom was an important feature of the twentieth-century ecumenical movement far before the official founding of the WCC at Utrecht in 1938. From the beginning the nature of the Kingdom's presence caused more conflict than did any other subject. The conflict centered particularly in the definition of the Kingdom and the implications for social involvement. Anglo-Saxon streams of the ecumenical movement, coming from the social-evolutionary views of the Social Gospel in America and Great Britain, tended to think of the Kingdom as a just and ethical society procured by the hard work of the Kingdom's people. Opposed to this position was the eschatological view of the German churches that had recently been influenced by the apocalyptic Kingdom of Schweitzer and Weiss. The Kingdom had nothing to do with this world; much less was it the work of humanity. It was a totally different and transcendent reality now only divinely evident in the hearts of its citizens. Clashes between these two views occurred in the early ecumenical conferences, such as the 1925 Universal Christian Conference on Life and Work held at Stockholm, Sweden.[53]

By the time of the founding of the WCC and its first General Assembly in Amsterdam in 1948, such eschatological battles had quieted down,

---

potential to be home to a whole spectrum of opinions, including the most radical. It is important, therefore, that the views of some members of some of the churches in the membership should not be taken as *prima facie* evidence for the direction of whole (cf. David L. Edwards, "Signs of Radicalism in the Ecumenical Movement," in *The Ecumenical Advance: A History of the Ecumenical Movement*, ed. Harold E. Fey, vol. 2, *1948-1968* [Philadelphia: Westminster, 1970], 373-445). Nonetheless, the general direction is not hard to detect from reports of the commissions and the general assemblies. Our discussion focuses on these sources.

53 Ernst Stähelin records the polarization of the two sides in the opening sermon of Anglican Bishop Frank Theodore Woods of Winchester and the reaction of the German Lutheran Bishop Ludwig Ihmels of Saxony. Woods had spoken of "the establishment of the sovereignty of Jesus Christ" and of the setting up of "the Kingdom of God on earth," to which Ihmels countered: "Nothing could be more mistaken or more disastrous than to suppose that we mortal men have to build up God's kingdom in the world" (Stähelin, *Die Verkündigung des Reiches Gottes*, 7:565-67; 568-70). See also D. J. Smit, "Kingdom of God," in *Dictionary of the Ecumenical Movement*, ed. Nicholas Lossky et al. (Grand Rapids: Eerdmans, 1991), 567-68; Nils Ehrenström, "Movements for International Friendship and Life and Work 1925-1948," in *The Ecumenical Advance: A History of the Ecumenical Movement*, vol. 1, *1517-1948*, ed. Ruth Rouse and Stephen Charles Neill, 2d ed. (Philadelphia: Westminster, 1967), 547; W. A. Visser 'T Hooft, "The Mandate of the Ecumenical Movement," in *The Uppsala Report 1968: Official Report of the Fourth Assembly of the World Council of Churches Uppsala July 4-20, 1968*, ed. Norman Goodall (Geneva: WCC, 1968), 314.

partly because of the advance of the mediating position that saw some presence of the future apocalyptic Kingdom in the world and partly because of World War II. The war had sufficiently doused the evolutionary optimism of the Social Gospel side, and the "otherworldly" side had become convinced of the world's need for the healing message and works of the church. The war-ravaged world now more than ever needed a unified front from Christ's people. Eschatological differences subsided beneath the favorite ecumenical axiom that "Doctrine divides, service unites."[54] Nevertheless the deeper issues of the conflict remained. Did world history have a divine purpose to which it was being drawn, or was history merely the backdrop to the real work of God, that of saving his people? When the official answer to these questions would come twenty years later, it would only confirm that the issue was already decided in the WCC's day-to-day quest of unity and renewal: the social-evolutionary side had won. The Kingdom of God was present and progressively being manifested in the ethical works of its citizens.[55]

The studied answer to the question of the nature of history appeared from the 1967 meetings of the CFO in Bristol, England. *God in Nature and History*, largely the work of the Dutch theologian Hendrikus Berkhof, addressed the question as to "whether the God of the Bible has any relation to the modern scientific [evolutionary] world-view, or has anything to say to the feelings of either optimism or pessimism which it creates in the hearts of contemporary men."[56] *God in Nature and History* contends

---

54 For a history of the WCC, see volumes of *The Ecumenical Movement,* ed. Fey, Rouse, and Neill, especially Willem Adolf Visser 'T Hooft, "The Genesis of the World Council of Churches," in *The Ecumenical Movement,* 1:697-724; Jean-Marc Chappuis, "The World Council of Churches: A Tentative Historical, Cultural and Theological Interpretation of Its Recent Development," in *The Nature of Church and the Role of Theology: Papers from a Consultation Between the World Council of Churches and the Reformed Ecumenical Synod, Geneva 1975* (Geneva: WCC, 1976), 30-44; and more briefly, Donal Dorr, *The Social Justice Agenda,* 63-82.

55 The status of the eschatological discussion in the 1930s and 1940s is noted by W. A. Visser 'T Hooft, "The General Ecumenical Development since 1948," *The Ecumenical Movement,* 2:21.

56 The text of *God in Nature and History* can be found in Günther Gassman, ed., *Documentary History of Faith and Order 1963-1993,* Faith and Order Papers no. 159 (Geneva: WCC, 1993), 289-311. On *God in Nature and History* see also Geiko Müller-Fahrenholz, "Salvation History," in *Dictionary of the Ecumenical Movement,* 898; Meredith B. Handspicker, "Faith and Order 1948-1968," in *The Ecumenical Movement,* 2:153.

that Christendom has been embarrassed by the evolutionary worldview and has typically and weakly answered its challenges either by denying the facts of science (fundamentalism) or the essence of the Christian faith (modernism), or by "limiting God's work to the inner life and to existential decision . . . denying his relations to the visible realities of nature and history (pietism, theological existentialism)."[57] By contrast Christianity should affirm the biblical message of God's relationship with nature and his intentions for history. Nature, history, and consummation are inseparable links of the chain of creation. In Israel's religion God used nature to bring understanding. Historical events like the deliverance at the Red Sea were means by which Israel gained knowledge of the covenant-keeping God.[58] The New Testament reveals the intricacies of this chain in the life-events and mission of Jesus Christ. He is the supreme historical revelation of the God who will consummate the creation with a display of glorious work *in history*.[59]

God's primary aim in history is the salvation of man. This goal however does not exclude God from working with nature in history because man's life is "embedded in the processes of nature . . . there is a continuous correlation between both. God's salvation has wider dimensions than the existential one."[60] Thus, man partakes in a universal history; secular and sacred histories join as one movement towards realization of God's goal, the final consummation of his reign, the Kingdom of God.[61] In solidarity with that end the church has an ethical thrust within history. Awareness of involvement with the universal history

> inspires men to react against all kinds of social, racial and economical discrimination and to strive with all their strength for world peace and world co-operation. In all this can be seen realizations of God's purposes for this world, signs of the coming Kingdom.[62]

---

[57] Gassman, *God in Nature and History*.
[58] Ibid., 292.
[59] Ibid., 294 (emphasis added). The consummation of the creation is a *"far higher work than creation*, far more than only the restoration of an original situation" (295; original emphasis).
[60] Ibid., 302.
[61] Ibid., 306-7.
[62] Ibid., 306.

The Kingdom's signs in the present history are both discontinuous and continuous with the consummation: discontinuous because this present history travails in sin and therefore does not approximate the glorious existence of the final consummation; continuous because "it may be believed that our works in the Church of Christ (1 Cor. 3:14) and our cultural achievements (Rev. 21: 24, 26) will be used as building-stones for the Kingdom of God."[63]

God in Nature and History establishes at a theological level two features important to the WCC's relationship to the Kingdom. First, the effacement of the boundaries between an evolutionary world history and salvation history gives great significance to "salvific" acts in history as contributory to that evolutionary process. What exactly might constitute such salvific acts is another matter, but it is nonetheless significant in the WCC that history be seen as progressing towards the goal of the Kingdom. Second, mention of the church's present actions as "signs of the Kingdom" is a common theme in the WCC's publications and is agreeable to most at the various points of the eschatological continuum, but the possibility that our "cultural achievements will be used as building-stones for the Kingdom of God" appears to go farther. It and statements like it that repeatedly come from the WCC have been a major point of contention for the WCC's critics.

The Kingdom as Measure and Motivation

The eschatological goal of the consummation in the Kingdom serves the two purposes of measure and motivation in the WCC. As a measure, the eschatological Kingdom of justice, peace, and freedom is the standard by which all Kingdom signs performed by the church are judged. These are the acts the church must seek to do in a world marked by injustice, war, and oppression. As a motivation, the Kingdom's inexorable draw of history toward itself encourages its people to optimism as they work. Their work is compelling and necessary. The twin themes of the Kingdom's motivation and measure punctuate the WCC's publications, particularly since the second General Assembly in Evanston, Illinois, in 1954, which

---

[63] Ibid., 309.

met under the theme "Christ—the Hope of the World." These statements from *The Evanston Report* give insight to the centrality of the Kingdom for the standards and motivations of the WCC's actions.

> It is certain that the perfect unity of the Church will not be totally achieved until God sums up all things in Christ. But the New Testament affirms that this unity is already being realized within the present historical order. By the power of His resurrection, Christ has granted this grace to His Church even now, and the signs of His work are discernible to him who has eyes to see.[64]

> The Church partaking through the Holy Spirit in the life of its Head is assured of the fulfillment of His work. The messenger of the unlimited grace of Christ looks towards the consummation of the Kingdom in which His redeeming love shall have achieved its full intention.[65]

> This troubled world, disfigured and distorted as it is, is still God's world. He rules and overrules its tangled history. In praying, "Thy will be done on earth as it is in heaven," we commit ourselves to seek earthly justice, freedom and peace for all men. Here as everywhere Christ is our hope. . . . We can therefore live and work as those who know that God reigns, undaunted by all the arrogant pretensions of evil, ready to face situations that seem hopeless and yet to act in them as men whose hope is indestructible.[66]

As it entered the turbulent 1960s, the WCC's own manifestations of the Kingdom evolved with the spirit of the age. The General Assembly at Uppsala in 1968 was a major turning point in the WCC's metamorphosis from a reflecting body to an acting one, as it challenged member churches to a new openness to the world for the causes of the Kingdom. Declarations affirming God's preferential option for the poor and the oppressed came very close to those made by the Catholic bishops in Medellín earlier

---

[64] W. A. Visser 'T Hooft, ed., *The Evanston Report: The Second Assembly of the World Council of Churches 1954* (New York: Harper & Brothers, 1955), 88.

[65] Ibid., 107.

[66] Ibid., 131.

that same year, and WCC action was initiated against South Africa in the struggle to combat racism.[67]

The surge to action crescendoed ideologically in the 1970s through the 1973 CWME Assembly at Bangkok, Thailand, which met under the theme of "Salvation Today." The assembled delegates pushed to enlarge the conception of salvation beyond the pietistic notions of a reconciled relationship with God to include any experience of the eschatological Kingdom's justice and peace in history. Biblical salvation was to be modeled after the shalom of God in the Old Testament with wholeness in every sphere of life. "Salvation is Jesus Christ's liberation of individuals from sin and all its consequences. It is also a task which Jesus Christ accomplishes through His church to free the world from all forms of oppression."[68]

The WCC's attention to the Kingdom came with grand circumstances into the 1980s with the next Assembly of the CWME in Melbourne, Australia, in 1980 under the theme: "Your Kingdom Come."[69] Plenary addresses and Section reports entertained topics as "The Kingdom of God and Human Struggles," "The Church Witnesses to the Kingdom," "The Church— Sign of the Kingdom," "Good News to the Poor," and "The Eschatological Royal Reign of God," all affirming the historical dimension of the Kingdom and the church's role in its work as unmasking the idolatry of corrupt institutions and economic systems, humbling the proud, seeking justice for the oppressed and redemption from captivity.[70]

The Kingdom in Unity and Renewal

The decision in 1982 for the CFO to undertake a new study on "The Unity of the Church and the Renewal of the Human Community" has

---

[67] See particularly the report of Section IV—Towards Justice and Peace in International Affairs, in *The Uppsala Report*, ed. Norman Goodall, 57-72. For an assessment of the impact of the Uppsala Assembly, see Philip A. Potter, "A Call to Costly Ecumenism," *EcuR* 34 (1982): 332, and Chappuis, "The World Council of Churches," 31-32.

[68] *Bangkok Assembly 1973: Minutes and Report of the Assembly of the Commission on World Mission and Evangelism of the World Council of Churches December 31, 1972, and January 9-12, 1973* (Geneva: WCC, 1973), 102; cf. 64-66.

[69] *Your Kingdom Come: Mission Perspectives: Report on the World Conference on Mission and Evangelism Melbourne, Australia 12-25 May 1980* (Geneva: WCC, 1980); Gerald H. Anderson, ed., *Witnessing to the Kingdom: Melbourne and Beyond* (Maryknoll, N.Y.: Orbis, 1982).

[70] Ernst Käsemann, "The Eschatological Royal Reign of God," in *Your Kingdom Come*, 61-71.

meant a new exposition of the Kingdom and its relationship to the original goals of the WCC. The initial stage of the study appeared in Faith and Order Paper Number 130, *Church Kingdom World: The Church as Mystery and Prophetic Sign,* in 1986, in which numerous papers reiterated the Kingdom's eschatological nature and the church's function as its historical anticipation.[71] The most significant essay relating the Kingdom itself to unity and renewal was written by Jan Milic Lochman of the University of Basle and was titled "Church and World in the Light of the Kingdom of God."[72]

Lochman's presentation of the Kingdom for the CFO seeks to avoid many of the overstatements so characteristic of the Kingdom's conflictual history in the WCC, while at the same time laying the theological groundwork for Christian unity and the renewal of the world. He echoes familiar themes of Dietrich Bonhoeffer as to the past mistakes of otherworldliness and secularity for the Kingdom. The Kingdom is neither a "paradise of the heart" for the escape of earthly tribulations, nor is it the interpretive dead-end of "some earthly goal of the church."[73] The New Testament, Lochman says, lays down the ultimate nature of the Kingdom as dynamic. It was summarized centuries ago by Origen: In the Gospel the Kingdom of God is Christ himself *(In evangelio est Dei regnum Christus ipse).* The Gospel is "basically the good news of the coming kingdom of God, of the liberating promise and claim of that kingdom."[74] The promise means earthly possibilities because the Kingdom is for the poor and every member of the human race in their need. To earthly realities the Kingdom comes in earthly realities: "[The Kingdom] approaches these realities in as earthly a way as could possibly be imagined: biologically, economically, historically and materially."[75] The Gospel of the Kingdom demands from the beginning

---

[71] See for example Gennadios Limouris, "The Church as Mystery and Sign in Relation to the Holy Trinity—In Ecclesiological Perspectives," in *Church Kingdom World: The Church as Mystery and Prophetic Sign,* ed. Gennadios Limouris (Geneva: WCC, 1986), 42; and Dumitru Staniloae, "The Mystery of the Church," in *Church Kingdom World,* 56-57.

[72] Jan Milic Lochman, "Church and World in the Light of the Kingdom of God," in *Church Kingdom World,* 58-72.

[73] Ibid., 59.

[74] Ibid., 61.

[75] Ibid., 66.

conversion to its claims, which means defiance to all the power structures of a cosmos alienated from the Kingdom.

> [W]e should and can pray: "Thy kingdom come!" This is a "word of defiance." Certainly not one which wipes out as if by magic the oppressive circumstances we have referred to but one which does bring them within the force field of the kingdom of God and thereby relativizes them and robs them of their seeming ultimate validity.[76]

The perspective of the Kingdom establishes a dialectic between the church and the world. On one hand, by means of the Kingdom the world and the church share the same ultimate destiny and in this they are united, but on the other hand, the church is not the world and retains her distinct mission to the world prior to the end of history.[77] The means of this mission in the present is the pneumatological emphasis of the Kingdom. Romans 14:17 in conjunction with 1 Corinthians 12:13 sustains the pneumatological emphasis of the Kingdom in the church as well as identifying the direction of the church's efforts. The Kingdom dynamic of the Spirit directs the church toward unity in itself, "Jews or Greeks, slaves or free," all were made to drink of the one Spirit and unity in the world. "Every form of 'apartheid' is sin—indeed, in this correct sense, the sin against the Holy Spirit."[78]

Lochman's more moderate understanding of the Kingdom, in comparison to the radicalism of the General Assemblies and the CWME documents, demonstrates the sometimes schizophrenic nature of "ecumenical theology" and thereby offers some justification for caution in evaluating WCC theology.[79] Whether they be extreme or moderate, individual voices in the WCC cannot be taken uncritically as representative of the whole body. Nonetheless, the specter of utopianism does seem to be fairly pervasive in the WCC understanding of the Kingdom. Frequent talk of the

---

[76] Ibid., 67.

[77] Ibid., 68.

[78] Ibid., 71.

[79] As Hertz notes, ecumenical theology is by nature conflictual (Hertz, "An Investigation of Ecumenical Theology," 406-8), and this no doubt contributes to the wide range of views on the Kingdom in the theology of the WCC.

church's "building the Kingdom" and the "utopian vision" abounds in WCC Assembly reports and plenary addresses, despite denials of utopianism by WCC apologists.[80] Several other streams of evidence also converge on this utopian vision in the WCC, giving us the group's tenor as far as the Kingdom of God is concerned.

First, the triumph of the Social Gospel group has been fully realized in the prevailing definition of the Kingdom in ecumenical circles. In the recent *Dictionary of the Ecumenical Movement,* Smit concludes: "generalizing, one can say that the notion of the kingdom as an ideal society, characterized by equality, justice, and freedom, has gradually been accepted."[81] The consistent anthropomorphic tone of such a definition speaks against the biblical, theological tone of the Kingdom *of God* and the christological tone of the Kingdom *of Christ.* The ecumenical vision of the

---

[80] See the statements of human effort building the Kingdom in *Faith in the Midst of Other Faiths: Reflections on Dialogue in Community,* ed. S. J. Samartha (Geneva: WCC, 1977), 56, 140; *Bangkok Assembly 1973,* 80; and the report of the Section on "Structures of Injustice and Struggles for Liberation," in *Breaking Barriers: The Official Report of the Fifth Assembly of the World Council of Churches, Nairobi, 23 November-10 December, 1975,* ed. David M. Paton (London: SPCK; Grand Rapids: Eerdmans, 1976), 100-19, which, as one reviewer says, "assumes that man can be liberated from the 'structures of injustice' and 'other destructive powers' but does not acknowledge clearly that the new liberated order will be subject to further injustice or corruption. Evil appears to reside exclusively in the external forces rather than in the human heart" (Ernest W. Lefever, *Nairobi to Vancouver: The World Council of Churches and the World, 1975-1987* [Washington, D.C.: Ethics and Public Policy Center, 1987], 7-8). Pauline M. Webb, former vice chairman of the WCC Central Committee, said in an essay to preview Bangkok '73: "The aim of the Section on Salvation and Social Justice will be to understand how the message of salvation in Christ . . . takes the inevitability out of the injustice of our present national and international institutions and liberates mankind into the possibility of achieving that new order in which the kingdoms of this world indeed become the kingdoms of our God and of His Christ" (Pauline M. Webb, "Salvation Today," *This Month [Ecumenical Press Service]* 33 [December 1972]: 3. Utopianism is denied in the WCC by Hertz, "An Investigation of Ecumenical Theology," 415. For more on utopianism in the WCC, see Peter Beyerhaus, "A Biblical Encounter with some Contemporary Philosophical and Theological Systems," in *In Word and Deed: Evangelism and Social Responsibility,* ed. Bruce J. Nicholls (Grand Rapids: Eerdmans, 1985), 173-76; and Dale Vree, *On Synthesizing Marxism and Christianity* (New York: John Wiley & Sons, 1976), 37ff.

[81] Smit, "Kingdom of God," in *Dictionary of the Ecumenical Movement,* 567. See also the supposition that the WCC's goal of a "responsible society" "stem[s] from the expectation of the Kingdom of God, from the ethos of the Old Testament, and from the appearance of the new humanity in Jesus Christ" (Goodall, *Uppsala Report,* 310).

Kingdom so broadened in terms of just social circumstances is vulnerable to denying the biblical necessity of the personal affirmation of the lordship of Jesus, the King, to be in the Kingdom.[82]

Second, the earthly realization of the Kingdom in this age by human hands is supported by the broadened definition of salvation hammered out in Bangkok at the CWME Assembly in 1973. Two things tend to happen when salvation is equated completely with being "whole, healed, fed, clothed, integrated, forgiven, reconciled to God and man":[83] (1) the urgency of spiritual salvation becomes proportionately diminished,[84] and (2) visions of complete salvation in this age by human attention to physical needs are encouraged. Scripture raises two problems, however, from such a compression of the Kingdom's "not yet" into its "already." First, Jesus' own

---

[82] The thrust of the ecumenical dialogue with non-Christian faiths in the name of the Kingdom could be admissible of this point. Stanley J. Samartha, former director of the WCC's Programme on Dialogue, appears to diminish the finality of Christ when he writes, "Unless one is prepared to forgive one's brother or sister, one cannot expect to be forgiven by the King when he wishes to settle accounts with his servants (Matt 18:23-35). And on the day of the last judgment when the King speaks to those at his right hand and those at his left (Matt 25:31-46), strangely enough, the line of demarcation is not between Christians and those who do not profess to be Christians. Christians do not find themselves slightly ahead of the line by virtue of their previous acquaintance with Jesus Christ. . . . As Christians we are possessed by God's love, but God's love is not an exclusive possession of Christians. There is considerable evidence that the children of the Kingdom may be rejected and replaced by others—'given to a nation producing the fruits of it' (Matt 21:43)" (Stanley J. Samartha, "The Kingdom of God in a Religiously Plural World," *EcuR* 32 [1980]: 160-61).

On the denigration of personal conversion to God through Christ versus collective conversion to the social agenda, note also the paranoid concern over the spread of "depoliticized" Christianity by WCC protagonist Donal Dorr, who suggests that the sole aim of such fundamentalist, sometimes Pentecostalist, sects "is to counter the growing commitment of Christians for the struggle for liberation" (Dorr, *The Social Justice Agenda*, 82).

None of the many New Testament passages about the Kingdom speak of the Kingdom's presence apart from confession of faith. Defining the Kingdom's presence in terms of just and free social conditions alone blurs the distinction of God's general benevolent will according to his own nature and the presence of his Kingdom (Ronald J. Sider and James Parker III, "How Broad Is Salvation in Scripture?" in *In Word and Deed*, ed. Nicholls, 103-4).

[83] Pauline Webb, "Salvation Today," 2.

[84] Bangkok '73 received strong criticism from evangelical circles for this. See *The Evangelical Response to Bangkok*, ed. Ralph Winter (South Pasadena: William Carey Library, 1973); and Harvey T. Hoekstra, *The World Council of Churches and the Demise of Evangelism* (Wheaton: Tyndale House, 1979).

ministry of the Kingdom falls short of this vision. Though Jesus is the model claimed by ecumenical theology, Jesus himself never gave a program of social action.[85] He never gave this kind of social salvation to anyone in his own ministry (nor did the apostolic church), nor was this kind of salvation the expectation of any first-century Jew for the present age.[86] Second, evolutionary triumphalism runs aground on Christianity's *theologia crucis*. This aspect of Christian thought argues that the presence of the eschatological Kingdom is manifested in this age through Christian suffering. Power through weakness as modeled in the suffering of the crucified Messiah is at odds with dependence on the power structures of this world to achieve salvific ends.[87] The New Testament shows the focus of the primitive church to have been personal and spiritual. Announcement of liberation from guilt, access to the Holy Spirit, and fellowship with God attest to the triumph of grace not power.[88] The *theologia crucis* is of course not antithetical to good deeds in service of the world, which are necessary to the proclamation of grace, but it does redirect the church's focus to the center of New Testament Christianity, the cross.

---

[85] I. Howard Marshall, "The Hope of a New Age: The Kingdom of God in the New Testament," *Themelios* 11, no. 1 (1985): 9; R. T. France, "Liberation in the New Testament," *EvQ* 58, no. 1 (1986): 3-23; Doug Brewer, "The Kingdom of God: Significant Recent Developments and Some Educational Implications" *JChrE*, Papers 98 (September 1990): 49-50.

[86] Note the third concentration point of the 1980 CWME at Melbourne, "Thy Kingdom Come." When the Melbourne assembly concludes "to announce the Good News to the poor is to call them to become protagonists, to organize themselves to claim the promises of the kingdom," it goes beyond Jesus (*Thy Kingdom Come*, 229). That is, Jesus did tell the poor the promises of the Kingdom (e.g., Matt. 5:5, 6), but he did not say they were necessarily fulfilled in this age. Every Jew of the first century knew the societal promises to be for the age to come, where injustice, oppression, and partiality would reign no more (E. P. Sanders, *Judaism: Practice and Belief 63 BCE-66 CE* [Philadelphia: Trinity Press International, 1992], 279-302). Jesus admits his personal adherence to this belief as well (Mark 10:30).

[87] See Pierre Bühler, *Kreuz und Eschatologie. Eine Auseinandersetzung mit der politischen Theologie, im Anschulß an Luthers theolgia crucis*, HUT 17 (Tübingen: J. C. B. Mohr [Paul Siebeck], 1981), and Hendrikus Berkhof, *Christ the Meaning of History*, trans. Lambertus Boorman (Grand Rapids: Baker, 1979), 104-6.

[88] See here Theo J. W. Kunst, "The Kingdom of God and Social Justice," *BS* 140/558 (1983): 113; David G. Kibble, "The Kingdom of God and Christian Politics," *Themelios* 7, no. 1 (1981): 25; Clowney, "The Politics of the Kingdom," 304-5; and Brewer, "The Kingdom of God: Recent Developments," 50.

Third, the CFO document, *God in Nature and History*, lends itself to the utopian vision of some in the WCC. The document's opening stanzas with their ringing endorsement of the evolutionary world view in the sciences and humanities, the parallel criticism of Christianity's lack of interaction with it, the general effacement of the boundaries between world history and salvation history, and the tacit assumption that the evolutionary movement of the world and humanity is a positive one, all serve utopianism. Biblical Christendom, of course, is not inherently opposed to the evolution of history, and the movement and purpose of world history in itself does not demand triumphal utopianism.[89] The history of this world and its occupants is a dynamic entity, not a static one, and theologies that relegate history to the purpose of "waiting for the gathering of the elect" deserve this challenge from the CFO. There is, however, need for caution exegetically in contending that the history of this age is gradually evolving in the direction of the future Kingdom in any way other than chronologically. Moreover, it can be justifiably asked whether a century of ecumenical activism, for example, has anything to show of this world being more "saved," namely, more humanly whole, than it was one hundred years ago. The *prima facie* evidence argues that injustice, war, and inequality have not faded at all worldwide; they have just changed faces through the years.

That the WCC's vision of salvation as to content and timing is at best lopsided is apparent. Earliest Christianity as recorded in the New Testament did not share the same emphasis on social action.[90] Given that this phenomenon is only tacitly admitted in the WCC, it is important to get behind the variance itself to the underlying hermeneutical presupposition. Similar to the contextual methodology of the liberation theologies, the WCC believes its agenda to be a legitimate extension of *the process* attested

---

[89] The main author of the CFO's *God in Nature and History*, Hendrikus Berkhof, himself took the church's praxis of the Kingdom more in line with Christ's sufferings than his eschatological glory. The presence of the final Kingdom is felt in this age through the church's suffering persecution, apostasy, and competing doctrines of salvation (Hendrikus Berkhof, *Christ the Meaning of History*, 104-6).

[90] Though early Christianity appears more interested in proclamation and conversion, it did have some concern for physical needs and doing good works (Eph. 2:9-10; Titus 2:14; 3:14). By comparison to the WCC, however, it was politically passive and started first with the needs in the church (Gal. 6:10; 1 Tim. 5:9).

by the New Testament. Ernst Käsemann articulated this belief in his plenary address before the General Assembly at Melbourne in 1980, and he demonstrates the service some streams of New Testament scholarship have been to ecumenical theology. Käsemann first noted the undeniable "plurality of theological systems" and corresponding "pluriformity" in the Christian community of the first century: "There has never been in the church any empirically provable unity in theology or in organization."[91] This situation grants a mandate for Christians centuries later who might not find their theology or particular form in the New Testament: "These facts," he states, "still have precise implications for us today. Understood rightly, they permit, indeed demand, theological insights for the contemporary situation of Christianity."[92] Even though the WCC's social-political focus is not matched by *any* of the plural theologies or forms of the New Testament church, an observation Käsemann fails to make, this is not the critical issue. Justification for the WCC's agenda does not need to be found in the New Testament writings themselves; it comes from partaking of the same process as the early Christians, that is, a contextualized process. Taking this road, the WCC inherits the same weakness as liberation theologians when it comes to claims for universality and objectivity of theological pronouncements.[93] That is, the degree to which the WCC's locus of normativity is found in the perceived process behind the New Testament and not the New Testament itself is the degree to which relativity and subjectivity prevail over the WCC's theological product. Because Scripture is not normative in the WCC, the argument can be made that neither is WCC theology. The biblical control over what is Christian and what is not is reduced drastically and theology fails to persuade.

Over against such excesses, mediating voices for the Kingdom do exist within the WCC. Lochman has already been noted as a more moderate member of the CFO, though some aspects of his view still fit well with the

---

[91] Käsemann, "The Eschatological Royal Reign of God," 68-69.

[92] Ibid., 69.

[93] Hertz notes the importance of claims for universality and objectivity for a theology to become dominant. "No matter how particular the situation within which the theologian is working, it is inherent in theology to claim that what is taught is valid for all" ("An Investigation of Ecumenical Theology," 407).

WCC's overall thrust.[94] Emilio Castro, former director for CWME and former general secretary of the WCC, is also deserving of mention as a moderate voice in the WCC for the Kingdom. His apologetic works for the WCC to the evangelical, Roman Catholic, and Orthodox churches are more successful in maintaining the balance of work and proclamation, personal and collective conversion, in the Already and the Not Yet of the Kingdom.[95] It is truly unfortunate that voices like this appear to be in the minority of the WCC.

EVANGELICALISM

Contemporary evangelicals come from many denominational groups but are chiefly the product of three distinct religious movements.[96] The first movement, which contributed the basic doctrinal orientation, was the Protestant Reformation. The Reformers' emphasis on biblical doctrine and personal salvation is at the core of the claim to the name "evangelical," which comes from the New Testament word *euangelion,* meaning "good news" or "gospel." To this focus on the gospel was added the "convertive piety" of eighteenth- and nineteenth-century Pietism (including English Methodism), with its revivalism and concern for a conscious awareness of conversion. Finally, modern evangelicalism in its broadest sense as it will

---

[94] That Lochman still refers to conversion primarily in terms of commitment to a course of action with regards to the world will not satisfy the more pietistic members of his audience. See Lochman, "Church and World," 64-65.

[95] See Emilio Castro, *Sent Free: Mission and Unity in the Perspective of the Kingdom,* Risk book series no. 23 (Geneva: WCC, 1985), especially 46ff.; Castro, "Your Kingdom Come: A Missionary Perspective," in *Thy Kingdom Come,* 26-36; and the WCC edition of his doctoral dissertation from Lausanne, *Freedom in Mission: The Perspective of the Kingdom of God: An Ecumenical Inquiry* (Geneva: WCC, 1985).

[96] On the history of evangelicalism see Stanley J. Grenz, *Revisioning Evangelical Theology: A Fresh Agenda for the Twentieth Century* (Downers Grove, Ill.: InterVarsity Press, 1993), 22-35; Millard J. Erickson, *The Evangelical Mind and Heart: Perspectives on Theological and Practical Issues* (Grand Rapids: Baker, 1993), 13-29; George M. Marsden, *Fundamentalism and American Culture: The Shaping of Twentieth Century Evangelicalism, 1870-1925* (New York: Oxford University Press, 1980); William W. Wells, *Welcome to the Family: An Introduction to Evangelical Christianity* (Downers Grove, Ill.: InterVarsity Press, 1979).

be used in this chapter includes a reactionary element from the Fundamentalism of the late nineteenth and early twentieth centuries.[97] At its heart, *evangelical* refers to

> those who believe that all humans are in need of salvation and that this salvation involves regeneration by a supernatural work of God. Based upon his grace, this divine act is received solely by repentance and faith in the atoning work of Jesus Christ. Further, evangelicals urgently and actively seek the conversion of all persons world-wide to this faith. They regard the canonical Scriptures as the supreme authority in matters of faith and practice.[98]

Due to evangelicalism's theologically conservative nature, changes in matters of doctrine are generally slow to occur. For the Kingdom theme particularly this has meant little change in recent times. The writings of those like George Eldon Ladd and G. R. Beasley-Murray, presented in earlier chapters, continue to represent a great majority of evangelical scholarship on the subject of the Kingdom of God. But recently other evangelicals, including some outside the traditions of Ladd and Beasley-Murray, have produced works that discuss the Kingdom's application to the present time.

The Kingdom and Social Action: The Lausanne Congress (1974)

The Kingdom's social and political mandate for the nonevangelical groups of the WCC and political theologies did not go unheeded within evangelicalism, and evangelicals began to grapple with the social implications of the Kingdom.

Social and political ethics is certainly not aberrant to the history of evangelicalism. In their zenith in the eighteenth and nineteenth centuries

---

[97] In its narrowest sense, evangelicalism is a post-fundamentalist phenomenon stemming from the late 1940s. Today this brand of evangelical occupies the middle ground between theological liberalism and fundamentalism. See here George M. Marsden, *Reforming Fundamentalism: Fuller Seminary and the New Evangelicalism* (Grand Rapids: Eerdmans, 1987). The theological orientation of this middle ground is expressed in *Evangelical Affirmations*, ed. Kenneth Kantzer and Carl F. H. Henry (Grand Rapids: Zondervan, 1990).

[98] Erickson, *Evangelical Mind and Heart*, 13.

of American history, evangelicals, driven by a postmillennial eschatology, were in the forefront of social reform, particularly in founding charitable and educational institutions. Some of this zeal dissipated, however, in the Fundamentalist-modernist controversy of the early twentieth century, where Christian social action more and more became the provenance of the Social Gospel. Increasingly the language of the Kingdom was used "to effect a quiet transfer from the gospel about Jesus to a programme based on the ideology of the progressive capitalism of the United States at that point in time," as Leslie Newbigin observes.[99] Mainly as a hedge against the tide of liberal theology associated with the Social Gospel, American evangelicalism's vision of social involvement was gradually dichotomized into "soul-winning" and social reformation, with the priority falling to the former.[100]

The year 1974 marked a renewed consideration of evangelical social responsibility in light of the Kingdom of God through the first International Congress on World Evangelization at Lausanne, Switzerland (Lausanne I).[101] The resulting document, the Lausanne Covenant, gives uncharacteristic prominence to evangelical socio-political involvement, and several of the papers read at the Congress devoted considerable attention to the theme of the Kingdom as the basis for such involvement.[102] Though

---

[99] Leslie Newbigin, *Sign of the Kingdom* (Grand Rapids: Eerdmans, 1981), 33.

[100] Bo Rin Ro, "The Perspectives of Church History from New Testament Times to 1960," in *In Word and Deed,* 33; see also David J. Bosch, "In Search of a New Evangelical Understanding," in *In Word and Deed,* 68-72; Athol Gill, "Christian Social Responsibility," in *The New Face of Evangelicalism: An International Symposium on the Lausanne Covenant,* ed. René Padilla (Downers Grove, Ill.: InterVarsity Press, 1976), 92-95; Brian Stanley, "Evangelical Social and Political Ethics: An Historical Perspective," *EvQ* 62, no. 1 (1990): 19-36.

[101] July 16-25, 1974. Lausanne I brought together 2,473 participants from 150 countries and 153 Protestant denominations.

[102] Social involvement is not completely foreign to such evangelical congresses. See the summary of the social perspectives of the evangelical meetings at Wheaton (1966), Berlin (1966), Frankfurt (1970), Devlali (India) (1970), and Chicago (1973) by Tokunboh Adeyemo, "A Critical Evaluation of Contemporary Perspectives," in *In Word and Deed,* 42-46. Lausanne I was uncharacteristic of former congresses in (1) the penitence expressed in article five of the Lausanne Covenant for evangelical neglect of social concern, (2) the adoption of "sociopolitical" instead of "social action" in the final document, (3) the addition of direct references to alienation, oppression, and

some observers saw Lausanne I's discussion of the Kingdom as a negative polemic aimed at the excesses of the WCC, that is to say, Lausanne was mostly interested in what the Kingdom is not,[103] several affirmations about the Kingdom should be noted from Lausanne I. The Kingdom is an eschatological reality inherently related to the earth and is now active in history.[104] Jesus Christ manifested the Kingdom in his proclamation and miraculous deeds and therefore is the foundation for the church's ministry in the world.[105] The Kingdom is a dynamic experienced now by spiritual regeneration, "even in view of the demands for social realization."[106] This regeneration is the result of repentance and faith, which are the two demands of the Kingdom. Repentance, however, includes ethics: "where there is no concrete obedience there is no repentance."[107] The sphere of the Kingdom's reality is all of life. Thus as Jesus was a king his Kingdom has political ramifications, not according to worldly political systems, but

---

discrimination, and the denunciation of evil and injustice, and (4) the promotion of the entire section on social responsibility from seventh position to fifth position in the final document (René Padilla, introduction to *New Face of Evangelicalism*, 11).

The official reference volume of Lausanne I is *Let the Earth Hear His Voice: International Congress on World Evangelization Lausanne, Switzerland: Official Reference Volume: Papers and Responses*, ed. J. D. Douglas (Minneapolis: World Wide, 1975). The fifteen articles of the Lausanne Covenant are on pages 3-9. Significant essays from the congress concerning the Kingdom contained in the reference volume are by René Padilla, "Evangelism and the World," 116-46; Peter Beyerhaus, "World Evangelization and the Kingdom of God," 283-302; Andrew J. Kirk, "The Kingdom of God and the Church in Contemporary Protestantism and Catholicism," 1071-82; and José Grau, "The Kingdom of God Among the Kingdoms of Earth," 1083-92.

[103] There is no doubt of the evangelical hesitation to equate the Kingdom with worldly politics. See Padilla, "Evangelism and the World," 117-18; Beyerhaus, "World Evangelization," 285ff. Beyerhaus refers to this as the Zealot mistake and the "Mission of Barabbas" (Beyerhaus, "World Evangelization," 290).

[104] Beyerhaus, "World Evangelization," 284; Padilla, "Evangelism and the World," 128.

[105] Padilla, "Evangelism and the World," 128; see Gill, "Christian Social Responsibility," 96.

[106] See Beyerhaus's definition of the Kingdom: "The kingdom of God is God's redeeming Lordship successively winning such liberating power over the hearts of men, that their lives and thereby finally the whole creation (Rom 8:21) become transformed into childlike harmony with his divine will" (Beyerhaus, "World Evangelization," 286).

[107] Padilla, "Evangelism and the World," 128.

according to grace and love.[108] The church, while it is not the Kingdom, is the Kingdom's messianic community approximating the reality of the Kingdom most closely on earth.[109] The church, therefore, is the Kingdom's sign destined for a "messianic ministry to the rest of the nations."

"Kingdom ethics" has developed into a distinct branch of evangelical social involvement since the first Lausanne Congress.[110] To the Kingdom's universal dimension in Christ's universal reign are usually added the concepts of the enemies against which citizens of the Kingdom must fight. The "powers" mentioned in the epistles are seen as referring to evil structures and systems of oppression, meaning that Christians must contend with evil on the personal and institutional levels. Some expressions of Kingdom ethics include a communal feature of the Kingdom that virtually identifies the church and the Kingdom. The church is the domain of the Kingdom in the present age; Christians should withdraw from the world ruled by Satan into the church and radically practice the ethics of the Kingdom among themselves.

As we shall see in the sections that follow, "Kingdom ethics" is just one indicator of evangelicalism's growing awareness of the Kingdom as a potential basis for social praxis in the modern world. Two factors appear to be driving such an awareness. One is the growing distance from the

---

[108] Padilla, "Evangelism and the World," 130. The Lausanne covenanters do not call the imperfect peace and justice which results from sociopolitical involvement "salvation" or the "Kingdom of God." This rhetoric has however appeared in some evangelical writings. See Ronald J. Sider's note to his own monograph, *Evangelism, Salvation, and Social Justice* (Bramcote, Notts.: Grove Books, 1977), 11, which contained this view, which Sider has since renounced (Sider, "How Broad is Salvation?" 107, n. 32).

[109] Beyerhaus, "World Evangelization," 288; see Peter Savage, "The Church and Evangelism," in *New Face of Evangelicalism*, 115-16.

[110] The other main evangelical approach to social ethics has been called "creation ethics." This starts with the assumption that the first commands given to humanity before the fall have not been rescinded. These commands address the topics of marriage, work, the state, the community, the Sabbath, and so on. Christians must work to uphold the divine perspective in these areas because they represent the Creator's will. On Kingdom ethics and creation ethics, see Oliver R. Barclay and Chris Sugden, "Biblical Social Ethics in a Mixed Society," *EvQ* 62, no. 1 (1990): 5-18; Barclay, "The Theology of Social Ethics: A Survey of Current Positions," *EvQ* 62, no. 1 (1990): 63-86; Michael Schluter and Roy Clements, "Jubilee Institutional Norms: A Middle Way Between Creation Ethics and Kingdom Ethics as the Basis for Christian Political Action," *EvQ* 62, no. 1 (1990): 37-62.

Fundamentalist-modernist conflict. It is only in the last couple of decades that the doctrine of the Kingdom has become safe enough, that is, free from liberal associations, for evangelicals to once again use it as the basis of a holistic ministry of the gospel. With the passage of time evangelicalism is more free to recover its roots in its own social and political ethics. Another factor is a growing acceptance of the Kingdom as Already and Not Yet within evangelical circles that previously had been resistant to it.[111] Evangelicals are trying to come to grips with the implications of the Already of the Kingdom of God in the present age. The theologically conservative nature of evangelicalism means all of this is a rather new direction for evangelicalism.[112] As evangelicalism forges ahead into this new territory it will do so in a way different from Roman Catholicism or the liberal Protestantism of the WCC.

In comparison to Roman Catholicism, the Lausanne Covenant demonstrates that evangelicalism understands with Protestantism in general the Kingdom's necessary freedom from the domain of ecclesiology. Evangelicals are able to treat the Kingdom as a theme in its own right, and what is more, give the Kingdom the supreme place it deserves from the biblical record. Bright was correct more than thirty years ago when he stated, "the concept of the Kingdom of God involves, in a real sense the total message of the Bible."[113] Evangelicalism recognizes this fact.

Conversely, a danger of this liberation from ecclesiology is in the church missing the powerful thrust the Kingdom has for the Christian ministry. As we have seen this is an element largely absent in twentieth-century

---

[111] The traditional resistance of Dispensationalism to the "already" of the Kingdom in any form is changing with the arrival of what is being called "Progressive Dispensationalism." Progressive Dispensationalism acknowledges a spiritual presence of the messianic Kingdom operative in the post-Pentecostal life of the church. See Robert L. Saucy, *The Case for Progressive Dispensationalism: The Interface Between Dispensational and Non-Dispensational Theology* (Grand Rapids: Zondervan, 1993); *Dispensationalism, Israel, and the Church: The Search for Definition*, ed. Darrell L. Bock and C. A. Blaising (Grand Rapids: Zondervan, 1992); and *Progressive Dispensationalism*, ed. C. A. Blaising and Darrell L. Bock (Wheaton, Ill.: Victor, 1993).

[112] L. D. Smith, "An Awakening Conscience: The Changing Response of American Evangelicals Toward World Poverty" (Ph.D. diss., American University, 1986), 387, 391.

[113] John Bright, *The Kingdom of God: The Biblical Concept and Its Meaning for the Church* (New York: Abingdon, 1962), 7.

evangelicalism through to the first Lausanne Congress. The liberals' social gospel had proven to be a greater force for Christian sociopolitical involvement since the turn of the century. Despite its awakened conscience for social ethics, a great majority of evangelicalism is still tempted to abandon the world to its destiny because of its premillennial eschatology that understands the world to be doomed.[114] The reality of the Kingdom's presence as well as its future must therefore penetrate deeply into the evangelical mind for evangelicals to realize fully that the beautiful, right, and noble in this age has real continuity with the age to come. The presence of some form of the Kingdom teaches that this world is not to be abandoned as purposeless or disgusting; it is rather the practice-hall for the symphony, the dress-rehearsal of the theater, the preface to the book.[115]

Evangelicalism's dominant premillennialism, on the other hand, encourages a healthy separation between the Kingdom's Already and its Not Yet which spares evangelical praxis from the snare experienced in the WCC. Unbalanced emphasis on the Kingdom's presence is a great temptation to collapse the Not Yet into the Already and confuse the Kingdom's *imperative* with its *indicative*. As Sturm has pointed out, when the Kingdom represents both the good society and the new creation which transcends the conditions of history, ambiguity and confusion as to the relationship of the two will be the results.[116] Though some have pointed out quite legitimately that evangelical Kingdom ethics tends to blur this line between indicative and imperative, specifically by confusing the *de facto* rule of Christ with his rule *de jure*,[117] relative to the WCC evangelicalism enjoys little doubt about the nature of its socio-political involvement with regard to the Kingdom of God.

---

[114] Bosch notes the potential cross-purposes of premillennialism and evangelical social involvement. Premillennialism can teach evangelicals to tolerate corruption and injustice, and even welcome them as signs of the end (Bosch, "In Search of A New Evangelical Understanding," 71-72; cf. also Peter Kuzmic, "History and Eschatology: Evangelical Views," in *In Word and Deed*, 141-47).

[115] Kuzmic, "History and Eschatology," 150-54.

[116] Douglas Sturm, "Praxis and Promise: On the Ethics of Political Theology," *Ethics* 92, no. 4 (1982): 749.

[117] See the comments of Schluter and Clements, "Jubilee Institutional Norms," 40-41.

Postmillennialism Revived: Theonomy

American evangelicalism of the last generation has also seen a modest resurgence of postmillennial eschatology with its optimism for the church's establishment of the Kingdom in the present age.[118] Postmillennialism, though it has claimed roots for itself back to the early church, experienced its zenith in American evangelicalism early in the twentieth century.[119] The reality of the First World War, however, shattered postmillennial optimism, and its popularity waned. Today very few evangelicals adhere to it formally, though many have articulated its beliefs on a popular level.[120]

---

[118] See John Jefferson Davis, *Postmillennialism Reconsidered* (Grand Rapids: Baker, 1986); Loraine Boettner, "Postmillennialism," in *The Meaning of the Millennium: Four Views,* ed. Robert G. Clouse (Downers Grove, Ill.: InterVarsity Press, 1977), 117-41. Classic postmillennialism includes five tenets, outlined by the *New Schaff-Herzog Encyclopedia of Religious Knowledge:* (1) through the preaching of the gospel and dramatic outpouring of the Holy Spirit Christian missions and evangelism will attain remarkable success, and the church will enjoy an unprecedented period of numerical expansion and spiritual vitality; (2) this period of spiritual prosperity, the millennium, understood as a long period of time, is to be characterized by conditions of increasing peace and economic well-being in the world as a result of the growing influence of Christian truth; (3) the millennium will also be characterized by the conversion of large numbers of ethnic Jews to the Christian faith (Rom. 11:25-26); (4) at the end of the millennial period there will be a brief period of apostasy and sharp conflict between Christian and evil forces (Rev. 20:7-10); and (5) finally and simultaneously there will occur the visible return of Christ, the resurrection of the righteous and the wicked, the final judgment, and the revelation of the new heavens and the new earth (cited by Davis, *Postmillennialism Reconsidered,* 11).

[119] On the history of postmillennialism see Davis, *Postmillennialism Reconsidered,* 16-22; Millard J. Erickson, *Contemporary Options in Eschatology* (Grand Rapids: Baker, 1977), 58-62; and Greg Bahnsen, "The Prima Facie Acceptability of Postmillennialism," *JChrRec* 3, no. 2 (1976-1977): 48-105.

[120] The revivalism of what came to be known popularly in American politics of the 1980s as the New Christian Right (cf. Steve Bruce, *The Rise and Fall of the New Christian Right: Conservative Protestant Politics in America 1978-1988* [Oxford: Clarendon, 1988]), a coalition of diverse groups most commonly associated with the Moral Majority and its leader, Jerry Falwell, offers a very postmillennial view of the future of Christian influence over the secular government. Numbered in this view, according to Jimmy Swaggert, should also be the organizations and teachings of Pat Robertson, Earl Paulk, Rex Humbard, Richard Roberts, and Robert Tilton, and their doctrines known as "The Dominion Kingdom," "The Kingdom Age," and the "Positive Gospel" (Jimmy Swaggert, "The Coming Kingdom," *Manna* 1, no. 1 [1988]: 3, 7-8). Robert G. Clouse has convincingly argued the case that the New Christian Right is postmillennial in its rhetoric but premillennial in doctrinal beliefs (Clouse, "The New Christian Right, America, and the Kingdom of God," *ChrSchR* 12, no. 1 [1983]: 1-16).

A relatively new group for which postmillennialism is an attendant doctrine is associated with groups like Chalcedon Ministries and is popularly known as Theonomy or Christian Reconstruction.[121] Key figures in the group are Gary North, Greg Bahnsen, David Chilton, James B. Jordan, Norman Shepherd, and R. J. Rushdoony. Members of the movement began publishing their views in the late 1960s and are anchored significantly in Rushdoony's *Institutes of Biblical Law*, published in 1973.[122] In their writings Theonomists claim the universal applicability of the Old Testament law for personal and social ethics (hence the derivation of their name). Jesus, for example, is said to have clearly taught the continued application of the law in Matthew 5:17–19.[123] Politically, the continuity of the law means a continuity between the civil government of Israel and the civil magistrates of all human society. Thus, the civil magistrate is supposed to enforce the injunctions of the Mosaic law, including retributions and penalties.[124] It is in correlation to this that Theonomists advocate a hybrid kind of postmillennialism.[125] They argue that the effect of God's law on his creation will mean the eventual establishment of the Kingdom in history.

---

[121] Theonomy finds current expression in *Christianity and Civilization*, the Institute for Christian Economics, the *Journal of Christian Reconstruction*, and the Geneva Divinity School Press of Tyler, Texas.

[122] R. J. Rushdoony, *The Institutes of Biblical Law* (Nutley, N.J.: Craig, 1973). Other significant Theonomist writings include R. J. Rushdoony, *The Foundations of Social Order* (Nutley, N.J.: Presbyterian and Reformed, 1972); and *Thy Kingdom Come* (Phillipsburg, N.J.: Presbyterian and Reformed, 1971); David Chilton, *Paradise Restored: An Eschatology of Dominion* (Tyler, Tex.: Reconstruction, 1985); Greg L. Bahnsen, *Theonomy in Christian Ethics*, rev. ed. (Phillipsburg, N.J.: Presbyterian and Reformed, 1984); Gary North, *Millennialism and Social Theory* (Tyler, Tex.: Institute for Christian Economics, 1990); North and Gary DeMar, *Christian Reconstruction: What It Is, What It Isn't* (Tyler, Tex.: Institute for Christian Economics, 1991).

[123] See the significant chapter on this passage in Bahsen, *Theonomy in Christian Ethics*, 39-86. Theonomists understand the ceremonial law to be fulfilled in Christ, so it is the moral and social ethic of the Old Testament that continues.

[124] John A. Spark, "Biblical Law: The Reconstruction of the Criminal Law: Retribution Revived," *JChrRec* 3, no. 2 (1976-1977): 128-38; Bahnsen, *Theonomy in Christian Ethics*, 317-472.

[125] In distinction from classic postmillennialism, Theonomists see more of a literal fulfillment of the Old Testament prophecies in the millennial Kingdom. They look for the church to establish a visible, earthly, theocratic Kingdom prior to the consummation of this millennial age (Bahnsen, *Theonomy and Christian Ethics*, 427-28).

> Postmillennialism . . . holds that God has provided the way for this
> conquest: His law. Every word that God speaks is law, it is binding on
> man. Grace, love and law are only contraries in a pagan view—in God
> they serve a common purpose, to further his Kingdom and his glory.[126]

In making disciples as Jesus commanded, the church is literally to put the nations of the world under the discipline of God's rules. The goal is nothing short of the world's complete conformity to God, which involves Christians' dominion over all ethical rebels, over nature, and over lawful subordinates.[127] Anything less than this goal is a denial of the Dominion Covenant given to God's people to subdue the earth on God's behalf.[128]

Tactically, Theonomists view education as the primary "program of conquest."[129] Discipling of the nations will take place when the whole counsel of God is preached and there is a detailed and comprehensive knowledge of God's revealed law. The program of education includes a reexamination of popular eschatologies of defeat and a recovery in the Christian community of the more optimistic stance found in the postmillennial "eschatology of victory." In the pagan community the program of education must take place through preaching the gospel to every person and teaching of the law to every person. Evangelism is to be "dominion-oriented," which means it is to be centered on the application of the law of God to the real problems of real people. When people are won to the Kingdom of God and discipled in the law of God, the Kingdom begins to permeate every sphere and institution, including church, state, family, economy, school, and farm. Books, newsletters, pamphlets, training programs, and Christian schools at all levels are the means to achieve the desired goals.

---

[126] Rushdoony, *Institutes of Biblical Law*, 126. See chapter eight, "The Kingdom of God," in Gary North, *Unconditional Surrender: God's Program for Victory* (Tyler, Tex.: Geneva Divinity School, 1985).

[127] Gary North, "The War Between Three Types of Religions," *Biblical Economics Today* 8, no. 1 (1985): 2.

[128] Theonomists denounce all other eschatologies as "defeatist" or "escapist" (Rushdoony, "Postmillennialism Versus Impotent Religion," *Journal of Christian Reconstruction* 3, no. 2 [1976-1977]: 122-27; North, "Three Types of Religions," 1-4). "Pessimillennialism" is another term of North's (*Millennialism and Social Theory*, 71ff.).

[129] See chapter nine, "A Strategy For Dominion," in North's *Unconditional Surrender*, 215-28.

As their tactics indicate, the fact that the Kingdom is already present and gradually taking full control of the world gives the postmillennialism of the Theonomist a certain clarity of purpose. The Kingdom is the final purpose for this age, and its advance is in the hands of its subjects. This almost complete collapse of the Kingdom's Not Yet into its Already, however, is precisely the undoing of postmillennialism in general and Theonomy in particular. Aside from the exegetical difficulties Theonomists have with their understanding of the continuity of the Mosaic law,[130] they suffer the incurable utopian fallacy in evidence in some parts of the WCC. The course of modern history, Theonomist's lack of a *theologia crucis*,[131] the lack of a biblical mandate for the church to "build" the Kingdom, and the posture of the apostolic church itself all inveigh against the utopian dreams of Reconstruction postmillennialism.

The Kingdom and Signs and Wonders

A third recent evangelical movement making significant use of the Kingdom in theology and praxis is the self-dubbed "Third Wave."[132] The Third Wave is international, conservative, and charismatic; it is centered in the Vineyard Ministries International, based in Anaheim, California, and led by John Wimber since 1977. Wimber was also the chief theologian in the movement's early years, though he would defer to others now.[133] He has written much on the Kingdom of God as the basis for the Vineyard's

---

[130] Meredith G. Kline, "Comments on an Old-New Error," *WestTJ* 41 (1978): 172-89; Norman L. Geisler, "A Premillennial View of Law and Government," *BS* 142 (July 1985): 250-56; Robert P. Lightner, "A Dispensational Response to Theonomy," *BS* 143 (July 1986): 228-45; Douglas E. Chismar and David A. Rausch, "Regarding Theonomy: An Essay of Concern," *JEvThS* 27, no. 3 (1984): 315-23.

[131] See for example Gary North, "Sociology of Suffering," in *Millennialism and Social Theory*, 210-37.

[132] Missiologist C. Peter Wagner applied the terminology after the two other great outpourings of the Holy Spirit in Western Christianity in this century. The first wave represents the Pentecostalism of the early twentieth century, and the second wave is the charismatic movement of the 1960s and 1970s. See his testimony of his own encounter with the Holy Spirit in *Power Encounters Among Christians in the Western World*, ed. Kevin Springer (San Francisco: Harper & Row, 1988).

[133] Among these would be Don Williams, Jack Deere, and Wayne Grudem.

ministry and as associated most notably with "signs and wonders" of the Holy Spirit.[134]

The Third Wave movement owes its theological understanding of the Kingdom to the writings of the evangelical scholar George Eldon Ladd. As Wimber testifies in the booklet *Kingdom Come,* Ladd's mediating position of the Already/Not Yet of the Kingdom came into his purview while he was on staff in the Department of Church Growth at Fuller Theological Seminary. It was when he read Ladd's *Presence of the Future* and *Crucial Questions About the Kingdom of God* in 1977 that Wimber realized for the first time that the Kingdom of God was for today.[135] He saw that the Kingdom was not just for the future millennium but that Jesus came to usher in the Kingdom now in the present age. Going beyond Ladd into the social praxis of the Kingdom,[136] Wimber saw that the signs, wonders, and miracles associated with the Kingdom's coming in Jesus should be manifested in the lives of Jesus' disciples today.[137] In the Great Commission of Matthew 28:19–20 Jesus is saying "Proclaim and demonstrate my Kingdom, just as I did and just as I trained my disciples to do."[138] There is a direct relationship between divine healings, casting out demons, dominion over nature, and

---

[134] Wimber's book *Power Evangelism,* with Kevin Springer (San Francisco: Harper & Row, 1986) is his most detailed theology of the Kingdom of God. See also Don Williams, *Signs, Wonders and the Kingdom of God: A Biblical Guide for the Reluctant Skeptic* (Ann Arbor, Mich.: Servant, 1989), and Wimber's many articles in *Equipping the Saints,* the quarterly publication of the Vineyard Ministries International.

[135] John Wimber, *Kingdom Come* (Ann Arbor, Mich.: Servant, 1988), 7.

[136] Ladd's own view on the praxis of the Kingdom is summarily presented in the *Presence of the Future* (278–304). He views the Kingdom as present through the inward and spiritual renewal of individuals, but he also claims to have opened the door for a more fully developed "social gospel" of how the Kingdom confronts evil, and he suggests this topic as fertile ground for further investigation. Wimber appears to have taken up Ladd's suggestion.

[137] Wimber, *Kingdom Come,* 33. Williams writes, "Rather than the thesis that Jesus reproduced his kingdom ministry in the apostles in order to authenticate revelation, we hold that Jesus reproduced his kingdom ministry in them in order that they might be the authoritative instruments of that kingdom for their world and generations yet to come. His design was not only that they bear his authority but also manifest his ministry" (Williams, *Signs, Wonders and the Kingdom of God,* 127).

[138] Wimber, *Kingdom Come,* 33.

the other signs, wonders, and miracles which filled Jesus' life and the presence of the Kingdom of God. Believers must be aware of this relationship and be more open to these miraculous demonstrations of the Holy Spirit's power in their lives and ministries.[139] In the name of the Kingdom Christians should seek and experience the same works of Jesus and his disciples.

Exegetically, the Third Wave's quest for the Kingdom's praxis in terms of the power of the Holy Spirit has much to commend it. As we have noted at other points of our study, this idea has the support of Jesus' own ministry at Matthew 12:28, Paul at Romans 14:17, and the writer of Hebrews at 6:5. In the New Testament perspective, Jesus' own status as the *autobasileia* was keenly manifested by his relationship with the Spirit and the Spirit's subsequent manifestation of miracles through him. The Kingdom is present in the signs the Holy Spirit performs; the Kingdom's presence is a dynamic, spiritual power. Questions will always be raised to the Third Wave as to the precise nature and purpose of the Spirit's power for the church today, especially given its popular context and lack of theological sophistication in general.[140] But the emphasis on looking for the Kingdom's praxis in the work of the Holy Spirit seems justifiable.

---

[139] Wimber believes that Western Christianity has gradually lost sight of the supernatural manifestations of Kingdom power since the Enlightenment and the rise of rationalism.

[140] Frequently criticisms of the Third Wave's emphasis on signs and wonders mention the Johannine denunciation of the need of signs (John 20:29: "Blessed are those who have not seen and yet believed"), the biblical pattern of signs and wonders functioning mainly as a prelude to the gospel making successful inroads into pagan cultures, and the covenantal context of the disciples' command to heal and exorcise in Matthew 10 (a favorite passage of the Third Wave); that is, the disciples were also commanded to go only to the Jews with their signs and wonders. See further Ken L. Sarles, "An Appraisal of the Signs and Wonders Movement," *BS* 145 (January-March 1988): 58-82; Craig L. Blomberg, "A Response to G. R. Beasley-Murray on the Kingdom," *JEvTS* 35, no. 1 (1992): 32-33; *Wonders and the Word: An Examination of the Issues Raised by John Wimber and the Vineyard Movement*, ed. James R. Coggins and Paul G. Heibert (Hillsboro, Kans.: Kindred, 1989); *Ministry and the Miraculous: A Case Study at Fuller Theological Seminary*, ed. Lewis B. Smedes (Pasadena, Calif.: Fuller Theological Seminary, 1987).

PART FOUR

Contribution to the
Study of the Kingdom

CHAPTER NINE

The Kingdom of God
in the Teaching of Jesus

The major task of this study is to follow the interpretation of the Kingdom of God to the present day, much the way Norman Perrin and Gösta Lundström did for their generation. At the time of Perrin's and Lundström's writings, New Testament and systematic studies of the Kingdom seemed poised to take off in new and promising directions; eschatology was on the forefront of everybody's mind. From their vantage point Perrin and Lundström, however, could only note the trajectories of these eschatological studies and leave the final verdicts to others. Thirty years later some of those trajectories have been fulfilled, and the verdicts are in as to how the last decades have advanced our understanding of the Kingdom that Jesus preached. It is against the background of the last generation of study that I now want to draw together the dispersed elements of my own view of Jesus' teaching on the Kingdom.[1]

At the outset of such a presentation, several things need to be said about method. As indicated throughout our study, I believe that the last thirty years have revealed some assumptions about method that have been useful for the study of the Kingdom in Jesus and some that have not. These assumptions include basic questions of historiography and how the Gospel data should be treated. The fundamental assumptions about method that underlie my own presentation of Jesus' teaching of the Kingdom are four. First, I assume a hermeneutic that is basically text-centered, as opposed to the reader-centered program utilized in the more literary critical methods

---

[1] Because most of the material for this chapter already exists in different places of this study, a complete repetition of those sources will not be made for every point. Key sources will be repeated in this chapter, along with referrals to the fuller citations as they appear in other contexts.

of the last generation. The Kingdom of God for Jesus cannot mean "whatever it means to the reader" if there is to be a hedge against relativizing the Kingdom. Second, the documents of the New Testament should be seen as fundamentally reliable in their presentation of Jesus' teaching. This includes not only their basic content but also the basic chronological arrangement of their data according to their status as complete narratives. Guelich is correct to contend that "the exegetical atomization of the Gospels leads to the distortion of the literary products."[2] Beyond the issue of exegetical distortion from purely literary studies of the Gospel pericopes, there is the issue of historiography. With Sanders it could be added that simply doing the history of individual sayings of the Kingdom will not tell us what we want to know about Jesus.[3] More needs to be heard from the study of all the facets of first-century life, including political and social realities, anthropological considerations, and economics. Third, Jesus should be allowed to speak as a genuine historical figure, a first-century historical figure who spoke to first-century Jews. This means that his message of the Kingdom should have real connections with what precedes him in Judaism as well as with what follows him in the movement that bears his name. Finally, the church that followed Jesus, the church that gave us both the Gospels and the epistles, should be assumed to be a true representative of what the historical Jesus taught about the Kingdom. Logically, their work

---

[2] Robert Guelich, "The Gospel Genre," in *Das Evangelium and die Evangelien*, ed. Peter Stuhlmacher (Tübingen: J. C. B. Mohr [Paul Siebeck], 1983), 219. The form-critical suppositions about the nature of the Gospels literature, I would suggest, have hampered the study of the Kingdom in Jesus' teaching. To study the Kingdom by first excising each Kingdom-pericope from its narrative context and then trying to probe the collective meaning of all the sayings yields a Kingdom of the lowest common denominator. In Matthew, for example, confusing conflicts arise if the "gospel of the Kingdom" (Matt. 4) is read in terms of the "mysteries of the Kingdom" (Matt. 13), the great banquet table of Matthew 8, the disciples ruling the twelve tribes (Matt. 19), and the Son of Man's glorious return (Matt. 24). As such conflicting passages are typically weeded out according to the method and subjectivity of the interpreter, the Kingdom also takes on a subjective appearance and we are left with the multiple variations of the Kingdom readily apparent in this study.

[3] E. P. Sanders stated fifteen years ago that "I think that the day is over when people could think that piously counting Aramaisms, or diligently seeking the earliest source, or fervently doing the history of individual pericopes, would tell us what we want to know about Jesus—his character and intent" ("New Testament Studies Today," in *Colloquy on New Testament Studies*, ed. Bruce Corley [Macon, Ga.: Mercer University Press, 1980], 15).

should be accorded the benefits due to the *first* followers of the historical Jesus. I would suggest further that a basic harmony can be demonstrated in their work, meaning that the message of the Kingdom in one of the Gospels is consistent with the Kingdom of the other Gospels and with the New Testament *in toto*. While there may be differences of emphasis in their theologies, the writers of the New Testament should be given the benefit of the doubt for maintaining the integrity of the Christian message they inherited from Jesus. We must not forget that they were the ones who were instructed by the risen Christ for forty days about the Kingdom (Acts 1:3), not we.

THE KINGDOM IN THE OLD TESTAMENT AND INTERTESTAMENTAL LITERATURE

To understand a first-century Jew's concern for God's rule we must first consider the Old Testament understanding of God's rule or Kingdom. At least two aspects of God's Kingdom are to be distinguished in the Old Testament.[4] First, the Kingdom of God in the Old Testament has an abstract and dynamic quality, the quality of a reign or a rule, the exercise of authority by God as the King. As the Deity, God exercises his reign (*malkuth*) or rule over the creation without successful challenge and has done so since the creation came into being. Expressions of this aspect of God's universal kingship are readily seen in the Enthronement Psalms (Psalms 47, 93, 95–99). God reigns in the face of every challenger and is the source of every earthly event. His rule is such that he uses all events of history to his own ends. As we have seen repeatedly in our study, this abstract connotation of a rule or reign is favored and emphasized by interpreters not only for the predominant Old Testament meaning of the Kingdom but also for Jesus' own meaning.

The second aspect of God's kingship in the Old Testament is tightly bound to the dynamic quality of God's rule. That is, God's reign naturally entails some consideration of the domain or territory where his rule is exercised. God's universal exercise of his sovereign will is manifested in a

---

[4] See here the discussions of Old Testament lexica *(malukah, malkuth,* and *mamlekah)* by Carmignac in chapter three.

concrete kingdom and through actual subjects. The realm logically cannot be separated from the reign, and it was not in the Old Testament.[5] Since the creation of the universe the arena or domain of God's rule has been all that was created. In biblical history God's universal reign was manifested specially in the midst of God's chosen people, the nation of Israel. Their liberation and constitution as a nation before God at the exodus was nothing less than a "theo-political act," as Buber has said.[6] The people of Israel were covenanted as Yahweh's "kingdom of priests and holy nation" (Exod. 19:6). God reigned as the King (Deut. 33:5), visibly exercising his dynamic rule in the land and people of Israel.[7] Thus, when the people of Israel later called for a monarchial king like the other nations surrounding them, it was a rejection of Yahweh's kingship over them (1 Sam. 8:5–7). Yahweh still reserved the right to choose the Israelite king who would rule as Yahweh's son over Yahweh's realm (1 Chron. 17:11–14). In this context of human vice-regency, the uniqueness of the Davidic rule in Israel occasioned a covenant between David and Yahweh which guaranteed the eternal, physical manifestation of Yahweh's dominion through David's seed over the land and people of Israel (2 Sam. 7:7-16).[8]

The theme of Yahweh's kingship manifested over the land and people of Israel appears again in the prophetic literature of the Old Testament. In and around the time of Israel's subjection by foreign powers the messages delivered by Yahweh's prophets called for comfort in the hope of Yahweh's future restoration of his Kingdom in Israel. Israel was to look forward to Yahweh's anointed one, who would again lead them in triumph, restore the fallen booth of David (Amos 9:11), and "set up a kingdom which will

---

[5] For the concrete, political expression of Yahweh's reign in the Old Testament, see also the discussion of the liberation theologians in chapter seven.

[6] Martin Buber, *The Kingship of God*, trans. Richard Schiemann (New York, N.Y.: Harper, 1967), 124ff.

[7] The Semitic concept of a king required first that he "safeguard the liberty of the state" (A. R. Johnson, "Hebrew Conceptions of Kingship," in *Myth, Ritual, and Kingship: Essays on the Theory and Practice of Kingship in the Ancient Near East and in Israel*, ed. S. H. Hooke [Oxford: Clarendon, 1958], 205). Yahweh, thus, exercised his kingship over Israel when he fought for them against the armies of Pharaoh at the exodus.

[8] See George Wesley Buchanan's discussion of Yahweh's kingdom in Israel as the *Davidic* Kingdom, which included a Davidic king on the throne in Jerusalem ruling over the land and people of Israel. (George Wesley Buchanan, *The Consequences of the Covenant* [Leiden: E. J. Brill, 1970], 58).

never be destroyed" (Dan. 2:44). Throughout the prophetic literature of the Old Testament the contents of this "hope" remained remarkably consistent. Gowan has summarized its contents: "God must transform the human person; give a new heart and a new spirit. . . . God must transform human society; restore Israel to the promised land, rebuild cities and make Israel's new status a witness to the nations. . . . And God must transform nature itself."[9]

Two matters of special import are not to be missed in the prophetic message to Israel. First was the "irreducibly national strain" embedded in the hope, as Patrick has noted.[10] The prophesied realm of Yahweh's reign was again to be manifested in a Jewish political state under a Davidic king in the land of Israel. Life on the land was at the very heart of the Old Testament view of the future.[11] This is a point admitted by virtually all the commentators of the Old Testament. The Jews looked for a revival of the former glory that was the Davidic kingdom. This nationalistic aspect of the promise should not, however, be seen as in any conflict with the universal dimensions of the Old Testament hope. The fact that Yahweh's rule would encompass all peoples need not dispute the Jewish character of that rule. Consider the juxtaposition of the universality of the hope and the Jewishness of the hope in Isaiah 2:2–4. It is to *Jerusalem* that the nations would come to learn the ways of God.[12]

Second, of great importance was the historical nature of the hope. As Rowland, Wright, and Collins have demonstrated, the hope of Israel was a historical hope and not a hope for the cataclysmic end of the world. Rowland summarizes,

---

[9] Donald E. Gowan, *Eschatology in the Old Testament* (Philadelphia: Fortress, 1986), 2.

[10] Dale Patrick, "The Kingdom of God in the Old Testament," in *The Kingdom of God in Twentieth-Century Interpretation*, ed. Wendell Willis (Peabody, Mass.: Hendrickson, 1987), 79.

[11] See Buchanan, *Consequences*, 136–49. The prominence of the physical life on the land highlights the holistic view of the Old Testament toward human life, namely, the physical cannot be separated from the spiritual. There was no eternal life without the land (Buchanan, *Consequences*, 145).

[12] The words of J. Ramsey Michaels, who comments on the universality and Jewishness of the Kingdom during the Intertestamental period, are worth our attention. He says, "The Kingdom in the book of Daniel, for example, or in the Pharisaic Psalms of Solomon from the first century BCE is universal in scope, yet no less Jewish for all its universality. It is the Kingdom of God, and at the same time the Kingdom of Israel" (J. Ramsey Michaels, "The Kingdom of God and the Historical Jesus," in *Kingdom of God in Twentieth-Century Interpretation*, 114).

God's rule and authority were ultimately to be manifested in the physical world. Salvation for a Jew was not primarily some mystical deliverance for the spirit to enter a private communion in the world beyond, but the manifestation on earth of God's authority over the universe and the setting right of all that was wrong.[13]

This is not to deny that at times there is "a confusing lack of system" to the prophecies of the Old Testament hope, but the intermittent prophetic unclarity should not be allowed to deflect the basic clear thrust of a historical, political, and ethnic Kingdom.[14]

For all the discussion to the contrary evident during the last generation (the New Hermeneutic and Perrin, for example), it can also be demonstrated that the physical, historical, and national hope of the Reign of Yahweh in Israel funded the literature of intertestamental Judaism. While it is true that the hope of intertestamental Judaism is typically more apocalyptic in the style of its presentation, that is, as to content it is more fanciful, cataclysmic, cosmic, and dualistic than the Old Testament, nevertheless the national and historic strain is still present. Writings like *Psalms of Solomon* 17, *Testament of Moses* 8–10, and *Sibylline Oracles* 3:47, 767 allow Collins to say of the Messiah's coming kingdom that "it is essentially the restoration of a national Jewish kingdom."[15] As Wright put it, the Jewish hope continued to concern the matters of "Temple, Torah, race, economy,

---

[13] Christopher Rowland, *Christian Origins: From Messianic Movement to Christian Religion* (Minneapolis, Minn.: Augsburg, 1985), 135. The historical nature of the hope underscores the nature of my use of the term "eschatological" throughout this chapter. An eschatological Kingdom is not, in my use of the term, an otherworldly, end-of-the-world, Kingdom that is usually associated with the term "apocalyptic." An eschatological or end-time event may have otherworldly or apocalyptic features, as in an earthly, historical Kingdom that would be funded and initiated by miraculous (otherworldly) events, but this miraculous initiation will not be used in this chapter to describe an "eschatological" Kingdom.

[14] On the sometimes unclear nature of Old Testament prophecy, see Dirk H. Odendall, *The Eschatological Expectation of Isaiah 40–66 with Special Reference to Israel and the Nations* (Philadelphia: Presbyterian and Reformed, 1970), esp. 126.

[15] Collins's comments were specifically in reference to *Psalms of Solomon* 17. See John J. Collins, "The Kingdom of God in the Apocrypha and Pseudepigrapha," in *The Kingdom of God in Twentieth-Century Interpretation*, 91. The late date of *Psalms of Solomon* should not be allowed to diminish the political nature of the national hope. Even though Camponovo uses the later date to say that the writer of *Psalms of Solomon* added political ideas to the intertestamental presentation,

and justice."[16] Hengel's and Schwemer's study of the Sabbath Songs similarly have demonstrated the persistence of these ideas in the desert community of Qumran. Yahweh's universal kingship as it was celebrated in the cult at Qumran looks forward to the eventuality of its earthly manifestation. "In heaven is eternally present what is expected for the earth in the future salvation."[17] In fact, political and national dreams appear to be so strong at Qumran that Hengel and Schwemer, like Camponovo on the *Psalms of Solomon,* postulate an artificial intensification of these ideas as foreign domination of Israel continued seemingly without end.[18]

Further evidence for an unending Israelite tradition of the manifestation of God's kingship in time is the presence of these concepts in Jewish literature that postdates the New Testament. Solomon Schecter's volume, for example, *Aspects of Rabbinic Theology: Major Concepts of the Talmud,* along with Strack's and Billerbeck's *Kommentar Zum Neuen Testament: Aus Talmud und Midrasch,* confirms the endurance of the national, literal hope of the Old Testament within Judaism.[19] Even the oft-quoted rabbinic admonition to take upon oneself "the yoke of the Kingdom" (*SLev* 18:6; *MekEx* 20:2), more than likely should be seen against this persistent hope for an earthly, messianic kingdom, rather than as an indicator of a

---

he also says that the Old Testament hope held the concrete expression of Israel's hope closely together with the dynamic reign of Yahweh (Camponovo, *Königtum, Königsherrschaft und Reich Gottes in den Frühjüdischen Schriften,* Orbis Biblicus et Orientalis 58 [Göttingen: Vandenhoeck & Ruprecht, 1984], 440-43). Far more likely is that instead of *Psalms of Solomon* adding the political element to the hope, its unbroken presence merely surfaces there more clearly than in other works.

[16] N. T. Wright, *The New Testament and the People of God* (Minneapolis, Minn.: Fortress, 1992), 285. See also Meier, *A Marginal Jew: Rethinking the Historical Jesus,* vol. 2, *Mentor, Message, and Miracle,* Anchor Bible Reference Library (New York, N.Y.: Doubleday, 1994), 245-65, and Buchanan, *Consequences of the Covenant,* 56-89, and *Jesus,* 15-24, for the national, historical Jewish hope in the intertestamental literature.

[17] Schwemer, "Gott als König und seine Königsherrschaft," in *Königsherrschaft Gottes und himmlischer Kult in Judentum, Urchristentum, und in der hellenistischen Welt,* ed. Martin Hengel and Anna Maria Schwemer, WUNT 55 (Tübingen: J. C. B. Mohr [Paul Siebeck], 1991), 117 (author's translation).

[18] Hengel and Schwemer, foreword to *Könighschaft Gottes,* 4.

[19] Solomon Schecter, *Aspects of Rabbinic Theology: Major Concepts of the Talmud* (New York, N.Y.: Schocken, 1961), 97-115; Hermann L. Strack and Paul Billerbeck, *Kommentar Zum Neuen Testament: Aus Talmud und Midrasch* (Munich: C. H. Beck, 1922-1928), 3:823-27.

purely dynamic, abstract understanding.[20] Investigations of the Kingdom of God in the Targumic literature done during the last generation also reveal the pervasiveness of these eschatological beliefs for Jews. Bruce Chilton's studies of the Targumic material show that Old Testament beliefs of the manifestation of God's kingship in Israel are present in the final editions of the Targums available to us today. Because he ultimately wants to deny the Old Testament Jewish hope as the meaning of the Kingdom in Jesus' teaching, Chilton is forced into the unlikely position of making the political, national Kingdom of the Targums purely a product of the fall of Jerusalem in A.D. 70.[21]

A final adduction that should not be neglected when discussing the ideas of the Kingdom in Jesus' day is the presence of Jewish eschatological hopes in the eschatology of the early Christian church. Even if one sets the New Testament aside for a moment, chiliasm was the dominant position among the ante-Nicene fathers, including Papias, Lactantius, Justin Martyr, the Pastor of Hermas, Barnabas, Irenaeus, Methodius, Commodianus, and Tertullian.[22] Jürgen Moltmann, with the help of several Lutheran scholars of the last century, has further brought to our attention the historical circumstances surrounding the demise of the early chiliasm in the Christian church. More precisely, that it was not the *usus* of the Jewish hope ("chiliasmus subtilis") that was eventually rejected in the Christian Church, but the *abusus* ("chiliasmus crassus") of the hope by heretics (e.g., Cerinthus), plus guilt by association with Montanism, that brought criticism upon millenarianism in Christian circles.[23]

---

[20] See Buchanan's suggestion that these statements should be seen merely as oaths of allegiance made to the national, temporal and earthly Kingdom that was coming in the future (George Wesley Buchanan, *Jesus: The King and His Kingdom* [Macon, Ga.: Mercer University Press, 1984], 23-24).

[21] Bruce Chilton, *A Galilean Rabbi and His Bible: Jesus' Use of the Interpreted Scripture of His Time*, Good News Studies 8 (Wilmington, Del.: Michael Glazier, 1984), 63-64.

[22] Thomas C. Oden, *Systematic Theology*, vol. 3, *Life in the Spirit* (San Francisco: Harper–SanFrancisco, 1992), 427. See also Hans Bietenhard, "The Millennial Hope in the Early Church," *ScotJT* 6 (March 1953): 12-30, and others cited in chapter six.

[23] Jürgen Moltmann cites the work of F. Delitzsch, J. C. K. von Hofmann, and C. C. Luthardt on this point (Jürgen Moltmann, *The Church in the Power of the Spirit: A Contribution to Messianic Ecclesiology*, trans. Margaret Kohl [New York, N.Y.: Harper and Row, 1977], 379, n. 14). It is further worth noting that all of the earliest critics of chiliasm, including Clement of Alexandria,

The ideas about the reign of Yahweh, as to both its dynamic and concrete aspects, that were current in the milieu of Jesus still reflect the core of the Old Testament belief about a restored Davidic kingdom. The visionaries of the Apocrypha and Pseudepigrapha dressed the belief differently, giving it an apocalyptic denouement, but the meaning was the same: Yahweh, the universal, sovereign King, would act mightily on the behalf of his people and return to them their ancestral glory. They would "practice their ancestral religion, with the rest of the world looking on in awe, and/ or making pilgrimages to Zion, and/or being ground to powder under Jewish feet."[24]

Such summary statements of the Jewish hope of the first century are very important as we now turn to the message of the Kingdom of God *(basileia tou theou)* that Jesus preached. They are important because they represent a very radically reduced list of options available for Jesus if he was going to use one of the ideas about the eschaton current in his day. The Judaism of the first century that is often portrayed in modern research as "kaleidoscopic" as to its beliefs and "lacking an orthodox center" may have been that way regarding the details of its other doctrines and practices,[25] but it was not that way about its basic hope for the future. Reading the intertestamental literature about the future will reveal much variety in the details but not in the fundamental nature of the Jewish hope for Yahweh's reign. It was political; it was historical; and it was rooted in the Old Testament. This was the hope of Jesus' day. His options therefore were only two: use his ancestral hope, or create his own. The option he ultimately took is the question we now must address.

Dionysius of Alexandria, and Athanasius, were prominent in the Alexandrian school, which championed a specifically allegorical hermeneutic. Chiliasm's literalistic eschatology was naturally resisted in this part of the empire.

[24] Wright, *People of God*, 285.

[25] For example, beliefs about the Messiah's person and work can vary greatly in the intertestamental literature. See James H. Charlesworth, "The Messiah in the Pseudepigrapha," *ANRW*, 19:1:188-218; Richard A. Horsley and John S. Hanson, *Bandits, Prophets and Messiahs: Popular Movements in the Time of Jesus* (San Francisco: Harper & Row, 1985), 88-92; *The Messiah: Developments in Earliest Judaism and Christianity*, ed. James H. Charlesworth (Minneapolis, Minn.: Fortress, 1992); *Judaisms and Their Messiahs at the Turn of the Christian Era*, ed. J. Neusner, W. S. Green and E. S. Frerichs (Cambridge: Cambridge University Press, 1987).

THE EARLIEST ANNOUNCEMENTS OF THE KINGDOM

In keeping with our stated method of approaching the Gospels as complete narrative units, we begin our discussion of Jesus' meaning of the Kingdom of God with its first appearances in the Gospel record. The Gospel of Luke is the starting point as it gives us the first glimpses of the Kingdom in the pronouncements surrounding the birth of Jesus. In the announcement to Mary by the angel Gabriel we understand that she will bear a son, Jesus, who would "have the throne of his father David, and he will reign *(basileusei)* over the house of Jacob forever; his kingdom *(basileias)* will never end" (Luke 1:32–33). Immediately the Old Testament, Davidic character of the Kingdom is apparent as this Son, Jesus, will realize the covenant made with David.[26] The Old Testament character of the hope is also visible in the Magnificat (Luke 1:46–55) and Zechariah's prophecy (Luke 1:67–79). Mary expresses the Jewish hope in her recognition of blessings for the humble (vv. 48, 52) and judgment for the enemies of Israel (vv. 51–54). In Zechariah's words the hope is for a spiritual and political deliverance (vv. 71–75).

The next appearance of the Kingdom in the Gospels, in the ministry of John the Baptist, is also antecedent to Jesus. Like that of Jesus (Matt. 4:17, Mark 1:15) and the disciples (Matt. 10:7), the message of John was "Repent. The Kingdom of heaven has drawn near" (Matt. 3:2). Several features of John's ministry indicate his correlation to the Jewish hope of the Old Testament, a correlation most scholars do not resist. First, in his own person he is the one to whom Isaiah the prophet referred when he said, "the voice of one crying in the wilderness, make ready the way of the Lord" (Matt. 3:3). Second, he is the one who carries on the line of the Old Testament prophets as their fulfillment (Matt. 11:13). Third, he is the one whom Jesus specifically identifies as Elijah "who was to come" before the Messiah, according to the prediction of the prophet Malachi (Matt. 11:14; 17:12; Mark 9:11-13; cf. Mal. 3:1; 4:5). Finally his message of repentance, especially when

---

[26] Raymond E. Brown has noted that the mention of "throne," "house," and "kingdom" in the announcement to Mary hearkens back to the first statement of the covenant Yahweh made with David in 2 Samuel 7:16 (Raymond E. Brown, *The Birth of the Messiah* [Garden City, N.Y.: Doubleday, 1977], 310-11).

read in concert with the Kingdom's near approach,[27] also signals to us the connection of his Kingdom with that of the Old Testament.[28]

Jesus' Proclamation of the Kingdom

The fact that Jesus appears on the pages of the Gospel record immediately after John, the herald of the advent of the Old Testament hope for Israel, sets us in the direction we should follow when considering Jesus' own message and ministry, at least initially. This spiritual lineage to John is further highlighted by the fact that Jesus himself offers no evidence that the Kingdom he announced was any different from the Kingdom of John's proclamation. In fact, as far as the Gospels are concerned, when he begins his ministry Jesus does not define the Kingdom at all, which is very significant considering his close connection to John and the eschatological options available to him. He simply repeats the message of John: "Repent. The Kingdom of God has drawn near" (Mark 1:15). Patrick catches the same significance for this simple announcement of the Kingdom that struck Reimarus centuries ago. Jesus uses Kingdom of God to call to mind all that his auditors knew

> about the coming intervention of God to redeem his people and pacify the world. . . . The expression itself gives a particular coloring to the denouement of history, namely a political and legal coloring. The whole of Scripture and tradition prepare for and are completed in a political state which God alone exercises sovereignty.[29]

---

[27] On the strength of W. G. Kümmel's discussion of the linguistic differences between *ēngiken* and *ephthasen,* most interpreters have seen a difference between the Kingdom's near approach *(ēngiken)* and its arrival *(ephthasen);* see W. G. Kümmel, *Promise and Fulfillment,* trans. Dorothea M. Barton [Naperville, Ill.: Allenson, 1957], 105-9; cf. also G. R. Beasley-Murray, *Jesus and the Kingdom of God* [Grand Rapids: Eerdmans, 1986], 75-80).

[28] Yahweh's reign would be manifested only to a prepared people. In the Old Testament repentance was the prerequisite to the restoration of the Israel (2 Chron. 7:12-22; Ezek. 33:7-20). John's message of repentance *(metanoia)* was the proclamation of an unconditional turning from all that was against God. See J. Behm, metanoevw *metanoeō, TDNT,* 4:1002.

[29] Patrick, "The Kingdom of God in the Old Testament," 71. Meier underscores the same point in *A Marginal Jew,* 270.

Beyond this simple, undefined proclamation of the Kingdom that begins Jesus' ministry, the Gospels give much evidence that Jesus initiates his ministry as the long-awaited Messiah of Israel's hope and that his Kingdom was the Kingdom of their hope.[30] The theme of fulfillment permeates Jesus' ministry from his application of Isaiah's messianic prophecy to himself in the synagogue (Luke 4:16–30, cf. Isa. 61:1–2)[31] to the report that John's disciples should take back to John the Baptist based on Isaiah 35:5 (Matt. 11:5).[32] Mark's programmatic statement in 1:15 includes the fulfillment theme as part of the proclamation itself: "the time is fulfilled and the Kingdom of God is at hand."[33] Jesus' message is the "gospel *(euangelion)* of the Kingdom" (Matt. 4:23), a phrase idiomatic in Matthew's Gospel and directly indicative of the Old Testament hope prophesied through Isaiah (Isa. 40:9; 41:27; 52:7; 61:1).[34] He proclaims himself as the Spirit-anointed one who would come in the future (Luke 4:18).[35] He announces the "favorable year of the Lord" in fulfillment of Jewish Jubilee eschatological hope

---

[30] See here the portraits of Jesus in the presentations of Harvey, Ladd, Sanders, et al. in chapter five, as well as those of the liberation theologians in chapter seven.

[31] Joseph A. Fitzmeyer sees Luke 4:16-30 as programmatic for Luke's Gospel on the same order as Mark 1:14-15 is for Mark (Joseph A. Fitzmeyer, *The Gospel According to Luke I-IX*, Anchor Bible Commentary [New York, N.Y.: Doubleday, 1981], 529).

[32] Matthew's stress on the fulfillment theme for Jesus is well known from his formulaic use of *plēroō* and its derivatives in 1:22; 2:15, 17, 23; 4:14; 8:17; 12:17; 13:14, 35; 21:4; and 27:9.

[33] Jesus' statement in Mark also sets a precedent for the New Testament literature in joining a Kingdom saying with a time element. See Werner H. Kelber, *The Kingdom of God in Mark* (Philadelphia: Fortress, 1974), 10-11.

[34] Gerhard Friedrich, *euangelion, TDNT,* 2:708-9.

[35] The role of the Spirit of God cannot be ignored as a key feature of the eschatological Jewish hope. In the Old Testament the Spirit is "the medium through which God's presence in the midst of his people becomes a reality" (Walther Eichrodt, *Theology of the Old Testament,* trans. J. A. Baker [Philadelphia: Westminster, 1961], 2:61). In the future age Yahweh's New Covenant would give his people greater experience of the Spirit (Jer. 31:33-34; Ezek. 36:26-27). The Spirit would be poured out in the end time as the cleanser and renewer who would establish righteousness (Isa. 32:15; Ezek. 18:31; 36:25ff.; 37:14; 39:29; Joel 2:28-32). The inaugurator of the future messianic rule, the Lord's servant, would be one specifically anointed by the Spirit for the accomplishment of this task (Isa. 11:2; 42:1; 48:16; 59:19-21; 61:1). The overall character of the future age in the Old Testament is thus wholly Spirit-conditioned in comparison to the present age, as Eichrodt again notes, "there is an advance from a picture of power working externally to one involving the innermost foundation of the personal life; man's relationship with God is no longer left to his own efforts, but is given him by the spirit. Because, however, all this is seen as

(Luke 4:19).[36] His message is authoritative (Matt. 7:29) and challenging to the religious and social hierarchy of his day (Matt. 5:20).[37] At this point the vision of Jesus' ministry only includes Jews (Matt. 10:5-7), and he chooses twelve disciples who he later says will one day judge the twelve tribes of Israel (Matt. 19:28).[38]

Jesus' Demonstration of the Kingdom

Tied very closely to Jesus' verbal proclamation of the Kingdom, but often neglected in the studies of Jesus' understanding of the Kingdom (e.g., the New Hermeneutic, Perrin, the New Literary Criticism), was Jesus' demonstration of the Kingdom in his miracles.[39] Though miracles themselves

---

the central miracle of the new age, the spirit as the living power of the new creation find its proper place in eschatology" (Eichrodt, *Theology of the Old Testament*, 2:59).

The New Testament places Jesus firmly in concert with this Spirit. He is the creation of the Spirit (Luke 1:35)—the divine Word united with the Spirit. At his baptism he is God's Spirit-anointed man, destined to cleanse, judge, and baptize the creation with the Spirit (Matt. 12:18; cf. 3:11, the prophecy of John). His ministry in word and deed is a manifestation of the Spirit (Matt. 12:28 and parallels; Acts 10:38), which is why rejection of the Spirit was the only issue of eternal consequence (Mark 3:28 and Matt. 12:31). His resurrection and exaltation crowns him as the Lord of the Spirit (Acts 2:33). His kingdom is entered through an act of the Spirit (John 3:5ff.), and it is experienced through the Spirit (Rom. 14:17). Jesus' church is empowered to preach by the Spirit (Acts 1:8). It works miracles through the Spirit (Rom. 15:18; 1 Cor. 12:7-10; Gal. 3:5; Heb. 2:2-3).

[36] See Buchanan's discussion of Israel's sabbatical theology in chapter five.

[37] For Jesus' place in the social-economic situation of first-century Palestine, see Horsley and others in chapter four.

[38] For a fuller discussion of the significance of the proclamation only to Israel see Ben F. Meyers, *The Aims of Jesus* (London: SCM, 1979), 133-36. On the significance of the selection of twelve disciples see E. P. Sanders, *Jesus and Judaism* (Philadelphia: Fortress, 1985), 98-106.

[39] Miracles are defined in the Gospel record according to their effect on those who witnessed them. Apart from modern philosophical notions that would see miracles as phenomena involving the abrogation or acceleration of "laws of nature," in the New Testament miracles were extraordinary actions that evoked awe and astonishment (cf. Acts 2:22). The Synoptic Gospels naturally designate them therefore in terms of *dynamis*. Miracles are "mighty acts" and "manifestations of power" (Birger Gerhardsson, *The Mighty Acts of Jesus According to Matthew*, trans. Robert Dewsnap [Lund: W. K. Gleerup, 1979], 18; G. H. Boobyer, "The Gospel Miracles: View Past and Present," in *The Miracles and the Resurrection* [London: SPCK, 1964], 32; Anton Vögtle, "The Miracles of Jesus Against their Contemporary Background," in *Jesus in His Time*, ed. Hans Jürgen Schultz, trans. Brian Watchorn [London: SPCK, 1971], 96-97). Augustine's definition of a miracle, cited by Brown, is "whatever appears that is difficult or unusual above the hope and power of them that wonder" (Colin Brown, *Miracles and the Critical Mind* [Grand Rapids: Eerdmans, 1984], 291).

are mute witnesses to Jesus' Kingdom, their presentation in the Gospels loudly proclaims the nature of the Kingdom Jesus announced. Specifically, they proclaim the eschatological reign of God anticipated in the Old Testament prophetic hope. Seven lines of evidence point to this conclusion about the miracles and we now consider them in some detail.

First, the close proximity of word and deed in Jesus' ministry provides for the interpretation of his deeds from the hope of the Old Testament. Matthew's juxtaposition of the miracles in chapters eight and nine and the authoritative words in the Sermon on the Mount show, as Held observed nearly a generation ago, that in Matthew Jesus is the Messiah of word and the Messiah of deed.[40] Mark begins his account of Jesus' ministry with Jesus' words and miraculous deeds (Mark 1:21–27) under the programmatic rubric of Mark 1:14–15. The witnesses of Jesus' deeds are "amazed" (1:27), just as they are with his words (1:22), rendering "impossible any clear division between his acts and teaching," as Mundle notes.[41] Luke's Gospel similarly unites Jesus' teaching and miracles through the paradigmatic use of the Isaiah prophecy Jesus fulfills in chapter 4:16–30. For Luke this announcement of fulfillment has reference not only to Jesus' proclamation of liberation and release, of which Luke has already made specific note at 4:15, but also to the previous demonstration of it by miraculous healings. So close is the connection of Jesus' teaching to his miracles that many have seen miracles as enacted or concrete parables, living examples of the content of Jesus' preaching.[42] Kallas makes the point well: "The miracles have precisely the same message as the words of Jesus. The message of Jesus concentrated on the announcement of the kingdom of God . . . and the miracles showed what the kingdom would be like."[43]

It is important at this point to also note the nature of miracles as wonders of the physical realm. As such they make a very important point for

---

[40] H. Held, "Matthew as Interpreter of the Miracle Stories," in *Tradition and Interpretation in Matthew* (Philadelphia: Westminster, 1963), 246.

[41] J. Mundle, "Miracle," *NIDNTT*, 2:623–24.

[42] Alan Richardson, *The Miracles Stories of the Gospels* (London: SCM Press, 1941), 86; Craig L. Blomberg, "The Miracles as Parables," in *The Miracles of Jesus*, ed. David Wenham and Craig Blomberg, Gospel Perspectives 6 (Sheffield: JSOT, 1986), 347.

[43] James Kallas, *The Significance of the Synoptic Miracles* (London: SPCK, 1961), 77.

understanding the words of Jesus about the Kingdom, just as the proclaimed word interprets the miracles. For their part, the miracles affirm that the Kingdom is a matter of the spiritual condition of the human heart and the physical condition of the human body and nature itself. They are *prima facie* evidence for a physical face to the Kingdom which is in general accord to the interrelatedness of physical and spiritual in the Jewish world view.[44] Beyond that, they demonstrate the fact that the physical side of the Kingdom is the literal fulfillment of what the prophets had written and proclaimed centuries before regarding the signs of the Kingdom's advent. When Jesus literally healed the lame, the blind, and the deaf, we can know that the prophets had not looked for just a spiritual allegory when they spoke of healing in the coming Kingdom. The Kingdom will not be fulfilled in the spiritual realm alone. The miracles, when juxtaposed to Jesus' teaching, are strong evidence that his ministry was literally derived from the Old Testament. It also points us, therefore, to the literal fulfillment of the other features of the prophetic hope, namely the promises to the Jewish nation and the whole creation.

Second, and most significant for a discussion of the Kingdom of God, is the connection of Jesus' miracles to the "central miracle of the new age," the Holy Spirit. Matthew and Luke both record the statement by Jesus that not only connects the Spirit to his own deeds, but also to the Kingdom. "But if I cast out demons by the Spirit [Luke: finger] of God, then the kingdom of God has come upon you" (Matt. 12:28; Luke 11:20). Miracles are the Spirit's work in the life of Jesus, and, as such, they continue the Old Testament tradition of Yahweh acting redemptively by the Spirit's miraculous power.[45]

Third, at many points the Gospel writers show how the particular miracles of Jesus hearken directly back to the Old Testament. For example, mention of Jesus healing the lame, deaf, blind, and raising the dead (Matt. 11:5) is typical of the Gospel miracle accounts and clearly draws from the promises of the coming new age recorded in Isaiah 26:19;

---

[44] See, for example, Buchanan's discussion of Israelite concepts of life as including life in history on the Promised Land of Palestine (Buchanan, *Consequences of the Covenant*, 136-49).

[45] See note 35.

29:18; 35:4–6; 42:18; and 61:1–2.[46] In Mark 7:32-35 the healing of the deaf mute and the releasing of his tongue from its "bond" is prefigured by the release from the oppressive bands predicted in Isaiah 58:6.[47] Jesus, who takes our infirmities and carries away our sickness (Matt. 8:17, quoting Isa. 53:4a), and who "heals them all" (Matt. 12:15) is Isaiah's Suffering Servant (Matt. 12:18–21, quoting Isa. 42:1–4).[48]

Fourth, the prophesied new age of salvation is also revealed by the occasion of many of Jesus' miracles. Several times the Gospel writers specifically note that Jesus performed many miracles of exorcism and healing on the Sabbath (Mark 3:1–6; Luke 13:10–17; 14:1–6; John 5:1–18; 9:1–14). These notations, plus Jesus' own challenge to the synagogue official about the woman with the bent back, "Should she not have been released from this bond on the Sabbath day?" (Luke 13:16), point to Jesus' miracles as the fulfillment of the eschatological Jubilee, the "favorable year of the Lord" of his proclamation (Luke 4:19). In the writings of the prophet Isaiah the year of Jubilee was an image associated with the eternal rest of the future age when all creation would be released from its captivity into the salvation of Yahweh (Isa. 58; 61:1–3). The subjects of Jesus' miracles experience in a provisional way the coming eternal rest that will be for all the creation.[49]

Fifth, the motivation of Jesus' miracles points to the Old Testament hope. Because Yahweh's salvation was restorative and liberating for his covenant people, the prophets naturally anticipated it as the supreme expression of his lovingkindness and mercy *(ḥesed)* under the covenant.[50] The coming new age would be the time when Yahweh's ultimate *ḥesed* would be revealed as he demonstrated his faithfulness to the covenant (Isa. 54:8;

[46] O. Betz and Werner Grimm, *Wesen und Wirklichkeit der Wunder Jesu* (Frankfurt: Peter Lang, 1977), 31.

[47] Ibid., n. 39.

[48] Held, "Matthew as Interpreter," 261. Held, interestingly, notes that Isaiah 53 is not about suffering or lowliness, but mighty works of power (262, n. 3).

[49] W. Grimm, *Weil Ich dich liebe. Die Verkündigung Jesu und Deuterojesaja* (Frankfurt: Peter Lang, 1976), 98-99; Betz and Grimm, *Wesen und Wirklichkeit*, 34-35; 35, n. 50; F. N. Davey, "Healing in the New Testament," in *The Miracles and the Resurrection*, 54.

[50] See Rudolf Bultmann, *eleos, TDNT,* 2:479-87; G. Schrenk, *dikaiosuneµTDNT,* 2:195.

55:3; Micah 7:20). Miracles, therefore, are particular and necessary expressions of God's covenant commitment and promise for the new age. The very idea of the in-breaking of divine love and kindness in the Kingdom without appropriate changes in the physical well-being of people was impossible under the righteous demands of covenant *ḥesed*.[51] It was, therefore, Jesus' covenant mercy *(eleos)* that the Gospel writers would often note as the motivation behind miraculous deeds (e.g., Matt. 9:13a; 20:30: 20:34). His miracles were not simply proofs for belief, but "they were rather the natural reaction of his spirit to sickness and suffering in the world and his desire for God's grace to be known in those he touched."[52]

Sixth, Jesus makes "open war" on the enemies of Yahweh's people by means of miracles. The Old Testament promise of the final Sabbath rest and the presence of God's eschatological *ḥesed* in the kingdom of the new age necessitated the destruction of the forces opposed to the divine order (Isa. 29:20; 35:4; 61:2). All the blessings of the age to come flowed out of the prior subjection of the people's enemies. In Isaiah 49:24–25 the prophet tells the captives they cannot be freed unless the mighty man is first subdued and Yahweh "contends with the one who contends with you." In the Gospels, Jesus' role as the one who contends with the enemy of Yahweh's people is the fundamental drama of his entire ministry.[53] In Matthew and Luke it is significant that the drama of Jesus' ministry opens in conflict with Satan in the temptations (Luke 4 and Matt. 4). In Mark 1:23–28 exorcism follows soon after the programmatic declaration of the Kingdom's near advent. The cries of the demons, "Have you come to destroy us?" (Luke 4:34; Mark 1:24) are naturally understood as tokens of the conflict. The conflict between the Kingdom of God and Satan is made clear in Matthew 12:28; Luke also reveals the Kingdom's nexus with exorcism in the account of the commissioning and return of the seventy (Luke 10). He notes that Jesus says that the ministry of the seventy as emissaries of the

[51] O. Betz, "Heilung," *TRE*, 14:766.

[52] Morton Kelsey, *Healing and Christianity* (New York: Harper & Row, 1973), 99.

[53] On Jesus' ministry as confrontation with the kingdom of Satan, see Howard Clark Kee, "The Terminology of Mark's Exorcism Stories," *NTS* 14 (1967-1968): 232-46; *Miracle in the Early Christian World* (New Haven: Yale University Press, 1983), 156-70; Rudolf Pesch, *Jesus Ureigene Taten?* (Freiburg: Herder, 1970), 151-155; W. Grimm, *Weil Ich dich liebe*, 88-93; R. Brown, "The Gospel Miracles," 187; Kallas, *Significance of the Synoptic Miracles*, 78 ff.

kingdom to the towns and villages (cf. Luke 10:9) let him see Satan "fall from heaven like lightning" (10:18). Further on in Luke 13:32, Jesus is able to summarize his whole ministry before the cross in terms of exorcism and healing: "I will drive out demons and heal people today and tomorrow, and on the third day I will reach my goal."[54] Finally, Jesus conquers the last weapon of Satan, namely death. Death is the ultimate enemy and stands in the ultimate position in Jesus' summary of liberating miracles in Matthew 11:5. For John the resurrection of Lazarus marks the climax of Jesus' ministry prior to his own Passion and resurrection.

Seventh and finally, Jesus' miracles bear on the fundamental eschatological problem of purity. The call to repent was rooted in the Old Testament, specifically in the prerequisite to Yahweh's visitation in the new age. The Kingdom would come only to a purified people. Ideas of purity, therefore, were woven deeply into the religious and social fabric of Judaism.[55] Beginning with the standard set out by Yahweh in the Mosaic law, "You shall be holy, for I the Lord your God am holy" (e.g., Lev. 19:2), Israel gained and maintained boundaries of cleanness and uncleanness which regulated all aspects of their life. The focal point of these boundaries was the temple, where Yahweh dwelt on earth. The prodigious, practical impact of all uncleanness was that one was denied entrance to the temple and shut off from the center of Israel's life.[56]

---

[54] The connection between exorcism and healing is not to be missed in the cosmic conflict, as the New Testament presumes that every malady and disorder of the creation is ultimately rooted in the chaos of Satan's kingdom. Jesus, therefore, understands that sickness can be related to Satan as well. The sick woman of Luke 13:10-16 was one "whom Satan has bound for eighteen years" (Luke 13:16). In Matthew the lines between disease and demons blur as *therapeuein* refers to healing diseases and also to casting out demons (Matt. 8:16; 10:8). Similarly with the nature miracles, Jesus' rebuke *(epitimaō)* of the storm (Mark 4:37-41) is the same as his rebuke of demons (Mark 1:25), which is the same as his rebuke of illness (Luke 4:39). See Grimm, *Weil Ich dich liebe*, 110; Gerhardsson, *Mighty Acts*, 33.

[55] On the purity system of Israel see Jacob Neusner, *The Idea of Purity in Ancient Judaism* (Leiden: E. J. Brill, 1973); Stephen Westerholm, *Jesus and Scribal Authority* (Lund: CWK Gleerup, 1978); G. Alon, *Jews, Judaism and the Classical World*, trans. Israel Abraham (Jerusalem: Magnes, 1977); Roger P. Booth, *Jesus and the Laws of Purity: Tradition History and Legal History in Mark 7*, JSNTSS 13 (Sheffield: JSOT, 1986); and Jacob Milgrom, "Purity and Impurity," in *Encyclopedia Judaica* (Jerusalem: Keter, 1971), 1405-14.

[56] On the significance of the temple, Neusner states, "The Temple supplied to purity its importance in the religious life. As the Temple signified divine favor, and as the cult supplied the nexus

Miracles touch the sensitive issue of purity in Jesus' ministry because it is precisely in his miracles that Jesus is in violation of the standards of purity of his day. In the first place, the primary subjects of Jesus' miracles were those deemed "unclean" in his day.[57] Beyond this, Jesus' ministry to the unclean compromised his own purity by the standards of his day.[58] Given the status of the purity system and its connection to the temple and God himself, in the eyes of those who enforced the system, Jesus' violation of purity standards constituted nothing less than an assault on the temple and Yahweh. This is the reason for the constant challenge from the Pharisees and Sadducees throughout Jesus' ministry. However, it is in his violation of their code that Jesus made his own powerful statement about purity in the Kingdom. In contrast to the Pharisees, who held to strict and defensive purity standards,[59]

---

between Israel and God, so purity, associated so closely to both, could readily serve as an image of either divine favor or man's loyalty to God. From that fact followed the assignment of impurity to all that stood against the Temple, the cult, and God: idolatry first of all. . . . All rites of purification aimed at one goal: to permit participation in the cult" (Neusner, *Idea of Purity*, 15, 118). On the importance of the temple to economic and political life in first-century Palestine, see Horsley, *Jesus and the Spiral of Violence*, 286ff.

[57] Gerhard Delling ("Botschaft und Wunder im Wirken Jesu," in *Der historische Jesus und der kerygmatische Christus*, ed. Helmut Ristow and Karl Matthiae [Berlin: Evangelische Verlagsanstalt, 1961], 397) notes that it is no mere coincidence that Jesus heals the blind, lame, and lepers, as well as the tax gatherers and sinners, given the purity system as evidenced in Josephus (*Jewish Wars* 6:425-27), Qumran (1Q Sa 2:3-9 and 11QTemple), and the rabbinic materials (*Men* 9:8). Neusner summarizes Josephus on the classes prohibited from the temple as (1) foreigners; (2) those with gonorrhea; (3) menstruating women; (4) anyone unclean by contact with a corpse; (5) lepers; (6) men not thoroughly clean from some other defect (*Idea of Purity*, 41).

[58] Some examples from Mark's account would be: Jesus touches lepers (1:41); he touches the woman with the issue of blood (5:25ff.); he enters the house where a girl lay dead (5:35-43); he touches her corpse (5:35-43); he heals a Gentile (7:24-30); he uses spittle in healing (7:31-36; 8:22-26); he heals on the Sabbath (1:29-31; 3:1-6); he fellowships with the unclean (2:15-17; 8:1-10). For a more complete enumeration of Jesus' offenses see David Rhoads, "Social Criticism: Crossing Boundaries," in *Mark and Method: New Approaches in Biblical Studies*, ed. Janice Capel Anderson and Stephen D. Moore (Minneapolis, Minn.: Fortress, 1992), 149-50; and Westerholm, *Jesus and Scribal Authority*, 67-69.

[59] The ground of the Pharisees' identity as a distinct sect was their belief that temple purity rites were normative beyond just the priesthood. Their particular views here were manifested in daily life around the taking of meals, which was supposed to be done in a state of ritual purity and only with others of similar "pure" status, and the careful giving of tithes and offerings. For a concise summary of first-century Pharisaism, see Klaus Berger, "Jesus als Pharisäer und Frühe Christen als Pharisäer," *NovT* 30 (1988), 231-37; see also Neusner, *Idea of Purity*, 65.

Jesus demonstrated an "offensive" holiness that was not threatened by the impurity of others.[60] Whereas the Pharisaic purity was something fragile that needed to be protected from pollution, Jesus, armed with the power of the Kingdom (that is, the Holy Spirit), crosses the boundaries of purity, reaches into the realm of the unclean, and, instead of being polluted himself, he makes the unclean to be pure. By means of his contact with the impure through his miracles, Jesus demonstrates that the purity of the Kingdom is not a matter of externals so that it can be threatened by something outside of the person. Purity of the Kingdom is something far more penetrating: it is an issue of the heart (Mark 7:15; Matt. 15:1-3; 25-28). This is why Jesus' healings were an outward sign of the forgiveness of sin offered from God (Mark 2:12; John 5:14).[61] Jesus, as bearer of the purity of the Kingdom, makes the external condition clean without suffering pollution himself; and he can go beyond that and heal the heart. The issue of the heart was why the purity of the temple cult came up short and received Jesus' condemnation. On the one hand, external observance may too easily overshadow demands God makes on the heart, and on the other, external demands are too simple a criteria for judging the heart.[62] So the Kingdom is inherently oriented towards purity, without which no one will see God, but it is a purity that operates in the deepest regions of the human heart, and Jesus' miracles are indirect testimony to that fact.

Summary

Our discussion of the nature of the Kingdom that Jesus first announces and demonstrates takes us inexorably to the Old Testament eschatological hope. In every way, through his preaching and demonstrations of divine power, Jesus is operating as the Coming One for whom Israel was to wait. The fulfillment theme of his preaching, the application of prophetic Scripture to himself, and the authority of his words dictate this verdict. Moreover, when we add to this Jesus' unique demonstrations of Spirit-power

---

[60] The concepts of offensive and defensive holiness are Berger's ("Jesus als Pharisäer).

[61] Betz, "Heilung," *TRE*, 14:766.

[62] Westerholm, *Scribal Authority*, 91; "Clean and Unclean," in *Dictionary of Jesus and the Gospels*, ed. Joel B. Green, Scot McKnight, and I. Howard Marshall (Downers Grove, Ill.: InterVarsity Press, 1992), 126-28; and Rhoads, "Social Criticism," 155-59.

which pointed to the new age through their own Old Testament antecedents, in their occasion (i.e., the Sabbath), motivation (i.e, covenantal mercy), and objects (i.e., the impure), the case becomes even more clear. At least at the initial stage of his ministry, Jesus appears to be taking the Kingdom according to the eschatological root present in Judaism. His Kingdom is the reign of Yahweh manifested historically, politically, spiritually, and nationally. It means ultimate rest, restoration, liberation, deliverance, and redemption for all of God's creation. For God's people it means the experience of this redemption in the whole person, in body (by miracles of healing, exorcism, and provision) and heart (by forgiveness). For the remainder of the creation, the redemption of Yahweh's reign means the final destruction of the chaotic principle which has been its cruel master since the advent of evil.

Jesus' miracles highlight one important feature of this general Old Testament understanding of the Kingdom visible in the inception of Jesus' ministry. Returning again to Matthew 12:28, we note that Jesus makes a remarkable statement about the Kingdom's presence in regard to his power to effect miracles, in this case exorcism. Jesus declares, "If I cast out demons by the Spirit of God, then the Kingdom of God has come upon you." Here we see the possibility of a broader domain of meaning for the *basileia* than simply the Jewish hope. Obviously, the visibly glorious, all-conquering reign of Yahweh as anticipated in the Old Testament was not there at that moment of the exorcism. What was there was the power of the divine Spirit working through the uniquely anointed Spirit-bearer, and this Jesus calls the Kingdom. Jesus, it would appear, makes room in his own initial understanding of the Kingdom for some idea of the reign or rule of God without particular reference to the realm or sphere of its concrete expression, similar to the dynamic and abstract concepts of Yahweh's reign and rule found in the Old Testament. In the New Testament *basileia* thus can also be a reference to Kingdom-power, in addition to the physical manifestation of that power in an eschatological Jewish realm.[63] Because of his unique anointing with the Spirit of power, the Kingdom's power was thus uniquely resident in Jesus, making Origen's designation of Jesus as the *autobasileia* not far from the mark: in the gospel the Kingdom of God

---

[63] Sanders makes this point in *Jesus and Judaism*, 236-37.

is Christ himself *(in evangelio est Dei regnum Christus ipse).* It also helps us understand Jesus' teaching of the Kingdom during the later periods of his ministry.

THE KINGDOM AFTER THE REJECTION OF THE KING

If the Kingdom of Jesus' original proclamation was the Jewish hope of the Old Testament, significant changes in this proclamation are evident as his ministry proceeds. For one thing this Kingdom which was initially proclaimed as near becomes near only in relation to certain events of the future.[64] For another, this Kingdom which was originally proclaimed publicly through the mouth of the herald after rejection becomes the matter of secrets and mysteries as the predominantly spiritual tone of Jesus' teaching becomes even more evident.[65]

The Mysteries of the Kingdom

Intimately associated with the Kingdom's proclamation is the element of human decision. For the Gospel writers, both the acts and the words of Jesus were intended to reveal the near approach of the eschatological Kingdom, but they were also intended to provoke a decision. Jesus did not come simply working wonders and teaching with new authority; he came demanding a response from his hearers. "Repent and believe" was the gospel

---

[64] In Luke 21:31 Jesus uses the same word *(engys)* he used at the beginning of his proclamation (Mark 1:15) to describe the Kingdom's nearness for a time in the future after the events of this age have run their course (see Matt. 24:33; Mark 13:29). Ridderbos has noted the change as well. "While at the beginning of his preaching all emphasis is laid upon the presence of the fulfillment, as is seen in connection with his miracles; at the end of the synoptic kerygma everything is again focused upon the future. The coming of the kingdom is then referred to in such an absolutely future sense as if it *had not* yet come, and the *parousia* of the Son of Man—the word *parousia* means arrival and not second coming!—is spoken of as if he were only a person of the future" (Herman Ridderbos, *The Coming of the Kingdom,* trans. H. de Jongste, ed. Raymond O. Zorn [Philadelphia: Presbyterian and Reformed, 1962], 468).

[65] As noted earlier in chapter five, a certain development in Jesus' ministry was often advocated by scholars of the Old Quest of the historical Jesus to account for the apocalyptic and religious elements of Jesus teaching. In the twentieth century T. W. Manson has also advocated some change in Jesus' ministry from the initial future, apocalyptic Kingdom to a Kingdom of personal salvation (T. W. Manson, *The Teaching of Jesus* [Cambridge: Cambridge University Press, 1931], 124-29; 135).

proclamation from the beginning, and Jesus' ministry polarized the crowds according to those who "had ears to hear" his message and those who did not. It is in response to growing rejection that we begin to see Jesus' use of the Kingdom change from his initial proclamation to one that now concerns the "mysteries of the Kingdom."

Matthew's Gospel makes this transition especially clearly.[66] Following two chapters where the rejection of Jesus' proclamation reaches its climax in rejection by the people, the leaders, and Jesus' own family,[67] Matthew 13 marks a pivotal point in Jesus' presentation of the Kingdom. On the same day (Matt. 13:1) in which rejection of his message and miracles reaches its zenith, Jesus is pictured as adjusting his proclamation in several ways. First, Matthew tells us Jesus now speaks to the crowds in "parables" (*en parabolais* [13:3]), which for Matthew is a new term to characterize Jesus' teaching. Prior to chapter 13, Matthew does not consider Jesus to use parables, but he reserves this term for that which begins now in light of Jesus' rejection.[68]

Second, the purpose of the parables as judgment for rejection is evidence for their transitionary nature. According to the Gospel record, a persisting condition of spiritual dullness merits Jesus' lack of clarity before the crowds. "Therefore I speak to them in parables; because (*hoti*) while seeing they do not see, and while hearing they do not hear, nor do they

---

[66] See Mark Saucy, "The Kingdom-of-God Sayings in Matthew," *BS* 151/602 (1994): 175-97.

[67] Jesus receives opposition prior to Matthew 11 and 12 (e.g., Matt. 9:34), but the force of the opposition reaches a high point in these chapters. Jesus reproaches his generation for their unbelief in John the Baptist (Matt. 11:16-19) and for their unbelief in him even in the face of his miracles (11:21-24). Chapter 12 shows the rejection of the Jewish leadership as they attribute his works of the Holy Spirit to the ruler of the demons (12:24). This chapter also has Jesus' own family seek to put him away because, as the Markan parallel makes clear, "he has lost his senses" (Matt. 12:46-50, cf. Mark 3:21).

[68] In light of the broad definition of *parabolē* usually understood by scholars, Matthew seems to create his own theory of parables. The parables of chapter 13 are somehow different in either method or content (or both) from anything else Jesus has said before. The likelihood of the parables being a different method of teaching is elicited from the disciples' question in verse 10. We note that they do not ask "Why do you speak to them in *these* parables?" which we would more reasonably expect if the difference now was only one of the crowds' inability to comprehend. Instead their question has the tone of "Why parables at all?" In Mark's Gospel such a theory of parables cannot be maintained, as he uses "parable" to describe Jesus' teaching prior to the mysteries of the Kingdom in chapter 4 (in 3:23).

understand" (Matt. 13:13). The crowds have proven themselves hardened and thus not suitable to know the subjects about which the parables teach. The citation of Isaiah 6:10 in verse fifteen only confirms their status in Jesus' understanding. Their eyes and ears do not admit truth because "they have closed their eyes."[69]

Finally, the content of these parables is specifically called the "mysteries" of the Kingdom of God (Matt. 13:13; Mark 4:11), which is especially significant given the context of rejection. If the parables of Matthew 13 and Mark 4 are given as judgment for hard-heartedness, then the probability increases that parables about the Kingdom are a means of concealing something from the crowds, because such parables have not appeared before in Jesus' ministry. Although most scholars reject any such distinction between the parables of the Kingdom and the rest of Jesus' general teaching ministry,[70] J. Arthur Baird's stimulating "pragmatic approach" to the exegesis of the mystery of the parables casts the issue in a different light.[71] Baird conducts his study on the premise that if the parables of the Kingdom were meant to conceal information from the crowds, then that intent would be borne out in Jesus' subsequent practice in the Gospels. Examination of the parables in the Synoptic Gospels reveals that specific

---

[69] The "hardening theory" of the parables is rejected by a number of scholars, who contend from rabbinic literature that parables are meant for enlightenment and that Jesus uses parables out of pity for the dullness of the crowds. His purpose is to enlighten, not judge. See C. F. D. Moule, "Mark 4:1-20 Yet Once More," in *Neotestamentica et Semitica*, ed. E. E. Ellis and M. Wilcox (Edinburgh: 1969), cited by J. W. Bowker, "Mystery and Parable in Mk 4:1-20," *JTS* new series 25 (1974), 301; J. Jeremias, *The Parables of Jesus*, trans. S. H. Hooke, rev. ed. (New York: Charles Scribners', 1966), 13-14. Some who argue for a hardening theory of the parables, as I have here, are Jack Dean Kingsbury, *The Parables of Jesus in Matthew Thirteen* (London: SPCK, 1969), 48-49; Bastiaan Van Elderen, "The Purpose of Parables According to Matthew 13:10-17," in *New Dimensions in New Testament Study*, ed. Richard N. Longenecker and Merril C. Tenney (Grand Rapids: Zondervan, 1974), 188; Rudolf Schnackenburg, *God's Rule and Kingdom*, trans. John Murray (New York: Herder and Herder, 1963), 187; and Dan O. Via, "Matthew on the Understandability of the Parables," *JBL* 84 (1965): 430-32.

[70] G. R. Beasley-Murray has a full listing of scholars who hold this position, to which could be added Ridderbos, *The Coming of the Kingdom*, 125; G. Finkenrath, "Secret," in *NIDNTT*, 3:503; Van Elderen, "The Purpose of Parables," 184; Schnackenburg, *God's Rule and Kingdom*, 188; James D. G. Dunn, "The Messianic Secret in Mark," *Tyndale Bulletin* 21 (1970): 113.

[71] J. Arthur Baird, "A Pragmatic Approach to Parable Exegesis: Some New Evidence on Mark 4:11, 33-34," *JBL* 76 (1957): 201-7.

"Kingdom" parables were in fact used this way by Jesus. More specifically, for the Synoptic Gospels Baird found that although Jesus told many parables to the crowds after Matthew 13 and Mark 4, very few of these parables were explained. Of the latter category of parables that were explained to the crowds, *none* of these parables is said explicitly to deal with the Kingdom of God.[72] Two things are implied from this for the Kingdom. First, it is specifically through certain Kingdom parables that Jesus does in fact deny understanding to the crowds and respond negatively to their hard-hearted rejection, as Matthew 13:11 seems to indicate.[73] Second, given the fact that Jesus does explain some parabolic teaching to the crowds, there seems to be a distinction between specifically "Kingdom" parables and the other parables. Thus, it would seem to be painting too broadly to simply say, as many do, that the mysteries of the Kingdom are synonymous with everything Jesus says and does.[74]

Leading us further in the direction that the mysteries of the Kingdom represent a change from Jesus' initial teaching is the stated content of the Kingdom parables in Matthew 13. Even a cursory look at the parables of

---

[72] Baird, "Pragmatic Approach," 206-7. See also Raymond E. Brown, *The Semitic Background of the Term "Mystery" in the New Testament* (Philadelphia: Fortress, 1968), 35, n. 110, who concurs with Baird's conclusions.

[73] In Matthew, for example, after the rejection of chapter 12, the crowds (including the rejecting leadership) understand only three parables specifically about the Kingdom (21:27-32; 33-40; 22:1-14), all of which explain how the Kingdom has been taken from them. Though Matthew 13:34 seems to indicate that Jesus told more Kingdom parables to the crowds, they must have been unexplained and enigmatic. Thus, no positive information about the Kingdom of God is revealed in parabolic form to those in rejection, though the disciples are privy to the meaning of *every* parable (cf. Mark 4:34).

[74] As does Kingsbury, for example (*Parables in Matthew Thirteen*, 44-45). Also contrary to the broad interpretation of the mysteries is the nature of the term itself. The meaning of *mystērion* in the Gospels is widely thought by scholars to derive from the Hebrew word *raz* in canonical (Dan. 2:18, 19, 27, 28, 29, 30, 47, 4:6) and noncanonical literature. It is a designation for the plan of God for the unfolding of the events of history which is hidden from human eyes and disclosed only by divine revelation. According to Bornkamm, in the New Testament the term "always has an eschatological sense," which would seem to be different from other subjects Jesus addressed, such as ethics (Bornkamm, *mystērion, TDNT,* 4:822; see also D. A. Carson, *Matthew,* Expositor's Bible Commentary [Grand Rapids: Zondervan, 1984], 306; and George Eldon Ladd *The Presence of the Future: The Eschatology of Biblical Realism* [Grand Rapids: Eerdmans, 1974], 222).

the Kingdom shows pronounced differences as the glorious, Jewish, Kingdom of the Old Testament promise is likened now to a grain of mustard seed or a morsel of leaven. Though many scholars would treat the results for the Kingdom in these parables more broadly to speak simply of the Kingdom's presence in Jesus' ministry,[75] the parables individually and pointedly say much more. In chapter thirteen they speak of the different responses to the word of the Kingdom (the parable of the sower) the future judgment of the Kingdom (wheat and tares, dragnet), the initial insignificance and secret but great growth of the Kingdom (mustard seed and leaven), and the great value and sacrifice required for the Kingdom (treasure and pearl).[76] It is in these details that the discontinuities between the Kingdom message of Jesus before and after his rejection stand in bold relief. Ladd observes such a limitation of the Kingdom was indeed new to Jesus' contemporaries and differed from the Old Testament's understanding of the Kingdom. He says, "That there should be a coming of God's Kingdom in the way Jesus proclaimed, in a hidden, secret form, working quietly among men, was utterly novel to Jesus' contemporaries. The Old Testament gave no such promise."[77]

The parables also clearly call for some sense of the presence of the Kingdom in this age. As we have already seen there is no question but that as it was first announced and demonstrated, Jesus felt that he and his ministry were the literal fulfillment of the promises of the Old Testament for the manifestation of Yahweh's reign over Israel. We have also seen that Jesus considered his ministry in the power of the Spirit to mean that Yahweh's reign had in fact come to earth. The *basileia*-language of Jesus is broad enough to include both the Kingdom as to its particularly Jewish manifestation, characteristic of the Old Testament hope, and the Kingdom as to its divine operation in power.[78] The parables of Jesus again readily point to the

---

[75] For example, see Kingsbury, *Parables in Matthew Thirteen*, 20.

[76] I have taken these interpretations of the parables from Robert H. Stein, *An Introduction to the Parables of Jesus* (Philadelphia: Westminster, 1981), 95, 105, 140, 142, respectively.

[77] Ladd, 225. See the same observation by D. A. Carson, *Matthew*, 307-8.

[78] Following the thought of Sanders, who states, "One need realize only that 'kingdom' does not always carry precisely the same meaning. The kingdom in the full eschatological sense could not be present, nor could it be entered into by individuals, but the meaning of the word can be stretched so that one can talk of the kingdom, in the sense of God's power, as present and extended to individuals in the present" (*Jesus and Judaism* [Philadelphia: Fortress 1985], 237).

latter sphere of meaning of the *basileia*. Evidently the power of the Kingdom that was present in Jesus would abide throughout the end of the present age separate and apart from its particularly Jewish manifestation. This is not to say that the original character of the Kingdom as Jewish, historical, and political was necessarily abandoned with the mystery-teaching of the Kingdom. Rending the physical from the spiritual is the nonchiliast's error, and, as we shall see in the following section, the error Jesus repudiates in his particular teaching of the Kingdom's futurity. However, the Kingdom's presence does mean that, as with the other features of the parables, the fulfillment of the Kingdom promises enters a new, unanticipated phase. The Kingdom could be said to be present in this age by means of its power. Thus, Jesus could teach the Kingdom could now be "entered" (Matt. 23:13) as people came into relationship with God by the power of the Spirit,[79] and that the Kingdom can be enjoyed now by the needy and the Gentiles (Matt. 21:43; 22:1–10; Luke 14:16–24).

The Futurity of the Kingdom

As the parables of the Kingdom introduce various limitations to the Old Testament concept of the Kingdom found in Jesus' initial teaching, they also point us towards another change in the message, that is, the Kingdom's futurity. We have noted earlier that in the message as it was initially proclaimed by John, Jesus, and his disciples, the Kingdom was near or "at hand," and that Jesus even taught about the presence of some form of the Kingdom. Nevertheless, the dominant teaching of Jesus about the Kingdom throughout his ministry and especially after his rejection was that the Kingdom had not yet "come" and that it would not come until some time in the future. This is the eschatological Kingdom of the parables associated with the return of the Son of Man that many of the Third Quest would circumvent by one means or another (cf. Matt. 13:43,

---

[79] Robert Recker explains that this verse and others like it teach a relationship with God, not a realm, so that one could not say with them that the Kingdom has come or been established on earth. The idea is similar to Paul's in Philippians 3:20. Those whose citizenship is in heaven with the King still wait for his return and the establishment of his Kingdom ("The Redemptive Focus of the Kingdom of God," *CTJ* 14 [November 1979]: 166). John 3:3-15 similarly teaches that one cannot enter the Kingdom without being born again, which also has antecedents in the Old Testament promised activity of the Spirit (Darrell L. Bock, "Current Messianic Activity and OT Davidic Promise: Dispensationalism, Hermeneutics, and NT Fulfillment," *TrinJ* 15 NS [1994]: 61).

Matt. 13:47–50).[80] It was the Kingdom that the righteous will enter on "that day" of judgment (Matt. 7:21–22, cf. 25:34), the Kingdom for which the disciples must pray would yet "come" (Matt. 6:10). It was the Kingdom where Jesus would again fellowship with the disciples as he did at the Last Supper (Mark 14:25; Luke 22:18), the Kingdom of the banqueting table (Matt. 8:12). It was also the Kingdom of the parable Jesus told the crowds in Luke 19 (vv. 11–27). At this critical moment, when Jesus is near Jerusalem and the crowds are anticipating the appearance of the Kingdom of their ancestral hope, Jesus makes it very clear that he must leave to receive his kingdom in a faraway land and then return to exercise his reign.[81] For the time being the glorious and physical manifestation of the Kingdom will be put off until the time of his return.[82]

But what kind of Kingdom was to come at the Son of Man's return? Jesus' later ministry and activity demonstrate he still had in mind the hope of his ancestors that had so colored the beginning of his ministry. Though the manifestation of the Kingdom that would immediately occupy was much more limited according to the parables and mysteries of the Kingdom, the coming Kingdom would still have a Jewish character, as Jesus continued to promise his disciples places of rulership over the twelve tribes

---

[80] See, for example, the presentation of Borg and others in chapter four. The connection of the return of the Son of Man and the parables is made clear in Jesus' interpretation of the parable of the wheat and the tares. The sons of the Kingdom will "shine as the sun in the kingdom" after the return of the Son of Man. The subject of coming judgment comes from the parable of the dragnet. For a defense of the authenticity of the Son of Man sayings, as well as their inherent connection to the Kingdom, see Beasley-Murray's discussion of Vielhauer's thesis (Beasley-Murray, *Jesus and the Kingdom*, 219-312).

[81] Jesus' use of *basileia*-language in the parable is significant. When the nobleman is said to go to a distant country to "receive a kingdom" *(labein heautō basileian)* for himself, Jesus demonstrates clearly the abstract, dynamic meaning of the Kingdom. The nobleman would receive the status of the king, but the expression of his status would not be manifest until his return to his domain. Thus the realm is also in the purview of the reign. See further Robert L. Saucy, *The Case for Progressive Dispensationalism: The Interface between Dispensational and Non-Dispensational Theology* (Grand Rapids: Zondervan, 1993), 95-96.

[82] As demonstrated by Witherington, Jesus' statements about imminence need not necessarily clash with other statements about the Kingdom's futurity as outlined here. When understood as a possible but not necessary imminence, there is room for both statements about the Kingdom's futurity and its imminence. See Ben Witherington, *Jesus, Paul and the End of the World: A Comparative Study of New Testament Eschatology* (Downers Grove, Ill.: InterVarsity Press, 1992), 36-44.

of Israel (Matt. 19:28, Luke 22:30).[83] It is the Kingdom that is still concerned with the social and political significance of the temple, as Jesus continues to directly confront the existing corrupt structures.[84] It is a universal Kingdom great enough to include the Gentiles (Matt. 21:43; 22:1–10; Luke 14:16–24), as the prophets had said. It is the Kingdom that would come in judgment of the enemies of Israel (Matt. 24, 25; Mark 13). It is the Kingdom that would manifest the Lord's dominion "as domain," as Mack describes the *prima facie* picture of Mark's Gospel.[85]

The miracles of Jesus also demonstrate the futurity of the Kingdom in their stated functions as signs (John 20:30, 31). A sign, understood through the tradition of the Old Testament, was something which pointed to something else. It either authenticates or predicts a coming event (e.g., Exod. 4:8–9; Isa. 7:14), but it was not that event.[86] In the Gospels the miracles of

---

[83] See also Jesus' teaching in Matthew 20:21-23 about places of honor for James and John in the future Kingdom.

[84] We have noted earlier the significance of Jesus' assaults on the temple by way of his miracles. In the Synoptic accounts of the temple cleansing during the passion week (e.g., Matt. 21:12-13), Jesus escalates and focuses his confrontation of the temple. Jesus' citation of the passage in Isaiah 56:7 also sets the place of the temple within the context of the eschatological hope of the Old Testament. Sanders correctly evaluates the significance of Jesus' actions relative to the eschatological hope. He notes that "the best explanation of Jesus' demonstrative action in the temple and his saying against the temple . . . is to be found in his eschatological expectation. The Kingdom was at hand, and one of the things which that meant was that the old temple would be replaced by a new" (Sanders, *Jesus and Judaism*, 77, cf. also 75).

[85] Burton L. Mack, "The Kingdom Sayings in Mark," *Forum* 3, no. 1 (1987): 18. Mack, of course, sees this picture as the result of several stages of development and not the view of the historical Jesus. Nevertheless he does point out the teaching of the Gospel if such schemes of development are not presumed. See also Borg's description of the "eschatological consensus" with the Kingdom's clear meaning: "it referred to the coming messianic kingdom, and/or the power (reign) of God by which that kingdom would be established" (Marcus J. Borg, "Portraits of Jesus in Contemporary North American Scholarship," *HTR* 84, no. 1 [1991]: 20). Borg attacks the eschatological consensus primarily via the authenticity of the Son of Man sayings, which, as already noted, is far from sure footing.

[86] Richardson, *Miracle-Stories of the Gospels*, 57; Brown, *Miracles and the Critical Mind*, 322-23. The "signs" that Moses performed have interesting parallel to those done by Jesus in that both were considered to be manifestation of the "finger of God" (Luke 11:20; Exod. 8:19). Buchanan has noted the parallel for the Kingdom, saying that just as the signs of Moses pointed to the future establishment of God's reign with his free people at Sinai, so the signs of Jesus point to the Kingdom's future establishment. The signs were expressions of the Kingdom's power, but were not the Kingdom *per se* (*Jesus*, 30-33).

Jesus and his disciples follow this pattern for the Kingdom by their provisional and signatory nature. Though they were proofs of the physical aspect of the Kingdom, Jesus' miracles did not accomplish the final rest and restoration of the Kingdom promised in the Old Testament. Those he had healed would again fall sick and die; the demons would escape complete subjugation until their "hour," and the creation would continue to suffer under the cosmic oppression of the evil one—all indications that the Kingdom was not yet established. There was a real disjunction between what Jesus' miracles were and what they pointed to. With Ridderbos we conclude,

> [miracles] indicate the coming of the kingdom and point to the cosmic palingenesis.... But they are not the beginning of this palingenesis, as if the latter were the completion of the miracles. For this palingenesis is something of the future world aeon; because it embodies the resurrection of the dead and the renewal of the world, it does not belong to the present dispensation. It even presupposes the precedence of the cosmic catastrophe.[87]

Summary

We have noted two significant developments of Jesus' understanding of the Kingdom in the later stages of his ministry. In response to rejection of the Kingdom Jesus first introduces the "mysteries of the Kingdom." According to the parables Jesus told, this development represented a significant limitation of the Kingdom as it was originally conceived by the crowds and as it was first announced by Jesus. The mysteries taught a realized manifestation of the Kingdom on the earth, but it was a manifestation very different from the Kingdom in the Old Testament Jewish hope. Second, as we have just seen, the Kingdom's futurity, even its contingent futurity, now also enters Jesus' ministry. The Kingdom that was first preached as "at hand" now becomes "at hand" only to certain, distant future events. It is still the Davidic Kingdom of the ancestral Jewish hope, but it would not come immediately through Jesus' ministry.

It is only when Jesus' ministry is investigated according to its narrative

---

[87] Ridderbos, *The Coming of the Kingdom*, 119-20.

context that both the mysteries of the Kingdom and the Kingdom's futurity realize their true significance in Jesus' teaching. One category need not indict the other, as is so often the case in modern research. Given the breadth of the Kingdom-language Jesus utilized, as well as the subsequent developments of Jesus' original proclamation, both mystery and futurity harmoniously coexist in a summary of Jesus' doctrine. The Kingdom can be present and active according to the description of the parables, and it can be the glorious promise of the Jewish ancestral hope coming one day as final fulfillment. Thus, the Gospels present one program for the manifestation of Yahweh's reign on the earth, but it is a program expressed in two phases. Rejection of the initial proclamation instituted Jesus' greater emphasis on phase one, the Kingdom as present in the power of the Spirit, while at the same time still retaining the promise of phase two, the Kingdom that will come in the future.[88]

THE KINGDOM AND THE CHURCH

A two-phased operation of the Old Testament Kingdom outlined here for the teaching of Jesus finds another voice in the teachings of Jesus' disciples after him. Since Luke tells us in Acts 1:3 that the disciples were tutored by the resurrected Christ for forty days on the Kingdom of God,

---

[88] The interpretation of Jesus' teaching I have presented here has been recently categorized as "progressive dispensationalism." The major difference of such a presentation, as against classic and revised dispensationalism, is that some initial fulfillment of the Davidic Covenant in the ministry of Jesus and the period of the church is allowed. The precise degree of fulfillment is still a matter of debate among the members of progressive dispensationalism, but the Kingdom plan of God is still allowed to retain better continuity from Old Testament to New Testament in the manifestation of the one Kingdom of God. It is not a plan of *many* biblical Kingdoms, as one might read from classic or revised dispensationalists (for example Ryrie and Walvoord, who are critical of Progressives because they "do not distinguish the various kingdoms in the Bible") (Charles C. Ryrie, *Dispensationalism*, rev. ed. [Chicago: Moody, 1995], 165; cf. John F. Walvoord, "Biblical Kingdoms Compared and Contrasted," in *Issues in Dispensationalism*, ed. Wesley R. Willis and John R. Master [Chicago: Moody, 1994]; 75-92). I have contended that the Kingdom of God is the progressive manifestation in creation of the one rule of the Almighty.

The major writings of progressive dispensationalists to date includes *Dispensationalism, Israel and the Church: A Search for Definition*, ed. C. A. Blaising and D. L. Bock (Grand Rapids: Zondervan, 1992); *Progressive Dispensationalism*, ed. C. A. Blaising and Darrell L. Bock (Wheaton: Victor, 1993); and Robert Saucy, *The Case for Progressive Dispensationalism* (1993).

it is unreasonable to suggest that they would adopt some other teaching immediately after the Ascension.[89] There must be real continuity between what follows Jesus and what he himself taught. Thus, the church teaches that there is some real manifestation of the promised Kingdom now in the presence and work of the Holy Spirit; and there is a future hope for the Kingdom to come in its fullness, a fullness that would accord with the Old Testament hope of Israel.[90]

The presence of the Kingdom in the power of the Holy Spirit is recorded in numerous places in the writings of the New Testament. Romans 14:17, for example, shows clear parallel with the teaching of Jesus about the Kingdom's presence in certain spiritual characteristics. Paul says, "the kingdom of God is not a matter of eating and drinking, but of righteousness, peace and joy in the Holy Spirit." Paul's statement to the Corinthians also echoes the Kingdom's presence in the current era through the spiritual power of the Holy Spirit in the Gospel.[91] In 1 Corinthians 4:20 Paul counters the haughty words of his opponents with a challenge to their power in the Spirit, because the Kingdom of God does not consist in words but in power.[92] The writer of Hebrews further adds to this concept in the men-

---

[89] It is doubtful that the disciples' instruction in the Kingdom of God only concerned eschatological matters. In light of Luke's consistent use in Acts of *basileia tou theou* for a summary of the whole Christian proclamation, it is evident that while the Kingdom surely did include matters of eschatology, it also summarized the whole Christian message about "Jesus as the Christ." See Acts 8:12; 19:8; 28:23, 31, and especially 20:24, 25, where Paul's declaration to the elders of Ephesus that he went about preaching the Kingdom of God (v. 25) is parallel to the thought that he solemnly testified to them "of the gospel of the grace of God."

[90] In the pages that follow I have left the detailed, traditional dispensational exposition of key passages (e.g., Rom. 9-11; 1 Cor. 15:24-25; Rev. 20:1-6) to others, in the hope of addressing more specifically the issues pertinent to progressive dispensationalism as it contrasts with traditional dispensationalism and other views asserting discontinuity between Jesus and the church that followed him.

[91] According to the context (1:18, 24; 2:4-5), the power Paul will test is the power of the Gospel made evident by the Spirit.

[92] It should also be pointed out from the context that 1 Corinthians 4:20 does not argue for a present established Kingdom, as if spiritual power were the final fulfillment of the promises to Israel in the Old Testament. Paul has just derided the haughtiness of the Corinthians who, although they act like they are already "reigning," really are not (1 Cor. 4:8). Paul would not deny their present reign and verses later assert a present Kingdom. Rather, according to Paul's general use, as we shall see later, the Kingdom for Paul here in First Corinthians, as C. K. Barrett says, "is always an eschatological concept (though sometimes brought forward into the present), and

tion of people having already "tasted . . . the power of the age to come" (Heb. 6:5). Regardless of the meaning of having "tasted" of these powers, the point is clear that people can experience some manifestation of the coming age already in this age.[93]

The Kingdom's futurity is also clearly seen in the church after Jesus. The first question of the disciples following their forty days of instruction on the Kingdom seeks a future and particularly Jewish manifestation of the Kingdom from Jesus. "Lord, is it at this time you are restoring the kingdom to Israel" (Acts 1:6)?[94] As Jesus answers (1:7-8), their error appears not to have been a question of the nature of the Kingdom, that is, that it was or was not the traditional Old Testament hope of Israel, but it was a question of timing and the concomitant need to wisely occupy themselves until the time is right.[95] That is, Jesus tells them, it is not for them to know the Kingdom's "when," and that in the meantime they should wait for the spiritual power to accomplish the work ahead of them. The near proximity of the promise of being baptized with the Spirit (Acts 1:5) also confirms the legitimacy of their question, especially in light of the

---

the *power* with which it works is the power of the Holy Spirit (cf. Rom. xiv. 17), by which God's purpose is put into effect and the future anticipated in the present" (*A Commentary on the First Epistle to the Corinthians* [New York: Harper & Row, 1968], 118).

[93] The two-age doctrine known to many authors of the New Testament alludes to the Old Testament messianic hope as expressed in Jewish pseudepigraphal literature. "This age" was the present time of unrighteousness, toil, and suffering lasting from the creation to the earth's passing away (cf. *1 Enoch* 48:7). The "age to come" meant the period of ultimate salvation, a new heaven and earth, and a fulfillment of Yahweh's promises to Israel. It was the time when the Gentiles were subdued and the Messiah would rule as king from his throne in Jerusalem. A fully developed two-age system is found in 4 Ezra 6:7-10, 20; 12:25; 14:10 dating to about A.D. 100. The two-age doctrine is known by Jesus in Matthew 12:32; Luke 16:8; 18:30 and Mark 10:30. The last two passages relate the age to come to the significant Johannine concept of eternal life, though John himself may also give voice to the two-age doctrine through his oft-used *ho kosmos houtos*. See John 8:23; 9:39; 11:9; 12:25, 31; 13:1; 16:11; 18:36 (H. Sasse, *aiōn*, *TDNT*, 1:205). The two-age system is found in Pauline literature at Galatians 1:4 and Ephesians 1:21.

[94] The disciples' use of the word "restore" *(apokathistaneis)*, according to Oepke, was a technical term for the messianic, political restoration of Israel to its own land (Albrecht Oepke, *apokathistēmi, apokatastasis, TDNT,* 1:388-89).

[95] The universalism of the Kingdom implied in the Gentile mission is not, as we recall, antithetical to the national concerns and hopes of Israel. The Kingdom of the Jewish expectation was both spiritual and national, *both* universal and ethnic (J. Ramsey Michaels, "The Kingdom of God and the Historical Jesus," 114).

messianic promises of Joel 2:28 and what they knew of the role of the Spirit in the new age.[96]

It is also evident that Jesus' answer to their question, his last words to them before his Ascension, did not succeed in changing the disciples' understanding of the Kingdom, if in fact that was their need. Peter again brings up the question of the future Kingdom for Israel in his sermon recorded in Acts 3. Addressing the absence of Jesus now, he says that the Christ must be in heaven until "the period of restoration of all things about which God spoke by the mouth of his holy prophets from ancient time" (Acts 3:21). The clear reference to the Old Testament hope of Israel's restoration shows again the correctness of the initial question of Acts 1:6 and the force of Jesus' answer then. As Jesus' answer concerned not the nature of the hope but its timing, so Peter now is explaining the new timing of the hope, not a radical reformulation of its nature. He and his Jewish brethren are still looking forward to the fulfillment of the ancient prophetic voice in Israel. The disciples, therefore, prove themselves to be attentive learners of the word of their Lord, not the stubborn of heart they are sometimes portrayed to be.[97] God's Kingdom for Israel was not yet there; it remained a hope for the future.

The other mentions of the Kingdom in the New Testament also assert that the Kingdom is something of the future. The Kingdom is something to be inherited (1 Cor. 6:9–10; 15:50; Gal. 5:21; Eph. 5:5; Col. 1:12–13; James 2:5), and while believers can recognize this inheritance by faith, and while they have a guarantee of this inheritance in the Holy Spirit, "this kingdom [the inheritance] embraces all those promises the fulfillment of which is yet future," as Eichler says.[98] As Jesus had taught his disciples, Paul also teaches that the reign of the believer with Christ is future. Because the

---

[96] For a fuller discussion of the meaning of the disciples' question, see Saucy, *The Case for Progressive Dispensationalism*, 268-71.

[97] Of the disciples' question in Acts 1:6, John Calvin said, "their blindness is remarkable, that when they had been so fully and carefully instructed over a period of three years, they betrayed no less ignorance than if they had never heard a word. There are as many errors in this question as words" (*The Acts of the Apostles, 1-13*, Calvin's Commentaries [Grand Rapids: Eerdmans, 1965], 29).

[98] J. Eichler, "Inheritance," in *NIDNTT*, 2:300.

Corinthian Christians were not yet "reigning" (though they inappropriately acted like it), it meant that he also was not yet reigning (1 Cor. 4:8). Far from being a king, Paul characterized his present situation as being a fool for Christ, weak, dishonored, "the scum of the earth, the refuse of the world" (1 Cor. 4:10–13). Rather than boast in his present reign Paul looked forward to the day when after the prerequisite sufferings (Acts 14:22) he would safely enter his heavenly kingdom (2 Tim. 4:18).[99]

The present activity of the risen and ascended Christ also leads us into the New Testament teaching about the futurity of the Kingdom. In conjunction with the New Testament's general restriction of the use of the *basileia*-language group after the Gospels,[100] is the parallel restriction of any clear reference to the risen Christ as "king" or as currently "reigning."[101] The fact that such terms were applied to the Christ from the predictions of the Gospel (Luke 1:33; 19:14), and that they again return to Christ in contexts of the future age (2 Tim. 2:12; Rev. 11:15, 17) suggests, by their absence for the present age, that Christ is not currently reigning as the messianic king today, and that the Kingdom is an entity of the future. That proponents of Christ's present reign also struggle for appropriate explanations for these biblical phenomena appears to confirm the improbability of their view.[102]

Lacking terminological justification for the present reign of Christ, it is sometimes offered that the *concept* of a presently reigning Christ is latent

---

[99] See the similar thoughts in 2 Peter 1:11.

[100] Although Luke used the word *kingdom* 39 times in the Gospel, it only appears 8 times in Acts. Excluding the Revelation, *kingdom* appears in the rest of the New Testament only 18 times, compared to 127 times in the Gospels. The cognate noun "king" and cognate verb "to reign" show similar patterns.

[101] The *ho basileus tōn basileuontōn* title in 1 Timothy 6:15 is seen by many as referring to God the Father, not the Son (e.g., I. H. Marshall, *Jesus the Saviour* [Downers Grove, Ill.: InterVarsity Press, 1990], 209). Even the reference *dei gar auton basileuein* (1 Cor. 15:25) is not without those who take it as a reference to a reign beginning at the Parousia. See W. Bousset, *Die Religion des Judentums im späthellenistischen Zeitalter*, 3d ed., HNT (Tübingen: J. C. B. Mohr [Paul Siebeck], 1926), 288; and H. Lietzmann, *An die Korinther I-II*, 4th ed., HNT (Tübingen: J. C. B. Mohr [Paul Siebeck], 1949), 81.

[102] See chapter 3 for the unlikelihood of *basileus* being subsumed under the *kyrios* or *christos* titles in the New Testament.

in the New Testament.[103] However, this notion cannot be sustained in light of the New Testament evidence. Three streams of evidence converge to suggest that such a concept is not the case, and by implication, that the Kingdom is an entity of the future. First, the concept of a reign is not unknown to the Bible, meaning that we are not at liberty to load the biblical terminology with our own ideas.[104] In Luke 19, the parable of the

---

[103] In his own version of the rapprochement progressive dispensationalism offers to nondispensationalism, Darrell Bock comes closest to the nondispensational position regarding Jesus' current administration of the Davidic throne. With nondispensationalists, Bock interprets the present activity of the ascended and exalted Lord based on the concept of a present "reign." He states: "The basic question for all approaches is this: does the Bible describe any current activity in conjunction with promise and beneficent authority that involves a regal function or an expression of executive, messianic authority? If it does, then is that not a reign, since a ruler is exercising sovereign authority on behalf of his subjects?" (Bock, "Current Messianic Activity," 64, cf. also his chapter, "The Reign of the Lord Christ," *Dispensationalism, Israel and the Church*, 37-67).

From the dispensational point of view, Charles Ryrie affirms that the major departure progressive dispensationalism makes from traditional dispensationalism is that "Christ, already inaugurated as the Davidic king at his ascension, is now reigning in heaven on the throne of David" (Ryrie, *Dispensationalism*, 167). In reality only the first part of the statement is characteristic of all progressive dispensationalists, because others, like Robert Saucy and myself, would make a distinction between the present enthronement of Jesus as the Davidic king and his exercise of that authority in a present reign. See Robert Saucy's discussion of these issues in *The Case for Progressive Dispensationalism*, 69-80.

[104] It is the burden of all who wish to assert a present reign that their concept of *reign* match that of the Bible. This task is particularly daunting when we realize that not only is *basileia*-language lacking for the present function of the exalted Christ, so is ruling/governing-language of any kind. None of the New Testament verbs within the semantic domain of ruling or governing considered by Louw and Nida are applied to the present status of Christ, except one instance of *hēgeomai* in 1 Timothy 1:12, where the apostle Paul thanks Christ for putting him in service. Those verbs of ruling or governing that are never applied to the exalted Christ include *archō*, *poimainō*, *krinō*, *kyrieuō*, *katakyrieō*, *exousiazō*, *katexousiazō*, *hēgemoneuō*, *basileuō*, *presbeuō* (*Greek-English Lexicon of the New Testament Based on Semantic Domains*, ed. Johannes P. Louw and Eugene A. Nida, 2d ed. [New York: United Bible Societies, 1989], 2:478-83). Speaking conceptually, this is a serious hurdle to those who would have Christ ruling now. Such evidence also makes more unlikely the case that 1 Corinthians 15:25 speaks of a present reign of the Lord Christ. If it does speak of a present reign, it is a very rare occasion in the New Testament concept of a reign. For exposition of 1 Corinthians 15:24-25 that does not see Christ's reign as a present phenomenon but a phenomenon for the Parousia, see Robert Saucy, *The Case for Progressive Dispensationalism*, 280-86.

The presence of the noun-forms of these verbs in the New Testament (e.g., Shepherd, Lord, etc.) and the obvious leadership of the exalted Christ his Church (e.g., Rev. 2-3; Eph. 4:7-11)

nobleman's return clearly associates the exercise of a reign with the king slaying his enemies who did not want him to rule over them (Luke 19:27). Similarly, in Revelation 17 and 19, when reigning terminology is again used of Jesus, the context is the exertion of coercive force against his enemies (Rev. 17:14; 9:15, 16). Such a posture of a reigning king towards his enemies also coheres to the general understanding of the functions of the king's reign in the ancient Near East. Passivity towards the enemies of ones' people was not the characteristic of the king (cf. Ps. 110:2).[105]

Second, the biblical concept of the exalted Christ's present function is not the concept of reign but the concept of intercession. The most frequently cited Old Testament passage in the New Testament, Psalm 110, is also the passage the New Testament writers used most in their meditations on the present activity of the exalted Christ. When we look at how this passage is used in the New Testament what we do not see is that it was used to assert a reign, though it was capable of doing so.[106] What we do see in the New Testament is that Psalm 110 was the basis of a current intercessory ministry of the risen Christ. This is true in Hebrews (8:1; 10:12–13; 12:2), Acts (2:33, 5:31; 7:55), and Romans (8:34), giving support to Argyle's statement that, "intercession is the essence of [Christ's] heavenly

means the evidence here about the nonreigning Christ cannot mean that he is currently inactive. The question is what this present activity should be called. As we shall see later, the New Testament seems to qualify Christ's present actions in terms of a priestly ministry rather than a kingly one.

[105] In ancient Israel the dominant role of the monarch was chief of the army. The conquest of all enemies, internal and external, was an essential function of the reign (Gerhard Delling, *hypotassō*, *TDNT*, 8:42; Ludwig Schmidt, "Königtum," *TRE*, 19:328, and H. Lesetre, "Roi," in *Dictionnaire de la Bible*, ed. F. Vigouroux [Paris: Letouzy & Ane, 1912], 5/1: col. 1122). See A. R. Johnson, who notes that the king's duty to maintain his domain ("safeguard the liberty of the state") is the first of the Hebrew kings' functions ("Hebrew Conceptions of Kingship," in *Myth, Ritual, and Kingship: Essays on the Theory and Practice of Kingship in the Ancient Near East and in Israel*, ed. S. H. Hooke [Oxford: Clarendon, 1958], 205). Per Beskow summarizes the functions normally associated with the concept of "king" as exalted judge, ruler, and conqueror (*Rex Gloria: The Kingdom of Christ in the Early Church* [Uppsala: Almquist and Wiksell, 1962], 38).

[106] Proponents of a present reign neglect the obstacle presented by Psalm 110:2 ("Rule in the midst of your enemies"), a statement that very clearly asserts the concept of a rule or reign on the basis of divine right, but one that is *never* utilized by the writers of the New Testament to speak of the present activity of the risen Christ. The explanation suggested by this lacuna in the New Testament is that, while the New Testament does assert an activity of the exalted king, it prefers not to delineate that activity in terms related to the ruling/reigning concept.

life."[107] Thus, what some want to call *regal* activity the New Testament calls *priestly* activity. Just any kind of regal activity does not automatically lay claim to the concept of rule or reigning, at least from the terminology and concepts of the New Testament. Without doubt the exalted Christ is active, but we should call this activity what the New Testament does. The New Testament calls it intercession. Reigning is left for another, future, time.[108]

Third, the New Testament positively associates the reign of Christ with the reign of his saints with him.[109] Such an association is significant, given

---

[107] A. W. Argyle, "The Heavenly Session of Christ," *Theology* 55 (1992): 288. D. M. Hay concludes that early Christians used Psalm 110 for one basic purpose: "to articulate the supreme glory, the divine transcendence of Jesus through whom salvation is mediated" (*Glory at the Right Hand: Psalm 110 in Early Christianity* [New York: Abingdon, 1973], 155). Hay's statement here confirms the application of his statement elsewhere that Psalm 110:1b does not "regularly express convictions about Christ reigning as royal lord in the present era" (*Glory at the Right Hand,* 91).

Hay's and Argyle's conclusions are borne out in the New Testament verbs within the semantic domain of *to intercede* (Louw and Nida, *Greek-English Lexicon,* 428). Of the two New Testament verbs in the semantic domain of *intercession* both are either directly or indirectly applied to the function of the exalted Christ. The word *entygchanō* is used directly of Christ in Romans 8:34 and Hebrews 7:25, and *hyperentygchanō* is only applied to the intercession of the Holy Spirit in Romans 8:26. The Spirit's intercessory function gives force to the idea that the bestowal of the Spirit is also an intercessory act of the exalted Christ, an act that would make the use of Psalm 110 in Acts 2:33-36 more specifically intercessory rather than simply regal (contra Bock, "Current Messianic Activity," 76-78). At any rate such a contrast in the New Testament concepts of intercession and rule/reign as they are applied or not applied to the exalted Christ make clear the case for the New Testament understanding of what we should call the present *regal* activity of the exalted Christ. It is intercession, not reign.

The objects of Christ's intercessory function also help establish the difference between the biblical concepts of reigning and interceding. In all of these verses cited from Acts, Romans, and Hebrews, the action of the exalted Christ is only towards his people. Because of the Session he grants repentance and forgiveness (Acts 5:31), gives the Spirit (Acts 2:33), and intercedes for us (Rom. 8:34). As we have noted earlier, however, in the New Testament concept of reign there is the focus upon the enemies of Christ (Luke 19:27; Rev. 17:14; 19:15-16). Towards his enemies the New Testament gives the idea of a passively waiting Christ (e.g., Heb. 10:12-13). See Mark Saucy, "Exaltation Christology in Hebrews: What Kind of Reign?" *TrinJ* 14 NS [1993)]: 50-58.

[108] The distinction between intercession and reign helps understand the shades of meaning of christological titles. The writer of Hebrews, for example, knows the concept of an intercessory "Lord" (cf. 1:10 and 8:1, where the Son's lordship establishes his place as intercessor [Mark Saucy, "Exaltation Christology," 59-60]), but not that of an intercessory "King." As we have seen, the rise of intercession/Lord language in the New Testament is also paralleled by the decline of ruling/King language.

[109] *Synbasileuō* is found in the New Testament at 1 Corinthians 4:8 and 2 Timothy 2:12.

that rule of Christ's saints is a future condition in both 1 Corinthians 4:8 and 2 Timothy 2:12. While such an association does not eliminate the possibility of a present reign of Christ without his saints,[110] it does complicate the picture of a present reign of Christ in the contexts of Revelation 20:4–6 and 1 Corinthians 15:24. If the reign of Christ in Revelation 20:4–6 is interpreted as an event of the present era, then its teaching of the coreign is in contradiction to Paul's teaching in 1 Corinthians 4:8 which plainly has no such coreign in the present. Similarly, if Christ is presently reigning, according to the much-used interpretation of 1 Corinthians 15:24, and scheduled to give up that reign at the Parousia, when would the saints reign with him?[111] Thus instead of clouding the issue for understanding the present status of the exalted Christ, the association of the reign of believers with the reign of Christ in fact helps clarify the issue and cannot be easily avoided.[112]

The doctrine of the Kingdom taught in the early church was one and the same as the doctrine taught by its Lord. The Old Testament hope of a messianic Kingdom on earth that would be historical and national, ethnic and universal, is revealed as coming in two stages. The first stage was the presence of spiritual power in the Holy Spirit under the intercessory ministry of a heavenly Christ, and the second stage in the future, visible return of the Lord in his glory to reign with his saints judging and putting his enemies under his feet. The first stage does not make the church to be the "revelation of the Kingdom" or even the "present reality of the coming eschatological kingdom."[113] Rather it suggests that we see the church as the sphere in which the coming eschatological Kingdom's power is active. This power of the coming Kingdom is today visible in the church.

---

[110] It is only clear in the New Testament that the believer's reign is always in reference to being with Christ, not vice versa.

[111] See Robert Saucy, *The Case for Progressive Dispensationalism*, 106, n. 79.

[112] Bock suggests that to ask the question of Jesus' reign is different from asking the question as to whether believers now reign with him. He proposes this bifurcation as a criticism of Robert Saucy's treatment of Christ's present reign (Bock, "Current Messianic Activity," 58, n. 8). However, when put in the light of Revelation 20:4–5 and 1 Corinthians 15:24, the coreign becomes determinative for the status of the reign of Christ.

[113] These are all phrases of some progressive dispensationalists that are noted and rightly criticized by Ryrie (*Dispensationalism*, 167).

BIBLIOGRAPHY

Adeyemo, Tokunboh. "A Critical Evaluation of Contemporary Perspectives." In *In Word and Deed: Evangelism and Social Responsibility,* edited by Bruce J. Nicholls, 41–61. Grand Rapids: Eerdmans, 1985.

Alfaro, Juan. "Reflections on the Eschatology of Vatican II." In *Vatican II: Assessment and Perspectives Twenty-five Years After (1962–1987),* edited by René Latourelle. Vol. 2, 501–13. New York: Paulist, 1989.

Althaus, Paul. *Der Brief an die Römer.* Das Neue Testament Deutsch. Göttingen: Vandenhoeck & Ruprecht, 1966, ad loc. Ro 13:11. Quoted in G. R. Beasley-Murray, *Jesus and the Kingdom of God* (Grand Rapids: Eerdmans, 1986), 344.

Anderson, Gerald H. *Witnessing to the Kingdom: Melbourne and Beyond.* Maryknoll, N.Y.: Orbis, 1982.

Anderson, H. "A Future for Apocalyptic?" In *Biblical Studies in Honor of William Barclay,* edited by J. R. McKay and J. F. Miller, 56–71. Philadelphia: Westminster, 1976.

Aquinas, Thomas. *Summa theologiae.* 3 vols. Edited by Instituti Studiorum Medievalium Ottaviensis. Ottawa: Garden City, 1961.

Armerding, Carl E., ed. *Evangelicals and Liberation.* Nutley, N.J.: Presbyterian and Reformed, 1977.

Ashton, John. *Understanding the Fourth Gospel.* Oxford: Clarendon, 1991.

Assmann, Hugo. *Theology for a Nomad Church.* Maryknoll, N.Y.: Orbis, 1976.

Augustine, Aurelius. *De catechizandis rudibus liber unus.* In *MPL,* vol. 40, *Patrologiae tomus sextus. S. Aurelii Augustini.*

_____. *De diversis quaestionibus LXXXIII liber unus.* In *MPL,* vol. 40, *Patrologiae tomus XL. S. Aurelii Augustini tomus sextus.*

_____. *De Trinitate libri XV.* In *MPL,* vol. 42, *Patrologiae tomus XL. S. Aurelii Augustini tomus octavus.*

_____. *Enarratio in Psalmum XCII.* In *MPL,* vol. 37, *Patrologiae tomus XXXVII. S. Aurelii Augustini tomus quartus. Pars altera.*

_____. *The City of God Against the Pagans.* Edited by T. E. Page et al. Translated by George E. McCracken et al. Loeb. Cambridge, Mass.: Harvard University, 1966.

Aune, David Edward. *The Cultic Setting of Realized Eschatology in Early Christianity.* Supplements to *NovT* 28. Leiden: E. J. Brill, 1972.

Bahnsen, Greg L. "The Prima Facie Acceptability of Postmillennialism." *JChrRec* 3, no. 2 (1976–1977): 48–105.

_____. *Theonomy in Christian Ethics.* Expanded edition with replies to critics. Phillipsburg, N.J.: Presbyterian and Reformed, 1984.

Bailey, J. W. "The Temporary Messianic Reign in the Literature of Early Judaism." *JBL* 53 (1934): 170–87.

Ballard, Paul. "The Kingdom of God and Christian Political Theory." *ModChu* NS 31, no. 4 (1990): 20–27.

Bammel, E. "The Revelation Theory from Reimarus to Brandon." In *Jesus and the Politics of His Day,* edited by E. Bammel and C. F. D. Moule, 11–68. Cambridge: Cambridge University Press, 1984.

Bangkok Assembly 1973: Minutes and Report of the Assembly of the Commission on World Mission and Evangelism of the World Council of Churches December 31, 1972 and January 9–12, 1973. Geneva: World Council of Churches, 1973.

Barbour, R. S. *Traditio-Historical Criticism of the Gospels.* London: SPCK, 1972.

Barclay, Oliver R. "The Theology of Social Ethics: A Survey of Current Positions." *EvQ* 62, no. 1 (1990): 63–86.

Barclay, Oliver R., and Chris Sugden. "Biblical Social Ethics in a Mixed Society." *EvQ* 62, no. 1 (1990): 5–18.

Barrett, C. K. *The Gospel According to St. John.* 2d ed. Philadelphia: Westminster, 1978.

_____. *Jesus and the Gospel Tradition.* Philadelphia: Fortress, 1968.

Barth, Karl. *Protestant Thought: From Rousseau to Ritschl.* Translated by Brian Cozens. New York: Harper & Row, 1959, 393. Quoted in Norman Perrin, *The Kingdom of God in the Teaching of Jesus* (London: SCM, 1963), 16.

Bauckham, Richard. *Moltmann: Messianic Theology in the Making.* Basingstoke, U.K.: Marshall Pickering, 1987.

Beardslee, William A. "Recent Literary Criticism." In *The New Testament and Its Modern Interpreters,* edited by Eldon Jay Epp and George W. MacRae, 175–200. Philadelphia: Fortress; Atlanta: Scholars, 1989.

Beasley-Murray, G. R. *The Book of Revelation.* The New Century Bible Commentary. Grand Rapids: Eerdmans, 1978.

_____. "A Century of Eschatological Discussion." *ExpTim* 64 (1952–1953): 312–16.

_____. *A Commentary on Mark Thirteen.* London: Macmillan, 1957.

_____. *Jesus and the Future: An Examination of the Criticism of the Eschatological Discourse, Mark 13, with Special Reference to the Little Apocalypse Theory.* London: Macmillan, 1954.

_____. "Jesus and the Kingdom of God." *BaptQ* 32 (1987): 141–46.

_____. *Jesus and the Kingdom of God.* Grand Rapids: Eerdmans, 1986.

_____. *Jesus and the Last Days: The Interpretation of the Olivet Discourse.* Peabody, Mass.: Hendrickson, 1993.

_____. "The Kingdom of God in the Teaching of Jesus." *JEvTS* 35, no. 1 (1992): 19–30.

_____. "Matthew 6:33: The Kingdom of God and the Ethics of Jesus." In *Neues Testament und Ethik,* edited by Helmut Merklein, 84–98. Freiburg/Basel/Vienna: Herder, 1989.

_____. "The Vision on the Mount." *Ex Auditu* 6 (1990): 39–52.

Belli, Humberto, and Ronald H. Nash. *Beyond Liberation Theology.* Grand Rapids: Baker, 1992.

Berger, Klaus. "Jesus als Pharisäer und Frühe Christen als Pharisäer." *NovT* 30 (1988): 231–62.

Berkhof, Herdrikus. *Christ the Meaning of History.* Translated by Lambertus Boorman. Grand Rapids: Baker, 1979.

Berkhof, Louis. *The Kingdom of God: The Development of the Idea of the Kingdom Especially Since the Eighteenth Century.* Grand Rapids: Eerdmans, 1961.

Berryman, Phillip. *Liberation Theology.* Philadelphia: Temple University Press, 1987.

Beskow, Per. *Rex Gloriae: The Kingdom of Christ in the Early Church.* Uppsala: Almquist and Wiksell, 1962.

Betz, O., and Werner Grimm. *Wesen und Wirklichkeit der Wunder Jesu.* Frankfurt: Peter Lang, 1977.

Beyerhaus, Peter. "A Biblical Encounter with Some Contemporary Philosophical and Theological Systems." In *In Word and Deed: Evangelism and Social Responsibility,* edited by Bruce J. Nicholls, 165–185. Grand Rapids: Eerdmans, 1985.

_____. "World Evangelization and the Kingdom of God." In *Let the Earth Hear His Voice: International Congress on World Evangelization Lausanne, Switzerland: Official Reference Volume: Papers and Responses,* edited by J. D. Douglas, 283–302. Minneapolis: World Wide, 1975.

Bietenhard, Hans. "The Millennial Hope in the Early Church." *ScotJT* 6 (March 1953): 12–30.

Biot, François. *Théologie du politique: Foi et politique elements de reflexion.* Paris: Editions Universitaires, 1972.

Black, M. "The Gospel and the Scrolls." In *Studia Evangelica III,* edited by K. Aland et al. Berlin, Akademie Verlag, 1964, 575. Quoted in G. W. Buchanan, *The Consequences of the Covenant* (Leiden, E. J. Brill, 1970), 14, n. 1.

Blackman, E. C. "New Methods of Parable Interpretation." *CanadJT* 15 (1969): 3–13.

Bleicher, Josef. *Contemporary Hermeneutics.* London: Routledge and Kegan Paul, 1980.

Bloch, Ernst. *Man on His Own: Essays in the Philosophy of Religion.* Translated by E. B. Ashton. New York: Herder and Herder, 1970.

_____. *Thomas Münzer als Theologe der Revolution.* Frankfurt: Suhrkamp, 1960.

Blomberg, Craig, L. "A Response to G. R. Beasley-Murray on the Kingdom." *JEvTS* 35, no. 1 (March 1992): 31–36.

_____. *Dictionary of Jesus and the Gospels.* Edited by Joel B. Green, Scot McKnight, and I. Howard Marshall. Downers Grove, Ill.: InterVarsity Press, 1992. S.v. "Healing."

Bloomfield, M. "Joachim of Flora: A Critical Survey of his Canon, Teachings, Sources, Biography, and Influence." In *Joachim of Fiore in Christian Thought,* edited by Delno C. West. Vol. 1, 29–92. New York: Burt Franklin, 1975.

Blue, Ronald J. "Major Flaws in Liberation Theology." *BS* 147 (1990): 89–103.

Blum, Georg Günter. *TRE.* S.v. "Chiliasmus."

Bock, Darrell. "Current Messianic Activity and the OT Davidic Promise: Dispensationalism, Hermeneutics and NT Fulfillment." *TrinJ* NS 15 (1994): 60–75.

Bock, Darrell, and C. Blaising, eds. *Dispensationalism, Israel, and the Church: The Search for Definition.* Grand Rapids: Zondervan, 1992.

Boettner, Loraine. "Postmillennialism." In *The Meaning of the Millennium: Four Views,* edited by Robert G. Clouse, 117–41. Downers Grove, Ill.: InterVarsity Press, 1977.

Boff, Clodovis. *Theology and Praxis: Epistemological Foundations.* Translated by Robert R. Barr. Maryknoll, N.Y.: Orbis, 1987.

Boff, Leonardo. *Erfahrung von Gnade. Entwurf einer Gnadenlehre.* Dusseldorf: Patmos, 1978, 221. Quoted in Reinhard Freiling, *Befreiungstheologien* (Göttingen: Vandenhoeck & Ruprecht, 1984), 15.

_____. *Jesus Christ Liberator.* Translated by Patrick Hughes. Maryknoll, N.Y.: Orbis, 1978.

_____. *Liberating Grace.* Translated by John Drury. Maryknoll, N.Y.: Orbis, 1979, 23. Quoted in Arthur F. McGovern, *Liberation Theology and Its Critics: Towards an Assessment* (Maryknoll, N.Y.: Orbis, 1989), 158.

_____. *Salvation and Liberation.* Maryknoll, N.Y.: Orbis, 1984.

_____. "Salvation in Jesus Christ and the Process of Liberation." *Concilium* 96 (1974): 87–91.

Boff, Leonardo, and Clodovis Boff. *Introducing Liberation Theology.* Translated by Paul Burns. Maryknoll, N.Y.: Orbis, 1986.

Boff, Leonardo, Gustavo Gutiérrez, Jon Sobrino, and Ignacio Ellacuría. *Latinamerica Press,* 1 May 1986. Quoted in Arthur F. McGovern, *Liberation Theology and Its Critics: Toward An Assessment* (Maryknoll, N.Y.: Orbis, 1989), 245, n. 42.

Bonhoeffer, Dietrich. *The Communion of the Saints.* Translated by R. Gregor Smith. New York: Harper and Row, 1963.

_____. *Letters and Papers from Prison*. London: Fontana, 1963.

Bonino, José Miguez. *Doing Theology in a Revolutionary Situation*. Philadelphia: Fortress, 1975.

_____. *Revolutionary Theology Comes of Age*. Philadelphia: Fortress, 1975.

Borg, Marcus. "Conflict as a Context for Interpreting the Teaching of Jesus." Ph.D. diss., Oxford University, 1972.

_____. *Conflict, Holiness & Politics in the Teachings of Jesus*. Studies in the Bible and Early Christianity 5. New York: Edwin Mellen, 1984.

_____. "Jesus and Eschatology: A Reassessment." In *Images of Jesus Today*, edited by James H. Charlesworth and Walter P. Weaver. Faith and Scholarship Colloquies 3, Florida Southern College, 42–67. Valley Forge, Pa.: Trinity Press International, 1994.

_____. *Jesus: A New Vision*. San Francisco: Harper & Row, 1989.

_____. "An Orthodoxy Reconsidered: The 'End-of-the-World' Jesus." In *The Glory of Christ in the New Testament*, edited by L. D. Hurst and N. T. Wright, 207–17. Oxford: Clarendon, 1987.

_____. "Portraits of Jesus in Contemporary North American Scholarship." *HarTR* 84, no. 1 (1991): 1–22.

_____. "A Temperate Case for a Non-eschatological Jesus." *Forum* 2, no. 3 (1986): 81–102.

Boring, M. Eugene. "The Kingdom of God in Mark." In *The Kingdom of God in Twentieth-Century Interpretation*, edited by Wendell Willis, 131–45. Peabody, Mass.: Hendrickson, 1987.

Bormann, Claus v., Ludwig Schmidt, and Henning Schröer. *TRE*. S.v. "Hermeneutik."

Bornkamm, Günther. *Jesus of Nazareth*. Translated by Irene and Fraser McLusky with James Robinson. New York: Harper & Row, 1960.

_____. *Jesus von Nazareth*. Stuttgart: W. Kohlhammer, 1956.

Bosch, David J. "In Search of a New Evangelical Understanding." In *In Word and Deed: Evangelism and Social Responsibility*, edited by Bruce J. Nicholls, 63–83. Grand Rapids: Eerdmans, 1985.

Bousset, W. *Die Religion des Judentums im späthellenistischen Zeitalter*, 3d ed. Tübingen: J. C. B. Mohr (Paul Siebeck), 1926.

Bowker, John. *Jesus and the Pharisees*. New York: Cambridge University Press, 1973.

Braaten, Carl E. "How New Is the New Hermeneutic?" *TToday* 22, no. 2 (1965): 218–35.

Brandon, S. G. F. *The Fall of Jerusalem and the Christian Church*. London: SPCK, 1951.

_____. *Jesus and the Zealots: A Study of the Political Factor in Primitive Christianity*. Manchester: Manchester University Press, 1967.

_____. "Tübingen Vindicated?" *HibbJ* 49 (1951): 41–47.

Braun, F. M. *Aspects nouveaux du problème de L'Église*. Fribourg: Librairie de l'Université, 1941.

Braun, Herbert. *Jesus. Der Mann aus Nazareth und seine Zeit.* Themen der Theologie I. Stuttgart: Kreuz, 1969.

_____. *Jesus of Nazareth: The Man and His Time.* Translated by Everett R. Kalin. Philadelphia: Fortress, 1979.

_____. *Qumran und das Neue Testament,* II. Tübingen: J. C. B. Mohr (Paul Siebeck), 1966.

Breech, James. *Jesus and Postmodernism.* Minneapolis: Fortress, 1989.

_____. "Kingdom of God and the Parables of Jesus." *Semeia* 12 (1978): 15–40.

_____. *The Silence of Jesus: The Authentic Voice of the Historical Man.* Philadelphia: Fortress, 1983.

Brewer, Doug. "The Kingdom of God: Significant Recent Developments and Some Educational Implications." *JChrE.* Papers 98 (September 1990): 41–54.

Bright, John. *The Kingdom of God: The Biblical Concept and Its Meaning for the Church.* Nashville: Abingdon, 1962.

Broer, Ingo. "Das Ringen Der Gemeinde um Israel: Exegetischer Versuch über Mt. 19,28." In *Jesus und der Menschensohn. Für Anton Vögtle,* edited by Rudolf Pesch and Rudolf Schnackenburg, 148–65. Freiburg/Basel/Vienna: Herder, 1975.

Brown, Colin. *Dictionary of Jesus and the Gospels,* edited by Joel B. Green, Scot McKnight, and I. Howard Marshall. Downers Grove, Ill.: InterVarsity Press, 1992. S.v. "Historical Jesus, Quest of."

_____. *Jesus in European Protestant Thought 1778–1860.* Grand Rapids: Baker, 1985.

_____. "Scripture and Christology: A Protestant Look at the Work of the Pontifical Biblical Commission." In *Perspectives on Christology: Essays in Honor of Paul K. Jewett,* edited by Marguerite Schuster and Richard Muller, 39–76. Grand Rapids: Eerdmans, 1991.

_____. "The Doctrine of the Trinity and the Shape of the Christological Question." Unpublished paper. Pasadena, Calif. January 1994.

_____. "The Unjust Steward: A New Twist?" In *Worship, Theology and Ministry in the Early Church: Essays in Honor of Ralph P. Martin,* edited by Michael J. Wilkins and Terence Paige. JSNTSS, 87, 121–45. Sheffield: Sheffield Academic Press, 1992.

Brown, R. E. "How Much Did Jesus Know?—A Survey of the Biblical Evidence." *CBQ* 29 (1967): 315–45.

Bruce, Steve. *The Rise and Fall of the New Christian Right: Conservative Protestant Politics in America 1978–1988.* Oxford: Clarendon, 1988.

Buber, Martin. *The Kingship of God.* Translated by Richard Schiemann. New York: Harper, 1967.

Buchanan, George Wesley. *Jesus: The King and His Kingdom.* Macon, Ga.: Mercer University Press, 1984.

_____. "Matthean Beatitudes and Traditional Promises." In *New Synoptic Studies: The Cambridge Gospel Conference and Beyond*, edited by William R. Farmer, 161–84. Macon, Ga.: Mercer University Press, 1983.

_____. *The Consequences of the Covenant*. Leiden: E. J. Brill, 1970.

Bühler, Pierre. *Kreuz und Eschatologie. Eine Auseinandersetzung mit der politischen Theologie, im Anschluß an Luthers theologia crucis*. HUT 17. Tübingen: J. C. B. Mohr (Paul Siebeck), 1981.

Bultmann, Rudolf. *History and Eschatology*. Gifford Lectures 1955. Edinburgh: Edinburgh University Press, 1957.

_____. *Jesus and the Word*. Translated by Louise Pettibone Smith and Erminie Huntress. New York: Scribner's, 1934.

_____. *Jesus Christ and Mythology*. New York: Scribner's, 1958.

_____. "New Testament and Mythology." In *Kerygma and Myth: A Theological Debate*, edited by H. E. Bartsch, 1–44. London: SPCK, 1953.

_____. "The Primitive Christian Kerygma and the Historical Jesus." In *The Historical Jesus and the Kerygmatic Christ*, edited and translated by C. E. Braaten and R. A. Harrisville, 15–42. Nashville: Abingdon, 1964.

_____. *Theology of the New Testament*. Translated by Kendrick Grobel. 2 vols. New York: Scribner's, 1955.

Bussmann, Claus. *Who Do You Say? Jesus Christ in Latin American Theology*. Translated by Robert R. Barr. Maryknoll, N.Y.: Orbis, 1985.

Butler, Christopher. *The Theology of Vatican II*. Sarum Lectures, 1966. London: Darton, Longman & Todd, 1967.

Butts, James, R. "Probing the Polling: Jesus Seminar Results on the Kingdom Sayings." *Forum* 3, no. 1 (1987): 98–128.

Caird, G. "Eschatology and Politics: Some Misconceptions." *Biblical Studies in Honor of William Barclay*, edited by J. R. McKay and J. F. Miller, 72–86. Philadelphia: Westminster, 1976.

_____. *The Language and Imagery of the Bible*. London: Duckworth, 1980.

Calvert, D. G. A. "An Examination of the Criteria for Distinguishing the Authentic Words of Jesus." *NTS* 18 (1971–1972): 209–18.

Camponovo, Odo. *Königtum, Königsherrschaft und Reich Gottes in den Frühjüdischen Schriften*. Orbis Biblicus Et Orientalis 58. Göttingen: Vandenhoeck & Ruprecht, 1984.

Cantley, M. J. *New Catholic Encyclopedia*. New York: McGraw-Hill, 1967. S.v. "Kingdom of God."

Capps, Walter H. *Time Invades the Cathedral: Tensions in the School of Hope*. Philadelphia: Fortress, 1972.

_____. "Vertical v. Horizontal Theology: Bloch–Dewart–Irenaeus." *Continuum* 5 (winter 1968): 616–33.

Cardenal, Ernesto. *Love in Practice: The Gospel in Solamentiname.* 4 vols. Maryknoll, N.Y.: Orbis, 1977–1984.

Carlson, Jeffrey, and Robert A. Ludwig, eds. *Jesus and Faith: A Conversation on the Work of John Dominic Crossan.* Maryknoll, N.Y.: Orbis, 1994.

Carmignac, Jean. "Conjectures sur les écrits de Qumrân." *Revue des sciences religieuses* 31 (April 1957): 140–68.

_____. "Les dangers de l'eschatologie." *NTS* 17 (July 1971): 365–90.

_____. *Dictionnaire de la Bible. Supplement.* Vol. 10. Paris: Letouzey et Ané, 1985. S.v. "Règne de Dieu. II."

_____. *Le mirage de l'eschatologie.* Paris: Letouzey et Ané, 1979.

_____. "La notion d'eschatologie dans la Bible et à Qumrân." *RQum* 7 (December 1969): 17–31.

_____. "Rectification d'une erreur concernant l'eschatologie." *NTS* 26 (1980): 252–58.

_____. *La Règle de la Guerre: Texte restauré, traduit, commenté.* Paris: Letouzey et Ané, 1958.

_____. "Roi, royauté et royaume dans la Liturgie Angélique." *RQum* 47 (1986): 178–86.

_____. *Les textes de Qumrân traduits et annotés.* 2 vols. Paris: Letouzey et Ané, 1963.

Casey, Maurice. *From Jewish Prophet to Gentile God: The Origin and Development of New Testament Christology.* Louisville, Ky.: Westminster/John Knox, 1991.

Castro, Emilio. *Freedom in Mission: The Perspective of the Kingdom of God: An Ecumenical Inquiry.* Geneva: World Council of Churches, 1985.

_____. *Sent Free: Mission and Unity in the Perspective of the Kingdom.* Risk book series 23. Geneva: World Council of Churches, 1985.

_____. "Your Kingdom Come: A Missionary Perspective." In *Thy Kingdom Come: Mission Perspectives: Report on the World Conference on Mission and Evangelism Melbourne Australia, 12–15 May 1980,* 26–36. Geneva: World Council of Churches, 1980.

Centensimus Annus. CNS Documentary Series. 16 May 1991.

Chapman, G. C. "Hope and the Ethics of Formation: Moltmann as an Interpreter of Bonhoeffer." *SR* 12 (1983): 449–60.

_____. "Jürgen Moltmann and the Christian Dialogue with Marxism." *JEcuSt* 18 (summer 1981): 435–50.

Chappuis, Jean-Marc. "The World Council of Churches: A Tentative Historical, Cultural and Theological Interpretation of its Recent Development." In *The Nature of Church and the Role of Theology: Papers from a Consultation between the World Council of Churches and the Reformed Ecumenical Synod, Geneva 1975,* 30–44. Geneva: World Council of Churches, 1976.

Charles, R. H. *Eschatology.* New York: Schocken, 1963.

Charlesworth, James H. "The Historical Jesus in Light of Writings Contemporaneous with Him." *ANRW.* 25, no. 1. Edited by W. Haase (1982): 451–76.

_____. "Jesus Research Expands with Chaotic Creativity." In *Images of Jesus Today,* edited by James H. Charlesworth and Walter P. Weaver. Faith and Scholarship Colloquies 3, Florida Southern College, 1–41. Valley Forge, Pa.: Trinity Press International, 1994.

_____. *Jesus Within Judaism: New Light from Exciting Archaeological Discoveries.* Anchor Bible Reference Library. New York: Doubleday, 1988.

_____., ed. *The Old Testament Pseudepigrapha.* 2 vols. New York: Doubleday, 1983.

Childs, James M., Jr. "Marxist Humanism and Hope of the Gospel." In *Christians and the Many Faces of Marxism,* edited by Wayne Stumme, 110–22. Minneapolis: Augsburg, 1984.

Chilton, Bruce. *A Galilean Rabbi and His Bible: Jesus' Use of the Interpreted Scripture of His Time.* Good News Studies 8. Wilmington, Del.: Michael Glazier, 1984.

_____. *The Glory of Israel: The Theology and Provenience of the Isaiah Targum.* JSOT, supplement 23. Sheffield: JSOT, 1982.

_____. *God in Strength: Jesus' Announcement of the Kingdom.* Studien zum Neuen Testament und seiner Umwelt, Series B, Vol. 1. Freistadt: F. Plöchl, 1979.

_____. Introduction to *The Kingdom of God,* ed. Bruce Chilton. Issues in Religion and Theology 5, 1–26. Philadelphia: Fortress, 1984.

_____. "Kingdom Come, Kingdom Sung: Voices in the Gospels." *Forum* 3, no. 2 (1987): 51–75.

_____. "The Kingdom of God in Recent Discussion." In *Studying the Historical Jesus: Evaluations of the State of Current Research,* edited by Bruce Chilton and Craig A. Evans, 255–80. Leiden/New York/Cologne: E. J. Brill, 1994.

_____. "Regnum Dei Deus Est." *ScotJT* 31 (1978): 261–70.

Chilton, Bruce, and J. I. H. McDonald. *Jesus and the Ethics of the Kingdom.* Grand Rapids: Eerdmans, 1987.

Chilton, David. *Paradise Restored: An Eschatology of Dominion.* Tyler, Tex.: Reconstruction, 1985.

Chismar, Douglas E., and David A. Rausch. "Regarding Theonomy: An Essay of Concern." *JEvTS* 27, no. 3 (1984): 315–23.

Cleary, Edward L. *Crisis and Change: The Church in Latin America Today.* Maryknoll, N.Y.: Orbis, 1985.

_____., ed. *Born of the Poor: The Latin American Church Since Medellín.* Notre Dame, Ind.: University of Notre Dame Press, 1990.

Clouse, Robert G. "The New Christian Right, America, and the Kingdom of God." *ChrSchR* 12, no. 1 (1983): 1–16.

Clowney, Edmund P. "The Politics of the Kingdom." *WestTJ* 61, no. 2 (1979): 291–310.

Cobb, John. *Process Theology as Liberation Theology.* Philadelphia: Westminster, 1982.

Coggins, James R., and Paul G. Hiebert, eds. *Wonders and the Word: An Examination of the Issues Raised by John Wimber and the Vineyard Movement.* Hillsboro, Kan.: Kindred, 1989.

Cohn, Norman. *Millennial Dreams in Action: Essays in Comparative Study.* Edited by Sylvia L. Thrupp. The Hague: Mouton, 1962.

Collingwood, R. B. *The Idea of History.* Oxford: Oxford University Press, 1946.

Collins, A. Y. "The Origin of the Designation of Jesus as 'Son of Man.'" *HarTR* 80 (1987): 391–407.

Collins, John. J., ed. *Apocalypse: The Morphology of a Genre. Semeia* 14 (1979).

_____. "The Kingdom of God in the Apocrypha and Pseudepigrapha." In *The Kingdom of God in Twentieth-Century Interpretation,* edited by Wendell Willis, 81–95. Peabody, Mass.: Hendrickson, 1987.

Cone, James H. *A Black Theology of Liberation.* Philadelphia: J. B. Lippincott, 1970.

Congregation for the Doctrine of the Faith (Cardinal Ratzinger). *Instruction on Christian Freedom and Liberation.* Vatican City: Libreria Editrice Vaticana, 1986.

Conyers, A. J. "The Revival of Joachite Apocalyptic Speculation in Contemporary Theology." *PerspRelSt* 12 (fall 1985): 197–211.

Conzelmann, Hans. *An Outline of the Theology of the New Testament.* Translated by John Bowden. New York: Harper & Row, 1969.

_____. *Jesus.* Translated by J. R. Lord. Edited by J. Reumann. Philadelphia: Fortress, 1973.

Cook, Michael L. "Jesus from the Other Side: Christology in Latin America." *TS* 44, no. 2 (1983): 258–88.

Costas, Orlando. *Christ Outside the Gate: Mission Beyond Christendom.* Maryknoll, N.Y.: Orbis, 1982.

Cox, Harvey. *The Secular City.* New York: Macmillan, 1965.

Cranfield, C. E. B. "Thoughts on New Testament Eschatology." *ScotJT* 35 (1982): 497–512.

Croatto, J. Severino. *Biblical Hermeneutics: Toward a Theology of Reading as the Production of Meaning.* Translated by Robert R. Barr. Maryknoll, N.Y.: Orbis, 1987.

Crossan, John Dominic. *A Fragile Craft: The Work of Amos Niven Wilder.* Biblical Scholarship in North America 3. Chico, Calif.: Scholars, 1981.

_____. *Cliffs of Fall: Paradox and Polyvalence in the Parables of Jesus.* New York: Seabury, 1980.

_____. *Finding Is the First Act: Trove Folktales and Jesus' Treasure Parable.* Semeia Supplements 9. Missoula, Mont.: Scholars; Philadelphia: Fortress, 1979.

_____. *In Fragments: The Aphorisms of Jesus.* San Francisco: Harper & Row, 1983.

_____. *In Parables: The Challenge of the Historical Jesus.* New York: Harper & Row, 1973.

_____. *The Dark Interval: Towards a Theology of Story.* Niles, Ill.: Argus Communications, 1975.

_____. *The Historical Jesus: The Life of a Mediterranean Jewish Peasant.* San Francisco: HarperSanFrancisco, 1991.

_____. "Literary Criticism and Biblical Hermeneutics." *JRel* 57 (1977): 76–80.

_____. *Raid on the Articulate: Cosmic Eschatology in Jesus and Borges.* New York: Harper and Row, 1976.

Cullmann, Oscar. *Christ and Time.* Translated by Floyd V. Filson. Philadelphia: Westminster, 1950.

_____. *Jesus and the Revolutionaries.* Translated by G. Putnam. New York: Harper & Row, 1970.

_____. *The Christology of the New Testament.* Rev. ed. Philadelphia: Westminster, 1963.

Cuthbertson, Malcolm. "The Kingdom and the Poor." *ScotBEv* 1, no. 4 (1986): 123–33.

Dalman, Gustaf. *The Words of Jesus.* Translated by D. M. Kay. Edinburgh: T & T Clark, 1909.

Daniélou, Jean. "La Session à la droite du Pere." *Studia Evangelica I,* edited by Kurt Aland et al., 689–98. Berlin: Akademie Verlag, 1959.

_____. *The Development of Christian Doctrine Before the Council of Nicea.* Vol. 1, *The Theology of Jewish Christianity,* translated and edited by John A. Baker. London: Darton, Longman and Todd, 1964.

Darshin, Wolfgang. "Bibliographische Hinweise zur 'Politische Theologie.'" In *Diskussion zur 'Politischen Theologie,'* edited by Helmut Peukert, 302–27. Munich: Christian Kaiser, 1969.

Dautzenberg, G. "Psalm 110 im Neuen Testament." In *Liturgie und Dichtung. Ein interdisziplinäres Kompendium,* edited by H. Becker and R. Kaczynski, 141–71. St. Ottilien: Eos, 1983.

Davies, W. D. *The Gospel and the Land.* Berkeley: University of California Press, 1974.

Davis, John Jefferson. *Postmillennialism Reconsidered.* Grand Rapids: Baker, 1986.

De Villiers, Pieter. "The Gospel and the Poor. Let Us Read Luke 4." In *Liberation Theology and the Bible,* edited by Pieter G. R. De Villiers, 45–76. Pretoria: University of South Africa, 1987.

de Jonge, Marinus. "The Christological Significance of Jesus' Preaching of the Kingdom of God." In *The Future of Christology: Essays in Honor of Leander E. Keck,* edited by Abraham J. Malherbe and Wayne A. Meeks, 3–17. Minneapolis: Fortress, 1993.

de Soto, Hernando. *The Other Path: The Invisible Revolution in the Third World.* Translated by June Abbott. New York: Harper and Row, 1989.

Delhaye, Philippe. "L'après Vatican II et la constitution de la Commission Théologique Internationale." *RTLv* 16 (1985): 288–315.

_____. "Memoirs of the First Five Years of the International Theological Commission." *L'Osservatore Romano,* 1 July 1976.

_____. "Paul VI et la Commission Théologique Internationale." *RTLv* 9 (1978): 417–23.

Delling, Gerhard. *TDNT.* S.v. *hypotassō.*

Dilthey, Wilhelm. *Gesammelte Schriften.* Stuttgart: Teubner, 1962.

Dodd, C. H. *The Apostolic Preaching and Its Developments.* London: Hodder and Stoughton, 1936.

_____. *The Founder of Christianity.* New York: Macmillan, 1970.

_____. *The Interpretation of the Fourth Gospel.* Cambridge: Cambridge University Press, 1954.

_____. *The Parables of the Kingdom.* 3d rev. ed. London: Nisbet, 1936.

Donahue, J. R. "Recent Studies on the Origin of 'Son of Man' in the Gospels." *CBQ* 48 (1986): 484–98.

Donahue, J. R., and Robert M. Fowler. "A Bibliography of the the Works of Norman Perrin." *JRel* 64 (October 1984): 548–57.

Dorr, Donal. *The Social Justice Agenda: Justice, Ecology, Power and the Church.* Maryknoll, N.Y.: Orbis, 1991.

Douglas, J. D., ed. *Let the Earth Hear His Voice: International Congress on World Evangelization Lausanne, Switzerland: Official Reference Volume: Papers and Responses.* Minneapolis: World Wide, 1975.

Douglas, Mary. *Purity and Danger: An Analysis of the Concepts of Pollution and Taboo.* London: Routledge & Kegan Paul, 1978.

Downing, F. Gerald. *Cynics and Christian Origins.* Edinburgh: T & T Clark, 1992.

_____. *Jesus and the Threat of Freedom.* London: SCM, 1987.

_____. *The Christ and the Cynics: Jesus and Other Radical Preachers in First-Century Tradition.* JSOT Manuals 4. Sheffield: Sheffield Academic, 1988.

Droge, A. J. "The Facts About Jesus: Some Thoughts on E. P. Sanders' *Jesus and Judaism.*" *Criterion* 26 (1987): 15–18.

Duling, Dennis, C. "Norman Perrin and the Kingdom of God: Review and Response." *JRel* 64 (October 1984): 468–73.

Dulles, Avery. *Models of the Church.* Garden City, N.J.: Image Books, 1974.

_____. "The Church as Eschatological Community." In *The Eschaton: A Community of Love,* edited by Joseph Papin, 69–104. Villanova: Villanova University Press, 1971.

_____. "The Meaning of Faith Considered in Relationship to Justice." In *The Faith That Does Justice: Examining the Christian Sources for Social Change,* edited by John C. Haughey, Woodstock Studies 2, 10–46. New York: Paulist, 1977.

_____. *The Reshaping of Catholicism: Current Challenges in the Theology of Church.* San Francisco: Harper & Row, 1988.

Dunn, James D. G. "Spirit and Kingdom." *ExpTim* 82 (1970–1971): 36–40.

Dupont, J. " 'Assis à la droite de Dieu': L'interprétation du Ps 110, 1 dans le Nouveau Testament." *Nouvelles études sur les Actes des Apôtres.* Lectio Divina 18. 210–95. Paris: Cerf, 1984.

Dussel, Enrique. "The Kingdom of God and the Poor." *IntRMiss* 68/270 (April 1979): 115–30.

Eagleson, John, and Philip Scharper, eds. *Puebla and Beyond: Documents and Commentary.* Maryknoll, N.Y.: Orbis, 1979.

Ebeling, Gerhard. *God and Word.* Translated by James W. Leitch. Philadelphia: Fortress, 1967.

_____. *RGG.* S.v. "Hermeneutik."

_____. *Introduction to a Theological Theory of Language.* Translated by R. A. Wilson. London: Collins, 1973.

_____. *The Nature of Faith.* Translated by Ronald Gregor Smith. Philadelphia: Muhlenburg, 1961.

_____. *The Problem of Historicity in the Church and Its Proclamation.* Translated by Grover Foley. Philadelphia: Fortress, 1967.

_____. *Theology and Proclamation: A Discussion with Rudolf Bultmann.* Translated by John Riches. Philadelphia: Fortress, 1966.

_____. "Time and Word." In *The Future of Our Religious Past: Essays in Honour of Rudolf Bultmann,* edited by James M. Robinson. 247–66. London: SCM, 1971.

_____. *Word and Faith.* Translated by James W. Leitch. Philadelphia: Fortress, 1963.

_____. *The Word of God and Tradition: Historical Studies Interpreting the Divisions of Christianity.* Translated by S. H. Hooke. Philadelphia: Fortress, 1968.

Economic Justice for All: Catholic Social Teaching and the U.S. Economy. Washington, D.C.: United States Catholic Conference, 1986.

Edward, Norman. *Christianity and the World Order.* New York: Oxford University Press, 1979.

Edwards, David L. "Signs of Radicalism in the Ecumenical Movement." In *The Ecumenical Advance: A History of the Ecumenical Movement,* edited by Harold E. Frey. Vol. 2, *1948–1968,* 373–445. Philadelphia: Westminster, 1970.

Ehrenström, Nils. "Movements for International Friendship and Life and Work 1925–1948." In *The Ecumenical Advance: A History of the Ecumenical Movement.* Vol. 1, *1517–1948,* eds. Ruth Rouse and Stephen Charles Neill. 2d ed., 545–96. Philadelphia: Westminster, 1967.

Eichler, J. *NIDNTT.* S.v. "Inheritance."

Eichrodt, Walther. *Theology of the Old Testament.* 2 vols. Translated by J. A. Baker. Philadelphia: Westminster, 1961.

Eisler, Robert. *IHSOUS BASILEUS OU BASILEUSAS (Die messianische Unabhängigkeitsbewegung vom Auftreten Johannes des Täufers bis zum Untergang Jakobs des Gerechten. Nach der neuerschlossenen Eroberung von Jerusalem des Flavius Josephus und den christlichen Quellen).* 2 Vols. Heidelberg: 1929–1930.

_____. *The Messiah Jesus and John the Baptist (According to Flavius Josephus' recently discovered "Capture of Jerusalem" and other Jewish and Christian sources).* Translated by A. H. Krappe. London: Methuen, 1931.

Eliade, Mircea. *Images and Symbols.* New York: Sheed and Ward; London: Horvil, 1961.

_____. *Myth and Reality.* Translated by Willard R. Trask. New York: Harper & Row, 1963.

Ellis, Marc H., and Otto Maduro, eds. *The Future of Liberation Theology: Essays in Honor of Gustavo Gutiérrez.* Maryknoll, N.Y.: Orbis, 1989.

Elmore, W. Emory. "Linguistic Approaches to the Kingdom: Amos Wilder and Norman Perrin." In *The Kingdom of God in Twentieth-Century Interpretation,* edited by Wendell Willis, 53–66. Peabody, Mass.: Hendrickson, 1987.

Epp, Eldon Jay. "Mediating Approaches to the Kingdom: Werner Georg Kümmel and George Eldon Ladd." In *The Kingdom of God in Twentieth-Century Interpretation,* edited by Wendell Willis, 35–52. Peabody, Mass.: Hendrickson, 1987.

Erickson, Millard J. *Contemporary Options in Eschatology.* Grand Rapids: Baker, 1977.

_____. *The Evangelical Mind and Heart: Perspectives on Theological and Practical Issues.* Grands Rapids: Baker, 1993.

Evans, Craig A. "Jesus' Action in the Temple: Cleansing or Portent of Destruction?" *CBQ* 51 (1989): 237–70.

_____. "Jesus of Nazareth: Who Do Scholars Say That He Is?" *Crux* 23/24 (1987): 15–19.

Falk, Harvey. *Jesus the Pharisee: A New Look at the Jewishness of Jesus.* New York: Paulist, 1985.

Farmer, Ron. "The Kingdom of God in Matthew." In *The Kingdom of God in Twentieth-Century Interpretation,* edited by Wendell Willis, 119–30. Peabody, Mass.: Hendrickson, 1987.

Farmer, W. R. *Jesus and the Gospel: Tradition, Scripture, and Canon.* Philadelphia: Fortress, 1982.

_____. *The Synoptic Problem.* New York: Macmillan, 1964. Corrected reprint, Dillsboro, N.C.: Western North Carolina, 1976.

Ferm, Deane William. *Third World Liberation Theologies: An Introductory Survey.* Maryknoll, N.Y.: Orbis, 1986.

Fierro, Alfredo. *The Militant Gospel: A Critical Introduction to Political Theologies.* Translated by John Drury. Maryknoll, N.Y.: Orbis, 1977.

Fitzmyer, Joseph A. *Scripture and Christology: A Statement of a Biblical Commission with a Commentary.* New York: Paulist, 1986.

Flusser, David. *Jesus.* Translated by Ronald Walls. New York: Herder and Herder, 1969.

France, R. T. "Liberation in the New Testament." *EvQ* 58, no. 1 (1986): 3–23.

Freiling, Reinhard. *Befreiungstheologien.* Göttingen: Vandenhoeck & Ruprecht, 1984.

Frye, Roland Mushat. "A Literary Perspective for the Criticism of the Gospels." In *Jesus and Man's Hope, II,* edited by Donald G. Miller and Dikran Y. Kadidian, 193–221. Pittsburgh: Pittsburgh Theological Seminary, 1971.

Fuchs, Ernst. *Hermeneutik.* Tübingen: J. C. B. Mohr (Paul Siebeck), 1970.

_____. *Marburger Hermeneutik.* Tübingen: J. C. B. Mohr (Paul Siebeck), 1968.

_____. *Studies of the Historical Jesus.* Translated by Andrew Scobie. Studies in Biblical Theology 42. Naperville, Ill.: Alec R. Allenson, 1964.

_____. "The Hermeneutical Problem." In *The Future of Our Religious Past: Essays in Honour of Rudolf Bultmann,* edited by James M. Robinson, 267–78. London: SCM, 1971.

_____. "The Parable of the Unmerciful Servant." In *Studia Evangelica I,* edited by Kurt Aland et al., 487–94. Berlin: Akademie Verlag, 1959.

_____. *Zum hermeneutischen Problem in der Theologie.* Tübingen: J. C. B. Mohr (Paul Siebeck), 1959.

_____. *Zur Frage nach dem historischen Jesus.* Tübingen: J. C. B. Mohr (Paul Siebeck), 1960.

Funk, Robert W. *Jesus as Precursor.* Semeia Supplements 2. Philadelphia: Fortress; Missoula, Mont.: Scholars, 1975.

_____. *Language, Hermeneutic and Word of God: The Problem of Language in the New Testament and Contemporary Theology.* New York: Harper & Row, 1966.

_____. *Literary Critical Studies of Biblical Texts. Semeia* 8 (1970).

_____. *Parables and Presence: Forms of the New Testament Tradition* Philadelphia: Fortress, 1982.

Funk, Robert W., Roy W. Hoover, and the Jesus Seminar. *The Five Gospels: The Search for the Authentic Words of Jesus.* New Translation and Commentary. A Polebridge Press Book. New York: Macmillan, 1993.

Gadamer, H.– Georg. "The Problem of Language in Schleiermacher's Hermeneutic." *JTChu* 7 (1970): 68–95.

_____. *Truth and Method.* 2d rev. ed. Translated by Joel Weinsheimer and Donald G. Marshall. New York: Crossroad, 1989.

Galilea, Segundo. *The Beatitudes: To Evangelize as Jesus Did.* Maryknoll, N.Y.: Orbis, 1984.

Galling, Kurt., et al. *RGG.* S.v. "Reich Gottes."

Gassman, Günther, ed. *Documentary History of Faith and Order 1963–1993.* Faith and Order Papers no. 159. Geneva: World Council of Churches, 1993.

Geffre, Claude. "A Prophetic Theology." *Concilium* 96 (1974): 7–16.

Geisler, Norman L. "A Premillennial View of Law and Government." *BS* 142 (July–September 1985): 250–66.

Gerhardsson, Birger. *The Mighty Acts of Jesus According to Matthew.* Translated by Robert Dewsnap. Lund: W. K. Gleerup, 1979.

Gibellini, Rosino. *The Liberation Theology Debate.* Maryknoll, N.Y.: Orbis, 1988.

Gilkey, Langdon. *Naming the Whirlwind: The Renewal of God-Language.* New York: Bobbs-Merrill, 1969.

Gill, Athol. "Christian Social Responsibility." In *The New Face of Evangelicalism: An International Symposium on the Lausanne Covenant,* edited by René Padilla, 87–102. Downers Grove, Ill.: InterVarsity Press, 1976.

Gilson, Etienne. *L'esprit de la philosophie médiévale.* 2d ed. 367–68. Paris, 1944. Quoted in M. Bloomfield. "Joachim of Flora: A Critical Survey of His Canon, Teachings, Sources, Biography, and Influence." In *Joachim of Fiore in Christian Thought,* edited by Delno C. West, vol. 1, 41, n. 57. New York: Burt Franklin, 1975.

Glasson, T. F. "Apocalyptic: Some Current Delusions." *LonQR* (1952): 104–10.

_____. *Jesus and the End of the World.* Edinburgh: St. Andrews, 1980.

_____. "The Kingdom as Cosmic Catastrophe." *Studia Evangelica III,* 187–200. Berlin: Akademie Verlag, 1964.

_____. "Schweitzer's Influence—Blessing or Bane?" *JTS* NS 28 (1977): 289–302.

_____. *The Second Advent: The Origin of the New Testament Doctrine.* London: Epworth, 1945.

_____. "The Temporary Messianic Kingdom and the Kingdom of God." *JTS* NS 14 (1990): 515–25.

Godsey, John D. *Preface to Bonhoeffer.* Philadelphia: Fortress, 1965.

Goodenough, E. R. "Kingship in Early Israel." *JBL* 48 (1929): 169–205.

Gottwald, Norman K. "Theological Issues in *The Tribes of Yahweh* by N. K. Gottwald: Four Critical Reviews." In *The Bible and Liberation,* edited by Norman K. Gottwald, 166–89. Maryknoll, N.Y.: Orbis, 1983.

_____. *The Tribes of Yahweh: A Sociology of the Religion of Liberated Israel 1250–1050 B.C.E.* Maryknoll, N.Y.: Orbis, 1979.

Gourges, M. *À la droite de Dieu: Résurrection de Jésus et actualisation du Psaum 110:1 dans le Nouveau Testament.* Paris: Libraire Lecoffre, 1978.

Gowan, Donald E. *Eschatology in the Old Testament.* Philadelphia: Fortress, 1986.

Grau, José. "The Kingdom of God Among the Kingdoms of Earth." In *Let the Earth Hear His Voice: International Congress on World Evangelization Lausanne, Switzerland: Official Reference Volume: Papers and Responses,* edited by J. D. Douglas, 1083–92. Minneapolis: World Wide, 1975.

Gray, John. "Hebrew Conception of the Kingship of God." *VT* 6 (1956): 268–85.

_____. *The Biblical Doctrine of the Reign of God.* Edinburgh: T & T Clark, 1979.

Grässer, Erich. "Norman Perrin's Contribution to the Question of the Historical Jesus." *JRel* 64 (October 1984): 484–500.

Gregory I. *Homilia XXXII.* In *MPL.* Vol. 76, *Patrologiae tomus LXXVI. S. Gregorii Papeaei tomus secundus.*

Gremillion, Joseph, ed. *The Gospel of Justice and Peace.* Maryknoll, N.Y.: Orbis, 1976.

Grenz, Stanley J. *Revisioning Evangelical Theology: A Fresh Agenda for the Twentieth Century.* Downers Grove, Ill.: InterVarsity Press, 1993.

Grenz, Stanley J., and Roger E. Olson. *Twentieth Century Theology: God & the World in a Transitional Age.* Downers Grove, Ill.: InterVarsity Press, 1992.

Grimm, Werner. *Weil Ich dich Liebe. Die Verkündigung Jesu und Deuterojesaja.* Frankfurt: Peter Lang, 1976.

Groh, John E. "The Kingdom of God in the History of Christianity: A Bibliographical Survey." *ChH* 43 (June 1974): 257–67.

Gutiérrez, Gustavo. *A Theology of Liberation.* Translated by Caridad Inda and John Eagleson. Maryknoll, N.Y.: Orbis, 1973.

_____. *The Power of the Poor in History.* Translated by Robert R. Barr. Maryknoll, N.Y.: Orbis, 1983.

_____. *We Drink from Our Own Wells: The Spiritual Journey of a People.* Translated by Matthew J. O'Connell. Maryknoll, N.Y.: Orbis, 1984.

Güttgemanns, Erhardt. *Candid Questions Concerning Gospel Form Criticism.* Translated by William G. Doty. Pittsburgh: Pickwick, 1979.

Hagner, Donald A. *The Jewish Reclamation of Jesus: An Analysis and Critique of Modern Jewish Study of Jesus.* Grand Rapids: Zondervan, 1984.

Haight, Roger. *An Alternate Vision: An Interpretation of Liberation Theology.* Mahwah, N.J.: Paulist, 1985.

Haight, Roger, and John Langan. "Recent Catholic Social and Ethical Teaching in Light of the Social Gospel." *JRelEth* 18 (1990): 103–28.

Handspicker, Meredith B. "Faith and Order 1948–1968." In *The Ecumenical Advance: A History of the Ecumenical Movement,* edited by Ruth Rouse and Stephen Charles Neill. 2d ed. with rev. bibliography, 143–70. Philadelphia: Westminster, 1970.

Harrington, Daniel J. *The New Dictionary of Catholic Social Thought.* Edited by Judith A. Dwyer. A Michael Glazier Book. Collegeville, Minn.: The Liturgical Press, 1994. S.v. "Kingdom of God."

_____. "Second Testament Exegesis and the Social Science: A Bibliography." *BibTB* 18 (1988): 77–85.

_____. "Sociological Concepts and the Early Church: A Decade of Research." *TS* 41 (1980): 181–90.

Harrington, W. J. "The Parables in Recent Study (1960–1971)." *BibTB* 2 (1972): 219–41.

Harvey, A. E. "Christ as Agent." In *The Glory of Christ in the New Testament*, edited by L. D. Hurst and N. T. Wright, 239–50. Oxford: Clarendon, 1987.

_____. *Jesus and the Constraints of History*. Philadelphia: Westminster, 1982.

Harvey, Van A. "Hermeneutics." In *Encyclopedia of Religion*, edited by Mircea Eliade. Vol. 6, 279–86. New York: Macmillan, 1987. 16 vols.

Haughey, John C. "Church and Kingdom: Ecclesiology in the Light of Eschatology." *TS* 29 (1968): 72–86.

Hay, D. M. *Glory at the Right Hand: Psalm 110 in Early Christianity*. SBL Monograph Series 18. New York: Abingdon, 1973.

Hayes, J. H. "The Resurrection as Enthronement and the Earliest Church Christology." *Interp* 22 (1968): 333–45.

Hefner, Philip. "The Concreteness of God's Kingdom: A Problem for the Christian Life." *JRel* 51, no. 1 (1971): 188–205.

Heidegger, Martin. *An Introduction to Metaphysics*. Translated by Ralph Mannheim. New Haven: Yale University Press, 1959.

_____. *Being and Time*. Translated by John Macquarrie and Edward Robinson. New York/Evanston, Ill.: Harper & Row, 1962.

_____. *On the Way to Language*. Translated by Peter D. Hertz. San Francisco: Harper & Row, 1971.

Hengel, Martin. *The Charismatic Leader and His Followers*. Translated by J. Greig. Edinburgh: T & T Clark, 1981.

_____. "Reich Christi, Reich Gottes und Weltreich im 4. Evangelium." In *Königsherrschaft Gottes und himmlischer Kult im Judentum, Urchristentum und in der hellenistischen Welt*, edited by Martin Hengel and Anna Maria Schwemer. WUNT 55, 163–84. Tübingen: J. C. B. Mohr (Paul Siebeck), 1991.

_____. *Was Jesus a Revolutionist?* Translated by William Klassen. Philadelphia: Fortress, 1971.

_____. *The Zealots: Investigations into the Jewish Freedom Movement in the Period from Herod 1 until 70 A.D.* Translated by David Smith. Edinburgh: T & T Clark, 1989.

_____. "Zur matthäischen Bergpredigt und ihrem jüdischen Hintergrund." *TRu* 52 (1987): 327–400.

Hengel, Martin, and Anna Maria Schwemer. Foreword to *Königsherrschaft Gottes und himmlisher Kult im Judentum, Urchristentum und in der hellenistischen Welt*, edited by Martin Hengel and Anna Maria Schwemer. WUNT 55, 1–19. Tübingen: J. C. B. Mohr (Paul Siebeck), 1991.

Hennelly, Alfred T. *Theologies in Conflict: The Challenge of Juan Luis Segundo*. Maryknoll, N.Y.: Orbis, 1979.

Herrick. *The Kingdom of God in the Writings of the Fathers*. Chicago: Chicago University, 1903.

Hertz, Karl. "An Investigation of Ecumenical Theology." *Mid-Stream* 19 (October 1980): 404–16.

Hiers, Richard H. *The Historical Jesus and the Kingdom of God: Present and Future in the Message and Ministry of Jesus.* Gainesville: University of Florida, 1973.

_____. "Interim Ethics." *Theology and Life* 9 (1966): 220–33.

_____. *Jesus and Ethics.* Philadelphia: Westminster, 1968.

_____. *Jesus and the Future: Unresolved Questions for Understanding and Faith.* Atlanta: John Knox, 1981.

_____. *The Kingdom of God in the Synoptic Tradition,* University of Florida Humanities Monograph 33. Gainesville: University of Florida, 1970.

_____. "Pivotal Reactions to the Eschatological Interpretations: Rudolf Bultmann and C. H. Dodd." In *The Kingdom of God in Twentieth-Century Interpretation,* edited by Wendell Willis, 15–34. Peabody, Mass.: Hendrickson, 1987.

Hodges, H. A. *Dilthey: An Introduction.* London: Kegan Paul, Trench & Trubner, 1944.

_____. *The Philosophy of Wilhelm Dilthey.* London: Routledge & Kegan Paul, 1952.

Hoekstra, Harvey T. *The World Council of Churches and the Demise of Evangelism.* Wheaton, Ill.: Tyndale House, 1979.

Holland, David Larrimore. "History Theology and the Kingdom of God: A Contribution of Johannes Weiss to 20th Century Theology." *BiRes* 13 (1968): 54–66.

Hollenbach, Paul W. "Recent Historical Jesus Studies and the Social Sciences." In *Society of Biblical Literature 1983 Seminar Papers,* edited by Kent Harold Richards, 61–78. Chico, Calif.: Scholars, 1983.

Hooker, Morna D. "Christology and Methodology." *NTS* 17 (1970–1971): 480–87.

_____. "On Using the Wrong Tool." *Theology* 55/629 (November 1972): 570–81.

Horsley, Richard A. "Ancient Jewish Banditry and the Revolt Against Rome, A.D. 66–70." *CBQ* 43 (1981): 409–32.

_____. "Bandits, Messiahs, and Longshoremen: Popular Unrest in Galilee around the Time of Jesus." In *SBL 1988 Seminar Papers,* edited by David J. Lull, 183–99. Atlanta: Scholars, 1988.

_____. "High Priests and the Politics of Roman Palestine: A Contextual Analysis of the Evidence in Josephus." *JStJud* 17 (1986): 23–55.

_____. *Jesus and the Spiral of Violence: Popular Jewish Resistance in Roman Palestine.* San Francisco: Harper & Row, 1987.

_____. "Jesus, Itinerant Cynic or Israelite Prophet?" In *Images of Jesus Today,* edited by James H. Charlesworth and Walter P. Weaver. Faith and Scholarship Colloquies 3, Florida Southern College, 69–97. Valley Forge, Pa.: Trinity Press International, 1994.

_____. "Josephus and the Bandits." *JStJud* 10 (1979): 37–63.

_____. "Like One of the Prophets of Old: Two Types of Popular Prophets at the Time of Jesus." *CBQ* 47 (1985): 435–63.

_____. "Popular Messianic Movements Around the Time of Jesus." *CBQ* 46 (1984): 471–93.

_____. "Popular Prophetic Movements at the Time of Jesus, Their Principle Features and Social Origins." *JStNT* 26 (1986): 3–27.

_____. "The Sicarii: Ancient Jewish Terrorists." *JRel* 59 (1979): 435–58.

_____. *Sociology and the Jesus Movement.* New York: Crossroad, 1989.

_____. "The Zealots, Their Origin, Relationships and Importance for the Jewish Revolt." *NT* 28 (1986): 159–92.

Horsley, Richard A., and John S. Hanson. *Bandits, Prophets, and Messiahs: Popular Movements in the Time of Jesus.* San Francisco: Harper & Row, 1985.

Howard, Roy. *Three Faces of Hermeneutics.* Berkeley: University of California, 1982.

Hull, John. *Hellenistic Magic and the Synoptic Tradition.* Studies in Biblical Theology 2, no. 28. Naperville, Ill.: Alec R. Allenson, 1974.

Hundley, Raymond. *Radical Liberation Theology: An Evangelical Response.* Wilmore, Ky.: Bristol, 1987.

Hunsinger, George. "The Crucified God and Political Theology of Violence: A Critical Survey of Jürgen Moltmann's Recent Thought, I." *HeythJ* 14, no. 3 (1973): 266–79.

_____. "The Crucified God and Political Theology of Violence: A Critical Survey of Jürgen Moltmann's Recent Thought, II." *HeythJ* 14, no. 4 (1973): 379–95.

James, G. Ingli. "The Autonomy of the Work of Art: Modern Criticism and the Christian Tradition." In *The New Orpheus: Essays toward a Christian Poetic,* edited by Nathan A. Scott Jr., 187–209. New York: Sheed and Ward, 1964.

Jeremias, Joachim. *Die Gleichnisse Jesu.* Zürich: Zwingli, 1947.

_____. *Jesus als Weltvollender.* Beiträge zur Förderung christlicher Theologie 28. Gütersloh: Bertelsmann, 1930.

_____. *New Testament Theology.* Translated by John Bowden. London: SCM, 1971.

_____. *The Parables of Jesus.* 2d rev. ed. Translated by S. H. Hooke. New York: Scribner's, 1966.

Joachim de Fiore, *Liber Concordie Novi ac Veteris Testamenti.* Venice, 1519.

Johnson, A. R. "Hebrew Conceptions of Kingship." In *Myth, Ritual, and Kingship: Essays on the Theory and Practice of Kingship in the Ancient Near East and Israel,* edited by S. H. Hooke, 187–210. Oxford: Clarendon, 1958.

Jones, G. V. *The Art and Truth of the Parables.* London: SPCK, 1964.

Josephus, Flavius. *The Jewish Wars.* Edited by T. E. Page et al. Translated by H. St. J. Thackery et al. Loeb. New York: G. P. Putnam's Sons, 1927.

Jüngel, Eberhard. *Paulus und Jesus. Eine Untersuchung zur Präzierung der Frage nach dem Ursprung der Christologie.* HUT 2. Tübingen: J. C. B. Mohr (Paul Siebeck), 1967.

Kahler, Martin. *The So-Called Historical Jesus and the Historic Biblical Christ.* Translated and edited by Carl E. Braaten. Philadelphia: Fortress, 1988.

Kallas, James. *The Significance of the Synoptic Miracles.* London: SPCK, 1961.

Kamlah, Eberhard. *NIDNTT.* S.v. "Spirit, Holy Spirit."

Kantzer, Kenneth, and Carl F. H. Henry, eds. *Evangelical Affirmations.* Grand Rapids: Zondervan, 1990.

Käsemann, Ernst. "The Eschatological Royal Reign of God." In *Your Kingdom Come: Mission Perspectives Report on the World Conference on Mission and Evangelism: Melbourne Australia, 12–15 May, 1980,* 61–71. Geneva: World Council of Churches, 1980.

_____. *Essays on New Testament Themes.* Translated by W. J. Montague. Philadelphia: Fortress, 1982.

_____. "Das Problem des historischen Jesus." *ZTK* 51 (1954): 123–53.

Keck, Leander. "Will the Historical Critical Method Survive? Some Observations." In *Orientation by Disorientation: Studies in Literary Criticism and Biblical Literary Criticism,* edited by Richard A. Spencer. Pittsburgh Theological Monograph Series 35, 115–28. Pittsburgh: Pickwick, 1980.

Kee, Howard Clark. *What Can We Know About Jesus?* Cambridge: Cambridge University Press, 1990.

Kelber, Werner H. "The Work of Norman Perrin: An Intellectual Pilgrimage." *JRel* 64 (October 1984): 452–67.

Kelsey, Morton. *Healing and Christianity.* New York: Harper & Row, 1973.

Kibble, David G. "The Kingdom of God and Christian Politics." *Themelios* 7, no. 1 (1981): 24–32.

Kingsbury, J. D. "Ernst Fuchs' Interpretation of Parables." *LuthQ* 22 (1970): 380–95.

_____. "Major Trends in Parable Interpretation." *ConcordTM* 42 (1971): 579–96.

_____. "The Parables of Jesus in Current Research." *Dialog* 11 (1972): 101–7.

Kirk, Andrew J. "The Kingdom of God and the Church in Contemporary Protestantism and Catholicism." In *Let the Earth Hear His Voice: International Congress on World Evangelization Lausanne, Switzerland: Official Reference Volume: Papers and Responses,* edited by J. D. Douglas, 1071–82. Minneapolis: World Wide, 1975.

Klappert, B. *NIDNTT.* S.v. "King, Kingdom."

Klein, Günther. "The Biblical Understanding of the 'Kingdom of God.'" Translated by Richard N. Soulen. *Interp* 26 (October 1972): 387–418.

Kline, Meredith G. "Comments on an Old-New Error." *WestTJ* 41 (1978): 172–89.

Kloppenburg, Bonaventura. *The Ecclesiology of Vatican II.* Translated by Matthew J. O'Connell. Chicago: Franciscan Herald, 1974.

Knoch, Otto. "Die eschatologische Frage, ihre Entwicklung und ihr gegenärtiger Stand." *BZ* 6 (1962): 112–20.

Koch, Klaus. "Offenbaren wird sich das Reich Gottes." *NTS* 25 (1979): 158–65.

_____. *The Rediscovery of Apocalyptic.* Studies in Biblical Theology, second series, 22. London: SCM, 1972.

_____. "What is Apocalyptic? An Attempt at a Preliminary Definition." In *Visionaries and Apocalypses*, edited by Paul D. Hanson, 16–36. Philadelphia: Fortress, 1983.

Kolden, Marc. "Marxism and Latin American Liberation Theology." In *Christianity and the Many Faces of Marxism*, edited by Wayne Stumme, 123–31. Minneapolis: Augsburg, 1984.

Kreck, Walter. *Die Zukunft des Gekommenen. Grundprobleme der Eschatologie*. Munich: Christian Kaiser, 1961.

Krentz, Edgar. *The Historical-Critical Method*. Guides to Biblical Scholarship. Philadelphia: Fortress, 1975.

Krieger, Murray. *A Window to Criticism*. Princeton: Princeton University Press, 1963.

_____. *The New Apologists for Poetry*. Minneapolis: University of Minnesota Press, 1956.

_____. *The Tragic Vision*. New York: Holt, Rinehart, and Winston, 1960.

Kroeber, A. L. *Anthropology: Race, Language, Culture, Psychology, Prehistory*. New York: Harcourt, Brace, 1948, 284. Quoted in John Dominic Crossan, *The Historical Jesus: The Life of a Mediterranean Jewish Peasant* (San Francisco: HarperSanFrancisco, 1991), 125.

Kromminga, D. H. *The Millennium in the Church*. Grand Rapids: Eerdmans, 1945.

Kunst, Theo J. W. "The Kingdom of God and Social Justice." *BS* 140/558 (1983): 108–16.

Kuzmic, Peter. "History and Eschatology: Evangelical Views." In *In Word and Deed: Evangelism and Social Responsibility*, edited by Bruce J. Nicholls, 135–64. Grand Rapids: Eerdmans, 1985.

Kümmel, W. G. "Die 'Konsequente Eschatologie' Albert Schweitzers im Urteil der Zeitgenossen." In *Heilsgeschen und Geschichte: Gesammelte Aufsätze*. Marburg: N. G. Elwert, 1965, 338. Quoted in Wendell Willis, "The Discovery of the Eschatological Kingdom: Johannes Weiss and Albert Schweitzer," in *The Kingdom of God in Twentieth-Century Interpretation*, edited by Wendell Willis (Peabody, Mass.: Hendrickson, 1987), 3.

_____. "Ein Jahrzehnt Jesusforschung (1965–1975)." *TRu* 41, no. 3 (1976): 197–363.

_____. *Jesus der Menschensohn*. Stuttgart: Steiner, 1983.

_____. "Jesuforschung seit 1965." *TRu* 43, no. 2 (1978): 105–61.

_____. *Promise and Fulfillment: The Eschatological Message of Jesus*. Translated by Dorothea M. Barton. Studies in Biblical Theology 23. Naperville, Ill.: Alec R. Allenson, 1957.

Küng, Hans. *The Church*. Translated by Ray and Rosaleen Ockenden. New York: Sheed and Ward, 1967.

Ladd, George E. *Crucial Questions About the Kingdom of God.* Grand Rapids: Eerdmans, 1952.

_____. "Historic Premillennialism." In *The Meaning of the Millennium: Four Views,* edited by Robert G. Clouse, 17–40. Downers Grove, Ill.: InterVarsity Press, 1977.

_____. *Jesus and the Kingdom: The Eschatology of Biblical Realism.* New York: Harper & Row, 1964.

_____. "The Kingdom of God: Reign or Realm?" *JBL* 81 (1962): 230–38.

_____. "The Life Setting of the Parables of the Kingdom." *JBiRel* 31 (1963): 193–99.

_____. *The Pattern of New Testament Truth.* Grand Rapids: Eerdmans, 1968.

_____. "The Place of Apocalyptic in Biblical Religion." *EvQ* 29 (1957): 94–100.

_____. *The Presence of the Future: The Eschatology of Biblical Realism.* A revised and updated version of *Jesus and the Future.* Grand Rapids: Eerdmans, 1974.

_____. "Why Not Prophetic-Apocalyptic?" *JBL* 76 (1957): 192–200.

Lane, Dermot A. *Foundations for a Social Theology: Praxis, Process and Salvation.* New York: Paulist, 1984.

Lapointe, R. "Hermeneutics Today." *BibTB* 2, no. 2 (1972): 107–54.

Lefever, Ernest W. *Nairobi to Vancouver: The World Council of Churches and the World, 1975–1987.* Washington, D.C.: Ethics and Public Policy Center, 1987.

Lepargueur, François Hubert. "Theologies de la liberation et theologie tout court." *NRT* 98 (1976): 126–69.

Lesétre, H. *Dictionnaire de la Bible.* Edited by F. Vigouroux. Paris: Letouzy et Ané, 1912–22. S.v. "Roi."

Levenson, Jon D. "Exodus and Liberation." *HorBibT* 13 (1991): 95–174.

Lietzmann, H. *An die Korinter I–II.* 4th ed. Tübingen: J. C. B. Mohr (Paul Siebeck), 1949.

Lightner, Robert P. "A Dispensational Response to Theonomy." *BS* 143 (July 1986): 228–45.

Limouris, Gennadios. "The Church as Mystery and Sign in Relation to the Holy Trinity—In Ecclesiological Perspectives." In *Church Kingdom World: The Church as Mystery and Prophetic Sign,* edited by Gennadios Limouris, 18–49. Geneva: World Council of Churches, 1986.

Lindars, Barnabas. *Jesus, Son of Man: A Fresh Examination of the Son of Man Sayings in the Gospels in the Light of Recent Research.* Grand Rapids: Eerdmans, 1984.

Lindbeck, George A. *The Future of Roman Catholic Theology: Vatican II—Catalyst for Change.* Philadelphia: Fortress, 1970.

Lindemann. A. *TRE.* S.v. "Gottesherrschaft."

Linnemann, Eta. *Gleichnisse Jesu. Einfuhrung und Auslegung.* Göttingen: Vandenhoeck & Ruprecht, 1961.

_____. *Historical Criticism of the Bible: Methodology or Ideology?* Translated by Robert Yarbrough. Grand Rapids: Baker, 1990.

_____. *Jesus of the Parables: Introduction and Exposition.* Translated from 3d ed. by John Sturdy. New York: Harper & Row, 1966.

Loader, W. R. G. "Christ at the Right Hand—Ps CX.1 in the New Testament." *NTS* 24 (1978): 199–217.

Lobkowicz, Nickolas. *Theory and Practice.* Notre Dame, Ind.: University of Notre Dame, 1968.

Lochman, Jan Milic. "Church and World in the Light of the Kingdom of God." In *Church Kingdom World: The Church Mystery and Prophetic Sign*, edited by Gennadios Limouris, 58–72. Geneva: World Council of Churches, 1986.

Löffler, Paul. "The Reign of God Has Come in the Suffering Christ: An Exploration of the Power of the Powerless." *IntRMiss* 68/270 (April 1979): 109–14.

Lonergan, B. J. F. *Insight: A Study of Human Understanding.* London: Longmans, 1958.

Lord, Elizabeth. "Human History and the Kingdom of God: Past Perspectives and Those of J. L. Segundo." *HeythJ* 30 (1989): 293–305.

Lundström, Gösta. *The Kingdom of God in the Teaching of Jesus: A History of Interpretation from the Last Decades of the Nineteenth Century to the Present Day.* Translated by Joan Bulman. London: Oliver and Boyd, 1963.

Mack, Burton L. "The Kingdom Sayings in Mark." *Forum* 3, no. 1 (1987): 3–47.

_____. "The Kingdom That Didn't Come." In *SBL 1988 Seminar Papers*, edited by David J. Lull, 608–35. Atlanta: Scholars, 1988.

_____. *The Lost Gospel: The Book of Q and Christian Origins.* San Francisco: HarperSanFrancisco, 1993.

_____. *The Myth of Innocence: Mark and Christian Origins.* Philadelphia: Fortress, 1988.

Mackey, J. P. *Jesus: The Man and the Myth.* London: SCM, 1979, 127. Quoted in Bruce Chilton and J. I. H. McDonald, *Jesus and the Ethics of the Kingdom* (Grand Rapids: Eerdmans, 1987), 59.

Maddox, Randy L. "Contemporary Hermeneutic Philosophy and Theological Studies." *RelSt* 21 (1985): 517–29.

Makkreel, Rudolf A. *Dilthey, Philosopher of the Human Studies.* Princeton: Princeton University Press, 1975.

Malina, Bruce J. "The Social Sciences and Biblical Interpretation." *Interp* 32 (July 1982): 229–42.

Mannheim, Karl. *Essays on the Sociology of Knowledge.* Oxford: Oxford University Press, 1952.

_____. *Ideology and Utopia.* New York: Harcourt, Brace and World, 1955.

Manson, T. W. "The Life of Jesus: Some Tendencies in Present–Day Research." In *The Background of the New Testament and Its Eschatology*, edited by W. D. Davies and David Daube, 211–21. Cambridge: Cambridge University Press, 1956.

Manson, T. W. *The Teaching of Jesus*. Cambridge: Cambridge University Press, 1931.

Marcus, J. "Entering into the Kingly Power of God." *JBL* 107 (1988): 663–75.

Marsden, George M. *Fuller Seminary and the New Evangelicals*. Grand Rapids: Eerdmans, 1987.

_____. *Fundamentalism and American Culture: The Shaping of Twentieth Century Evangelicalism, 1870–1925*. New York: Oxford University Press, 1980.

_____. *Reforming Fundamentalism: Fuller Seminary and the New Evangelicalism*. Grand Rapids: Eerdmans, 1987.

Marshall, I. Howard. *Dictionary of Jesus and the Gospels*. Edited by Joel B. Green, Scot McKnight, and I. Howard Marshall. Downers Grove, Ill.: InterVarsity Press, 1992. S.v. "Church."

_____. "The Hope of a New Age: the Kingdom of God in the New Testament." *Themelios* 11, no. 1 (1985): 5–15.

_____. *Jesus the Saviour*. Downers Grove, Ill.: InterVarsity Press, 1990.

Martin, Ralph P. "The New Quest of the Historical Jesus." In *Jesus of Nazareth: Saviour and Lord*, edited by C. F. H. Henry, 25–45. Grand Rapids: Eerdmans, 1966.

Marxsen, W. *The Beginnings of Christology*. Translated by P. J. Achtemeier and L. Nieting. Philadelphia: Fortress, 1979.

Mau, Rudolf. *TRE*. S.v. "Herrschaft Gottes."

McBrien, Richard P. *Catholicism*. Minneapolis: Winston, 1981.

_____. *The Church in the Thought of Bishop John Robinson*. Philadelphia: Westminster, 1966.

_____. *Do We Need the Church?* New York: Harper & Row, 1969.

McCarthy, Brian Rice. "Jesus, the Kingdom, and Theopolitics." In *Society of Biblical Literature 1990 Seminar Papers*, edited by David J. Lull. Society of Biblical Literature Seminar Papers Series 29, 311–21. Atlanta: Scholars, 1991.

McDonald, James I. H. "New Quest—Dead End? So What About the Historical Jesus?" In *Studia Biblica 1978*. Vol. 2, *Papers on the Gospels*, ed. E. A. Livingstone. JSNTSS 2. 151–70. Sheffield: JSOT, 1980.

McEleney, Neil J. "Authenticating Criteria and Mk 7:1–23." *CBQ* 34, no. 4 (1972): 431–60.

McGinn, Bernard. *The Calabrian Abbot: Joachim of Fiore in the History of Western Thought*. New York: Macmillan, 1985.

McGovern, Arthur F. "The Bible in Latin American Liberation Theology." In *The Bible and Liberation*, edited by Norman K. Gottwald, 467–71. Maryknoll, N.Y.: Orbis, 1983.

_____. *Liberation Theology and Its Critics: Toward An Assessment.* Maryknoll, N.Y.: Orbis, 1989.

McKnight, Scot. "Jesus and the Endtime: Matthew 10.23." In *SBL Seminar Papers 1986,* edited by Kent Harold Richards, 501–20. Atlanta: Scholars, 1986.

Mealand, David L. "The Dissimilarity Test." *ScotJT* 31 (1978): 41–50.

Meier, John P. *A Marginal Jew: Rethinking the Historical Jesus.* Vol. 1, *The Roots of the Problem and the Person.* Anchor Bible Reference Library. New York: Doubleday, 1991.

_____. *A Marginal Jew: Rethinking the Historical Jesus.* Vol. 2, *Mentor, Message and Miracle.* Anchor Bible Reference Library. New York: Doubleday, 1994.

Mercer, Calvin R. Jr. "APOSTELLEIN and PEMPEIN in John." *NTS* 36 (1990): 619–24.

_____. *Norman Perrin's Interpretation of the New Testament.* Studies in American Biblical Hermeneutics 2. Macon, Ga.: Mercer University Press, 1986.

_____. "Norman Perrin: A Scholarly Pilgrim." Ph.D. diss., Florida State University, 1983.

Merk, O. *TRE.* S.v. "Bibelwissenschaft."

Merkel, Helmut. "Die Gottesherrschaft in der Verkündigung Jesu." In *Königsherrschaft Gottes und himmlischer Kult im Judentum, Urchristentum und in der hellenistischen Welt,* edited by Martin Hengel and Anna Maria Schwemer. WUNT 55, 120–35. Tübingen: J. C. B. Mohr (Paul Siebeck), 1991.

Merklein, Helmut. *Die Gottesherrschaft als Handlungsprinzip. Untersuchung zur Ethik Jesu.* Wurzburg: Echter, 1978.

_____. *Jesu Botschaft von der Gottesherrschaft. Eine Skizze.* Stuttgarter Bibelstudien 111. Stuttgart: Katholishes Bibelwerk, 1983.

_____. *Studien zu Jesus und Paulus.* Tübingen: J. C. B. Mohr (Paul Siebeck), 1987.

Metz, Johann Baptist. *Theology of the World.* Translated by William Glen-Doepel. New York: Herder and Herder, 1971.

Meyers, Ben F. *The Aims of Jesus.* London: SCM, 1979.

_____. "Jesus's Scenario of the Future." *DRev* 109 (1991): 1–15.

Michaelis, Wilhelm. *Reich Gottes und Geist Gottes nach dem Neuen Testament.* Basel: Friedrich Reinhardt, n.d.

Michaels, J. Ramsey. "The Kingdom of God and the Historical Jesus." In *The Kingdom of God in Twentieth-Century Interpretation,* edited by Wendell Willis, 109–18. Peabody, Mass.: Hendrickson, 1987.

Migliore, Daniel. "Biblical Eschatology and Political Hermeneutics." *TToday* 26 (1969–1970): 116–32.

Miranda, José Porfirio. *Marx and the Bible: A Critique of the Philosophy of Oppression.* Translated by John Eagleson. Maryknoll, N.Y.: Orbis, 1974.

Moltmann, Jürgen. *The Church in the Power of the Spirit: A Contribution to Messianic Ecclesiology.* Translated by Margaret Kohl. New York: Harper and Row, 1977.

_____. *Creating a Just Future.* Translated by John Bowden. Philadelphia: Trinity Press International, 1989.

_____. *The Crucified God: The Cross of Christ as the Foundation and Criticism of Christian Theology.* Translated by R. A. Wilson and John Bowden. London: SCM, 1974.

_____. *The Experiment Hope.* Edited, translated, with a foreword by M. Douglas Meeks. Philadelphia: Fortress, 1975.

_____. *The Future of Creation: Collected Essays.* Translated by Margaret Kohl. Philadelphia: Fortress, 1979.

_____. Foreword to *Origins to the Theology of Hope,* by M. Douglas Meeks. Philadelphia: Fortress, 1974.

_____. *God in Creation: A New Theology of Creation and the Spirit of God.* San Francisco: Harper & Row, 1985.

_____. "God's Kingdom as the Meaning of Life and of the World." *Concilium* 108 (1978): 97–103.

_____. *Im Gespräch mit Ernst Bloch: Eine theologishe Wegbegleitung.* Munich: Christian Kaiser Verlag, 1976.

_____. *Jewish Monotheism and Christian Trinitarian Theology.* Translated by Leonard Swidler. Philadelphia: Fortress, 1981.

_____. *The Passion for Life: A Messianic Lifestyle.* Translated with an introduction by M. Douglas Meeks. Philadelphia: Fortress, 1978.

_____. "Politics and the Practice of Hope." *The Christian Century* 35, no. 3 (1970): 288–91.

_____. "Das Reich Gottes und die Treue zur Erde." *Das Gespräch* 49 (1963): 3–23.

_____. *Religion, Revolution, and the Future.* Translated by M. Douglas Meeks. New York: Charles Scribner's, 1969.

_____. *Theologie der Hoffnung. Untersuchungen zur Begründung und zu den Konsequenzes einer christlichen Eschatologie.* Munich: Christian Kaiser, 1964.

_____. "Theology in Germany Today." In *Observations on the "Spiritual Situation of the Age,"* edited by J. Habermas. Translated by A. Buchwalter. Cambridge, Mass.: MIT, 1984.

_____. *Theology of Hope: On the Ground and the Implications of a Christian Eschatology.* Translated by James W. Leitch. New York: Harper and Row, 1967.

_____. "Toward a Political Hermeneutics of the Gospel." *USemQR* 23 (1968): 303–23.

_____. "The Trinitarian History of God." *Theology* 78 (December 1975): 632–46.

_____. *The Trinity and the Kingdom: The Doctrine of God.* Translated by Margaret Kohl. San Francisco: Harper and Row, 1981.

_____. "Verschränkte Zeiten der Geschichte: Notwendige Differenzierungen and Begrenzungen des Geschichtsbegreiffs." *EvT* 44 (1984): 213–27.

_____. *The Way of Jesus Christ: Christology in Messianic Dimensions.* Translated by Margaret Kohl. San Francisco: HarperSanFrancisco, 1990.

Moltmann, Jürgen, H. Kremers, and L. Goppelt. *Evangelisches Kirchenlexikon.* Edited by Heinz Brunotte and Otto Weber. Göttigen: Vandenhoeck & Ruprecht, 1956–1961. S.v. "Reich Gottes."

Moltmann, Jürgen, and Jürgen Weissbach. *Two Studies in the Theology of Bonhoeffer.* Translated by Reginald H. Fuller and Ilse Fuller. New York: Scribner's, 1967.

Moore, Stephen D. *Literary Criticism and the Gospels: The Theoretical Challenge.* New Haven: Yale University Press, 1989.

Morse, Christopher. *The Logic of Promise in Moltmann's Theology.* Philadelphia: Fortress, 1979.

Moule, C. F. D. *The Birth of the New Testament.* London: A & C Black, 1962.

Mowinckel, Sigmund. *He That Cometh.* Translated by G. W. Anderson. New York: Abingdon, 1954.

Muller, Richard A. *Dictionary of Latin and Greek Theological Terms.* Grand Rapids: Baker, 1985. S.v. "regnum Christi."

Müller-Fahrenholz. *Dictionary of the Ecumenical Movement.* Edited by Nicholas Lossky et al. Grand Rapids: Eerdmans, 1991. S.v. "Salvation History."

Neely, Alan Preston. "Liberation Theology and the Poor: A Second Look." *Missiology* 17 (1989): 387–404.

_____. "Protestant Antecedents of Latin American Theology of Liberation." Ph.D. diss., The American University, 1977.

Newbigin, Leslie. *Sign of the Kingdom.* Grand Rapids: Eerdmans, 1981.

Newsom, Carol A. *Songs of the Sabbath Sacrifice: A Critical Edition.* Harvard Semitic Studies 27. Atlanta: Scholars, 1985.

North, Gary. *Millennialism and Social Theory.* Tyler, Tex.: Institute for Christian Economics, 1990.

_____. *Unconditional Surrender: God's Program for Victory.* Tyler, Tex.: Geneva Divinity School, 1985.

_____. "The War Between Three Types of Religions." *Biblical Economics Today* 8, no. 1 (1985): 1–4.

North, Gary, and Gary DeMar. *Christian Reconstruction: What It Is, What It Isn't.* Tyler, Tex.: Institute for Christian Economics, 1991.

Novak, Michael. *Will It Liberate? Questions about Liberation Theology.* Mahwah, N.J.: Paulist, 1986.

Nunez, Emilio A. *Liberation Theology.* Chicago: Moody, 1985.

O'Connell, Patrick F. "The Bishops, The Critics, and the Kingdom of God." In *Theology and the University,* edited by John Apczynski. The Annual Publication of the College of Theology Society no. 33, 87–116. Lanham, Md.: University Press of America, 1987.

O'Toole, Robert. "The Kingdom of God in Luke-Acts." In *The Kingdom of God in Twentieth-Century Interpretation,* edited by Wendell Willis, 147–62. Peabody, Mass.: Hendrickson, 1987.

Oden, Thomas C. *Life in the Spirit.* Systematic Theology, vol. 3 (San Francisco: HarperSanFrancisco, 1992.

Odendaal, Dirk. *The Eschatological Expectation of Isaiah 40–66 with Special Reference to Israel and the Nations.* Philadelphia: Presbyterian and Reformed, 1970.

Oepke, Albrecht. *TDNT.* S.v. *apokathistēmi, apokatastasis.*

_____. *TDNT.* S.v. *parousia.*

Osborne, Grant. *The Hermeneutical Spiral: A Comprehensive Introduction to Biblical Interpretation.* Downers Grove, Ill.: InterVarsity Press, 1991.

Otto, Randall E. "The Eschatological Nature of Moltmann's Theology." *WestTJ* 54 (1992): 115–33.

_____. *The God of Hope: The Trinitarian Vision of Jürgen Moltmann.* Lanham, Md.: University Press of America, 1991.

Padilla, René. "Evangelism and the World." In *Let the Earth Hear His Voice: International Congress on World Evangelization Lausanne, Switzerland: Official Reference Volume: Papers and Responses,* edited by J. D. Douglas. 116–146. Minneapolis, World Wide, 1975.

_____. Introduction to *The New Face of Evangelicalism: An International Symposium on the Lausanne Covenant,* edited René Padilla, 9–16. Downers Grove, Ill.: InterVarsity Press, 1976.

Palmer, Richard. *Hermeneutics: Interpretation Theory in Schleiermacher, Dilthey, Heidegger, and Gadamer.* Evanston, Ill.: Northwestern University, 1969.

Pannenberg, Wolfhart. *Basic Questions in Theology.* Translated by George H. Keim. 3 vols. London: SCM, 1970.

_____. "Dogmatische Thesen zur Lehre von der Offenbarung." In *Offenbarung als Geschichte,* edited by Wolfhart Pannenberg, 91–114. Göttingen: Vandenhoeck & Ruprecht, 1961.

_____. *Grundzüge der Christologie.* Gütersloh: Gerd Mohn. 1964.

_____. *Jesus—God and Man.* Translated by Lewis L. Wilkins and Duane A. Priebe. Philadelphia: Westminster, 1968.

_____., ed. *Revelation as History.* Translated by David Granskou. London: Collier, 1968.

_____. *Theology and the Philosophy of Science.* Translated by Francis McDonagh. Philadelphia: Westminster, 1976.

Paton, David, M., ed. *Breaking Barriers: The Official Report of the Fifth Assembly of the World Council of Churches, Nairobi 23 November–10 December, 1975.* London: SPCK; Grand Rapids: Eerdmans, 1976.

Patrick, Dale. "The Kingdom of God in the Old Testament." In *The Kingdom of God in Twentieth-Century Interpretation,* edited by Wendell Willis, 67–79. Peabody, Mass.: Hendrickson, 1987.

Patte, Daniel. *What is Structural Exegesis?* Philadelphia: Fortress, 1976.

Perrin, Norman. *A Modern Pilgrimage in New Testament Christology.* Philadelphia: Fortress, 1974.

_____. "Against the Current." *Interp* 19 (1965): 228–31.

_____. "Eschatology and Hermeneutics." SBL Presidential Address, 1973. *JBL* 93 (1974): 3–14.

_____. "Interpretation of a Biblical Symbol." *JRel* 55 (July 1975): 348–70.

_____. *Jesus and the Language of the Kingdom.* Philadelphia: Fortress, 1976.

_____. *The Kingdom of God in the Teaching of Jesus.* London: SCM, 1963.

_____. "The Modern Interpretation of the Parables of Jesus and the Gospel of Mark Today." *JRel* 52 (1972): 361–75.

_____. *The New Testament: An Introduction: Proclamation and Paranesis, Myth and History.* New York: Harcourt Brace Jovanovich, 1974.

_____. "The Parables of Jesus as Parables, as Metaphors, and as Aesthetic Objects: A Review Article." *JRel* 47 (1967): 340–47.

_____. *The Promise of Bultmann: The Promise of Theology.* Edited by Martin Marty. Philadelphia: J. B. Lippincott, 1969; reprint, Philadelphia: Fortress, 1979.

_____. *Rediscovering the Teaching of Jesus.* New York: Harper & Row, 1967.

_____. "The *Wredestrasse* Becomes the *Hauptstrasse*: Reflections on the Reprinting of the Dodd Festschrift." *JRel* 46 (1966): 296–300.

_____. "Wisdom and Apocalyptic in the Message of Jesus." In *Proceedings of the 108th Annual Meeting of the Society of Biblical Literature,* edited by L. C. McGaughty. Vol. 2, 543–570. Missoula, Mont.: Society of Biblical Literature, 1972.

Petersen, Norman R. *Literary Criticism for New Testament Critics.* Guides to Biblical Scholarship. Philadelphia: Fortress, 1978.

Phipps, W. E. "Jesus, The Prophetic Pharisee." *JEcuSt* 14 (1977): 17–31.

Pius IX. *Amantissimus.* In *The Papal Encyclicals.* Edited by Claudia Carlen. Vol. 1, *1740–1848.* A Consortium Book. 363–67. Wilmington, N.C.: McGrath, 1981.

Pius XI. *Mortalium animos. AAS* 20 (1928): 5–16.

Pius XII. *Mystici corporis. AAS* 35 (1943): 193–248.

Pixley, George V. *God's Kingdom: A Guide to Biblical Study*. Translated by Donald D. Walsh. Maryknoll, N.Y.: Orbis, 1981.

Polanyi, Michael. *Personal Knowledge*. Rev. ed. New York and Evanston, Ill.: Harper Torchbooks, 1964.

_____. *The Study of Man*. Chicago: University of Chicago, 1963.

Pope, Hugh. *Catholic Encyclopedia: An International Work of Reference on the Constitution, Doctrine, Disciplines, and History of the Catholic Church*. New York: Encyclopedia, 1913. S.v. "Kingdom of God."

Potter, Philip A. "A Call to Costly Ecumenism." *EcuR* 34 (1982): 332–44.

Prien, Hans-Jürgen, ed. *Lateinamerika: Gesellschaft, Kirche, Theologie*. Göttingen: Vandenhoeck & Ruprecht, 1981.

Quade, Quentin L., ed. *The Pope and Revolution: John Paul II Confronts Liberation Theology*. Washington, D.C.: Ethics and Public Policy Center, 1982.

Rahner, Karl. *Theological Investigations*. Vol. 6, *Concerning Vatican Council II*. Translated by Karl-H. and Boniface Kruger. Baltimore: Helicon, 1969.

Reimarus, Hermann. S. *The Goal of Jesus and his Disciples*. Translated with an introduction by G. W. Buchanan. Leiden: E. J. Brill, 1970.

_____. "Von dem Zwecke Jesu und seiner Jünger." In *Noch ein Fragment des Wolfenbüttelschen Ungenannten*, ed. Gotthold Ephraim Lessing. 1778.

Rengstorf, K. H. *TDNT*. S.v. *apostellō*.

Riches, John. *Jesus and the Transformation of Judaism*. New York: Seabury, 1983.

Riches, John, and Alan Millar. "Conceptual Change in the Synoptic Tradition." In *Alternative Approaches to New Testament Study*, edited by A. E. Harvey, 37–60. London: SPCK, 1985.

Ricoeur, Paul. *Conflict of Interpretations: Essays in Hermeneutics*. Evanston, Ill.: Northwestern University, 1974.

_____. *The Symbolism of Evil*. Boston: Beacon, 1969.

Ridderbos, Herman. *The Coming of the Kingdom*. Translated by H. de Jongste and edited by Raymond O. Zorn. Philadelphia: Presbyterian and Reformed, 1962.

Rikhof, Herwi. *The Concept of Church: A Methodological Inquiry into the Use of Metaphors in Ecclesiology*. London: Sheed and Ward, 1981.

Ritschl, Albrecht. *The Christian Doctrine of Justification and Reconciliation*. Edited by H. R. Mackintosh and A. B. Macaulay. Edinburgh: T & T Clark, 1900.

Ro, Bo Rin. "The Perspectives of Church History from New Testament Times to 1960." In *In Word and Deed: Evangelism and Social Responsibility*, edited by Bruce J. Nicholls, 11–40. Grand Rapids: Eerdmans, 1985.

Roberson, David. "Structuralist Criticism of the Parables: A Brief Response." In *Semiology and Parables: An Exploration of the Possibilities Offered by Structuralism for Exegesis*, edited by Daniel Patte. Pittsburgh Theological Monograph 9, 186–88. Pittsburgh: Pickwick, 1976.

Robinson, James M. *A New Quest of the Historical Jesus and Other Essays*. Philadelphia: Fortress, 1983.

_____. *A New Quest of the Historical Jesus*. London: SCM, 1959.

_____. "Hermeneutic Since Barth." In *The New Hermeneutic*, edited by James M. Robinson and John B. Cobb. New Frontiers in Theology 2, 1–77. New York: Harper & Row, 1964.

_____. "Jesus' Parables as God Happening." In *Jesus and the Historian*, ed. F. Thomas Trotter, 134–50. Philadelphia: Westminster, 1968.

Rowland, Christopher. *Christian Origins: From Messianic Movement to Christian Religion*. Minneapolis: Augsburg, 1985.

_____. *The Open Heaven: A Study of Apocalyptic in Judaism and Early Christianity*. New York: Crossroad, 1982.

Rowland, Christopher, and Mark Corner. *Liberating Exegesis: The Challenge of Liberation Theology to Biblical Studies*. Philadelphia: Fortress, 1990.

Rushdoony, R. J. *The Foundations of Social Order*. Nutley, N.J.: Presbyterian and Reformed, 1972.

_____. *The Institutes of Biblical Law*. Nutley, N.J.; Craig, 1973.

_____. "Postmillennialism Versus Impotent Religion." *JChrRec* 3, no. 2 (1976–1977): 122–27.

_____. *Thy Kingdom Come*. Phillipsburg, N.J.: Presbyterian and Reformed, 1971.

Russell, D. S. *Apocalyptic: Ancient and Modern*. Philadelphia: Fortress, 1978.

_____. *The Method and Message of Jewish Apocalyptic*. Philadelphia: Westminster, 1964.

Ryan, Samuel. "Your Kingdom Come." *SEAJT* 21, no. 1 (1980): 69–77.

Samartha, Stanley J., ed. *Faith in the Midst of Other Faiths: Reflections on Dialogue in Community*. Geneva: World Council of Churches, 1977.

_____. "The Kingdom of God in a Religiously Plural World." *EcuR* 32 (1980): 152–65.

Sanders, E. P. *Jesus and Judaism*. Philadelphia: Fortress, 1985.

_____. "Jesus and the Kingdom: The Restoration of Israel and the New People of God." In *Jesus, the Gospels, and the Church: Essays in Honor of William R. Farmer*, ed. E. P. Sanders, 225–39. Macon: Mercer University Press, 1987.

_____. *Judaism: Practice and Belief 63 BCE–66 CE*. Philadelphia: Trinity Press International, 1992.

_____. "New Testament Studies Today." In *Colloquy on New Testament Studies*, edited by Bruce Corley, 11–28. Macon, Ga.: Mercer University Press, 1980.

Sarles, Ken L. "An Appraisal of the Signs and Wonders Movement." *BS* 145 (1988): 57–82.

Saucy, Mark. "Exaltation Christology in Hebrews: What Kind of Reign?" *TrinJ* NS 14 (1993): 41–62.

_____. "The Kingdom-of-God Sayings in Matthew." *BS* 151/602 (1994): 175–97.

Saucy, Robert L. *The Case for Progressive Dispensationalism: The Interface Between Dispensational and Non-Dispensational Theology*. Grand Rapids: Zondervan, 1993.

Sauter, Gerhard. *Zukunft and Verheissung. Das Problem der Zukunft in der gegenwärtigen theologischen und philosophischen Diskussion*. Zürich: Zwingli, 1965.

Savage, Peter. "The Church and Evangelism." In *The New Face of Evangelicalism: An International Symposium on the Lausanne Covenant*, edited by René Padilla, 103–125. Downers Grove, Ill.: InterVarsity Press, 1976.

Schall, James V. *Liberation Theology in Latin America*. San Francisco: Ignatius, 1982.

Schecter, Solomon. *Aspects of Rabbinic Theology: Major Concepts of the Talmud*. New York: Schocken, 1961.

Schleiermacher, Friedrich D. E. *The Christian Faith*. Edited by H. R. Mackintosh and J. S. Stewart. Edinburgh: T & T Clark, 1928.

_____. *Hermeneutics: The Handwritten Manuscripts*. Edited by Heinz Kimmerle. Translated by James Duke and Jack Forstman. American Academy of Religion Texts and Translations 1. Missoula, Mont.: Scholars, 1977.

Schlosser, Jacques. *Le règne de Dieu dans les dits de Jésus*. 2 vols. Études Bibliques. Paris: J. Gabalda, 1980.

Schluter, Michael, and Roy Clements. "Jubilee Institutional Norms: A Middle Way Between Creation Ethics and Kingdom Ethics as the Basis for Christian Political Action." *EvQ* 62, no. 1 (1990): 37–62.

Schmidt, K. L. *TDNT*. S.v. *ekklēsia*.

Schmidt, K. L., Hermann Kleinknecht, Gerhard von Rad, and Karl G. Kuhn. *TDNT*. S.v. *basileus*.

Schmidt, Ludwig. *TRE*. S.v. "Königtum."

Schnackenburg, Rudolf. *The Church in the New Testament*. Freiburg: Herder; London: Burns & Oates, 1965.

_____. *God's Rule and Kingdom*. Translated by John Murray. New York: Herder and Herder, 1963.

_____. *The Gospel According to St. John*. New York: Seabury, 1980.

_____. *Sacramentum Verbi: An Encyclopedia of Biblical Theology*. Edited by Johannes B. Bauer. New York: Herder and Herder, 1970. S. v. "Kingdom of God."

Schreiter, Robert J. *Constructing Local Theologies*. With a foreword by Edward Schillebeeckx. Maryknoll, N.Y.: Orbis, 1986.

Schweitzer, Albert. *The Kingdom of God and Primitive Christianity*. Edited by Ulrich Neuenschwander. Translated by L. A. Garrard. New York: Seabury, 1968.

_____. *The Mystery of the Kingdom of God. The Secret of Jesus' Messiahship and Passion*. Translated with an introduction by Walter Lowrie. New York: Schocken, 1964.

_____. *The Quest of the Historical Jesus: A Critical Study of Its Progress from Reimarus to Wrede.* Translated by W. Montgomery. New York: Macmillan, 1968.

Schweizer, Eduard. *The Good News, According to Mark.* Richmond: John Knox, 1970. 45–46. Quoted in James H. Charlesworth, "The Historical Jesus in Light of Writings Contemporaneous with Him," *ANRW* 25, no. 1: 464.

Schwemer, Anna Maria. "Gott als König und seine Königsherrschaft in den Sabbatliedern aus Qumran." In *Königsherrschaft Gottes und himmlischer Kult im Judentum, Urchristentum, und in der hellenistischen Welt,* edited by Martin Hengel and Anna Maria Schwemer. WUNT 55, 45–118. Tübingen: J. C. B. Mohr (Paul Siebeck), 1991.

Scott, Bernard Brandon. *Jesus, Symbol-Maker for the Kingdom.* Philadelphia: Fortress, 1981.

Scroggs, Robin. "The Sociological Interpretation of the New Testament: The Present State of Research." *NTS* 26 (1980): 164–79.

Seal, Welton, O. Jr. "Norman Perrin and his 'School': Retracing a Pilgrimage." *JStNT* 20 (February 1984): 87–107.

_____. "The Parousia in Mark: A Debate with Norman Perrin and 'His School.'" Ph.D. diss., Union Theological Seminary, 1981.

Segundo, Juan Luis. "Capitalism—Socialism: A Theological Crux." *Concilium* 96 (1974): 78–92.

_____. *Jesus of Nazareth Yesterday and Today.* Vol. 1, *Faith and Ideologies,* translated by John Drury. Maryknoll, N.Y.: Orbis, 1984.

_____. *Jesus of Nazareth Yesterday and Today.* Vol. 2, *The Historical Jesus of the Synoptics,* translated by John Drury. Maryknoll, N.Y.: Orbis, 1985.

_____. *The Liberation of Theology.* Maryknoll, N.Y.: Orbis, 1976.

_____. *Theology and the Church: A Response to Cardinal Ratzinger and a Warning to the Whole Church.* New York: Winston, 1985.

Sharkey, Michael, ed. *International Theological Commission: Texts and Documents 1969–1985.* With a preface by Joseph Cardinal Ratzinger. San Francisco: Ignatius, 1989.

Sider, Ronald J. *Evangelism, Salvation, and Social Justice.* Bramcote, Notts.: Grove Books, 1977.

Sider, Ronald J., and James Parker III. "How Broad Is Salvation in Scripture?" In *In Word and Deed: Evangelism and Social Responsibility,* edited by Bruce J. Nicholls, 85–108. Grand Rapids: Eerdmans, 1985.

Simon, U. E. "Eternal Life in the Fourth Gospel." In *Studies in the Fourth Gospel.* Edited by F. L. Cross. London: A. R. Mowbray, 1957.

Sjöberg, Erik. *TDNT.* S.v. *pneuma.*

Skydsgaard, Kristen E. "The Church as Mystery and as People of God." In *Dialogue on the Way,* edited by George A. Lindbeck, 145–74. Minneapolis: Augsburg, 1965.

_____. "Kingdom of God and Church." *ScotJT* 4 (1951): 383–97.

Smedes, Lewis B., ed. *Ministry and the Miraculous: A Case Study at Fuller Theological Seminary.* Pasadena, Calif.: Fuller Theological Seminary, 1987.

Smit, D. J. *Dictionary of the Ecumenical Movement.* Edited by Nicholas Lossky et al. Grand Rapids: Eerdmans, 1991. S.v. "Kingdom of God."

Smith, D. M. "A Review of Marcus Borg, *Jesus: A New Vision.*" *Forum* 5, no. 4 (1989): 71–82.

Smith, L. D. "An Awakening Conscience: The Changing Response of American Evangelicals Toward World Poverty." Ph.D. diss., The American University, 1986.

Smith, Morton. *Jesus the Magician.* New York: Harper & Row, 1978.

Sobrino, Jon. *Christology at the Crossroads.* Translated by John Drury. Maryknoll, N.Y.: Orbis, 1978.

_____. "La centralidad del 'Reino de Dios' en la teología de la liberacíon." *Revista Latinamericana de Teología* (San Salvador) (September–December 1986): 248–65.

Sölle, Dorothee. *Political Theology.* Translated by John Shelley. Philadelphia: Fortress, 1974.

_____. "Resistance: Toward a First World Theology." *ChrC* 39 (July 1979): 178–82.

Spark, John A. "Biblical Law: The Reconstruction of the Criminal Law: Retribution Revived." *JChrRec* 3, no. 2 (1976–1977): 128–38.

Springer, Kevin, ed. *Power Encounters Among Christians in the Western World.* San Francisco: Harper & Row, 1988.

Stähelin, Ernst. *Die Verkündigung des Reiches Gottes in der Kirche Jesu Christi. Zeugnisse aus allen Jahrhunderten und allen Konfessionen.* 7 vols. Basel: Friedrich Reinhardt, 1957–1964.

Staniloae, Dumitru. "The Mystery of the Church." In *Church Kingdom World: The Church as Mystery and Prophetic Sign,* edited by Gennadios Limouris, 50–57. Geneva: World Council of Churches, 1986.

Stanley, Brian. "Evangelical Social and Political Ethics: An Historical Perspective." *EvQ* 62, no. 1 (1990): 19–36.

Stanton, G. N. *The Gospels and Jesus.* Oxford: Oxford University Press, 1989.

Stein. Robert H. "The 'Criteria' for Authenticity." In *Studies of History and Tradition in the Four Gospels,* edited by R. T. France and D. Wenham. Gospel Perspectives 1. 225–63. Sheffield, JSOT, 1980.

Stevenson, Eileen. "Some Insights from the Sociology of Religion in the Origin and Development of the Early Christian Church." *ExpTim* 90 (1979): 300–5.

Stoldt, Hans–Herbert. *History and Criticism of the Marcan Hypothesis.* Translated and edited by Donald Niewyk. Macon, Ga.: Mercer University Press, 1980.

Strack, Hermann L., and Paul Billerbeck. *Kommentar Zum Neuen Testament: Aus Talmud und Midrasch.* Munich: C. H. Beck, 1922–1928.

Sturm, Douglas. "Praxis and Promise: On the Ethics of Political Theology." *Ethics* 92 (July 1992): 733–50.

Sullivan, Clayton. *Rethinking Realized Eschatology.* Macon, Ga.: Mercer University Press, 1988.

Suro, Robert. "The Writing of an Encyclical." In *Aspiring to Freedom: Commentaries on John Paul II's Encyclical 'Social Concerns,'* edited by Kenneth A. Myers, 159–69. Grand Rapids: Eerdmans, 1988.

Swaggert, Jimmy. "The Coming Kingdom." *Manna* 1, no. 1 (1988): 3–8.

Talbert, Charles H., ed. *Reimarus: Fragments.* Translated by Ralph S. Fraser. Philadelphia: Fortress, 1970.

Tanner, Norman P., ed. *Decrees of the Ecumenical Councils.* Original text established by G. Alberigo et al. Vol. 2, *Trent to Vatican II.* London: Sheed and Ward; Georgetown: Georgetown University Press, 1990.

Tertullian, Quintus Septimus. *De exhortatione castitatis.* In *MPL.* Vol. 2, *Patrologiae Tomus II. Quinti Septimii Florentis Tertulliani tomus secunda. Pars secunda.*

_____. *De jejuniis.* In *MPL.* Vol. 2, *Patrologiae Tomus II. Quinti Septimii Florentis Tertulliani tomus secunda. Pars secunda.*

The Challenge of Peace: God's Promise and Our Response. A Pastoral Letter on War and Peace. Washington, D.C.: United States Catholic Conference, 1983.

Theissen, Gerd. "'Wir haben alles verlassen' (MC. X.28). Nachfolge und soziale Entwurzelung in der jüdisch-palästinischen Gesellschaft des 1. Jahrhunderts n. Chr." *NovT* 19 (1977): 161–96.

_____. "Historical Skepticism and the Criteria of Jesus Research *or* My Attempt to Leap Across Lessing's Yawning Gulf." *SJT* 49, no. 2 (1996): 147–76.

Thiselton, Anthony C. "The New Hermeneutic." In *New Testament Interpretation,* edited by I. Howard Marshall, 308–33. Grand Rapids: Eerdmans, 1977.

_____. *New Horizons in Hermeneutics: The Theory and Practice of Transforming Biblical Reading.* Grand Rapids: Zondervan, 1992.

_____. *The Two Horizons: New Testament Hermeneutics and Philosophical Description.* Grand Rapids: Eerdmans, 1980.

Thomas, Richard W. "The Meaning of the Terms 'Life' and 'Death' in the Fourth Gospel and in Paul." *ScotJT* 21 (1968): 199–212.

Thompson, Marianne Meye. "Eternal Life in the Gospel of John." *Ex Auditu* 5 (1989): 35–55.

Turner, Max. "The Spirit and the Power of Jesus' Miracles in the Lucan Conception." *NovT* 33:2 (1991): 124–52.

Tuttle, H. N. *Wilhelm Dilthey's Philosophy of Historical Understanding: A Critical Analysis.* Leiden: E. J. Brill, 1969.

Van Der Loos, Hendrick. *The Miracles of Jesus.* Leiden: E. J. Brill, 1965.

Vermes, Geza. *Jesus and the World of Judaism*. Philadelphia: Fortress, 1983.

_____. *Jesus the Jew: A Historian's Reading of the Gospels*. New York: Macmillan, 1973; rev. ed. Philadelphia: Fortress, 1981.

_____. *The Religion of Jesus the Jew*. Philadelphia: Fortress, 1993.

Via, Dan O. "Kingdom and Parable: The Search for a New Grasp of Symbol, Metaphor, and Myth." *Interp* 31 (1977): 181–83.

_____. *The Parables: Their Literary and Existential Dimension*. Philadelphia: Fortress, 1967.

Vielhauer, P. *Gottesreich und Menschensohn in der Verkündigung Jesu. Aufsätze zum Neuen Testament*. Munich: Christian Kaiser, 1965.

Vincent, Ph. I. "Les 'theologies de la liberation.'" *NRT* 98 (1976): 109–25.

Visser T' Hooft, Willem Adolf. "The General Ecumenical Development Since 1948." In *The Ecumenical Advance: A History of the Ecumenical Movement*, edited by Harold E. Frey. Vol. 2, *1948–1968*, 1–26. Philadelphia: Westminster, 1970.

_____. "The Genesis of the World Council of Churches." In *The Ecumenical Advance: A History of the Ecumenical Movement*. Vol. 1, *1517–1948*, edited by Ruth Rouse and Stephen Charles Neill. 2d ed. with rev. bibliography, 697–724. Philadelphia: Westminster, 1967.

_____. "The Mandate of the Ecumenical Movement." In *The Uppsala Report 1968: Official Report of the Fourth Assembly of the World Council of Churches Uppsala July 4–20, 1968*, edited by Norman Goodall, 313–23. Geneva: World Council of Churches, 1968.

_____., ed. *The Evanston Report: The Second Assembly of the World Council of Churches 1954*. New York: Harper & Brothers, 1955.

Vivas, Eliseo. *The Artistic Transaction*. Columbus: Ohio State University Press, 1963.

_____. *D. H. Lawrence: The Failure and Triumph of Art*. Evanston, Ill.: Northwestern University, 1960.

Viviano, B. T. *The Kingdom of God in History*. Wilmington: Michael Glazier, 1988.

_____. "The Kingdom of God in the Qumran Literature." In *The Kingdom of God in Twentieth-Century Interpretation*, edited by Wendell Willis, 97–107. Peabody, Mass.: Hendrickson, 1987.

Vree, Dale. *On Synthesizing Marxism and Christianity*. New York: John Wiley, 1976.

Wainwright, Geoffrey. *Eucharist and Eschatology*. New York: Oxford University Press, 1981.

Walker, W. O. "The Son of Man: Some Recent Developments." *CBQ* 45 (1983): 584–607.

Walther, Christian. *Typen des Reich-Gottes Verständnisse*. Munich: Christian Kaiser, 1961.

Walton, Robert C. "Jürgen Moltmann's Theology of Hope." In *Liberation Theology*, edited by Ronald H. Nash, 139–86. Milford, Mich.: Mott Media, 1984.

Webb, Pauline M. "Salvation Today." *This Month* 33 (December 1972): 1–3.

Weigel, "The New, New Things: Pope John Paul II on Human Freedom." *American Purpose* (May–June, 1991): 33. Quoted in Humberto Belli and Ronald H. Nash, *Beyond Liberation Theology* (Grand Rapids: Baker, 1992), 54.

Weiss, Johannes. *Jesus' Proclamation of the Kingdom of God.* Translated and edited by Richard H. Hiers and David L. Holland. Philadelphia: Fortress, 1971.

_____. *Die Predigt Jesu vom Reich Gottes.* Göttingen: Vandenhoeck & Ruprecht, 1892.

Wells, William W. *Welcome to the Family: An Introduction to Evangelical Christianity.* Downers Grove, Ill.: InterVarsity Press, 1979.

Wenham, David, and Craig Blomberg, eds. *Gospel Perspectives 6: The Miracles of Jesus.* Sheffield: JSOT, 1986.

West, Delno C., and Sandra Zimdars-Schwartz. *Joachim of Fiore.* Bloomington, Ind.: Indiana University Press, 1983.

Wheelwright, Philip. *The Burning Fountain.* Bloomington: Indiana University Press, 1968.

_____. *Metaphor and Reality.* Bloomington: Indiana University Press, 1962.

Wiebe, Ben. "Interpretation and Historical Criticism: Jürgen Moltmann." *RestQ* 24 (1981): 155–66.

Wilcox, Max. "Jesus in the Light of His Jewish Environment." *ANRW.* 25, no. 1. Edited by W. Haase (1982): 131–95.

Wilder, Amos. "Albert Schweitzer and the New Testament." In *In Albert Schweitzer's Realms,* edited by A. A. Roback. Cambridge, Mass.: Sci-Art, 1962.

_____. *The Bible and the Literary Critic.* Philadelphia: Fortress, 1991.

_____. "Eschatological Imagery and Earthly Circumstance." *NTS* 5 (1958): 229–45.

_____. *Eschatology and Ethics in the Teaching of Jesus.* New York: Harper and Brothers, 1939; reprint of rev. ed. 1950. Westport, Conn.: Greenwood, 1978.

_____. Foreword to *The Kingdom of God in Twentieth-Century Interpretation,* edited by Wendell Willis, vii–x. Peabody, Mass.: Hendrickson, 1987.

_____. *Jesus' Parables and the War of Myths: Essays on Imagination in the Scripture.* Edited by J. Breech. Philadelphia: Fortress, 1982.

_____. "Kerygma, Eschatology, and Social Ethics." In *The Background of the New Testament and Its Eschatology,* edited by W. D. Davies and David Daube, 509–36. Cambridge: Cambridge University Press, 1954; reprint, Facet Books Social Ethics Series 12. Philadelphia: Fortress, 1966.

_____. *The Language of the Gospel: Early Christian Rhetoric.* New York: Harper & Row, 1964; reissued as *Early Christian Rhetoric: The Language of the Gospel.* Cambridge, Mass.: Harvard University Press, 1971.

_____. "New Testament Hermeneutics Today." In *Current Issues in New Testament Interpretation,* edited by W. Klassen and G. F. Snyder, 38–52. New York: Harper, 1962.

_____. "Scholars, Theologians and Ancient Rhetoric." SBL Presidential Address, 1955. *JBL* 75 (1956): 1–11.

_____. "*Semeia* An Experimental Journal for Biblical Criticism: An Introduction." *Semeia* 1 (1974): 1–16.

_____. "The Word as Address and the Word as Meaning." In *The New Hermeneutic,* edited by J. M. Robinson and J. Cobb. 198–218. New York: Harper, 1964.

Williams, Don. *Signs, Wonders and the Kingdom of God: A Biblical Guide for the Reluctant Skeptic.* Ann Arbor, Mich.: Servant, 1989.

Williams, James G. "Neither Here Nor There: Between Wisdom and Apocalyptic in Jesus' Kingdom Sayings." *Forum* 5, no. 2 (1989): 7–30.

Willis, Wendell. "The Discovery of the Eschatological Kingdom: Johannes Weiss and Albert Schweitzer." In *The Kingdom of God in Twentieth-Century Interpretation,* edited by Wendell Willis. Peabody, Mass.: Hendrickson, 1987.

Wimber, John. *Kingdom Come.* Ann Arbor, Mich.: Servant, 1988.

Wimber, John, with Kevin Springer. *Power Evangelism.* San Francisco: Harper & Row, 1986.

Winter, Ralph, ed. *The Evangelical Response to Bangkok.* South Pasadena: William Carey Library, 1973.

Witherington, Ben, III. *The Christology of Jesus.* Minneapolis: Fortress, 1990.

_____. *Jesus, Paul and the End of the World: A Comparative Study of New Testament Eschatology.* Downers Grove, Ill.: InterVarsity Press, 1992.

Wrede, William. "Die Predigt Jesu vom Reiche Gottes." In *Vorträge und Studien.* Tübingen, 1907, 88. Quoted in Helmut Merkel, "Die Gottesherrschaft in der Verkündigung Jesu," in *Königsherrschaft Gottes und himmlischer Kult im Judentum, Urchristentum und in der hellenistischen Welt,* edited by Martin Hengel and Anna Maria Schwemer, WUNT 55 (Tübingen: J. C. B. Mohr [Paul Siebeck], 1991), 124.

Wright, N. Thomas. *Christian Origins and the Question of God.* Vol. 1, *The New Testament and the People of God.* Minneapolis: Fortress, 1992.

Wright, N. Thomas, and Stephen Neill. *The Interpretation of the New Testament 1861–1986.* New York: Oxford University Press, 1988.

Young, F. "A Cloud of Witnesses." In *The Myth of God Incarnate,* edited by J. Hick, 18. London: SCM, 1977. Quoted in G. R. Beasley-Murray, *Jesus and the Kingdom of God* (Grand Rapids: Eerdmans, 1986), x.

Your Kingdom Come: Mission Perspectives: Report on the World Conference on Mission and Evangelism Melbourne, Australia 12–25 May 1980. Geneva: World Council of Churches, 1980.

S C R I P T U R E   I N D E X

AUTHOR INDEX

SUBJECT INDEX

Abrahamic Covenant: 181
Already/Not Yet Consensus: xvii,
 xxviii, xxix, xxx, xxxvi, 18, 21, 160,
 187-195, 255, 262, 277, 290, 304
Angels: 122
Anti-semitism: 224, 225
Apocalypticism: xxii, xxiii, xxvi-xxvii,
 3, 8-9, 46, 62, 63, 74-76, 131, 145,
 147, 150, 155, 188, 218, 313, 336;
 see also Kingdom in
 Intertestamental Literature;
 and language: 118
 and the Jewish War: 102-103, 135
 in Gospels: 134-135
 decline of apocalyptic interpretations: 145, 146
 Jewish Apocalypticism: 107, 113,
 120, 127, 174-175, 179, 188, 254;
 see also Kingdom in
 Intertestamental Literature
Apostolic church:
 and eschatology: 116
 and social action: 257-262, 291
 and the Kingdom: 48, 50, 53-56,
 80, 82, 91, 107, 221-223, 256, 258,
 260-261;
 see also Kingdom of God in the
 Pauline corpus under Rome: 259
 see also Hellenism

Ascension/Exaltation: see Jesus Christ
Base communities: 237, 243;
 see also Liberation Theology
Biblical Theology: 212
Capitalism: 238, 239
CELAM II: 234
CELAM III: 235
Charismatics: 304
Chiliasm/Millennialism: 225, 232,
 299-300
Christology: 168-169, 198, 224, 230,
 233, 246
Church: see also Kingdom of God and
 human activity/social issues
 and Kingdom: 115-116, 266, 268-
 269, 270-271, 285, 286, 292, 293
 under Constantine/Triumphalism:
 224, 225, 230, 234, 267
Congregation for the Doctrine and
 Faith: 236-237, 271
Consistent Eschatology: xxxi, 11, 118,
 159, 165, 166, 171, 281
Contextualization: 244
Counter Reformation: 267
Criteria of Authenticity: 75-76, 192,
 194, 195;
 see also Critical Methodologies
Critical Methodologies:
 Form Criticism: 29, 64, 75, 76,

401

First printed in Great Britain in 2013
By Amazon.co.uk, Ltd., Marston Gate.

l

World Rights, The Feldstein Agency.

The author, Gayle Eileen Curtis
asserts her moral rights to be identified as the author of this work
www.wilfredginge.co.uk

ISBN-13: 978-1482558043

www.thefeldsteinagency.co.uk

1

For Christopher, with all my love

MEMORY SCENTS

BY

GAYLE EILEEN CURTIS

6

Prologue

Norfolk 1950

I don't want another cup of tea or coffee, a sandwich, piece of cake or another person to say to me they are sorry. Sorry for what?

The word sorry, at first, caused quite a lot of confusion in my head. Were they sorry that my daughter had died or that she'd been murdered or that they'd committed the evil deed? How can someone else be sorry for another's death unless they were somehow to blame? I was always led to believe that sorry was used when you had done something wrong. Sorry, sorry, sorry. If I heard it again, I'd be committing murder myself. I'd had my fill of that tiny self satisfying word, especially today.

All I wanted to do was sit in my daughter's bedroom on my own, undisturbed and forgotten about for a few hours. I knew I was being rude, flouting the unwritten laws of funeral etiquette, but I didn't particularly care. All those people downstairs, paying their respects, coping with their own grief as well as contemplating mine; talking in hushed voices as a mark of respect or as if they were frightened of startling the grief stricken.

But what could be more startling than being told your seven year old daughter had been found murdered. Snatched and then strangled. Five minute wonder for a sick perverted killer. To then be told by the police that they were doing everything they

7

could. Well, everything they could didn't include bringing my daughter back alive, exactly as she was, untouched, innocent.

The last few weeks had been filled with statements and remarks, as if I wasn't there or too fragile to have a conversation with. And sometimes it was as if I was devoid of feelings, as our home had been searched, family and close friends questioned.

And now the day had come to bury our child. I felt like I'd reached a milestone, the top of the mountain. I knew that getting to this day and enduring the funeral meant I could then grant myself this time. It had become a long awaited piece of light relief. A tiny spark, albeit minute, of something to look forward to. I desperately wanted to award myself this time to steal away, to lie in my daughter's bed, her childlike sanctuary, and interact with no one but me; wishing I was an infant again.

I needed to still my mind, face my thoughts. I'd cringed at every stark, raw vision as it entered my head. It had dawned on me that it would be better to make an attempt to face them. They were something I would have to live with for the rest of my life. It was like being given a box full of films that you had to carry around with you forever. Like another limb, a useless, damaged, painful one.

My thoughts flittered from the funeral, to her tiny body lying amongst the leaves. Grey skin, tinged with blue. Her body distorted, broken like a discarded doll. The top half of her body exposed, apart from her grey cardigan, just covering her arms. 'Remember me' etched on her torso. Her skin purple and livid where the cuts had been made, with a kitchen knife, the police had said.

I hadn't been to see where they'd found her; I was already haunted by the visions in my imagination. The scenarios kept turning in my troubled head, tormenting myself, wanting to feel every bit of it. Surrender to the nightmare, which is what I'd stolen myself away for, to completely wallow in the horror of it all. In the hope that I would come out the other side a bit stronger and saner? My logic here was to do with knowing that bottling things up made everything so much worse and letting the floodgates open would make me feel so much better. It was a long shot and one that I knew wouldn't leave me feeling much different than what I felt now. But a fraction of relief was far better than none at all. So my logic was to face all those abhorrent visions in my head, fearlessly and courageously, with the hope that I would somehow desensitize it all.

I sighed as my mind drifted to the image of her lying in her coffin, her tiny hands clasped peacefully across her chest. A far cry, I'm sure, from the violent position that she'd been found in. I'd clasped her cold, lifeless little hands and become obsessed with them thereafter. Any parents most frequent memories are of their child's hands, from birth onwards. There are so many photographic memories of them completing new activities as they learn and grow, relying on those funny little spindles to guide them and keep them safe. They are a part of them learning so many new things, touching and feeling their way forward. The best memory of those little hands for me was of them simply holding mine. The night before her funeral I'd woken up crying and felt a tiny hand in mine and saw the outline of a small figure beside me in the dark. I wasn't dreaming; I'd felt her presence; saw it with the help of the moonlight through the window.

I sighed again, kicked off my shoes and sat heavily on the bed. I stood up again, lifting my skirt, hitching my nylons down over my legs and feet. I loved that feeling of freedom after I'd been trussed up in layers and then crippled my feet in high heels. If only everything could be so easily released. So trivial a thought, when my mind rapidly moved back to the reality of the situation and what lay ahead of me. I swung my legs on to the bed and wriggled my toes. I leaned back on the wooden head board and clasped my hands together as they rested on my lap. I pulled her dusky pink eiderdown over my legs, tucking it under my thighs, wanting to feel cocooned, comforted. A thought dawned on me and I pulled my arm behind me and under her pillow. There they were, still folded, waiting for her return home to wear for bed; her tiny soft pink checked pyjamas. Waiting patiently to be filled and warmed up. I pulled them out and buried my face in the gentle fabric and took in the scent left by my daughter.

As I leant back on the head board, tears flooding my eyes again, I felt something jutting in my back. I let my hand search under the pillow and pulled out a book. A book that we were reading together – *Alice's Adventures in Wonderland* – she'd marked the page by folding it over at the corner, something I often scolded her for. I stared at the book for quite some time, running my fingers over the silver lettering that had been embossed in the pink hardback cover. It was ironic really that we should be sharing this fictional little girl's adventure together when, so abruptly, we had arrived at a crossroads where my daughter was taken down another path, a different journey to mine. Somewhere I wasn't permitted to go. She'd woken up that day not expecting to go on that particular adventure much like I'm sure Alice had when she'd fallen down the rabbit hole. Only, my daughter's adventure was over and wasn't anything like the one in the book we had been reading.

I gripped the book and her pyjamas, savouring the scent left behind. It conjured up a clear, strong picture of her in my mind, and I wanted to stay there forever. I didn't want to cry dramatically or rock backwards and forwards with my head in my hands. I just wanted to step off the world for a while and sit with the knowledge that my daughter had been murdered. That she would never be coming back. Growing up or growing old. She had ceased to exist. A decision I had no power over, one that had been taken out of my hands and placed in the palms of another.

CHAPTER ONE

Norfolk 1989

Dear Alice,

I don't know why I'm writing you this letter but I am at a loss to know what to do. It's a year to the day that you went missing from our lives, and we don't even know where you are or what has happened to you.

The world around us appears to have creaked back into action and life goes on, but not for us my darling. I feel that if I move on, I'll somehow be accepting your fate, and I can't bear to think what that might be.

We haven't touched your bedroom since you left, but to clean it and keep it tidy. I've washed your bed linen every week as normal so that it's nice and fresh for when you come home.

You're getting quite a collection of Jackie magazines now; I've been and fetched them every week from the village shop as you would have done. I've often thought that I might bump into you there doing the same as me. But that would be silly because you would have come home to us if that was the case.

You must have changed a lot in a year; you'll be fifteen in a couple of months and it doesn't seem possible. Daddy and I often try to imagine what you would look like now and if we would even recognise you. But that's a silly thing to think because we couldn't mistake our beautiful girl.

I can't express to you darling how much we all miss you and how we've felt our hearts breaking every single day.

Loving you always

Mummy xxx

Norfolk 1998

Chrissie lugged another box from the sitting room and dumped it into the kitchen of her new home. She was fatigued and almost at the point of giving up for the day. She could feel every tendon and muscle in her body and her feet were buzzing and sore from all the physical wear and tear.

She linked her fingers behind her back and stretched her arms feeling the immense relief right through to her bones. Deciding it was time for a break she made a cup of coffee and went out into the garden to survey the property she'd bought just over a week ago. Chrissie walked across the grass to sit on an old swing that was hanging from an apple tree. She swung aimlessly round causing her coffee to splash down the side of the mug. She studied the Norfolk red brick of the cottage that seemed to have lost its lacklustre since she'd very first viewed it. A familiar feeling of knowing the house filtered through her causing an uneasy detachment from her present life. A fluttering of fear stirred in the pit of her stomach and she wasn't sure if it was regret or just apprehension at her new circumstances. It had been a huge decision to move four hours away from the area she'd grown up in; leaving her family and friends behind. Divorce had been the trigger causing her to become aware that she needed to get out of her comfort zone and embrace the unexpected. She'd barely given it much thought apart from the fact that she'd be moving so far away from her stepchildren, family and friends. It helped that she had moved to a place where she'd spent all her childhood holidays with her parents and siblings.

Chrissie yawned, threw the last dregs of her coffee on to the grass and made her way into the house. She wanted to get some more boxes unpacked and pictures up to give the house more of a homely feel. As she walked through the small cottage door the darkness covered her whole being like misty rain. She hadn't realised how quickly it had turned dusk. It had blanketed the cottage in a thick, sad, darkness, making it quite apparent that there had been no life in it for quite some time. Chrissie wasn't fazed by this, as she'd gotten used to being on her own. What with the divorce and all the dark lonely evenings that had brought her. And anyway she wasn't alone; she had her three beautiful cats.

After an hour of mainly moving items from one room to another, unable to make a decision about where to put anything, she lit candles and turned the oven on to heat up some supper. Cats were fed, dinner underway and the television was flickering in the background and suddenly the house seemed to smile, glad of the company.

Eventually, after some supper and half an hour spent arranging her bedroom, Chrissie snuggled down with Lewis, Harry, and Rosie, her somewhat confused and unsettled felines, and slipped into a deep and peaceful sleep.

The morning appeared as quite a shock and Chrissie woke up wondering where she was and where she'd been. The night had passed in a flash with lots of dreams full of faces she didn't recognise, which were now drifting from her mind. They swirled like steam, disappearing into the atmosphere as she pulled herself into an upright position in the bed.

She swung her still aching body out from underneath the warm quilt and threw on a comfy sweater over her pyjamas. She stretched and made her way down the stairs to make a hot drink.

The house felt different this morning, slightly drab, and there was a strong cloying smell of damp. Outside wasn't much better, but then it was to be expected being five hundred yards from the sea.

She tried not to allow the atmosphere to affect her and decided over a cup of coffee that she would spend the day making the sitting room cosy and homely. Hopefully then she could get some work done and concentrate on the new book she'd just started writing.

Chrissie opened the kitchen door to the garden and breathed in the salty, fresh cold air. Lewis wound his body round her legs as she wandered across the uneven grass, almost tripping her up. She never worried about her cats wandering off, she'd moved so many times and they were so fond of her that they just accepted their new surroundings. Chrissie bent down and picked him up with one hand. He immediately climbed onto her shoulders and curled his silky black body around the back of her neck. Slightly stooped, she continued her exploration of the garden. She reached some thick undergrowth that she pushed her way through. Lewis chirruped and chattered to her as she eventually came across a wooded area that led to a narrow stream. She'd seen it before when she'd viewed the property, but not from this end of the garden. It was just as beautiful as she had remembered, even though it was an overcast day. Through the evenly spaced trees the sparkling stream flowed, the field acting as an embankment. The views were breathtaking and she stood for many minutes taking it all in, as Lewis purred in her ear.

Chrissie looked around her and noticed a small ivy covered brick building through the trees. Intrigued, she made her way across the soft undergrowth towards the odd looking building. On closer inspection it looked very much like a miniature chapel, mainly because of its pointed roof. Most of the tiles were missing and there were lots of saplings growing out of it. Above the door was a small hole cut in the brick. Inside it contained a discoloured old bell which had taken on the shade of the concrete it was set in.

As Chrissie approached the unhinged cracked wooden door, the temperature seemed to plummet, which made her pause. She put it down to her overactive imagination; she had a habit of thinking too much, which was what made her such a good novelist. But in certain circumstances it occasionally frightened her out of her wits. Being in a wooded area in front of a derelict building was causing a whisper of a chill to creep over her skin. She stopped for a second to focus her mind to the fact that she was standing in the bottom of her garden in front of an old brick shed. The house and garden she'd viewed and fallen madly in love with all those weeks ago

Pausing dispersed her irrational feelings and she began to move again towards the rickety old door. It was definitely colder and there seemed to be complete silence, as if someone had pressed a switch and turned off the countryside. Even Lewis had stopped purring. She felt his body tighten around her neck and a soft growl was emanating from the pit of his throat. This only caused her senses to heighten again as she felt Jack Frost tip toeing up her spine. However freaked out she was, she still had a need to find out what was behind the door, knowing that would then stop all this silliness. After all, it was just an old shed and Lewis was only picking up on her irrational fear. But Lewis continued his growl and had started to sit up, digging his claws into her shoulder. Chrissie reached her hand up to stroke him but he ducked from it, his big green eyes like marbles, intent on staring at the shed door.

As she pushed the door with her foot and her hand, it was all too much for him and he leapt from her back growling and hissing. Chrissie flinched at his claws leaving her shoulders; her skin prickled with goose-bumps. She peered inside the shed, her heart was pounding and every hair on her arms was standing to attention. As her eyes got used to the light all she could see was an empty building with a few young trees sprouting out of the top. The floor was made up of soil, which would explain the cold damp feeling in the air. As she strained her eyes to the back of the building, she became aware of some piles of logs but that was all she could see. She had a sudden need to look behind her, which only revealed the wooded area, just as still as it was before. It was as if it had been pulling faces at her behind her back and she'd almost caught it.

"It's just an old wood shed," she muttered to herself over and over again as her body relaxed and her heart slowed down. She could feel a sweat flashing all over her body and a warm heat rising up her face as she walked away and headed back to the house. Lewis had completely deserted her and she cursed him as she gingerly made her way across the garden. She kept thinking how silly it was to get in such a tizzy over a stupid old wood shed. But she was walking quicker than normal, eager to get inside and close the door. What a drama over nothing. But

19

even though she was telling herself this, there was something niggling in the cellar of her mind. There had been a strange familiarity about going into that shed, a flash of a memory, a smell, and a feeling that she couldn't quite grasp. Whatever it was, it wasn't sitting very well with her. She physically shuddered as if to mentally shake the feeling off and steered her mind to emptying boxes and heading back towards the house.

As she made her way through the wooded area and back to the bumpy lawn, she glanced up at the cottage and as she did so she lost her footing on the uneven grass and stumbled forward onto her hands. On pushing herself up from the ground her vision had flashed across the front of the cottage and in that split second she saw a small figure of a child, standing on the doorstep, and she almost stumbled forward again, as she looked back at it. But when she did so, there was nothing there. Having composed her balance, Chrissie stood still on the grass and stared, then looked around her. Then stared again. Icicles dripped down her back and a sick feeling crept through her stomach and into her heart. This wasn't how she'd imagined it. She hadn't even got through a month in her new home and she was already feeling frightened and homesick.

Chrissie sat on the damp grass for a few minutes while she rationalized her mind. She didn't care for the fact that the wetness from the ground was seeping through her trousers. She was more concerned about how tired and stressed she appeared to be and what a huge factor it was playing in all of this. She felt a bit like a child refusing to give in to exhaustion. But she didn't want to kid herself. Moving house was supposed to be one of the most stressful things you could go through in your life. Along with getting divorced. She knew perfectly well what stress could do to a tired mind and body.

Feeling newly composed, she put it all down to the fact that she'd frightened herself in the wood shed. She rolled over onto her knees to make it easier to stand up. Taking a deep breath and feeling much better she stomped back in the house and began unpacking boxes. It took her a while to settle to it, and there remained an obsessive urge to keep looking behind her. But she turned the radio on and erratically hummed her way through it until the atmosphere seemed to have lifted. The problem was that however much Chrissie tried to convince herself that the figure hadn't existed, the more the little child became clearer in her head. She kept seeing flashes of a little girl in the cinema of her mind, with straggly bobbed dirty blonde hair, wearing a smock style dress covered in a loud pink and turquoise pattern with a pinafore. Not dissimilar to the type of thing she had worn as a child. But this little girl was barefoot and very dirty. There was also something peculiar about her eyes, but Chrissie hadn't been close enough to see properly. She pushed the vision away and busied herself, until a creek from the front door made her gasp and jump at the same time.

"Oh sorry, I didn't mean to frighten you!" said a friendly faced woman who was looking round the door.

"I live in the white cottage down the track, the Old Dairy? We're your most immediate neighbours, my husband Tim and I, albeit two hundred yards or so away. I'm Grace. I just wanted to say hello and see if there was anything you needed. I am so sorry; I gave you quite a fright didn't I?"

"Gosh, sorry…come in, come in…I'm just a bit jumpy today. Think it's just the move and everything" replied Chrissie, getting her breath back and feeling relieved that the woman standing in the doorway was actually a real solid human being.

"How are you settling in? You've made a lot of progress, seeing as you only arrived last week." Grace said looking around at the already cosy sitting room.

Chrissie could tell that she'd moved into a typical village where she presumed no one missed a thing. She decided to be friendly but not reveal too much.

"Well, not really but I'm getting there. Would you like a cup of tea or coffee? I'm Chrissie by the way."

"Oh… um… yes that would be nice, as long as I'm not stopping you. I did just pop by to say hello and see if you needed anything."

"Not at all, I'd be glad of a break to be honest."
They stepped into the garden while the kettle was boiling and chatted as if they'd known one another for years.

"I tell you what? I've got a nice bottle of wine in the fridge…."

"That'd be nice, but it's a bit early isn't it…?" Grace said glancing at her watch.

"No! It's Saturday afternoon and I haven't celebrated my moving in yet."

"Ok, why not…"

Chrissie smiled at the warm amiable lady who she knew would become her first friend in the village. Maybe she was just being friendly and not the nosy neighbour that Chrissie had first judged her to be.

Chrissie tied back her straggling brown hair with a band that she had wrapped around her wrist and went to the kitchen to get the drinks. Grace followed her.

"So how are you finding this strange old house?"

Chrissie frowned at her and then smiled. She had a lovely warm face with small features apart from her soft brown eyes, which were huge and accentuated by her blonde hair. In fact she was extremely tiny in form, Chrissie realised as she took in the physical outline of her new companion. She reminded her of her mother a little bit; she was about the same age.

"Sorry, I didn't mean strange…because it's lovely, but…" Grace said, trying to recover herself.

"Its fine," Chrissie raised her hand to reassure the nervous woman, "I know exactly what you mean. It is strange but carries a lovely charm with it. Let's go back outside and enjoy the last of the summer weather."

They chatted like old friends once Grace had relaxed and Chrissie was glad of the company. It seemed to lift the spirit of the whole house and garden. It was almost dark by the time Grace left and they'd drunk a whole bottle of wine.

"I better get back; I only popped out for five minutes."

"I'm sorry it's my fault, enticing you with white wine! Will your husband be worried?'

"No, he won't be back yet, he's gone on one of his fishing trips with his friends and afterwards they always end up in the local pub. Which reminds me. Most Sundays we all pop there at lunch time for a few drinks and sometimes lunch, for whoever can't be bothered to cook. Do you fancy joining us? Get you properly ensconced in the village?"

"Yeah...I'd like that, thank you, that's really kind."

They hugged each other and then said their farewells feeling warm and light-hearted at the prospect of their new friendship. Chrissie pulled her cardigan tightly around her and wandered back into the house. She really felt like they'd picked up where they left off. Then she realised what she had just thought. Left off from where? They'd only just met. It had suddenly turned cold and feeling slightly uneasy again, Chrissie wanted to get the lamps and the television on in the house before her imagination got the better of her again.

CHAPTER TWO

Norfolk 1982

Lucy cycled her usual route she followed at the same time every day to the village shop. The sun had crept through the clouds and was warming the freshly sprinkled rain. The dirty spray from her bicycle wheels was soaking her white socks and splattering muddy water up her shins. She marvelled at the colours reflecting off everything and how sparkly everywhere looked, as it always does when the sun arrives after the rain.

Lucy smiled to herself as she thought about the youth disco she was going to that night. She couldn't believe her Mother had agreed to let her go. She was so protective of her and at fourteen she was beginning to develop a more social personality and she'd wanted her to loosen the apron strings. With her head full of outfits and friends she wasn't concentrating on her bicycle when the tyre burst and caused her to come off the quiet country road and skid into a field. For a few seconds the world seemed to turn upside down.

Once everything stopped moving and she managed to untangle herself from her slightly mangled bike Lucy was able survey the damage. A few bruises were appearing on her grazed legs and there was a throbbing in her elbow, which she had landed on.

But this was nothing in comparison to what she would look like in a few hours time. Unfortunately, while Lucy was examining the cut on her arm, she was unaware of the gloved black figure approaching her. Or the rope and sack they were carrying or the red car that she would be bundled into, that was parked in the field behind the hedge.

There wasn't much of a struggle, Lucy was very slight and being caught unawares hadn't given her much of a chance.

Her bicycle was neatly leant up against the hedge, out of view of the road, and the rain began to pour again, washing away any trace of Lucy on the muddy track.

*

Norfolk 1998

Grace was comfortably ensconced in her favourite tatty armchair in the kitchen, staring at the dead and empty fire place. A draft was occasionally circling her feet and scuffing up the ashes in the grate. She was falling into the depths of her mind, like a deep sea diver moving softly through the chilling water. Grace's thoughts were becoming colder and colder as time ticked on. Images of children intruded her mind, pricking her conscience and sending a wave of pain across her heart.

The sound of her husband Tim coming through the old cracked latch door brought her quickly back to the surface, giving her the emotional bends. He turned on the kitchen light causing her to squint and jolt her mind back into the present.

"Whatever are you doing sitting in the dark like that? You almost gave me a fright." he said, resting both hands on the arms of her chair and leaning in to look at her perfectly formed, childlike face.

Grace could smell the warm deep scent of rum on his breath and her stomach turned in revulsion as the bristles of his grey moustache kissed her on the lips.

Tim pulled away from her and studied her face, just in time for her to plaster her usual well practiced false smile on.

"You alright gal?"

"Yep, I'm fine. I was just out visiting our new neighbour and thought I'd have five minutes in the chair when I got back. I must have nodded off; too much wine I should expect. You know what that does to me," she said, scraping her chair back across the rickety stone floor, causing him to move away from her. She pushed passed him and busied herself with the supper.

"Get on well did you?"

"Yes, we did actually. She's really nice."

"Good for you. What's for supper? I'm starving!" he said, hanging his coat up behind the door and wandering into the sitting room to put the telly on.

"I'm making a curry," Grace called after him.

And that was pretty much the end of their conversation for the rest of the evening. Grace's hatred towards him had simmered in the pit of her stomach for over a year. She'd not liked him much after thirty years of being treated like a second class citizen and having to put up with his selfish, tedious ways, although this wasn't what had caused her hatred towards him. But her feelings were beginning to bubble dangerously close to the surface. As she prepared the supper, she tried to get a grip of herself and her thoughts. Meeting Chrissie had unsettled her for some reason. Her face was all too familiar and it had brought back flashes of the past. She poured herself another glass of wine; the only thing that would get her comfortably through another excruciating evening with Tim.

It had taken all the will she had not to walk out on him almost a year ago, but Grace felt that she could do a better job if she stayed. She'd come so far. Having to share a bed with him, a table, even a drink; it all repulsed every cell of her body. But she was going to have her revenge and get away with it because like everything else in Grace's life, when she set her mind to do something she made sure she carried it out.

Unfortunately, Grace hadn't discovered he was having an affair or that he had a secret life with someone else. But a different personality, that involved children. She'd found out that Tim was a murderer, a child killer in fact. It wasn't information she was unsure of, and it certainly wasn't something you discovered about your partner every day. She only wished he had been having an affair. That was the grim reality Grace had discovered about him over a year ago. And it didn't matter how much she thought about it or pondered over it, it was still there, set in stone because she couldn't turn back the clock and erase the irreversible damage that he'd caused.

*

Dear Alice,

Daddy is talking about us having a holiday in Spain. He says we need to get away and that we can't stay here forever, hoping that you'll walk through the front door. I don't want to go but there is a part of me that thinks we may feel differently after a holiday. I've barely been out since you left for fear of missing you, but maybe he's right. Are you really going to walk through the door after ten years?

I've spent all this time dreaming of it, imagining you every day, opening that door and shouting your greetings. I've even imagined you as you would be now, grown up. Your beautiful blonde hair stylishly cut; stopping in on your way home from work to tell us about your day. Every day I wake up and go to the window...but you're never there.

I'm sorry darling; I promised I wouldn't get maudlin in my letters to you.

Daddy painted your bedroom last weekend in a gorgeous shade of apple green. We've put everything back where it was but we wanted to give it a spring clean because it was getting a bit dusty in there.

I've been thinking about starting an art course to try and pick up my painting again. I've found a really good home studies course, but Daddy says I'd have to go to college to do it properly and you know how I feel about going out to new places. I can just about cope with visiting Nana and Granddad at the retirement home, let alone anything else. He thinks I'd benefit more from the course if I went to college and mixed with other people. I'll think about it a bit longer.

Nana and Granddad are settling in well by the way and getting used to their new surroundings. They're still arguing as much as ever! Granddad says he's going to buy his own microwave meals because he hates the food there and thinks the wardens are trying to poison him.

That's all my news for now my beautiful darling and I'll write again soon.

Loving you always – Mummy

*

NORFOLK 1998

Tim sniffed hard at the small child's T-shirt that he had screwed up in his hands and then took another swig of his rum bottle. Even though the item of clothing smelt of the sheds that it had lived in for fifteen or more years, he could still occasionally catch a whiff of the child's smell that he so adored. He had always been fascinated by the smell of children, especially when they lost that baby smell and gained the smell of school and hormones. It comforted and eased him in a way that nothing else could. Everything had a particular scent to Tim and the first thing he did when he discovered something new was to sniff it. He saw it as an invisible label; like looking at an object and observing its colour or shape.

Tim liked nothing more than sitting in his shed with a bottle of rum and reminiscing over his box of souvenirs. They were what he called, his 'memory scents'. He'd thought of this nickname whilst he muttered to himself about all the boxes of children's clothes and toys he had stored one day when he was in his shed. He tried to preserve the scents by putting each one inside a polythene bag, as though he was vacuum packing them. Each time he held one and smelt it, it conjured up memories of the short time he'd spent with that particular child. Tim felt they were celebratory, happy times in his life, filled with excitement and thrills. Another conquest gained through planning and hard

31

work and a pat on the back for not getting caught. The only blessing to each child being dead was that they weren't alive to reflect on the horror that he had put each one through.

The particular child's T-shirt that he was pondering over wasn't one of his favourites. But he always started off with the lower impact items and then ended his session in the shed with the items that had the most recent smells and the most vivid memories.

The T-shirt belonged to one of his earlier victims; a small boy with a strangely angelic face which had captured Tim's attention. Tim didn't know why he'd murdered him; he usually went for girls and grabbing the small boy hadn't been anything sexual. It was in the early days and he put it down to a bit of practice and the fact that six year old Jonathan had been quite happy to talk to him. And quite happy to get into Tim's car and quite happy to go and look at some puppies that didn't exist. Jonathan played along amicably with the game, until he realised what Tim was going to do to him. But to Tim's disappointment he died quite quickly and he put that down to him being small for his age, and not the fact that the frayed rope was extremely tight around Jonathan's neck.

He breathed in deeply and tried to recapture the boy's smell so that he could revel for a little while in that fond memory. But it was becoming distant and it only just triggered a feeling and a memory, like a wasted spark trying to reignite a dead fire. It was slowly being replaced with a musty stale odour and the scent of turpentine which was found in most sheds.

The police had discovered that particular victim, which had been another thrill for Tim. He loved it when they found one of the bodies, but there was also something thrilling about the body they had never uncovered. It was a huge power game to Tim; he'd laid out a knotted web of a puzzle for the police to untangle, with a few prizes here and there. But there was one body he wanted no one to ever find. It made him feel as if he was keeping the game alive. He didn't want the police thinking they'd completed a part of it; he wanted them to be forever wondering, the same as he wanted the families to keep hoping, and then he would revel in what he'd caused when their precious children were found. There was a feeling of tragedy and despair and Tim was so sick and twisted that he absorbed himself in it. He loved watching the families on the television, appealing for anyone with any information to come forward. The feeling of power and adrenaline that rushed through his body was immense. The knowledge that he was the only one who knew what had happened to that particular child. Being the only person in the whole world made him feel like he could rule it.

But there was one family who didn't know what had happened to their little girl. They had a good idea, but Tim got a kick out of the fact that they didn't know for sure.

Alice had been special, partly because she was to be his last victim for the time being and also because she had the strongest scent of all. Alice not only had the scent of a child turning into a teenager but she had traces of her Mother's perfume on her clothes, which reminded Tim of his own Mother.

He often wondered whether this was where he got his urges from; having been brought up by a woman who was one minute over protective and emotionally smothering and then the complete opposite end of the scale; cold, dismissive and distant.

The problem with Tim's box of tricks was that all the items were slowly losing their scent. Even Alice's pretty embroidered cardigan.

A warm exciting feeling began to stir in the pit of Tim's stomach as he screwed the cap on his rum bottle and thought about where his next memory scents would come from.

*

Chrissie ambled down to the local pub at lunchtime on Sunday and felt quite relieved when she spotted Grace in the distance. She didn't fancy entering a close knit village pub on her own. She could just tell it would be one of those pubs where they'd all stop talking, put down their drinks and stare at the stranger who'd dared to enter their domain. She waved frantically and Grace half heartedly raised her hand and nodded in acknowledgement. Chrissie was a bit uncertain as she approached Grace and her husband as to whether she'd made a mistake coming along. Grace seemed a bit subdued and not at all how she'd been yesterday. Chrissie scolded herself for her over-sensitive nature and put it down to it being Sunday and maybe they'd had a late night.

Grace gave Chrissie a brief hug and then introduced her to Tim. He wasn't what Chrissie had expected at all. She'd imagined a large man, the life and soul of the party with evidence of it written on his face. But instead, she was faced with a fairly short person, of not quite medium build, from what she could gather under his checked shirt and jeans, and a full head of floppy salt and pepper hair and a moustache to match. His face was very well lined but not, thought Chrissie, from laughter. His small brown eyes seemed to be dark pools of nothing. As he shook Chrissie's hand he breathed in through his nose, very strongly lifting his head to lock eyes with hers. Chrissie frowned at him and decided he was very strange indeed. She saw Grace watching her face and quickly smiled and exchanged pleasantries with him. Maybe that's why Grace was a bit subdued; having to put up with him, thought Chrissie.

"Are you ok? Is it still alright for me to join you?" Chrissie said as they entered the pub.

"Yes, course it is!" Grace gave Chrissie's arm an affectionate squeeze. "Sorry. I'm a bit subdued today. Had a few more glasses of wine when I got home last night, which I've now decided was not a good idea!"

"I nearly did that," Chrissie laughed, 'but I'd frightened myself so much during the day that I thought I ought to get some supper and myself to bed compos mentis!"

"What did you frighten yourself over?" Grace asked, walking over to a table and pulling out some chairs so that they could all sit down. The pub was empty apart from a couple of regulars in the corner, who they politely said hello to while Tim got the drinks.

"Oh it's nothing I'm sure. Just tiredness I think." Chrissie didn't want to appear like a tall story teller. She wasn't keen on sharing ghost stories with people she didn't know too well, just in case they thought it was a load of rubbish or they were terribly religious and found it offensive.

"I remember now! You nearly jumped out of your skin when I knocked on the door. That didn't look like nothing to me. What had you seen?"

Chrissie relayed her story of the previous day's events to Grace and then reluctantly to Tim who joined them with the drinks half way through.

"Well its obvious why you saw that little girl," said Tim smugly, "it'll be because of that child killer who committed murder in the village, committed offences over quite a long period."

Chrissie and Grace both turned to stare at him, but not for the same reasons.

"What child killer?" asked Chrissie; the tiny hairs on her arms lifting at the words.

"Oh, it was years ago now but there was someone going around the area topping children. Some of them were found not far from the village and one of them was in your garden." Tim said with a slight smirk wavering on his lips.

Chrissie's blue eyes were the size of saucers and she had begun to feel slightly sick.

"Stop it Tim, that's enough!" Grace leaned in his face, the words coming out a bit sharper than she'd meant them to.

"Well someone's bound to tell her sooner or later, it may as well be us," Tim leaned back in his chair with his pint, thoroughly enjoying the attention he was getting, "Yeah, they reckon the one found in your garden was strangled with an old dog chain, very grim business. But as I said it was a very long time ago."

"Just ignore him Chrissie, he's winding you up." Grace tried to dilute the situation. She glared at Tim, unable to believe how cocky and arrogant he was being. Grace tried to distract everyone by handing out menus.

"But its true isn't it, what you're telling me?" Chrissie wanted to continue the conversation; she was feeling very unnerved. It wasn't just what Tim was telling her that was making her feel uneasy; it was the odd flashes that had passed the screens of her mind. She was unable to interrupt them long enough to see what they were or work out what they meant.

"Yes, it is true Chrissie but it all happened a very long time ago and the family that lived in the house before you had a very happy time there. You were just very tired my love and your mind can play tricks on you when you feel like that. Now let's change the subject and order some food before the crowds get here."

And that's exactly what they did; talked about something else. But it didn't change anything for any of them because all three had their minds set on the same subject and all three of them were feeling completely different emotions to each other. One was frightened, one was furious, and the other was full of anticipation.

CHAPTER THREE

Dear Alice,

I found a box of your old toys in the attic yesterday and it set me off on one of my bad days again. Daddy is still insisting that we go on holiday but I just can't do it, Alice. And the very thought of it is making me feel ill. What if I missed you? What if the one time that I don't get up in the morning to look out of the window, you appear at our door?

Daddy has even mentioned selling up and moving away but that is just unbearable to think about. We have hope, which is something other families don't have. There is always hope my darling and I think its this that somehow keeps me alive and enables me to get through each day.

Aunty Jenny brought round some pictures of your cousin Emily's wedding. They're gorgeous and were all taken in black and white. Nana and Granddad managed to go, and there are some lovely pictures of them dancing together. We have chosen the ones we want and framed a couple and put them in your bedroom for you. They look nice against the newly painted walls.

I think that's another reason I'm having such a bad day. The photos are beautiful but they were just another reminder of what you would have looked like had it been your wedding day. You and Emily are so alike.

Daddy says I should go and see a therapist to talk about how I'm feeling. He thinks it will help me to move on. But apart from my bad days, I'm fine Alice. I'll never get over it, but then who would having lost their precious daughter? No not lost, not lost, not lost! I don't know why I said that my darling Alice, please forgive me.

I don't need to move on. I am here in the present, living each day without you, without my beautiful daughter, but I know one day that you'll walk through the door and we will make up for all the time we've lost together.

Loving you always – Mummy

*

Norfolk 1984

Jody was happy to go with the nice man because he'd promised to find her mother, who she'd lost in the commotion of the Christmas shoppers. Her mother had told her not to run off but she'd been distracted in the large store by the little Russian dolls that were on display. She wanted one of those so badly and she'd written about it in her letter to Father Christmas. Her mother had helped her put it together and they'd added lots of other things to the list of items including a copy of The

Velveteen Rabbit and a pram to push her teddy around in. She was filled with magical excitement at the thought of it all, as if Christmas was a brand new invention and she would be one of the first to experience it. Until today, where the excitement had melted like snow and had been replaced by a sickly fear. She had run and pushed through people and turned in circles searching for her mother's familiar face. Eventually she had found herself near the main doors and had walked straight into the man's legs as if they were fated to meet.

The man's hands were large and warm around her tiny cold one and he smelled like her father.

Jody chatted away to him, totally distracting herself from the fact that he had walked her out of the department store and down the street to his car. They looked like any other father and daughter shopping for mother a few days before Christmas and went unnoticed by the passing public, who smiled at the pretty five year old who appeared to be chatting to her father.

By the time they reached the car it was too far away for Jody to hear the panicked shouts of her mother out on the street. A mother who was already filled with a heavy dread and fear as she turned round and round in the street, frantically calling for her little girl in the busy town; knowing all too well that there was a child killer on the loose.

*

The suffocating heat and stench of over-boiled vegetables and urine hit Tim in the face as he was bleeped through the double doors of Poppy Field's retirement home. He was used to it after visiting his Mother religiously every week for the past eight years.

She'd had a series of strokes when she was sixty seven and never fully recovered. The doctors had put it down to the stress of losing her husband and suddenly being on her own. But Tim felt as though it wasn't the fact that she was 'being' on her own, it was the fact that she had to 'cope' on her own after a life with a husband who saw to her every whim.

Daphne had actually grown up in a working class family with lots of siblings, all living hand to mouth, appreciating every tiny little luxury that rarely came their way. Luxuries that wealthy families took for granted. She didn't fit into her family at all and they looked upon her as a stranger. They felt that she had ideas of grandeur. There wasn't much resemblance with any of them, physically or mentally. Daphne held herself differently, daydreamed often and read books, which was unheard of in the household. She came from generations of a repetitive theory, a school of thought that you accepted what you were given, 'your lot' as it was so aptly put.

The community she lived in frowned at her attitude of wanting to improve her situation. So she was generally an outcast and no one was surprised or pleased when she met Jack Charlesworth, a very wealthy lawyer. They fell in love quite quickly and Daphne fled as fast as she could, not realising that she may have just used Jack as a scapegoat to get away from her circumstances. She loved him, but not as he loved and adored her. As his adoration grew stronger throughout their marriage, Daphne's love turned into bitter resentment for him. The life she'd spent years wishing for hadn't turned out to be the one she wanted after all and she made him suffer for it. Money didn't buy you happiness or put right life's tragedies, she'd found that out the hard way. But as horrible as she was to him he still loved her, until the day he suffered a massive heart attack in his green house at the unripe age of seventy. Daphne had seen it more as an inconvenience than a tragedy, which was really how she'd treated him their entire married life.

But, as Jack had adored her, so did Tim. However frequently she pushed him away, he went running back, seeing her in his younger days as an independent and powerful woman instead of the bitter, twisted person he was to see her as later in his life.

And this is where she'd ended up; Poppy Field's retirement home. She'd more or less recovered from the strokes eight years previously but was deemed too unstable to live alone. Tim thought that a lifetime of being waited on hand and foot had left her fragile and slightly pathetic; a side to her that very few people glimpsed. So Tim had been quite happy to keep her in the retirement home. As much as he adored his Mother, he didn't want her interfering with his life and spoiling his routine. He had learnt only too well from her that you treated people like you treated your possessions. Getting them out when it suited you and then putting them away when they grew tiresome. So Daphne was safely ensconced in the box that Tim had put her in; boxed with a memory scent like everything else in his life.

There was something quite repulsive and sinister about Tim's relationship with his Mother. He had this sickly sweet affection for her and treated her as one of his prized possessions. He also revelled in the fact that their roles had reversed. It suited Tim very well to have her in a retirement home where he could pick her up and drop her, as she had done to him so often when he was a child. A part of him saw it as payback in the warped little depths of his mind.

He remembered so often how his mother went out for hours on end and left him with the housekeeper, Dora. She would put him in the cellar because he was being a nuisance. This was where Tim heightened his sense of smell. Dora would turn up the wireless to drown out his cries, leaving him unable to hear or see anything in the pitch black cellar. However much he strained his eyes to adjust to the light, hoping and waiting for shadows to become apparent, nothing happened. It was thick, damp and dark blackness all around him, so Tim improved the only sense he had left because there was nothing else to do. If he closed his eyes and imagined hard enough he could pretend he was somewhere else. He got so good at it that sometimes he fell asleep. He used smelling as a guessing game and would see what he got right when Dora deemed it necessary for him to come out of the dark. He would guess what they were having for dinner, which perfume from her dressing table his mother was wearing, whether his father was on his way home or not. All this he achieved from his sense of smell.

It was no good telling his mother that Dora made his life a misery when she went out; he just ended up being punished again for telling tales.

Tim wandered down the corridor carrying the white carnations that he took her every week. Daphne glanced at him as he walked into her private bedroom. She turned back to the window that she was sat next to. Tim kissed her on the cheek, smelling stale perfume with undertones of decay and laid the flowers on her portable table.

"Hello Mother, how are you today? Shall I put your flowers in a vase?"

"You ask me that every bloody week that you come here. Have you got nothing else to say to me?"

"Having a bad day, Mother?" he said, putting his arm around her shoulder and giving her a squeeze. She shrugged him off; a look of repulsion streaking her thickly made up face.

Daphne never passed a day without her makeup. She put on lashings of powder that made her look ghostly white, black liquid eyeliner that crumbled once dry on her tissue paper eyelids, along with her lumpy mascara. A bold layer of cerise pink lipstick was put on last, which always leaked into her stained, lined lips. The headband that she used to keep her hair out of the way of this ritual was replaced with a turban. Her makeup routine was the only time she didn't wear it. She thought this gave her the look and air of a movie star but it just made her look freakish and harsh.

"And how's that lovely wife of yours doing; still too busy to come and see her Mother in law?" Sarcasm dripped from her mouth.

"Don't start that again. You know how busy she is and she always sends her love. Anyway she thinks it's nice for us to spend some time on our own. I don't want to share you with anyone."

"Yes, yes, yes! Can you go and sit on the bed; I don't want you smothering me." She said, swatting him away like a dirty germ ridden fly.

Tim sat down on the edge of the bed and watched her as she scowled out of the window. It was to be one of those visits again. The ones that made him feel like he did as a child. Only, the difference was, he was an adult and it made him feel like strangling her.

*

James banged on Chrissie's bathroom door, startling her and causing her to spill water over the edge of the bath.

"Come on Mother, hurry up, you know what the water does to your wrinkly skin!"

"I was just getting out. And don't call me Mother, it makes me feel old!"

"You are old!" said James wandering downstairs to make a cup of tea.

"What time did Kate say her train was coming in?" Chrissie called down to him, choosing to ignore his last comment. It was an ongoing joke between them because there were very few years separating Chrissie and her step-children. Their Father, Marcus was fifteen years older than Chrissie. She'd always got on well with them because she had never posed as a replacement Mother. They had a perfectly good one as far as she was concerned and whom she got on well with. Chrissie had no intention of playing mother to two young adults who weren't much younger than she was. So they saw her more as an older sister, which was why they thought it was funny to wind her up by calling her 'Mother'.

"James?!" she called again, but he couldn't hear her above the noise of the boiling kettle and the blaring radio that he'd switched on.

Chrissie shivered as she stood up and grabbed a warm towel off the piping hot rail. She was so thankful that the previous owners had installed central heating and replaced the kitchen and the bathroom in the time that they had lived there. Something she'd dreaded having to do. It needed a lot of cosmetic work but they'd done all the expensive stuff. Grace had told her that the last owner was in the Armed Forces and he had been posted away, taking his family with him. Chrissie had looked at so many cottages, but they all needed too much work, and she didn't want a brand new home because she found them characterless. Just as she was about to give up, having decided that it wasn't meant to be, there had been a phone call from the estate agents. They told her that there was a cottage that had just come on the market and the couple needed a quick sale.

Chrissie knew as soon as she stepped out of the car that she wanted it. She loved the old Norfolk red brick which looked deep in colour in the midday sun, and the pretty overgrown front garden. Stocks and roses crowded the path that beckoned her to the front porch. It all held a familiar feeling with it. A feeling she couldn't pin point but had decided was her gut reaction telling her that it was the right house.

Chrissie dried herself with the soft towel, soothing her skin which was prickled, having stepped out of the warmth and comfort of her steamy bath. The latch on the door clicked up and the door creaked open, startling her again, causing her to quickly cover her naked body with the towel.

"James, I haven't finished!" she screeched, looking up at the empty doorway.

But there was no reply and no James stood at the bathroom door.

"James….?' Chrissie called, feeling her heart begin to pound; her skin prickling from fear, rather than a chill, that was creeping over her body. Chrissie stood in her bathroom staring at the space left by the door; cold water was running down her body as it dripped off her hair.

"Did you call me?" James appeared in the doorway, startling her yet again.

"Cover yourself up, I don't wish to…." He stopped, seeing her pale face. "Chrissie are you alright?"

"Um, yeah, did you open the bathroom door?"

"No, I've been downstairs making a cuppa. What an earth is wrong?"

"Nothing, I probably didn't shut the door properly, and it swung open and made me jump."

"You dozy old bag! Get some clothes on for god's sake and hurry up and get downstairs; I've just made a brew."

"Enough of the old!" Chrissie shouted light heartedly after him as he made his way down the winding staircase. But she didn't feel light hearted, not one little bit. She felt silly getting so worked up about a door but it was the feeling that it had left her with that bothered her the most. She knew she'd shut the bathroom door properly because since she'd moved into the house, doors opening on their own had become a frequent occurrence. This had caused her to become almost obsessive about checking them.

When James and Kate rang to tell her that they were coming to stay for a couple of days, she'd tried to stop herself sounding too hysterical. The relief that had swept through her was palpable. Almost every day she had spent in the house there had been some incident or another that had either frightened her or made her waste time wondering whether she had caused it herself. Especially after what Grace and Tim had told her at the pub. Hearing about the murders of all those children, particularly one that was found in her garden, had really freaked her out.

There had been things left on the kitchen work top that she knew she hadn't removed from the fridge, pictures falling off the wall for no reason, the television changing channels of its own accord and the most frightening one of all was when the dial moved on the radio. Chrissie had been unpacking some boxes and listening to her favourite radio station when it had suddenly become high pitched and crackly. She went into the kitchen to see what had happened, and as she began fiddling with the aerial she had spotted the dial turning backwards and forwards as if someone was tuning it.

Most of the time the house felt warm, homely and familiar, and these were the times that Chrissie really felt she'd made the right decision. And that the future was full of exciting things. But at some point during each day, a cold blanket descended on the cottage like a layer of snow; silent and chilling.

It left her feeling sick and fearful and wanting to jump into her car and drive far away from the whole place.

These extreme changes in atmosphere were causing Chrissie to have conflicting emotions. She enjoyed and looked forward to each day in her new house because at times she felt elated. But she also dreaded anticipating the change in atmosphere that could appear at any time. So, gradually and very slowly Chrissie was becoming a nervous wreck; like a large screw being turned inside her head. The offer of some company was grabbed with both hands because Chrissie naively convinced herself that it would all stop for a couple of days.

CHAPTER FOUR

NORFOLK 1955

Daphne unscrewed the cap of her flask and inhaled the metallic smell of strong sweet tea that wafted towards her nose.

It was a beautiful summer's day and it was promising to be really warm by the afternoon. She was pleased to be outside for a change. When the weather was bad, Daphne spent time in the library or a café. But she preferred to be in the fresh air, it made her feel free. Something she didn't feel in her life in general. When she was at home with Tim and Jack, in their big house, with their acre and a half of garden, she felt trapped like a rabbit in a hutch.

So, most days during the summer holidays Daphne asked Dora their housekeeper to watch over Tim.

They were some of the best days of her life and some of Tim's worst, something she was oblivious to. Lost in her own world, she never once questioned why Tim hated the summer holidays, unlike other children, who loved them.

Daphne leant back on the bench, crossed her feet and breathed deeply. Relief flooded her. She came out most days to be alone, think and reflect. It was like a whole new life she'd created outside her old one. This had been imperative to the well being of her family, even though they were unaware of her other life.

It had been on a day a few months previously when she thought her head would explode like a ticking bomb. It had scared her, what she might do to Tim, she'd become so distressed. So she'd called on Dora to look after him for a few hours. And it was like someone had turned a tap on. She'd run to the park that day, sobbing all the way there in the rain, wanting so desperately for things to be different.

That day had been the first of many and a tiny spark of an idea had ignited in her head. She decided that in order for her to be able to function in her role within her family, she would go out whenever she could. So, Daphne approached Dora with an agreement. Dora was paid extra to stay on and look after Tim and she wasn't to breathe a word of it to anyone. If Jack ever asked, she would just tell him that she'd been out visiting or shopping and Dora had agreed to baby sit. He had no idea how often or how long she was out; he was always at work. She couldn't tell Jack she wanted a Nanny because he'd then enquire where she was going. Dora just thought that Daphne was having an affair, one that she was glad of because it was lining her pockets and her lifestyle.

The agreement worked for many years and Daphne was eternally grateful for the lifeline she'd been thrown. It had saved her from committing suicide and taking her son with her. It had only meant to be until Tim started school full time but then

Daphne had found herself calling on Dora during the school holidays.

Daphne became a familiar face to people after a while, visiting the same places. Frowning, inquisitive looks had turned into cheery hellos and a brief passing of time. Those people knew her as Daphne and no one else and she found this immensely liberating. She'd picked a town roughly fifteen miles away where she could safely immerse herself. No one there had any idea that she had a son and a husband at home. They knew nothing about her, thought she was a loner. She liked it that way, it was comfortable and familiar and it made her feel whole and complete.

There was no guilt involved for Daphne; she knew she needed this life to be able to continue with the other one. Leaving either life wasn't an option for her. She'd made her bed and she would lie in it, now, more comfortably than before. Had she been aware of what Tim was going through while she was away from him, she would have felt very different.

And as Daphne now sat on the bench sipping her tea and enjoying the peace, her son was sat in a pitch black, damp cellar, wishing for the entire world that his mother would come home and rescue him.

*

Norfolk 1998

"There was no need for you to tell Chrissie all that nasty business about the murdered children. What on earth were you thinking? She's only just moved in and she's trying to get used to the place. Thanks to you, she's probably frightened out of her wits!"

"Oh shut up, you stupid woman! Someone was bound to tell her. You know what the gossip's are like in the village, I've done her a favour." Tim said, opening the fridge door to see if there were any leftovers to quell his hunger. Drinking beer at lunch time always made him hungry, even if he had already eaten at the pub.

"And what makes you think that you were the right person to relay that information?" Grace searched his face for any sign of a nervous reaction.

"Just being neighbourly. If I'd have left it to the gossips she would have heard some half baked story more frightening than the truth, which would have had her packing her bags and leaving. At least what I've told her is a matter of fact, without all the bullshit with it."

"I can't understand why you would think that anything could be more frightening than the truth of all that happened to those poor little souls. And what makes you an expert on delivering the facts?"

Grace leant on the kitchen worktop and folded her arms. She scrutinized his face while he busied himself with some bread and cheese, but to no avail. Not a flicker; he was as cool and calm as normal. This only made her more agitated and she needed to watch her step. The last thing Grace wanted to do was to let him know that she knew what he'd done all those years ago. She wasn't frightened of him killing her, just the fact that he might do it before she got the pleasure of doing it to him first.

Grace felt she had already experienced the worst kind of fear and pain that any human being could go through. She wasn't worried about dying; that would be a time to go to sleep and be put out of the misery that she'd endured through her lifetime. No, dying was a luxury. There had been a time when she'd wanted that experience to happen sooner rather than later. That had been the day her daughter had died in a terrible accident. She'd felt that she'd died right there and then with her on the day the police knocked at her door. Dying, for Grace felt like it would have been a light relief from the horrendous nightmare that she was about to go through.

She remembered an unconscious thought fleeting through her mind when she saw the two officers walking up the path; that they'd come to tell her that Tim was dead. Not her precious daughter.

Nadine had been playing in the garden of an old derelict house and hadn't seen the open cess pit. The police said they thought that Nadine had been playing whilst waiting for her friend who lived next door. A dog walker had seen her there and had told her to move on saying it was dangerous but she'd ignored him. It was when he heard her screams after he'd got some way past her that he knew something bad had happened and alerted the police from a phone box. He searched for Nadine with the help of her friend Pauline and Pauline's Father, who had heard the commotion because he was working nearby. They almost fell down the cess pit themselves, it was so well camouflaged.

That day had happened almost ten years ago but it was as clear as the minutes passing now. She could even remember the warm sunshine peeking through the rain clouds making them look like they were lined with silver. But there was no silver lining that day or any of the days that had followed for Grace. Tim had dealt with his grief in his own selfish way. Leaving her for days on end to lose himself in his sailing and then coming back for such a brief time she hardly noticed he was there. Even though she yearned for some support, she realised looking back she hadn't wanted it from him. All the times she'd screamed at him that he wasn't there for her, she actually realised in her quieter, less hysterical moments that he had done exactly what she wanted, which was to leave her alone. How could she gain any sort of comfort from someone she thought was emotionless and weak?

So Grace was looking forward to the luxury of dying but not until she'd had the pleasure of killing Tim first and making it look like a tragically sad accident.

This comforting thought passed through her mind as she watched him sink his teeth into the bread and cheese he'd prepared for his supper.

*

Tim found himself wandering past his shed and down the garden path and through the gate. He didn't quite know what he was doing but he knew where he was going.

He was becoming increasingly bored with his boxes of memory scents; the smells were fading fast. Until he worked out what he was going to do next he needed to occupy himself with something else and that was to have a bit of fun.

Chrissie had made a huge mistake telling him about her little problem. He laughed to himself at how women were so over-emotional and stupid; couldn't keep anything to themselves, not like men. Tim thought he was especially good at it. He knew that the only way to continue enjoying what you were doing was to keep your mouth shut. He believed that the only person you could ever trust was yourself.

And that was why Tim had got away with all his gruesome activities. He'd not told a soul, not even his Mother, with whom he shared the most secrets.

He contemplated this little gem of information about himself as he walked down the dimly lit lane towards Chrissie's house. He wanted to go and sit in his favourite shed at the bottom of her garden, so that he could think about what he was going to do next. That particular old shed held fond memories for him and there was still a faint smell from the past that he could detect if he breathed in hard enough.

It was time to plan some excitement and by the time Tim finished, Chrissie would have a perfect understanding of the meaning of fear. Tim would make sure she would feel like she had completely lost her mind.

It would be a part pay back for the spectacular escape she had made when she was a child. It had taken him a while to work out the familiarity of her. The smell was similar to that of when she was younger, but only a hint. It was her eyes that had given her away. Those fascinatingly beautiful blue eyes that almost looked like they were coloured lenses because they were so bright. Tim recognised her when they were talking about her house, and from her scared expression. He couldn't place her in that capacity at first, not until she mentioned she had holidayed with her parents in the village for many years as a child. It caused a memory to flash across his mind. He remembered that scared look very well, and what a beautiful little child she'd been.

Chrissie was on holiday with her family and Tim had watched her for almost a week, waiting to pounce on her as soon as her family left her alone. There were three little girls but he'd only been interested in her. Partly because of her alluring eyes but also because she'd passed him innocently in the local post office, leaving a scent behind her that had captivated him. A child like smell mixed with washing powder and soap and a slight scent of unwashed hair with remnants of the sea.

Tim was slightly worried she was on to him; why else would she have moved here? He was so conceited; he couldn't imagine anyone making a decision that didn't concern him being taken into account. Even though Chrissie hadn't appeared to have known who he was, Tim needed to keep an eye on her and make sure she didn't put two and two together. Logically he couldn't see how she could link him to anything because he had never let her see his face back then.

Luckily for Tim, on this occasion he had picked the night time to abduct Chrissie. If he hadn't, she would have been able to give the police a full description of his face. Tim was usually the last person that his victims saw, but he hadn't been Chrissie's. He remembered her being a strong little thing, not wanting to give up without a fight. He was surprised at her will to live. His other victims had given up after what Tim saw as only a tiny struggle, pathetic and weak. The fact remained, it had been pure fear that had caused their bodies to fail in their functioning, that and Tim's rough handling.

That particular night, he'd gone into the garden of the holiday cottage where Chrissie and her family were staying.

He'd observed whilst watching her and her family that Chrissie would go back outside after she'd got ready for bed and sit on the old swing in the garden. Her mother regularly called her in but she ignored her until she was physically marched upstairs to bed.

Tim thought the best way of enticement would be to make a noise like an animal to draw the little girl to the gate. It worked and with very little effort he grabbed the tiny six year old, clamped his hand over her mouth and took her a little way down the track to a nearby back garden where he knew of an old unused shed. He knew it was quiet there, because it was so far away from the house that it belonged to.

It was to be that same house and garden that Chrissie bought, many years later.

It was all as simple as that, in those few seconds that any parent whose child has gone missing wishes they could rewind. Those missing minutes that can never be repeated.

Luckily for Chrissie it all back fired on Tim because, being used to taking children during the daylight, the night time seemed to have short-footed him. So, while he was trying to deal with a small child who was kicking but unable to scream, he didn't notice the slight step into the old shed and as he stumbled forward he lost his grip of her and Chrissie made her escape. She ran and ran and somehow managed to get back to the holiday cottage where her mother was frantically searching the garden for her.

For the first time in his life, Tim had been scared. He rushed back to his house hoping that no one was in, so that he could hide his panic.

The house had thankfully, been empty, because Grace was at a Women's Institute meeting. This enabled Tim to turn on the lights, get something in the oven, and generally make it look like he had been there all evening. Tim knew that the whole place would be crawling with police in a matter of minutes; especially as they were on the hunt for a child killer. That was the only time he scolded himself for being stupid and genuinely felt he may have blown the whole thing.

Within half an hour he was back to his usual calm, cold self and when the police knocked on the door to let him know what had happened he looked like any other normal citizen who had spent an evening in on his own. The problem was Tim was so clever that he'd managed to convince the entire village that he was a pillar of the community. He'd been a serving police officer since he was old enough to join up. A local bobby, trustworthy and friendly, prepared to go that extra mile for someone else and always keeping a watchful eye over everyone's children.

CHAPTER FIVE

Dear Alice,

I think I've managed to convince Daddy to go on holiday without me. I know I'm going to miss him dreadfully but I just can't bring myself to leave the house. He knows I wouldn't enjoy it anyway. I'd be constantly wondering what was happening here. There in body but not in mind as they say. He refused at first and said he wouldn't go at all but he needs a holiday desperately. He sees it as a way of moving on and I suppose we all deal with things differently, but it's not a way forward for me. The thought of it is just pure torture.

Anyway, I was reading an article the other day about how some people can suffer amnesia from shock or a bump to the head. In some cases they go wandering off, not remembering who they are. Sometimes, after a few years they just come to, and go looking for their real families. It gave me fresh hope because you were on your own that day, and you could have easily fallen over and bumped your head without anyone knowing.

The whole thing made Daddy cross and I've promised not to mention it again. Daddy is convinced that you're not coming back and that the only thing that would have caused you to leave us would be if you were dead. But I would know that as a mother, and I've never felt it, not like other people who have lost a child.

I know you wouldn't leave us intentionally because I know how happy you were. And you certainly wouldn't have left your beloved little dog, Tilly.

I'm sorry for running on again my darling, but I've felt that the whole situation has consumed me lately. Maybe this is a sign that you are near and that we will see you soon. I don't just feel it, I know it.

I cut the article out and put it in your scrap book with all the other cuttings for you to read when you get home.

Loving you always

Mummy xxx

*

NORFOLK 1956

The scent of Dora and the warmth of the range cooker that they were sat next to in the old familiar kitchen were making Tim sleepy. He was sat on Dora's lap; his head leant against her breast, as she read from his favourite story book. His tiny fingers were entwined in her soft blonde hair, as he twirled the golden locks round and round. He loved the feel of her silky, waxen, shiny hair on his hands. It was something he should have been doing with his mother, but she was hardly ever around and he'd grown used to Dora as a substitute.

They'd had a lovely day together. Tim had skipped into town with her in the sunshine and she'd bought him a packet of sweets. He'd even heard her humming to herself on the way. It was the first day he could remember in his short little life that she hadn't scolded him or snapped at him. She was in one of her better moods.

Whatever had caused this gaiety in Dora was to be short lived but Tim wasn't old enough to know this familiar pattern of events. Launching him off her lap and across the kitchen was the result of him snagging her hair with a hang nail. Dora's temper brought out her true roots, the posh clipped accent she used to impress Daphne and Jack evaporated as quickly as fading breath on glass.

"You stupid little bastard!" she screeched at Tim as he hit the far kitchen wall and crumpled in a heap on the floor, shocked and astounded, as ever, at the personality change in her.

"Get up!" she said, rubbing her neck where he'd snagged her hair.

"I'm sorry..."

"Get up, I said." This was said more quietly but with a sinister tone in her voice, which scared Tim more than anything. She was bent over and moving towards him slowly, as he desperately scrambled to pull himself off the floor and stand up straight. He closed his eyes, not wanting to meet hers, and crossed his tiny legs, hoping she wouldn't see the dark stain appearing on his trousers. But urine began to drip loudly on the unforgiving linoleum floor.

Dora stared at the wet patch and then back at Tim, a look of disgust shadowing her face. She grabbed him sharply by the arm, her temper getting the better of her, and dragged him screaming to the cellar door. As she thumped down the steps dragging him behind her, his small legs couldn't keep up and he fell twisting his arm in her grip. She continued regardless, his body thumping down the concrete steps as if she was a child again dragging a rag doll. She swung him around and flung him on the soot and dirt covered floor.

Back in the kitchen, Dora leant her hands on the kitchen sink and stared out of the window, trying to calm her breathing and her rage.

Tim's crying could be heard through the floor in the kitchen, which only served to irritate her more. She poured herself a large gin and tonic and went outside for a cigarette so she couldn't hear him. Jack was away on business and Daphne would be out until late, so she wasn't concerned about anyone coming back. She more or less lived in the house, she was there far more than Tim's parents and she'd begun to treat the house like it was her own.

Two hours later, a tear and urine stained Tim was removed from the cellar and put into a hot bath and scrubbed clean. Afterwards, she put him to bed and finished reading the story that had been interrupted earlier. It was as if nothing had happened. Dora looked in every way the angelic young beauty that she always portrayed to Daphne and Jack. It was the perfect calm setting for when Daphne eventually came home.

*

Norfolk 1998

Chrissie wandered along the beach, deep in thought, looking very troubled. There were all sorts of scenarios running through her head, but the light sea air seemed to be helping. Just lately she'd felt safer outside her house than she had in it. The sheer panic that engulfed her when there was a change of atmosphere at home had caused her on a few occasions to run outside and sit on the swing. The swing was where she felt safe. And whatever it was that she thought was chasing her inside, outside felt like an expanse of escapism.

There had been a new turn of events just recently and it had caused her to call her best friend Sarah. She needed to feel that someone was there with her and, not knowing many people in the village, the telephone seemed like the next best option.

Chrissie had been unable to hide her alarm and begged Sarah to stay on the line and keep talking. This obviously worried Sarah greatly and, after talking with Chrissie for almost two hours until the commotion died down, she insisted that she would get some time off work and drive over to her for a few days as soon as she possibly could. She'd wanted to get in the car that night and drive over to Chrissie, but had been ordered in no uncertain terms not to. Chrissie assured Sarah that she would call on Grace if things got unbearable. Sarah felt that 'unbearable' had already been reached but didn't like to say, in case it unsettled Chrissie further.

Not only were there things going on in the house but to add to Chrissie's hysteria there were unexplained activities going on outside. The night it started she hadn't had too bad a day apart from the interference with the radio, but that was becoming a normal occurrence for her, and the atmosphere in the house hadn't dropped to its normal level.

Whatever it was that was going on outside seemed to have a knock on effect of aggravating the activities indoors. She wasn't sure what she had heard at first because every time Chrissie turned down the television it appeared to stop. But then it continued so she switched the TV to standby and waited. Then she heard it. A scratching at the window which she thought might be one of the cats. But after a quick look around she located all three. The scratching got louder and it sounded like a razor blade being dragged across the window, which caused Chrissie to shiver uncontrollably, even though she was sweating with fear. The cats began to stir and a low deep growling could be heard coming from their tiny bodies. In her panic Chrissie had checked the back and front doors were locked and in doing so had briefly peered out of the small window to the door. She couldn't see anything and wasn't brave enough to pull back the curtains and look out of the windows. She'd made that mistake the other night when she thought she'd heard something, only to have been frightened out of her wits at the sight of her own haunted reflection.

So she had curled up on the sofa with a blanket and the television turned up loud until it passed. When she thought the noise had stopped she began to feel brave enough to turn on the outside light and venture upstairs to look out of her bedroom window. At first she didn't notice what was strange in the garden until she walked away and then turned back. It reminded her of one of those picture quizzes where you have to spot the odd thing out.

The air was completely still that night although it hadn't felt like that with all the noise and the strained atmosphere inside her home. She'd imagined there to be a raging storm outside, but it was as still and quiet as most other late summer evenings. Everything in Chrissie's garden was perfectly still, even her cottage garden plants. What was glaringly obvious when she turned back to have another look was the swing hanging from the tree. And unlike everything else, it was swinging backwards and forwards with quite some force. Chrissie tried to suppress the bile that flooded her throat, before she ran to the toilet. She only just made it to the bathroom, in order for her body to express all the pent up fear of the past few weeks in the only way it knew how. Anyone else would have called the police or left the house screaming but Chrissie was used to paranormal activity. She and her sisters had been brought up in an old rectory where it was a normal occurrence. She knew the difference between that and an intruder. Or so she thought.

The freedom of walking along the beach in the light autumnal breeze was a huge relief to Chrissie as she waited for Grace to meet her for a chat. She spotted her in the distance, walking confidently across the beach car park towards her. She was unsure whether to tell her any more of what had happened, partly because she didn't want to appear obsessed with the whole thing, having only just met her, and because she wasn't sure if she wanted to hear any more grim details about these child murders. She found it strange that she hadn't remembered hearing about them when she was younger, seeing as she'd holidayed here for many years as a child.

"Hello!" called Grace cheerfully to her as they approached one another. "Oh, dear, you don't look your best, are you coming down with something?'

"Thanks very much!" Chrissie said, giving Grace a brief hug and kiss on the cheek.

Grace laughed and returned her greeting.

"I'm not feeling too good as it happens. I've not been sleeping very well. But I'm sure a lovely walk along the beach will blow the cobwebs away."

"Have you had some more problems at the house?" Grace asked.

"Yes and I can't understand it. I feel like I'm going round the bend! I had my step-children to stay for a few days and I thought it would all stop while they were here or that I'd realise I'd been seeing things. But it all continued and what really freaked me out was that James and Kate experienced it as well. They couldn't get away quick enough."

"So do you really think it's haunted?" said Grace, beginning to feel slightly uncomfortable.

"Well, I can't think of any other explanation. Maybe the things that are being moved are simply me misplacing items, but the radio dial turning and the television switching channels are definitely nothing to do with me."

"Perhaps you've got an electrical fault; it might be worth getting someone to have a look at it all."

"Oh come on Grace, you and I both know that the previous owners had all that major work done before I got there. And it's not just the electrical things; the latch doors keep opening on their own and the atmosphere and temperature in the house plummets for no reason. I think it's got something to do with that child Tim was telling me about." Chrissie was tentative, having not wanted to bring the subject up, but talking about her problem had stirred a curiosity inside her to know the facts.

"Don't take too much notice of what Tim says. He thinks he's laying out the bare facts to people when in fact they're probably slightly exaggerated; typical of a policeman."
Chrissie paused briefly from walking.

"I didn't realise Tim's in the police?"

"Was, in the police, he's retired now; done his time."

Chrissie nodded and watched the other woman's expression change into what looked like disappointment. She waited, expecting her to continue with what she was saying but there was a long pause. As if by saying anything further about her husband, she'd let out too much information. And actually Chrissie was right; Grace felt that if she ever started talking to anyone about her marriage with Tim, she'd never be able to stop. And it was a much bigger trauma than Chrissie could ever anticipate.

"But there was a child found in my garden wasn't there?" said Chrissie wanting to pick up the conversation again.

"Yes there was, but I don't think it has anything to do with the problems in your house. Her body was found near the old shed right at the end of your garden, quite a distance from the house. I think they actually discovered her in that stream that passes the bottom of your land. Poor little love."

"What, my shed? The one I told you about? Why didn't you tell me at the time?"

"Because I didn't want to frighten you. Cause you to panic unnecessarily and put two and two together and come up with five like you're doing now."

Grace stopped and turned to face her friend, who looked even more haunted than she had when she'd first arrived.

"Look Chrissie, let's not talk about it; you don't need to know the gory details. Let's talk about how we can solve your problem. Hey?"

Chrissie looked like she was about to cry; a mixture of fatigue and fear almost visibly washed over her. Grace suddenly felt very protective of Chrissie; there was a strange responsibility for her. Grace felt almost like she was partly to blame for all the catastrophic nightmares that her husband had caused. There were still new consequences to his actions, like ripples in the water appearing endlessly. And Grace felt she needed to fix what little she could.

"But don't you think if I know all the details then I'll be able to make some sense of what's happening. Just because that little girl was found at the bottom of my garden doesn't rule out the fact that she could be haunting my house. Maybe, if I trace it all back and find out who lived in the house before the previous owners, I might be able to find out what happened in the house during the time these murders took place. You did say there was more than one child, didn't you?"

"Yes, there was more than one child. I think there were eight or nine altogether," said Grace, continuing to stroll again as they talked. It was going to be an uncomfortable conversation but Grace managed to detach what she knew about her husband from the whole story. That was her business, and something she didn't want another living soul to know. Not if she was to successfully complete her plan.

So Grace composed herself and relayed all the facts she knew about the children who had left this world in a way that no living creature should have to endure.

*

NORFOLK 1984

Jennifer had been so excited about the birthday party she was having after school that she didn't think twice when her friend's father had stopped her on her way home from school. He told her that her mother had asked him to take her in his car to the local café for a birthday treat. Make sure she got there safely.

She knew Tim quite well, having been to his house to play with his daughter, Nadine many times. Her mother had told her not to go off with strangers or even talk to them. But Tim wasn't a stranger so that made it alright.

When he locked the car door so she couldn't get out and drove in the opposite direction which took them down some desolate Norfolk back roads, she started to worry.

"Where are we going? That's not the way into town."

"You didn't seriously think I was going to actually take you to the café did you?" Tim glanced at her in the back of the car; his face having changed completely.

"But where are we going?" Jennifer's face was a mixture of surprise and confusion. Her first thought was that her mother had organised a bigger party for her at the village hall and kept it a secret. But fear was creeping through her stomach, telling her that all was not well.

"And I wouldn't waste your time trying to get out of the car, it's got child locks." He said, spotting her hand moving towards the handle.

Jennifer, who had just turned eleven that day, stared back at the complete stranger who she had made the mistake of getting into the car with. The fear had reached her throat, twisting it and causing her mouth to sporadically open and close in an effort to make a noise. Her hand was white from the grip on the car door handle and she seemed incapable of movement, as the reality of who he was dawned on her. All she kept thinking was why it had to be her, and of all days her birthday.

Jennifer's downfall had been her beautiful green eyes and curly dark hair. Her skin was as white as a lily; making her red lips and emerald green eyes stand out. She was striking and that was what had attracted Tim to her. Every victim was picked carefully but usually because they had aesthetically struck a chord inside him. A bit like two people meeting each other for the first time and falling madly in love. But not the warped, twisted, sinister way that Tim loved his victims.

Feeling warmly satisfied, Tim took some time to watch Jennifer laying in the little copse surrounded by trees, his choice of a bed for her. It was well hidden down a more or less unused back road and along a track that not many people knew about. He rolled a cigarette from his tobacco tin as he observed her like a work of art.

She looked even more beautiful now than she had when she'd been alive. Her green eyes were still sparkling, but now glazed; they held a snap shot of the fear she had endured only moments previously.

Death fascinated him. The way a person's eyes altered, showing no emotion, becoming empty, coloured oval shaped glass. Tim loved that part, when he could reflect on the stillness of his victim like a photo in an album. All his snapshots were logged safely in the dark cellar of his mind. The added bonus was that he got to keep a memory scent as well as a picture.

Jennifer lay in her cold, damp grave, her body mostly naked apart from her school cardigan that Tim had decided to put back on her after he'd taken her shirt. Mud caked her nails where she had grabbed at the ground in an attempt to get away from him. Those fingers that had been so frenetic moments earlier now lay motionless like a statues, as if they would crack and break under the slightest movement. Her distorted tiny body, paler than when she'd been alive, now lay broken like an old doll. A grey blue shade was beginning to colour her white skin. Her tiny neck was in an unnatural position where Tim had broken it from strangling her so hard.

*

A few weeks later Tim knocked hard on Jennifer's mother's door, as he and his colleague removed their police hats as a mark of respect.

"I hate doing this." His workmate said, gripping his hat as if it might transport him to another time and place.

"So do I, mate." Tim could see Marion, Jennifer's mother coming towards them through the frosted glass door. He discreetly glanced at his watch. All Tim could think about was getting this over and done with and going on his lunch break.

A tearful Marion opened the door, a tissue already gripped to her mouth.

"You've found her haven't you…Oh god no…not my Jennifer!"

Marion's legs buckled from underneath her and she fell against the porch door frame, as she took in the two police officers faces, knowing it wasn't good news. Tim grabbed her before she completely collapsed and managed to get her into her living room.

His colleague, Paul busied himself in her kitchen, glad to have been allocated the job of making her a strong cup of tea.

Tim made her comfortable on the sofa and explained how a gamekeeper had stumbled across a body on his estate. The police believed it to be that of Jennifer. Tim told her how she or another member of her family would have to formally identify Jennifer's body and that it would probably be best if it was someone other than her because Jennifer had been put in a shallow grave but more or less left out in the extremities for several weeks.

Tim then let Paul take over for a bit, while he busied himself calling members of her family and her local doctor so that he could prescribe her something to calm her down.

Marion wept and wept like she'd never stop; her heart was slowly and painfully breaking. She'd become a widow two years previously and now she'd lost her only child. She'd known something had happened to Jennifer when she hadn't come home

78

from school that day. She knew she wouldn't have missed her birthday party for the world.

Marion had watched the clock in the kitchen as she'd flitted around the dining table laying out plates of homemade sausage rolls, pretty coloured biscuits, and cheese on sticks.

` She'd wanted it to be so special for her. Jennifer's last birthday had been filled with sadness because it was her first birthday after her father had died of cancer. His diagnosis had left him with a death sentence of six weeks, and he had deteriorated rapidly. Before Marion and Jennifer knew it they were standing by his grave saying their goodbyes to him.

Jennifer had just begun to enjoy life again; accepting that her father wasn't coming back, but that he would always be watching over her. So Marion had wanted her to have a birthday party that she would never forget. Not just marking her birthday but also a fresh start. But now it would be a birthday that Marion would never forget, for all the wrong reasons.

While Marion had been busy preparing the table she had assumed that Jennifer was held up by excited friends and maybe stopped off at one of their houses on the way home. Something she forbade her to do without informing her where she would be and what time she would be home. But because Marion was distracted with the party and it being Jennifer's birthday she'd let it pass, just this once, assuming she'd got caught up receiving more birthday gifts. She was such a popular girl.

When the party guests arrived with no Jennifer in tow and no news of her since they'd all left school, she knew that something was wrong. She also knew after the first night that Jennifer was missing that she was never coming back. Jennifer would never leave her like that and not tell her where she was going. She wouldn't leave her mother's side since her father had died. She was such a caring and protective little girl, sometimes Marion had felt, in her deepest moments of grief that they had swapped roles and Jennifer had mothered her instead of the other way around.

It still didn't make the news relayed to her by the police officers any easier. Even though she knew Jennifer's fate already, there was still that glimmer of hope she had clung onto every day. And now it was all over.

CHAPTER SIX

Norfolk 1998

Chrissie sat at her writing desk mulling over the information that Grace had told her about the murders of all the children. She needed to concentrate on her writing but it kept going round and round in her head. It wasn't only the horror of the story that she couldn't let go of but there was also something nagging her about it all. She was sure it was in some way connected to the strange episodes she was having in her house. Grace hadn't offered much information about who had lived in the house over the years, just that she remembered it being a holiday home for a time. What Chrissie was really shocked at was that no one had been caught for the crimes. Apparently the police hadn't even come close to it. Whoever it was had been extremely clever and left no evidence. The only consistent piece of information the police had was that the murderer took a souvenir from the body, usually an item of clothing, and that all the victims were children and they had all been sexually assaulted before being murdered. The police thought it was a local man because whoever it was knew the area very well, always choosing secluded places normally down the country roads that formed a bridge between villages. It made Chrissie shudder to think there was some creep on the loose who hadn't been made to pay for his crimes. Not that Chrissie could think of any type of punishment that would make up for what had happened to those poor little souls and their families. Grace had told her how it had affected the area dreadfully and even though it had all happened a long time ago it was still a very sore subject. Especially in the villages that each child came from; it was still so fresh in their minds.

What Chrissie couldn't understand was why she wasn't able to recall anything about the murders. Even though she was a child when they'd happened, and she'd only visited the area on holiday, she surely would have remembered them being talked about, or it being on the news? Another strange thing Grace had told her was that the murders suddenly just stopped. There was talk in some of the villages that whoever committed the crimes had either died or moved away. But then if they'd moved away, they surely would have continued murdering in another area. Maybe the murderer was dead. Not a bad thing, thought Chrissie to herself, although, if it had been a member of her family she would have wanted the bastard publicly tortured and hanged.

The phone rang, startling her and interrupting her thoughts.

"Hello, Mum. How are you?"

"I'm fine thank you, darling and how are you? I was just ringing to see how you were settling in to darkest Norfolk."

Chrissie took a deep breath and mentally counted to ten. She wasn't going to tell her mother what had been going on in the house, which would only serve to give her the pleasure of saying "I told you so".

"Very well, thank you, Mother. I've got some bits and pieces to do here but the previous people did the main work which has made it all a lot easier. The areas lovely and I've made a couple of friends already.'

"Oh how lovely for you darling. Your Father and I are hoping to come and visit you before Christmas. Is the house habitable?"

"Yes, its fine Mother," Chrissie rolled her eyes to the heavens, "and it'll probably be completely sorted by the time you and Dad get here. While you're on the line Mum, do you remember anything about a series of child murders that happened in this area? It was quite a few years ago but some of them would have been about the time we came down here on holiday."

The line went quiet and Chrissie wondered if they'd been cut off.

"Mum, are you still there?"

"Yes, darling...I'm just trying to remember...I can vaguely recall something about it. Why?"

"Oh nothing really, it's just something that was being discussed in the pub the other night and I wondered why I couldn't recall anything about it. It was obviously a major enquiry."

"Yes, yes it must have been…oh sorry darling I must go there's someone at the door. Daddy sends his love, speak soon…"

"Oh, ok, by Mum. Love to you all too…" she found herself saying to a dead line.

Sylvia didn't have anyone at her door at all, and she'd remembered, as if it were yesterday, what Chrissie was asking her about. How could she forget that her precious daughter could have so easily been one of the victims?

That was one of the reasons why she and Peter, Chrissie's father, hadn't wanted her to move there. But Chrissie had seen it as another one of their over protective episodes. They had often wondered if they should have told her when she got older, because for some strange reason Chrissie quickly forgot about the whole incident, which had been a blessing in disguise. They had watched her like a hawk and taken her to the doctors for regular checkups after the attack. The doctor had told them it was quite common for a child to temporarily erase a frightening memory from their brain due to shock. And that was exactly what Chrissie had done. So, throughout her life she had been unaware of why her parents and her sisters were so protective of her. She had often complained that they suffocated her, when actually it was because they were all still living through the terrible awareness that things could have been so awfully different and that they felt incredibly blessed to have her with them.

They had all been heart broken when she announced she was moving away and even more distressed when she told them where she was going. But they couldn't protect her forever and while they were suffocating her with their love, they all knew that they were slowly losing her.

Sylvia had thought it was best she didn't know the truth because she was frightened of how it would affect her daughter's life. Chrissie was such a free spirited child; a trait that Sylvia was glad hadn't been shocked out of her by that horrible incident. She just hoped and prayed that after the telephone conversation they'd just had, her memory didn't come flooding back.

*

Dear Alice,

I dreamt about you again last night, but it felt different to what I normally dream.

You were in your favourite night dress. You know the white one with the embroidered panel down the front? You'd worn it the night before you went away.

Anyway, you were standing in a clearing, surrounded by trees with a field behind you. You were beckoning me to come towards you.

We hugged and hugged for what seemed like an age. It was so real Alice! The feeling has stayed with me all day like a scent that clings to your skin. I could even smell your beautiful blonde hair. We didn't speak, just held each other. The relief I felt in my sleep was incredible and I was quite upset when I awoke. I felt free for the first time in so many years. Like this massive weight had lifted from me. Of course, when I first awoke I didn't know where I was because the dream was so vivid. I ran into your bedroom knowing I was going to see you laying there asleep. But then reality hit me like an iron wall. I sat on your bed for a long time wishing I could swap it all for my dreams.

Daddy told me to go back to bed and get some more sleep, which was what I did in the hope that I would see you again. But there was nothing.

The sleep did me good though, because when I awoke again I realised how lucky I was to have that dream. I feel that it is another sign. I think it was you letting me know that we will see you again very soon, a bit like a premonition.

Daddy is still trying to talk me into going on holiday with him, but when I suggested to him about taking one of his fishing friends with him I think he realised that I'm not going to budge on my decision, especially not after this. It isn't that Daddy doesn't love you darling. It's just his way of dealing with it all.

Anyway, he seems to be resigned to the fact that I won't go on holiday with him and he's thinking about taking your Uncle Tim with him instead.

Loving you always xxx

NORFOLK 1998

Tim sat in his draughty old shed and, pulling his coat tighter around him he took a large slurp of his hot toddy, the ratio of which was more rum than coffee. The weather had suddenly turned cold because of the bad winds whipping across from the sea. It felt like winter already and it was only September. The wind whisked around the shed making a noise that could be mistaken for people whispering outside. But Tim was familiar with these old noises caused by the wind tunnel that was their garden. When Grace and he had first lived there and he was just beginning to collect his memory scents and store them in his new shed, he'd thought it was a ghost haunting him. He chuckled at this thought, remembering how naïve and impatient he'd been in his younger days in comparison to the confident and relaxed person he was now.

He needed time to sit and think about his options because he was becoming very bored. Retirement had done Tim no favours whatsoever, and more to the point it wouldn't help the local community if he decided to continue with his old games. Not that this little fact bothered his conscience.

Tim needed to think carefully about the whole thing even though his urges had been getting unbearable. He had managed to take the edge off that though, by stealing a few items of clothing here and there. His best ones had been from Chrissie's place. Her smells held a special mixture of memories for him. She was connected to the past, from a time that had been filled with excitement and danger for him. Sniffing her clothes was a bit like smelling all his victims at once from a fresh scent altogether. Although he was still sore about the fact she hadn't become another of his conquests. But he had to be grateful for what he could get at the moment and she was a link to tide him over for the time being.

He loved the power he had of frightening her and the fact that he could so easily get into her house without her knowing and rifle through her linen basket; stealing various items of clothing. He had so far taken a couple of vest tops and an old cardigan because it was small and reminded him of a child's pullover. Tim never took underwear. He'd never been a knickers man unless they were on little girls. The smell of a woman had never turned him on and actually only served to repulse him. So Chrissie's dirty underwear had been removed from her linen basket with a look of disgust on his face, like he was removing a dead mouse from a trap. He'd never been able to understand those types of men who took so much pleasure from smelling women's knickers. Even going as far as buying them from people who advertised in magazines. They were dirty perverts as far as he was concerned.

The problem Tim had was that he realised there had been an element of luck involved when he had played his games and got away with it. He knew that he was incredibly clever; bordering on genius he liked to think. But if he hadn't been in the police force he knew he would have been looked at closely like every other man in the area and remembering lies as you wove them would have made the whole process much harder. As he often reflected on it, it had all been fairly straightforward and easy; he'd felt like a child in a sweet shop. There was one little problem he had with it being so many years on, and that was the discovery of DNA. He was always very careful not to leave anything behind anywhere but he knew now that with technology becoming so advanced, low copy DNA evidence would soon be utilised within the forensic world, he'd read about it. It wasn't too much of a problem for him because he wasn't registered on the national database anyway, not having a criminal record. But even so, he had to be careful.

The other factor that he was worried about was the CID department and all the new police officers that he didn't know. He'd started in the police force extremely young and had served his thirty years. Most of the officers he'd worked with were also retired or had left on ill health. The new crowd were much more on the ball than when he'd been a serving police officer. In the days when he served the community it was much more laid back, especially in the villages. If you misbehaved you got a clip round the ear or a warning. Whereas now, it wasn't just the community that was watched but you and your colleagues too; everyone was under suspicion. The fresh blood wouldn't take any notice of anyone telling them that he was a respectable, retired policeman who had served his community well.

His mind drifted backwards and forwards like a swaying ship. Jonathan, Alice, Nadine....

His thoughts flitted back to Chrissie, and he chuckled to himself as he remembered seeing her frightened face squashed up against the tiny window of her front door; full of panic and shock. If she'd had any common sense, she would have turned her indoor lights off and looked out of her window. He thought everyone knew that you could see into someone's house when they had the lights on, and they couldn't see out unless they turned them off. He'd almost fallen over with laughter when he'd seen her scream at her own reflection. Scraping a razor blade on her windows was working a treat, but he needed to be careful that he didn't get seen there. Luckily, Grace had come home from Chrissie's the other day, saying that she had her friend Sarah arriving for a few days, so he stayed well clear. It would also look like she'd lost the plot if she told her friend about the experiences and there didn't appear to be any evidence of it.

A few days break from Chrissie's house would give him time to plan what he was going to do next.

*

NORFOLK 1987

"I'll meet you in the garden of that old derelict house, where we went the other day? I can't talk to you at yours, I can't risk anyone hearing." Nadine pushed her mouth closer to the receiver as she said the last sentence. "Yes, I'm fine. Honestly. I'll see you tomorrow. We can get in the house through the back door; some old tramp that was living there wrenched it open. Ok? I'll see you in the morning."

Nadine hung up the phone in her parent's bedroom and peered round the door to see if anyone was lurking before she ventured out.

She crept across the hallway quietly so she could get to her room without anyone noticing. She checked again before closing her bedroom door behind her; the only person she hadn't wanted to hear that conversation had been her father.

Unfortunately for Nadine, that one and only person had been eavesdropping on her phone call, standing in the shadows of the study. He had crept outside the door and heard every word. He'd been watching her like a hawk since he'd caught her in his shed. He hadn't been sure of what she'd seen at first, she wasn't giving much away. But he'd felt a definite change in her attitude towards him. She'd sulked in her bedroom more than normal and had been distant and vague, distracted. Grace had put it down to hormones or that she was coming down with something.

Nadine might have been hormonal on account of her age but she definitely wasn't coming down with anything. She was so shell shocked by what she'd seen in her father's shed. She'd looked in almost every box in there. At first she hadn't realised what they were, but then she came across some items she recognised as belonging to one of her friends. That and the blood stains had given the game away.

If she'd run into the house as she'd first intended after making the discovery, she'd probably have survived. But Tim had caught her on her way out of the shed door. Both startled at the sight of each other. The look on his face had made him appear unrecognisable to her and it had frightened her to the core. He didn't have to say anything, that one look in the dusky light of the evening was enough to scare her into silence in case she had discovered his secret.

Grace assumed Tim had scolded her badly for going in his shed and encroaching on his privacy.

Nadine had kept it to herself for quite a few days. There had been a several occasions when she'd approached Grace to tell her but nothing would come out of her mouth and Tim was usually hovering nearby.

She had to talk to someone about it, which was why she'd organised to meet up with her friend.

It had been a race between good and evil. In those few days that she was trying to work things out in her head, Tim was plotting how he could get rid of her.

Unfortunately, he won the race, Nadine had spent too long mulling it over. It was all too huge for her to cope with and she'd had no idea what to do with the information she'd discovered. Apart from knowing that she had to report him, her father.

She'd arrived at the tumble down house early, mainly due to nerves. She wandered round the garden, scuffing up old bits of pottery while she waited for her friend.

She didn't see or hear Tim coming up behind her.

She managed a few muffled screams through his large fingers that were clamped around her mouth, as he dragged her across the rough waste land. As he pushed her into the cess pit and took his hand off her mouth she screamed out 'No!'

Tim made himself scarce, as the dog walker who had passed her earlier heard her scream and ran to her aid. The cess pit was well camouflaged and it was a few hours before Nadine's body was actually found.

CHAPTER SEVEN

Norfolk 1998

Grace was becoming increasingly worried about the strange change in her husband's behaviour. He'd always behaved oddly, but there had been something different about him for the last few weeks. He seemed to be distracted a lot more than normal, and he was frequently absent, not telling her where he was going. It was beginning to unnerve her because it hadn't occurred to her before that he might start looking for more potential victims again. He'd stopped all that as soon as his mother had gone into a retirement home. It had triggered something in his twisted little brain. Grace didn't understand what, but it was the only traumatic thing that had happened to him personally and she couldn't think of another explanation. It had to be personal to affect Tim, because if it wasn't, then he was his usual cold-hearted self. Not that he showed that side of himself to anyone except Grace and his victims.

Grace thought back to the day she'd caught Tim out and the utter shock that still engulfed her as the reality had unfolded in her mind in slow motion.

It had been over a year ago and Tim had been behaving particularly oddly. Grace knew things weren't right between them and hadn't been for many years. He hadn't been near her for months, so she naturally assumed that he was having an affair. She'd searched around the house one day, but found no evidence of another woman. Then she thought about his shed; the precious place that no one was ever allowed to go. She remembered Nadine being really upset because Tim had scolded her badly for catching her in there. She sulked in her bedroom for days and Grace had wondered then why he was so touchy about it. The shed was kept under lock and key and Tim claimed after the incident with Nadine that it was his own private domain. The only place he said he had where he could get away from nagging women. After that he kept his keys on him at all times.

Grace had forgotten about the shed for many years, understandably, because of Nadine's accident overshadowing it all. But when Grace thought he was acting strangely, she remembered how sensitive he was about his shed.

Tim probably hadn't been acting any different to normal; it was just that his personality was more noticeable to Grace because she was looking for a way out. An excuse to leave him; but not the excuse she was going to be dealt.

It had taken a long time to get the keys from him without him knowing. She'd had to wait for him to go on one of his fishing trips with his mates and come home fairly well oiled. She laid on a hearty meal and plenty more drink for him when he got home. The idea was that he'd fall asleep, drunk in front of the television. Giving her time to get the keys and nip down to the shed.

At first when she looked around the cramped old shed, she was surprised at how tidy he kept everything. She'd imagined it to be like any other shed, full of useless old tools, gadgets and dirty magazines. But Tim's shed was different, once you looked passed all the usual things like the lawn mower, garden shears, and cans of turpentine. There were boxes neatly stacked on all the shelves that surrounded the walls of his shed. They were all marked with coloured labels; so all the boxes with blue labels were stacked together, and all the ones with red labels were in their own place and so on and so on. She made a mental note to remember to put the boxes that she took down, back in their rightful place. She didn't want to risk him finding out that she'd ever been in there just in case she didn't discover anything.

Unfortunately, Grace decided to look in the boxes that were hidden under the wooden worktop that Tim had installed in there for what she assumed was potting. They were unmarked and easily accessible to her even though they were pushed out of the way. It took her a few seconds to realise what she was looking at in the boxes. At first she thought they were boxes full of old stained rags, which she thought might be covering up some love letters or photographs; but then she rifled through one of them and found a small soft toy bunny at the bottom. She took it out and stared at it. She remembered thinking how odd it was because she hadn't recalled Nadine having one like it. Then, as she shone the torch on the items she had mistaken for rags she realised that they weren't stained with varnish or wax but what looked like dried blood. Each item she pulled out was a piece of child's clothing; some were inside polythene bags. Vests, school shirts, cardigans, knickers, even hair bands. Some were stained with blood and some weren't. She had passed each item through her hands as if her arms didn't belong to her anymore and it all began to slot into place.

Grace's immediate reaction had been to march straight inside the house and confront the bastard or call the police. She didn't know which. The sad thing was that she wasn't surprised that he could do such a thing, she was just totally devastated and shocked that he had. She had wondered, fleetingly when each child was found, if he had anything to do with it. But she'd quickly pushed it from her mind, scolding herself for having such an abhorrent thought. There had been no logical reason why she should think that about him. Tim was a complete arsehole at home but whatever he was, she always saw him as an excellent police officer. Never in her wildest dreams did she think he was capable of anything so evil. He'd even come home from work and ranted to her about what a sick and twisted bastard the murderer must be and how he and his colleagues didn't know what they'd do to him if they caught him. Unfortunately, it had all been a very clever piece of acting.

Looking back, she'd been glad of the fact she'd discovered his secret while he was pissed. It left her time to think because she was unable to talk to him while he was passed out on the settee.

Grace had always felt prison was far too good for child killers and paedophiles. And as she had begun to think as rationally as she could that night in the shed, she realised that this was the perfect way to get rid of him for good. Tim had always told her the best way to get away with murder was to make it look like the victim had committed suicide. So, that's exactly what she intended to do with him. She just wasn't quite sure when and how. She'd had plenty of time to think about it because she hadn't been worried about him hurting anyone else. The last tragic victim had been ten years ago. And that had been her sister's daughter, Alice. That discovery had hurt her most of all and she wanted revenge so much that she thought it would consume her. The sand timer appeared to be running out though, and Grace didn't want the risk of another victim because that would most definitely be something she couldn't live with on her conscience. Living with the guilt that she'd let him walk free for a year, while she figured out what to do with him, was bad enough.

*

NORFOLK 1983

Tim had placed himself strategically in his car on the sea front with a full view of the beach. He was right at the end of the harbour so he could see everyone on the beach and also had a clear view across the road and along the parade of shops. He'd been over to the newsagents to buy a newspaper and a pasty. Firstly, to make it look like he was just a normal man passing the time in his car having a lunch break. And secondly, so that on his way back from the shop he could check that the sun was shining in the right direction, shielding any view through the windows so that the car appeared to be empty. This was all for the purpose of having full view of all the families arriving for a day out with their children. It was the summer holidays and the coast was crawling with them; Tim's favourite time of year.

He sat in the hot car for hours watching over his paper. The heat and oily stench in the car, which now mixed with his sweat and bad breath didn't seem to bother him like it would anyone else. He was used to being shut in stifling areas for great lengths of time, another skill he had his mother to thank for.

The heat and his lunch laying heavy in his stomach were causing him to feel sleepy. Even though child watching was one of his favourite activities, he was growing bored.

That was until he spotted his next victim, like a sparkling jewel amongst some faded beads. Tim sat up abruptly. He scrambled for the dial so that he could pull up his seat which he'd previously lowered to a reasonable nap level.

Everything and everyone else turned a shade of grey, like a black and white television screen with one person standing out in vibrant colour. That one person flying towards Tim's vision as if she'd been miraculously magnified was twelve year old Jacqueline. She lived further up the coast in the next village with her mother and father and her older brother, so Tim had never encountered her before.

She was walking down the steps to the beach with her family, her gangly frame exposed to the sun, wearing only shorts and a vest top. Apart from being tall and slender for her age, which Tim found immensely attractive, it was her extremely long vibrant red hair that had caught his eye. It was down to her waist, making her appear even taller than she actually was. The tones of her hair sparkled in the afternoon sun, accentuating her deep cornflower blue eyes.

To Tim, she was a stunning object of desire and he wanted her. To anyone else she was a pretty, kind hearted, innocent little girl.

He had made up his mind the moment he set eyes on her that he would pursue her until he got his way.

Jacqueline had gone from having her life spread out endlessly before her to a limit of a few days in a matter of seconds. A decision made by a stranger who was play acting god, with an ego the size of the universe.

No one told Jacqueline or her family that she had only a few days to live. Tim didn't give her that privilege, or any of his victims for that matter. Her father had taken a week off work to spend with his children and wife. They spent the days, carefree in the coastal sunshine, oblivious to the sinister stranger lurking in the back ground like the grim reaper.

Tim effortlessly snatched her as she was walking from the village where she lived to go and meet her brother, who got up before the light of day to go fishing in a nearby pond. Jacqueline had taken to joining him when she got up; leaving their parents to enjoy a lie in before they dragged them up for another day out.

Jacqueline's memory scents had been particularly special to Tim. He normally took one item of clothing and a toy if they had been carrying one. Getting a toy as well as a piece of clothing was a real treat to Tim. Toys carried stronger, different smells. Mainly because they'd come from the child's bed.

In this case though he'd taken Jacqueline's vest top, and pulling her beautiful mane of red hair together, he cut it along the nape of her neck. He tied the pony tail in the middle with the hair bobble she'd been wearing.

He sat on the soft ground next to Jacqueline's twitching, cold body and buried his face in her hair and sniffed hard. He was so astounded by its beauty that it brought a tear to his eye. It glistened golden against the rays of light that were shining through the trees in the small wood where he had dragged its owner.

A blackbird landed on one of the branches near Tim, startling him at first. The bird cocked its head at the sight laid in the clearing as if it had seen it all before. Life and death. A dead girl, lying awkwardly over some tree roots, half naked. With a man sat next to her holding a long piece of golden hair as if he'd discovered the most precious thing in the whole world. To Tim, the line between life and death was flimsy and fickle, all part of the game he was playing.

*

NORFOLK 1998

For the first time since Chrissie had been in her new home, she'd had a completely incident free day. Sarah was arriving in the morning and she wanted to make sure it was as homely as possible.

She didn't know what the cease in activity was about, but she wasn't going to complain about it. For some reason the cottage had taken on an air of calm within its walls and the peace inside was tangible. Chrissie had spent the day soaking up the calm atmosphere, albeit slightly apprehensively. She had got used to it changing so dramatically, but today it all felt different somehow.

She'd felt safe enough to have the doors open and allow some fresh sea air to weave its way around the stagnant old cottage. Perhaps that was what had made the difference, she'd thought to herself as she put flowers in vases, lit oil burners, and unpacked the rest of her books.

She'd not seen a soul that day and had thoroughly enjoyed having some fairly nerve free time to herself.

Opening a bottle of wine and sitting down at her kitchen table with a steaming plate of pasta and fresh shellfish from the local shop, Chrissie let her new home envelope her. She'd even felt comfortable enough to play some music on her stereo, something she hadn't done since she'd arrived, having found comfort and company in the television. She had felt the noise from it had drowned out the spirits that haunted her.

The only thing that made her jump out of her chair that evening was the sudden rush of cats through her open kitchen door, as they made chase with one another in the slightly breezy late summer evening.

*

After a shockingly peaceful night's sleep, Chrissie, having finished making the cottage as homely as possible, sat outside with a cup of coffee and watched her garden.

She loved the transitional stage between summer and autumn where both seasons amicably merged, celebrating the end of one and the beginning of the other.

As she sipped her coffee, Chrissie glanced down towards the bottom of the garden and debated whether or not to venture into the shady area to the old brick shed. The fresh atmosphere of the house had encouraged her to explore her surroundings and wholeheartedly embrace her property without fear.

It all appeared to be peaceful and silent and the only way to conquer it all was to face it and alter the atmosphere herself. After all, this was her house now, and whatever had happened before was in the past and that was where she wanted it to stay.

Feeling a bit more assertive, Chrissie began to wander across the grass, making a mental note of the plants and flowers as she went by, as if by acknowledging them she would be sweeping a new ownership over the entire house and garden.

As she approached the bowed trees which led to the clearing down to the stream she couldn't resist the urge to quickly look behind her. But there was nothing, no horrible feeling, no cold atmosphere, nothing.

Chrissie made her way slowly through the trees, ducking slightly to avoid catching her hair in the branches. There was the stream and the old brick shed which was secretly disguising itself as a chapel. And that's all she could detect, except for the slight anticipation in the pit of her stomach.

Braver still, Chrissie went towards the shed and put her hand on the large metal latch. She turned it and pushed the decrepit door forwards and stared into the empty darkness. A cold, damp breeze swept passed her face and apart from the birds singing and the slight rustle of the leaves in the trees, there was a gentle silence.

Chrissie breathed a sigh of relief and leaned forward to grab the latch on the door and pull it shut. The door seemed to be caught on the floor of the shed and as Chrissie yanked it forward she looked up and noticed the top of the door had come off its hinge.

A vision, albeit brief, swept across her mind and the hairs on her arms lifted, magnetised by the sudden memory. It was of her falling through that very door and scrabbling on the ground in a panic, followed by a need to escape. From what or who she didn't know. Even though the flash in her mind had been brief, she was aware of a feeling that came with the vision that someone else was there. Someone, who she was desperately trying to escape. She sought the comfort of the cottage and ran rather than walked back to the house.

CHAPTER EIGHT

In the morning Chrissie started preparing the dinner for the evening ahead. She just about had time to make a nice autumnal casserole for the slow cooker before her friend Sarah arrived. She'd put the previous night's incident down to another psychic vision. Considering it had unnerved her somewhat, she'd still managed to have a fairly peaceful night's sleep.

She didn't want to dwell on it too much for fear of bringing back a horrible atmosphere or attracting spirits. She didn't understand it all, but it had made her wonder whether or not someone from beyond the grave was trying to lead her to the guilty party.

She shook the thought from her mind and concentrated on the job at hand. A knock at the door made her realise how jumpy she'd become again.

"Goodness me, you gave me a fright! You're early..." said Chrissie, flinging the door open to an equally startled Sarah.

"And you look like you've been caught doing something you shouldn't. Come here!"

They hugged for quite some time and there was more to their embrace than two old friends who hadn't seen each other for a while. Sarah was hugging her friend to give her comfort as though she'd just rescued her from falling down a cliff. Chrissie felt this emotion from her, and allowed Sarah to comfort her. The tears started and she felt like they'd flow forever.

"Come on, let me get in and I'll make us a nice hot drink and then you can tell me all about it," said Sarah, shivering as she entered the strange cottage, unsure whether it was just from what she'd been told or a genuine sense of foreboding.

After Chrissie had explained wearily every little detail of the activities that had been haunting her, Sarah insisted on a tour of the old house. They avoided the garden for the time being because Chrissie was feeling rather uneasy again. Postponing the garden had relieved Sarah. She hadn't liked the sound of the old brick shed that looked like a chapel, not if the house was anything to go by. Sarah didn't say anything to Chrissie, not wanting to frighten her anymore than she was, but the house had the most awful atmosphere and Sarah couldn't understand what charm anyone could possibly see in the place. The garden and the look of the cottage, she accepted, was very attractive, but once inside it gave off a feeling of terrible foreboding.

"Right," said Sarah, pulling out a chair at the kitchen table and plonking herself down in it, "we need to work out whether or not these feelings are coming from you or from an outside influence."

"What do you mean? Of course it's an outside influence. I'm not making it up."

Chrissie stared meaningfully at her best friend, praying that after all she'd told her she wasn't going to say it was all in her mind.

"Calm down." said Sarah, making herself more comfortable in her chair and tucking her blonde hair behind her ears, "I didn't mean that at all. What I meant was it could be a memory from your past that is being stirred by these surroundings or there is some sort of spirit trying to reach you with a message. I suspect it is the latter after you told me about the child that was found at the bottom of the garden."

"How could it be something from my past? I'd know about it, surely?"

"Not necessarily. All our memories are logged somewhere in our brains, but we aren't always capable of accessing them. Sometimes due to fear we block them. I wasn't actually talking about memories from this life, but maybe you're experiencing something that has come from a past life. And I did just say I don't think that is the cause."

"I don't know what to think anymore. Oh God, I feel like I'm going mad! You know when you feel like you're just about keeping it all together but one little thing could cause you to tip over the edge?"

Chrissie put her head in her hands, and Sarah sat quietly, deep in thought watching her, whilst she drained the dregs of her tea cup.

'Why don't you have a therapy session with me while I'm here?' Sarah rubbed Chrissie's arm, trying to comfort her friend.

"Do you think it'll work or will I just be stirring up more trouble?" Chrissie squeezed Sarah's hand and got up from the kitchen table to get herself some tissue from the downstairs toilet, so she could blow her nose. She wasn't sure she believed whole-heartedly in what Sarah did even though she was a professional hypnotherapist, Chrissie found some of her views hard to grasp.

"Of course it'll help, I'm not saying it'll be easy and it might reveal some things that you may have to confront and deal with, but if you don't..."

A loud scream caused Sarah to throw back her chair and run to Chrissie who was still in the toilet.

"What is it!?" Sarah grabbed Chrissie.

"It's ok... I'm ok," Chrissie stuttered through gasps as she gripped her chest, "it's a bloody great black spider..."

"You frightened the living day lights out of me! I thought there was a headless figure in here or something!' she laughed and put her arm around her friend.

"Now, that's not funny." said Chrissie.

"And neither is your irrational fear of spiders..."

*

Tim watched his mother as she rattled on about the issues she had with the staff in the retirement home. He couldn't quite fathom how you could so passionately love someone but detest them at the same time. He hadn't even loved his own daughter like he loved his mother. Loved her yes, but not with the intensity that he did his mother. He'd never been able to understand that paternal bond that all his friends talked about. He just remembered having these strange, confused feelings for her, knowing that she was his daughter and he was supposed to feel this overwhelming love for her. And he'd assumed when she was born that it would be similar to the love he felt for his mother. He'd waited and waited, but nothing, other than a growing feeling of fondness because he thought she looked a little bit like him. But then she'd betrayed him and whatever love he'd had for her had dissipated like early morning mist. Unbeknownst to Tim, she couldn't have looked anything like him; it wasn't possible, as she didn't belong to him.

"You haven't listened to a word I've said have you? I don't know why you bother coming to visit me at all if you're just going to sit there and stare at the wall."

"I was listening Mother, I always do. I've told you before that if you've got a problem with the staff here then you must make a complaint to the manager when you see her."

"And what good is she going to do, pray tell? She's just as useless as them. Don't worry about it, Timothy, I'll ask Eve when she comes to visit." Daphne gave Tim one of her scathing looks and continued taking out her anger on the innocent blood orange she was peeling.

"What's she been visiting you for?"

"Her in laws have moved in here and we bumped into each other. When she pops in on them, she often comes to see me as well, if you must know."

"Grace never said."

"Why would she? It's none of her business. So, tell me son, what have you been doing with yourself? Nothing you shouldn't, I hope?" Daphne concentrated on the task in hand, not wanting to meet Tim's empty gaze.

"Oh, nothing much, just the odd boat trip to do a spot of fishing…" Tim glanced at his watch. He was finding the visit quite strained and terribly boring.

"If you need to be somewhere, just go. I don't want your pity and I certainly don't want you sitting here when you've clearly got other more pressing things to do."

"Ok, Mother, I'll see you next week." Tim chose to ignore his mother's sarcasm and seized the opportunity to leave. He kissed her on the top of her head, harder than he'd meant. For a second he thought she was going to topple forward off her chair, but she didn't. She just stayed where she was as if rigour mortis was paying her a visit.

Tim couldn't believe how much older she looked compared to other people of her age. There wasn't even any disease speeding up the ageing process. She'd smoked up until a few years ago, and now, she was stooped and pruned like a wizened old woman.

He could have understood it if she'd had a hard, poverty stricken life filled with worries. But apart from one trauma that had happened before he was born, she'd lived a life which many people could only hope for.

While Tim was busy filling his head with thoughts of his mother, she was doing exactly the same about him.

Daphne sat for quite some time in her little chair, staring at the segments of her blood orange, as if she had revealed the answer to all life's problems inside that one piece of fruit.

*

"I thought we'd go outside today, Daphne, get some fresh air?"

"Is it cold out, dear?"

"No, it's unseasonably warm, which is why it'd be nice to take advantage of it while we can. I'll fetch you a chair."

Daphne pulled back the net curtain with her spindly fingers, smiling to herself. She loved her time with Eve, lived for it. It made her realise how much she'd longed for another daughter for all those years. And Eve had done more for her in the few months she'd been visiting than Tim had his entire life. She listened and cared, which was all Daphne wanted.

It was an unlikely match having listened to what Grace had told her about her mother-in-law over the years. But most of this had been Tim filling Grace's head with lies in order for her to hate his mother as much as he did.

But a bond had formed that couldn't be explained. Daphne had been wandering in the garden of the retirement home and had found Eve sitting on the bench deep in thought. Daphne had joined her, remembering her vaguely from family parties and the odd outing. A connection had formed from there on in.

Eve admired Daphne's truthfulness and direct manner. This was viewed by other people as harsh and spiteful. But Eve knew where she stood with her and there was an element of this within Eve as well. They both had an ability to be truthful however much it offended others and people didn't like it. It amazed both of them how people said they wanted honesty but when they were it was met with a frosty offended attitude. Neither could understand why people wanted to be lied to. This caused them to be loners in the world. The only friends they would ever have would be like minded people.

They'd spotted this trait in one another during some banter, not long after they'd first sat on the bench together. Daphne had made some clipped, waspish comment at her. She'd waited for the usual expression of hurt, anger or dismay and instead was faced with a smile and a look of fellowship. Eve had quipped right back at her and there then formed a bond.

Personality traits weren't the only things that welded them together.

Eve carefully manoeuvred the wheelchair through the open door.

"Why would you make doorframes so narrow?"

"When they knew it was for a retirement home and it needs to use wheelchairs? You say it every time, Eve!"

"Well, it's becoming a ritual. I've said it so many times that if I don't you might get wedged in the door forever!"

"You stupid girl, hurry up and get me into that sunshine. At this rate it'll be Christmas."

"Have you seen Tim this week?"

"Only his usual habitually forced visit. Don't know why he bothers."

"A mixture of guilt, habit and love, I should think."

"Oh I'm not daft enough to think that he loves me, Eve. That's long gone."

"What makes you think that?"

Daphne paused to breathe in the fresh air as Eve burst out of the double doors and into the sunshine. She likened it to being resuscitated and she savoured every moment, seeing as she spent most of the time stuck in her private room on the premises.

"Well, it finished when he met your sister, not that we were ever close when he was at home. I never bonded with him you see. He adored me, mainly because I wasn't there much. He mistook it for love though; his motherly figure was Dora who looked after him most of the time. I suppose I would have been diagnosed with post natal depression in this day and age. Couldn't cope with being a mother to him, missed my daughter dreadfully."

Eve remembered Grace telling her that Daphne had lost a baby girl before Tim came along.

"But don't all children love their parents? Just because you weren't there much doesn't mean he didn't love you."

"Tim's different though, sweetheart. He'll tell you he's always loved me but whatever was there seemed to diminish when Grace came along. I'm not blaming her Eve; it would have happened whoever had come along. However prepared you are for it, it still cuts you like a knife. It made me realise how ineffectual I'd been when he was growing up."

Eve paused in front of some rose bushes so that Daphne could touch the flowers. She loved roses; they were her favourites in the whole landscaped garden. Eve often pondered that Daphne wasn't dissimilar to a rose, strong, honest, robust, with prickly thorns depicting her truthfulness.

"But that's not what happens to all people who get married. My brothers were still close to our mother, they still loved her."

"I know that," Daphne waved a bejewelled hand causing her rings to turn on her twiggy like fingers, "but we're talking about Tim, dear. He isn't capable of loving more than one person

115

at a time. He focuses on an obsession. I suspect he doesn't love your sister anymore if the truth be known."

Eve was slightly shocked by this last statement; she assumed everything was ticking along nicely with Grace.

"You mean he's in love with someone else? Who?"

"That's what worries me, dear."

Eve pondered on what she'd just heard. The more Daphne told her about Tim, the stranger Eve thought he was. She had never seen this side of her brother in law. As she walked along the pretty garden, pushing Daphne in her chair, she marvelled at the various factors which made up people's personalities, like complex mathematical shapes.

*

NORFOLK 1988

Alice was in her bedroom, getting changed for the fourth time that day. She was meeting a friend, a boy from school, in a matter of hours and the panic of what to wear had gripped her. They were going to the end of term disco and she wanted to get it right. He was the most popular boy in the school and there were plenty who would have wanted to be in her shoes.

She couldn't make up her mind whether or not to stop at her Aunt Grace's house on the way there. She often popped in for a chat, which was something she had done more frequently since Nadine's accident. She was extremely close to Grace and had been to her cousin too. She'd taken the news of Nadine's accident very hard and she liked to check in on her aunt to make sure she was ok. They had bonded more tightly in their grief and Alice could tell, even though she was young, that her Uncle Tim wasn't terribly supportive.

Unsure of whether she had time, but so excited because she wanted to show Grace her outfit and get her opinion, she changed her mind several times whilst getting ready. That one tiny decision was to determine the rest of Alice's life. Live or die, live or die, live or die. What seemed to her a mere trivial choice was actually a massive universal one, only, Alice didn't know it. Choice 'A' had the 'life' tag in its box, and choice 'B' had the 'death' tag with it.

Unfortunately, she unwittingly opened the lid of box B, and stepped into the film set of the last few hours of her life. And like Alice falling down the rabbit hole, once she'd opened the lid, she was committed.

Alice made her way to her aunt's house, after saying goodbye to her anxious mother. It was the first time her parents had let her go to a school disco, especially with a boy. But she was fifteen now, and they felt they had to loosen the apron strings at some point.

It was a beautiful summer evening, and Alice almost skipped down the road to her fate. She stopped at the crossroads and looked left and right. It was to be her last chance to change her mind. Left was a slow stroll, with time to stop at the village shop for some sweets, a quick chat with the owner, Mrs. Newton, and then on to meet Jeremy at the playing field. Right was down the road a hundred yard and right again onto the bumpy track leading to the back door of Auntie Grace's, where no one was there apart from her Uncle Tim.

CHAPTER NINE

Norfolk 1998

Dear Alice,

It saddens me to write this letter, and I don't really know how to tell you, but I think I'll just have to come out with it.

Daddy has decided that it would be best if we separated for a little while, and he has gone to live somewhere else. He's renting a small cottage in the next village, so it gives us some space between us. It's close enough though in case I need him for anything.

I don't know how to feel about it really, or what to say to you. I suppose it was always on the cards if I'm honest. We both want different things and neither of us can meet in the middle. I just hope you understand, darling. One thing we do want you to know is that we don't blame you at all. It's just something that often happens between couples. They grow apart.

Even though we'll be living apart, darling, we will still both be here for you when you come home. And we love you just the same, even though we're not together. I still pray every night that you'll come home again.

Loving you always xxx

*

"Dad, come over here, I've found something!"

"What have you found now? Another piece of pottery I suppose?"

Carl Meakin wandered over to the clearing where his daughter was standing with her hand on her hip and one foot on the spade she was using to dig with. Attitude oozed from her and she raised an eyebrow at her father's comment.

"No, not 'another' piece of pottery, I've found a necklace actually." Jessica said, with emphasis. She'd been out metal detecting with her dad for most of the day. They'd got permission from the farm owner, on the condition that he had a share in whatever they found. They'd started the day as always, quite optimistically, only to get towards tea time, tired, and a bit fractious with one another. He was fed up of her showing him pieces of flowery pottery and she with him for calling her over to look at rusty bits of metal.

Carl examined the tarnished piece of jewellery, soil caked in its links.

"Well, that's a bit of a find, girl! It's not very old, but I think its silver, and it's got a nice semi precious stone on it. Where'd you find it?"

"Down there in that hole in the clearing," Jessica said, feeling quite chuffed with her treasure. "I think there must have been a small pond there, but the sun has dried the water up."

"Yeah, there is normally water in there; it's called a 'mere'. You can tell by the cracks in the soil, and the slightly different shade of dirt. Let me look."

Carl stepped down the slight embankment into the empty mere and peered into the large hole his daughter had dug.

"You should have marked out a patch with your spade like I told you to; you've dug far too wide."

"I know Dad. You say that every time we come out."

"Well, I wouldn't have to if you did what I asked. You're all over the ruddy place. You start with a square foot each time and then if you find anything..."

"Yeah, yeah, I know, you can widen the square. God, Dad we're not professionals – Dad what is it?'

"I'm not sure yet love, pass me my trowel."

Carl had noticed some strange, familiar shapes at the bottom of the hole his daughter had dug. They were like pieces of stone embossed in the flat damp pit, all linked together. Something you wouldn't notice whilst you were digging, but was quite obvious when you observed it from above. Carl scuffed the soil off one of the lumps with his boot and a creamy colour began to appear.

"Dad?" Jessica passed her father the trowel.

"Just a minute, please!"

"Alright, alright!" Jessica sighed and wandered over to the patch her father was working on.

Carl jumped out of the dried up mere and stared down at the base of the hole. It appeared to be the outline of a human body. Lying almost like a curled up foetus. Carl stepped around the hole to view it from another angle, trying to convince himself that it was an animal. But it didn't matter which way he looked at it, it was what it was, the remains of a human being. The wiggly outline of the necklace his daughter had found was still imprinted in the mud. Jessica had, without realising it, dug down into someone's grave. An eerie feeling crept through Carl's stomach and into his throat. This wasn't a proper burial site, so why would the remains look like they were lying in a foetal position?

"Jessica, can you go and get my phone out of the truck please?"

"Yeah, why, what's the matter?" Jessica had noticed her father had turned an odd shade. "Have you found something really exciting? Are we going to be millionaires? You've found the King John's treasure haven't you? I knew it was crap about it being in the Wash–"

"No Jessica, don't come over here, just get me the phone." Carl began to climb back up the embankment to prevent his daughter walking over.

"I want to see, what is it? Dad, you're scaring me…"

"No, just for once will you do as I ask!"

Jessica didn't argue with him, she'd never seen her father like this before, and scuttled to the truck to get the phone.

"Whatever you do, don't go back over to the hole you've dug, sweetheart. I don't want you to see it, and you mustn't tread near it. Ok?" His voice softened to try and keep her calm.

"Why Dad, please tell me what you've found, you're as white as a sheet?" Jessica's eyes filled with tears, her father was frightening her.

Carl didn't know how else to say it, without scaring her. He certainly didn't want his sixteen year old daughter looking into the grave she'd dug up. It'd give her nightmares for years, something he was sure he would be having for the next few weeks.

"I think, we've uncovered a grave, and I need to call the police and get them to come out and check it over. Nothing to panic about, it's fine."

Jessica dropped the dirt encrusted necklace as if it had suddenly glowed like a red hot coal. Carl bent down and picked it up, noticing his daughters look of horror.

"It's probably all above board, sweetheart and has been there for hundreds of years. Now, why don't you pour us the last of the coffee from the flask and I'll give the police a quick ring."

"But you said that the necklace wasn't very old."

"I don't think the necklace you found has anything to do with it, so sit down there and drink your coffee."

*

NORFOLK 1965

The boxes were all laid out neatly on the floor of Tim's bedroom. He sat before them, proud of the little treasures he'd stolen.

Each one had been achieved by stealing from people in the village as a dare with his friends. Only, the difference was that Tim's friends ditched theirs, the thrill having gone once they'd won the game and achieved it without getting caught.

They looked up to Tim, even though they thought he was a bit strange. But he'd gained kudos at school because of his talent for being the best thief.

His little trophies meant more to him than they did to the other boys; this was what made him such a good thief. He badly

124

wanted what he was stealing, like a magpie with its beady eye on a prize. Tim's trophies were significant of his increasing power.

He often sat in his bedroom and surveyed his handiwork, the excitement rising in his stomach. All the boxes looked the same so he had no idea which box held which items. He'd play a guessing game sometimes when he'd nothing better to do, or when Dora had ordered him to stay in his room. He knew better from past experience not to disobey her. She always managed to come up with a punishment that was worse than the last.

This was one such occasion. His father was at work and it was the summer holidays. Severe rain had put pay to any play time activities outside with the other boys, and Dora couldn't bear him coming home with dirty sodden clothes on. That just warranted another punishment.

He began to play his game of guessing the items in the boxes after he'd mixed them all up. He heard Dora running up the stairs giggling. Her foot fall was followed by a much heavier one and her laughter trailing behind a far deeper anonymous male voice.

Tim hated those days trapped in his room, trying desperately to drown out the noises he could hear coming from his parent's bedroom. Noises he didn't quite understand but which he knew would anger his mother and father greatly, had they come home and caught Dora. There was no point in him telling them; his mother scolded him if he bothered his father after work and he'd long given up telling his mother anything.

She just accused him of lying, making things up because he wanted her to come home. She was incapable of showing him any attention other than what she really had to. So he moved his affections to his possessions.

When he got really lost in his game, he could look at each item, smell it and drift into another world of memories. Making up games about where the item had come from. He had quite a collection building up and some of the things he had stolen were quite valuable. He had fine pieces of jewellery, brooches, rings, tie pins, silk scarves and gloves, hats and ties, underwear and blouses. Summer was the best time to steal from people. They tended to leave doors open and things laying about ready to be lifted. That was Tim's logic, if people took more care of their things and really wanted them, they wouldn't leave them out to be stolen. It was ingrained in him, a form of conditioning he got from his mother, that possessions were to be stored away. Tim took this school of thought to include people.

*

NORFOLK 1987

Alice excitedly picked at the layers of tape holding the floral paper wrapped around the box, while her parents busied themselves making tea and toast. It was Alice's birthday and she was sat at the kitchen table ploughing through her cards and

126

gifts. The one that meant the most to her was the one her father had given her. The one she'd left until last. Eve and Jon, her parents, usually gave her a present that was from both of them. They'd still followed this tradition but Jon had wanted to get her something special that he'd chosen and was solely from him.

This had really touched Alice. She knew that dads didn't really get involved in going shopping and choosing presents, it didn't seem to be in their nature. So the idea her father had chosen something especially for her had filled her with excitement.

"Oh Dad, how much tape did you use, I can't get it off!"

"I didn't want you snooping around before your birthday and peeking. Like you do with your mother's loose wrapping."

"Well, there's no danger of that here. Can you pass me the scissors please?"

"Careful you don't mark the box, I'll have to take it back to the shop once you've opened it."

Alice's face dropped. "Why?"

"Don't wind her up on her birthday, Jon!" Eve gave him a swipe on her way to the table with a pot of tea.

"Dad!"

"Oh, just hurry up and open it. The suspense is killing me! I'm not used to all this malarkey." Jon pulled out a chair and joined his daughter at the table.

Silence descended in the room apart from the snipping of scissors as Alice desperately tried to prize open the tightly wrapped little box, a pained expression on her face. This was rapidly replaced with a look of elation when she finally opened the box and saw the beautiful pendant and chain hanging from the blue velvet cushion inside, a smile was quickly followed by tears, which was then chased with a scream.

Alice jumped up and flung herself onto her father's lap.

"Do you think she likes it, Eve? I was hoping to get a refund."

"Daddy!" Alice slapped his arm, and then showered his face in kisses, "I love it! It's the best thing ever! I love you!"

"And I love you too, sweetheart."

*

Norfolk 1998

"Where are you going in such a hurry?"

"I'm going over to Eve's; Alice's remains have been found."

Grace glanced at Tim to see his reaction; a shadow passed across his face. She wouldn't have noticed it if she hadn't been married to him for so long. But there was a definite flicker of an emotion, although she was unsure of which one. She glared at him with pure burning hatred and repressed the urge to smash open his skull like a walnut in a nutcracker.

"Alice has been found? Are they sure it's her?"

"Of course they're sure, even you should know that! They've done all the tests. A local man and his daughter were out metal detecting and found her a few days ago," Grace snapped at him.

"Oh dear. Poor Eve. Does Jon know?"

This last sentence was said with such insincerity that Grace could only stare at him for a few moments. She was at such a loss to know what to say to him or quite any idea as to what to do.

"I don't know, Tim, I should imagine so. Why don't you go over there and see if he needs some support. My main priority, at the moment, is my sister. She was bad enough before Alice was found, goodness knows what this will do to her.'

Tim almost fell into the kitchen chair as he watched the back of his wife head out of the door. He was wondering who the hell had found her and why they'd been in such a secluded spot. He didn't need to worry about that though, he just needed to act as if he knew nothing about it. That would be fairly easy for Tim, it'd happened such a long time ago that he'd become almost completely detached from it. What he most definitely needed to do was to clear out his shed. The police would be re-opening all the cases, once they connected Alice to the others, and they would probably search the whole village again, especially now they had all that new blood at the station.

He sat for a while, trying to gauge how he felt about it. Alice had been the one that he'd carefully buried, not wanting her to be found. The mere used to dry up in the summer and he knew that years of climate change would cause it to be permanently filled with water, but he hadn't anticipated the particularly hot summer they'd had. But then, why would he? He'd buried her quite deep in the ground, in the middle of nowhere, where no one ventured. Or so he'd thought. And he'd more or less forgotten about her, apart from the lovely memory scent he had of her.

She had looked like an angel when he'd laid her in his home made wooden box. He'd caught her stirring slightly just before he sealed the lid and realised she wasn't dead. But he didn't have time to mess about and he knew the lack of air in the box underground would finish her off fairly quickly, if the hyperthermia didn't get to her first.

He wasn't worried about the police finding any of his DNA; he was too careful to leave anything. The bonus for any psychopath was having an Obsessive Compulsive Disorder in cleanliness. Anyway, she'd been under the ground for far too long for there to be anything of any significance left.

The best thing he could do was to burn all the boxes of memory scents and get himself over to his brother-in-law's house and pretend like he cared. He'd have to get his thrills in some other way for the time being and Chrissie would provide plenty of those. His arrogance had reached nauseating new levels and he wasn't worried one tiny bit that he might get caught. He'd gotten away with it for this long, who was going to catch him out now?

CHAPTER TEN

"Four, three, two, one, and now I want you to look down at your feet and when you're ready, tell me where you are?"

Sarah watched Chrissie as she floated into hypnosis and waited for her to settle and answer her question. Chrissie would either be transported into a significant time in a past life, or one more recent.

"I'm standing on a grassy cliff....no shoes...the sun is warm. We're having a picnic." Chrissie's voice came out raspy and shallow and slightly childlike.

"Who are you with?" Sarah kept her voice soft and gentle so as not to startle her out of her hypnosis.

"My Mum and sisters…. Dad's gone to the shop for ice creams. Mum's playing catch with us…"

"Who are you?"

"Christine, I'm Christine."

"Ok, Christine, I want you to go to the next significant point in your life."

Chrissie stirred slightly under the blanket that Sarah had put over her to keep her warm.

"Where are you now Christine?"

"I'm…I'm on the swing…"

"Where is the swing?"

"In the garden....but it's not our house. It's dark...Mum's calling me for bed...but I don't want to come in."

"Whose house are you at?"

Sarah watched her friend begin to stir under the blanket; her brow furrowed and she was starting to make peculiar noises.

"Christine, where are you?"

But Chrissie seemed unable to speak and her head was swaying from side to side as if she was trying to get away from something. Her hands began to grip the blanket and tears sprung from her eyes; all that was coming out of her mouth was muffled crying.

"It's alright Christine, I'm going to touch your arm and then count backwards from ten and bring you safely back into this room. Ten...nine...eight...seven..."

Chrissie started to calm as she slowly returned back to the comfort of her living room, and her own surroundings.

"Don't sit up just yet sweetheart. Stay where you are for a few minutes and take some deep breaths."

Sarah went into Chrissie's kitchen and poured them both a glass of water. When she went back into the room, Chrissie was sitting on the sofa and rubbing her face.

"Are you ok?"

"I think so. That was really strange."

"You got as far as the swing and then you became really distressed, which is why I bought you back. What happened?"

"It was so weird, because I was there and aware of being here at the same time. Is that normal?" Chrissie asked, gratefully taking the glass of water from Sarah.

"Yes, it's your physical self keeping a connection with the here and now." Sarah said, trying to be patient with her friend, but eager to know what had happened.

"I seemed to be reliving a very vivid memory, or so I thought, but I heard an animal noise by the gate in the garden where the swing was and the next thing I knew there was a large gloved hand over my face. It was horrible." Chrissie started to cry again.

"That's awful, did you know who it was?" Sarah handed Chrissie a tissue.

"No, but it was definitely a man. He was dragging me along what I felt was a dark track or alleyway. It was pitch black and I just remember feeling really frightened and being unable to scream. As I was coming back into the room, I could hear my mother calling me." Chrissie blew her nose and stared at Sarah as if she had an explanation for it all.

"Why would I have a memory of my childhood merged with what must be a past life?"

"I'm not so sure that it was a past life. You referred to yourself as Christine, which was what you were called as a child."

"But I would remember something like that, surely? Could it have been something paranormal?"

"What do you mean?"

"Well, I know it sounds weird, but could it have been a spirit showing me something that happened to them."

"It could be, but didn't you say it was a memory from your childhood?"

"Yes, I remember the house vaguely. It could have been a holiday home we stayed in."

"I hate to tell you this Chrissie, but you may have just recalled a memory from your childhood that you blocked out."

Chrissie pondered on this information while Sarah made them both some fresh coffee.

"It can't be. My parents would have told me. Wouldn't they?"

"Not necessarily. It could explain their protectiveness of you."

"Hang on a minute, there's just one small problem with this whole thing! If that was a memory from my childhood, then how am I still here?" Chrissie said, jumping up from the sofa and joining her friend in the kitchen.

"What do you mean?"

"I wouldn't be alive now would I?"

"What makes you think this memory ended in death? Perhaps you got away?"

"No, no. I think it was one of the murdered children trying to show me something. I need to explore the village to try and trigger my memory." Chrissie drained her coffee cup. Her brain was working overtime, a feeling of excitement was creeping through her body and she really felt like she was onto something.

Sarah looked on with concern; she wasn't convinced it wasn't a memory Chrissie had stirred up in this life. Or maybe a past life had merged with this one. She hadn't seen it before in all the years she had been a therapist, but it was a possible explanation.

*

Dear Alice,

So, this is it my darling. Now I finally know what happened to my little angel after all these years. And now that I know, it seems the only realistic explanation. It's funny how you can see it all so clearly when you're given the true facts.

I feel like someone's dropped me into an ice cold ocean, which has awoken me. Woken me from the world I've lived in for ten years, where you walk through the gate and up the path to the front door.

I think I preferred that world. Although I knew deep down you were never coming home. In my moments of panic when time passed and I constantly went to the window, I knew you'd never be there.

Ignorance is bliss, or so they say. Well, I wouldn't go that far, but I wish I could stop all the clocks and the world, so I can stay in that time where you come home. That's a poem I think...can't remember. Who cares? I can't even recall how I felt before. The atmosphere has engulfed me.

I thought I'd feel relieved, but I don't. I just feel like it's all over; over forever. I used to envy the other parents in the village who'd lost their child. Awful I know, but they had something that I never had in this whole tragic mess. They had the knowledge of what had happened to their children, instead of spending every moment going over the same scenario, and then inventing new ones to chew over.

Being privy to that information, albeit horrific, felt to me like you could somehow try and move on with your life, if that's at all possible. Not having to wonder, and at some point reaching a time of acceptance. Something you have no control over has changed forever, so the only solution is to live your life the best way you can.

But I don't envy those parents anymore, not with the news I now have. It's just a different type of nightmare, worse than the last, and full of unanswered and unthinkable questions. A different set of scenarios to play in the cinema of my mind, and I don't want to see the reruns. But they'll play and play, and no amount of crying or time is ever going to change anything.

Loving you always and forever xxx

137

*

NORFOLK 1998

"How's your sister?"

"As to be expected."

"Have the police said anymore?"

"Not really." Grace said crisply. She was in no mood for a conversation with Tim.

"Oh. I went to see Jon. He seems to be handling it ok, said he knew all along."

"Good for Jon."

"Have I done something wrong, Grace?"

"Bloody hell Tim, it's not all about you all the time! My sister's just found out what's happened to her daughter after all these years. Give me a break!"

"Ok, ok!" Tim put his hands up defensively. "I was only saying."

Grace busied herself putting wet laundry into the tumble dryer, and then began rifling through the cupboards and fridge.

"What are you doing?"

"I'm going to stay with Eve for a few nights, and I need to take some food and clean bed linen with me." Grace resumed her search for the makings of a cottage pie.

"What? Leave me here on my own?" Tim attempted a forlorn look.

"I'm sure you'll survive. I'm just going to make this and wait for the washing to dry, and then I'll be off."

"Oh, is that for me?" Tim was enjoying winding her up. He was perfectly capable of looking after himself; he'd done it enough times on his boat trips. He was looking forward to having the house to himself. He just wanted to get a rise out of her before she left; another one of his kicks.

"Don't!" Grace glared at him, as she pointed a gleaming kitchen knife she was using to chop onions, in his direction.

"Alright, alright! I'll have to order in a takeaway." Tim threw over his shoulder as he walked into the sitting room to watch the rest of the football.

Grace stood there for a time, staring at the space where her husband had been. As if staring would cause her to suddenly wake up and discover that the whole thing had never happened, and that Nadine was upstairs in her bedroom and Tim had died in some freak accident. And Alice was at home with Eve and Jon. But life wasn't like that. While she was enjoying this vision, another film was playing in her mind. One where she had walked from the kitchen into the sitting room and plunged the knife so hard into Tim that it pierced the sofa underneath. Then she began wondering how she would get rid of the stains and his sorry corpse. And, she mused, she quite liked the sofa and he wasn't worth it. No, no, no, it was far too messy and not something that would look remotely like suicide. She snapped back into reality and continued chopping. Her sister needed her right now, and that's what she had to concentrate on. She'd have plenty of time when Eve was settled into bed to think about Tim's exit from this world.

*

NORFOLK 1988

`

Alice had appeared to stop breathing several times while she endured the rape of her fifteen year old body. And it was rape in every sense of the word. Tim was so violent with his niece that the shock caused unconsciousness similar to a drug induced trance. Every time she became aware of her physical self and the horror of what was happening, she was sick. Which only resulted in Tim becoming more intolerant and cross with her; he appeared to be angry and euphoric at the same time. At one point she thought she was going to choke on her own vomit, because Tim had rammed tissues into her mouth as a way to stem the flow of sick. This only served to make her gag even more, the tissue turning to soggy pulp in her mouth.

Tim didn't like human waste of any kind, it repulsed him, and he wasn't going to let it spoil his long awaited moment with her.

What she thought was going to be her last memory, was of her Uncle Tim looking down on her. She was standing on the other side of the room watching herself, one of those out of body experiences that she'd heard and read about.

She watched her uncle with his hands around her tiny neck, squeezing the last bit of life out of her. Her eyes bulged out of her porcelain coloured face, blood, spittle, and vomit drying around her nose and mouth.

She stood in the corner watching this scenario and prayed to die. She swayed like a piece of driftwood washed up on the shore. Backwards and forwards, backwards and forwards.

Alice thought she was in her bedroom on the floor when she woke up. It was cold and so dark that even the widening of her eyes made no difference to the light. The memories of what had happened suddenly stung her like a swarm of bees and reawakened the physical pain in her body. Even her skin hurt.

Alice tried to move to get up off her bedroom floor and turn the light on, but the bang and pain of her head hitting some wood made her realise she wasn't where she thought she was. Confusion hit her at first, and then she thought that maybe she was dreaming. The flash of her out of body experience flew in front of her eyes, and for a split second she thought she might be in hell. The pounding of her heartbeat and the goose bumps on her skin told her she was very much alive.

Alice knew she was naked even though her body felt so alien to her. She was freezing cold and breathing was becoming harder and harder. She tried again to sit up, but the same thing happened. A noise like the sound of crumbling plaster fell on her. She moved her hands beside her to feel what she was laying on. It felt like floorboards, rough and covered in splinters.

As Alice became more and more conscious and able to move her body, she quickly realised she was in a large box, which she suspected was in the ground. Her limbs came into contact with every side of it as she moved around; small insects began to crawl across her sensitive skin as they found their way through the gaps. And she soon discovered it was soil that was falling on her through the cracks in the wood, not plaster.

Panic hit her like a lightning strike and she screamed from the bottom of her soul. But she soon realised no amount of clawing and screaming was going to save her.

Alice gave up after what seemed like hours; her hands throbbed from banging the lid of the box and her fingers were sticky with blood from clawing at the wood. This had only served to cause more soil to drop through the cracks.

Waves of panic washed over her and she cried and cried.

She managed to lie on her side and pull her knees up to her chest in an attempt at comforting herself. She wept for her mother and father who'd be wondering where she was. The tide of panic set in again, and she knew they'd never find her. When the tide went out Alice prayed someone would rescue her, but this tiny glimmer of optimism was short lived and after a few hours Alice began to pray again for Death. He was the only being that was going to save her from this horrific nightmare. But there would be no standing at the crossroads deciding whether to turn right or left. Not once he'd lifted her from the box; his path would take her down a dead end. But right now that pathway held the hope of comfort and eternal sleep.

She slipped in and out of consciousness only to repeat the nightmare of realising where she was over and over again.

Eventually, Death came to collect her. And Alice died, imagining she had fallen asleep safe and warm in her mother's arms, with the necklace that her father had bought her for her birthday in the palm of her hand.

CHAPTER ELEVEN

Norfolk 1998

Chrissie and Sarah had searched most of the small coastal village. There were plenty of familiar areas, but not the place that was in Chrissie's subconscious. She felt like she was hitting a brick wall at every turn. She'd called her mother before she'd left the house but she wasn't there, so Chrissie had left a message. She had no luck with either of her sisters, they were out too. She wanted to talk to them about her session with Sarah to see if there was any light they could shine on it. It was mainly to satisfy Sarah's theory of it all, and their absence only further proved to Chrissie that this wasn't the path she needed to follow.

"I'm a great believer in finding things when you're not looking for them, and we seem to be going around in circles." Sarah pulled the sleeves of her sweater over her hands as a chilly wind began to whistle down the street. "Why don't we stop in that lovely café we just passed and have a coffee?"

"Ok, but can we just try that track again? The one where we turned right, but could have turned left as well?" Chrissie wanted to explore every little area before she gave in; a foible that was every part of her nature and one that sometimes infuriated her friends.

"But doesn't that way take us back towards your house? Why don't we do that after we've had a coffee, via the beach? Come on Chrissie, I'm gasping here!"

Sarah grabbed Chrissie's arm to stop her striding so she could show her friend that she meant it.

Chrissie shrugged and sighed.

"Ok, you're right. We need a break. It can't hurt to stop for a few minutes. Come on."

Sarah watched her stride towards the café, slightly worried Chrissie was letting this whole thing take over. Once they were nicely ensconced in the seaside café, and Sarah could slip her shoes off and discover her feet again, she decided it was time for a little chat.

"Do you think it might be better to just wait until all this unfolds naturally?" Sarah made an attempt at diplomacy, not something she was used to.

"You think I'm becoming obsessed with it, don't you?" Chrissie said, adding more sugar to her cup.

"No....but I think you could be in danger of becoming so. I don't disbelieve what you're saying about the activity in the house, and maybe someone is trying to tell you something, but surely it would be a clearer message if there was one?"

"But maybe the message is clear and I'm just not getting it – and what about the therapy session?'

"Well, you know my thoughts on that. I really do think you need to speak to your mother."

145

"Look, you've always told me to go with my gut feeling and I really feel that someone is trying to show me something. I suppose it has become somewhat all consuming, because there's been so much going on in the house." Chrissie suddenly seemed to come back to reality for the first time in weeks. It was as if she'd woken up from a very long sleep.

Sarah read her mind.

"Have you done much writing lately?"

"Do you know, you've just made me realise how much I've allowed this whole thing to dominate my thoughts. I've written bits and pieces, but I've been unable to concentrate for any length of time and I'm so tired. It's a good thing I don't have a deadline at the moment. I'm supposed to use this time to settle into my new surroundings, which is exactly what I haven't done much of either."

"I didn't make you realise anything, you did that by yourself, which isn't a bad thing. Most of us spend time consumed by various matters, living in the past or the future instead of concentrating on the present. So now you've come to this realisation, why don't we go and do some of that 'settling' in together? You need to familiarise me with the area anyway, seeing as I'm moving here as soon as I've found somewhere to buy.'

There was a long pause before Chrissie answered, she was unsure if she'd heard her properly. "You're moving here?"

"Yes. I've been thinking about it for a long time and you being here made up my mind. I need a change. I only moved to London because of work. Now that I'm setting up on my own, I can go where ever I want. I like it here actually, it has a nice energy. And let's face it, if I still want to move here after the ghoulish tales you've told me, there must be something enchanting about it!"

"That's brilliant news! Bloody hell! How long ago was it when we lived so near each other?"

"Far too long, and you obviously need someone here to keep you on the path of sanity, and obviously I'm the best person for the job."

"Ha, ha, very funny! But you're right – this place does hold some sort of enchantment, even though it freaks me out most of the time!" Chrissie laughed, standing up and putting her chair in. She felt much more light hearted. It had done her the world of good coming into the café. It wasn't just the change of scenery; it was the atmosphere there as well. The café was nothing special to look at, but it had an ambience that most places lacked. It could have been passed off as a 1930's railway café, with its steamy windows, metal teapots and wafts of homemade soup and pastries.

Chrissie stared at Sarah and smiled as she watched her friend carefully putting her coat on.

"What? Have I got cheese scone stuck to my face?"

"Not a chance of that, you looked like you hadn't eaten for a week! No, I was just thinking how you have a miraculous way of knowing what other people need, even when they can't see it themselves."

"Huh, not so good when it comes to analysing myself though."

"Oh, I don't think you do a bad job. When you become aware you're not learning anything from your current situation, you suddenly make a huge life changing decision, where most people would just stay in the same place. I love that about you."

"Coming from the woman who just made a massive move on her own after making the brave decision to get a divorce." Sarah linked her friend's arm as they made their way towards the sea front.

"Yes, and you're now doing the same thing, only you've done it loads of times."

"It's easier for me to make this move though, because I know I'm going to be near my best friend."

They squeezed one another's arms and then both jumped as a car beeped and pulled up by the side of the road. Chrissie could see someone looking at her through the rear view mirror.

"Oh, it's Grace!" Chrissie said, running over to the passenger side window which Grace had wound down.

"Hello! How are you? You haven't met my friend Sarah. Sarah this is Grace, Grace this is…" Chrissie stopped as she took in Grace's pale face.

"My sister has had some really bad news…well, we all have really…. Hello Sarah, sorry, that was very rude of me."

"Not at all, you're obviously in shock. Is there anything we can do?" said Sarah, pushing her head through the car window with Chrissie's.

"Whatever's happened?"

"My niece, Alice went missing ten years ago, and someone has just found her remains…the police say it's her…"

"Oh no, Grace that's awful! Do they know what happened to her?"

"No…no, not yet. The police suspected at the time it could have been to do with the other murders in the area, but…they're not sure."

Chrissie felt a sensation like ice cold water trickle down her back.

"Grace…that's just…awful."

"Is there anything we can do? Where are you going now?" Sarah almost demanded, always the one to organise and help.

"No, no, thank you. I've just been home to get food and clothes and I'm now making my way over to stay with my sister for a few days. Her husband just left her so it's an especially…well you can imagine." Grace said, gripping the steering wheel and checking her rear view mirror for traffic.

"Well, that's just…"

"Anyway, Grace,' said Chrissie, nudging Sarah and cutting her off mid-sentence, knowing exactly what she was going to say about Grace's brother-in-law. Chrissie didn't think that giving unasked for opinions was the way forward under the circumstances, "you must let us know if you need anything. Anything at all. And we are so sorry for your news."

"Thank you Chrissie, I'll be in touch when I get home."

"Ok Grace."

They both waved her off and then stood there for a while, watching Grace's car drift up the road.

"You look perplexed, what are you thinking?" Sarah began walking again and after a few seconds Chrissie fell into step beside her.

"Well there are two things, one much less significant than the other."

"What? That Grace's insignificant brother-in-law buggered off and left her sister?"

"No, no, no, although that is awful, but we actually don't know the circumstances of that situation. And anyway Missy, being a therapist you should know better than to judge when you have no background information. For all you know Grace's sister could be a right cow."

"Yep, she could be, but it's unlikely isn't it?"

"And how do you come to that very narrow minded conclusion?"

"It's not narrow minded, it's logical. You really like Grace and speak highly of her, and so it's very unlikely that her sister is going to be the complete opposite. Anyway, we digress, what were you going to say?"

"Sometimes I really worry about your 'logic' mind. Well, firstly, and it isn't anything to do with the situation, it's just made me realise something about my therapy session."

Chrissie stopped, so she could give more thought to what she was about to say.

"There was a smell that lingered with me after my session, but I wasn't really aware of it until now. It was the faint smell of menthol sweets. It was a bit like Fisherman's Friends. Do you know what I mean?"

"Yes. Lots of people get that. It's because you're exploring the subconscious, so you can carry something with you afterwards, such as a smell, and not be aware of it until later when that memory is triggered. You might find you remember more about the whole thing as time goes on. Your brain will fill bits and pieces in at various times; giving you a bigger picture. What has that got to do with Grace?"

"What I actually meant was do you know the smell I'm talking about?"

"Oh, yeah, yeah I know what Fisherman's Friends smell like."

"Well, when I leaned in Grace's car, I got a faint smell of them and realised the smell had been with me since my session. I

151

had a flash of something as well, but I don't know what that was. It was more a feeling."

"There's obviously stuff that's going to come out from your session. What was the other thing you were going to say?"

Chrissie and Grace made their way down the sandy steps and onto the sparkling shell encrusted beach. The late summer sun was glowing orange and pink shades onto the clouds, making everything glisten.

"Grace and I have had quite a few long discussions about the murders in this area…."

Chrissie stopped to think again, while Sarah stared at her friend in anticipation, trying to be patient.

"What I can't understand is why she never told me about Alice?"

"Why do you think she didn't?"

"I really don't know. But it feels a bit strange, kind of like she's holding a lot of things back."

"Perhaps she finds it too difficult to talk about. Or, like she said, they aren't sure if it's connected. Some people don't like to talk about personal things."

"It could be, but I don't get that feeling. She's a very warm and open person. Although, she and her husband Tim make a very odd match. I find him really strange and I don't think she's particularly happy with him."

"Well, a feeling is a feeling and you must take notice of it. Maybe she'll tell you more when you see her."

"Yes, probably. Anyway, I'm doing it again."

"What?"

"Talking about all that stuff."

"It doesn't matter, I find it interesting and two brains mulling it over are far better than one. I think the key is not to let it consume you."

"Precisely. So, let's get home and I'll prepare dinner while you tell me all about your plans to move here."

*

Grace didn't know why she'd felt the need to pull the car over and tell Chrissie her news. She supposed it was due to shock and an overwhelming feeling to just tell someone what had happened. As if she was going to rescue them all from the awful nightmare they were in, erasing it out for them. Like deleting a screen full of words and changing the whole story. But Grace knew it didn't work like that because they were the ones floating out on the choppy sea, whilst the world carried on around them, as they slowly became dots on the horizon.

But there was more to it than just wanting to share her awful news. She'd spotted Chrissie in the street and it wasn't in Grace's nature to stop the car and tell someone something, especially when they were with someone she didn't know. She'd normally wait even under such tragic circumstances. But she'd felt it was important to tell Chrissie, and she did know why deep down. Grace was finding the secret about Tim almost too much to bear. And the news of Alice had only heightened the urge to tell someone. Grace was torn between telling the police and following through with her plans. She carried an awful guilt around, knowing she was privy to information so many people were desperate to know. And would she really go through with her plans? It had been over a year already. She'd often visualised doing it to see if she was really serious about it. Most of the time she was, but then she had moments of feeling really scared and aware of how huge it was to take another person's life, however evil they were. To take someone else's fate into your own hands seemed quite an arrogant decision to make. Perhaps telling Chrissie wouldn't be as monumentally explosive as she thought. Maybe Chrissie would agree with her plans once she knew the full story?

No, no, no! What was she thinking? Grace nearly collided into the back of a stationary car; she was so engrossed in her thoughts. It jolted her back to reality, and after the car had screeched to a halt, she became starkly aware of what she'd just thought, and knew she must keep quiet.

The key to getting rid of anyone, alongside making it look like suicide, was not to tell another soul. Tim had taught her that. Times changed, people's views altered and then you had to trust them not to tell anyone. The only person you could really rely on was yourself. Grace stopped herself again; she was beginning to sound like Tim. What on earth was happening to her?

She banged her hands on the steering wheel as if to jolt herself out of it, and pulled into the familiar drive of her sister's house.

All was quiet when she went in. She called to Eve but there was no reply.

She unloaded the bags onto the kitchen table and made her way through the house looking for her.

She stopped at the foot of the stairs and listened carefully, thinking that she was probably upstairs having a sleep. Eve hadn't slept since she'd heard the news about Alice.

Grace made her way up the stairs, but Eve wasn't in her room as she'd first thought. A slight spark of panic ignited in her stomach.

"Eve?"

She thought perhaps she'd gone out, but then Eve rarely went anywhere.

"Eve?" She called a bit louder as she began opening the doors to each room.

The spark was now turning into a flame and making its way from her stomach to her heart.

"EVE!!"

The last and only room she hadn't looked in loomed at the end of the corridor, like the forbidden door to the Secret

Garden. Only, she didn't feel what lay behind it would be a pleasant surprise.

She moved slowly down the corridor as the door appeared to magnify in front of her. The carpet and walls became noticeable for the first time in years and Grace realised nothing had been changed since Alice went missing. The house was trapped in a time warp, with Eve in it, while everything moved on in the outside world. Or maybe it was the other way around.

Tentatively her hand came out to reach for the door handle. Her entire body filled with dread at what might be on the other side.

She seemed to float through the next few moments, as if a gentle breeze was blowing her into the room to stand next to her sister, who was lying in a ball on her daughter's bed.

Grace's hand went to her throat as she tried to gulp in air.

"Oh Eve...no Eve." She whispered like a small child.

Eve stirred on the bed, and her eyelids slowly pulled apart; sticky from crying herself to sleep.

"Bloody hell Eve!" Grace launched herself on the bed and picked her tiny sister up in her arms and sobbed.

"Grace...? What's happened?"

Grace couldn't speak, she was so relieved.

"Grace you're frightening me, what's happened?"

"I thought you were...I thought you'd..." Grace looked at the bottle of sleeping tablets on the bedside table and Eve followed her gaze.

Oh Grace. No....no! I came in here for a sleep. I took a tablet because I knew you'd be a while and I'm having trouble sleeping on my own. I just wanted to feel close to her."

Grace and Eve wrapped their arms around each other, and looking like identical twins began to cry for the last ten years that had passed without Alice.

*

Tim watched the sparks spitting from the bonfire he'd lit in the garden. It was dusk and he'd questioned whether it was normal to have one at this time of day. He didn't want to draw attention to himself, especially as he didn't normally burn his rubbish.

The glow of the fire warmed the front of his body and lit up his face. To anyone who didn't know, he looked like any normal man enjoying a bonfire after a hard day's work in the garden. But to know him for what he was, he was more like the devil incarnate floating up from the flames.

He sniffed the air, trying to detect any trace of a smell from the memory scents that he was burning. There were no scents; they had gone a long time ago, not far behind their owners. But Tim convinced himself there was an aroma in the air. He'd almost forgotten himself when he came out of the shed, and nearly opened the boxes to smell each and every one of them, one last time. But he'd remembered he was out in the open, albeit in his garden, but still visible to the neighbours. It was imperative that it looked like he'd had a clear out and was simply burning his rubbish.

He had felt a certain attachment to all the memory scents he had kept over the years. A bit like a child not wanting to get rid of a much loved collection of old toys.

He watched the flames fold and marry perfectly with the boxes, as one by one he gave each victim their second funeral; apart from Alice of course.

There had been no funeral for Alice's parents, or a time to say goodbye to their daughter, because they'd had nothing to say farewell to until now.

Tim didn't care about this though; it was of no significance. To him, funerals were just an excuse for people to be dramatic in public, crying because they felt guilty for not appreciating that person while they were alive. He didn't understand why people were so shocked by death. Everyone had to die, that was a sure fact that everyone grew up knowing. Once you were born you had begun the process of dying.

He felt slightly bereft, watching the fire, but not for his victims, but rather for the fact this era of his life was now over.

A tiny idea was beginning to form in Tim's head. If he could persuade Grace to move house they could set up somewhere else. No one would suspect a thing. It would take him out of the enquiry and enable him to set up a new life, and to gather new memory scents.

Come to think of it, if Grace wouldn't come with him, he'd go it alone. There was nothing between them anymore, even Grace would agree with that.

Tim sipped the beer that he was holding and stared into the flames that were showing him all sorts of visions of his new life. There was, however, one thing he hadn't yet thought of. His mother.

*

Grace tucked the blanket around her sister, who had eventually made her way downstairs and curled up on the sofa. She kissed her forehead.

"I'll make you a cup of tea. Do you want me to turn the television on for you?"

"No, but a cup of tea would be nice thanks."

Eve wanted to think about the last few days. Having a cry had helped ease things and she was slightly surprised at the change in her emotions. She didn't normally cry much, because to her crying had meant an admission and acceptance of Alice not returning. But she had realised it was just a way of releasing strong emotions when things got to be too much to bear.

"How are you feeling?" Grace handed her a cup of tea.

"I don't know really. I thought I would feel a tiny bit relieved and similar to the way I felt all those years ago. But I don't at all. It's a different kind of grief and now another nightmare to face."

"Is there some way you can try and focus on remembering Alice how she was? How you have been doing these past few years? I know its hard Eve, but she died ten years ago; it's just that you didn't know about it. Please don't torture yourself all over again." Grace knew she sounded callous but she wanted Eve to skip the awful nightmare and move forward, because she was scared of the massive effect it would have on her. She knew there was an element of guilt hidden in her words as they came out of her mouth.

"What? So, you think I should just forget it and get on with my life?" Eve's tone was deep and dark.

"I'm not saying that Eve. I'm not taking away the magnitude of what has happened, but I don't want it to destroy you anymore than it has done. I really think you ought to go and see a counsellor." Grace knew she was treading on volcanic ground. But someone had to say something; her sister had allowed this to eat her away for far too long.

"So, because you come into my house and assume I've topped myself and then I cry over my daughter whose remains have just been found, you think I need professional help?"

"Oh come on Eve. I know I jumped to the wrong conclusion, but you can't blame me? Look at what you've been through?"

Grace knew she had to turn this around otherwise her sister would snap. She felt like she was trying to control a saucepan of simmering milk from boiling over.

"There is nothing wrong with going to a counsellor for help with your problems, especially after what you've been through."

"I don't want any help from strangers. I will deal with this in my own way, as I have done for the last ten years. No one can fix this, not even a professional." Eve sipped the sugary, toffee coloured tea.

"Alright." Grace cringed at Eve's clipped tone; her face stung as if she'd been slapped. Eve obviously felt no one had been there for her. She had retreated back into her shell again; protecting herself from everything and everyone.

"What would really help me right now would be the police ringing to tell me that they'd caught the bastard who did this."

Grace fidgeted in her chair, as a wave of guilt passed through her, and the enormity of the secret she was keeping slapped her around the face, and not for the first time that day. It didn't go unnoticed.

"You know something, don't you?" Eve eyed her sister beadily.

"What? No! What made you say that?" Grace tried desperately to look calm.

"The police have told you something you're not allowed to tell me. Tim knows doesn't he?"

"Don't be daft! If I knew anything I'd tell you. Why would they speak to Tim about anything?"

"Oh I know how it works in the police. They all stick together. You told me yourself he used to tell you things that other people weren't privy to."

"Eve, look I know…"

"Don't try and fob me off Grace, just tell me what you know."

"I honestly don't know anything Eve. Really, if I did I would tell you. Come on you're being silly, you know I wouldn't keep anything from you."

Grace squeezed her sister's leg, as if by doing so it would give her lie some sort of truth.

Eve held her sister's gaze, searching her face for clues. There was something there. Even if it didn't have anything to do with Alice, there was definitely something on her sister's mind. But she was too exhausted to pursue it.

Grace's mind moved like a piece of driftwood, in and out of the shore, wanting to tell Eve, keeping it to herself. Telling her, not telling her, until the driftwood finally settled on the shore and the tide went out. The urge was gone to unburden herself, and she was left with a feeling of determination to rid the world of her sick and twisted husband.

*

Even though Tim didn't particularly care much for Grace's company, it kept him occupied for certain periods of time. Her absence had left him with boredom on his hands and time to whistle like the wind around the village and over to Chrissie's house.

It was time to have some fun. If Chrissie had any doubts about her house being haunted, then she certainly wouldn't after tonight.

A little sapling of an idea had grown in Tim's mind, and he began to chuckle at the thought of it. The tiny idea eventually turned into a clear visualisation in his head.

He crept silently around the back of Chrissie's house. He'd come along the track and past his favourite shed. He had the weather on his side, because even though it was quite a warm, clear moonlit night, the breeze blowing off the sea was quite strong and would impair anyone's hearing in a draughty old house like Chrissie's.

All the lights were off and it was the early hours so Chrissie and her friend were most probably in bed. He glanced up at the bedroom windows. Two were open.

Tim crept over to the patio area and as quietly as possible he picked up the garden table and carried it across the grass to place it near the stream in a sheltered clearing right at the bottom. Then he went back for two of the chairs. Once they were in place and sheltered in front of some trees, he searched through the bag of items he'd brought with him, until he found what he was looking for with the help of his torch.

With his gloved hand he placed a child's book on the table. Perfect.

Then he moved back up to the house, checking the windows as he went, for any sign of movement. He made his way towards Chrissie's washing line which was tied from her outhouse and reached along to a large tree. On there he pegged some children's clothes. He stifled a laugh; his excitement was beginning to bubble over.

His last stop was the shed. Tim's favourite shed. There, he planned to hang an old dolly by its neck from the rafters with a noose made from a frayed piece of rope. He felt like an excited child playing hide and seek, filled with the anticipation of someone catching him.

Only, Tim wasn't a child and this was no game. Tim crept backwards down the garden, viewing his handy work, as he made his way towards the shed.

He lifted the rickety old door up from the floor as he pushed it open, because he remembered the hinge having come away and he wanted to keep the noise to a minimum. He shivered as he felt the cold stale air rush to his body.

Something made him look over his shoulder. A feeling, a memory, he didn't know what, but a change in the atmosphere was very slowly making the elated excitement in Tim's stomach turn to sand and slip through the timer.

He shone the torch out of the doorway, but there was nothing there. He shrugged and carried on with the task in hand.

Once he'd hoisted the doll where he wanted it, he shone the torch around the shed to make sure he hadn't left anything. Switching it off he picked up his bag, not wanting to step out of the shed with it on, just in case someone was lurking about.

He turned towards the shed door to adjust his eyes to the altered light. The moon was shining quite brightly and there was a silvery blue light cast over everything.

As his pupils dilated, he suddenly became aware of the outline of something in the doorway. He held his breath, his heart beginning to thump, thump, thump.

There seemed to be a strange kind of whimpering coming from whatever it was, and Tim let out a huge stifled breath as he realised it was either a fox or a stray dog. He turned on his torch to get the measure of what he needed to swat out of the doorway.

But it wasn't a dog or a fox that faced Tim in the doorway of the shed. It was a small child. A child he very much recognised.

Tim became aware of his heart again and gripped his torch. He opened his mouth, but nothing came out; his throat was like sand paper.

The little girl stood in front of him crying, her eyes wide and haunted.

He'd remembered the floral pinafore she was wearing. It was an item he'd just thrown on the bonfire along with all the other memory scents.

What he couldn't comprehend, as he tried to move his feet, which seemed to have turned into lead weights, was that the little girl who stood in front of him was dead. He knew he wasn't mistaken because he was the one who had killed her, with the help of a dog chain. He'd then thrown her into the stream at the bottom of the very garden he was standing in.

CHAPTER TWELVE

"I had some really vivid dreams last night. Did you sleep well?"

"Fairly well. Kept thinking I could hear things but it was just the wind." Sarah said, pulling up a chair at the kitchen table.

"I was back in that garden. Where I was when I had my regression therapy? And I had that same feeling and smell."

"Did you go any further with it than you did in your session?"

"A little bit I think. I was being dragged somewhere but then I woke up in a sweat." Chrissie poured tea for them both from the pot she'd brewed.

"Are you any closer to working out if it's a memory or a psychic vision?"

Chrissie fidgeted in her chair.

"No. I still think it's a psychic vision.' Chrissie's voice was clipped. Sarah thought it was best not to push it, so she kept quiet. They both stared into the atmosphere, each in their own little worlds.

They were transported back to the kitchen table by the telephone ringing. Chrissie, jolting herself back to the present, answered it.

"Hi Mum. Have you and Dad been busy?"

"Hello darling. Yes, we've been out and about…are you alright?"

"Yes fine thanks. I've got Sarah here at the moment." Chrissie wandered into the lounge with the phone and stared out into the garden.

"Oh that's nice dear. Give her our love. Was there any reason for your message?"

"No not really. Just had some regression therapy with Sarah and it threw up some stuff we thought may have come from the past. It's nothing, don't worry about it. I've sorted it out in my head."

"Alright darling. I'll let you get back to Sarah. I expect you've got a lot to catch up on."

Chrissie totally missed the fact her mother hadn't asked her about her regression, as she was too distracted by the absence of her garden table and two chairs. She hadn't been sure what was different about the garden when she'd first looked, but the two lonely chairs that were left behind had given it away.

She hung up the phone and went into the kitchen to tell Sarah but she was already staring out of the kitchen window.

"Sarah, something strange is going on in the garden."

"You're telling me. Have you seen what's hanging off your washing line?"

Sarah's voice sounded distant and small.

Chrissie was becoming familiar with the presence of Jack Frost. He seemed to be a permanent fixture on her shoulder, ready to tip toe down her back whenever he deemed it necessary.

Chrissie wrenched on her Wellington boots and bravely went outside to face whatever it was.

There was a thin low mist billowing across the garden and the day was overcast and dull. Chrissie pulled her dressing gown around her for warmth and went over to the washing line to get a better look at what was hanging from it. She turned to look at Sarah through the kitchen window but she was in the porch getting her shoes on so she could join Chrissie in the garden.

They both turned very pale and it wasn't just from the cold.

"Did you notice the table and chairs?"

"No, what?" Sarah spun round. Being unfamiliar with the garden she hadn't noticed anything was missing.

As Sarah turned to look at the empty space on the patio, she saw something moving out of the corner of her eye. The swing hanging from the tree had begun to move as if there was someone sitting on it. She was sure it hadn't been swinging when she came out. She grabbed Chrissie's arm, making her turn around and look.

"Oh my god, Sarah! Get back in the house!"

The two women scrabbled for the front door. Out of breath, they stood in the kitchen staring at one another.

"Now do you see what I mean?"

"Yes. But are you sure that's paranormal activity and not some head case trying to frighten you?"

"And who would do that around here? No one knows me apart from Grace. Maybe it's a puzzle"

"What? A baby's clothes on a washing line? And how do the table and chairs fit in?" Sarah filled up the kettle to make a strong cup of tea.

"Whoever it was killed children, didn't they? But I'm lost on what the table means. Where is my table anyway?"

Chrissie peered out of the window again and shuddered. It was hard to see right down the garden due to the mist. She scanned it from side to side, struggling to see anything. But as her eyes adjusted she began to make out a shape near the trees.

"Come on Sarah. We're going for a walk."

"Are we?" Sarah was cautious and didn't fancy going back outside.

"Just to the bottom of the garden."

"Can't we have a cuppa first?"

"Come on! I need you with me."

They found the table and chairs as Tim had left them with the child's book placed on the top. Everything was damp from the mist and dew.

"But how did an iron table and chairs get down here?"

"How do we explain any paranormal activity? Whatever it is it's obviously trying to get my attention." Chrissie shivered again.

"I really think you should call the police, Chrissie."

"It's not what you think it is, Sarah. Trust me on this one. It's a feeling. I know someone's trying to get a message to me. I've just got to work out what it all means."

Chrissie turned around and stared at the shed. The door was open, which was unusual. She was sure she'd shut it the last time she'd been down here. She moved over to it, feeling the usual flush of sweat prickle her forehead as her heart began to beat faster.

She held onto the frame and leaned into the dark, damp room, staring into the gloom to adjust her eyes. Everything was as it had been before. She reached for the door latch and wrenched it as best she could to the frame.

"Where does that lead to, down there?"

"Where?"

"Down the side of the shed. Look," said Sarah, pushing her way through the shrubbery.

"Oh! I don't know. I hadn't noticed it before."

Chrissie started to follow Sarah along the path, pushing down the tangle of tumbleweed as she went.

"We can't go too far, Sarah. We aren't even dressed and I don't think this is part of my garden."

"Who's going to come down here?" said Sarah, pressing her friend to keep going. They walked for quite a distance, delayed slightly by the sprouting plants in their way.

Sarah stopped, causing Chrissie to walk into her.

"What is it?"

"There's a row of cottages up ahead and what looks like the back gardens leading to them. Look, up on the right."

Chrissie squinted.

"Oh yeah. Must be my other neighbours. Can we go back now? This is still freaking me out."

"Let's just go a bit further and then we'll turn back."

Chrissie was feeling extremely peculiar and she didn't like it one bit.

As they got closer to the row of cottages, Chrissie had a strange feeling of déjà vu sweep across her vision.

"Bloody hell, Sarah! That looks like the cottage in my regression."

Sarah stopped and turned to look at Chrissie.

"Are you sure? I had a feeling we needed to keep going. Come on!"

And there it was, the swing hanging from the tree in the middle of the garden with the tiny gate and the path leading to the French windows.

Several visions flashed across Chrissie's mind and a familiar scent of Fisherman's Friend floated up to her nostrils.

"I don't like this, Sarah. This is really freaking me out. I'm going back."

Chrissie turned and made her way up the track, leaving Sarah behind. She said hello to a man in his garden who she hadn't noticed before.

As she stomped along the track a thought suddenly occurred to her. She turned back, meeting Sarah a little way down the path.

"Excuse me? Sorry to bother you, but could you tell me who used to live in the cottage at the end of this row?"

The man looked up from his rake and regarded her oddly as he took in her dressing gown and Wellingtons.

"Well now my beauty. No one really."

Chrissie stared at the weathered old man, waiting for him to continue.

He pulled his cap forward and leaned back as if to stretch.

"Well someone must have at some point?'" Chrissie was becoming impatient.

"No, no, no! That's a holiday home, love, has been for donkey's years."

"Oh…well thanks."

Chrissie and Sarah turned to leave.

"What business is it of yours anyway?"

Chrissie pushed her hands into her dressing gown pockets.

"No business really. I've just moved into the house a few hundred yards through there," Chrissie nodded towards the direction of her cottage, "just getting to know the village a bit better."

"Oh ah, the detached place with the stream at the bottom?"

"Yes that's right. I'm Chrissie, by the way, and this is my friend Sarah."

"Oh, right."

"And you are?" Chrissie extended her hand over the old man's fence.

The man just stared at it and for a second Chrissie thought he was going to carry on raking his garden.

"The name's Redvers. Reddy." He shook her hand firmly.

"Nice to meet you, Reddy."

"You want a know anythin' about the village you're welcome to pop in on me 'n the wife anytime."

"Thank you very much. I'll bear that in mind."

Reddy dibbed his cap and continued with his gardening. Chrissie and Sarah took this as their cue to leave and made their way down the path.

"The people here are friendly in an odd kind of way. Bit abrupt but they seem sincere."

"You've only met a couple of people!" Chrissie laughed.

"He wasn't the chattiest of men."

"No. but I'm sure his heart's in the right place. He's a local so he's bound to be suspicious."

"Right. Well. I need to digest all this weird information and I'm gasping for a cup of tea and some breakfast."

"Yes, absolutely. Come on." Chrissie linked Sarah's arm.

"Are you alright?"

"I think so. I'm getting used to the creepy goings on and I suppose I don't find them as shocking as I did when I first moved here. Either that, or I'm still in shock."

"You can become slightly desensitized when you have recurring shocks. I think in this case it's not a bad thing."

They wound their way around the shed, both shivering at the same time, even though the sun had emerged from the greyness and drunk up the dew, which in turn had warmed the mist away. It was promising to be a better day than it had started out to be.

"What's that?" Sarah stopped in her tracks pulling Chrissie up with her.

"What's what?"

"That. Look over there!" Sarah pointed and then began to move towards the stream.

Chrissie looked to where Sarah was pointing. She could see something pale sticking up in the grass.

Chrissie's hand flew to her throat.

"Oh my god, Sarah! Don't go any closer it's a....oh god no!"

Sarah didn't take any notice and carried on towards the stream.

She let out a scream and turned to Chrissie with a look of horror on her face.

Chrissie ran over to her, glancing down the embankment.

"Oh shit! I thought….it was…"

"I know, me too." Sarah said, taking deep breaths and holding onto Chrissie's dressing gown. After they'd calmed themselves, Chrissie leant down and picked up the battered doll that was laying half in the stream.

It had looked an awful sight and at first glance they'd thought it was a baby's body. It was so grim, tangled in the long grass with its head floating in the water. One eye was missing and the other turned into its head and the reflection of the water had magnified it, making it look quite a sight to any passer by.

"I really do think you ought to call the police. This doesn't appear to have anything to do with the supernatural at all. This is a prank being played by someone. Somebody who knows you're new here." Sarah shivered, wrapping her dressing tighter around her body.

"I'm not phoning the police just yet, I need to think about it all. I can't shake off the feeling that it's a message, as bizarre as it seems."

Chrissie and Sarah collected the doll, the book and the clothes and made their way back to the house.

"I've had enough for one day. Can we lock the doors and stay in?" said Sarah, looking rather pale and ill.

"I think that's a brilliant idea." Chrissie linked her arm through Sarah's as they wandered up the garden, glad of each other's company.

"I still think you ought to inform the police, Chrissie."

"I'll think about it."

*

Tim found himself standing in the stream at the bottom of Chrissie's garden. He was exhausted, having walked around the village several times. He was unshaven with bruised rings around his tired eyes. The bottle of rum he was carrying was almost empty and he was in a complete drunken oblivion. Whenever he turned around the little girl in the pinafore was behind him. She sobbed and sobbed, occasionally tugging at the back of his coat to try and gain his attention. But she had his full attention, only he didn't want to face her. He had tried all night since he'd scrambled out of the shed to get away from her. He'd even gone home and locked all the doors but she was still there. Crying, crying, crying.

He thought the only way to escape it was to go out of the house with his bottle of rum. He'd walked up and down the beach several times, but she'd persisted almost as if she'd stepped into his conscience. Like a reflection in the mirror, she would never leave.

As the sun was coming up he'd staggered his way over to the stream. To her resting place, to see if that would break the spell.

But she stood on the bank sobbing, managing the odd words he could just make out, which were "want" and "Mummy".

He screamed to the pink streaked skies for help, a pathetic sight. And for the first time since he was a child he experienced the feeling of how small and insignificant he was. Just how his mother had made him feel. The realisation hit him like a door slamming in a strong wind; there was a much larger force than him to be reckoned with.

Looking skyward made everything spin and he staggered, almost losing his footing. As he looked down to steady himself he stared at a pair of hands, which he didn't recognise as his own at first. They were dripping in thick, cloying blood.

The scream from his mouth woke him.

He sat up abruptly, unsure of where he was at first. Sweat was pouring over his body. He scrambled for the light while he tried to swallow and dampen his dry mouth.

Just a dream, he kept telling himself as the flick of the switch lit up the room. He moved to lie back down and compose himself but there she was again, the girl in the pinafore, sobbing at the bottom of his bed. One eye blackened and cut, the other completely red where he'd pushed his fingers so hard into her tiny face.

NORFOLK 1987

Karen had had a lovely time with her grandparents. She'd stayed with them overnight for the first time in her short life. Her parents lived only a few miles along the coast, but it had seemed too daunting to stay overnight before. Her grandparent's house was so big and imposing, especially to a child.

She'd woken up earlier than she normally did and had decided to get herself dressed. Her grandparents were still in bed and the house was much too quiet for a five year old. Boredom got the better of her and she decided to go outside and finish playing the game she'd been busy inventing the day before.

It was a tea party for monkey and rabbit. The table and chairs were at the bottom of the garden near the stream, just as she'd left them. Her plastic tea set and her picture books lay out on the table.

Karen placed monkey and rabbit on the chairs and began to play her game.

She hadn't been expecting a fourth person for tea and she hadn't laid the table accordingly for her unexpected visitor.

179

*

Norfolk 1998

Grace pushed her way through the front door, her bags catching on the frame, causing her to back track. She swore as she sidled in and dropped her luggage on the hall floor. Looking up she noticed how dark it was in the house and there was a strange smell emanating towards her. Registering that it was brilliant sunshine outside, it dawned on her there was something wrong.

Wandering through the rooms, she opened all the curtains. The house was a mess. Dirty crockery in the sink and the dishwasher looked like it hadn't been turned on since she'd left, five days ago.

She sighed, desperately trying to stifle the anger bubbling up inside her. On opening the lounge curtains and turning to face the room she was sharply confronted by Tim's presence.

"What the bloody hell is going on here?"

There was a grunt from the sofa as Tim tried to prize open his bloodshot eyes.

"Couldn't you have tried to keep the place tidy in the short time I was away? Obviously it was too much to ask!"

Grace stormed out of the lounge, unable to discuss it with him for fear of caving his skull in with the empty rum bottle that lay on the floor beside a congealed plate of food.

"Lazy bastard!" She spat at him as she left the room.

It hadn't passed her by that he looked an absolute mess. It was out of character for him not to tidy up after himself; he was so obsessed with cleanliness that it drove Grace to distraction. But after seeing how devastated her sister was over the last few days, she was past caring. Maybe he was finally going round the twist. Perhaps his conscience had paid him a visit after all these years.

"Grace! Grace....come on!" Tim staggered into the kitchen and almost fell onto her.

"Oh my god, you stink! Go and have a shower."

"Grace...I've been so...lost without you!" he slurred and pulled at her jacket.

"Piss off, Tim! I mean it! Just piss off!" She pushed him and he fell backwards hitting his head on the kitchen cupboards.

It knocked him out cold. She stood there for quite some time holding her breath while she stared at him. She was wondering if she'd killed him but there was nothing in her being urging her to check for any signs of life.

Eventually there was movement from his chest and he groaned. It occurred to her how easy it had been to push him. If she'd done it a bit harder she might have killed him there and then.

She imagined how she would feel now if it had been a reality. How she'd go straight back to her sister's and pretend she hadn't returned to the house yet. That he'd got extremely drunk and slipped on some water in the kitchen; a tragic accident in their tragic family. It would have been all over as easy as that. But it wasn't. And Tim wasn't dead. And she was back in her house.

Grace felt surprisingly chirpy for the rest of the day. She left Tim on the kitchen floor to sleep it off and she tidied the whole house from top to bottom.

A beautiful realisation was surging through her, like the buds of a plant unfurling. She could kill him quite easily and make it look like an accident. All she had to do was encourage him to keep drinking. It was perfect.

CHAPTER THIRTEEN

When Tim woke up from his drunken stupor, he wasn't quite sure where he was. His first view was of a cupboard, and as his eyes focused he realised it was the kitchen where he lived. He tried to move his cold body off the floor. He ached from head to toe, quite literally and imagined he felt like someone who had been in a car crash.

He had no recollection of what had happened, but as he got to his feet and rubbed his head he noticed the kitchen was tidy and there were fresh suds in the sink.

A bizarre thought entered his head. Maybe someone had broken in and cleaned up. He often had stupid thoughts when he was hung over.

It took him a few minutes as he sloped around the house to realise that Grace had been home. The thing was, he couldn't remember falling over in the kitchen. He thought he'd slipped on the floor Grace had mopped and it seemed the most likely explanation.

He looked around the house but Grace was nowhere to be seen. He could feel a strong irritation creeping through his body. Why wasn't she here to nurse him better?

He got into bed so he could try and get some sleep. This proved a much harder task than he thought. He couldn't shut down.

Flashbacks of the previous two days were appearing as a jumbled mess in his mind.

A vision of Karen kept sliding into his head and he turned from one side of the bed to the other, desperate to rid his mind of the awful vision. But the vast amount of alcohol in his system had over stimulated his body.

His urge for some sympathy and the battle he was having in his mind got the better of him. Grace wasn't around so the only other place to go was his mother's.

*

Chrissie had just waved Sarah off when she spotted Grace coming down the track towards her house.

"Sorry Chrissie, you're still in your dressing gown!"

"Don't be silly, it's lovely to see you. Come in. Sarah's just left and I haven't got my arse in gear yet. Coffee?"

"Oh. I should have rung first. You've probably had your fill of company. I'll call back another day." Grace turned in the door to leave.

"Excuse me I'll be the judge of that. You don't need to ring first. Now get your bottom back in here right now!"

Chrissie grabbed Grace's shoulder and marched her into the kitchen. It wasn't until she pushed her onto a kitchen chair that she realised Grace was crying.

"What's all this? Oh Grace, come here!"

Grace stood up and Chrissie held her in her arms. She seemed so small and vulnerable compared to what she normally appeared to be.

Grace had felt so elated after she'd finished cleaning the house, but fatigue had gotten the better of her and she'd collapsed with a bang. She'd suddenly become aware again of how monumentally huge the whole thing was. She nearly voiced this to Chrissie without thinking.

"It must be so hard supporting your sister when you're grieving too, you poor thing."

"I just...I...can't...I..."

"It's alright Grace. There's plenty of time. Just take some deep breaths."

Chrissie patted her friend's hand, her heart tightening at the sight of her in such distress. The whole situation was so tragic.

Grace composed herself while Chrissie made a pot of coffee. She took off her coat and hung it on the back of one of the kitchen chairs. The draught from the coat wafted a smell under Chrissie's nose. Fisherman's Friend. There it was again.

Chrissie paused as visions she couldn't quite grasp flashed across her mind. She sniffed hard to try and recapture it.

185

"Are you ok?" Grace asked, wiping her nose with an old tissue she had up her sleeve.

"Yes. Sorry. For some reason I keep getting a waft of some sort of menthol sweet. Fisherman's Friend I think. It's triggering all sorts of memories. I had some regression therapy with my friend Sarah. The one who was staying here? Ever since then, well...anyway, you don't need to hear all about that. Tell me what's been happening."

"It is Fisherman's Friend. That's Tim's wax jacket. He keeps them in his pocket. It was the first coat to hand in this awful weather. What came up in the therapy?"

Grace knew she was being nosy, but she had a strong urge to find out for some reason. It would also distract her from talking about herself. It was a mixture of not wanting to say too much in her emotional state and revealing her shaky, mixed up mind. She felt like an old rag doll that had been sewn up over the years, only to come undone again. Something she could ill afford at the moment. She had to keep the seams together.

*

Daphne eyed Tim beadily over her bowl of congealed apple crumble and custard. The smell of it, mixed with urine and disinfectant, was causing Tim's face to flush from holding down the contents of his stomach.

"Why have you come to see me looking like that?" Daphne's hand flicked towards him, catching the edge of the bowl. The spoon clattered against it causing Tim to flinch. It echoed right through to his very core.

"I wanted to see you. Does it matter what I look like? Can't I just pop in on you now?"

"Not looking like that you don't. It's not how I brought you up."

"We both know exactly how you brought me up, don't we Mother?" Tim spat, leering slightly across her dinner tray. "Or shall I rephrase that. Didn't bring me up."
Daphne chose to ignore this.

"Been up to your old tricks again, Tim? Was that my fault as well? I know what's got to you, my boy. They've found that girl. Grace's niece."

Tim was caught speechless for a start. Not sure how to take what she'd said. He ignored it and chose to turn the conversation around. He'd come here for some comfort, although, he now realised he'd been chasing her for that all his life. A picture of who he wanted her to be which never actually matched who she truly was. This had caused him to be permanently disappointed. Not accepting her for who she was had set him up for failure time and time again. Why hadn't he noticed before? Maybe the alcohol had made it all clear.

187

"I am a bit upset Mother. It's been an awful time for the whole family. We've been busy supporting Eve and of course, Jon."

Daphne paused to observe him. After a few minutes she clapped her gnarled old hands together, like two pieces of bracken.

"Well done son. I'm sure you'll pass it off to the police when they come and question you. You can't pull the wool over my eyes though."

They stared at each other for a very long time, neither one wanting to be the first to give in.

"I don't know what you're talking about, Mother. You're obviously in one of your moods. So I'll leave you for now and I'll come back when you're feeling better."

Tim got up rather unsteadily and left the room without even saying goodbye properly.

"I know you better than anyone." She whispered to herself.

Tim more or less ran from the building. He couldn't cope with her today. He reassured himself she was just testing him. Who would believe a mad old woman in a retirement home? But his hangover and past events were making him feel dark and uneasy.

*

Grace listened carefully to Chrissie's news about what she'd found in the garden and the regression therapy she'd had.

"This is getting really serious Chrissie."

"Tell me about it. I've barely slept since I've been here. Does any of what I've told you fit....oh, Grace. That was really insensitive of me. I'm so sorry."

"It's fine. Don't worry. You'd be amazed at how many people feel they've said the wrong thing. When my daughter died, people actually crossed the street so they didn't have to talk to me. They just didn't know what to say. I'd rather people put their foot in it than say nothing at all."

"I didn't know you had a daughter." Chrissie's voice was small and distant. The tragedy in Grace's family just got worse.

"I just assumed that you and Tim didn't want children or perhaps couldn't have any. What happened to her?"

Grace fiddled with the old bit of crumbling tissue she'd found tucked in her sleeve.

"She had an accident. A terrible accident whilst she was out playing with a friend." Grace paused and took a deep breath, not used to discussing Nadine with anyone. "She fell into a cess pit, the entrance of which was hidden in a derelict garden. There was nothing anyone could do."

"That's awful, Grace, what with Alice as well."

"Yes, well. At least I have a tiny amount of comfort in the fact that Nadine died relatively quickly, and not at the hand of a monster, something my sister must live with."

"I can't imagine comfort from anything, at a time like that."

"No. Quite." Grace took a deep breath and straightened herself in her chair, physically ironing out the pain in her heart.

"So, where are these things you found in your garden?"

"Are you sure you want to look at them?"

"Yes. Two heads are better than one and I know more about what happened back then than you do. I might be able to shine some light on it." Grace hated lying to Chrissie but she had to go along with it all.

"I really do feel that someone is trying to get through to me about the murders. And I'm more determined than ever to piece it all together. Tim said something about one of the victim's being found in my garden. Is that true?"

Grace flinched at hearing Tim's name.

"Yes it is I'm afraid. A little girl called Karen. She was very young. Five or six I think."

"Whoever it was really was sick." Chrissie shook her head. "What I can't understand is how the police never came close to finding the culprit, especially with so many victims in more or less the same area."

Chrissie went into the utility room to get the child's book and clothes. She decided it was best not to show Grace the doll with the broken face, under the circumstances.

"A criminal mastermind."

Grace's sarcasm was lost on Chrissie.

"Do you think so?"

Grace didn't answer. She was staring at the items Chrissie had in her hands. She could feel the blood literally draining from her face.

There was silence as she went through the motions of looking through them. She couldn't let on to Chrissie that they were Nadine's. She lingered, trying to think of something to say.

"Are you ok, Grace? You've gone awfully pale. Let me get you some water."

Grace was so close to telling Chrissie everything, for what reason she wasn't sure. Maybe she was looking for an ally; someone to help her rid the world of the bastard, a friend to lean on so she didn't feel so impossibly alone.

Grace was trying to swallow the fact that Tim had been in Chrissie's garden causing mischief with their precious daughter's childhood possessions. How much further would the man go?

"I'm fine, Chrissie, just a little tired. You won't throw these things out will you?"

"No, of course not. I thought you were going to pressure me into going to the police. That's what Sarah thought I should do when I first found them."

Grace leafed through the hard back book Nadine had loved so much as a child. Tears sprung to her eyes.

"And now?"

"I don't know really. I know she thinks you should always follow your gut feeling. And that's what I'm doing."

"Go with your gut feeling, Chrissie. The police won't take much notice I wouldn't have thought. I don't think these things belong to one of the victims."

Grace felt bad saying this to Chrissie, knowing that any good friend would tell her to report it.

"It is really weird though isn't it? Where could they have possibly come from? I mean, I've heard of people experiencing paranormal activity but nothing like this, especially not with a stranger's possessions. Sarah says it could be some kind of poltergeist, but I don't even want to think about that."

Grace was deep in thought again. A tear trickled down her face.

"I'm sorry, Grace. My mouth runs ahead of my mind sometimes."

"It's not you, Chrissie. I'm just very emotional. I want to hear about it, I really do. I may be able to help you solve the puzzle so please don't hide it from me."

Chrissie reached across the table and squeezed Grace's hand, unable to hold back her own tears.

*

After Grace left, Chrissie was relieved to have some time on her own. She sat on the sofa and stared at the book she'd found on her garden table.

"Bedtime Stories," she said out loud to the room, as if it might come back with some answers. She flicked through the pictures. They were ironic really, depicting another world. A whimsical world where there was Good and Evil. A place where Good always triumphed over Evil, not like in reality.

Just as she was pondering on these thoughts, the phone rang.

"Hello, darling. It's Mum."

"Hi Mum, are you alright? Is Dad alright?" Chrissie suddenly panicked, not used to hearing from her mother two days in a row.

"Yes, everything's fine. I wanted to talk to you about something. Have you got a minute?"

"Yes, several. What's wrong?"

"Nothing's wrong, there's just something I need to tell you."

"Mother, you're frightening me. What is it?"

Sylvia relayed everything that had happened on that awful night at the holiday cottage when Chrissie was snatched. The line at Chrissie's end went quiet for a very long time.

"Chrissie, darling? Are you ok?"

Chrissie slumped back on the sofa; nausea rising in her stomach.

"Why didn't you tell me?" Chrissie almost whispered.

"I'm so sorry, Chrissie. You suffered some sort of amnesia afterwards. The doctor said it was because of the shock and for the time being was for the best. We just wanted you to have as normal a childhood as possible after that awful incident."

"Did he touch me? Did he...you know?"

The line was quiet again.

"Did he touch me?!" Chrissie shrieked down the phone.

"Not as far as we know. We don't know if it was a man, darling. It was dark and you didn't have a description. You just said you thought it was a man and he smelt funny. Darling, we kept it from you because we love you."

"So, did the police think it was the person who killed all those children?" Chrissie snapped at her.

"They couldn't be sure. There was a huge police hunt but they couldn't find anything. The point is, darling, you survived."

"I know that Mother, but you can't just ring me with this monumental news and expect me to immediately focus on the bright side."

"But you mustn't dwell on 'what ifs'."

"You've obviously had plenty of time to get used to this information over the years, where as I haven't. So please allow me to have some time to adjust to what you've just told me, instead of doing what you always do – stick a plaster on it and hope it'll go away!"

Chrissie slammed the phone down. Her mother had the good sense not to phone back, thinking it was best to leave her daughter to calm down.

Chrissie felt so angry. But she didn't quite know who with. She could see why her family had kept it from her, although it was typical of them. But then maybe all their protectiveness over the years had stemmed from this incident. She needed time for all this information to filter through her mind.

The thought that as a child she might have been so close to such an evil monster made her feel physically sick. Her mother was right. She was immensely lucky to have got away.

A thought dawned on her. The shed. The memory of the flashback flooded her mind. That was why it was all so familiar. Perhaps that's where he had taken her. She shivered, thinking of poor little Karen, who probably took her place. She didn't want to sit with those thoughts. It was all too much. She decided to get dressed and sort out the jumble of her mind by walking along the beach.

*

"I went to see Chrissie today, you know, my friend in the village?"

"Oh yeah."

"She's still having some really strange things happening at the house and it's now spread to the garden."

"Really." Tim was dead pan and sarcastic. He didn't even look up from the newspaper crossword he was doing.

Grace continued to channel hop. She needed to choose her words carefully.

"She found some children's clothes and a book in the garden. She's not sure whether to go to the police, what with everything that's happened with Alice."

That got his attention. The paper lowered slightly.

"It was really strange. For a few minutes after she showed me what she had found I thought they were Nadine's things."

"What has that got to do with Alice and why would she go to the police?"

"All this activity in the house; I suppose she thinks it's got something to do with all those murders from years ago. She thinks one of the victims is trying to get a message to her about the killer."

Tim chuckled and continued with his crossword.

"It would be amazing if it did though." Grace pressed further.

"If it did what?"

"The messages from beyond the grave; if they led her to the killer."

"Grace, I don't know what you're waffling on about. The police won't take any notice of your nutty friend, especially if she keeps going on about silly ghost stories."

He looked quite calm. Grace couldn't tell if she'd rattled him or not. But then she supposed that was how he'd managed to become a serial killer.

She had without realising it rattled him quite a bit. He hadn't thought of the scenario that Chrissie might go to the police. He didn't want them tracing the items to his house. It was drinking too much that had caused him to make that error. He had to keep a clear head, especially when there was a new police investigation going on.

"Will they open up a full investigation like they did all those years ago?" Grace asked, trying to sound naive.

"I should imagine they have done already." Tim muttered almost under his breath.

Grace settled on a repeat of an old drama programme, as a slightly uncomfortable silence landed in the room.

"Better get the sheds cleared out." Grace said, keeping her eyes on the television screen.

The paper lowered again.

"What's that got to do with anything?" Tim's voice became dark and cold.

"Oh, nothing. I was just thinking the other day we ought to have a clear out before the winter sets in. Tidy the garden up a bit."

Grace knew she needed to go steady. She could see it had hit a nerve with him and she didn't want to push him too far.

*

"I know you're very angry with us at the moment, darling. But I've just called to tell you we did what we thought would be best for you at the time. We decided to tell you because we didn't want you finding out through someone else, especially as you were having some therapy.

Daddy and I were so thankful every day that you were spared, and we still are. We didn't want it to be a black cloud over our lives. So we tried to carry on as normal. It made us appreciate all three of you so much more, even though we didn't think that was possible. It wasn't an easy decision to make, not telling you. And I know you think we've suffocated you over the years, but now you know why. Anyway…that's all I wanted to say on the matter. We love you very much and we hope you can see our reasons for keeping it from you…."

Chrissie turned off the answer machine. Despite the situation, she chuckled to herself. Her mother had sounded so matter of fact and defensive. She did that when she was wounded.

Chrissie, having calmed somewhat, called her mother back to put her mind at rest. The fresh air from the sea had done her the world of good.

They had a much better conversation about it all even though Chrissie still felt extremely sore and upset. It was as if someone had allowed her into a room of memories where the door had been locked for so many years.

Her mother was right. It served no purpose to dwell on "what ifs". She hadn't been aware of it for so many years and had got along in her life quite happily. Something her mother thought she wouldn't have done had she remembered the awful incident.

But she couldn't whole heartedly throw herself into this carefree attitude. She needed some time. Every moment she thought about what could have happened, her stomach turned over. She felt like she'd been rescued from falling off a cliff, but she was still standing on the edge. Each time she looked over her shoulder she was staring down a sheer drop.

Chrissie decided to call Sarah before she settled down for the night. She wanted to let her know she'd been right about the childhood memory. She still couldn't believe it. A whole part of her life seemed to have been erased; like a piece of puzzle that didn't belong in the whole picture.

The anger Chrissie felt earlier began to bubble up inside her. It made her realise who she was angry with. The person who'd tried to snatch her. How dare they? How dare they put her and her parents through that awful trauma? Her lovely, kind parents who'd strived to give her and her siblings a magical childhood. Something that, in Chrissie's opinion, should be set in stone, not something you had if you were lucky. And how dare they try to cut her life short; what right had they to make that decision.

` These feelings gave her the determination to work out the messages she was being given and the will to work out who it was who committed these abhorrent crimes.

*

Grace knocked at her sister's door but there was no answer. She'd brought her some shopping, knowing she wouldn't have been out of the house. She put the bags down on the door step and let herself in. All was silent apart from the buzz of the refrigerator.

She went through the rooms calling her, but there was no answer. She remembered the last time she'd freaked out and scolded herself for even thinking it. Eve was just upstairs taking a nap.

She switched on the kettle to make a hot drink for them both and began to unpack the shopping, whilst reassuring herself everything was fine. But the atmosphere felt heavier than usual and she couldn't shake off the feeling of foreboding. She scolded herself again and finished putting the shopping away.

As Grace put the last of the things in the fridge and cleared the kitchen table of bags, she noticed an envelope with her name on it.

At first she thought Eve had gone for a walk and left her a note. But then the logical side of her brain told her that Eve would have scribbled on a piece of paper, rather than go to the trouble of putting it in an envelope.

A sick feeling began to rise from the pit of her stomach as she opened the carefully folded letter.

Dear Grace,

I'm so sorry....

Grace didn't get any further. She scrambled up the stairs so fast she fell up them. She recovered herself immediately and within seconds she was barging through Alice's bedroom door.

A loud scream made her jump. She turned around to see who it was and then realised it had come from her mouth.

Eve was laid on Alice's bed, a deathly shade of white. For what felt like a few seconds Grace was rooted to the spot.

Brain in gear, she checked for a pulse, but she was shaking so much, she wasn't sure if she could feel one or not. She ran downstairs to call for an ambulance. She tried to calm her breathing so she could relay the address to the operator on the end of the phone.

"Grace? Whatever's happened? I heard a terrible scream."

Grace turned in the hallway to find Eve's next door neighbour, Dennis. He was a close friend of the family and a retired Detective Inspector. He'd been at the forefront of all the murder investigations and had been a huge support to their entire family during their time of need.

"Oh Dennis, she's upstairs....she's in Alice's bedroom..."

Dennis sprinted up the stairs two at a time with Grace following closely behind him.

"Christ, Eve!"

"Is she still alive, Dennis?" Grace said, as Dennis checked Eve for a pulse.

"There's a faint pulse." He leaned his face near to hers to see if he could feel her breath on his cheek.

"It's weak, but she's still with us." Dennis moved her carefully into the recovery position in case she was sick. He picked up the bottles of tablets she'd taken, and examined the labels.

"Just try and keep calm, Grace, the ambulance will be here in a minute."

"Oh god, Dennis! What was she thinking?"

Grace sat on the end of the bed, her head in her hands.

"She's not been right since Alice went Grace. You know that."

"But to get in this...that's the ambulance!" Grace raced back downstairs to guide them to the correct house, not wanting to waste a second.

Grace and Dennis followed the ambulance to the hospital, leaving the crew space to bring Eve back to life.

"Try not to worry, Grace. I don't think she's taken enough. She's in the right hands now."

"But I wasted time making a drink and unloading the shopping," Grace sobbed, "I just thought she was having a nap as normal."

"You've got nothing to reproach yourself for. It was inevitable it would come to this, she's been in such turmoil."

"If it was inevitable, Dennis, then I should have looked after her better."

"Look, you can't watch someone twenty four hours a day. She'd have found a way at some point."

"I clearly wasn't watching enough. I just assumed Jon was on top of it all. But now, as I reflect on recent events, he obviously wasn't."

"Grace, you need to remember you had your own loss to deal with. In my experience, when people plan this sort of thing, they've gone beyond accepting any sort of help."

They parked out the front of the hospital and watched as the ambulance crew deftly unloaded Eve and rushed her through the emergency doors. Grace and Dennis followed. They were sent to the family room by an austere but friendly nurse, despite Grace's protests to be with her sister.

"Let them do their jobs, Grace. Sit there and I'll get you a drink."

Grace was going over and over things in her head. Her mind was like a washing machine running through a cycle. Round and round. All she kept thinking was what if she'd reported Tim or followed through with her plans earlier. Maybe this wouldn't have happened.

Perhaps Eve would have coped better knowing who it was, even though it would have been such a shock finding out it was her brother in law. This thought caused little sobbing noises to escape her mouth; she was so knotted up with it all. When Dennis came back in with their drinks she was rocking backwards and forwards in one of the weather beaten chairs.

Dennis put the cups down and grabbed Grace by her shoulders.

"Grace, this is not going to help Eve!"

"You don't understand," Grace sobbed again, "you don't understand."

"Hey, come on. It's ok. She'll be alright." He sat next to her and pulled her body towards him. She gripped his shirt, having always found him more of a comfort than Tim. She relaxed in his arms and cried and cried.

Once she'd calmed, Dennis got her to drink the coffee he'd brought. She seemed to be much calmer after she'd released all her pent up emotion.

She smiled at Dennis and then frowned as she looked at his tired face.

"Are you alright? You don't look your usual sprightly self."

"I'm just tired, Grace. Too much golf and gardening."

"Are you sure that's all it is? You look a bit pale."

Dennis was the picture of health. He was in his fifties, the same as Grace, and as the years had been kind to her, so they had to him. He'd had his fair share of admirers over the years and he was the healthiest police officer Grace had ever known. In her experience they were usually overweight smokers with a drink problem. But she'd known Dennis long enough to know there was something weighing heavy on his mind.

"Honestly. I'm fine. By the way I've called Jon and he's on his way. I tried Tim as well, but there's no answer."

"Thanks Dennis, but I don't want him here."

"Good job I didn't get hold of him then."

"I'm not being ungrateful. He's just the last person I want to see at the moment."

"Not getting on?"

"Just the usual. You know what we're like; you've known us long enough."

Grace almost choked on the words. What she'd wanted to say was, "he's a fucking bastard and I want him to suffer a slow and painful death and never see him ever again", but this was hardly appropriate.

Dennis half chuckled and sighed to himself.

"You've never had what could be called a 'blissful' marriage, have you?"

"Far from it, Dennis. Far from it."

"My parents were like you two. Bickered all the time, but really loved each other. When my mother died, my father was a broken man."

"Oh, I wouldn't go that far, Dennis. There's no love lost between Tim and me."

Dennis frowned.

"Is he really that bad, Grace?" Dennis laughed, "I'll take him on another fishing trip. We haven't been for a while; get the old boy out of your hair for a bit."

Dennis nudged Grace, trying to cheer her up, which probably wasn't going to work under the circumstances.

"That would be great. Give us a break from each other."

"You've got a lot on your plate at the moment. You're bound to rub each other up the wrong way."

Dennis patted Grace's knee.

The doctor that had been dealing with Eve came into the room.

Grace held her breath. Good news or bad, doctors always appeared to have that sombre "I have tragic news" look on their faces.

"We have managed to stabilise Eve's condition, but she's in a very fragile state. We don't believe enough has been absorbed into her system to cause any permanent damage to her organs.'

"So, will she be alright?"

"We've stabilised her, as I said, and she's in the best place. You found her just in time. She's very lucky"

"But surely, if she hasn't taken enough to do any permanent damage to her organs, then she hasn't taken enough to kill herself?"

"It's a little more complicated than that. If Eve hadn't been found then the tablets would have completely dissolved into her system, which could have been fatal. We have managed to pump quite a lot out of her stomach. Now we have to let her body do the rest. She's being monitored."

"Can we see her?"

"The nurses are just getting her settled into a side room on the Sandringham ward. Give them a few minutes and then you should be able to go and see her. Only for a few minutes though, she's very weak."

The doctor nodded reassuringly, smiled and left the room.

"They never seem to answer the bloody question." Grace frowned.

"Sounded pretty clear to me. She's very bloody lucky."

"Let's hope she sees it that way when she comes round."

CHAPTER FOURTEEN

Chrissie had been lying awake for quite some time. She was watching the sun come up through her bedroom window. It was slowly lighting up her garden and giving it a warm glow.

Strangely, she'd had the best night's sleep since she'd lived in the cottage. After the shock of the news from her mother and all the pieces she'd linked together, she'd thought that would have caused her to have a very bumpy journey through the night. But it was quite the opposite and she felt very calm. It was as if by solving part of the mystery, her mind could relax. Like she'd let go of something.

Everywhere felt calm. Chrissie knew it hadn't stopped there. That there would be another part to the puzzle she would have to solve. She promised herself that from now on she wouldn't rule out any possibilities, however outrageous they were or however much she didn't want them to hold any truth. She'd done that over the regression therapy and Sarah had turned out to be right.

Since the session and her mother telling her what had happened, the memory had become clearer in her head. Little bits and pieces were coming back to her, mainly about that particular holiday, rather than anything to do with the actual incident. Most of what she remembered was of it being very dark and that she'd felt absolutely petrified.

A thought hit Chrissie like an electric shock. Something her mother had said replayed in her head.

"You just said you thought it was a man and he smelt funny..."

What smell?

Chrissie ran downstairs to call her mother. It was some time before Sylvia answered the phone and Chrissie wondered if she was still in bed.

"You're up and about early, darling. Are you alright?"

"What smell did I say he had?"

"Sorry?"

"You said yesterday that I thought it was a man who snatched me and he smelt funny. Did I say what smell?"

"Oh, yes. Umm...let me think...it was something herbal, but I can't remember what. It was such a long time ago. Darling, I hope you're not torturing yourself with all this?"

"No Mum. I just need to work something out. Was it Fisherman's Friend?"

"That rings a bell. It might have been. Why is it so important?"

"My therapy session brought up the memory of a smell and it's been bugging me. It was Fisherman's Friend."

"Oh. Well. Do you feel better now?"

"I do now I know what it is. I'm just not sure I know what it means."

"Probably nothing, darling, I'm sure there are hundreds of people who ate and smelt of those sweets. You must remember that you were very young at the time and memories get muddled. Now go and do something nice with your day and try not to dwell on it."

Chrissie had decided not to tell her mother about what had happened in the garden. It would only worry them. They wouldn't think it was someone with a message from beyond the grave. They'd think it was some psycho stalking her. They'd only talk her into phoning the police, or worse still, call them themselves.

Chrissie's mind rested on this thought. Having dismissed the regression therapy theory that it was a childhood memory and not a past life, maybe she shouldn't ignore this either. After all, Sarah and Grace had suggested it might not be a paranormal message.

A really disturbing thought entered her mind. If it was the serial killer who had snatched her, was he still in the village, and had he recognised her? Had all the paranormal activities been a clever trick in order for him to frighten her? She plonked herself down on the sofa after turning on the television. She needed some background noise, some attachment with the real world to drown out the eerie atmosphere that was descending on the house again.

She went through all the people she'd met since she'd arrived in the village. Then she went back over the paranormal activity. Some of it couldn't have been orchestrated. But then, when she thought about it, some of it could have. Did someone know about the paranormal activity and think it'd be funny to frighten her further?

For some reason Chrissie's mind kept picturing Grace's kitchen, a clear vision in her head. Grace and her husband Tim were the only people who knew about the incidents, unless they'd told someone else about it, which was doubtful.

Chrissie's mind settled on Tim. Fisherman's Friend. No. He wouldn't play games; he's a retired policeman; Grace's husband.

But the more Chrissie's mind settled on Tim, the more he felt familiar to her.

*

What was she waiting for? Grace didn't know. After the day's events she had become acutely aware of the knowledge she had about Tim. If a friend confided in her and told her this story, she'd scream at them from the steeples that they had to go to the police. But this was her and not someone else.

The guilt was beginning to weigh heavily on her. She'd kept the information to herself for over a year, even though it only felt like a few weeks. Sometimes when she thought about it all, she felt completely in control and confident she was doing what she believed was only right and just. But a lot of the time she felt like a frightened little child who was completely out of their depth. And that maybe she'd spent the last year hiding away from the truth. Not wanting it to come out because of the repercussions it would cause. She soon snapped out of it, knowing she wasn't that much of a coward. She wouldn't have kept the information to herself purely because of the fear of everyone knowing it was her husband and the stigma that carried.

Grace kicked the bottom of the bed with her heels. She was sitting in Alice's bedroom, having left Eve to rest. Dennis had dropped her off. She didn't ask him in, just told him she needed some time on her own.

She'd eventually got through to Tim and then wondered why she'd bothered. He hadn't been fazed by any of it. She told him she didn't know when she'd be home. He'd said nothing.

Her resolve returning, Grace began to think about her plans. She found this immensely therapeutic and it kept her mind focused; a means to an end, a life for everyone again without Tim.

She got up from the bed and turned Alice's bedside lamp on and the over head light off. She didn't like glaring main lights on in rooms. Apart from making the atmosphere impersonal and stark, it brought back sad memories for Grace.

She remembered when her mother had died, how she and her siblings had sat around the family kitchen table, the main light glaring down on them all, the bulb high-lighting everything like a big fluorescent pen marking out a sentence. They had sat there to discuss things after their mother's death, and again after her funeral, and again when they were sorting out her paper work. All under the overhead light and it had made it seem so stark and raw.

It was one of those things in life Grace hated. She remembered being distracted because the whole time she sat there, all she could think about was turning the light off and putting the lamps on. Making it cosy, just as it had always been. She supposed it was because she needed the comfort, wanting things to stay the same, as if by turning the lamps on it would flick another switch.

After she'd turned the lamp on, Alice's bedroom felt totally different. Grace sat on the bed and closed her eyes. She imagined Alice walking through the door with a cup of hot chocolate and a book, ready to jump into bed and read. Alice loved books. She and Nadine had always swapped novels.

Grace opened her eyes and stared around the room. It was exactly how Alice had left it. Apart from the fact everything was faded, the posters, the spines of books, photographs and curtains. It was as if they'd faded out alongside Alice.

Grace casually opened the small bedside cabinet. A pile of envelopes cascaded onto the floor. They were all addressed to Alice.

She picked one up. It was sealed. She tried another, frowning. They were all sealed and franked.

Grace didn't want to pry, but she was intrigued that all these letters had been sent and put away unopened. She looked at the dates.

As far as she could tell, all the letters had been sent after Alice went missing. Why hadn't her sister opened them?

Grace tapped an envelope on her hand, trying to decide if she should open some. She didn't normally read people's letters, but she was concerned that they might hold some important information.

They all looked like they'd come from the same person; they were identical apart from the sizes and colours. The address on the front of each envelope had been typed, so she couldn't glean any clues from that.

She was surprised the police hadn't found these in their investigations, especially as the case had been reopened. She decided it could be important and ran downstairs with a handful to open over a steaming kettle.

There was no soft lighting in the kitchen, so she had no choice but to use the glaring one over the kitchen table. It was to be another sad memory stored in her mind, tinged yet again with the starkness of the light.

She made herself a hot drink and then kept re-boiling the kettle so she could steam open each letter. She sat down at the kitchen table and examined one of the envelopes again before she removed its contents. She was still undecided. She was very particular about privacy and didn't like it when anyone encroached on hers.

Curiosity and anxiety got the better of her. She pulled the carefully folded paper from one of the envelopes. A familiar feeling rose in her stomach. Some miniature paper stars and hearts dropped onto the table.

She opened the letter and began to read. Then she looked at another and another. They were all from Eve. One of them was a birthday card to Alice with a silver charm bracelet in it. They were all decorated with something and were so lovingly written. Some even had photographs of family events.

Grace thought she would choke on the lump in her throat. An immense sadness descended on her like a veil. She gulped down the tears; she was so exhausted from crying.

Once she'd finished her drink, she put all the letters and items back in their envelopes. Another wave of guilt passed over her. She felt bad for opening the letters and stealing a private moment that Eve had been sharing with her daughter.

She took the letters back upstairs and put them in Alice's bedside cabinet where she had found them. She flicked through the other envelopes to see if they were all the same. They all matched.

Perhaps Eve had felt that by posting them, it would break some sort of spell and bring Alice home. Grace had no idea. It dawned her that there was quite a lot she hadn't known about her sister. Eve had been right when she'd implied she'd coped with it all alone. Grace's face stung with shame. She'd been so wrapped up in her own grief for her daughter and her niece that she hadn't been there for Eve. It was something they could have shared, a grief that would have brought them closer together. Instead, Eve had turned to the only person there was and that had been Daphne. But as Grace had shut away her pain of losing Nadine, she'd not really wanted to approach Eve's over Alice. She'd done exactly what she despised in other people, avoided the issue. Not wanting to talk about it, because it was all a bit too dreadful. She'd been happy using the excuse that Jon was there supporting her and they wouldn't want busybody do-gooder's interfering in their private time.

This was Grace realised, what she had wanted, to shut everyone out. Deal with it the way she thought best, stoically and privately. The awareness of the fact that this behaviour may have resulted in her not having dealt with her daughter's death at all began to creep over her skin. She physically shook herself and her guilt away, something she would have to face at a later date. Feeling herself coming undone again, she jumped up off the bed.

She looked in Alice's wardrobe. Her clothes were still hanging in it, just as they had done all those years ago. Grace felt a pain shoot across her heart. She pulled back the clothes to reveal piles and piles of Jackie magazines, all dated after Alice went missing.

"Oh Eve." Grace whispered, realising the enormity of her sister's pain.

There were some boxes neatly stacked on the shelf at the top of the wardrobe. She pulled them down and looked inside. They were all filled with unopened letters, all addressed to Alice. Grace looked all over the bedroom and found boxes and boxes of the same thing. Hundreds and hundreds of love letters Eve had sent her daughter in the hope she would one day come home and read them.

A thought dawned on her. She was sure the police would want to search Alice's bedroom again. She didn't want them going through these. She decided to bag them up and put them away somewhere. She didn't want her sister dealing with that. They'd open and read every single one of them.

She knew exactly where they could be kept safe. Dennis would understand.

She decided to take them over there that evening, just in case the police turned up first thing in the morning. He wouldn't mind. He'd told her if she needed anything or felt like a night cap, she only had to call.

The letters were safely put away at Dennis's, a task which had taken them both a couple of trips back and forth because there were so many boxes. Then they sat together in his living room and had a night cap. The trouble was that one night cap led to another, and another, which then led to something else.

*

Tim had drunk too much again. The longer Grace stayed away, the more bored he became. There was a strange atmosphere between them that was unnerving him. He felt like he was losing her, even though nothing tangible had changed. The truth was, Tim had lost her a long time ago, he just hadn't noticed. Mainly because she was always there and he'd taken her for granted.

The days and nights she was away left a void and a feeling their marriage was over. Tim was feeling quite bereft about it all. He'd never have imagined he would feel like that about Grace; she just irritated him most of the time.

Tim shrugged as he sat at the kitchen table and picked at the label on the almost empty rum bottle. When he thought about it, it seemed that ever since Chrissie had turned up, Grace's attitude had changed. It was shortly after that she'd turned distant and cold.

Typical bloody women, he thought to himself, sitting around gossiping and convincing each other that there was a better life elsewhere; the grass was greener and all that.

Tim sighed, bored with himself and his life in general. But however bored he was, he wasn't about to go to Chrissie's again and start messing about. The last time had been enough. He knew that drink had a lot to answer for, but he knew what he'd seen and it was no drunken illusion. Never in all his time as a police officer had he seen anything like that. He didn't believe in it. Load of old clap trap, he thought normally, rum or no rum.

He had been tempted to go round there when Grace had told him that Chrissie might go to the police. Shake her up a bit to make sure she kept her mouth shut. But he'd reasoned with himself that he'd deny all if the police traced anything back to him. He'd just say that someone must have stolen the clothes from him and Grace, or that they were being set up. He doubted she'd go to the police anyway; she thought it was ghosts playing tricks with her.

Tim chuckled to himself. There was only one woman he needed to sort out, and that was his mother. He didn't need her mouthing off about him, especially if she was going round the twist and having spontaneous outbursts. He couldn't have anything said about him that might connect him to the murders. Even if it did sound ludicrous, someone might just take notice if she went on about it for long enough.

Once the police connected Alice with the other murders, there'd be a massive investigation, which would spread nationally. The urge to move away and start a new life overwhelmed him again. It was becoming more and more apparent to him there were more positive points to going than there were to staying.

He had no memory scents, which was his first reason. He'd even burnt the ones he'd stolen from Chrissie, and in light of what happened last time he was in her house, there'd be no chance of getting anymore.

He could start all over again if he moved away. Get some new memory scents. Take himself out of the picture before things got too heavy with the police.

His mind wandered back to his mother and settled like a gnat on a potential piece of flesh. What he couldn't work out was how she knew what he'd done. He'd searched her face for a clue, because he hadn't been sure if she was calling his bluff. That it was just a wild guess because she knew him so well. It must have been. How else could she know?

It was a mother's intuition, Daphne thought as she sat in her magnolia overdosed room, watching the telly. Coupled with the fact she knew him so well, she'd been able to piece it all together. She had seen his elation each time a body was found. His excitement when he relayed the details to her, and how he revelled in the facts.

All through his life he'd stolen obscure items of clothing from people. She just thought it was a phase he was going through and it would pass as he got older. But it didn't.

Ever since she'd told him about his sister Verity being murdered when she was seven, before he was born, he'd become obsessed with clothing. She'd kept Verity's bedroom as it was the day she was taken. Not a thing was touched, even her clothes still hung in her wardrobe, the pain so great that Daphne couldn't face getting rid of them. She'd caught him in there a few times, sniffing her clothes. The door had been locked throughout his childhood and the room passed off as a storage area, but after they'd told him the truth she'd permitted him in there once to have a look. After that, he'd regularly stolen the key so he could unlock the door and go inside the mysterious room. She put it down to him grieving for the sibling he'd never had.

He'd had an unusual fascination with the details of his sister's murder, wanting to visit the library to read newspaper cuttings. This was the only way he learned the facts of what had happened because Daphne wasn't prepared to discuss it with anyone. She'd only told him when he turned twelve because she didn't want him finding out from someone else, and he seemed to be mature enough to take the news. She told herself she hadn't wanted him poisoned by it as a child; for him to be aware of the black cloud that hung over the family. The real reason had been because it was all too painful for Daphne to speak of.

When the police reported that each child had a piece of clothing missing, she'd had a feeling. It had felt like being plunged into a pool of ice cold water. But that idea of knowing had quickly altered in her mind, as denial set in.

She knew the thrill he got out of producing his own crime; she could see that much. And in some perverse way, she thought he could justify his acts, because it was keeping the local police force busy, a bit like a manufacturer producing the goods. An atrocious thought to have, but she knew how his mind worked. She had thought of every excuse conceivable, anything to protect her son and herself from this whole ghastly mess.

Then her denial took over, convinced her she was wrong about it all, and she'd swatted it away like an annoying fly.

It was the discovery of Alice's body that had stirred it all up again. She knew the area they'd found her remains very well. It had been the area that had given the game away. That and how he'd reacted to what she'd said when he visited the other day.

The place where Alice had been found was, to anyone else, just a rural piece of woodland. No footpaths or bridleways marked out. You wouldn't know it was there unless you stumbled across it accidentally.

And that's exactly how Daphne had discovered it, chasing the family dog when they were all out for a walk and a picnic. It had become a favourite place for them. Undisturbed, unspoilt.

His reaction to her words the other day had almost broken Daphne's heart. She'd seen it all in his eyes, those eyes she knew so well, because they were like looking into her own.

Her dilemma now was where to go from here? He was still her son after all. But Daphne saw herself as an upstanding moral citizen and she remembered only too well the pain she had suffered all those years ago when it had happened to her. Ironic she should be the mother of a victim and then perpetrator years later.

Thinking of his privileged upbringing, she wondered how he'd turned out to be such an abhorrent human being.

Because I wasn't given enough attention, Tim thought to himself.

He was pondering over his bottle of rum why he hadn't achieved more in his life. He was convinced it was his mother's fault, always leaving him with Dora who shut him away for hours in the cellar. When his mother was there she was always entertaining people and telling him to go to his room and stay out of the way.

His father was hardly around so it was unlikely he'd ever known. He remembered so clearly the times when Dora had left him with some friend or another, while she went off on "business". He realised now, looking back, that "business" had been her having an abortion.

She'd always told him, but he'd never understood.

"I've got some business to clear up," she'd leer at him; "I don't want a little bastard like you, do I?"

The words moved around in his head, as clear as if they'd just been said to him. Dora had been like a mother to him and it had cut him like a knife. She'd picked him up and dropped him as she'd pleased. All he'd wanted was some attention from his mother. And his father, who was so wrapped up in his work he didn't have a clue what was going on. He always knew his mother had been so disappointed he'd been a boy and he could never live up to Verity. She always gave him a look of dismay and dissatisfaction, even when she was being kind to him. As the years had gone by she'd become more bitter and twisted.

The memories were jumbled. One thing was clear to him; he'd been such a horrible child she hadn't wanted anymore. He thought about all the lost siblings he had never had the chance to know.

Somehow, and it was hard to tell when it had happened, but Tim's emotions towards his mother had shifted. Drained away like water through a sieve. Tim put it down to his survival instinct kicking in, which may have happened when he realised she knew his secret. And now he just felt cold emptiness for her, as he did for most people he'd ever known. He needed that detachment towards her in order to get rid of her without remorse.

*

Chrissie knocked on Grace's back door, tentatively. She didn't like calling round to people unannounced, but she'd been out for a stroll and found herself nearby.
Thinking Grace was out and not wanting to risk Tim answering, she began to walk away. When it opened and he peered through the gap like a wizened old man, Chrissie jumped slightly and the hairs on her arms began to rise.

He looked dreadful, and for a few seconds Chrissie found herself staring at him.

"Yes?" he snapped at her.

"I'm Chrissie, Grace's friend. We met in the pub for lunch?" Chrissie was a bit taken aback by his rudeness.

"Yeah?"

"Um, well….I just called by on the off chance that Grace was in? But I see she's not. I'll call round another time." Chrissie moved to walk away again, not wanting to be near him any longer than necessary. She hadn't remembered him being so vile.

Tim opened the door a bit wider. "She's at her sister's house, if it's urgent."

"No, it's not urgent. I was just wondering how she was." Chrissie said, staying rooted to the spot. She suspected he smelt as bad as he looked.

"I can give you directions if you want to go over there. Come in for a minute."

Tim hadn't wanted to invite her in when she'd first arrived; he'd got a stinking hangover. But her perfume and the smell of her body were riding on the breeze that had travelled through the open door and now he was desperate to get her inside and smell her.

"It's fine, thank you. I'll see her another time." Chrissie shoved her hands in her coat pockets and turned on her heel.

"Why don't you come in for a bit and wait for her. She'll be back soon." He hadn't a clue when she'd be back, but he was willing to try anything to get her in the house, his urge to smell her getting the better of him.

Chrissie turned, frowning at him.

"No. Thank you. Just tell her I called." Her voice was clipped, but she managed a smile.

"Suit yourself." He muttered and slammed the door.

"Weirdo." Chrissie said back to him through the closed door. She shivered. There was something really peculiar about him. As she closed the gate behind her, Grace pulled up in the car.

"Oh Chrissie, am I glad to see you! What a spot of luck."

"I know what great timing. Tim did ask me in to wait for you. He said you wouldn't be long."

"Did he?" Grace frowned.

"Yes, but I told him I'd call another time." Chrissie noticed the frown and she didn't want Grace to think Tim had been suggestive.

"Well, actually, he wouldn't know because I didn't tell him. I've just popped back for some things."

Chrissie continued to frown.

"Don't worry, I'll tell you everything later. Have you got time to come in with me, and then I'll take you back to my sister's?"

"Err...yes, yes ok."

"Oh sorry, I'm being terribly bossy. Was it a flying visit?"

"No, not at all. I was hoping for a pot of tea and a chat?"

"I can do better than that. How about supper and a bottle of wine? If you haven't any plans?"

"At your sister's?" Chrissie didn't want an evening with Tim.

"Oh god yes. I wouldn't inflict him on you any longer than necessary." Grace flicked her hand towards the house.

"Yes, that'd be lovely!"

"Good, I could do with the company. Right, let's get this out of the way. Excuse my husband and please excuse the mess he will have left the house in."

Chrissie waved her hand and told her friend not to worry, as she followed her back up the path to the house.

"Hello, again." Tim leered at Chrissie more from the amount of rum he'd had than from anything else.

Grace glared at him.

"I've just come back to get some fresh clothes and things."

"Oh, I thought you were coming home?"

"No."

"Oh."

They stared at each other for quite some time, which made Chrissie feel very awkward. She looked at Grace's face and saw an absolute look of hatred. It changed the look of Grace altogether and it unnerved Chrissie slightly.

"Shall I make myself useful and put the kettle on?" Chrissie said, trying to break the excruciating awkwardness.

Tim and Grace broke away from their silent conversation.

"Yes, that's a good idea, Chrissie. I won't have one, but I'm sure Tim could do with a strong coffee." Her voice was clipped and she didn't take her eyes away from him.

"Thank you, Chrissie. I'll have a cup of tea." Tim looked at Grace pointedly.

"Right then I'll sort that out while you do what you need to do."

Chrissie walked between them in the hope it would shatter the invisible frosted screen that was hovering in the middle of them. Tim sniffed hard as she walked passed. Grace glared at him harder and Chrissie stopped in her tracks. A flash of the pathway at the bottom of her garden down the side of the shed flittered across her vision. She shook it off, putting it down to another random flashback. Sarah had told her she'd get those.

Grace went off to pack some more things while Chrissie made herself and Tim a hot drink. Chrissie could feel Tim staring at her and she was desperately trying to think of something to say to break the silence. The atmosphere was unbearable. It didn't help that all the curtains were shut, making the place look dingy, coupled with the fact it looked like it had been burgled.

Chrissie placed two mugs of steaming tea on to the old kitchen table where Tim was sat. Chrissie prayed as she gripped her mug for Grace to be quick.

"So, have you settled in Chrissie?"

' "Yes, just about." Chrissie wasn't one for making small talk to people she didn't like, so she picked up the newspaper that was laid on the table.

"Do you want to do the crossword while you're at it?" Tim leered at her again, throwing a pen in her general direction. It rolled off the table and onto the floor. Chrissie glared at him and reached down to pick it up. As she did, he leaned down towards the floor with her and sniffed her hair. Her hand hovered over the pen as the memory of him flooded her vision, like the shock of cold water hitting her skin.

Her fingers felt for the pen as she looked up into his face.

The smell, his voice, everything, it was all slotting into place and the film began to run freely in her mind, without the pauses and the editing.

She quickly composed herself, wanting to digest the information without him noticing. Not that he was capable of noticing anything, the state he was in.

Grace breezed back in, dispersing the icy moment.

"Are you ok?"

"Yes. Fine. Why?" Chrissie was finding it hard to take her eyes off Tim.

It was all too huge to digest. She can't have just discovered something in a few seconds that the police had spent years trying to work out. She must be getting muddled with someone else. She was finding it hard to connect the information that if he'd snatched her when she was a child that could quite possibly make him the serial killer. Or was she mistaken? She couldn't be sure of anything at that moment.

"Are you ready?" Grace's voice broke her train of thought.

"Yes, I'm ready." She wanted to tell Grace she needed to go home, but the words wouldn't come out of her mouth. Something inside Chrissie was urging her to go with Grace. She needed to talk to her, to glean some sort of information from her without her knowing what she was doing.

"Get this place cleaned up." Grace snapped at Tim on her way out of the door.

"I'm going fishing at the weekend. I'll do it when I get back." He slurred, not bothering to get out of his chair.

"Oh do what you like!" Grace snapped, and slammed the door.

Chrissie's mind was whirring, flitting from one memory to the next, as she felt Grace's footsteps behind her on the path. They got into the car, both silent.

Chrissie reasoned with herself that the Fisherman's Friend and the rum smell could belong to anyone. But there was something else. A familiarity when she'd got close to him.

"Has Tim said something to you?"

"Um...Sorry?"

"Tim. Has he upset you?" Grace was trying to figure out the change in her friend.

"No not at all. Sorry Grace, he just reminded me of someone. Have you left him?"

The question startled Grace at first and it was a few seconds before she answered.

"I'm not sure. I think I've done it without realising it."

Grace filled Chrissie in on what had happened with her sister as they made their way to her house. Chrissie was finding it hard to pay attention to what was being said, but as Grace rested on telling her about Tim, she noticed a change in her tone.

Chrissie was beginning to wonder if Grace knew what her husband had done, but then she realised what a ridiculous thought that was. If she knew she would have reported him, surely?

Chrissie physically shook herself; the whole thing was ridiculous. He was a retired police officer, an upstanding member of the community. He didn't even look like a serial killer, Chrissie thought to herself. But then it dawned on her; what was a serial killer supposed to look like?

"Are you sure you're ok?" Grace said, again.

"I'm fine. I just had some news from my parents that disturbed me a bit."

"Oh. What?" Grace pulled the car into her sister's drive.

"I told you about the regression therapy and all that? Well, Sarah told me it could be a childhood memory, a theory that I dismissed until my mother phoned. But it turns out its true, only I got away. From whoever snatched me, I mean."

Grace was silent as the information penetrated her mind.

"You're Christine, the one that got away." Grace's voice was almost a whisper. It was all rushing to her like a head on collision.

"How did you know that?"

"It was all over the papers. Why hadn't I connected it before?" Grace was talking to herself more than to Chrissie.

"That's why you're so familiar to me. I recognise you from the pictures."

A flurry, a bit like a snow storm flittered through Chrissies mind and fragments of memory melted as they landed in her head.

They sat in silence for some time before they made their way into the house. There was so much said in that silence. They were both going over the same thing in their heads, only from completely different directions. But eventually their minds would bring them onto the same path. It was just a matter of time, which of them was going to say it out loud first.

Grace sighed, knowing they both knew the same thing.

CHAPTER FIFTEEN

For what he thought was the last time, Tim pressed the buzzer on the double doors of the retirement home. One of the usual voices greeted him over the intercom; Veronica, the home manager. But instead of buzzing him in as she normally did when she heard his name, she asked him to wait there.

Tim frowned, wondering what was going on. Perhaps one of the residents had had an accident, he thought. Tim could see Veronica coming down the corridor, an air of authority wafting around her. He found her a little bit intimidating, which was unusual for Tim. She was always dressed in a power suit, immaculate nails, makeup, and blonde hair tied up in a chignon. She looked totally out of place there. She would have looked more fitting in an expensive restaurant.

"Hello Tim. Step into the office, would you?" She was pleasant, but there was obviously something very wrong.

All sorts of things were moving through his mind, but he wasn't panicking. He thought perhaps she'd died, and they'd been trying to get hold of him while he was on his way there.

Veronica proffered for him to take a seat, as she positioned herself in front of a large leather bound desk.

"Is there something wrong, Veronica?" Tim put on his best calm and concerned voice and linked his hands on his lap like a vicar might.

Calculated cash sums were already running through his head.

"I'm really sorry to have to tell you this, Tim..."

Tim didn't hear anything else Veronica said. Elation was sweeping over him. The old witch had finally died of her own accord. That was until he caught the last words out of Veronica's mouth.

"...she doesn't want to see you at the moment."

"Sorry, what did you say?"

"Unfortunately, your mother doesn't want to see you at the moment. We have to respect her wishes, Tim. Did you have some sort of difficulty with her last time you were here?"

Tim snapped back to reality.

"No. Why? What did she say?" Tim's face appeared to darken.

"She has just requested not to see you at the moment. She's made an official request, which means I can't let you in to see her. I'm really sorry."

"Well, she's obviously had another stroke or she's going senile."

"I'm afraid not. The doctor's been in to see her and he says she's doing quite well and appears to be of sound mind."

"Appears to be? That's not good enough. I want some more tests done. You can't stop me seeing my own mother." Tim was becoming irate. His brain was trying to grasp the concept that someone, a woman, was telling him what to do.

"It's not us, Tim. Your mother has requested we don't let you in and we have to respect that."

"I don't have to respect anything. She's my mother, for fuck's sake!" Tim banged his fist on the desk, causing Veronica to flinch slightly.

She looked at him properly for the first time since he'd arrived and noticed how rough he looked. Unclean, unshaven and there was a smell of stale alcohol wafting across the desk to her nostrils with each word he spat.

"I don't know and I don't want to know what problems you've had with each other, but I suggest you go home and call us in a week's time. See what the situation is then." She stood up, walked to the door and gestured for him to leave. She didn't like his aggressive behaviour and wanted him off the premises as quickly as possible. She was starting to see what Daphne had been talking about.

"You can't do this! She can't do this!" Tim shouted.

It had no effect. Veronica continued to stand by the door, willing him to leave.

Tim gave in, feeling like a scolded child under her glare.

"Bitch!" he spat at her as she saw him out of the main doors.

She alerted the other staff to his behaviour and made sure that under no circumstances was he to be let into the building. She had felt something really sinister from him, something she hadn't noticed before.

Tim used the incident as another excuse to drink himself into oblivion. He'd taken his anger out on the house by throwing a few things around when he got home. Some of his anger and violence was aimed at Grace too.

The rum coursed through his veins, making everything feel better. It was the hangovers and tiredness that made him feel violent and vicious. The alcohol calmed him down, taking him by the hand and leading him to the drunken fuelled daze he liked to exist in.

He sat at the kitchen table trying to work out a way of getting to his mother. He wasn't allowed to talk to her and he didn't know what she'd said to the people in the care home, so breaking in to the place wasn't an option. They'd know it was him and he didn't want to draw attention to himself.

Verity's face swam in front of his vision. Picture after picture of her smiling, her with his mother, her with his father, pictures of happier times when he wasn't around, when Verity was still very much alive. It ran through his head that he'd have killed her had she still been around today.

"Verity, fucking Verity!" he shouted to the blank wall.

It was the losing that infuriated him more than anything, the fact that his mother had got there first. She was one step ahead of him and he hated that. He had never liked anyone getting one over him.

As the rum mellowed him, he realised he needed to appeal to her better nature. He was, after all, the apple of her eye, well, the only apple left. Once he got back in her good books, he'd be allowed to see her again. It wouldn't take long for her to give in, he just needed to play his cards right.

The only way he could get through to her was to write her a letter. She liked letters; she'd be impressed by that. He was sure they'd pass a letter on to her in the retirement home, especially if he posted it. They wouldn't know it was from him until she opened it.

That night, Tim sat at his kitchen table and wrote the most heartfelt letter he'd ever written in his life. Convincing himself as he did so, that it was all an act to reach his ultimate goal.

*

Grace had stayed at Chrissie's for the weekend. They needed time in each other's company for Grace to be able to relay everything she needed to Chrissie.

Grace had started with the beginning of her marriage and led right up to what she found out about Tim all those months ago. She felt it was important for Chrissie to know everything from the start to fully understand her future plans for Tim.

Chrissie had listened attentively as Grace had relayed every little detail. They spent most of the weekend going through every imaginable emotion together. Finding out Tim had tried to snatch Chrissie and that she had briefly known Nadine and Alice, had linked them together more so than they had been before.

Had someone else told Chrissie they knew their husband was a serial killer she'd have run from the house and straight down to the nearest police station. But this was different, as things always were when they affected you personally. Grace had shown her the bigger picture, and she now felt like she'd watched a horrible film. Only this was real. And Grace had convinced her that her way was the better way of dealing with it all.

Chrissie had never thought in her wildest dreams that she would ever plot to take another person's life. But in her eyes, he wasn't worthy of living.

Chrissie thought that going out of the house and away from their big secret, she'd wobble and reality would hit her. But it didn't. She felt the same about it when she was around other people as she did when it had first been talked about.

She was still feeling a cocktail of emotions: anger, disgust, devastation and sadness, but also a strange feeling of relief. It was as if she'd always been aware of the whole situation, which she probably had in her subconscious. She was desperate to talk to Sarah about it and she hated keeping secrets from her but she knew she could never tell another soul. Grace had been very clear about that.

Her relationship with Grace had changed along with her relationship with the house. It was no longer a house to her, but a home as well. Both had grown much stronger in a matter of days, and the secret she now shared with Grace would bind them forever.

An atmosphere had descended on the house which Chrissie recognised from when she first viewed it. Whatever it was that had been haunting her had stopped, and there was a tranquillity that had landed like a summer mist. Chrissie put this down to the fact that all the blanks had been filled in, as if it had pushed her onto the path she was about to take.

Chrissie and Grace had realised they were cut from the same mould. Their minds followed the same thought processes. When they discussed killing Tim, it appeared to be a fairly straight forward process. And as the days passed, the thought of it became less and less shocking. It was easier to digest because it involved him having an accident.

Unfortunately for Tim, his drinking habits hadn't gone unnoticed by either of the women and this was what they had decided to use to make his death look like an unfortunate accident. They had agreed to go ahead with their plans once Tim came back from his fishing trip. He was going to have a drink fuelled tragic accident.

Grace didn't really need Chrissie's help doing it, she just wanted her support. Telling Chrissie everything had felt like the most natural thing in the world, and the relief had been immense. It hadn't worried her that she might tell someone or report it to the police. Grace was past caring, she just wanted the whole sorry situation to be over. But it wasn't the reason she'd told Chrissie. She'd told her because she trusted her. Something she'd not felt about anyone for a very long time. There was also a feeling of Chrissie being a stepping stone to her daughter; a link to the past, a much happier time.

Grace also felt that Chrissie needed to know, after she'd found out she was the little girl that Tim had tried to turn into one of his victims. She knew their support for each other would last a lifetime.

Even though they had spent most of the weekend talking about such a sinister subject, Grace had enjoyed the best few days she'd had in years. She felt free. Not as free as she'd feel once she got Tim out of her life, but even so, she felt better.

The weekend was coming to a close and Grace decided it was time to get back to Eve's house; she'd be coming home soon. The police, having been there the last few days had assured her they had finished their investigations for the time being.

She needed to go back and start letting the neighbours know she'd left Tim. That living with an alcoholic had become so unbearable. It would give her a good alibi, when his twisted, broken body was found at the bottom of their stairs. A lonely alcoholic whose wife had left him, being unable to cope, he'd drunk himself into a stupor and lost his balance on the stairs.

Everyone would understand her leaving him as no one liked him much anyway; they were just too polite to say. His drinking hadn't gone unnoticed in the village either. It was all a perfect build up for there to be no suspicion about his death.

CHAPTER SIXTEEN

Dear Mother,

I don't understand your reasons for refusing to see me, but I must respect your decision. I am writing to you because I have no other way of communicating and I am desperate to reach you.

I want you to know how much I love you. Our relationship hasn't always been easy, I know that. But you are the closest person to me. You know me better than anyone and you understand me more than anyone ever has.

I want you to remember, Mother, that we are one and the same. I am merely a male version of you. Please know that whatever I do, I do it because of my love for you.

I can't live with the knowledge you hate me. Please, Mother.

Your ever loving son

Tim

Grace gripped the kitchen table, turning her fingers white she was so filled with rage at the news that had just been relayed to her. David Croxton, the family liaison officer, poured her a glass of water, reading her response as upset and shock.

The atmosphere in Eve's kitchen was solemn. David Croxton and his colleague PC Ian Walsh stared at the floor. Here they were again, delivering this poor woman and her family yet more bad news, and they felt desperately sorry for her.

"Is there anyone we can call for you?" David said to Grace, as she loosened her grip on the table and fell rather than sat on one of the kitchen chairs.

"No. Yes, actually. Yes. But I'll do it. I have a friend who will come over. Are you sure they searched the whole area?"

"They've been searching for more than two days, Grace. The weather is too bad to continue. It's extremely unlikely…under the circumstances…"

Grace nodded and put her hand up to stop the policeman talking.

"I'd like to be left alone please."

Grace needed to think, and sympathetic faces were of no help to her whatsoever.

"We'll be in touch if there's any further news. In the meantime you know the number to call if you need anything." He hesitated. "We will have to come and ask you some questions, Grace, when you're feeling up to it."

David gently pushed the leaflets about bereavement counselling across the table towards Grace.

"Oh, piss off!" was what she wanted to say to the two officers, but she managed to keep it to herself.

After the door closed behind them, Grace took in the feeling which was always left by having uniformed people in the house. Even when they weren't delivering bad news, a feeling of anticipation was always left behind. That was probably what made them good police officers.

Grace got up from the table and phoned Chrissie, asking her to come over. Chrissie had been waiting patiently since the weekend for any news. Grace hadn't wanted her to come over until she knew anything. She'd wanted the time on her own to think about the fact that Tim might be dead.

It wasn't the news he was dead that had upset her when the officers had arrived. It was the sickening letter to his mother they'd found left on Grace's kitchen table at home. Coupled with the fact that it appeared to be a suicide note and the bastard had got there before Grace did.

She, like him, didn't like people being one step ahead of her. She couldn't think properly, she needed to air it.

Chrissie burst through the door within minutes of the phone call.

"Have they found him?"

"No, they've called off the search. They say the weather is too bad. They don't think there's any possibility of finding him alive now."

"Are you ok?" Chrissie walked over to Grace and put her arms around her.

"Silly question. Of course you're not ok. Can I do anything?"

Grace picked up the alleged suicide note and handed it to Chrissie. She waited while her friend read it silently behind her. Chrissie slumped into one of the kitchen chairs.

"Bloody hell," was all Chrissie could manage.

"I know. What a bastard, hey? The police want to know if I knew of any reason why he might want to kill himself."

"Did you have any idea he was building up to this?"

"No. I might have if I hadn't had Eve to think about. But even then I'm not sure. This just isn't Tim. He wouldn't kill himself; he regarded himself too highly to do anything like that."

Chrissie held Grace's limp hand which was laid on the table. She stared at her as if seeing her for the first time since she'd walked in. Both arms were resting on the table with her palms supine. She looked like she was meditating.

A smile crept onto Grace's mouth. Chrissie thought she was going to start crying and as she rushed to get a tissue out of her pocket, Grace began to laugh.

"Grace?!"

"Oh, come on, Chrissie! He saved us a job. The bastard's dead!"

"Even so." Chrissie looked around, at who she didn't know, just in case someone heard their conversation.

"Just before I called you, I'd got myself all caught up in the fact I hadn't been the one who'd killed him. That he'd got there first and taken that away from us all as well. I was so angry. But it just dawned on me that it doesn't matter. The point is, we're all free, and he can't hurt anyone else. I've just been lowering myself to his standards, by plotting to kill him."

"Well, I wouldn't go that far." Chrissie frowned, unable to think of Grace as being on the same level as Tim.

"The point is, Chrissie. He's gone. Dead. It doesn't matter if he killed himself or if it was an accident. The bastard's dead!"

The word "dead" appeared to be highly amusing and Grace started laughing all over again, which infected Chrissie with the same fit of giggles. Their laughter filled the room, something the house hadn't been used to for a very long time. It seeped into every room, including Alice's, as if someone had spray painted it with light.

"I think I'm going to like it here!" Chrissie managed to say through the laughter. This caused a new fit of the giggles and they continued until they were both wiping their streaming eyes. But the laughter was soon followed by tears. It overwhelmed Grace and the enormity of it all hit her.

"I should have told the police when I first knew shouldn't I?"

"Why do you think that?' Chrissie was shocked at the change of emotions.

"Because I've deprived those families of having a choice. They might have wanted him to go to prison. Now they might never know who killed their children."

Chrissie banged her hand on the table, making Grace flinch in her seat.

"That's enough! You are not responsible for this and what would it have achieved in the long run? We went over all this at the weekend and we agreed that a protected life in prison was not what he deserved. It was taken out of your hands, thankfully, and it's over."

"I know."

"Look forward, Grace, not back. Concentrate on you for a change. Eve's coming home soon and she needs you to help her get through all this." Chrissie got up to give her a hug.

"I know you're right. But what I don't want to happen is for Tim to be made into a hero because he died at sea in a tragic accident."

"How is that ever going to happen?" Chrissie asked bewilderment plastered all over her face.

"You're forgetting that it's only you and me who know about Tim. You know what people are like when someone dies, especially in a village."

"I'm confused. You told me that no one liked him."

"They don't. But people's views of someone can change completely when that person dies. Even if they think he committed suicide, they'll make up some tragic story about him."

"So, what are you trying to say? Are you going to tell the police what he's done?"

"I might not need to. Apparently, they paid him a visit before he went on his fishing trip with Dennis. They asked him a few questions about the disappearance of Alice. They told him that it was ok to go on his fishing trip, but he wasn't to leave the country and they'd be back on Monday with a search warrant."

"Bloody hell, Grace! But you'll get into trouble for not telling them! Why didn't you tell me this before?"

"Because I've been getting it straight in my own head. All of it."

"I know, I'm sorry. I didn't mean to snap at you. But this is huge. Do you think they've found something from Alice's remains?"

"I don't know. They won't tell me anything like that. This is why I'm starting to wonder if he did actually commit suicide. That would be typical of Tim. He'd definitely kill himself rather than face the consequences."

"Oh Grace, what are you going to do?"

"I don't know yet. One thing I do know is that when they search the house and garden, they're going to find all the boxes he kept. They'll know straight away it was him."

"But you can't tell them you knew. You'll go to prison."

"Oh I've got no intention of telling them I knew about it. I'm not going to prison for that bastard. I'll deny it all and tell them the marriage broke down years ago. I just hope his death was somewhere near the suffering he put his victims through."

"I doubt it. It's most likely he drowned and that's supposed to be the most painless and calm way to die. I can't imagine wanting to kill myself…oh, Grace I've done it again!"

Grace put her hand up to quieten her friend.

"Stop worrying about what you're saying. It's fine. Most people can't imagine doing it. I felt a bit like doing it when Nadine died and for quite some time afterwards."

"What changed?"

"I couldn't actually see myself physically doing it. I'm a bit of a coward deep down. And then the feeling started to fade away. Mainly because I found a friend I could talk to and trust."

Chrissie blushed. "You must have other friends in the village?"

"I do. But no one I've ever felt I can trust. It was difficult being a copper's wife. There were certain expectations and complaining about him wasn't one of them. I had better friends who lived away but no one close by. Meeting you felt almost like meeting Nadine again after all these years, you so remind me of her, of what she would have become. She'd be about your age now."

"Well, I feel very privileged to be your friend and you have been a great comfort to me, being new to the village."

They sat quietly for a few minutes sipping their cold cups of tea.

"Do you have any idea what you're going to do?"

"No. Just sit tight for now and weather the storm."

The irony of this comment brought on a fresh bout of laughter, even though the situation was far from funny.

CHAPTER SEVENTEEN

The last thing Tim had been aware of was sitting on the deck of the boat with Dennis, enjoying a drink. Now everything was black and cold and he couldn't move. His head was pounding. He thought perhaps Dennis had put him to bed because he was so drunk. But the bunks on the boat weren't anywhere near as uncomfortable as where he was laying now.

He tried to sit up but his arms were stuck to his sides and he only managed to bang his head on something hard, which did not help his impending hangover at all.

Fear and nausea began to creep through his stomach and up into his throat. There was something wrong. Very wrong indeed. He shouted to Dennis but there was no answer.

After quite some time wriggling and trying to move from his situation he began to wonder if perhaps he'd died. But he quickly decided he couldn't have because he wouldn't be able to feel the pounding in his body, which was causing him a lot of discomfort. Then he wondered if, in his drunken state, he'd fallen over in the cabin and somehow wedged himself under one of the bunks. Or maybe they'd been caught in a storm and the boat had thrown them around. On this thought he tried to move sideways, but he was jammed tight.

He could hear someone moving around.

"Dennis? Mate? What's going on?"

Still no answer.

He tried desperately to keep his heavy eyes open and his spinning head still so he could think clearly. He racked his painful head to try and work out what had happened. He remembered fishing with Dennis for most of the day. They didn't catch much because the weather was too changeable. They'd eaten a measly fish supper on account of their unlucky catch and then chatted over a few drinks. Flashes of Dennis's face near his, passed fleetingly across his mind's eye.

He began to sweat and he was finding it hard to breath. He stared into the blackness to try and adjust his eyes to the light but it didn't work. Where ever he was, it was pitch black. He felt as if he was tightly wrapped in something. He had worked out quite quickly that he was in a very tight, small place because his breath was circulating back to his nostrils, coupled with the fact he could barely move.

The smell of his warm, stale alcoholic breath was turning the insides of his stomach. He was catching another smell in his nostrils apart from stale alcohol and that was stale urine. He tried to move again but it was pointless. He began calling again but there was no answer. He knew he was still on the boat as he could feel the movement and vaguely hear the lapping of the water.

A sick feeling rose in his stomach, so much so that bile reached his mouth. He turned his head to vomit, which was all he was able to do. He desperately needed to sit up but his reflex reaction to vomiting had proved to him again that he was unable to do so.

He hadn't felt this hung-over for ages, not even after his most recent benders.

He coughed and spluttered, trying desperately to clear his throat. His arms were flexing automatically, as they would have if they'd been free to allow him to sit up properly, but they were stuck fast to the sides of his body.

He began to feel as if he'd been flipped over. Everything was circulating in his mind's eye, making the sickness even worse. The movement of the boat and the lapping of the waves were almost unbearable. But as unbearable as it was, Tim had to endure it. After a few minutes of panicking, he passed out.

When he awoke again a couple of hours later, he opened his eyes to daylight and found himself gasping as fresh sea air hit his lungs. Relief flooded him as he realised it had all been a bad dream. Until he became aware of the fact he still couldn't move.

He looked from side to side, only to be faced with rough wooden slats. He tried to glimpse down his body but pushing his chin down to his chest and straining his eyes brought on a new wave of nausea. All he could see was that he was wrapped in black tape and was in a wooden box.

The familiar feeling of fear that was there before burst into his mind like an unwanted visitor.

"Help!"

"I wouldn't bother if I were you, Tim." Dennis's frame appeared, blocking the sun light from Tim's eyes. "No one will hear you out here. It's just you and me."

"What's going on mate? Is this some kind of joke?" The relief at seeing Dennis's face was almost tangible in his voice.

Dennis laughed. "Trust me, Timothy. This is no joke. Or perhaps you find killing children absolutely hilarious?"

Sweat pricked Tim's forehead and his mouth opened and closed like a fish trying to take in air.

"Not so funny now though, is it Timothy?"

"I….don't…..come on Dennis, this is ridiculous. I haven't killed anyone."

Tim thought that acting casual would get him out of this awful situation.

"Oh dear, Timothy. I hope you're not mocking my intelligence again?" Dennis tutted and walked up and down the deck, back and forth past Tim's box.

"Do you like your box, Timothy? I tried to model it on the one I imagined you put Alice in. The absurd thing is you helped me load it onto the boat. You even helped me unload all the provisions from your very own coffin."

"Dennis, please? Get me out of here. We can talk about it. Whatever it is that's on your mind."

"What? Talk about all the children you've killed, including my daughter." Dennis kicked the box.

"Your daughter? You don't have any children."

255

"Oh, Timothy! You're not the sharpest tool in the box, are you? If you'll excuse the pun," He laughed again, "but then that's probably why you were only ever a PC."

Dennis continued to wander around the box. He put his hands into his jeans pockets, beginning to enjoy himself.

"Did you really, seriously think you'd get away with it?"

"Get away with what?"

"You're doing it again, Timothy." Dennis squatted down and leaned into Tim's face. "Listen to me, you fucked up little bastard, you haven't got a choice about what happens next. So I suggest you start telling me the truth."

Tim had only ever heard Dennis talk like that when he was dealing with paedophiles or rapists at work; his voice was dark and angry and it frightened him. He knew he was in trouble.

"I really don't know what you're talking about, Dennis. Come on! We've known each other for years. You can't seriously think I'd do something like that? I worked on those cases. Get me out of here and we'll talk about it over a drink."

"You did door to door enquiries, Tim. I'd hardly call that 'working' on the cases."

"Whatever. Just get me out of here. I'm an innocent man."

"Oh dear, Timothy. You're making me really angry now. I know and have known for a while that you killed those children. I've just been trying to work out what I was going to do with you; prison's far too good for the likes of you."

256

Tim knew then that the chances of him getting out of this situation alive were slim, so he tried to buy himself some time in the ridiculous hope someone might pass them and realise what was going on.

"What did you mean when you said one of the children was your daughter?"

"Come on, Timothy! You must know that Nadine was mine?"

"Nadine? My Nadine?"

"Yes, that Nadine, but not yours, mine."

"But she can't be yours."

"Oh she was mine alright, which is the main reason you're in that box. Nobody hurts my flesh and blood and gets away with it."

Tim thought about what Dennis had said. There was no point in telling him she wasn't his – it would only serve to make him even angrier. It didn't surprise him; Tim had known deep down she belonged to Dennis. He often caught glimpses of him in her face. When he'd found out that Grace had had an affair with Dennis all those years ago, it hadn't taken him long to work out the mathematics of it all. Yet he'd convinced himself it wasn't true.

"You know I didn't kill her mate, it was a terrible accident."

"We both know that's not true. There wasn't any evidence but I knew it wasn't an accident. That she'd been killed

257

by the same person who killed the other children. I just didn't know who it was at the time. But it didn't take me long to start getting suspicious. You got rid of her because she found out your dirty secret."

"That's not true! I loved Nadine, and even though..."

"Do you know something, Tim? I don't want or need to hear your bullshit or your pathetic reasons for killing all those children. I'm just going to tell you what's about to happen."

"How did you know it was me?" Tim tried to change tack and thought that by admitting it, he'd give himself a better chance. Appeal to Dennis's better nature.

"How did you know it was me?" Dennis mimicked Tim's pathetic child like voice.

The hysteria in Dennis's voice was beginning to really unnerve Tim.

"I didn't really. It was just a hunch to begin with. Copper's nose. This caused me to watch you for a while. Then I had a cosy little chat with Grace over a few night caps, just after Eve tried to take her own life. She told me all about the dirty, sordid secrets you were keeping in your shed. She said she'd discovered them about a year ago."

Tim registered this information. Waves of fear drifted backwards and forwards in his body in time with the movement of the boat. He was finding it hard to let his mind rest on anything other than the fact he might die.

"If she found out all that time ago then why didn't she report me or say anything?"

"Because, Timothy. Grace thinks like me, and she wanted to deal with you in her own way."

"You mean she's in on this sick plan?"

"Well…..sort of. She had her own plans for you but I couldn't be sure she wouldn't get caught. So…I thought we'd go on a nice fishing trip together. I don't want the love of my life going to prison once I've got rid of you, do I Timothy?"

"She doesn't want you, she never wanted you!" Tim spat, jealousy raging through his veins.

"Well, actually Tim, she does. We've rediscovered something while you've been busy getting pissed all the time. Thanks to Eve in a strange way. If she hadn't tried to take her own life then…well, who knows? They say that don't they? When one door closes another door opens. Although, your situation is more like that poem….*triumph and disaster, and treat those two impostors just the same*…or something like that. You get the general gist of it."

"You're lying! You bastard!" A mixture of vomit and spittle splattered across Tim's chin as he screeched at Dennis.

Dennis was enjoying himself now. He'd hit a nerve. Tim didn't like having anyone or anything taken away from him. He saw everything around him as his own possessions. His memory scents. Only, this time he didn't have a choice.

"Here's what's going to happen, Timothy. I'm going to put the lid on your special bed, seal it and then push you over board. Then you will sink to the bottom of the sea on account of the very thoughtful air holes I've placed in the box. And no one will see you ever again."

This last statement renewed Tim's panic like an electric shock and he squirmed again, desperately trying to get free.

"I'd save your energy for your breath, Timothy. You're going to need it." Dennis laughed deeply.

"After a couple of hours, I'm going to call out an emergency on the radio, saying that I've only just got out of bed, on account of a boozy night, and I can't find you anywhere. They'll be a search which will be called off on account of a storm in about a day and a half. I'll pretend to be devastated. Everyone will believe me and no one will have to think of you ever again. And I'll live happily ever after with your wife. Does that sound fair, Timothy?"

"You won't get away with this! They'll find me, someone….please Dennis? Please?" Tim began to cry, his face red with shame. He'd never cried in front of anyone apart from his mother and Dora.

"Oh, come now, Timothy. It's only fair after what you put all those children through. Just be thankful your death will be far quicker than any of theirs was, especially Alice's. I did think about sailing you out to one of the small islands and burying you alive. But then that would make me as bad as you." He laughed again.

"You are as bad, if you do this!" Tim sobbed like a small child, snot running down the side of his face.

"I don't think so, Timothy. Have you forgotten what you did to all those children? Do I need to remind you?" Dennis leaned in Tim's face.

"No. I thought not."

"Dennis, please? Don't do this! Let me go and I'll move away. You and Grace can have the house to yourselves. I won't cause you any trouble. I'll just leave quietly."

Dennis picked up the lid to the box and placed it over Tim as if he'd pressed the mute button to his mouth. As if Tim didn't exist and Dennis was merely sealing a crate of fishing gear.

He ignored Tim's protests. He'd dealt with enough tossers at work to know how to switch off from them when they protested about being arrested or going down to the cells.

Dennis lifted the lid back up, remembering something.

"Thank you, thank you, thank you!" Tim gasped, "I knew you wouldn't do it."

"Wrong, Timothy! I found something in your coat pocket that might come in handy. There you go. Nighty, night, Timothy!" Dennis threw a packet of Fisherman's Friends onto Tim and banged the lid back down.

He chuckled to himself. Tim's Fisherman's Friends weren't going to help him out of this situation.

Dennis took a few moments to think about what he was doing. Relief and panic swept through him simultaneously, albeit briefly.

*

Eve peered around the door of Daphne's room to see if she was in.

"Hello? Daphne?" she spoke gently in case she was asleep; she didn't want to startle her.

Daphne was sat in her chair, staring out of the window, her back to the door.

"Hello Eve, I haven't seen you for a while. How are you?"

Eve wandered in slowly and laid the flowers she'd brought for Daphne, on her table. She was still feeling fragile after recent events.

"I'm ok, thanks."

Daphne turned from the window to look at her.

"Oh my goodness, have you been poorly? You look ashen."

Eve perched herself on Daphne's bed and examined the old woman's troubled face.

"And you've been crying. What's wrong?"

There was a long pause as they both locked eyes with one another.

"Memories sweetheart, that's all. Now then, I asked you first."

Eve took a deep breath. "It all got the better of me Daphne. That's all."

Eve chose not to tell her she'd tried to kill herself. It wasn't that she couldn't, she just didn't have the energy to talk about it. She was bored of her life being one trauma after another and she was slightly ashamed that the last one had been self inflicted. It was like a perpetual nightmare.

Daphne reached out to Eve and grasped her hand.

"I know sweetheart, I know. You feel like your whole world's collapsed, like someone's catapulted you off it and there's no point going on." She patted her hand.

Eve stared at her, sensing she was going to say more.

Daphne picked up the fresh roses Eve had cut from the garden and buried her face in their fragrance.

"They're beautiful. Your garden?"

"Of course. I didn't steal them!" Eve laughed.

"Well you never know dear, I thought you might have taken a fancy to old Mrs. Newark's prize flowers on the way!"

They laughed together. For a moment the atmosphere lifted but was soon smothered by the dense emotion that had been there moments before.

"My daughter, Verity was murdered. Seven years old she was. I didn't want to go on, after they found her, didn't see the point really." Daphne sat back in her chair and gazed out of the window. She was mentally travelling back in time, back to an era she'd locked away since it'd happened.

"I had no idea…I mean I remember Grace saying you lost a baby before Tim was born but…"

"I've never talked about it, that's why you didn't know. It became too unbearable. The longer I left it, the harder it was, so in the end I locked it away."

Eve stared at her. Shocked she'd become so close to this woman and had never known she'd experienced the same awful trauma. Something began to shift inside Eve. She knew of the other people in the area who had lost their children in the same way but they had seemed distant because she didn't know them well enough. It had made her feel terribly lonely. And here she was sat in front of someone who was carrying the same battle scars as her. A kind of relief flooded her, causing her to blush with embarrassment. It wasn't something she'd wish on anyone but she was glad of the company in her lonely, cold world.

"Did they catch who did it?"

"Oh yes. He was caught a few months afterwards, hanged for it."

Eve frowned.

"It was 1950. The death penalty was still punishment for murder."

"How did that feel? Knowing who it was and seeing them hang for what they'd done."

Daphne turned away from the window to look Eve in the eye.

"Empty. It made me feel empty. At first there was a strong urge to see him get what he deserved. I wanted him to feel the fear he'd put Verity through. I wanted to kill him with my own hands. But then it was all over and there was nothing. I knew it was for the best, that he wouldn't be able to harm anyone else. But he was free of it all and we were the ones left with the whole nightmare he'd caused."

Eve nodded, understanding totally what she was saying. She'd run through the scenario in her head many times after Alice went missing. Not that she had ever voiced it out loud, that would have meant admitting Alice had been murdered. Death was the easy option in her eyes, which was why she'd tried to end it all only a few days earlier.

"I know there's no excuse for what he did, but was there any explanation?"

Daphne sighed, her eyes watery with tears.

"She smelt nice, he said; took her school shirt as a souvenir. He mutilated my beautiful little angel all because she smelt nice. All I could think about afterwards was that we were halfway through 'Alice's Adventures in Wonderland'. It's strange what goes through your mind when you're in shock."

"I'm so sorry…"

265

Daphne flinched at the words she hadn't heard for so long, hadn't wanted to hear, especially not from Eve. She put her hand up to stop her saying anything else.

"But I am Daphne, you've listened to me endlessly talking about Alice, which must have been excruciating for you, and you never said a word."

"It wasn't the right time to tell you and I wasn't sure if I was right."

Eve frowned at this last sentence, wondering if she had missed part of the conversation and they were now talking about something else.

"Eve, I've got something to tell you and I need you to listen carefully. Don't interrupt me. I can tell you, now he's dead."

"Who's dead? Daphne, what are you talking about?"

"Tim, who do you think?"

"Tim's dead? Dead? Don't be daft, Daphne!" She stared at her, for the first time seeing her as a fragile old woman. She wondered for a few moments if she was going senile.

"Yes Eve. It was all over the news. Lost at sea on one of his fishing trips, you must know, Grace called me. Where ever have you been?"

*

266

After the dramatic events of the last few days, Chrissie had felt much more settled in her new home. She couldn't quite believe Tim was actually dead and she wasn't totally sure how she felt about it all. Everything that had happened since she'd lived in the house was hitting her like pelting hailstones. She'd been so bombarded, she could have been told that the village was being wiped out by a plague and she would probably have shrugged it off.

In the last couple of days she'd had time to digest it all. She felt relieved and fairly calm but there was still a slight uneasiness surrounding her. The activity in the house had almost stopped but there were still a few strange things occurring. The radio continued to have a mind of its own and things kept going missing. She'd spoken to Sarah about it over the phone, which had resulted in her inviting herself over for a few days, firstly to support Chrissie, and also to take the opportunity to do some house hunting.

Sarah had felt that the ongoing activity could be caused by Chrissie's anxiousness or maybe an unsettled spirit not willing to move on. She'd promised her some therapy sessions during her stay to help her to come to terms with it all. Chrissie was having a problem going into the garden, especially down the bottom near the shed.

The trouble was, it didn't matter how many times Sarah told her it was all ok, something still wasn't sitting right with her.

She couldn't shake off the overwhelming feeling that someone was trying to get through to her. She brushed the thought away as if she was swatting an insect from her arm; she just needed to let go of it all.

She busied herself preparing supper for Sarah's arrival, trying to concentrate on the task in hand. A movement outside caught her eye and she put down her vegetable peeler and strained her eyes to see through the window.

It was hard to see, the rain was thrashing down and the clouds had shed a premature darkness over everything. Thinking it was probably the wind blowing the trees, she continued peeling her potatoes, taking deep breaths to calm herself.

There was a creaking noise from the far end of the house which caused her to drop her peeler again. She went to the kitchen door to see if it was Sarah; she was beginning to feel uneasy. She strained her eyes to look through the window of the stable door. She was hoping to see car lights coming from the drive at the end of the house, so that she could explain it all away, but there was nothing. Telling herself she was being silly, Chrissie locked the door. Better to be on the safe side. Glancing up at the garden as she turned the key, she caught sight of someone sitting on the swing. She quickly glanced back but there was no one there. The swing was moving violently backwards and forwards as if it was possessed by the wind. Chrissie could have sworn she saw a child sitting on it. She shivered and rubbed her arms, taking a few moments to scan the garden. A shadow

268

passed the small door window and it wasn't coming from the outside. The screeching of a wooden chair across the tiled kitchen floor startled her. Chrissie turned slowly.

"Hello Christine."

There sat a very soaking, dripping, dirty Tim.

CHAPTER EIGHTEEN

Dennis and Grace held each other tightly for what seemed like forever.

"Do you know what my first thought was when the police knocked on the door?"

Dennis kissed her forehead. "No, what?"

'That you were dead or missing too. I was more worried about that than I was about Tim."

Dennis got up to get them both a drink.

"You know they'll find him don't you? Alive I mean."

"No, the police called round yesterday and said it was unlikely now."

"Grace, listen to me. I'm telling you, he'll be found alive."

Grace was digesting this news; she wasn't thinking about why or how but the fact she'd felt quite elated by the thought that he was dead. Grace sat down on Dennis's sofa, her head in her hands. The heavy feeling she had carried for so many years began to descend over her body like a black cloud. After quite some time she took a deep breath that seemed to started at the very bottom of her stomach.

"What happened on the boat trip, Dennis? I mean really? I thought you said you were going to deal with it – not that I wanted you to."

"And I have dealt with it. I let him think he was going to die; gave him a taste of his own medicine." Dennis saw Grace's look of dismay, "The one thing I've learnt from being in the police force is that death is the easiest way out for someone like Tim."

"But we agreed."

Dennis laughed and sat down next to her on the sofa.

"I didn't agree anything. I just said I didn't want you to worry about it and to leave it to me."

"But I didn't want you dealing with it. I could have made it look like a simple accident and it would have been better for everyone concerned. He's my stupid alcoholic husband." Grace knew she was being childish which wasn't becoming for a woman of her age but she couldn't help herself, the disappointment was so great.

"I'm really sorry, Grace, but he still is." Dennis laughed.

"I'm glad you find this all so amusing!" Grace started to cry.

"Listen to me. He's had the most horrible experience of his life; one he'll never forget. Very soon he's going to wake up on someone else's boat, which is moored in the harbour about a mile from here, further along the coast, with an empty rum bottle in his hand, totally unscathed, apart from being a bit smelly and dirty."

"But why, if you were going to make him suffer, why didn't you just finish him off?"

271

"Because my darling, death is too kind for him and in the next few days the police will find evidence to convict him of all the murders he committed. I for one want to see him in court. He's going to prison for a very long time, which is where, I suspect, he'll end his days. This way we can all live with a clear conscience."

Dennis searched Grace's face to see if she understood what he was saying. He needed her to think about it all rationally; otherwise the consequences could be horrific.

"I nearly did do it you know? I came so close to pushing the box I'd put him in over the side of the boat."

"You put him in a box?" Grace sipped the brandy Dennis had poured her.

"Sure did. Frightened the living daylights out of him; he actually wet himself."

A smile crept across Grace's mouth, nudging her eyes to follow suit. They sat in silence for a while.

"I told him about Nadine."

Grace stayed very still, unable to look at him.

"He tried to deny he'd killed her but when he realised I was going to throw him overboard, he just gave in."

Grace felt as if the room and everything in it, including her insides, was rushing away from her.

"Can you repeat that?" It came out more as a whisper and Grace felt for a moment that the words had come from someone else. "What did you just say?"

272

Dennis watched the colour drain from her face and then the enormity of what he'd said dawned on him.

"Nadine. Oh Grace, please tell me you knew? I thought when we talked the night you brought Alice's letters over you knew he'd killed her. I thought it was your main reason for wanting to get rid of him."

"I was going to do it for Alice, for all the others. He can't have killed Nadine. It was an accident." Grace stared at him, waiting for him to tell her he'd made a mistake.

"It was recorded as an accident but there was a strong feeling throughout the station that she may have been murdered. The dog walker who heard her scream also heard some muffled noises and he thought she shouted at someone."

"Yes, she shouted for help."

"No Grace, there's a difference between shouting to someone and shouting at them. The witness couldn't be sure and we knew it wouldn't stand up in court. I'm so sorry Grace, I thought you knew. I suppose I assumed Tim told you all the details of the case. Of course he wouldn't have. How silly of me to even think it."

"Well, he wasn't ever going to reveal that little bit of information, was he? He knew I would have pushed for further inquiries; that I might have worked out what he'd done."

"Are you ok?"

"I don't know. I just feel numb and...I don't know. I just don't know." Grace fell into Dennis's arms and cried.

273

She cried herself to sleep while he stroked her hair. Then he gently moved her onto the sofa and covered her with a blanket, while he made them both some lunch.

He knew she'd go through all sorts of emotions and she'd still want to kill Tim for a time, but he knew he'd done the right thing. He knew from experience that all those families would want to see justice, would want to see the face of the person who killed their child. It helped people through the grieving process; a face and a name, a real life human being. He knew Grace would see this in time and he understood what she was feeling. He also knew strong emotions would fade over time and eventually the guilt would set in regardless of what that person had done. Moral standards always got in the way and there was a lot of truth in the saying that two wrongs don't make a right. He didn't feel he had the right to make that decision on behalf of all those parents who may have different views.

Even though he knew it was the correct and clear way forward he was still left with the urge to have pushed Tim over the edge of the boat and the satisfaction that would have brought. But he consoled himself with the fact that coppers were hated in prisons; if Tim had ever thought about killing himself in the past, he'd soon be wishing he'd done it before now.

He just hoped Grace was stable and strong enough to get through the next few weeks of gossip and nosy reporters.

*

Grace placed the handset back in its bed and with a frown contemplated where her sister could have got to. She'd spoken to the hospital and they'd discharged her that morning. It was now mid-afternoon. Grace had been waiting to go and pick her up. She'd been on pins since her conversation with Dennis. She'd more or less sat by the phone, willing it to ring and the person on the other end to tell her they'd found and arrested him. But there had been nothing.

Every avenue she'd followed to try and keep herself busy had led to a dead end. Dennis had told her to act normal, play ignorant and keep herself occupied. Now she was worrying about where Eve had got to. She'd rung round everyone she could think of but no one had seen her. She couldn't believe the hospital had just let her go without checking if she was with someone. A rather no-nonsense nurse had told her tersely over the phone that you couldn't watch someone twenty four hours a day and they'd seen this sort of thing before. In other words, thought Grace, if she was going to do it, she'd find a moment. Not exactly what she wanted to hear when the hospital had no information on her whereabouts. But this wasn't primarily what she was worrying about. She knew that Eve wouldn't try it again, she'd hit rock bottom and she was slowly on her way back up.

What was concerning her was the vision of Tim in the back of her mind, drifting around like a piece of wood on the water. She shook it off realising there was no reason for Tim to go looking for Eve or for her to go searching for him, for that matter. She reassured herself that once he came to, he'd find his way home first, before going anywhere else, and by that time the police would have caught up with him.

It suddenly dawned on her like light bursting through a crack in the curtain. Daphne. That was it. She'd gone to see Daphne. Grace was aware of how close they had become. She couldn't understand why, she thought the old woman was vile and always had done.

She jumped up from where she'd been sitting in Eve's kitchen, grabbed her keys and was out of the door in seconds. She wasn't quite aware of what she'd do when she got to the retirement home; she just knew she needed to go there. She hadn't seen her for a long time and felt that after the false news she had delivered her, she owed her a visit.

Daphne had seen all about how Tim had gone missing on the news. Grace had called her with the developments but the phone call had been strained, neither woman having much to say to the other. Grace felt a twang of guilt that Daphne had been told her son was dead, in light of the fact that he actually wasn't. Although, she hadn't appeared to be overly distraught but then it wasn't easy to tell over the phone. Grace thought maybe she hadn't understood; Tim had said he thought she was losing the plot.

She pushed open the doors of Poppy Field's as she was buzzed in and ran down the corridor. Just before she got to Daphne's room she slowed down and walked. There wasn't any point in causing a panic and she wasn't quite sure why she was in such a hurry. Something was wrong, she could feel it.

"Daphne?" Grace tapped on her door which was ajar. There was no answer.

"Daphne, its Grace can I come in?" At first she thought there was something wrong with her; there were strange noises coming from her chair. Then she wondered if she'd had another stroke. She wandered into the room and leaned over the chair Daphne was sat in.

"Oh Daphne..." Grace pulled another chair up close to the fragile old woman and sat down. She picked up her bony hand and gave it a gentle squeeze. Grace sat quietly with her mother in law and allowed her to cry. She'd never seen her like this before, not even when Jack died. She'd always thought her a strange old fish; cold and harsh. But looking at her now was like sitting with someone else. Someone she knew, not a stranger, which is how Grace had felt towards her in all the years she'd been married. The woman sat in front of her now had emotion in her face, making her look softer, more vulnerable.

Grace suddenly realised she'd never spent the time making an effort to get to know her. She'd always taken Tim's word that she was a vile human being. Eve obviously saw someone different.

This thought reminded her why she was there and a shot of panic entered her heart.

"Has Eve popped in for a visit today?" Grace kept her voice light and casual.

Daphne looked up at Grace, squeezing her hand slightly.

"What is it, Daphne?"

"I've told her everything."

"What do you mean you've told her everything?"

"Everything."

CHAPTER NINETEEN

Chrissie was frozen to the spot; three things were circulating around in her head. Firstly, she thought that the person sat in her kitchen was dead but he appeared to be very much alive. Secondly, she was going to die. And thirdly, it had been him trying to scare her out in the garden all along.

Chrissie looked from him to the clock on the wall, which seemed to be ticking louder than normal, warning her that her time was almost up. She prayed that for the first time in Sarah's life she wouldn't be late. The silence gave her time to think, to work out how she could get out of the situation alive.

She lifted her arm slowly up her back to try and reach the key behind her in the lock. She was watching Tim the whole time. He continued to stare at the table, picking at an old candle wax mark. She expected him to say something else but he didn't. Her fingers found the key and she held her breath as she desperately tried to get her fingers to work without making too much noise. She bit her lip hoping beyond hope that the latch wouldn't fly back, making a loud clunk like it usually did. She mentally pictured herself turning quickly, opening the door and running out. She felt slightly like she had done as a child when she and her sisters had been playing chase with one another and she was trying to get away from them. Only this wasn't a game and she felt much, much worse.

Tim continued to pick at the table and stare at nothing; his eyes were glazed; he'd stepped into another world. She could hear the thumping of her heart beating in her ears, almost in time with the loud ticking of the clock.

Clunk, click. She grabbed the door handle; a whimpering escaped her lips as she heard the screeching of Tim's wooden chair across the tiled kitchen floor. She banged the door against the wall and ran screaming down the path that led to the bottom of the house, the driveway, the footpath, the whole time anticipating a hand grabbing her. She daren't look behind her; she just knew she had to keep going. Get into an area where there were other people. She didn't want to knock on anyone's door; she couldn't risk them not answering. Great gulps of breath were straining her chest and neck.

She kept going until she got to the seafront and dared to turn and look behind her before she stopped running. She'd had an idea when she got to the main street in the centre of the village that maybe Tim wasn't following her; she couldn't hear his foot fall behind her. She hadn't wanted to risk it though just in case it was wishful thinking. She looked behind her; there was no one to be seen in the pouring rain, only the passing traffic. She placed her hands on her knees to catch her breath; the rain was pelting down on her, running down her face. She turned around and around frantically looking for him, expecting him to jump out and grab her.

A car beeped and screeched to a halt on the side of the road, startling her. It was Grace. Chrissie checked around one more time before she got in the car. Once inside she pressed the central locking and stared at Grace, her eyes wide and full of fear.

"You're soaked. What on earth are you doing out in this weather?"

"I...I...Tim..." Chrissie was still trying to catch her breath. She was shivering, shaking, crying and absolutely petrified all at the same time. "Tim's at mine...Tim...I'm not seeing things...I promise."

"Shit! We need to phone the police, Chrissie. Is he still there?"

"No. I don't know. He came in the house. I thought he was going to hurt me." Chrissie's breath was coming back and she was finding it easier to talk and breathe.

"Are you ok? He hasn't hurt you has he?" Grace looked Chrissie up and down.

"No, I got out and just kept running." Chrissie wiped her face on the sleeve of her damp sweater. "I thought the police said he was dead?"

Grace sped off while Chrissie stared through the car windows looking for Tim. She was waiting for Grace to continue what she was saying.

Grace glanced at her. "Sorry Chrissie I'm looking for Eve, the hospital discharged her and I haven't been able to find her. I'm getting really worried."

"I assume you've looked in all the likely places she would go?" Chrissie was still shivering.

"Yes but no one's seen her. At least I know she's not with Tim." Grace paused as she digested her own words. "Oh my god! You don't think he's already seen her?"

All Chrissie could do was stare at her; she needed to think.

"Right, ok. Let's think about this logically, I'm sure she's fine. There's no reason why Tim would have come across her."

"I'm not so sure. The thing is Chrissie, there's quite a lot that's come to light the last couple of days and I haven't had a chance to tell you. Let me get you back to Eve's. We can check to see if she's there, find you some warm clothes and then I'll ring the police."

*

Tim wandered through the open door and out into Chrissie's garden. The rain seemed to be coming down in sheets; the grass under foot was already beginning to drown with the amount of water that had already fallen. Tim lifted the collar of

282

his coat, tucked his hands in his pockets and made his way across the garden to Chrissie's swing. He sat down on it and gently pushed himself.

In his mind he was twelve again and not in Chrissie's garden but in the garden of his childhood. He was back in the moment when his mother had sat him down and told him the truth about his sister, Verity. She hadn't died when she was a baby as he'd always been led to believe. She had been murdered when she was seven. It was a day that had changed his entire life forever.

There was a room in the house he was always forbidden to go in and it was kept locked. Daphne had told him it was a storage room and wasn't to be played in. But that day, Daphne had unlocked the door to the mysterious room and allowed him to enter. It was Verity's bedroom, his sister's. He remembered when he walked into that room how the mysteries of his short life had all become clear in that one moment. A bedroom to a life he'd never known about, a life he hadn't been permitted to know; one that had existed before him.

The room was similar to a scene in a museum, except the life like plastic figures were missing.

He'd been allowed in there that one and only day, with Daphne. It was a clear and vivid memory that had stayed with him all his life. He hadn't been allowed to touch anything; he was just allowed to have a look. It had been Daphne's way of making it real for him, to hopefully dampen the shock of finding out the truth about his sister. She and Tim's father had wanted to protect him, so that his childhood wasn't tainted with the ghastly truth they had to live with. This had only proved to have the opposite effect, and in truth the real reason had been that it was too painful for either of them to talk about.

Before Tim was permitted to go into the room, he wouldn't have been shocked to see Verity lying on the bed, a preserved waxen effigy in the little time warp his mother was exposing him to.

As he twirled round on the swing he clearly saw the memory of watching his mother standing in Verity's bedroom, checking that everything was in its place. He'd wondered at the time if she was looking to see if Verity had come back and moved something, a sign she might still be around somewhere. He could still recall the clinking of the keys in his mother's hand, tears filling her eyes as she moved forward to shake the dusky pink eiderdown. Everything was clean and tidy and perfectly placed. Tiny hand printed roses flecked the walls, the rugs on the floor were flat as if they'd been painted on, their fringes immaculately straight on all sides.

Tim had looked around and noticed how everything had been carefully chosen. Perfectly picked for Verity, unlike his own room which looked like it had been made up for an unexpected guest.

It hadn't been the fact his mother had told him his sister had been murdered that bothered him. It had been the realisation that he'd come face to face with his competition. His sibling rival.

He'd always known there had been something untouchable standing in his way; he just hadn't realised the extent of what it had been. It was like finding a missing piece of an old puzzle long since packed away; a vital part of the whole picture.

Verity was the reason his mother didn't want him. His mother and father had had a life with her before him. He realised this whenever he had revisited this memory. He'd been too young at the time to understand it all then; too young to analyse it. Re-running the footage throughout his life had made it become clearer in his mind.

It had been raining the day she told him, as it was now, soaking him as he sat on the swing under the willow tree. Huge droplets of water were sliding off the leaves and landing on his head, as though he was being smacked by hundreds of tiny cold hands.

He'd become aware as he grew up that his mother and father had tried to recreate their life after Verity, but it had backfired on them because Tim had been born a boy. And from that day forward he had never been wanted. His feelings the day he'd stood in Verity's room, had been a mixture of disappointment, pain and anger. Verity had upped the stakes and even though she wasn't alive, Tim had felt she very much was.

Competing against a dead baby had been hard enough but a murdered, pretty, clever little girl had seemed almost impossible.

He and his mother had stood in Verity's bedroom for what seemed like hours. He had mainly watched his mother's reaction, studied her heartbroken face. Devastated and contorted at the loss of her first born, still in that era, locked in a time when Verity was still alive. He'd stretched out his hand, hoping beyond hope she'd clasp it with her own. Instead, she did something that caused a crack to run through the centre of his tiny heart; she flinched. Then she busied her hand with finding a tissue in her sleeve so that she could wipe the tears from her face.

Tim pushed himself off the swing, his salt and pepper hair plastered to his head by the rain water. He took a deep breath and began walking down the garden to the old brick shed. His special shed.

A car pulling into the driveway jerked him into the present day, causing him to stop in his tracks.

CHAPTER TWENTY

Grace had arrived back at Eve's with a much shaken Chrissie. There was still no sign of her sister, although she had been back at some point because Grace noticed her bags in the hallway. She checked round the house but she was nowhere to be seen. This had eased her concern; her hospital luggage showed there was some sign of life, but Grace was still worried. She called the police telling them that Tim was very much alive and had paid her friend a visit, giving her quite a fright. They told her to stay exactly where she was while they looked for him, and a police officer would be over to them soon. They also promised to send some police officers out to look for her sister. Grace played ignorant to the fact she knew anything about Tim, but the officer on the other end of the phone sounded far too serious for it to be purely to do with Tim's disappearance. She knew the news was all over the police station and they'd be pleased if they did find him alive. A case could be put together and some sort of justice would be done. It made Grace realise that Dennis had been right; death was far too easy an option for Tim. She just hoped they had enough evidence to convict him for the rest of his life.

Grace put the phone down on the kitchen table, mentally deciding she would tell the police that her mother in law had told her everything that day. It was something Daphne had agreed with her. They'd shared their secrets that afternoon and bonded in the process. Grace hadn't been sure about using her as a scapegoat, even though Daphne had insisted, but now, as she clicked the red button on the phone, she surrendered to the offer. For the first time in many years, she felt safe and protected, pleased that someone else was shouldering some of the responsibility.

She got Chrissie a warm sweater and blanket out of Eve's airing cupboard and, after settling her with a hot drink, brought her up to speed with everything that had happened.

"It just gets worse, Grace. I couldn't make it up to write about." Chrissie sipped her hot sweet tea, still shaken from her encounter with Tim. Being in such close proximity to him had brought back a barrage of feelings and fears from the past.

"I know. It's a lot to take in. I still can't quite believe it myself."

"Oh my god!" Chrissie jumped up, throwing the blanket off her shoulders. "Sarah is coming over tonight; she's probably at mine already!"

"Oh shit! Quick, ring her!" Grace thrust the phone into Chrissie's hand.

After several attempts and no answer from Sarah's phone, the two women decided to jump in the car and go straight to Chrissie's house and wait for her. They didn't want to think about the various scenarios that could face them all, and they weren't prepared for the one they hadn't even thought of yet.

It was a strange sight as they pulled down the track towards Chrissie's house. There was no way they were going to be able to park in her driveway. There were police cars everywhere; some of them still had their lights flashing. Chrissie sat bolt upright in the car and strained her neck to see what was going on. The sight of Sarah's car caused a jolt of shock to pass through her. She jumped out of the car before Grace had stopped moving, and ran up the driveway. She was stopped by a police officer before she'd even got halfway to the house.

"What's happening?" Chrissie desperately tried to see passed the young police officer.

"I'm afraid you can't go in there."

"It's my house! Is Sarah in there?"

The police officer was slightly taken aback and he wasn't quite sure what to do or say next. He was new to the job and his lack of experience and confidence showed in his worried face.

"Wait there, I'll just go and get someone."

Grace had joined her and they were waiting patiently in silence, both straining on tip toe to see what was going on.

After what seemed like half an hour but actually only a few minutes, a plain clothed officer came out of Chrissie's house.

"Hello. I'm Detective Sergeant Jane Spencer." She flashed some identification in front of their startled faces.

"Are you Christine Newman?"

"Yes." Chrissie's voice sounded small and quiet. So she tried again after clearing her throat. The Detective Sergeant stared at her like a strict school teacher chastising a child; her serious blue eyes boring into Chrissie, letting her know that time was of the essence.

"Yes, I'm Chrissie."

Chrissie pulled her shoulders back and stood tall, preparing herself for the shocking news she was anticipating; like a sea wall waiting for a strong tidal wave.

"Can you come into the house please; we need to ask you some questions."

A prickling sensation was beginning to spread across her neck, threatening to burst into a rash; nausea was rising in her stomach.

"Where's Tim?" Grace said. Seeing Chrissie's distress, she squeezed her arm.

"And you are?" Detective Sergeant Jane Spencer peered at Grace as if she'd only just realised she was standing there.

She wasn't at all friendly and Grace could completely understand how she'd got to the position she was in. Everything about her was cold; from her short blonde hair right down to her pale grey trouser suit.

"I'm his wife, Grace Charlesworth."

The Detective leant back slightly, unable to hide her surprise.

"You need to come in as well, there's been an incident concerning your husband."

At this last comment, Chrissie and Grace stared at each other, both with the same panic stricken faces. They followed the Detective Sergeant Jane Spencer into the house.

*

The rain had finally stopped and the sun was bursting through the early evening clouds, touching everything in its sight with an orange glow. The wind blowing off the sea was making it hard for Sarah to hear what Tim was saying. It was vital she heard every word and responded to him in the right way.

Tim was stood on a grassy verge on top of a cliff, not far away from the edge. He was talking to Sarah, who was a few feet away from him, oblivious to the fact he was surrounded by police, albeit quite a distance from him.

He was in another world again, a different era, another time and place. All he could see was Sarah, only to him she wasn't Sarah, she was his mother. Daphne was dressed in a pretty, floral 1950s dress, which was white and splashed with vibrant cerise pink roses. A navy clutch bag was clasped in her gloved hands, which were crossed and tucked, as always, under her breast. A navy shrug matched her navy shoes and her shiny

291

bleached blonde hair was perfectly pinned on top of her head. She looked exactly as she always did, with her immaculate makeup, like she'd just stepped off a film set.

It hadn't taken Sarah long to work out that the man in front of her thought she was someone else and it was likely to be his mother. She'd seen it many times with the clients she counselled.

She'd found Tim in Chrissie's garden, although she didn't know it was him. She'd been told by Chrissie that Tim had died whilst out on a weekend fishing trip. She'd approached the stranger to ask him what he was doing, but he'd just stared at her, a glazed look in his eyes. She'd noticed Chrissie's door was wide open, panic had hit her and she'd run all over the house looking for her. Half peeled potatoes on the table and the radio blaring caused Sarah to think she'd left the house in a hurry. She called the police and then followed Tim from a distance, as he wandered aimlessly down the garden. She thought there might be a chance he would lead her to Chrissie. Her instinct was telling her it was Tim, but logic was telling her she was wrong.

And now here she was, standing on top of a cliff, her blonde hair whipping and irritating her face, pretending to be some strange man's mother so that he didn't jump off the cliff.

"Dora shut me in the cellar while you were out. She said I'd been naughty but I wasn't, was I Mother?"

"Of course you weren't. You've always been a good boy." Sarah hadn't any idea who this Dora was but she was going along with it anyway.

"Why did you leave me then?" He was crying now, sobbing like a small child, snot running down his lip.

"I didn't leave you, sweetheart. I'm here."

Tim edged backwards, causing Sarah to put her hand out to him, fearful that if he took any more steps he'd be falling into oblivion.

"Don't lie! You were never there. You didn't want me!"

Sarah couldn't help feeling there was a parent somewhere, living or dead, who was responsible for this mess, someone who should have been facing up to all this crap instead of her. She thought of the evening she was supposed to be having with Chrissie and how much she'd been looking forward to it. Curled up on the sofa with a glass of wine, a hot meal and her best friend, a far cry from what she was doing now. Sarah made a mental note that when she moved here she wouldn't actually offer her services within the village; perhaps she'd stick to ten miles distance from it.

"Come over here towards me so we can talk about this properly."

Tim stared at what he saw as his mother, unsure whether to move towards her or not. Daphne stretched out her arms towards him, encouraging him to come forwards. Tears were dragging her makeup down her face like an unusual art technique on brilliant white paper.

"But you don't love me; you always wanted Verity instead of me."

Sarah was beginning to lose her patience. She didn't want to be standing on a cliff, the cold wind chilling her bones, trying to coax some crack pot from jumping to his death. As heartless as this thought was, in her experience they usually ended up finishing themselves off, one way or another, especially when the damage was so deeply ingrained. But she knew she had to keep talking to him, he may have some knowledge of where Chrissie was, and she was her main concern at the moment. She was hoping he'd just frightened Chrissie, causing her to flee from the house, and that she was tucked up somewhere safe and warm. Her instinct said so, but it was also telling her she needed to keep this man alive, whatever state he was in.

"I loved you both the same and I still do very much. Now please, darling, come away from the edge."

This was the worst sentence Sarah could have uttered to Tim. Being unaware of the facts and having to ad lib as if she was on a stage playing a part she hadn't rehearsed, Sarah had unintentionally flicked a switch in Tim's head.

He took a deep breath and stepped backwards, his foot sliding through the air instead of hitting the earth, and he was gone.

Sarah screamed and ran forward; she hadn't actually anticipated him going through with it right there and then. The next thing she knew there was a blur of police officers running towards her and the cliff's edge.

CHAPTER TWENTY-ONE

Eve found herself outside Grace's gate, which was the entrance leading to the front of her cottage. The house where the man who'd killed her daughter lived. Alice probably came through this gate the night she died, thought Eve, full of innocence and trust, not for one moment imagining her Uncle Tim would hurt a hair on her head. She shook the image from her mind and it dispersed into the background ready, Eve was sure, to reappear at a later date.

She'd been back to her own home a couple of times that day, hoping to see Grace, but there had been no one in. She had been occupied with many other things and assumed that Grace would be at her own house sorting out Tim's affairs. She'd been putting off going to Grace's house all day, it was the last place she wanted to be, but the concern for her sister had grown throughout the day and she knew she had to put her own needs aside for the time being and offer her some support. She was astounded at the amount Grace had had to cope with while she'd been in hospital. A spark of guilt prodded her heart as she thought of her own self inflicted trauma.

Eve was unsure about all the information she had received that day; she supposed she was feeling a bit numb. The feeling of shock and horror hadn't lasted very long, as if it had hit the surface of her body but had been unable to penetrate it.

There had been a weird sense of comfort that had replaced all those feelings, an odd sense of relief that it had been a family member, someone they all knew, rather than a stranger. It was something she could get the measure of, having known him for so many years, although she realised she hadn't known him very well. It didn't stop her feeling angry or outraged or guilty that she hadn't spotted it, but it was preferable to seeing a blank figure in her mind's eye. She couldn't explain these strange feelings, so she was just accepting them as they greeted her. Any sort of comfort at the moment was a light relief from the storm that had been raging on inside her for so many years.

The news that had upset her the most had been hearing that Tim was dead; she had so many things she wanted to say to him, scream at him. For a short while she'd wanted to be the one who had killed him, in a violent and painful way, not the way she imagined, where the sea swallowed him up, filling him with salty water and calming him within minutes to drift into an eternal sleep.

She'd spent quite some time with Daphne after being told everything she knew. They'd cried together, having tried to make sense of it all; Daphne blaming herself and Eve telling her she wasn't to.

After she'd left Daphne she'd spent the rest of the day on her own; she needed time to think. She'd walked for most of it; had gone to the area where Alice had been found, forcing herself to face it all. Then she'd made her way to the beach for a walk and to take in the fresh cold sea air. Even though the news that day had been mind blowing, she felt different for the first time in a very long time.

Something had shifted inside her, she no longer felt in absolute desperate despair; having some answers to such monumental questions had somehow liberated her. And even though she was still hurting and completely aware she would have many more feelings to deal with, she was free. All in the space of a few hours she'd been thrown into moving forward with her life. No waiting for Alice to come home, no wondering anymore.

After walking for quite some time before being forced to stop in a cafe due to the ferocity of the rain, Eve decided to go and see her husband Jon. He had the right to know what she had been told, and she wanted to talk to him more than anyone else. They had shared a beautiful human being, whom they had produced together; Alice had been a part of both of them.

His face went from shock to concern to love when he saw the small figure of his wife on his doorstep. Her light brown hair was tied back from her face, showing up the unusually dark brown eyes she shared with her sister, Grace. Those eyes now had a spark of life in them; they'd been like flat pieces of granite since Alice had gone missing. She looked like someone had breathed the elixir of life into her lungs, saving her from dying out altogether.

After she told him all she knew, he was understandably distressed and she stayed with him, letting him talk it all out. It was roles reversed for the first time in their married life; he had always comforted and protected her and he'd become so heavy with it he'd had to leave for the sake of them both.

By the end of their tears and conversation together, they had found an equal footing, a way forward to working on their future together.

Having laid many things to rest that day, Eve wanted to see her sister. And here she was stuck at the gate like a statue, unable to lift the latch with her stone fingers and walk up the garden path to the front door. She felt ridiculous. Especially after all the hurdles she'd faced that day, this should have been relatively easy. She knew she'd have to go in there at some point and she knew that Tim wasn't there anymore.

Just as she was mustering up the courage and feeling like her whole body was turning from stone to flesh again, a police car pulled up behind her.

"Are you Eve Thomlinson?" the officer called through the wound down window.

Eve turned slowly from the space she had occupied for many minutes, dread filling her entire being. Grace had been missing all day and fear was now reaching out and gripping her throat.

"Yes...why?"

"Your sister, Grace has been looking for you. I've just had a message on my radio saying she's at a Christine Newman's house. She's quite worried about you. Jump in and I'll take you over there."

Relief flooded her and it felt like it was leaking into her bones. The feelings startled her slightly, it dawned on her that she hadn't had any feelings about anyone else since Alice had gone missing.

The journey in the police car gave her time to reflect on how dead her life had been. She suddenly felt very ashamed; Alice wouldn't have wanted her to live her life like that, and she'd only just realised it.

*

Chrissie, Sarah, Grace and Eve spent the evening after their eventful day talking right into the small hours. It was an odd combination, seeing as they weren't all familiar with each other, and at times was awkward and excruciating but it worked. They shared many emotions together and it caused a bond to form that would last for the rest of their lives.

The fire was lit, the outside world had been shut out quite some time ago and stiff drinks were flowing along with the conversation. They were all completely exhausted but somehow managed to stay awake to counsel one another.

For the first in a very long time Chrissie's house took a deep breath and let out a very large sigh, as a veil of serenity and peace landed on the whole area, dispersing the cold, sinister atmosphere as easy as someone blowing on a dandelion head.

*

The guilt had been too overwhelming for Daphne to bear, and she had passed away two years to the day since she had unburdened everything she'd known about Tim. But aside from her despair she had lived the best two years of her life. Not only had she gained a friendship with Eve and Grace, but she developed one with Chrissie and Sarah too. Chrissie had wanted to interview her for research for her new book and Sarah, having newly arrived in the village, had wanted to come along and get to know a few people. For Daphne it had been like gaining four daughters where she had lost one. They consoled her through her bad moments, telling her she wasn't to blame for Tim's behaviour. But it didn't matter how many times she heard it, she still felt guilty. He had been right about the fact she hadn't wanted him. He'd arrived far too soon after they had lost Verity, well too soon in Daphne's eyes. She had been unable to bond with him and she remembered so clearly feeling like a child being given a new toy to replace a much loved old one. Only, this hadn't been a toy she'd been dealing with and she was no

301

longer a child. The bond she had expected and thought every mother was supposed to feel hadn't arrived.

People had thought a boy had been better than having another girl, which they thought would highlight the fact she wasn't Verity and could never replace her. A boy signified a fresh start, a new chapter in her life, but Daphne didn't feel any of those things, she'd just felt more miserable than before and worse still, she'd felt trapped.

Over and over in her head she would run memories, wondering if she could have tried harder, spent more time with him, loved him more.

She knew that Verity's murder had been the trigger for all the crimes Tim committed, but she had been the catalyst for it all by making him feel so unwanted and unloved.

Eve and Grace told her time and again that if Verity hadn't been murdered she wouldn't have felt like that towards him, so therefore it had been the fault of the monster who'd cruelly taken her daughter. They assured her he wouldn't have been aware of her feelings, that lots of mothers went through the same thing, only it was diagnosed as post-natal depression today rather than ignored as it was back then. It wasn't an excuse for him to go round killing innocent children; everyone had a choice in life, no matter how badly they had been treated.

Even Daphne telling them she suspected Dora of abusing Tim couldn't convince them that it was all her fault, or how horrible she felt she'd been to him because she simply didn't like him. They loved her and couldn't imagine she would intentionally hurt anyone, even with her harsh prickly exterior.

Sarah even tried to talk to her on a professional level, to reassure her that at all times she would have done the very best she could for her son and she wasn't to blame herself any longer; that they had both been victims of tragic circumstances. There was no rhyme or reason for it and Daphne beating herself up wouldn't change any of it one little bit.

Absolutely nothing would convince Daphne otherwise; it eased the guilt and softened the pain for her but it didn't dissolve it. It was something no one could take away from her and she knew they were just being kind. The guilt of her son's actions would stay with her forever. Daphne felt after all was said and done, she and Jack had chosen to bring him into the world, and it had been their duty to guide him in the right way.

Their support and loyalty helped her though and it was like having her daughter back with her again, only in four separate people. She felt extremely privileged to have them around her, fussing over her, genuinely interested in what she had to tell them.

Daphne passed away peacefully with all four of them around her. She was no longer scared or bitter about her life and she left, feeling quite peaceful and ready to go home.

*

Tim was found guilty of the murders of Jody, Karen, Jennifer, Jacqueline, Lucy, Jonathan, Nadine and Alice. He was sentenced to life in prison for each murder.

He had survived his attempted suicide because he hadn't anticipated the ledge that broke his fall halfway down to the sea. And it quite literally broke his fall, by snapping his spine in two places, leaving him paralyzed for the rest of his life.

His pleas of insanity at the time of the murders had fallen on deaf ears and he was removed from the court after a long hearing. There wasn't one parent, family member or friend in the area who wished he'd died that day on the cliffs. Everyone wanted him to serve his sentence in full for the rest of his life, because they knew how much he wanted death to come and relieve him.

He was put on a hospital wing in prison and watched by the staff determined to keep him alive. He appealed against his sentence, much to the shock of everyone concerned, but it was understandably thrown out of court. He felt that the sentence was immensely unfair because he'd been damaged as a child, but as the judge had pointed out to him on his day of sentencing, he'd had a choice. Everyone has the freedom to choose their actions.